Contemporary Practice With Young People Who Sexually Abuse

Evidence-based Developments

Edited by
Martin C. Calder

RHP

Russell House Publishing

First published in UK in 2011 by:

Russell House Publishing Ltd.
58 Broad Street
Lyme Regis
Dorset DT7 3QF
Tel: 01297-443948
Fax: 01297-442722
e-mail: help@russellhouse.co.uk
www.russellhouse.co.uk

Published simultaneously in North America by:

The NEARI Press
New England Adolescent Research Institute
70 North Summer Street
Holyoke
MA 01040
Tel: 413-540-0712
www.nearipress.org

British Library Cataloguing-in-publication Data:

A catalogue record for this book is available from the British Library.
ISBN: 978-1-905541-74-4

Typeset by TW Typesetting, Plymouth, Devon

Front cover art by Stacey Laura Calder

Printed by CPI Group, Eastbourne

Contents

Dedication

To my best friend and wife, Janet, for her patience and loyalty
over and above the call of duty

To my beautiful daughters, Stacey Laura and Emma Anne

About the Contributors

The Editor

Martin C. Calder MA, CQSW has worked in the field of child protection and child welfare for over 25 years. He is now an Honorary Research Fellow with Durham University. Martin has written and published extensively around policy and procedural issues in the child care field as well as the development of accessible, evidence-based assessment tools for frontline workers. Martin has written extensively in the area of young people presenting with sexual behaviour problems. Further details of his work are accessible at www.caldertrainingandconsultancy.co.uk

The Contributors

Libby Ashurst served as a uniformed police officer and then as a detective in a UK police force. Following this service she qualified with a B.Sc. in psychology and a master in Applied Forensic Psychology. Currently she is completing her PhD at Queens University Belfast where she is conducting research into an innovative simulated training model for improving professional practice for front line practitioners in Social Services. As well as being a senior practitioner (Forensic psychologist in training) for Barnardo's Young Peoples Therapeutic Service, Belfast where she carries out assessment and treatments with young people presenting with SHB and forensic mental Health. Additionally, she works with the PSNI in an immersive training environment assisting them to develop skills in the application of Emotional Intelligence in Critical Incidents.

Dr Nicholas A.J. Bankes is an independent psychotherapist, consultant, supervisor and trainer. He has worked as a child protection specialist since 1989. He is currently Clinical Director of A.C.T (Ireland), an assessment, consultation, therapy and training service in the field of sexual abuse in the Republic of Ireland and Oak Lodge Residential and Fostering Services Ltd. for children in care. Previously he had developed assessment and therapeutic services for adolescent and adult perpetrators of sexual abuse in the UK. Dr Bankes' interests are in the area of staff care and supervision.

Ann Brady has been managing the Halt Project for Glasgow City Council for four years. This is a community resource that works with children and young people who display a range of problem sexual behaviours. It is located within the city's child protection services and offers assessments and therapeutic interventions as well as providing a range of services to professionals, including consultancy and risk management advice and guidance. In 2005 she co-authored a chapter, 'The

Extra Dimension: Developing a Risk Management Framework' in *Children and Young People Who Sexually Abuse: New Theory, Research and Practice Developments*, edited by Martin C. Calder (2005). She is currently writing a practice manual on risk management, assessment and intervention in collaboration with Christine McCarlie, independent social worker. Prior to working at thne Halt Project, Ann worked with children and young people who had been traumatised.

Joanne Butterworth has been working for the past seven years at The Cornerstone Project in Salford. It provides therapeutic interventions to children and young people who have suffered sexual abuse, or who exhibit problematic sexualised behaviours. She also works with families, safe carers and multi-agency professionals; provides consultation and delivers training in relation to sexual abuse and communicating with children. Joanne has been a qualified social worker since 1997 and has worked extensively with disabled children and their families. She has developed group work programmes for children and young people with learning disabilities in relation to issues of sexual health and personal safety. In 2010 Joanne was awarded Salford City Council's Employee of the Year and went on to win the Local Government Worker of the Year award for her work with young people. Joanne.butterworth@barnardos.org.uk

Peter Clarke is the Director of Glebe House Therapeutic Community, a voluntary sector service that works residentially with older teenagers who have a history including sexually harming behaviour. He is a qualified social worker and holds an MA by research from University of East Anglia. He has over 20 years experience working in Therapeutic Communities and in direct clinical work with young people who have sexually harmed. Petner is currently a member of the Association of Therapeutic Communities Executive Committee (ATC) and the Chair of the Anglia Branch of the National Association for the Treatment of Abusers (NOTA). Peter is currently undertaking a PhD at Durham University with a focus on the development of standards for specialist residential provisions working with sexually harmful behaviour.

Dana Costin, PhD CPsych is a registered clinical and forensic psychologist who specialises in the assessment and treatment of adolescents who have sexually offended, children and adolescents who have experienced trauma, children exhibiting sexualised behaviours, youth in conflict with the law, and their families. She regularly provides consultation, training, workshops, and conference presentations regarding this work. Dr Costin maintains a private practice in the Toronto area, and also provides consultation to various programs in and around the Toronto area: Halton Trauma Centre, Turning Point Youth Services, Youth Connections Residential Program, Wallenberg Residential Centre, Griffin Centre, and the Hospital for Sick Children's Tele-Psychiatry Program. She also provides training at the Ontario Police College several times per year.

Tracey Curwen holds a doctoral degree in Applied Developmental Science from the University of Toronto and she is currently Assistant Professor in Psychology at Nipissing University in North Bay, Ontario. In addition to her research regarding risk assessment and prediction for repeated sexual behaviour problems, Dr Curwen is also investigating causes of child sexual behaviour problems.

Julian Dunn qualified as a social worker in1989. He worked as a probation officer for ten years specialising in working with adult sex offenders. He has worked within the UK South East region developing individual and groupwork programmes for adults and adolescents that have sexually harmed. He has been associated with the SWAAY organisation for over 19 years and is currently manager of the therapeutic team. He has presented seminars and workshops in the UK and Europe.

Bernadette Fahy is a registered social worker and has been practising in the field of child protection for 16 years. She has trained as both a general and psychiatric nurse and is a qualified counsellor. She has been working with children and adolescents who display sexually harmful behaviour for over 12 years and has been involved in the development and delivery of specialist training to professionals about children and young people who display sexually harmful behaviour. She currently works for the NSPCC and is an associate lecturer at Plymouth University.

Nicola Gilderthorp BA (Hons) MSc is a forensic psychologist in training at SWAAY. She has six years experience working in various capacities with adolescents who have suffered, as well as perpetrated sexual harm. This has been in the context of residential work, delivering individual therapeutic interventions and facilitating and observing group work programmes (social and emotional competency, offence-specific, and relapse prevention) as well as conducting psychometric and risk assessments. She has also undertaken research evaluating the effectiveness of the SWAAY treatment programme in impacting upon anger management difficulties in a group of adolescent males who have sexually harmed. Prior to working at SWAAY Nicola undertook some volunteer work with a youth offending team, which involved supervising and supporting adolescents with reparation tasks.

Dr Sharon Hall has recently completed ESRC funded doctoral research on the topic of working holistically with young people who have sexually harmed others. Her research included an internet survey of practitioners and a fieldwork placement within a Youth Offending Team where she interviewed young people, a parent, volunteers, staff and external professionals. Sharon now works as a lecturer in Working with Children, Young People and Families at Newman University College in Birmingham, including teaching on Safeguarding and Risk. She plans to develop her research in work with families and multi-agency teams. Previously Sharon worked as an Integrative Therapist with young people who had sexually harmed. She was employed by Birmingham Youth Offending Service within a specialist holistic team, drawing on her professional background in dramatherapy. She has also worked as a dramatherapist with adults and as a carer within a local authority children's home.

Nicole Hickey MSc is a forensic research psychologist with nearly 20 years experience in both research and clinical settings. She currently works in the Academic Unit of Child and Adolescent Psychiatry, Imperial College London, but has previously worked at Rampton high secure psychiatric hospital; the Forensic Psychiatry Research Unit, Queen Mary's College London, and the Young Abuser's Project. Her research interests include risk assessment measures, juvenile offending, and sexual offending.

Dr Nina Josefowitz, Ph.D., C.Psych. is a psychologist in private practice and part time faculty in the Department of Adult Education and Counselling Psychology at OISE/University of Toronto. Dr Josefowitz has a particular interest in the treatment and forensic evaluations of individuals who have experienced breaches of fiduciary duty, including childhood sexual abuse, domestic violence, sexual harassment and physical abuse. She has appeared in court on numerous occasions. Dr Josefowitz has been a Council member of the College of Psychologists, and President of the College. In addition she offers training programs in CBT to mental health agencies throughout Ontario. Dr Josefowitz has published and presented at professional conferences on a wide number of topics including trauma, CBT and ethical issues in the practice of psychology. She recently published a chapter on 'Confidentiality' which will appear in D. Evans (Ed.) *The law, standards of practice and ethics in the practice of psychology.* 3rd edition. Toronto: Emond Montgomery (publishing date fall 2011).

Tom Leversee, LCSW, has over 36 years of clinical and administrative experience in the Colorado Division of Youth Corrections (DYC) and in private practice, including over 27 years of experience working with sexually abusive youth. Tom published the *Moving Beyond Sexually Abusive Behavior* group therapy curriculum through the NEARI press and co-edited/authored the recently released 3rd edition of *Juvenile Sexual Offending: Causes, Consequences, and Correction* with Gail Ryan and Sandy Lane. Tom also has publications in a journal and chapters in numerous books. Tom was presented the National Adolescent Perpetration Network's 'Pioneer Award' in 2005 for his '21 years of unique contributions to prevent perpetration of sexual abuse'. Tom retired from DYC in

July of 2008 and is currently an adjunct professor at the Graduate School of Social Work at the University of Denver. He is a member of the Colorado Sex Offender Management Board and also provides consultation, training, and clinical services for youth who have committed sexual offenses.

Robert E. Longo, LPC, NCC is Director of Clinical Training, and Director of the Stress Reduction Clinic & Biofeedback Lab at Old Vineyard Behavioral Health Services; Winston-Salem, NC; a private for profit psychiatric hospital treating male and female adolescents, sexually abusive males, and both a child and adolescent acute care unit and an adult acute care unit.

Melissa Maltar, MSW, RSW is a registered Social Worker in private practice. She holds a Master of Social Work degree from the University of Toronto and a Bachelor of Social Work degree from Ryerson University. Since 2003, Melissa has specialized in community-based work with adolescents who have sexually harmed, children and adolescents who have experienced trauma, children who display problematic sexual behaviour problems, and their families. She has developed specialized assessment and treatment skills in these areas and has provided trainings, workshops, and presented at national and international conferences related to this work. Melissa also provides consultation to sexual abuse specific programs in children's mental health organizations across Southern Ontario. Prior to 2004, Melissa worked within the violence against women sector supporting survivors of sexual assault, woman-abuse, and their children.

Christine McCarlie has been a social worker for over 24 years. During the last 15 years she has been specialising in the field of children and young people displaying sexually problematic behaviours. She both managed and developed the Halt Project, which is a well established resource and highly regarded throughout the UK and abroad. For the last five years Christine has worked independently providing training, consultation and direct work for a number of local authorities as well as providing consultation to a number of specialist projects in Scotland. She has developed a risk management framework and protocol that is being used by several authorities across Scotland. She is also an associate trainer for AIM2. In 2005 she co-authored a chapter, 'The Extra Dimension: developing a risk management framework' in *Children and Young People Who Sexually Abuse: New Theory, Research and Practice Developments* edited by Martin C. Calder (2005). She is currently writing a practice manual on risk management, assessment and intervention in collaboration with Ann Brady, Glasgow City Council.

Dr Brent J. Oneal is a licensed psychologist and certified sex offender treatment provider in Washington State. He earned a PhD in Clinical Psychology from Washington State University and completed his internship/residency and post-doctoral fellowship through the University of Washington School of Medicine, with his post-doctoral fellowship emphasis in forensic clinical psychology. He currently holds a faculty appointment in the Department of Psychiatry and Behavioral Sciences at the University of Washington School of Medicine and Clinical Privileges at Child Study & Treatment Center. Dr Oneal has over nine years of direct forensic and clinical experience including specialised forensic psychological evaluation and sexual offense evaluation/treatment. He is presently the Treasurer for the Washington Association of Treatment for Sexual Abusers, is a former board member of that organisation, and holds professional memberships in a variety of organisations including the American Psychological Association, American Psychology-Law Society, and the Association for the Treatment of Sexual Abusers. He has published and presented work in the areas of forensic evaluation, risk assessment, developmental psychology, scale development, sexual-offense-specific evaluation and treatment, and medical psychology. Dr Oneal currently maintains a private practice in Seattle, WA, and specialises in a variety of forensic and clinical activities. In addition, he presently works as a court evaluator through inpatient psychiatry at Harborview Medical Center and as a contract psychologist for WA DSHS/DVR conducting psychological and neuropsychological evaluations.

Tim Plant B.A. Hons, Diploma in Social Work, Diploma in Nursing Studies, Registered Nurse Learning Disabilities (RNLD). Since qualifying in 1998, he has worked as a learning disabilities nurse in residential and community settings with adults and children. Tim is currently employed by Salford Royal Foundation Trust as a Paediatric Learning Disabilities Nurse, providing behavioural advice and support to families of children with severe learning disabilities and autism. His professional development interests include local policy initiatives regarding the behavioural, health and developmental needs of young people with severe learning disabilities and autism.

Kevin M. Powell, Ph.D. has been working with at-risk children, adolescents, and their families for over two decades in a variety of settings including schools, outpatient youth service agencies, inpatient hospital, and correctional facilities. He is the Clinical Director and a licensed psychologist at Platte Valley Youth Services Center, a 132-bed youth correctional facility in Colorado. He is also an adjunct assistant professor at Colorado State University in the Department of Psychology. In addition, Dr Powell provides trainings to mental health professionals, teachers, direct care staff, and other youth service providers on the topic of strengths-based interventions for working effectively with at-risk youth, including those with sexual behavior problems. He can be contacted through his website at www.kevinpowellphd.com

Mr Prescott is the Past President of the Association for the Treatment of Sexual Abusers (ATSA), and edited of that organisation's newsletter, *The Forum, from 2002-2007*. He is currently that newsletter's Review Editor. Mr Prescott is a charter member of the International Association for the Treatment of Sex Offenders and has also served on the board of directors for Stop It Now! an organisation dedicated to the prevention of sexual abuse. Mr Prescott is also a member of the Motivational Interviewing Network of Trainers (MINT) an international organisation devoted to a client-centered guiding method for exploring with clients how and why they might change. Mr Prescott has published seven books on the assessment and treatment of people who have sexually abused. He has written a number articles and book chapters in these areas as well. Mr Prescott is on the International Advisory Board for the *Journal of Sexual Aggression* and a Section Editor for the formative journal *Motivational Interviewing: Training, Research, Implementation, Practice*. He currently writes articles for the monthly NEARI Press Newsletter.

Siegi A. Schuler, PhD Candidate, RSW is a registered social worker who specialises in the assessment and treatment of children and adolescents who have experienced trauma, children who display problematic sexual behaviour, adolescents who have sexually offended, at-risk youth and youth who are in conflict with the law, and their families. He has considerable experience working with both community-based and residential programs, and has provided ongoing consultation, training, and presentations regarding his work. Siegi maintains a private practice in the Toronto area, is the Consulting Clinical Director at the Halton Trauma Centre, and provides consultation to Youth Connections Residential Program, the Hospital for Sick Children's Tele-Psychiatry Program, and the National Ballet School. Siegi also teaches a number of Masters-level courses in the Faculty of Social Work at the University of Toronto.

Dr Therese Skubic Kemper earned a Ph.D. in Clinical Psychology from Florida State University. As a graduate student, she worked extensively as a clinician and researcher with the Florida State University Specialized Treatment Program, which provides therapy and assessment services for incarcerated male adolescents, including sexual offenders. She is currently a Licensed Clinical Psychologist in Florida and has continued her work with the Specialized Treatment Program as a researcher, clinician, and clinical supervisor. Dr Skubic Kemper has published and presented work in the areas of juvenile sexual offender classification, sexual offender recidivism, nonsexual criminal behavior in sexual offenders, institutional adjustment of delinquent youth, and the use of empirically supported treatments. She is a member of the American Psychological Association and Association for the Treatment of Sexual Abusers.

Richard Swan has worked in children's social care in the UK for 22 years as a social work practitioner, manager and trainer. Over the last 12 years he has specialised in investigative assessment and therapeutic interventions with children and young people at risk of harm having undertaking additional post qualifying training at the Tavistock Clinic, London, the University of Sussex and the University of East London. Since 1999 Richard has developed a specialist interest in the provision of assessment and treatment services for children and young people who harm sexually. Between 2003 and 2006 he managed ACT (Assessment, Consultation and Therapy) a specialist community-based service. Between 2006 and 2007 Richard worked as a Senior Clinical Therapist at the Lucy Faithfull Foundation. Richard is an associate trainer for the AIM Project, Manchester – a national charity which delivers training regarding young people who sexually harm to agencies across the UK and Ireland.

Mette K Whittaker BSc (Hons) MSc, DipForPsy is a chartered forensic psychologist at SWAAY and is registered with the Health Professions Council. She has seven years experience of working with adolescent males who have suffered, as well as perpetrated sexual harm. This has been in the context of residential work, group and individual therapeutic interventions (social and emotional competency, offence-specific, and relapse prevention) as well as through conducting psychometric and risk assessments. She has also developed a motivational intervention for the use with young people and has implemented this programme with both adolescent sexual and non-sexual offenders. In addition she has undertaken research into the extent to which treatment affects psychometric change in a group of adolescent males who have sexually harmed as well as into the empathic ability of adolescent child abusers. Prior to commencing the work with adolescents, Mette spent four years working as a community support worker with adults with mental health problems, learning disabilities, drug dependency and challenging behaviours.

Dr James R. Worling, Ph.D., C.Psych. is a clinical and forensic psychologist who has worked extensively with adolescents who sexually offend, and their families, since 1988. During this time, he has presented many workshops internationally, and he has written a number of professional articles and book chapters regarding the etiology, assessment, and treatment of adolescent sexual offending. In addition to his full-time consulting and clinical practice, he is presently an associate faculty member at the University of Toronto, and he serves on the Editorial Boards for *Sexual Abuse: A Journal of Research & Treatment* and *Child Abuse & Neglect*.

Introduction

Martin C. Calder

This book is entirely free-standing, but builds on five earlier books about young people who sexually abuse. (Calder 1999, 2002, 2005, 2007). Details of the earlier books are at the end of this introduction.

This latest volume reflects both the desire to consolidate what we know about what works and what doesn't work as well as some of the contemporary cutting edge research and thinking in this challenging area of work.

I have endeavoured to assemble contributors from different disciplines and work bases from several countries to try and capture the best of current thinking as well as some of the continuing dilemmas. I have continued not to change the language used to reflect some of the variations in practice and research and the cross-validation of many salient points is self-evident to the reader as they work through the chapters. This means that

- Chapters from British-based authors are in British English, while chapters from authors based in North America are in American English, and so on.
- Some chapters will be contextualised in systems of service delivery that are specific to the country in which their authors are practicing. Of course, the specifics of system options within the UK, for example, differ from those within the US. However, in all chapters, the articulated principles of practice are universal. I therefore encourage readers to modify any suggestions about systems for service delivery according to the system in which they operate, which will allow them to follow the authors' practice advice without needing to alter their intent.

In this book, as in my previous ones, the drive is to furnish busy frontline staff with the latest thinking and materials to inform their practice. Happy reading and application . . .

The previous books can all be obtained from www.isbs.com in North America, and from www.russellhouse.co.uk everywhere else. They are:

Previous edited volumes

Working with Young People who Sexually Abuse: New Pieces of the Jigsaw Puzzle (1999)

Introduction: How to Begin the Assembly Process.
Martin C Calder, Child Protection Co-ordinator, City of Salford Community and Social Services Directorate

Chapter One: Causal Explanations: Filling the Theoretical Reservoir.
Kevin J Epps, Forensic Clinical Psychologist, Glenthorne Youth Treatment Centre, Birmingham

Chapter Two: The Case for Paraphilic Personality Disorder: Detection, Diagnosis and Treatment.
Frank I MacHovec PhD, Christopher Newport University, Newport News, VA

Chapter Three: CASPARS: Clinical Assessment Instruments That Measure Strengths and Risks in Children and Families.
Jane F Gilgun PhD, Professor of Social Work at the University of Minnesota

Chapter Four: Recovery Assessments With Young People Who Sexually Abuse.
Mark S Carich PhD, Big Muddy Correctional Center, State of Illinois Department of Corrections
Matt Lampley BS, Intern at Big Muddy River Correction Center and Graduate student at Southern Illinois University at Carbondale

Chapter Five: Attachment and Intimacy in Young People Who Sexually Abuse.
Spencer Santry, The Tizard Centre, The University of Kent at Canterbury
Gerard McCarthy, Principal Clinical Child Psychologist, North Somerset

Young People who Sexually Abuse: Building the Evidence Base for your Practice (2002)

Broad practice issues

Therapeutic Communities: A Model for Effective Intervention With Teenagers Known to Have Perpetrated Sexual Abuse.
Peter Clarke, Glebe House Children's Home, Cambridgeshire

Developing Focused Care: A Residential Unit for Sexually Aggressive Young Men.
Dr Andrew Kendrick, Department of Social Work, University of Dundee
Ranald Mair, Head, Geilsland School, Beith, Ayrshire

Accreditation of Work and Workers Involved in Providing a Service to Children and Young People Who Sexually Abuse.
Colin Hawkes, Young Abusers Project, London

Residential Standards of Care for Adolescent Sexual Abusers.
Robert Freeman-Longo, Director of Special Programming and Clinical Training, New Hope Treatment Centers, Summerville, SC

Groupwork With Parents of Children Who Have Sexually Harmed Others.
Simon Hackett, Centre for Applied Social Studies, University of Durham
Paula Telford and Keeley Slack, Kaleidoscope Project

Assessment issues

An Integrated Systemic Approach to Intervention With Children With Sexually Abusive Behaviour Problems.
Lucinda Rasmussen, Assistant Professor, San Diego State University

The Assessment of Young Sexual Abusers.
Dr Eileen Vizard, Consultant Child and Adolescent Psychiatrist, Young Abusers Project, London

South Asian Adolescent Sex Offenders: Effective Assessment and Intervention Work.
Kamran Abassi and Shabana Jamal, Probation Officers, Pakistani resource Centre, Manchester

Abused and Abusing: Work With Young People Who Have a Dual Sexual Abuse Experience.
Simon Hackett, Centre for Applied Social Studies, University of Durham

Treatment issues

A Holistic Approach to Treating Young People Who Sexually Abuse.

Robert E Longo, Director of Special Programming and Clinical Training, New Hope Treatment Center, Summerville, SC

Family Work With Adolescent Sex Offenders.
Carol Barnes, Family Therapist, SWAAY and Gareth Hughes, Kneesworth House Hospital

Management of Programme Pitfalls in Juvenile Sex Offender Treatment.
Edward Wieckowski and Curtis R Grant, Virginia Department of Juvenile Justice, Hanover
Charles E Hodges, Poplar Springs Hospital

A Proposal for Comprehensive Community-Based Treatment of Female Juvenile Sexual Offenders.
Dr Darlene Williams PhD, Psychological Management Group, Tampa, Florida and Mark Buehler, Licensed Clinical Social Worker

Management issues

Structural Changes in the Management of Young People Who Sexually Abuse in the UK.
Martin C Calder, Child Protection Co-ordinator, City of Salford Social Services Department; Lecturer in Social Work, University of Salford; and Independent Social Work Trainer and Consultant

Forensic Foster Care for Young People Who Sexually Abuse: Lessons From Treatment.
James Yokley, Metrohealth Medical Center and the Twelve Inc, Cleveland, OH
Sarah Boettner LSW, The Twelve Inc, OH

The Community Management of Young People Who Sexually Abuse.
Dr Tony Baker, Baker and Duncan Consultancy, Ashwood Centre, Woking, Surrey

Outcomes

Research on the Development of Sexually Abusive Behaviour in Sexually Abused Males: The Implications for Clinical Practice.
Arnon Bentovim, Consultant Child Psychiatrist, SWAAY, Berkshire and Director, The London Child and Family Consultation Service, Harley Street, London

Factors Associated With Recidivism in Juvenile Sexual Offenders: A Study of Serious Offenders.
Michael Miner, Assistant Professor, Department of Family Practice and Community Health, University of Minnesota

Emotion-focused Therapy and Children With Problematic Sexual Behaviours.
Professor Jane Gilgun PhD, University of Minnesota, Kay Rice and Danette Jones, St. Paul, MN

Sexual Offending and Sexual Behaviour Problems: Treatment With Multisystemic Therapy.
Elizabeth J Letourneau and Dr Cynthia Cupit Swenson, Family Services Research Center, Medical University of SC

Mode Deactivation Therapy: Cognitive-Behavioural Therapy for Young People With Reactive Conduct Disorders or Personality Disorders or Traits Who Sexually Abuse.
Jack A Apsche, The Pines Behavioural Studies Treatment Program, VA
Serene R Ward Bailey MA, Private Practice, lake View Psychotherapy

Management issues

The Extra Dimension: Developing a Risk Management Framework.
Christine McCarlie and Ann Brady, The Halt Project, Glasgow

The Use of Sex Offender Registration With Young People Who Sexually Abuse.
Robert E Longo and Martin C Calder

Outcomes

Family Reunification in Cases of Sibling Incest.
Jerry Thomas and C Wilson Viar III, Consulting and Training Services, Memphis

Sex Offender Treatment in a Juvenile Correctional Setting: Program Description and Nine-Year Outcome Study.
Edward Wieckowski, Dennis Waite, Relana Pinkerton, Elizabeth McGarvey and Gerald L Brown, Virginia Department of Juvenile Justice, Hanover

Working With Children and Young People Who Sexually Abuse: Taking the Field Forward

Chapter 1 Introduction
Martin C. Calder Director, Calder Training and Consultancy having recently left his Child Protection Operational Manager post with Salford City Council.

Chapter 2 Just How Different are They? Diversity and the Treatment of Young People with Harmful Sexual Behaviours.
Simon Hackett, Reader, School of Applied Social Sciences, Durham University.

Chapter 3 A Study of the Experiences of Black and Asian Young People Whose Behaviour is Sexually Harmful.
Baseer Mir, Children's Services Manager, NSPCC and Elleen Okotie, G-Map.

Chapter 4 Using Typologies to Individualise the Assessment, Treatment and Supervision of Sexually Abusive Youth.
Tom Leversee Cordinator, Sex Offense Specific Services, Colorado Division of Youth Corrections.

Chapter 5 The Good Lives Model of Rehabilitation: Reducing Risks and Promoting Strengths with Adolescent Sexual Offenders.
Rachael Collie, Cinical Pychologist, Victoria University. Tony Ward, Formerly Director, Kia Marama Sexual Offenders' Unit, Rolleston Prison, New Zealand. Lesley Ayland, Cinical Psychologist and Bill West, Senior Therapist, WellStop, New Zealand.

Chapter 6 Emerging Personality Disorders in Sexually Harmful Young People.
Graeme Richardson, manages a Psychology Team, NHS Forensic Mental Health Service For Young People.

Chapter 7 The Relationship Between Deviant Arousal and Sexual Recidivism in Adolescent Sex Offenders.
Robert J.W. Clift, Psychology Assistant, Heather M. Gretton Program Director and Gordana Rajlic, Research Assistant, Youth Forensic Psychiatric Services, British Columbia.

Chapter 8 Working with the Families of Children and Young People Who Sexually Harm: It Shouldn't be an Optional Extra.
Tess Johnson, and Jane Scott, Children's Services Practitioners, and Paula Telford, Manager, Kaleidoscope (NSPCC) Team.

Chapter 9 Young People with Learning Disabilities Who Sexually Abuse: Understanding, Identifying and Responding from Within Generic Education and Welfare Services.
Rachel Fyson, Lecturer in Social Work, University of Nottingham.

CHAPTER 1

Examining Risk of Youth who Sexually Offend

Therese Skubic Kemper and Brent J. Oneal

Juvenile sexual recidivism: risk and risk assessment

The need to understand juvenile sex offender recidivism risk is greater than ever before. Little is known about the characteristics or behaviors that increase a young person's risk for sexual reoffense, and as a result, legal decision-makers and treatment providers are casting a wide net of criminal sanctions and lengthy treatment requirements to minimise harm to the public. This, in combination with the recidivism patterns of juvenile sex offenders, including relatively low rates of sexual recidivism and high rates of non-sexual recidivism, suggest that a careful and empirically-based evaluation of the response to and treatment of juvenile sex offenders is in order (Letourneau and Miner, 2005).

It is widely assumed that many or most adolescent sexual offenders are at high risk to reoffend sexually. However, large, well-conducted studies fail to support this assumption. Though reported rates of sexual recidivism are influenced by length of follow up, treatment history, and recidivism definitions (eg conviction, criminal charges, etc.) measured rates are consistently low and rarely above 15 per cent (see Caldwell, 2002 and Reitzel and Carbonell, 2006). Recent meta-analyses have reported average juvenile sexual recidivism rates of 7 per cent (Caldwell, 2010) and 12 per cent (McCann and Lussier, 2008). In addition, another meta-analysis reported sexual recidivism rates of 7.4 per cent for youth who participated in treatment and 18.9 per cent for those not receiving treatment over an average follow-up of nearly five years (Reitzel and Carbonell, 2006). These data suggest that the vast majority of juvenile sexual offenders are *unlikely* to sexually reoffend. However, experts in the area agree that the consequences of reoffense are serious for both victims and offenders, and therefore emphasise the importance of improving the ability to accurately identify both the low-risk offenders and the small group of high-risk offenders. Improved accuracy in risk assessment will help prevent unnecessary negative consequences (ie lengthy treatment, family separation, legal restrictions) for those who pose little risk and will help allocate resources more efficiently to the youth with the greatest need.

At this time, however, there is no empirically validated measure of risk for juvenile sexual recidivism. As a result, clinicians, judges, probation officers, and others asked to provide estimates of risk have generally used one or more of these less than ideal approaches: estimate risk using clinical judgment; use risk assessment instruments designed for adults; or use one of the few risk measures designed for adolescents. Each of these poses somewhat different problems for a well-intentioned evaluator, but ultimately results in inaccurate, invalid, or tentative conclusions. First, the data on the accuracy of clinical judgment are clear (Dawes, Faust, and Meehl, 1989; Hanson, 2000; Hanson and Morton-Bourgon, 2009; Prescott, 2004): clinicians typically do not outperform structured, actuarial methods; they may attend to interesting but irrelevant factors; their accuracy is only slightly above chance levels, and they do particularly poorly (ie lack sensitivity) when predicting low base rate events. Second, research has shown that several measures developed to assess sexual recidivism among adults have moderate predictive accuracy with adult offenders (Hanson and Morton-Bourgon, 2009; Langton et al., 2007) but, despite potential similarities in recidivism risk factors, little is known about their reliability and validity in juvenile samples. Specifically, few measures (eg Static-99; Hanson and Thornton, 1999) have included juveniles in the development or validation samples and there are no data indicating that the items, scoring procedures, or risk level designations are applicable to juveniles. In fact, differential performance of these measures between rapists and child molesters (Looman and Abracen, 2010), differences between adolescents and adults on the stability of key characteristics assessed by many of these measures (eg sexual deviance) and automatic discredit for young age on some measures provide clear evidence that use of these instruments with juveniles is risky and will likely result in inaccurate conclusions. To highlight the importance of considering developmental constructs in the juvenile sexual reoffense risk assessment process, results of a relatively recent study (Viljoen et al., 2008) demonstrated that even among the juvenile sexual reoffense risk tools, there are significant differences between younger and older adolescents. Third, the use of measures designed specifically for adolescents is undoubtedly a step in the right direction. However, despite good adherence to accepted strategies in test development (eg Prentky and Righthand, 2003) and ongoing research, the goal of establishing an empirically validated actuarial measure of sexual recidivism in adolescents has been elusive and none of the measures currently available have consistently demonstrated adequate predictive validity. Nonetheless, two commonly used risk assessment tools, the Juvenile Sex Offense Assessment Protocol-Second Edition (J-SOAP-II) and the Estimate of Risk of Adolescent Sexual Offense Recidivism (ERASOR) have demonstrated predictive validity in some studies (eg McCoy, 2007; Rajlic and Gretton, 2010). Overall, however, there are significant empirical limitations for assigning youth to risk levels (eg low, medium, high) using responses or scores from these instruments. Despite this, evaluators are often asked to go beyond the scope of the measures and make risk level determinations that are used in clinical and legal decision-making.

Given that the three best available options for risk assessment are inadequate, there is a strong demand for an instrument that will do the job adequately. Two key ingredients are needed on which to build such an instrument: knowledge of recidivism base rates and knowledge of recidivism predictors. As described above, sexual recidivism base rates are relatively well-established. In contrast, studies examining predictors of risk have been scarce and generally the results have been inconsistent and inconclusive, which has created a formidable barrier to the development of risk assessment tools. With a goal as important as the prevention of sexual abuse, it may be surprising that so little is known about risk factors. There are three primary reasons for the relative lack of knowledge: low base rates of sexual recidivism, the heterogeneity of juvenile sex offenders, and methodological issues of existing studies, each of which will be discussed in turn.

It is extremely difficult to identify reliable predictors of low base rate events such as juvenile sexual recidivism. With a base rate of approximately 15 per cent, research samples of over 300 youth would be required to find only 50 recidivists, which is barely enough to conduct any meaningful statistical analysis. Furthermore, the heterogeneity of juvenile sex offenders, which will be discussed in more depth shortly, decreases the ability to find consistent patterns or characteristics among recidivists, particularly in small samples.

Similarly, low sexual recidivism base rates make it exceedingly difficult to establish the predictive validity of risk assessment measures and accurately identify youth who are at a high risk to reoffend. As described in greater detail elsewhere (DiCataldo, 2009; Meehl and Rosen, 1955; Waller, Yonce, Grove, Faust, and Lenzenweger, 2006) optimal conditions for predictive validation occur when events have base rates near 50 per cent. In these cases, an instrument needs only to have a minimal degree of predictive accuracy in order to improve upon a chance prediction. Challenges arise with low base rate events such as juvenile sexual recidivism because instruments must be extremely accurate in order to improve upon an automatic clinical prediction of 'no recidivism' that has an accuracy rate of 85 per cent or higher, assuming a 15 per cent base rate (DiCataldo, 2009; Quinsey, Harris, Rice, and Cormier, 1998). As discussed above, low base rates inhibit the identification of reliable recidivism predictors, which in turn, limits the ability to develop an instrument that is useful for predicting recidivism.

The heterogeneity of juvenile sex offenders also contributes to difficulty in identifying risk factors for sexual recidivism (DiCataldo, 2009). Despite differences in levels of delinquency, sexual interests and deviance, psychological diagnoses, and a wide variety of additional factors that may impact recidivism risk, these youth are often combined in research studies, treatment, and in policy decisions as if they were a homogeneous group. As noted above, this practice, particularly in research, decreases the ability to identify patterns or characteristics relevant to recidivism risk. It is likely that specific risk factors operate differently for different subgroups of offenders and that important findings are clouded by sample diversity.

This has contributed to a number of attempts to identify valid subgroups of juvenile sex offenders

(Butler and Seto, 2002; Butz and Spaccarelli, 1999; Hunter et al., 2003; Worling, 2001). Characteristics including personality (Worling, 2001) physical force (Butz and Spaccarelli, 1999) and non-sexual offense history (Butler and Seto, 2002; van Wijk, Mali and Bullens, 2007) have been used to classify young offenders. However, when subgroups are formed on the basis of these characteristics, they often do not differ on other relevant characteristics, including treatment outcome or recidivism rates, thereby limiting their validity and clinical utility. One exception is a study that revealed a clinically meaningful distinction between youth who commit only sexual offenses (sex-only offenders) and youth who commit sexual *and* non-sexual offenses (sex-plus offenders), by way of demonstrating differential predictive validity of both the JSOAP-II and ERASOR (Rajlic and Gretton, 2010).

The common method of classifying juvenile sex offenders by victim age has also been met with limited success, despite its utility in classifying adult sex offenders. Some consistent differences have been found between youth who victimise children and those who victimise peers or adults on variables such as victim characteristics, (eg relationship and gender; Fehrenbach et al., 1986); sexual abuse history (Awad and Saunders, 1991; Ford and Linney, 1995; Worling, 1995) and non-sexual conduct problems or crime (Ford and Linney, 1995; Kemper and Kistner, 2007; Richardson, Bhate, and Graham, 1997). However, in order to be clinically useful, a classification system should identify subgroups that differ on psychologically meaningful variables (Kemper and Kistner, 2010; Mann, Hanson, and Thornton, 2010) that are related to the development and maintenance of offense-related behavior, response to treatment, and importantly, recidivism risk. Research has failed to show that victim age-based subgroups consistently differ on any of those important outcomes. Regarding sexual recidivism, some studies have reported higher rates of sexual recidivism in juveniles who offend children (Kahn and Chambers, 1991; Vandiver, 2006) but others reported higher rates in those who offend peers or adults (Nisbet, Wilson, and Smallbone, 2004). Three studies have not found statistically significant differences in sexual recidivism rates between the two groups (Hagan and Cho, 1996; Kemper and Kistner, 2007; Parks and Bard, 2006) despite trends in two of these studies (Kemper and Kistner, 2007; Parks and Bard, 2006) showing somewhat higher

recidivism rates in the group with offenses against children. Thus, the heterogeneity of juvenile sexual offenders and the inability to date to identify meaningful subgroups are significant obstacles to the identification of valid and reliable predictors of sexual reoffense risk.

Methodological limitations also contribute to the inability to draw conclusions about risk factors for juvenile sexual recidivism. First, there are considerable inconsistencies across studies on the measurement and operational definitions of both risk factors and recidivism (McCann and Lussier, 2008), making cross study comparisons difficult. For example, criteria and data sources for determining whether events are considered to be acts of recidivism range from unofficial reports (self-report or clinical judgment) to stringent and official findings (criminal sanctions or criminal records/conviction) and these differences have been found to impact reported recidivism rates (DiCataldo, 2009). Second, follow-up periods are typically short, but range from several months to over 15 years. Though some studies suggest that a high proportion of reoffenses will occur shortly after release or treatment termination (see DiCataldo, 2009), research also shows a strong positive relationship between length of follow-up and recidivism rates (Caldwell, 2002). Therefore, it is unclear exactly how variations in follow-up periods have influenced reported recidivism rates and the ability to identify meaningful predictors. Third, the infrequent use of standardised tests and measures to assess constructs of interest is problematic (McCann and Lussier, 2008) and contributes to the variability in the measurement of risk factors. Fourth, criteria used to assign youth to subgroups, particularly victim age-based subgroups, vary widely across studies. Though results from one study indicate that this may not be particularly problematic, more research is needed to determine how variations in offender classification impact findings regarding recidivism rates (Kemper and Kistner, 2010). Fifth, low sample sizes limit statistical power, leaving the conclusions that can be drawn from many studies tentative at best. Finally, lack of appropriate control groups (eg untreated youth, non-sexual offending delinquents, non-delinquent youth) give a narrow view of the true picture of juvenile sexual crime and fails to provide insight into the unique risk juvenile sex offenders and specific subgroups pose for sexual recidivism.

Though the obstacles to identifying risk factors are numerous, recent studies have pointed to several variables that show promise in their link to sexual recidivism. For example, one review indicated that deviant sexual interest (ie interest in prepubescent children and/or sexual violence) prior criminal sanctions for sexual offenses, multiple victims, stranger victims, social isolation, and failure to complete treatment have been linked in at least two studies to sexual reoffense and that there have been no contradictory findings reported (Worling and Langström, 2006). Though more than a small handful of studies is needed to draw conclusions about risk factors, the data thus far are promising and the similarity of many of these variables to those that predict risk in adults suggests they are worthy of further examination.

The results of individual studies provide a good launching point, but meta-analyses are also needed to clarify the predictive utility of specific variables and the strength of their relationships with recidivism (McCann and Lussier, 2008). However, few attempts at this have been made (Cottle, Lee and Heilbrun, 2001; Hanson and Morton-Bourgon, 2005; Heilbrun et al., 2005; McCann and Lussier, 2008). In 2001, Cottle and colleagues attempted a meta-analysis of sexual recidivism in delinquent youth; however, they discovered only eight relevant studies and due to between-study variability in the risk factors assessed, they were unable to perform the meta-analysis. Heilbrun and colleagues (2005) conducted a meta-analysis of nine studies and their findings indicated that young offenders, those who committed noncontact initial sex offenses, and those who victimised acquaintances showed an increased likelihood of sexual reoffense. A more recent meta-analysis included 18 studies and found that a history of sexual offenses; a history of non-sexual offenses; older age at intake; use of threats or weapons during a sex offense; offense against a male; offense against a child or adult, as opposed to a peer; and offense against a stranger were significantly related to sexual recidivism (McCann and Lussier, 2008). However, few variables had three or more studies that were used in computation of the effect sizes and it is noteworthy that their findings regarding offender age and victim relationship are in direct contrast to what was reported by Heilbrun and colleagues. These contrasting findings between inclusive and well-conducted studies highlight the difficulties researchers have had in drawing conclusions about risk factors for juvenile sexual recidivism.

Of interest is that almost all of the variables identified by the studies above are offense related variables that are static, historical, and unchangeable even with treatment (eg offense history, offender age, etc.). Though unchangeable, it is important to know whether those are related to risk, particularly if they improve the ability to distinguish between low- and high-risk offenders. However, the high personal and economic costs of providing intense, long-term treatment to juvenile sex offenders places an ethical duty on treatment providers to be knowledgeable of and provide treatment targeting factors that can be changed or otherwise managed through compensatory strategies (Mann, Hanson, and Thornton, 2010). These risk factors, often called dynamic risk factors or criminogenic needs, when targeted in treatment are a clinician's best bet for impacting recidivism risk (Hanson et al., 2009; Vieira, Skilling and Peterson-Badali, 2009). As noted above, risk factors influencing juvenile sexual recidivism are not well understood, but based on the adult and juvenile literature, at least two dynamic factors appear to be both related to recidivism and promising points of intervention: sexual deviance and antisociality.

Sexual deviance is generally understood as a combination of cognitive, physiological, and behavioral processes indicating sexual arousal to and preference for unconventional sexual stimuli and behavior such as pre-pubescent children or sexual violence. Although experts in the field would likely agree that a relatively small proportion of juvenile sexual offenders prefer deviant stimuli and are driven to offend by sexual deviance (see Letourneau and Miner, 2005) there is undoubtedly a group for whom these statements are true. Sexual deviance is a robust predictor of sexual recidivism in adults (Hanson and Bussière, 1998; Hanson and Morton-Bourgon, 2005) but developmental considerations and measurement difficulties have made this an elusive construct in adolescents.

The primary problem in assessing sexual deviance in adolescents is the fluid nature of adolescent sexual arousal and interest, which is in contrast to the relative stability of these in adults (Hunter, Goodwin, and Becker, 1994; Prescott, 2004). This fluidity makes it exceedingly difficult to determine how long deviance in adolescence will maintain its predictive value and alternatively, whether a youth who shows little evidence of deviance at the time of the assessment will develop deviant interests over time. Another problem in assessing sexual deviance in adolescents lies in the nature of the assessment. Self-report is prone to bias due to lack of insight, embarrassment, or a host of other factors related to self-presentation. Clinician ratings rely heavily on behavioral observations and knowledge of sex offense history, which do not necessarily reflect sexual preferences or underlying deviance (see Kalmus and Beech, 2005). Physiological measures, such as the penile plethysmograph (PPG) are popular for assessing deviance in adults, but even these are not without their problems. For example, research has shown that physiological response, arousal, interest and behavior are not inextricably linked (Kalmus and Beech, 2005) and that responses on these measures can be intentionally manipulated (DiCataldo, 2009). Furthermore, there are numerous ethical concerns about the use of these measures with adolescents, related to both the fluidity of adolescent arousal and the practice of showing sexually explicit, deviant stimuli to adolescents.

Despite these problems in measuring sexual deviance, several researchers have examined its relationship to sexual recidivism in adolescents. Though there is conflicting evidence regarding the utility of PPG measurements (Clift, Rajlic, and Gretton, 2009; Gretton et al., 2001) both self-reported and therapist-rated deviance have been empirically linked to recidivism in adolescent samples (Kenny, Keogh, and Siedler, 2001; Worling and Curwen, 2000). Furthermore, sexual deviance has held up in two meta-analyses as a significant predictor of adolescent sexual recidivism over periods of five to nine years (Hanson and Morton-Bourgon, 2005; McCann and Lussier, 2008). Relatively few studies, low effect sizes, and broad operational definitions make it difficult to determine its true predictive value, but these findings suggest avenues for further examination.

The use of clear operational definitions of deviance, multiple assessments over time, and multi-method assessment procedures are essential for furthering the understanding of this topic. Specifically, this will allow for the development of a clear picture of the specific types of thoughts, behaviors, and attitudes that are linked to recidivism risk. These can then be the focus of interventions, including reducing the rewarding nature of deviant fantasies, providing opportunities for appropriate sexual behavior, or challenging distortions related to deviant attitudes.

Because juvenile sexual offenders are often viewed as distinct from juvenile non-sexual offenders, the role of antisociality in sexual recidivism is often overlooked in favor of sexual deviance and other sex-specific explanations such as abuse history. However, emerging research with both adults and juveniles suggests that for many, sexual offending is but one manifestation of general criminality or antisociality (Lussier, LeBlanc, and Proulx, 2005; Seto and Lalumière, 2006). This is supported by findings that a large proportion of sexual offenders, including juveniles, have histories of non-sexual conduct problems and crime that are more extensive than their histories of sexual behavior problems and crime (Kemper and Kistner, 2007; Lussier, 2005).

In a meta-analysis of sex offender recidivism, antisocial orientation (eg antisocial personality, psychopathy, lifestyle instability, substance use, rule violations, etc.) was second only to sexual deviance in its relationship to sexual recidivism for both adults and adolescents (Hanson and Morton-Bourgon, 2005). Similarly, in a meta-analysis including only juveniles, McCann and Lussier (2008) found that antisociality, defined as non-sexual offense history, number of previous convictions, use of threats or weapons, psychopathy, antisocial personality, aggression, lack of discipline, and drug use, was a significant predictor of sexual recidivism over an average follow-up period of 10 years.

As with sexual deviance, more research is needed on the precise aspects of antisociality that increase recidivism risk, but the available data have important implications for the risk assessment and treatment of juvenile sex offenders. It forces treatment providers and risk assessors to challenge their assumptions about juvenile sex offenders and look beyond sexual deviance as a marker of risk. It also suggests a wide variety of potentially treatable factors that could be addressed with these youth. Antisocial attitudes, aggression, substance use, and impulsivity are often secondary treatment targets to sex offense specific factors such as accountability and victim empathy, neither of which has been found to independently predict reoffense. These data suggest, however, that attention to antisociality may be as or more important as attention to sex specific issues in the treatment of some juvenile sex offenders. This point is emphasised by the results of a recent study that revealed that antisociality was a statistically significant moderating factor for the predictive validity of two commonly used sexual reoffense risk assessment tools (Rajlic and Gretton, 2010). In other words, for some populations of adolescents who sexually offend (ie antisocially inclined youth), the typical methods of evaluating risk for sexual reoffense are not at all adequate.

Finally, though caution must be taken in automatically making downward extensions to juveniles, research on adults can also provide useful information on potentially fruitful areas of juvenile risk factor and sexual recidivism research. In contrast to what is known about juveniles, risk factors for adult sexual recidivism are relatively well-established. With careful consideration of developmental factors, examination of the risk factors described above (sexual deviance and antisociality) and others relevant for adults (Mann et al., 2010), such as intimacy deficits, problem-solving skills, hostility, and the ability to appropriately cope with emotions, is a potentially worthwhile endeavor.

The role of treatment participation

Though data are limited, research to date indicates several important findings regarding the relationship between participation and progress in treatment and juvenile sexual reoffense risk assessment. First, studies suggest that failure to complete treatment is related to sexual recidivism (Worling, Littlejohn, and Bookalam, 2010) and that sexual recidivism rates are lower for youth who participate in treatment than for those who do not (Gretton et al., 2005; Reitzel and Carbonell, 2006; Walker et al., 2004; Worling and Curwen, 2000). Second, research suggests that risk of reoffense may be lessened for some youth through participation in sex offense specific treatment, whereas other youth may benefit from treatment focused on delinquency more broadly. Specifically, sex offense specific cognitive behavioral treatment (CBT) models, which focus on supportive attitudes and beliefs, age-appropriate socialisation and dating skills, relapse prevention, and victim empathy appear to reduce risk of reoffense (Reitzel and Carbonell, 2006; Walker et al., 2004). However, for youth who present with a proclivity for general antisociality and engage in sexual misconduct within the context of a broader range of delinquent acts, multisystemic treatment approaches (eg Multisystemic Therapy) may be particularly effective (Borduin and Schaeffer,

2002). What appears to be forthcoming is that sex offense specific CBT may be the treatment of choice for youth who commit exclusively sexual offenses but multisystemic models, developed for antisocial youth, are indicated for those who commit both sexual and non-sexual acts of delinquency. Third, though the 'active ingredients' of treatment are not particularly well established and specific aspects of treatment have yet to be empirically wedded to reoffense risk, commonly applied treatments have shown a meaningful impact on modification of treatment targets. For example, Eastman (2004) found that youth in sex offense specific treatment demonstrated some positive changes in their empathy levels and showed significant positive changes in their level of cognitive distortions about sexual abuse, sexual knowledge, and attitudes about sexual behavior.

The links between treatment participation, progress, and recidivism are not well established, but available information is encouraging. An in-depth examination of several factors are needed to clarify this relationship, which will in turn assist in improving both treatment delivery and risk assessment. First, an examination of personal (ie personality, offense characteristics, antisocial attitudes) and situational (ie treatment setting) factors that impact treatment progress and outcomes is needed. Second, structured treatment progress tools that operationalise and examine key ingredients of sexual offense specific interventions are needed. A recently developed instrument, the Treatment Progress Inventory for Adolescents who Sexually Abuse (TPI-ASA; Oneal et al., 2008) is showing promise toward this end (Kemper, Oneal, and Drew, 2009). However, more research on the psychometric properties of the TPI-ASA and its relationship to emerging risk assessment tools (eg JSOAP-II or ERASOR) will help identify the key ingredients of treatment and better determine the relationship between youth's progress on treatment targets and sexual recidivism risk. Third, studies that examine the differing treatment needs and performance of different types of offenders (ie high and low risk; highly antisocial and more pro-social; sexually deviant and non-deviant) will also be valuable in uncovering the role of treatment in risk assessment and risk management.

Without these types of studies, it is difficult to determine how to use treatment to modify risk and unless treatment is targeting risk-relevant factors, it will do little good for the youth or potential victims. While we are ultimately arguing for a refined analysis of the relationship between treatment and recidivism risk, this is not to minimise the positive life impacts, such as improved self-efficacy and social competence, that may also come to youth who actively engage in sex offense specific treatment.

Rethinking risk assessment: non-sexual recidivism

Extensive attention is paid to improving the ability to predict juvenile sexual recidivism. Often overlooked, however, is the need to attend to non-sexual recidivism as part of a comprehensive risk assessment. Sex offenders, both adult and juvenile are often believed to be specialists with a unique propensity to commit sexual crime. Though this is certainly true for some offenders, there is emerging evidence that many adult sex offenders are generalists, committing both sexual and non-sexual crimes, which is driven by general antisociality and criminal deviance (Lussier et al., 2005).

A similar refocus of attention is slowly taking place with juvenile sex offenders. Up to 80 per cent have a history of non-sexual crime and up to 25 per cent have three or more non-sexual offenses on record (Fehrenbach et al., 1986; Ryan et al., 1996; Kemper and Kistner, 2007; Seto and Lalumière, 2006), which is clearly in contrast to the view that these youth specialise in sex crimes. More importantly to the focus of risk assessment, however, is what the data show regarding recidivism. The general consensus is that juvenile sex offenders as a whole are more likely to recidivate with non-sexual rather than sexual crime, no matter what criteria are set for recidivism (eg re-arrest, conviction, etc.). A review of individual studies reported that, on average, non-sexual recidivism was six times more likely than sexual recidivism in samples of juvenile sex offenders (Caldwell, 2002). In addition, two meta-analyses found juvenile sexual recidivism rates of just over 12 per cent compared to non-sexual recidivism rates of 20 per cent (unspecified non-sexual; Reitzel and Carbonell, 2006) to 61 per cent (nonviolent, non-sexual; McCann and Lussier, 2008), with recent individual studies reporting rates between 30 per cent and 50 per cent (Kemper and Kistner, 2007; Vandiver, 2006; Waite et al., 2005). Few would argue that assessment of sexual recidivism risk is unimportant; however, these data show that non-sexual recidivism has a potentially greater impact on both the re-offending youth and the community that bears the social and economic costs of reoffense. In the interest of service to the youth and community, assessment, identification, and treatment of juvenile sex offenders who are likely to commit non-sexual crimes is essential.

Highlighting the lack of attention to this area, neither recent meta-analysis on juvenile sex offender recidivism (McCann and Lussier, 2008; Reitzel and Carbonell, 2006) reported on predictors of non-sexual recidivism. However, an earlier meta-analysis (Hanson and Morton-Bourgon, 2005) found that antisocial orientation (eg antisocial personality, psychopathy, substance abuse, lifestyle instability, history of non-sexual offenses) predicted non-sexual recidivism in a subset of juveniles. These factors are remarkably similar to variables that predicted non-sexual recidivism in meta-analyses of general recidivism in delinquents: prior delinquency (Loeber and Dishion, 1983), prior criminal history (eg age at first law contact and first commitment, number of prior commitments), and important dynamic factors such as ineffective use of leisure time, delinquent peers, and substance abuse (Cottle et al., 2001).

These findings have two broad implications. First, strategies used for assessing risk in general delinquents may be useful for a large proportion of juvenile sexual offenders, given the substantial overlap in risk factors for general recidivism. For example, the Youth Level of Service/Case Management Inventory (YLS/CMI; Hoge et al., 2002) has been shown to be a valid short-term (ie six months) measure of risk, needs, and protective factors for juvenile offenders (Holsinger, Lowenkamp and Latessa, 2006; Marczyk, Heilbrun, Lander and DeMatteo, 2003; Schmidt, Hoge and Gomes, 2005) and may prove useful for the many sexual offenders at risk for, or with histories of non-sexual delinquency. Second, the fact that variables related to antisociality predicted both sexual and non-sexual recidivism has both risk assessment and treatment implications. Though sex specific risk factors should generally be of focus, the antisociality related risk factors can potentially help increase accuracy of prediction, though more research is needed to determine how this information can be used optimally. Also, treatment geared towards these criminogenic needs, in addition to sex specific needs, may help increase the efficiency of treatment by reducing the risk for recidivism more broadly.

Measurement of recidivism risk

Despite, or perhaps because of, the significant barriers to uncovering predictors of adolescent sexual recidivism, there is a strong demand by clinicians, legal professionals, and policymakers for a risk assessment tool for adolescent sex offenders. Numerous efforts have focused, in part, on other areas in which relative success in risk assessment has been achieved. In the assessment of violence (see Campbell, French and Gendreau, 2009) and in the assessment of recidivism risk for adult sex offenders (see Hanson and Morton-Bourgon, 2009) actuarial methods, which combine data in an objective and empirically derived fashion (Meehl, 1954; Prescott, 2004) have become the gold standard. With actuarial scales, scores or risk estimates are tied to probability estimates of recidivism that were established by observing the known recidivism rates for groups of offenders with similar scores on the instrument. Though not without critics, actuarial methods are generally viewed as a marked improvement over unstructured and error prone clinical judgment, as they are easy to use; perform adequately with low base rate events, where clinicians typically do poorly; and reduce interference by irrelevant factors (see Prescott, 2004).

A few noteworthy attempts have been made at developing actuarial scales for juveniles but all have encountered a similar 'chicken and egg' dilemma, particularly related to sexual recidivism: a measure is needed to identify potential recidivists but a good number of recidivists is needed in order to develop and refine the measure. This has prevented the development of a true actuarial scale to date, but several measures show promise. A brief review of these measures will be provided here, but in depth descriptions of the development and validation studies can be found elsewhere (DiCataldo, 2009; Prentky and Righthand, 2003; Righthand et al., 2005; Worling, 2004).

The most widely used risk assessment measure for juvenile sex offenders is the Juvenile Sex Offender Assessment Protocol-II (J-SOAP-II; Prentky and Righthand, 2003). This is a 28-item checklist with four scales:

1. Sexual Drive/Sexual Preoccupation
2. Impulsive/Antisocial Behavior
3. Intervention
4. Community Stability/Adjustment

designed for use with 12 to 18 year olds with a history of sexually coercive behavior (adjudicated or non-adjudicated). It has relatively good psychometric properties (see Prentky and Righthand, 2003 and DiCataldo, 2009) has Static (Scales 1 and 2) and Dynamic Factor scales (Scales 3 and 4) and correlates with the YLS/CMI, a measure of juvenile offenders' risks and needs.

Despite the use of scientifically sound procedures in development and validation, only tentative support has been found for its predictive validity. Though low base rates have generally limited the evaluation of the predictive validity of the instrument, a recent study with somewhat higher than average base rates of sexual recidivism (30 per cent for pre-adolescents over four years and 23 per cent for adolescents over three years) found the total score distinguished between recidivists and non-recidivists (Prentky et al., 2009). Prentky and colleagues also found some support for the predictive validity of the Static and Dynamic factors scores. Another recent study found that the total score did not predict sexual or non-sexual recidivism, but found that it was related to non-sexual aggression during treatment (Viljoen et al., 2008). Of note, is that the average time to recidivism in this study was over eight years, which is far beyond the time frame the J-SOAP-II is intended to predict. Other studies examining the predictive utility of subscales found that the Impulsive/Antisocial Behavior scale predicted general recidivism (Waite et al., 2005) and the Sexual Drive/Preoccupation Scale (along with the total score as noted above) predicted non-sexual aggression during treatment (Viljoen et al., 2008). Finally, as aforementioned, the recent study conducted by Rajlic and Gretton (2010) revealed predictive validity of the J-SOAP-II total score and three scale scores (Impulsive/Antisocial Behavior, Intervention, and Community Stability/Adjustment) in predicting sexual reoffense for sex-only but not sex-plus offenders. The authors of the J-SOAP-II note that continued validation research along with evolving knowledge about adolescent risk assessment will inform future revisions to the instrument, with the goal of eventually providing probabilistic (actuarial) estimates of recidivism risk.

In the manual, the authors explicitly note the limitations of the instrument and recommendations for appropriate use. First, because of the high stakes associated with risk assessment, the J-SOAP-II should be used as part of a comprehensive assessment rather than used in isolation. Second, the J-SOAP-II is an empirically informed guide rather than an actuarial instrument and cut-off scores for risk designation are not provided due to a lack of empirical data on which to base them. In other words, designating a youth as low, medium, or high risk on the basis of J-SOAP-II scores is an inappropriate use of the instrument. Rather, the authors recommend reporting ratio scores that reflect the 'amount' of risk rated as present for each scale. Third, the manual also states that adolescents are 'moving targets' who are constantly 'in flux.' Therefore, regular reassessment (ie at least every six months) is necessary for conceptualising relevant risk factors operating at a specific point in time.

The second most popular measure of juvenile sex offender risk assessment (DiCataldo, 2009; McGrath, Cumming, and Burchard, 2003) is the Estimate of Risk of Adolescent Sexual Offense Recidivism Version 2.0 (ERASOR (2.0); Worling and Curwen, 2001). The instrument assesses 25 risk factors, the majority of which are dynamic areas and potential treatment targets. Risk factors are grouped into five categories: Sexual Interests, Attitudes, and Behaviors; Historical Sexual Assaults; Psychosocial Functioning; Family/Environmental Functioning; and Treatment. It is for use with 12 to 18 year olds who have committed a sexual assault and is designed to be completed as part of a thorough clinical assessment. The psychometric properties, such as inter-rater reliability and internal consistency are good (Worling, 2004) and it correlates with the YLS/CMI and the Psychopathy Checklist: Youth Version (Viljoen et al., 2009).

There have been few studies conducted with the ERASOR and as a result, there is little, but growing, evidence to support its predictive validity. A preliminary examination of the predictive validity showed that the total score may assist in discriminating between adolescents who continued committing sex offenses after being detected and sanctioned from those who desisted after detection and sanction (Worling, 2004). A more recent study found that ERASOR total scores were unrelated to sexual recidivism but moderate support was found for the use of structured clinical judgments of risk level (low, moderate, or high) formed on the basis of ERASOR ratings (Viljoen et al., 2009).

Furthermore, the authors of this study indicated that of the instruments examined in their protocol (ie PCL:YV, ERASOR, YLS/CMI, and Static-99) the ERASOR showed the most promise in predicting adolescent sexual reoffending. Moreover, as noted above, a recent study revealed strong predictive validity of the ERASOR total score and three risk domains (Historical Sexual Assaults, Psychosocial Functioning, and Family/Environmental Functioning) in predicting sexual recidivism in a sample of sex-only, but not sex-plus, offenders (Rajlic and Gretton, 2010). In addition, the ERASOR total score predicted non-sexual recidivism in the sex-only offenders and both the Psychosocial Functioning and Treatment domains predicted non-sexual recidivism in the sex-plus offenders.

Similar to the J-SOAP-II, cautionary notes and appropriate uses of the ERASOR are provided in the manual, a few of which are highlighted here. First, assessment of multiple domains of functioning, using a multi-method and multi-informant approach, is recommended as part of a comprehensive assessment that includes the ERASOR. Second, the ERASOR is described as an instrument that relies on empirically guided clinical judgment in formulating risk estimates. As with the J-SOAP-II, there are no empirically established cut-offs for assigning risk levels. Clinical judgment, taking into account the number and combination of risk factors, is used to formulate a risk estimate of low, moderate, or high. Third, the manual highlights that the results of an assessment will become obsolete over time and/or with a change in any of the assessed risk factors. Assessment results are valid for one year at the most and should not be used to address questions related to longer-term risk (Worling, 2004).

Recommendations

The consequences of risk estimates for juvenile sex offenders can be severe and long lasting. The lack of an empirically validated system often leaves evaluators with the task of answering questions, making predictions, and providing recommendations that are nearly impossible to back up with definitive data. This is problematic for the assessor, the youth, and the community. The following recommendations are therefore provided for the conceptualisation, assessment, and communication of risk with juvenile sex offenders.

First, clinical judgment alone should not be used to estimate risk (Vitacco et al., 2009) but at the same time, evaluators should be aware of and communicate the limitations of the available empirical data. Second, evaluators should be knowledgeable about base rates of recidivism and the factors relevant to recidivism risk. Assumptions about base rates and risk factors are often in contrast to empirical data and it is the responsibility of the evaluator to possess this knowledge and communicate it clearly. Third, risk of both sexual and non-sexual recidivism should be considered, and formally assessed when clinically indicated. Though the consequences of sexual recidivism are serious, so are those of non-sexual recidivism, which is far more common. It is the responsibility of evaluators and treatment providers to take this into account and use it when making recommendations for case management or treatment services. Fourth, both static historical risk factors as well as dynamic factors suitable for intervention should be assessed. Fifth, evaluators should be intimately familiar with the coding rules and scoring procedures for instruments included in their assessments; however, evaluators should also never score an instrument without referring to the scoring manual, regardless of their level of familiarity with the instrument. Ideally, evaluators should practice scoring the measure and establish inter-rater reliability with seasoned evaluators prior to using a risk assessment measure independently. Sample coding exercises for the ERASOR are available from the author to assist evaluators in familiarising themselves with the instrument and scoring procedures (Worling, 2006). Sixth, evaluators should know the strengths and limitations of various risk assessment instruments and stay within the scope of the measure's abilities. Seventh, assessments should be conducted within a developmental context and as a result, be limited to short-term predictions. A variety of physical, psychosocial, and cognitive changes occur during adolescence (Worling and Langström, 2006) and two of the most significant predictors of recidivism to date, sexual deviance and antisociality, show significant instability between adolescence and adulthood. Furthermore, most recidivism research has been conducted with relatively short follow-up periods. For these reasons, estimates of risk should be short-term and re-evaluation of risk should occur at least yearly. Finally,

evaluators should clearly specify the presence and absence of both risk and protective factors (Worling and Langström, 2006) that contribute to a risk estimate. The combination of these factors should be used to generate an overall picture of a youth's level of risk. Specific and individualised recommendations should then follow from the findings.

References

Awad, G. and Saunders, E. (1991) Male Adolescent Sexual Assaulters: Clinical Observations. *Journal of Interpersonal Violence*, 6, 446–60.

Borduin, C.M. and Schaeffer, C.M. (2002) Multisystemic Treatment of Juvenile Sexual Offenders: A Progress Report. *Journal of Psychology and Human Sexuality*, 13, 25–42.

Butler, S. and Seto, M. (2002) Distinguishing Two Types of Adolescent Sex Offenders. *Journal of the American Academy of Child and Adolescent Psychiatry*, 41, 83–90.

Butz, C. and Spaccarelli, S. (1999) Use of Physical Force as an Offense Characteristic in Subtyping Juvenile Sexual Offenders. *Sexual Abuse: Journal of Research and Treatment*, 11, 217–32.

Caldwell, M.F. (2002) What We Do Not Know About Juvenile Sexual Reoffense Risk. *Child Maltreatment*, 7, 291–302.

Caldwell, M.F. (2010) Study Characteristics and Recidivism Base Rates in Juvenile Sex Offender Recidivism. *International Journal of Offender Therapy and Comparative Criminology*, 54, 197–212.

Campbell, M.A., French, S. and Gendreau, P. (2009) The Prediction of Violence in Adult Offenders: A Meta-Analytic Comparison of Instruments and Methods of Assessment. *Criminal Justice and Behavior*, 36, 567–90.

Clift, R.J., Rajlic, G. and Gretton, H.M. (2009) Discriminative and Predictive Validity of the Penile Plethysmograph in Adolescent Sex Offenders. *Sexual Abuse: A Journal of Research and Treatment*, 21, 335–62.

Cottle, C.C., Lee, R.J. and Heilbrun, K. (2001) The Prediction of Criminal Recidivism in Juveniles. A Meta-Analysis. *Criminal Justice and Behavior*, 28, 367–94.

Dawes, R.M., Faust, D. and Meehl, P.E. (1989) Clinical Versus Actuarial Judgment. *Science*, 243, 1668–74.

Dicataldo, F. (2009) *The Perversion of Youth: Controversies in The Assessment and Treatment of*

Juvenile Sex Offenders. New York, NY: New York University Press.

Eastman, B.J. (2004) Assessing The Efficacy of Treatment for Adolescent Sex Offenders: A Cross-Over Longitudinal Study. *The Prison Journal*, 84, 472–85.

Fehrenbach, P. et al. (1986) Adolescent Sexual Offenders: Offender and Offense Characteristics. *American Journal of Orthopsychiatry*, 56, 225–33.

Ford, M. and Linney, J. (1995) Comparative Analysis of Juvenile Sexual Offenders, Violent Nonsexual Offenders, and Status Offenders. *Journal of Interpersonal Violence*, 10, 56–70.

Gretton, H. et al. (2001) Psychopathy and Recidivism in Adolescent Sex Offenders. *Criminal Justice and Behavior. Special Issue: Psychopathy and Risk Assessment*, 28, 427–49.

Gretton, H.M. et al. (2005) The Relationship Between Psychopathy, Treatment Completion, and Criminal Outcome Over Ten Years: A Study of Adolescent Sexual Offenders. in Calder, M.C. (ed.) *Children and Young People Who Sexually Abuse: New Theory, Research, and Practice Developments*. Lyme Regis: Russell House Publishing.

Hagan, M. and Cho, M. (1996) A Comparison of Treatment Outcomes Between Adolescent Rapists and Child Sexual Offenders. *International Journal of Offender Therapy and Comparative Criminology*, 40, 113–22.

Hanson, R.K. (2000) *Risk Assessment*. Beaverton, OR: Association for the Treatment of Sexual Abusers.

Hanson, R.K. et al. (2009) The Principles of Effective Correctional Treatment Also Apply to Sexual Offenders. A Meta-Analysis. *Criminal Justice and Behavior*, 36, 865–91.

Hanson, R.K. and Bussière, M. (1998) Predicting Relapse: A Meta-Analysis of Sexual Offender Recidivism Studies. *Journal of Consulting and Clinical Psychology*, 66, 348–62.

Hanson, R.K. and Morton-Bourgon, K.E. (2005) The Characteristics of Persistent Sexual Offenders: A Meta-Analysis of Recidivism Studies. *Journal of Consulting and Clinical Psychology*, 73, 1154–63.

Hanson, R.K. and Morton-Bourgon, K.E. (2009) The Accuracy of Recidivism Risk Assessments for Sexual Offenders: A Meta-Analysis of 118 Prediction Studies. *Psychological Assessment*, 21, 1–21.

Hanson, R.K. and Thornton, D. (1999) *Static 99: Improving Actuarial Risk Assessment for Sex Offenders*. Ottawa: Corrections Research, Department of the Solicitor General of Canada.

Heilbrun, K., Lee, R. and Cottle, C. (2005) Risk Factors and Intervention Outcomes: Meta-Analyses of Juvenile Offending. in Heilbrun, K., Goldstein, N.E. and Redding, R. (eds.) *Juvenile Delinquency: Prevention, Assessment and Intervention*. Oxford: Oxford University Press.

Hoge, R., Andrews, D.A. and Lescheid, A. (2002) *Youth Level of Service/Case Management Inventory: YLS/CMI Manual*. Toronto: Multi-Health Systems.

Holsinger, A.M., Lowenkamp, C.T. and Latessa, E.J. (2006) Predicting Institutional Misconduct Using The Youth Level of Service/Case Management Inventory. *American Journal of Criminal Justice*, 30, 267–84.

Hunter, J.A., Goodwin, D.W. and Becker, J.V. (1994) The Relationship Between Phallometrically Measured Deviant Sexual Arousal and Clinical Characteristics in Juvenile Sexual Offenders. *Behaviour Research and Therapy*, 32, 533–8.

Hunter, J. et al. (2003) Juvenile Sex Offenders: Toward The Development of A Typology. *Sexual Abuse: A Journal of Research and Treatment*, 15, 27–48.

Kahn, T. and Chambers, H. (1991) Assessing Reoffense Risk With Juvenile Sexual Offenders. *Child Welfare*, 70, 333–45.

Kalmus, E. and Beech, A.R. (2005) Forensic Assessment of Sexual Interest: A Review. *Aggression and Violent Behavior*, 10, 193–217.

Kemper, T.S. and Kistner, J.A. (2007) Offense History and Recidivism in Three Victim-Age-Based Groups of Juvenile Sex Offenders. *Sexual Abuse: A Journal of Research and Treatment*, 19, 409–24.

Kemper, T.S. and Kistner, J.A. (2010) An Evaluation of Classification Criteria for Juvenile Sex Offenders. *Sexual Abuse: A Journal of Research and Treatment*, 22, 172–90.

Kemper, T.S., Oneal, B.J. and Drew, C. (2009, October) *Psychometric Properties of The TPI-ASA in A Sample of Adjudicated Adolescents*. Poster Presented at The Annual Research and Treatment Conference of The Association for the Treatment of Sexual Abusers, Dallas, TX.

Kenny, D.T., Keogh, T. and Seidler, K. (2001) Predictors of Recidivism in Australian Juvenile Sex Offenders: Implications for Treatment. *Sexual Abuse: A Journal of Research and Treatment*, 13, 131–48.

Langton, C.M. et al. (2007) Actuarial Assessment of Risk for Reoffense Among Adult Sex Offenders: Evaluating the Predictive Accuracy of the Static-2002 and Five Other Instruments. *Criminal Justice and Behavior*, 34, 37–59.

Letourneau, E.J. and Miner, M.H. (2005) Juvenile Sex Offenders: A Case Against the Legal and Clinical Status Quo. *Sexual Abuse: A Journal of Research and Treatment*, 17, 293–312.

Loeber, R. and Dishion, T. (1983) Early Predictors of Male Delinquency: A Review. *Psychological Bulletin*, 94, 68–99.

Looman, J. and Abracen, J. (2010) Comparison of Measures of Risk for Recidivism in Sexual Offenders. *Journal of Interpersonal Violence*, 25, 791–807.

Lussier, P. (2005) The Criminal Activity of Sexual Offenders in Adulthood: Revisiting the Specialization Debate. *Sexual Abuse A Journal of Research and Treatment*, 17, 269–92.

Lussier, P., Lablanc, M. and Proulx, J. (2005) The Generality of Criminal Behavior: A Confirmatory Factor Analysis of the Criminal Activity of Sex Offenders in Adulthood. *Journal of Criminal Justice*, 33, 177–89.

Mann, R.E., Hanson, R.K. and Thornton, D. (2010) Assessing Risk for Sexual Recidivism: Some Proposals on the Nature of Psychologically Meaningful Variables. *Sexual Abuse: A Journal of Research and Treatment*, 22, 191–217.

Marczyk, G.R. et al. (2003) Predicting Juvenile Recidivism With the PCL:YV, MAYSI, and YLS/CMI. *The International Journal of Forensic Mental Health*, 2, 7–18.

McCann, K. and Lussier, P. (2008) Antisociality, Sexual Deviance, and Sexual Reoffending in Juvenile Sex Offenders. A Meta-Analytic Investigation. *Youth Violence and Juvenile Justice*, 6, 363–85.

McCoy, W.K. (2007) *Predicting Treatment Outcome and Recidivism Among Juvenile Sex Offenders: The Utility of the J-SOAP-II and ERASOR in an Outpatient Treatment Program* (unpublished doctoral dissertation) Sam Houston State University, Huntsville, TX.

McGrath, R.J., Cumming, G.F. and Burchard, B.L. (2003) *Current Practices and Trends in Sexual Abuser Management: The Safer Society 2002 Nationwide Survey.* Brandon, VT: Safer Society Press.

Meehl, P. (1954) *Clinical Versus Statistical Prediction: A Theoretical Analysis and A Review of The Evidence.* Minneapolis, MN: University of Minnesota Press.

Meehl, P. and Rosen, A. (1955) Antecedent Probability and The Efficiency of Psychometric Signs, Patterns, and Cutting Scores. *Psychological Bulletin*, 52, 194–216.

Nisbet, I., Wilson, P.H. and Smallbone, S.W. (2004) A Prospective Longitudinal Study of Sexual Recidivism Among Adolescent Sex Offenders. *Sexual Abuse: Journal of Research and Treatment*, 16, 223–34.

Oneal, B.J. et al. (2008) Initial Psychometric Properties of a Treatment Planning and Progress Inventory for Adolescents Who Sexually Abuse. *Sexual Abuse: A Journal of Research and Treatment*, 20, 161–87.

Parks, G.A. and Bard, D.E. (2006) Risk Factors for Adolescent Sex Offender Recidivism: Evaluation of Predictive Factors and Comparison of Three Groups Based Upon Victim Type. *Sexual Abuse: A Journal of Research and Treatment*, 18, 319–42.

Prentky, R.A. et al. (2009) Predicting Risk of Sexual Recidivism in Juveniles: Predictive Validity of The J-SOAP-II. in Beech, A.R. Craig, L.A. and Brown, K.D. (eds.) *Assessment and Treatment of Sex Offenders: A Handbook.* New York, NY: John Wiley.

Prentky, R. and Righthand, S. (2003) *Juvenile Sex Offender Assessment Protocol-II (JSOAP-II) Manual.* Retrieved August 27, 2010 From http://www.ncjrs.gov/pdffiles1/ojjdp/202316.pdf

Prescott, D.S. (2004) Emerging Strategies for Risk Assessment of Sexually Abusive Youth: Theory, Controversy, and Practice. *Journal of Child Sexual Abuse: Research, Treatment, and Program Innovations for Victims, Survivors, and Offenders*, 13, 83–105.

Quinsey, V.L. et al. (1998) *Violent Offenders: Managing and Appraising Risk.* Washington DC: American Psychological Association.

Rajlic, G. and Gretton, H.M. (2010) An Examination of Two Sexual Recidivism Risk Measures in Adolescent Offenders: The Moderating Effect of Offender Type. *Criminal Justice and Behavior*, 37, 1066–85.

Reitzel, L.R. and Carbonell, J.L. (2006) The Effectiveness of Sex Offender Treatment for Juveniles as Measured by Recidivism: A Meta-Analysis. *Sexual Abuse: A Journal of Research and Treatment*, 18, 401–21.

Righthand, S. et al. (2005) Factor Structure and Validation of the Juvenile Sex Offender Assessment Protocol (J-SOAP) *Sexual Abuse: Journal of Research and Treatment*, 17, 13–30.

Ryan, G. et al. (1996) Trends in a National Sample of Sexually Abusive Youths. *Journal of The*

American Academy of Child and Adolescent
Psychiatry, 35, 17–25.

Richardson, G., Bhate, S. and Graham, F. (1997)
Cognitive-Based Practice With Sexually
Abusive Adolescents. in Hoghughi, M., Bhate,
S. and Graham, F. (eds.) *Working With Sexually
Abusive Adolescents.* Thousand Oaks, CA: Sage.

Schmidt, F., Hoge, R.D. and Gomes, L. (2005)
Reliability and Validity Analyses of the Youth
Level of Service/Case Management Inventory.
Criminal Justice and Behavior, 32, 329–44.

Seto, M.C. and Lalumière, M.L. (2006) Conduct
Problems and Juvenile Sexual Offending. in
Barbaree, H.E. and Marshall, W.L. (eds.) *The
Juvenile Sex Offender.* New York, NY: The
Guilford Press.

Van Wijk, A.P., Mali, S.R.F. and Bullens, R.A.R.
(2007) Juvenile Sex-Only and Sex-Plus
Offenders: an Exploratory Study on Criminal
Profiles. *International Journal of Offender Therapy
and Comparative Criminology,* 51: 4, 407–19.

Vandiver, D.M. (2006) A Prospective Analysis of
Juvenile Male Sex Offenders. Characteristics
and Recidivism Rates as Adults. *Journal of
Interpersonal Violence,* 21, 673–88.

Vieira, T.A., Skilling, T.A. and Peterson-Badali,
M. (2009) Matching Court-Ordered Services
With Treatment Needs. Predicting Treatment
Success With Young Offenders. *Criminal Justice
and Behavior,* 36, 385–401.

Viljoen, J.L. et al. (2008) Assessing Risk for
Violence in Adolescents Who Have Sexually
Offended. A Comparison of the J-SOAP-II, the
J-SORRAT-II, and SAVRY. *Criminal Justice and
Behavior,* 35, 5–23.

Viljoen, J.L. et al. (2009) Assessment of Reoffense
Risk in Adolescents Who Have Committed
Sexual Offenses. Predictive Validity of The
ERASOR, PCL:YV, YLS/CMI, and Static-99.
Criminal Justice and Behavior, 36, 981–1000.

Vitacco, M.J. et al. (2009) Assessing Risk in
Adolescent Sexual Offenders:
Recommendations for Clinical Practice.
Behavioral Sciences and The Law, 27, 929–40.

Waite, D. et al. (2005) Juvenile Sex Offender
Re-Arrest Rates for Sexual, Violent Nonsexual
and Property Crimes: A 10-Year Follow-Up.
Sexual Abuse: Journal of Research and Treatment,
17, 313–31.

Walker, D.F. et al. (2004) Treatment Effectiveness
for Male Adolescent Sexual Offenders: A
Meta-Analysis and Review. *Journal of Child
Sexual Abuse,* 13, 281–93.

Waller, N.G. et al. (eds.) (2006) *A Paul Meehl
Reader. Essays on The Practice of Scientific
Psychology.* Mahwah, NJ: Lawrence Erlbaum
Associates.

Worling, J. (1995) Sexual Abuse Histories of
Adolescent Male Sex Offenders: Differences on
the Basis of the Age and Gender of their
Victims. *Journal of Abnormal Psychology,* 104,
610–13.

Worling, J. (2001) Personality-Based Typology of
Adolescent Male Sexual Offenders: Differences
in Recidivism Rates, Victim-Selection
Characteristics, and Personal Victimization
Histories. *Sexual Abuse: Journal of Research and
Treatment,* 13, 149–66.

Worling, J.R. (2004) The Estimate of Risk of
Adolescent Sexual Offense Recidivism
(ERASOR): Preliminary Psychometric Data.
*Sexual Abuse: A Journal of Research and
Treatment,* 16, 235–54.

Worling, J.R. (2006) Coding Examples for the
ERASOR (Estimate of Risk of Adolescent
Sexual Offense Recidivism, Version 2.0)
Thistletown Regional Centre, Ontario Ministry
of Children and Youth Services.

Worling, J. and Curwen, T. (2000) Adolescent
Sexual Offender Recidivism: Success of
Specialized Treatment and Implications for
Risk Prediction. *Child Abuse and Neglect,* 24,
965–82.

Worling, J.R. and Curwen, T. (2001) *The ERASOR:
Estimate of Risk of Adolescent Sexual Recidivism*
(Version 2.0) Toronto, ON: Safe-T Program,
Thistletown Regional Centre.

Worling, J.R. and Langström, N. (2006)
Assessment of Criminal Recidivism Risk With
Adolescents Who Have Offended Sexually: A
Review. *Trauma, Violence, and Abuse,* 4, 341–62.

Worling, J.R., Littlejohn, A. and Bookalam, D.
(2010) 20-Year Prospective Follow-Up Study of
Specialized Treatment for Adolescents Who
Offended Sexually. *Behavioral Sciences and The
Law,* 28, 46–57.

CHAPTER 2

Evidence for Working Holistically With Young People who Have Sexually Harmed

Sharon Hall

Introduction

This chapter draws heavily from doctoral research exploring the implications and benefits of holistic working with young people who have sexually harmed others. The first aim of the study was to identify broadly accepted meanings of working holistically with young people who have sexually harmed. Further investigation explored the associated benefits, challenges and implications for holistic working in practice with these young people. Evidence for the research was drawn from a wide literature base as well as original survey responses, interviews and observation in a Youth Offending Team in the Midlands, UK. A number of issues relating to Evidence-Based Practice were prominent throughout the study and these will be highlighted throughout the chapter. This work was supported by the Economic and Social Research Council [grant number 2006-00236].

The chapter will begin with a brief location of the topic within the literature, judging that the more specialist audience will be aware of major developments within the field of working with young people who have sexually harmed. The idea of working holistically will be introduced, with a range of theoretical bases arranged in the author's original holistic spectrum. The choices of methods for the research will be described, followed by a summary of the findings from the study. Four main themes will be presented, namely: seeing the whole young person; working with wider family and peers; working in a multi-agency way; and using a range of creative methods. Benefits, challenges and implications from each of these areas will also be discussed, leading into recommendations for practice and policymakers. Some suggestions for further research will be followed by a conclusion summarising the work so far completed.

Context and literature base

Complexity across disciplines

Early responses to young people who have sexually harmed need to be extrapolated from the history of youth offending (eg Children Bill, 1908: Home Office, 1968), historical recognition of child abuse (eg Corby, 2006; Butler-Sloss, 1988) and the treatment of adult sex offenders (eg McAlinden, 2007; Finkelhor, 1986). More recent scholarship regarding young people who have sexually harmed includes responses from the youth justice field, from social work research and from child and adolescent mental health workers and this reflects the cross-disciplinary nature of the professionals who may be involved with these young people. The lack of clear guidance from the Government over who has responsibility for these young people and their entitlement to specialist services or mental health services has led to a range of service provision.

In England and Wales, Youth Offending Teams hold responsibility for young people who have been convicted of sexual offences, and may have some involvement with others who are not convicted but are assessed by early intervention panels or receive preventative work. Children's Services (social work teams) are likely to be involved with young people who have sexually harmed but not been charged or convicted, but their involvement may be brief and may focus on protecting a victim rather than working with the young person. Some young people who have sexually harmed may be referred by professionals to specialist services or mental health services, particularly in areas where few cases occur or when a case is considered to be particularly concerning. Geographical variations may lead a young person to receive a therapeutic service, a criminal justice sentence, social work support, a mixture of these or none of the above (Long, citing Hackett, 2010).

Need for clarity on buzzword 'holistic'

The word 'holistic' is used within all of these different professional contexts as part of how staff should work with young people who have sexually harmed (Hackett et al., 2003; DoH/Home Office, 2006; Bannister, 1998; Longo, 2002; Morrison and Henniker, 2006; Corby, 2006; Smith, 2007). The importance of working holistically with young people who have sexually harmed was agreed by managers involved in Hackett et al.'s (2003) Delphi study. The statement:

> *The approach to these children and young people should be based on a developmental and holistic philosophy of intervention that addresses nonsexual needs as well as specific sexual risks.*
>
> Hackett et al., 2003: 28

received 97 per cent agreement and a median response of 10, indicating the strongest possible agreement. The need to work holistically was highlighted alongside abuse-specific and multi-modal work within the Department of Health and Home Office guidance regarding effective treatment with young people who have sexually harmed (DoH/Home Office, 2006). Elaboration of the term holistic here was limited to a brief statement about promoting 'the physical, sexual, social and emotional well-being' (ibid., 45) of the young people while the multi-modal heading was used to include work with the young person's carers. However, many references to holistic from the literature include family work as well as the use of different methods of working. This supported the case for a more robust definition of holistic work before the benefits, challenges and implications could be explored.

Different models from literature

Early mentions of holistic responses to young people who have sexually harmed are included in a chapter by Hackett et al. (1998) as well as being used by Ryan (1997) to describe the wider developmental and contextual realities of treatment advocated by the US National Task Force on Juvenile Sexual Offending (1993). The first outright presenter of an holistic approach to treating young people who have sexually harmed was Longo (2001, 2002) who developed his work with adults and adaptation of the relapse prevention model to include work looking at mind, body, spirit and the emotional self (see Lakota Medicine Wheel: Warne, 2005) and addressing four universal needs of belonging, generosity, mastery and independence (Brendtro et al., 1990).

Longo's (2002, 2004) model emphasises how holistic treatment focuses on wellness and healing the whole person. It integrates different models and theories into the process of treatment including knowledge of young people's learning styles, understanding feelings and the importance of a healthy therapeutic relationship. Longo also advocates the use of experiential therapies delivered by trained and experienced clinicians including 'role plays, drama therapy, art therapy, music therapy, and exercises used to build trust and explore family issues' (Longo, 2002, 228). The importance of including family work is also acknowledged, as is the addressing of a young person's victim experiences; however, the main emphasis is on seeing the individual young person as a whole.

Summarising the difficulties with traditional approaches, Collie et al. (2007: 53) state concern that 'risk management rehabilitation fails to provide an holistic theory of sexual offending that is sensitive to the developmental and contextual needs of young people'.

They present the Good Lives Model as an alternative theory of rehabilitation, being a strengths-based model. Central to the model is the notion that all human beings act to meet inherent human needs or 'primary human goods'. While the ten main needs areas are different to the four areas identified by Longo there is some overlap, and the overall impression of focusing on positive attributes and goals for the individual as a whole is similar. Again, ways of incorporating and augmenting other relapse prevention and self-regulation models are presented, but within a 'meaningful and holistic way of making sense of past offending and a future *good life* without offending' (Collie et al., 2007: 58). The balance of risks and goods is argued to be vital to meet the psychological needs of the young people.

The word 'holistic' here describes the integration of theories, and is also used to describe a thorough, wider understanding of human behaviour as well as an overall theoretical approach. Some mention is made of the adolescents' ecological contexts, but in contrast to other models which will be presented, the focus is again very much on the whole individual young person.

Another way of seeing the fuller context of the young person is using the dual approach proposed by Bannister (1998) where she describes therapy addressing both the child's harmful sexual behaviour and own victim experiences, instead of using two therapists which might reinforce the 'splitting' in their own behaviour. The other dual aspect of the approach is identified in the deep involvement of the child's carer who helps the child in stopping the 'steps to abuse' and may jointly work with the therapist in providing sex education and building the child's self-esteem. Bannister also mentions the effective use of creative techniques including art work, physical and vocal expression and story-making.

In the same volume, Hackett et al. (1998) define an holistic framework for sibling abuse work which brings together three strands of healing the victim, healing the 'young abuser' and healing the family. The primary importance of work with the victim is placed centrally, and this is offered by a separate but connected worker to the therapist working with the young person who has sexually harmed. Hackett et al. suggest that work with the family has been over time perhaps 'the weakest part of practice in the field' (1998: 169) and discuss the challenges in addressing concepts of acknowledgement, responsibility and accountability within the family as well as questions regarding reconciliation. Bentovim (1991) also briefly mentions young people as perpetrators within a family system of sexual abuse, expanded in Bentovim (1998) where he proposes a 'Family systemic approach to work with young sex offenders' (Bentovim, 1998: 119).

An even greater focus on the family context is seen in Multi-Systemic Therapy (MST), which is outlined for use with young people who have sexually harmed by Letourneau and Swenson (2005). While not explicitly using the word holistic, the ecological framework in which they present the young person as embedded can be seen as another approach with an holistic emphasis, seeing the whole context. Ecological approaches including MST have roots in theories from Bronfenbrenner (1977) where a young person is considered within nested systems which can be presented as widening concentric circles ranging from family to the macro society. In MST, the main treatment modality is intensive home-based therapist support to a young person's caregivers to deliver structured exercises targeting agreed goals, and the emphasis is on

building strengths and protective factors within the systems where a young person is living. This contrasts with approaches which require the removal of a young person to an external placement where they are treated with other young people which is argued to be iatrogenic, that is, actually increasing negative behaviour.

In contrast to Longo's (2002) model, Multi-Systemic Therapy does not prioritise the therapeutic relationship between the therapist/worker and the young person:

> *the MST model assumes that the relationship between therapist and child is neither necessary nor sufficient to obtain favourable clinical outcomes. Although therapists should have a good working relationship with the child, the primary relationship for the therapist is with the caregiver(s) who is the manager of the child's ecology and exerts the greatest amount of influence.*
> Letourneau and Swenson, 2005: 256

Another key difference between Multi-Systemic Therapy and the holistic models described so far is the insistence on the use of interventions that have empirical support 'such as the cognitive-behavioural therapies, behaviour therapies, pragmatic family therapies, and certain pharmacological interventions (eg for attention deficit, hyperactivity disorder)' (ibid., 260). The authors are keen to demonstrate the effectiveness of MST as a treatment in randomised controlled trials and this rigorous testing requires strong treatment fidelity and quality assurance.

Looking at a young person's wider family and environment are two of the domains of the AIM model, another approach which is described as holistic. While AIM stands for Assessment, Intervention and Moving On, an early priority of the project was the development of initial and comprehensive assessment tools (Morrison and Henniker, 2006). The assessment tools require information gathering across four domains: the developmental, family/carers and environment, deliberately following the *Framework for the Assessment of Children in Need and their Families* (DoH, 2000) and an additional domain of 'Offence Specific'. Evidence is gathered to demonstrate concerns and strengths in each of these domains, using criteria of available research-informed indicators of risk and others based on a consensus of clinical judgement.

Another key emphasis from the AIM model is the importance of interagency and multi-agency procedures, partnership, involvement and training, within an overall holistic philosophy:

The strong holistic philosophy underpinning the AIM approach, for example, the use of the terms 'strengths and concerns' as core constructs, was also powerful in gaining practitioner support and enthusiasm. It seemed that for some practitioners this represented a rekindling of lost or submerged professional ideals.

Morrison and Henniker, 2006: 47

This over-arching holistic philosophy is similar to that in the Good Lives model above, with an emphasis on strengths which is common to the AIM approach, the Good Lives model and Multi-Systemic Therapy. The benefits of framing goals positively and utilising and building up pre-existing strengths, protective factors and resilience are key to a number of strengths-based approaches which have become popular in social work (Saleebey, 1996; Powell et al., 1997) and have also had some influence in youth justice (Clark, 1996; Corcoran, 1997). Some of these cite roots in Solution Focused therapy (de Shazer, 1988) but the breadth of 'strength-based' approaches well outstrips this possible beginning. However, none of these models focus on strengths to the extent of excluding concerns, needs or risks, but instead seek balance within an holistic context.

A further model for consideration of holistic work with young people who have sexually harmed is proposed by Durham (2006). His framework considers the widest social context of any, moving from the individual through the family out to a political and social context and including organisational principles such as gender and sexuality as well as emphasising power relationships and language. Durham seeks to offer an holistic view of 'why we have sexual abuse in our society and why it is mainly committed by males' (Durham, 2006: 22) as well as going on to propose a 'holistic and flexible practice intervention schedule' (ibid.).

These different holistic models can be represented as segments of an holistic spectrum (Figure 2.1), with the main axis from left to right varying with whether the focus of the work is on all aspects of an individual or a wider emphasis on society. For clarity the extremes at each end of the spectrum are also pictured but these do not fall within the holistic spectrum. An earlier version of this diagram was included in the researcher's Master's research (Hall, 2007).

Both ends of this holistic spectrum can be seen in a definition from Rich:

Treating the whole child means treating different aspects of the pathology presented by the juvenile in treatment, but it also means recognising the array of forces at play in the lives of each individual child or adolescent.

Rich, 2003: 449

His chapter on 'Treating the Whole Child in a Whole-Minded Manner' seeks to incorporate approaches from public health, criminology, mental health, personal competency, social environment and social psychology. Another broader approach to working holistically with young people who have sexually harmed can be seen in the article by Bentovim (1998) where he describes 'systemic' work. Bentovim's definition of systems-thinking includes three different issues:

- a philosophy of observation which includes the context as well as the object of concern
- an approach to treating problems in context which includes families and those concerned with them
- a number of methods of treatment

Bentovim, 1998: 120

These issues from a family therapy perspective include seeing the whole context of the individual (the left hand of the spectrum) as well as including families and other professionals (the right hand side of the spectrum). Bentovim also mentions a range of treatment methods which have been emphasised within different theories across the spectrum. Morrison's (2006) 'tentative definition' of holistic work also includes the totality of needs alongside the partnership with others:

A holistic approach seeks to understand and address the YP/child's sexually problematic behaviour within the totality of his/her context and needs, by working in partnership with the young person/child and his/her significant others including family, school, and social support network to promote the healthy and sustained development of the young person/child.

Morrison, 2006: 358

Fitting in to wellness, whole assessment, preventative agendas

In addition to theories from the field of tackling sexual harm, holistic working can also be seen to be located within wider movements key to social work, health, education and youth justice. The Department of Health *Framework for Assessment* (DoH, 2000) outlines how a thorough view of the young person within their family and community context should inform assessment and was issued jointly with the Department for Education and

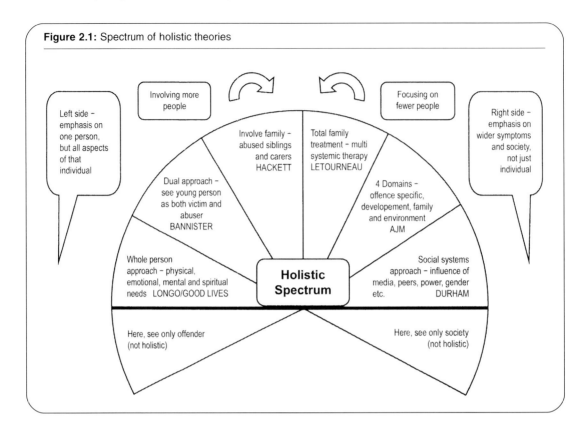

Figure 2.1: Spectrum of holistic theories

Employment and the Home Office. Wellness models in health have been linked to diverse cultural ideas of whole person care and healing (Weaver, 2002; Leung et al., 2009). A focus on wellness or well-being and the importance of preventative measures for children and families is promoted by Prilleltensky and Nelson (2000) and this can be seen to be rising in emphasis within UK Government policy in particular the *Healthy Children, Safer Communities* (DoH et al., 2009) document. After stressing the importance of preventing offending by early intervention and improved mainstream services this document also advocates the use of holistic assessments and utilising family and community links. Similar mentions of well-being, prevention and early intervention also feature prominently in the *Healthy Lives, Brighter Futures* (DoH/DCSF, 2009) document.

Challenges within what is evidenced, funded, known

These and other key Government documents also place a strong emphasis on evidence and

evidence-based practice. The dominance of evidence-based practice within medicine is undeniable and appropriate in considering measurable effects of drugs and standardised treatments. However, the superiority of evidence-based methods in social fields including psychology, social work and youth justice is more open for debate (Webb, 2001; Wilcox, 2003). No programme or treatment method can be reproduced as precisely as a particular dose of a particular drug, and human factors such as relationships, sensitivity and engagement will all influence the effectiveness of any intervention. Standardised Sex Offender Treatment Programmes (SOTPs) have become typical within adult treatment; however, the use of randomised controlled trials to demonstrate effectiveness with adult sex offenders has recently been called into question by Marshall and Marshall (2007). Moreover, the individual needs of developing children and adolescents have been stressed in arguing against treating young people as mini-adult sex offenders (Hackett et al., 2003).

The relative infrequency of reoffending by young people who have sexually harmed makes it difficult to demonstrate conclusively the effectiveness of any treatment programme. This is compounded by the fact that additional measures regarding observation and controls on behaviour are alternative likely causes of behaviour change. Additionally the ethical arguments against leaving any group without treatment to be a 'control group' prohibit any randomised controlled trials with these young people. This has led to a paucity of evidence regarding 'what works' with young people who have sexually harmed, and the lack of any validated actuarial instrument for assessing risk of sexual harm by juveniles (Parks, 2007). Further trials into Multi-Systemic Therapy and other treatment methods and assessment tools should not be ignored, but the question of how conclusive any such evidence can be remains. Instead a broader approach to evidence seems advisable, sharing good and effective practice and seeking a range of positive outcomes for young people. This can be considered more in line with social work and education aims than a simple 'avoid reoffending' aim, although similar objectives should lead to reduced offending as well as addressing needs and promoting strengths. The need for measurable outcomes may be pushed by funding bodies and management but such outcomes should reflect a range of progress in areas like family relationships, emotional coping and social skills as well as a lack of further incidents of sexual harm. The priority for this research was to understand practice now and how this could be improved rather than a trial of a particular holistic method, recognising the diversity of holistic practice.

Rationale for methods chosen

The aims of understanding meanings of holistic working and identifying benefits and implications in practice indicated the need for subjectivist research with an element of practice observation. Positivistic methods such as experiments or closed question surveys are not expected to reveal nuances of meaning to individuals but instead focus on facts and measuring. Interviews and observation allow a much more thorough review of opinions and actions in relation to topics, but risk being seen as very specific to one location or subject team. A mixed methodology was chosen to combine the benefits of semi-structured interviews and observation with an initial broader open question

survey. This strategy sought to draw meanings and key themes from a wider group of respondents from a range of agencies across the country, in combination with a careful review of the literature. These themes were then explored in more detail within one local team, with interview responses being complemented with observation of practice and meetings.

Data collected included completed surveys, interview transcripts, a field journal, copies of anonymised documents, emails and contact records as well as data-sets of cases of sexual harm and all YOT referrals over the past three years. The main analysis strategy used was Grounded Theory (Glaser and Strauss, 1967) which develops findings grounded in the data through a process of line-by-line analysis, the development of codes and themes and on-going comparison of themes with data by processes of writing memos and further data collection. Themes found from the survey were discussed during the interviews and used to lead discussion around associated benefits, challenges and implications of the work. Theoretical saturation was achieved for the meanings of holistic work; however, the findings relating to the challenges and implications of holistic work could be seen as more tentative. Within a longer research period these further findings could have been scrutinised and developed with more input from other professionals.

Findings – what is holistic, four key themes but an integrated whole

Development of main themes

The initial development of main themes was drawn from the results of the survey which presented a number of statements regarding holistic working for agreement or disagreement by respondents. The three statements identified as most important were that:

- Working holistically means having a broad perspective – seeing the whole young person.
- Working holistically means working with the young person's family as well as with the individual.
- Working holistically means having a multi-agency partnership approach rather than one agency.

Other statements which received strong agreement emphasised good communication, stressed the need for addressing wider system issues and preventative work as well as the importance of addressing the young person's victim experiences. The themes were also compared to open responses to questions about holistic work which led to the fourth separate main theme summarised by the statement:

• Working holistically means using creative and alternative treatment techniques.

One respondent disagreed with this statement, while four respondents were ambivalent. Further opinions on this subject were found in a wide range of responses to the statement:

• Working holistically means using only evidence-based methods.

Around half the respondents disagreed or strongly disagreed with this statement, while other respondents were ambivalent (around a fifth), agreed (around a quarter) or strongly agreed (two respondents). Later findings suggested that some of this divergence of opinions may have been due to different understanding of the term 'evidence-based methods' as will be described later in this chapter.

These four inter-connected main themes provide a definition of holistic working with young people who have sexually harmed, as shown by the survey responses and supported by the interviews conducted at the Youth Offending Team and with associated professionals. These were seeing the whole young person, working with wider family and peers, working in a multi-agency way and using a range of creative methods. These four themes, with connecting arrows representing the need for communication and connections between the areas are presented in Figure 2.2.

The need for a whole, integrated picture was evident in defining holistic working as well as when assessing the young person and their wider context. Dictionary definitions of holism and holistic stress the whole being greater than the sum of parts, and a contrast with atomism which typically reduces something to a sum of separate, quantifiable components (cf *Asset*, YJB, 2006). Colley (2003) also promotes consideration of an integrated whole in her research into holistic youth mentoring. Throughout the analysis and theory-building a repeated concern was that while separating elements can be useful for diagrams and explanations, putting young people

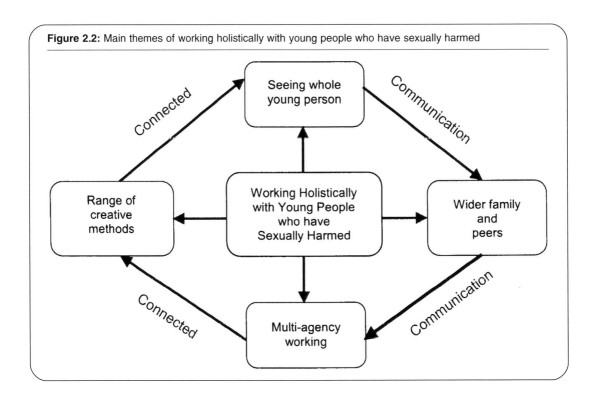

Figure 2.2: Main themes of working holistically with young people who have sexually harmed

and their families or aspects of young people into boxes is generally unhelpful.

Seeing the whole young person

Perhaps the most frequently repeated message from the research was the need to consider the whole young person and not simply their offending or harmful behaviour (see Hackett et al. 2003; Longo, 2002; Creeden, 2005). One experienced YOT worker explained how working holistically means:

> *... treating the individual, basically I hate this label of 'young offender'. I think we work with young people who commit offences, and I think we have to remember that they have a whole range of needs ... it's about looking at the individual as a whole person, not just attaching that label 'offender', but thinking about how they are as pupil, friend, sister, teenager, member of society.*

The importance of recognising the range of needs and strengths present for each individual young person was stressed, both in terms of being respectful of the young human being and in terms of identifying the most necessary areas for help and change. In setting out what was meant by the 'whole young person', a selection of models was compared, including the Good Lives Model (Ward and Stewart, 2003), Human Givens (Griffen and Tyrrell, 1997), the Lakota Medicine Wheel (Warne, 2005), 6 Dimensions of Wellness (Hettler, 1976), the Indivisible Self (Sweeney and Myers, 2003) and the Wheel of Wellness (Witmer et al., 1998). After identifying some similarities the decision was made not to 're-invent the wellness wheel' but rather to adapt a familiar model, creating a diagram based on the seven developmental areas from the *Common Assessment Framework* (CWDC, 2010) incorporating elements from other models and the research findings.

The consideration of the harmful sexual behaviour is seen as a clear part of this picture, but in order to work holistically this needs to be in balance with other areas. Addressing a young person's experiences of being a victim of abuse was also seen as crucial by many staff and this is included under the emotional and social development segment. Different sections will be more significant for individual young people but all should be considered to gain a full picture. The presentation of internal and external factors allowed the inclusion of factors from the other CAF triangle sides, and more research areas. This model does not focus on offending behaviour to the same extent as the AIM model (Morrison and

Henniker, 2006) or *Asset* (YJB, 2006) and will be less useful than these in evaluating future risk of offending. However, it provides an overview of the whole young person who has sexually harmed, their needs and the surrounding context.

The rationale developed for seeing the whole young person included the need to respect the young person's autonomy and individuality as well as seeing the strengths and positives which could be enhanced and used for the future. In addition, a broad view of the young person allowed the range of needs, vulnerabilities and problems to be assessed as well as giving insight towards understanding the roots of the harmful behaviour and ways to reduce future risks. This broad view was seen to increase the effectiveness of the work in helping the young person, protecting potential future victims and improving outcomes while acting within a framework that supports respectful, anti-oppressive practice and includes a focus on strengths and protective factors.

Challenges to seeing the whole young person included a likely reluctance from the young person to share or disclose some of their whole person (see Lambie, 2005) as well as possible attitudes and prejudices from staff who might label the young person and not see their full strengths or potential (see Fyson, 2007). Further challenges come from systems which prioritise offence reduction, public protection and basic compliance and from restrictions to time with young people, resources and access to specialists.

Working with wider family and peers

The theme of working with a young person's family was seen to combine *working with* (to help) the family, addressing the family's needs and *working with* (alongside) the family seeing them as co-workers able to support the young person. One therapist expressed the range of influences from family members, both positive and negative:

> *Winnicott's role of the child, the family and the outside world ... that is central to how I work with children and young people ... They are themselves first, [then] whether they still live with their family or not, they still come from a family and that family has an influence, for good, indifference or ill (my emphasis).*

The theme incorporates the systemic view of a young person being embedded in a family and wider social networks (see Letourneau and Swenson, 2005; Bronfenbrenner, 1977) and follows on from the consideration of family and

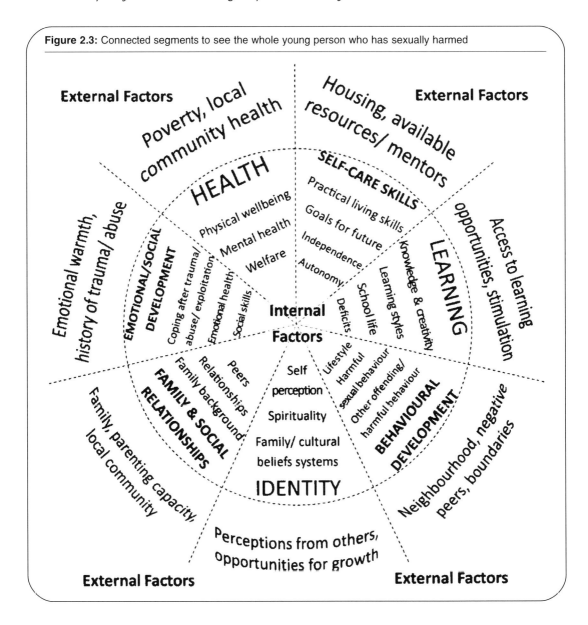

Figure 2.3: Connected segments to see the whole young person who has sexually harmed

social relationships being a segment in seeing the whole young person (Figure 2.3). During analysis five views of family influence were identified, as presented in Figure 2.4.

Again, caution is stressed against the placing of any family in any one box, since most families can be considered in at least three of these areas. Perhaps the areas could better be described as different ways professionals may view families, as they were derived predominantly from interviews with professionals. To give an extreme example, even a family considered dangerous

may contain a non-abusive parent who could act as an expert in directing work with that family, and this would bring both extremes of the diagram into play with the same family.

The idea that parents are likely to be part of the problem and therefore part of the solution was argued by Johnson and Doonan (2005), particularly looking at harmful behaviour by younger children. The role of families being part of the problem and part of the solution for *Children in Trouble* was also emphasised in this more general report (Hayden, 2007).

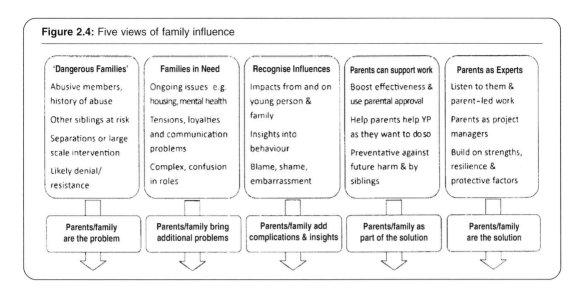

Figure 2.4: Five views of family influence

'Dangerous Families'	Families in Need	Recognise Influences	Parents can support work	Parents as Experts
Abusive members, history of abuse	Ongoing issues e.g. housing, mental health	Impacts from and on young person & family	Boost effectiveness & use parental approval	Listen to them & parent-led work
Other siblings at risk	Tensions, loyalties and communication problems	Insights into behaviour	Help parents help YP as they want to do so	Parents as project managers
Separations or large scale intervention	Complex, confusion in roles	Blame, shame, embarrassment	Preventative against future harm & by siblings	Build on strengths, resilience & protective factors
Likely denial/resistance				

Parents/family are the problem	Parents/family bring additional problems	Parents/family add complications & insights	Parents/family as part of the solution	Parents/family are the solution

The central category, where families and young people are seen to impact each other in ways that can be positive and negative will be the case in virtually all situations, and this was the sub-theme raised most consistently across all interviewees. Either side of this category are sub-themes of Families in Need (see Children's Act, 1989, sec 17) and Families who can Support Work, and these were the next most mentioned within the interviews. The level of need identified from the families or support offered by the families can be seen as moderate, and most families of young people who have sexually harmed will present some needs and some potential to support the young person. The extreme levels of need and support/control are represented by the 'Dangerous Families' (see Dale, 1986) and Parents as Experts categories at each end of the diagram. Around half of those interviewed mentioned serious risks or histories of abuse within families while around a quarter talked about parents being the experts or needing to lead the work.

Similar patterns were found from a young person's peers, considered another key influence contributing potential strengths as well as difficulties. Working holistically necessarily includes consideration of the young person's family, and usually to a lesser extent their peers, in terms of assessing needs, risks and strengths as well as understanding contributing factors and recruiting allies to help a young person.

Working in a multi-agency way

The need for improvement in multi-agency working is a frequent recommendation of serious case reviews, including the *Childhood Lost* (Bridge Child Care Development Service, 2001) report which identified serious shortcomings in what should have been the co-ordinated supervision of a young man, DM, who had sexually harmed and went on to murder a child. The survey, observation and interview study found that contributions from a range of agencies are seen as essential for holistic working with young people who have sexually harmed, both to gain the full picture of the young person's and their family's needs and strengths, and to support the young person and their family. A police officer at the YOT explained:

> I'd say [my] team [work holistically] ... in terms of, resources are shared, the actual geography if you like ... all in a cluster together so they actually talk to each other ... If you're going to work holistically then obviously then communication is essential to that as a process. Collaboration in terms of, it could be resources, it could be in terms of shared best practice.

Good connections and communications between agencies are again seen as vital to an holistic approach, both within a multi-disciplinary YOT team and with external agencies. The range of professionals linked to key segments within the whole young person diagram (Figure 2.3) have different targets and priorities (outlined in *Every Child Matters*, Chief Secretary to the Treasury, 2003) and the need to promote shared values and clarity of roles came through strongly. Findings relating to multi-agency working were found to be linked to three main sub-themes: values, clarity and resources, and these echoed findings from the literature regarding a number of challenges to multi-agency working in child protection (Atkinson et al., 2005; Charles and Stevenson, 1990; Morrison, 1992).

The statutory guidance *Working Together to Safeguard Children* (HM Government, 2006, 2010) sets out how agencies should work in partnership to meet local authorities' obligations to safeguard and promote the welfare of children, including those who have abused others. The guidance includes the need for a multi-agency assessment as well an overall multi-agency approach:

> . . . *including youth justice (where appropriate), children's social care, education (including educational psychology) and health (including child and adolescent mental health) agencies and police.*
>
> HM Government, 2010: 303

Further recommendations include maintaining clear frameworks and consultation between Local Safeguarding Children Boards and YOTs for assessment, decision-making and case-management; separately addressing both the needs of victims and the needs of the young people who have abused. This guidance also states that the long-awaited 'cross-government service delivery framework for young people who display sexually harmful behaviour is due for publication in early 2010' (ibid.). A national framework or strategy, strongly recommended by the *Childhood Lost* report (Bridge Child Care Development Service, 2001) had been cried out for by Morrison (1999) and the early NCH (1992) Report. The multi-agency Government team tasked with the development of this strategy seem to have had their own difficulties in working together leading to repeated delays and the framework being still pending at time of writing.

Hackett et al. (2003) reported how improved inter-agency co-ordination was the second most frequently desired improvement (by 35/111 YOTs) following a 'miracle' question (the first was local specialist provision). Fewer than half the YOTs and other services reported that formal inter-agency protocols about work with young people who have sexually abused had been agreed locally, and around 40 per cent of YOTs and other services had negotiated local multi-agency agreements about provision of services for these young people. A considerable lack of consistency was found across the UK in the holding of child protection meetings and multi-agency meetings. Further multi-agency training was also considered desirable in many cases, the effectiveness of which was supported by Carpenter et al. (2010).

Using a range of creative methods

The final main theme found to be necessary for holistic working with young people who have sexually harmed was the use of both a variety of methods to engage the young person, and the specific use of creative methods such as art, drama, multi-media and practical activities. One YOT worker explained:

> *I would suggest to work holistically was to look at it from all different angles, as a worker I believe you need to . . . continually strive to look for better ways of working . . . for instance, where a young person has not had much education, therefore they struggle with literacy and numeracy, the work we should do with them shouldn't be paper based. I feel, we should do stuff, maybe drawing work, we should be doing more hands on work with them, doing things with media, taking them away from the office environment.*

Activities advocated by professionals and the young people included examples of Visual learning, Auditory learning, Reading/writing learning and Kinaesthetic learning (VARK) (Fleming, 2010). While recent research has questioned the evidence base for individuals having any one more effective learning style (Coffield et al., 2004; Annison, 2006) the idea that people may benefit from using different styles and ways of learning has both popular and critical support (Fadel et al., 2008; Ginns, 2005). Some methods were seen to benefit or suit the young people in comparison with others which perhaps suited professionals, management or the general public. The importance of engaging the young people was seen to be key to building a relationship and facilitating effective work.

The influence of evidence-based practice was considered under this theme and found to be understood differently by many professionals. Some professionals described practice which examined criminal evidence or recorded evidence of work completed rather than effective practice guided by an evidence-base. The demands of management and funding bodies for work to be based on evidence were discussed but scepticism remained regarding the quality or amount of evidence available and the underlying agendas of those promoting it. One senior YOT worker shared the opinion:

> *I think it's crucial to keep up to date with research, and I think that we should base our practice on the latest research. I also think it's quite important to have quite a sceptical eye and to remember that things do go in fashions and that kids don't fit into boxes . . . I think we have to use Evidence Based Practice as the basis of what we do, but we also have to remember . . . that young people are individuals.*

This view balances the need to keep aware of research while emphasising the other holistic concerns of seeing the whole young person. Other staff discussed the way that using evidence helped to access funding and permission for activities and several staff mentioned the Professional Certificate for Effective Practice and the McGuire Principles (McGuire and Priestley, 1995) The more general term of 'effective practice' has appeal since all workers would want their practice to be seen as effective. It could be maintained that much of the argument behind using creative methods is for practice to be accessible and engage the young people, thereby being effective. While YJB National Standards focus on assessment by reductions in offending and completing orders, the Key Elements in Effective Practice series does include a focus on engagement of young people (YJB, 2008) although this summary acknowledges the lack of research into this area.

Further discussion of evidence and effective practice brings in not just the influence of managers and policies but also the way these are led by a need for public accountability. An experienced YOT worker considered the historical and political influences of research as well as the increasing pressures of public opinion:

> *We have to have research into what is effective, but we've also got to be aware that a lot of research is misused, is manipulated by the YJB . . . There's a whole range of research out there that says we don't have to have such a controlling system, that a lenient system is just as effective . . . but I think that we now live and work in a society that is much less forgiving . . . we're expected to be much more accountable to the public*

The lack of a broad evidence base for work with young people who have sexually harmed leads to the necessary reliance on practice experience and more general research into work with these and other young people with complex needs Additionally some suspicion of evidence agendas

and manipulation (as found by Wilcox, 2003) reduces adherence to requirements that work is evidence-based.

The limitations of evidence for effective interventions with young people who have sexually harmed raise the question of whether a controlled outcome study for holistic work with these young people is feasible or desirable. Even if a definition of holistic work such as that provided by these four main themes was agreed, the range of practice and necessarily individualised interventions recommended for young people would prevent a straightforward comparison between an holistic approach and 'standardised treatment', as experienced by Smallbone et al. (2009). I would also argue that good practice does not necessarily require an evidence base if it is grounded in ethical reasoning. The choice to promote anti-discriminatory practice does not depend on the acceptance of randomised controlled trials showing that racist, sexist or homophobic practice increase recidivism. Instead collective ethics and wisdom lead to changes in practice because this is the humane thing to do, and the reader is invited to consider whether the benefits of holistic practice outlined below provide a similar ethical reasoning.

Benefits of holistic working with young people who have sexually harmed

Holistic working brings benefits throughout the assessment and intervention stages of work, and these should lead to benefits as overall outcomes of the work. At the assessment stage, an holistic approach should ensure that the young person is viewed respectfully as a human being with both strengths and needs. An holistic approach will examine the range of influences on the young person from within their family and the wider community including peers. During an holistic assessment some of the roots of the young person's behaviour will be revealed as well as the range of needs experienced by the young person and their family. Strengths from the young person and their family will also be usefully identified.

Moving on to the intervention stage, an holistic approach will seek to address the needs of the young person and their family as effectively as possible. This will generally require involvement from other professionals since the needs will be wider than the sexual harm concerns. Support from the young person's family will contribute to assisting the young person effectively, and holistic interventions will seek to utilise the power of positive family reinforcement. A range of creative methods will increase engagement and effectiveness of the work.

In terms of outcomes, an holistic approach should benefit the young person and their family by ensuring their needs are addressed, their strengths and protective factors are boosted and they can move towards a positive future. An holistic approach will also benefit the public by using insights and thorough work to protect future victims while sharing resources to be cost-effective. The crucial nature of this work was stressed by one YOT worker:

> I think the [Multi Agency Public Protection Arrange-ments] system . . . has done a lot to improve multi-agency working and it's made other agencies very much more aware of their duty to provide resources for this group of people, children . . . [It's important] for public protection issues, because these young people, if they're worked with and made to feel safe at an early age, I believe, are much less likely to become dangerous adults . . . I think society has a duty and should be putting more money into this particular area to protect them and to protect the public in the future.

Here an holistic approach by agencies working together to address the range of needs is seen to prevent future harm to children.

Challenges related to holistic working with young people who have sexually harmed

The study also revealed a wide range of challenges to holistic working with these young people from the young people themselves, from their families, from staff members and from Government and policy sources. These are summarised in Figure 2.5.

In some situations the challenges faced were seen to inhibit holistic working, including some custodial and residential placements. Additionally the unstable funding arrangements for some specialist teams and bureaucratic demands on staff to 'cover themselves' and spend a lot of time on paperwork were seen to further limit the provision of an holistic service.

One further consideration was the need for a targeted response which can be considered in contrast to a fully holistic approach. Following a thorough holistic assessment, in some cases a more specific, limited response may be

appropriate, particularly when the assessment has indicated a low level of needs and risks. This fits into the need for a measured and appropriate response and was not argued to be any kind of rejection of the principles of an holistic approach.

Implications of holistic working with young people who have sexually harmed

An understanding of the benefits and challenges of holistic work with young people who have sexually harmed led to the identification of a number of implications from this study for future policy and practice. These comprise two main strands: necessary responses following better recognition of the needs of the young people and their families, and improvements to tackle some of the challenges inherent to the work. These strands are shown in Figure 2.6.

An holistic view of the needs of the young people and their families will frequently lead to the identification of areas which require intervention from other agencies, reiterating the multi-agency emphasis. Recognition of common factors in the history of young people who have sexually harmed will suggest areas where preventative work would be helpful, including better services for young people who have witnessed domestic violence, been abused or been involved in sexual exploitation. The importance of good closure following emotive work was also stressed by a number of interviewees.

Other challenges were seen to have implications for changes in practice and policy, as seen on the right hand side of the diagram. Findings indicated the need for further training, both relating to creative methods but also general awareness-raising with associated professionals. The need for better inter-agency relationships included increasing shared values, clarity in roles and communication and better sharing of resources. Clearer policies were seen as essential, both on a local and a national level with associated commitment of staffing and financial resources. In order to improve effective practice, better sharing of 'what works' as well as more research into effective treatments were identified as necessary. Additional awareness-raising amongst professionals and the general public were also seen to be desirable, incorporating better training and preventative work within schools.

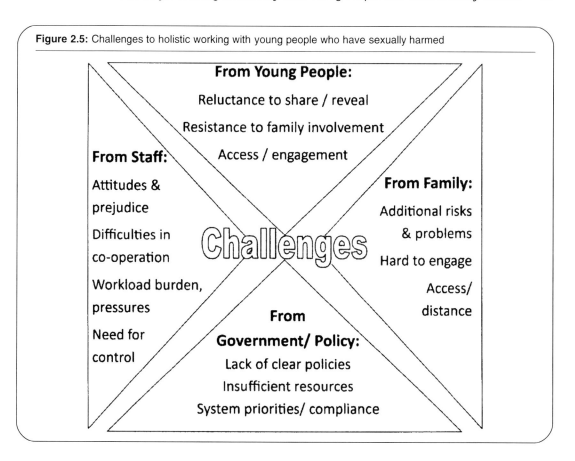

Figure 2.5: Challenges to holistic working with young people who have sexually harmed

Recommendations for practice and policy

These recommendations will be shared with the research participants but are also considered relevant to other professionals and policymakers seeking to advocate holistic practice with young people who have sexually harmed.

Assessment of young people who have sexually harmed should be holistic

The on-going assessment process will require input from the young person, their family and other professionals and should aim to get a broad view of the whole young person, including their individual needs and strengths. In addition to understanding the harmful sexual behaviour and any other offending behaviour, the assessment should consider the young person's health, learning, family and social relationships, emotional and social development, self-care skills and personal identity. Commitment from a multi-agency team should be gained to work to address the needs and risks identified as well as seeking to boost the strengths and protective factors present in the young person and their family and peers environment.

Intervention work with young people who have sexually harmed should be holistic

Following on from an holistic assessment, intervention work should also be delivered in an holistic manner. In some low concern cases, limited targeted intervention may be pursued where this is considered most beneficial for the young person and their family as a whole. However, where serious concerns and needs have been identified, an holistic approach should involve the young person, their family and other key professionals wherever possible. Holistic work will address the whole young person, will seek to support and gain support from the young

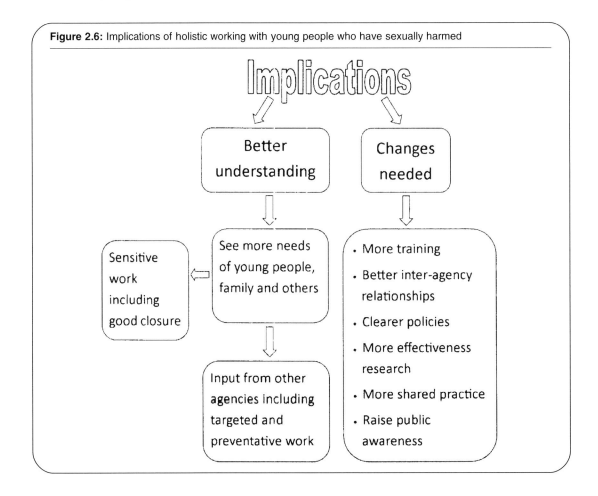

Figure 2.6: Implications of holistic working with young people who have sexually harmed

person's family, will involve workers from a range of agencies and will utilise a range of creative methods.

Further training is needed across agencies regarding young people who have sexually harmed

In order to provide a more holistic service, better inter-agency involvement requires training across social work, education, health, residential care, police and YOTs. Aims should be raising awareness about factors contributing to sexual harm by young people and ways of working together to address it. Staff need to be aware of local and national policies and supported to give time to relevant intervention and preventative work. Challenging attitudes which seek to avoid the issue or harshly judge the young people is important to increase commitment to attending meetings, sharing information and making

appropriate referrals. Improved awareness will increase confidence in effective working and reduce short-sighted decisions to refuse to work with a young person or to exclude them from educational or other opportunities.

Clearer policies regarding sexual harm by young people

Local YOT teams and Child Safeguarding Boards should have clear policies regarding young people who have sexually harmed to ensure a fair and balanced service is provided. Inter-agency protocols should include time for thorough assessments before sentencing and should seek to include young people who do not proceed through the court process. Access to specialists should be available according to the needs and risks identified and where necessary joint funding should be pursued via a multi-agency forum.

National policies should address the inequalities across provision for young people who have sexually harmed and ensure that services are adequately funded and accessible. Sharing of best practice should be encouraged at a national level while further research into effective practice also continues. A national audit of young people who have sexually harmed may be necessary to understand the distribution of cases including severity and to ensure that the highest concern young people are receiving the most intensive service. The use of residential treatment should be reviewed to discover whether this is the most appropriate service for the young people or whether it has been chosen by authorities with sufficient funding or without appropriate local services. Where residential treatment is seen as the best option every effort should be made to include the young person's family in some treatment and with good reintegration where possible.

More shared practice and effectiveness research

Policies at a local and national level should include the encouragement of sharing best practice and practical research into what helps young people and their families. Websites including those hosted by the Youth Justice Board and the NSPCC may be sources of good practice sharing and these should be developed with access available to a wide range of professionals. Training events should also include sharing of good practice while intervention manuals could be developed with integral feedback systems, perhaps issued in a 'beta version'. Knowledge from specialist training and resources should be cascaded throughout local authorities with more staff holding training remits to pass on what they have learnt. Research into effective interventions should be facilitated at a local level as well as wider clinical studies using links between training institutions and practice centres. Further consideration of the feasibility and desirability of an 'evidence-base' for holistic working should include the inherent ethical arguments for respectful work which acknowledges a young person's wider context, strengths and needs.

Raising awareness and preventative work

Increasing public awareness of sexual harm including harm by young people fits within a wider agenda of acknowledging abuse of children and seeking to prevent it. National campaigns by organisations such as the NSPCC, Barnardo's and Action for Children are seeking to increase recognition that harm to children is usually not from strangers but from people known to the child, and this could be expanded to include from young people as well as adults. Responsible journalism could increase understanding rather than simply sensationalising cases and demonising paedophiles. This would require a level of co-operation from services who would need to balance carefully the confidentiality of individual young people and their families with the need to raise more general awareness.

Preventative work within schools and with specific young people considered to be at higher risk of causing sexual harm deserves further support. Simple guidelines about ok and not-ok touching should be integral to early relationships education, with more information about the law and consequences of sexual behaviour being given to older children and teenagers. A culture encouraging talking about unwanted sexual contact and promoting responsible dating behaviour should increase reporting of sexual harm and offences. Effective earlier intervention with younger perpetrators should protect further victims as well as helping to address the wider associated needs of the young person. While most young people will not go on to reoffend, preventing any young perpetrator from becoming an adult sex offender could protect an unknown number of child victims. Intervening while a young person is still developing has the greatest hope for change and saves much greater future spending on the incarceration, treatment and supervision of adult sex offenders. The cost of good preventative work is one society cannot afford *not* to pay.

Further research indicated

Further discussions and interviews with local or other professionals testing out the findings of this research would add generalisability and allow the benefits, challenges and implications to be considered more robust findings. Interesting findings relating to links with sexual exploitation or staff attitudes to evidence-based practice could be further developed with additional questions or carefully selected interviewees. More integrated research with a team could explore efforts to work in a more holistic manner using more participative, action-research methods. Inter-agency relationships could also be usefully examined in this way. A different focus on working holistically to reduce sexual harm would necessarily include more investigation of preventative work and work with victims of sexual harm. More young person-centred research with carefully negotiated access to young people who have sexually harmed could allow further understanding of what young people find helpful and their motivation to involve or exclude other family members in intervention work.

The importance of effective practice and evidence-based practice deserves further exploration within the wider fields of youth justice and social work, not simply in terms of trials to demonstrate the effectiveness of specific intervention methods but considering more basic questions of the dominant agendas, the ethical foundations, the choices of measurable outcomes and perhaps 'what helps' rather than 'what works'. A review of the Professional Certificate of Effective Practice course and more scrutiny of training provided and interventions used would be useful to assess the standards being applied to identify effective practice and how influential these are in front-line practice. Critical evaluation of any new Government strategies regarding young people who have sexually harmed and their implementation would also be significant research comparing the importance of an holistic approach with new guidelines, priorities and available resources.

Conclusion

The study identified broadly accepted meanings of working holistically with young people who have sexually harmed, filling a gap in knowledge around this popular but vaguely defined concept. A thorough theoretical base with a spectrum of holistic approaches was gained from the literature and a broad collection of sources were analysed to identify themes grounded in the data. The four main areas identified: seeing the whole young person, working with wider family and peers, working in a multi-agency way and using a range of creative methods received good confirmation from professionals within the field and are supported in the literature. The integrated combination of these areas is necessary

to allow an holistic approach which is more than the sum of parts, just as an holistic view of the whole young person is more than the sum of identified areas of needs and strengths.

Each theme presented associated benefits, challenges and implications of an holistic approach. These original findings would benefit from further confirmation through future research but connections can be drawn with other related literature regarding effective multi-agency working, involving family members and developing effective practice. Finally, recommendations have been made for further research and developments of policy and practice on a local and national level. An holistic approach to understanding the topic of 'working holistically with young people who have sexually harmed' has been attempted, using a range of research methods to view a wide picture of the research area and seeking to triangulate findings to gain integrated and robust findings. Such a broad topic will always merit further exploration but a thorough assessment is an important first stage. The challenge remains to proceed to intervention and put more holistic work into practice.

In terms of 'evidence' for working holistically with young people who have sexually harmed, this chapter has presented a review of existing evidence from literature as well as original findings from qualitative research. Multi-Systemic Therapy has perhaps the most promising empirical evidence base in terms of intervention methods with young people who have sexually harmed, and this methodology has been demonstrated to include many aspects of an holistic approach, particularly in terms of seeing the young person within family and other systems. However, other holistic approaches bring further contributions to ethical arguments for holistic work which can be seen as influential in practice despite the absence of a specific 'evidence-base'. While 'holistic' and 'evidence-based practice' are both terms interpreted widely and causing some confusion amongst practitioners, the growth of holistic practice has perhaps the stronger foundations in social work and therapeutic values. Having fewer dissenters and increasing dominance in everyday practice, holistic practice is forging ahead and leaving evidence-based practice to catch up. Perhaps there will be studies in the future to demonstrate empirically the superiority of interventions which treat 'young offenders' as human beings and see their wider context, strengths and needs as important, alongside the needs of victims and protecting the public. Fortunately this study (and that of Hackett et al., 2003) showed that the majority of UK practitioners have already come to these conclusions.

References

Annison, J. (2006) Style Over Substance? A Review of The Evidence Base for the Use of Learning Styles in Probation. *Criminology and Criminal Justice*, 6: 2, 239–57.

Atkinson. M., Doherty, P. and Kinder, K. (2005) Multi-agency Working: Models, Challenges and Key Factors For Success. *Journal of Early Childhood Research*, 3: 1, 7–17.

Bannister, A. (ed.) (1998) *From Hearing to Healing: Working with the Aftermath of Child Sexual Abuse*. 2nd edn. Chichester: Wiley.

Bentovim, A. (1991) Clinical Work with Families in Which Sexual Abuse Has Occurred. In: Hollin, C. and Howells, K. (eds.) *Clinical Approaches to Sex Offenders and their Victims*. Wiley.

Bentovim, A. (1998) Family Systemic Approach to Work with Young Sex Offenders. *The Irish Journal of Psychology*, 19: 1, 119–35.

Brendtro, L., Brokenleg, M. and Van Bockern, S. (1990) *Reclaiming Youth At Risk: Our Hope for the Future*. Bloomington: National Education Service.

Bridge Child Care Development Service (2001) *Childhood Lost: Part 8 Case Review, Overview Report DM*. Hay-on-Wye: The Bridge Publishing House Limited.

Bronfenbrenner, U. (1977) Toward an Experimental Ecology of Human Development. *American Psychologist*, 32: 7, 513–31.

Butler-Sloss, E. (1988) *Report of the Inquiry into Child Abuse in Cleveland 1987*, Cmnd 412. London: HMSO.

Carpenter, J. et al. (2010) *Outcomes of Interagency Training to Safeguard Young People: Final Report to the Department for Children, Schools and Families and the Department of Health*. DCSF. http://www.dcsf.gov.uk/research/data/uploadfiles/DCSF-RR209-FinalCopy.pdf [Accessed 17/06/10].

Charles, M. and Stevenson, O. (1990) *Multi-disciplinary is Different!* Nottingham: University of Nottingham.

Chief Secretary to the Treasury (2003) *Every Child Matters: Green Paper*. London: HMSO.

Children's Workforce Development Council (2010a) *The Common Assessment Framework for Children and Young People: A Guide For Practitioners*. http://www.dcsf.gov.uk/everychildmatters/resources-and-practice/IG00063/.

Children Act 1989.c.41. OPSI http://www.opsi.gov.uk/acts/acts1989/plain/ukpga_19890041_en

Children Bill 1908. Hansard http://hansard.millbanksystems.com/commons/1908/feb/10/children-bill-1

Clark, M. (1996) Brief solution-focused work: A strength-based method for juvenile justice practice. *Juvenile and Family Court Journal*, 47: 1, 57–65.

Coffield, F. et al. (2004) *Learning Styles and Pedagogy in Post-16 Learning*. London: Learning and Skills Research Centre.

Colley, H. (2003) Engagement Mentoring for Socially Excluded Youth: Problematising an 'Holistic' Approach to Creating Employability through the Transformation of Habitus. *British Journal of Guidance and Counselling*, 31: 1, 77–99.

Collie, R. et al. (2007) The Good Lives Model of Rehabilitation: Reducing Risks and Promoting Strengths with Adolescent Sex Offenders. In: Calder, M. (ed.) *Working with Children and Young People Who Sexually Abuse*. Lyme Regis: Russell House Publishing.

Corby, B. (2006) *Child Abuse: Towards a Knowledge Base*. 3rd edn. Maidenhead: Open University Press.

Corcoran, J. (1997) A Solution-oriented Approach to Working with Juvenile Offenders. *Child and Adolescent Social Work Journal*, 14: 4, 277–88.

Creeden, K. (2005) Integrating Trauma and Attachment Research into the Treatment of Sexually Abusive Youth. In: Calder, M. (ed.) *Children and Young People Who Sexually Abuse: New Theory, Research and Practice Developments*. Lyme Regis: Russell House Publishing.

Dale, P. (1986) *Dangerous Families: Assessment and Treatment of Child Abuse*. London: Tavistock.

DCSF and DoH (2009) *Healthy Lives, Brighter Futures: The Strategy For Children and Young People's Health*. http://www.dh.gov.uk/prodconsum_dh/groups/dh_digitalassets/documents/digitalasset/dh_094397.pdf

DoH (2000) *Framework for the Assessment of Children in Need and their Families*. London: DoH.

DoH and Home Office (2006) *The needs and effective treatment of young people who sexually abuse: current evidence.* London: DoH.

DoH, DCSF, Ministry of Justice and Home Office (2009) *Healthy Children, Safer Communities.* London: DoH.

De Shazer, S. (1988) *Clues: Investigating Solutions in Brief Therapy.* New York: Norton.

Durham, A. (2006) *Young Men Who Have Sexually Abused: A Case Study Guide.* Chichester: Wiley.

Fadel, C., Lemke, C and Metiri Group (2008) *Multimodal Learning Through Media: What the Research Says.* [Online] Cisco Education white paper, Cisco Systems. http://www.cisco.com/web/strategy/docs/education/Multimodal-Learning-Through-Media.pdf

Finkelhor, D. (1986) *A Sourcebook on Child Sexual Abuse.* Newbury Park: Sage.

Fyson, R. (2007) Young People with Learning Disabilities Who Sexually Abuse: Understanding, Identifying and Responding from within Generic Education and Welfare Services. In: Calder, M. (ed.) *Working with Children and Young People Who Sexually Abuse.* Lyme Regis: Russell House.

Ginns, P. (2005) Meta Analysis of the Modality Effect. *Learning and Instruction,* 15: 4, 313–31.

Glaser, B. and Strauss, A. (1967) *The Discovery of Grounded Theory: Strategies for Qualitative Research.* New York: Aldine Publishing Company.

Griffin, J. and Tyrrell, I. (1997) *Psychotherapy, Counselling and the Human Givens.* Chalvington: European Therapy Studies Institute.

Hackett, S., Masson, H. and Phillips, S. (2003) *Mapping and Exploring Services For Young People Who Have Sexually Abused Others.* NSPCC. http://www.nspcc.org.uk/Inform/research/Findings/mappingandexploringservices_wda48266.html

Hackett, S., Print, B. and Dey, C. (1998) Brother Nature? Therapeutic Intervention with Young Men who Sexually Abuse their Siblings. In: Bannister, A. (ed.) *From Hearing to Healing: Working with the Aftermath of Child Sexual Abuse.* 2nd edn. Chichester: Wiley.

Hayden, C. (2007) *Children in Trouble: The role of families, schools and communities.* Basingstoke: Palgrave Macmillan.

Hettler, W. (1976) *Origins of the Hettler 6 Dimensional Model* http://www.hettler.com/OriginsoftheHettler6DimensionalModel.mht

HM Government (2010) *Working Together to Safeguard Children.* http://publications.education.gov.uk/eOrderingDownload/00305-2010DOM-EN.PDF

Home Office (1968) *Children in Trouble.* Cmnd 3601, London: HMSO.

Johnson, T. and Doonan, R. (2005) Children With Sexual Behaviour Problems: What Have We Learned in the Last Two Decades? In: Calder, M. (ed.) *Children and Young People Who Sexually Abuse: New Theory, Research and Practice Developments.* Lyme Regis: Russell House.

Lambie, I. (2005) You Can Get an Adolescent to Grunt but You Can't Make Them Talk: Interviewing Strategies with Young People Who Sexually Abuse. In: Calder, M. (ed.) *Children and Young People Who Sexually Abuse: New Theory, Research and Practice Developments.* Lyme Regis: Russell House.

Letourneau, E. and Swenson, C. (2005) Sexual Offending and Sexual Behaviour Problems: Treatment with Multi-Systemic Therapy. In: Calder, M. (ed.) *Children and Young People Who Sexually Abuse: New Theory, Research and Practice Developments.* Lyme Regis: Russell House.

Leung, P. et al. (2009) Towards Body-Mind-Spirit Integration: East Meets West in Clinical Social Work Practice. *Clinical Social Work Journal,* 37: 4, 303–11.

Long, J. (2010) *Hidden Problem of Children Sexually Abusing Children.* File on 4. BBC, 16/03/10. http://news.bbc.co.uk/1/hi/programmes/file_on_4/8570303.stm

Longo, R. (2001) *Paths To Wellness: A Holistic Approach and Guide For Personal Recovery.* Holyoke: Neari Press.

Longo, R. (2002) A Holistic Approach to Treating Young People who Sexually Abuse. In: Calder, M. (ed.) *Young People Who Sexually Abuse: Building the Evidence Base for Your Practice.* Lyme Regis: Russell House.

Longo, R. (2004) An Integrated Experiential Approach to Treating Young People Who Sexually Abuse. *Journal of Child Sexual Abuse,* 13: 3/4, 193–213.

Marshall, W. and Marshall, L. (2007) The Utility of The Randomised Controlled Trial For Evaluating Sexual Offender Treatment: The Gold Standard or an Inappropriate Strategy? *Sexual Abuse: Journal of Research and Treatment,* 19: 2, 175–91.

McAlinden, A. (2007) *The Shaming of Sexual Offenders.* Oxford: Hart.

McGuire, J. and Priestly, P. (1995) Reviewing What Works: Past, Present and Future. In: McGuire, J. (ed.) *What Works: Reducing Offending.* Chichester: Wiley.

Morrison T. (1992). Managing Sex Offenders: The Challenge for Managers. *Probation Journal.* 39: 3, 122–8.

Morrison, T. (1999) 'Is there a strategy out there?' Policy and management perspectives on young people who sexually abuse others. In: Erooga, M. and Masson, H. (eds.) *Children and Young People Who Sexually Abuse Others: Challenges and Responses.* London: Routledge.

Morrison, T. (2006) Building a Holistic Approach in the Treatment of Young People Who Sexually Abuse. In: Longo, R. and Prescott, D. (eds.) *Current Perspectives: Working with Sexually Aggressive Youth and Youth with Sexual Behavior Problems.* Holyoke: Neari Press.

Morrison, T. and Henniker, J. (2006) Building a Comprehensive Inter-Agency Assessment and Intervention System for Young People Who Sexually Harm. In: Erooga, M. and Masson, H. (eds.) *Children and Young People Who Sexually Abuse Others: Current Developments and Practice Responses,* 2nd edn. London: Routledge.

National Children's Home (1992) *The Report of the Committee of Enquiry into Children and Young People Who Sexually Abuse Other Children .* London: NCH.

National Task Force on Juvenile Sexual Offending (1993) Revised report. *Juvenile and Family Court Journal,* 44: 4.

Parks, G. (2007) Emerging Data for Risk Prediction and Identification of Offender Sub-groups. In: Calder, M. (ed.) *Working with Children and Young People Who Sexually Abuse.* Lyme Regis: Russell House.

Powell, D. et al. (1997) A Strength-Based Approach in Support of Multi-Risk Families: Principles and Issues. *Topics in Early Childhood Special Education,* 17: 1, 1–26.

Prilleltensky, I. and Nelson, G. (2000) Promoting Child and Family Wellness: Priorities for Psychological and Social Interventions. *Journal of Community and Applied Social Psychology,* 10: 2, 85–105.

Rich, P. (2003) *Understanding, Assessing and Rehabilitating Juvenile Sexual Offenders.* Chichester: Wiley.

Ryan, G. (1997) Creating an 'Abuse-Specific' Milieu. In: Ryan, G. and Lane, S. (eds.) *Juvenile Sexual Offending: Causes, Consequences and Correction.* 2nd edn. San Francisco: Jossey-Bass Publishers.

Saleebey, D. (1996) The Strengths Perspective in Social Work Practice: Extensions and Cautions. *Social Work,* 41: 3, 296–305.

Smallbone, S., Crissman, B. and Rayment-McHugh, S. (2009) Improving Therapeutic Engagement with Adolescent Sexual Offenders. *Behavioral Sciences and the Law.* 27: 6, 862–77.

Smith, R. (2007) *Youth Justice: Ideas, policy, practice.* 2nd edn. Cullompton: Willan.

Sweeney, T. and Myers, J. (2003) *The Indivisible Self: An Evidence-Based Model of Wellness.* Greensboro: Author.

Ward, T. and Stewart, C. (2003) Criminogenic Needs and Human Needs: A Theoretical Model. *Psychology, Crime and Law,* 9: 2, 125–43.

Warne, D. (2005) Traditional Perspectives on Child and Family Health. *Paediatric Child Health,* 10: 9, 542–44.

Weaver, H. (2002) Perspectives on Wellness: Journeys on the Red Road. *Journal of Sociology and Social Welfare,* 29: 1, 5–15.

Webb, S. (2001) Some Considerations on the Validity of Evidence-based Practice in Social Work. *British Journal of Social Work,* 31: 1, 57–79.

Wilcox, A. (2003) Evidence-based Youth Justice? Some Valuable Lessons from an Evaluation for the Youth Justice Board. *Youth Justice,* 3: 1, 21–35.

Witmer, J., Sweeney, T. and Myers, J. (1998) *The Wheel of Wellness.* Greensboro: Authors.

Youth Justice Board (2006) *Asset.* http://www.yjb.gov.uk/Publications/Scripts/prodView.asp?idproduct=203andeP

Understanding and Applying Typologies in the Context of a Holistic Model for the Treatment of Sexually Offending Juveniles

Tom Leversee

Introduction

When this author first engaged in specialised treatment with sexually offending juveniles in the early 1980's, treatment and supervision planning was simpler. The adult model that was applied to juveniles at that time supported a narrow and specialised 'one size fits all' treatment and supervision approach. Juveniles who had committed sexual offenses were seen as significantly different from juveniles who engaged in non-sexual delinquency. Normal adolescent development was not viewed as particularly relevant to the understanding of and interventions with this population. Programs were more likely to have relatively prescribed treatment expectations and fixed time frames for the completion of treatment. The field today looks quite different. Recidivism research has exposed the fallacy of the 'no cure' philosophy and informed hope for many sexually offending juveniles to move to a non-abusive, healthy, and normative path of development. Sexual recidivism across the different studies ranges from approximately five to 14 per cent (Alexander, 1999; Reitzel and Carbonell, 2006; Caldwell, 2007; Worling, Litteljohn, and Bookalam, 2010). While sexual reoffense recidivism rates for youth who participate in treatment is low, recidivism rates for engaging in non-sexual reoffending are higher, ranging from 22 to 28.51 per cent (Worling, Litteljohn, and Bookalam, 2010; Reitzel and Carbonell, 2006).

Risk reduction and risk management are foundational to the overall goal of preventing future sexual offending. Risk assessment and treatment planning that targets the dynamic risk factors associated with sexual offending and other conduct problems is essential to risk reduction and risk management. However, a narrow risk reduction/management framework is not sufficient in addressing the wide range of risk and treatment/supervision needs and the dynamic nature of adolescent development. The risk reduction/management model does little to assist youth in learning to live healthy pro-social lives. Prescott and Longo (2007) proposed the need to recast the best features of risk reduction/management models in an holistic context of sexual, social, and spiritual development, as well as the natural push of young people to develop the 'good life' for themselves. That is, treat the whole person by not only addressing risk factors but also promoting health. The challenge is to protect community safety by identifying, treating, and effectively managing those youth at highest risk to re-offend while at the same time facilitating low to moderate risk youth in returning to a more normative path of development (Chaffin and Bonner, 1988; Leversee and Pearson, 2001).

An holistic model is informed by the diverse developmental and dynamic factors associated with juvenile sexual offending and other non-sexual conduct problems. *Typology research* has differentiated juveniles who have committed sexual offenses in regard to patterns of offending, personality characteristics, etiology, and the identification of what is driving the sexually abusive behavior and other conduct problems. While the main focus of this chapter will be to discuss typology research, work with juveniles unfolds within the context of the dynamic nature of *adolescent development*. The adolescent years are defined by dynamic growth and development that takes place within the contexts of family, school, neighborhood, and peer group. The prevalence and impact of *co-occurring mental disorders* are factors from the standpoint of to what degree they are contributing factors to offending and their impact on amenability to treatment and healthy functioning. *Trauma-informed care* models are progressing in response to advances in the understanding of brain development and the impacts of neglect and trauma on the brain. This chapter will discuss the importance of the areas highlighted above in regard to understanding and intervening in juvenile sexual offending.

Adolescent development

The place of normal adolescent development in informing placement, treatment, and supervision starts with its role in maturation and behavioral change. The adolescent years (approx age 12 to 20) are marked by dramatic changes in many facets of life (Lerner and Steinberg, 2009). This dynamic maturational process includes changes in the physical, cognitive, social, emotional, and moral domains. In order to be effective, treatment interventions must match the adolescent's developmental status in these domains. The increasing knowledge of brain development deserves a special mention as it relates to understanding and intervening in juvenile offending. The more recent knowledge that the development of the neocortex continues up until the mid 20s informs professionals that these higher cognitive processes are not fully developed in adolescence. Relative to adults, this translates to adolescents demonstrating less efficient processing speed, including working memory, decreased judgment, and less ability to anticipate consequences (Yager, 2005). Powell (2010a) points out that children and adolescents appear to be using more of the rapid response, emotional region of the brain, and that brain development into adulthood facilitates improved ability to think before acting and change abusive behavior patterns. This knowledge has increased our understanding of adolescent behavior, particularly as it relates to self regulation and adolescent culpability (Steinberg and Haskins, 2008).

The ecological model (Bronfenbrenner, 1979, 1989) informs that child and adolescent development is the product of the continuous dynamic interaction between the youth and the experience provided by the family and social context that includes school, neighborhood, and peer group (Davies, 2004). Resiliency research (Werner and Smith, 1992) has illuminated the role of protective factors in supporting positive adaptation within the context of significant adversity. Protective factors are factors in the child or the environment that mitigate risk by reducing stress, providing opportunities for growth, or strengthening coping capacities

(Davies, 2004). Examples of protective factors include improved parent/child relationship, extended family support, school mentors and pro-social friends, involvement in extracurricular activities, and community safety. An holistic model not only targets empirically supported risk factors associated with offending but seeks to mitigate developmental and contextual risk factors and enhance protective factors. Multisystemic Therapy is an example of a family and community based approach that has strong research support in the treatment of general delinquency and has been identified as a potentially effective means of treating juvenile sexual offending (as cited in Saldana, Swenson, and Letourneau, 2006).

Typologies

Typology research offers a foundation for identifying the differential static and dynamic risk factors and personality characteristics associated with offending. O'Brien and Bera (1986) developed the most utilised early typologies of adolescent offenders, consisting of seven categories. Each category considered motivational, psychological, and situational factors that contribute to sexual offending behavior. The categories ranged from the younger adolescent attempting to explore and experiment with developing sexual feelings to the adolescent who displays an acute disturbance of reality testing and has a history of psychological, family and substance abuse problems.

More recent typology research (Becker, 1988; Hunter et al., 2003; Hunter, 2006, 2008; Miner, 2010; Richardson et al., 2004; Worling, 2001) has differentiated subtypes of youth based on patterns of offending, etiology, personality characteristics, and the identification of what is driving the sexually abusive behavior and other conduct problems. A synthesis of the typology research (Leversee, 2007, 2010a, 2010b) supports a differentiation between those sexually abusive youth characterised by:

- deficits in psychosocial functioning
- general conduct problems and delinquency
- pedophilic interests

The synthesis of the typology research presented here is not sufficient to explain all of the individualised developmental and dynamic risk factors associated with juvenile sexual offending and other non-sexual conduct problems. Although there is some notable convergence in the research, there are no empirically validated typologies of juveniles who have committed sexual offenses. There is a great deal of diversity within the different subtypes and youth may manifest characteristics of more than one subtype. While typology research helps to illuminate the diversity of this population, it is important it is not misapplied in adopting a 'cookie cutter, one size fits all' approach to the treatment and supervision of each subtype.

Deficits in psychosocial functioning

Becker (1988), Hunter et al. (2003), Hunter (2006, 2008) and Miner et al. (2010) identified specific characteristics which differentiate youth who choose child victims versus those who offend against peers/adults. In contrast to this, Richardson, Kelly, Graham, and Bhate (2004) and Worling's (2001) research did not indicate any strong link between specific youth profiles and victim selection based on age. However, the findings of all of these researchers were relatively consistent in delineating subtypes of youth characterised by deficits in psychosocial functioning.

Becker (1988) described the youth whose impaired social and interpersonal skills contribute to the molestation of younger children for sexual gratification and social interaction. Hunter (2006, 2008) described the 'socially impaired-anxious and depressed' youth who engages in transient sexual offending predominately against children. The sexual offending of these youth is seen as a form of adolescent experimentation and an attempt to satisfy unmet intimacy needs in compensation for psychosocial deficits that impair the development of healthy peer relationships. Miner et al. (2010) focused on attachment anxiety and found that adolescents who sexually offend against children to meet their intimacy needs do so not only because of a desire for interpersonal closeness but also because of a fear of rejection. They may also experience a preoccupation with sexuality.

Richardson et al. (2004) identified the 'Submissive' group as passively dependent on others, excessively compliant with rules, deferring to authority, and subsuming his needs to the wishes of others. Richardson and associates' 'Dysthymic/Inhibited' group are described as apathetic and lacking in motivation

to socialise with peers and likely to experience a sense of failure in relationship with peers. Worling (2001) characterised the 'Overcontrolled/Reserved' youth as initiating offending behaviors, in part, as a result of their shy and rigid interpersonal orientation, resulting in limited access to intimate relationships with peers. Worling's 'Unusual Isolated' group are described as emotionally disturbed and insecure and as characterised by a peculiar presentation and social isolation. These youth's awkward personality features may inhibit their ability to develop and maintain healthy and intimate relationships with consenting peers.

Characteristics that are relatively consistent across these research groups are the following: a lack in self-confidence and feelings of inadequacy; expectations of peer rejection and ridicule; increased levels of generalised and particularly social anxiety; social avoidance and isolation; and mood problems. Their motivation for turning to younger children could be explained in part by their apprehension and avoidance of social/sexual contact (Hunter, 2006; Miner et al., 2010).

Seto and Lalumiere's meta-analysis (2010) found the following risk factors that would appear to be associated with deficits in psychosocial functioning:

- social isolation
- significantly higher anxiety in general and social anxiety
- low self-esteem

The findings on social isolation suggest that social problems play a role but not necessarily because of social incompetence. Seto (personal communication, 2010) proposed that the social isolation may have more to do with engagement in peer relationships than inability, but that the direction in which that flows is unclear. It may be the case that for some adolescents the measures of peer relationships fail to tap into the fact that they are less interested in peers and more interested in young children, for developmental, emotional, or sexual reasons. This could include socially immature adolescents who feel more comfortable and, in some senses, have more in common with younger children than their peers. Sexual reasons could include pedophilia and sexual anxieties regarding interactions with peers.

The author has found some commonalities in regard to the developmental pathways and cognitive-emotional processes of youth characterised by deficits in psychosocial functioning (Leversee, 2008). The lack of social confidence, feelings of social inadequacy, and social anxiety and avoidance frequently have their origins in social histories characterised by peer rejection, alienation, and social isolation. Deficits in self-esteem and social efficacy are reflected in negative basic beliefs about self and relationships. The emotions associated with these beliefs include rejected, unloved, insecure, inadequate, lonely, and sad. These youth may report that engaging younger children in social/sexual behavior is associated with experiencing feelings of acceptance, emotional connection, and safety; feelings that are lacking in relationships with same age peers.

Case example – Josh

Josh sexually offended against pre-pubescent children. His history of non-sexual conduct problems and delinquent behavior was relatively minor. Josh identified rejection as his most powerful emotional precursor to offending. In reflecting on his middle school years, Josh described himself as a skinny and long-haired youth who wore glasses and was an 'easy target for peers'. He disclosed that peers called him names, picked on him a lot, and didn't want to be his friend or 'hang out' with him. Josh stated that, 'nobody wanted me around . . . I would go to a party and people would start joking about me.' He described his response as pretending that it didn't bother him and reported that he responded by withdrawing from the group or the area. Josh identified his core beliefs as, 'nobody loves me . . . I'm a loser . . . ugly . . . worthless . . . no self esteem.' Josh disclosed that he 'wanted a girl friend' but did not believe girls his own age would go out with him. In addition to rejection, he reported feeling unloved, inadequate, hopeless, insecure, and abandoned. Josh also reported that he started experiencing depression during this period of time. Josh attributed his inability to get along with youth his own age and his ability to get along with children as eventually leading to his sexual offending against children. He stated that, 'little children always wanted me around . . . didn't reject me . . . didn't judge me'. Josh identified the needs met through associating with and offending against children as feeling wanted, connected, and loved.

Treatment

The treatment needs of youth characterised by deficits in psychosocial functioning includes:

- sex offense specific treatment
- skills building
- providing opportunities for growth and strengthening coping capacities in the context of family, school, and peer group.

The degree and intensity of sex offense specific treatment interventions can be guided by the overall risk and the degree of sexual drive and preoccupation. Hunter and associates (2003) place emphasis on the importance of addressing deficits in self-esteem, self-efficacy, and social competency. A strengths-based approach can enhance self-esteem and self-efficacy by recognising youth's strengths, exceptions to problems, and providing opportunities for success experiences and mastery (Powell, 2010b; Worling, 2001) incorporated *Skillstreaming the Adolescent* (Goldstein and McGinnis, 1997) and recommended beginning and intermediate social skills including 'joining in', 'expressing your feelings', 'standing up for your rights', and focused on the outward expression of affect.

Youth who manifest significant social anxiety and avoidance can benefit from cognitive behavioral treatment to address maladaptive cognitions. Exposure therapy focuses on the need to take social risks and engage in activities and relationships with same age peers (Hunter 2006, 2008; Worling, 2001). This is facilitated utilising a collaborative approach that includes the involvement of the family, school, and peer group in supporting the practice and mastery of targeted skills. In addressing healthy sexuality, Brown and Schwartz (2006) describe a program that creates opportunities for learning social, courtship, and dating skills in supervised community-based social activities. This program encourages youth to overcome social anxiety and prepares the youth with role plays about social and dating situations.

General conduct problems and delinquency

Convergence in the typology research (Becker, 1988; Hunter et al., 2003; Hunter, 2006, 2008; Miner, 2010; Richardson et al., 2004; Worling, 2001) also delineates a subtype whose sexual offending is part of a broader pattern of non-sexual conduct problems and whose personality characteristics are more similar to those associated with generally delinquent youth.

Referencing Moffit's Developmental Taxonomy of juveniles who had engaged in delinquent behavior, Hunter and associates (2003; Hunter, 2006, 2008) identified a subgroup of sexually offending youth, described as Life Course Persistent, characterised by lifestyle delinquency. These youth have a broader range of non-sexual delinquency, an early onset to conduct problems, and are more likely to sexually offend against peers and adults with more violent forms of coercion. Life Course Persistent youth are characterised by traits such as egotistical-antagonistic masculinity, defined as aggressively seeking interpersonal dominance, and hostile masculinity. Hostile masculinity is defined as a constellation of beliefs that a masculine identity involves power, risk-taking, toughness, dominance, aggressiveness, honor-defending, competitiveness, impersonal sexuality (Miner et al., 2010) and viewing of females in a negative and pejorative manner supportive of rape myths (Hunter, 2008). This personality characteristic may manifest in the use of more gratuitous violence in the sexual offenses. The etiological factors associated with this subtype include the highest incidence of physical abuse by father/stepfather and the highest exposure to male modeled antisocial behavior, including domestic violence and male relative substance abuse (Hunter et al., 2003; Hunter, 2006, 2008). It is important to note that Moffit's research found that the Life Course Persistent youth constituted only five to six per cent of juveniles who engaged in delinquent behavior.

Miner (2008) found few differences between those youth who had sexually offended against peers/adults and non-sexual delinquents. Both groups were likely to have dismissive attachment styles, characterised by an avoidance of intimacy, devaluation of relationships, and striving to maintain autonomy. Richardson et al. (2004) described the Antisocial subtype as the closest to a pure conduct disorder and characterised these youth as indifferent to the feelings and welfare of other people and as frequently disregarding social rules, the rights of others, and the consequences of their actions. They may be impulsive, self-indulgent, and excessive in the expression of their emotions and desires. Family life is associated with parental rejection and conflict. Richardson et al. (2004) suggests that this subtype is similar to Worling's Confident/Aggressive group, characterised as confident, self-centered, outgoing, aggressive, and sociable.

Richardson et al. (2004) also identified a Dysthymic/Negativistic group, who exhibit both internalising and externalising symptoms, with the externalising symptoms being predominant. Internalising symptoms include a very negative self-perception, low self-esteem, and low self-confidence in relation to peers. Dysthymic mood may be chronic and incapacitating. Externalising symptoms consist of intimidating others, strong feelings of resentment about limitations, indifference to the feelings and rights of other people, and deficits in self-control. These youth experience distress about family relationships. Richardson suggests this subgroup resembles Worling's (2001) Antisocial/Impulsive group, who are described as likely to have a propensity for rule violations and to be characterised as anxious, unhappy, and rebellious.

Hunter (2008) identified the 'Adolescent Onset-Experimenters' and described the sexual offending of these youth as a transient form of adolescent experimentation. They are less delinquent and have not been exposed to high levels of violence and substance abuse associated with Life Course Persistent youth. They are generally less psychosocially and psychosexually disturbed than other subgroups. This subgroup has fewer victims than Hunter's other subgroups and is relatively comparable to Richardson et al's (2004) 'Normal' prototype, described as presenting with relatively minor personality difficulties as compared to the other groups. None of the Expressed Concerns or Clinical Syndrome scales on the MACI were clinically significant in the 'Normal' subgroup.

Clinical experience reveals that sexually abusive youth who are more generally delinquent may present with a higher degree of anger and are more likely to have documented and self-reported histories of impulsive and assaultive behavior, authority problems, fighting, and use of drugs and alcohol (Leversee, 2008). Their patterns of non-sexual delinquency and conduct problems often have an earlier onset and are more extensive and pervasive than their sexual offending. Burton and Meezan (2004: 51) hypothesise that, 'sexual offending and rule breaking is a logical progression when they become developmentally focused on their sexuality – they see no reason not to break the rules, and have been taught that rule breaking is a way to fulfill their desires'. Consistent with the research on juvenile delinquency, these youth are more likely to manifest delinquent attitudes, values, beliefs and associate with delinquent peers (Latessa, 2005).

Case example – Mike

Mike sexually abused his seven-year-old niece at the age of 16. He described his motive as revenge for his older sister allegedly sexually abusing him when he was a child. Charges were reportedly not pursued in another state when he engaged in sexual contact with 13-year-old female when he was 17. Mike stated that she lied about her age. With the exception of engaging in frottage while utilising buses, there was no documented or self-reported engagement in other sexual paraphilias. Mike's non-sexual delinquent history included assaults, armed robbery, breaking and entering, selling drugs, truancy, and suspensions and expulsions from school. Mike was previously in residential placement in New York due to conduct problems and was also being treated for depression. While in residential placement, he demonstrated significant behavioral problems including verbal abuse, aggressive posturing/intimidation, and insubordination/oppositional behaviors. Mike's family history was reportedly characterised by physical and sexual abuse, neglect, and parental antisocial behavior.

Mike's basic beliefs were consistent with his history of child maltreatment and a more general antisocial orientation and included:

- If I want something, I'll take it.
- Nobody can tell me what to do . . . I'm my own boss.
- No one is going to disrespect me.
- If people control me, I get hurt. Therefore, no one is going to control me.
- I learned not to trust a lot of things that people tell me.
- Every time I get close to somebody, they pull away . . . it always happens.
- I'm going to do whatever I wanna do.
- I wasn't scared of nothing.

Mike reported being very easily triggered to anger. He stated that, 'anger has been there since I was a kid, I can't remember not being angry . . . always been there . . . I'm used to it . . . like a part

of me.' Mike went on to say that, 'the only feeling I'm comfortable showing is anger'. He reported becoming 'really upset over really tiny things'. Mike identified the feelings underlying his anger as sad, depressed, anxious, aggravated, and irritable. He stated, 'I can feel like crying and will show it with anger.' Mike's strengths included being intelligent, articulate, and artistic. He was able to demonstrate some degree of social competence, hadn't completely given up on adults, and exhibited some motivation for a pro-social lifestyle.

Treatment

Juveniles whose sexual offending is part of a broader pattern of conduct problems and delinquency represent a wide range in regard to the degree of delinquent orientation and the risk for future sexually abusive and non-sexual conduct problems and delinquency. Treatment and supervision planning should be individualised to reflect this diversity.

Overall, this subtype of youth may require delinquency-focused treatment interventions (Prentky and Righthand, 2003; Worling, 2001; Hunter et al., 2003; Hunter, 2006, 2008). Edward Latessa (2005) identifies the major set of risk factors/treatment targets for juvenile delinquents as follows:

- antisocial attitudes, values, and beliefs
- associating with delinquent peers and isolation from pro-social others
- temperamental and personality factors including weak socialisation, impulsivity, restless aggressive energy, egocentrism, below average verbal intelligence, a taste for risk, and weak problem-solving/self-regulation skills
- familial factors that include criminality and a variety of psychological problems including: low levels of affection, caring, and cohesiveness; poor parental supervision and discipline practices; and outright neglect and abuse
- low levels of personal educational, vocational or financial achievement

The more delinquent youth may require a high degree of structure and accountability in order for them to begin to take responsibility for and change their delinquent cognitive-behavioral patterns. The beliefs and cognitive emotional states associated with the justification of abusive and delinquent behavior, possibly including egotistical antagonistic masculinity and hostile masculinity, need to be identified and altered through the use of cognitive restructuring. Hunter (2006) emphasises the importance of strong adult male role models and mentors who can challenge the cognitive-behavioral patterns associated with hostile masculinity and aggressive interpersonal dominance and model healthy masculinity. Psycho-educational interventions that address appropriate sexual boundaries, non-abusive sexual behavior, healthy sexuality, and healthy masculinity are also recommended (Latessa, 2005; Prentky and Righthand, 2003; Hunter, 2006). Worling (2001) recommend instruction on skills categorised as 'Alternatives to Aggression' (Goldstein and McGinnis, 1997). Aggression Replacement Training (ART) (Goldstein, Glick, and Gibbs, 1998; Glick, 2006) has been identified as a preferred evidence-based institutional program for delinquent youth (Greenwood, 2008). ART treats aggressive and violent prone youth with a curriculum that includes social skills, anger control, and moral reasoning components. As stated above, Multisystemic Therapy is an evidence-based ecological model based on addressing the multi-determined nature of antisocial behavior in adolescents using home-based services and intervention in the school and community (as cited in Saldana, Swenson, and Letourneau, 2006).

Pedophilic interests

Becker (1988) found there were a minority of sexually offending youth who showed a well-established pattern associated with sexually deviant stimuli. Hunter, Figueredo, Malamuth, and Becker (2003) identified a small subset of juveniles who target children and may have a more fixated interest, indicative of early onset pedophilia. The highest levels of deviant sexual arousal have been found in juveniles who exclusively target young male children, specifically when penetration is involved (Hunter and Becker, 1994; Marshall, Barbaree and Eckles, 1991). In general, the sexual arousal patterns of these youth appear more changeable than those of adult sex offenders, and relate less directly to their patterns of offending behavior (Hunter and Becker, 1994; Hunter, Goodwin, and Becker, 1994). Related to assessing arousal patterns, Prentky (2001) notes that the fluidity of sexual preference in adolescence raises the question as to whether we can capture a stable snapshot. There is some research to support a connection between deviant sexual arousal and sexual victimisation. Hunter et al. (2003) found that a history of non-coercive sexual victimisation by non-relative males was associated with sexual perpetration against a male child. Worling (2004) cited research that found that in some cases, deviant arousal may have been shaped by long-term abuse that involved fear, violence, and physiological arousal.

Hunter (2008) found those youth with pedophilic interests could be differentiated by antisocial versus non-antisocial orientation. The 'Pedophilic Interests/Antisocial' youth show many of the characteristics of the 'Life Course Persistent' youth and may need more of an adult lifetime management model. The 'Pedophilic/Non-Antisocial' youth do not appear to be pervasively delinquent and their prognosis may be favorable. They may benefit from specialised cognitive behavioral and pharmacological treatments, including arousal reconditioning.

One youth with whom this author worked had engaged in sexually abusive behavior toward male and female children. An Abel assessment found an extremely high degree of sexual interest in young males between the ages of two to four and eight to ten. This youth reported that approximately 80 per cent of his masturbation fantasies involved males between the ages of 9–13. He had been sexually abused at the age of seven by a 12-year-old male with the sexual contact involving anal intercourse.

Treatment

As stated above, those youth characterised by pedophilic interests in combination with an antisocial orientation need a higher level of external supervision and monitoring. Covert sensitisation is a technique in which youth are taught to pair their sexually abusive fantasies with mentally aversive stimuli in order to interrupt the pleasurable association they have previously experienced. Vicarious sensitisation involves participants listening to individualised crime scenarios, based on their offense and fantasies, and then being exposed to aversive video vignettes depicting a range of negative consequences that could result from sexually abusive behavior (Faniff and Becker, 2006). Satiation therapy involves utilising deviant thoughts in a repetitive manner to the point of becoming satiated with the very stimuli that has previously been used for arousal (Becker, 1990). The technique utilises both verbal, involving repeating statements to the point of boredom (Becker, 1990; Becker et al., 1988) and masturbatory satiation (Hunter and Santos, 1990). The penile plethymograph (PPG) may be utilised in conjunction with the above techniques in order to establish a baseline of the deviant arousal pattern and as a post test to assess to what degree the youth has been able to master techniques to suppress deviant arousal.

Co-occurring mental disorders

Typology research identified the prevalence of mood and anxiety related symptoms in the different subtypes. Kavoussi et al. (1988) found in an outpatient sample of sexually abusive youth that 20 per cent had some symptoms of adjustment disorder with depressed mood and close to seven per cent had Attention-Deficit Hyperactivity Disorder (ADHD). Becker et al. (1991) found that 42 per cent of their sample experienced major depressive symptoms. In a sample of 9–14-year-old boys with sexual behavior problems, Shaw et al. (1993) found that 50 per cent had an anxiety disorder and 35 per cent suffered from a mood disorder. Cavanaugh, Pimenthal, and Prentky (2008) studied a sample of 667 boys involved with social services, most who came from 'highly dysfunctional' families and had experienced a high degree of physical, psychological, and sexual abuse as well as neglect. The authors found that 66.7 per cent had ADHD, 55.6 per cent Post Traumatic Stress Disorder, and 49.9 per cent had a Mood Disorder. Approximately a quarter used drugs and about one-fifth consumed alcohol.

In some cases, the symptom profile of these disorders may be contributing factors to the sexually abusive behaviors. Becker (1988) identified adolescents who are compromised by a psychiatric condition that interferes with the ability to regulate and inhibit aggressive and sexual impulses. Sexually abusive behavior may reflect compensatory behavior secondary to depression and associated low self-esteem and hopelessness (Ryan and Lane, 1997). Dailey (1996) identifies youth whose obsessive-compulsive disorders appear to drive paraphilic behaviors. This author has evaluated youth in

whom the hyper-sexuality and impulsivity associated with mania appeared to have been an important precursor to a sexual offense. Co-occurring mental health problems may also impact amenability to treatment and interfere with adaptive functioning and the ability of the youth to move toward a more normative path of development.

Treatment

It is essential to identify and treat more pervasive developmental delays, neurological problems, significant substance abuse, mood instability, depression, suicidal ideation, trauma related anxiety, and disorders of thinking or reality testing. The Revised Report from the National Task Force on Juvenile Sexual Offending (1993: 69–70) articulates the following important assumptions in regard to the treatment of youth with co-occurring mental disorders:

- Some co-occurring disorders may impede the juvenile's ability to successfully participate and progress in offence specific treatment.
- Some co-occurring disorders may require stabilisation prior to acceptance into offence specific treatment programs. Examples include psychotic symptoms, substance abuse, suicidal ideation, affective disorders, PTSD, etc.
- Specialised inpatient, outpatient, and aftercare treatment programs for youth with multiple diagnoses should be included in the continuum of services for sexually abusive youth. Such programs must integrate management of chronic psychiatric disorders and specialised, offense specific treatment either within the psychiatric program or in a congruent fashion with other programs that are available.
- Pharmacological intervention may be necessary in cases in which associated depression and anxiety significantly impact on the youth's functioning and amenability to treatment.

Dialectical Behavioral Therapy (DBT) (Linehan, 1993) is a promising mental health treatment designed to treat severe and chronic multi-diagnostic patients. The four primary components of the skills training portion of DBT are core mindfulness, interpersonal effectiveness, emotional regulation, and distress tolerance. The use of DBT has been found to result in significant reductions with suicidal teen's symptoms including anxiety, depression, interpersonal sensitivity, and obsessive-compulsive symptoms patterns (Miller et al., 1996). Improvements were also found in confusion about self, impulsivity, emotion dysregulation, and interpersonal difficulties. The cognitive behavioral chain utilised in DBT as well as the skills based focus is congruent with the goals and methods of sex offense specific treatment.

Trauma informed care

Scientific advances studying the impacts of child maltreatment on the brain have significant implications for understanding and treating traumatised children and adolescents. 'Traumatic and neglectful experiences cause abnormal organisation and function of important neural systems in the brain, compromising the functional capacities mediated by these systems' (Perry, 2004: 29). Teicher et al. (2003) describe child maltreatment as promoting an alternative neural 'stress response pathway' that may enhance the emergence of psychiatric illness and behavioral problems. The environment of persisting threat associated with childhood trauma and the resulting exposure to high levels of stress hormones results in an altered baseline state of arousal, characterised by a physiological state of persisting alarm and increased reactivity. This plays a major role in maladaptive behavioral and cognitive problems that may include hypervigilance, impulsivity, anxiety, affect regulation problems, and sleep problems (Perry, 2006). Teicher et al. (2003) propose that the stress related effects on the brain may impact on the control of aggressive, oral, and sexual behaviors, formation and recollection of emotional memory, the triggering of the fight or flight response, and the development of Post-Traumatic Stress Disorder.

Research has found significant relationships between youth's sexual victimisation experiences and the sexually abusive behavior perpetrated by the youth in regard to the type of sexual contact, gender, relationship, modus operandi, and severity of acts (Veneziano et al., 2000; Burton, 2003). Ryan (1989) described parallels in victim outcomes and offender triggers as it relates to power and control behaviors, irrational thinking, irresponsible decision-making, deviant sexual arousal, aggression, and preoccupation with or reenactment of one's own victimisation. Gil and Johnson (1993) describe the sexually reactive child whose sexual behavior problems are in response to having been sexually and possibly physically abused at a young age. The sexual behaviors are likely to be advanced far beyond age expectations, patterned and increase over time, and often associated with other conduct problems. Finkelhor (1987) identified the behavioral manifestations of traumatic sexualisation as including sexual preoccupations and compulsive, precocious, and aggressive sexual behaviors. Similar characteristics may be found in sexually abusive youth. One older adolescent whom this author evaluated was sexually abused by his biological father up until the age of five. He subsequently engaged in an extensive history of sexualised behaviors including sexual contact with other children, sexually offending against children when he became an adolescent, involvement in multiple paraphilias, and extensive sexual acting-out with peers in residential settings. When asked about the impact of his being sexually abused, he stated that it 'totally changed the way I saw the world . . . from that point on things were different'. He went on to say that while a normal five year old would think about toys and ice cream, 'all I could think about was sex'. He reported that this high degree of sexual drive and preoccupation has been consistent since his early sexual victimisation.

Treatment

The evolving knowledge about the brain has implications for the power of experiences and interventions to change an individual's adaptive functioning. Research on neuro-plasticity informs that the brain can be neurologically altered (use-dependent alterations) through the youth's exposure to environments that are consistent, predictable, nurturing, and encourage the repetitive practicing of healthy emotional regulation strategies (Perry, 2006).

Trauma treatment emphasises the importance of physical and psychological safety. In an unsafe or threatening environment, youth will continue to manifest the physiological and psychological reactivity and cognitive, emotional, and behavioral patterns they perceive as necessary to survive in a 'malevolent world'. In a safe environment, youth can begin learning coping skills to decrease and de-condition anxiety and arousal levels, enabling them to tolerate work on past traumatic experiences and begin to alter the way they view themselves and their world (van der Kolk et al., 1996).

Treatment with traumatised youth must first regulate the brainstem's sensitised and dys-regulated stress response systems. Once these systems are more regulated, a sequence of developmentally appropriate enrichment and therapeutic activities can be implemented (Perry, 2006). Interventions that can decrease hyperarousal and emotional reactivity include: relaxation, meditation, yoga, dancing, drumming, music, massage, biofeedback, neurofeedback, art, drama, occupational therapy, Eye Movement Desensitisation and Reprocessing (EMDR), Dialectical Behavioral Therapy (DBT) and other cognitive-behavioral treatments, and psychopharmacology (Perry, 2006; Linehan, 1993; Creeden, 2006; Longo, 2009, 2010; Fentress, 2005). These interventions help improve self-awareness and self-regulation skills, often in conjunction with changes in thinking, emotions, and behavior. Treatment utilises multi-sensory (auditory, visual, tactile, kinesthetic) 'whole brain' teaching (Creeden, 2007). Providing a 'safe place', weighted blankets (deep pressure), and sensory rooms accompanied by soothing music may also be helpful (Creeden, 2005).

Once youth have acquired some self-monitoring and self-regulation skills to decrease anxiety and arousal levels, they can work to alter the way they view themselves and their world. Van der Kolk (2003) emphasises the importance of processing and integrating trauma memories into conscious mental frameworks. Youth seek to gain a deeper understanding by creating a coherent narrative (autobiographical story) as a means of discovering the origins of the cognitive and emotional precursors to offending. Parallels between the outcomes of past trauma and triggers for abusive behavior include feelings such as anxiety, fear, abandonment, rejection, shame, helplessness, and powerlessness (Ryan, 1989). Gaining insight and awareness can have a powerful impact and be a first step toward being open to corrective experiences that challenge dysfunctional and abuse-supportive thinking and moderate the emotional pain/triggers (Leversee and Ryan, 2010).

Conclusion

The history of the juvenile sexual offending field reflects an evolution from a narrow, specialised approach to a more holistic model that recognises the complex and multi-determined nature of juvenile sexual offending and other non-sexual conduct problems and delinquency. An holistic model understands the diverse developmental and dynamic factors associated with offending and strives to be both comprehensive and individualised in assessment, treatment, and supervision planning. Adolescent development, typology research, co-occurring mental health problems, and trauma-informed care are important areas that inform our work. As we continue to expand and refine our knowledge, it should always be applied in a manner that recognises the unique characteristics and treatment and supervision needs of each youth.

References

Alexander, M. (1999) Sexual Offender Treatment Efficacy Revisited. *Sexual Abuse: A Journal of Research and Treatment*, 11: 2, 110–16.

Becker, J.V. (1988) Adolescent Sex Offenders. *Behavior Therapy*, 11, 185–7.

Becker, J.V. (1990) Treating Adolescent Sex Offenders. *Professional Psychology, Research and Practice*, 21, 362–5.

Becker, J.V., Kaplan, M.S. and Kavoussi, R. (1988) Measuring the Effectiveness of Treatment for the Aggressive Adolescent Sexual Offender. *Annals of the New York Academy of Sciences*, 528, 215–22.

Becker, J. et al. (1991) The Incidence of Depressive Symptomatology in Juvenile Sex Offenders with a History of Abuse. *Child Abuse and Neglect*. 15: 531–6.

Bronfenbrenner, U. (1979) *The Ecology of Human Development*. Cambridge, MA: Harvard University Press.

Bronfenbrenner, U. (1989) Ecological Systems Theory. In Vasta, R. (ed.) *Six Theories of Child Development: Revised Formulations and Current Issues*. Greenwich, CT: JAI.

Brown, S.M. and Schwartz, J.D. (2006) Promoting Healthy Sexuality in Sexually Abusive Youth. In Longo, R.E. and Prescott, D.S. (eds.) *Current Perspectives: Working with Sexually Aggressive Youth and Youth with Sexual Behavior Problems*. Holyoke, MA, NEARI Press.

Burton, D.L. (2003) The Relationship between the Sexual Victimization of and the Subsequent Sexual Abuse of Male Adolescents. *Child and Adolescent Social Work Journal*, 20: 4, 277–96.

Burton, D.L. and Meezan, W. (2004) Revisiting Recent Research on Social Learning Theory as an Etiological Proposition for Sexually Abusive Male Adolescents. *Journal of Evidenced Based Social Work.* 1, 41–80.

Caldwell, M.F. (2007) Sexual Offense Adjudication and Sexual Recidivism among Juvenile Offenders. *Behavioral Science.* 19: 2, 107–13. (Online Issue)

Cavanaugh, D.J., Pimenthal, A. and Prentky, R. (2008) A Descriptive Study of Sexually Abusive Boys and Girls-Externalising Behaviors. In Schwartz, B.K. (ed.) *The Sex Offender: Offender Evaluation and Program Strategies Volume VI.* Kingston: Civic Research Institute.

Chaffin, M. and Bonner, B. (1998) 'Don't Shoot, We're Your Children': Have We Gone Too Far in our Response to Adolescent Sexual Abusers with Sexual Behavior Problems. *Child Maltreatment: Journal of the American Professional Society on the Abuse of Children.* 3: 4, 314–16.

Creeden, K. (2005) *The Brain's Part in Juvenile Sexual Offending.* Presentation to the National Adolescent Perpetration Network Annual Conference, Denver, CO.

Creeden, K. (2006) Trauma and Neurobiology: Considerations for the Treatment of Sexual Behavior Problems in Children and Adolescents. In Longo, R.E. and Prescott, D.S. (eds.) *Current Perspectives: Working with Sexually Aggressive Youth and Youth with Sexual Behavior Problems.* Holyoke, MA: NEARI Press.

Creeden, K. (2007) *Brain Functioning and Dynamics Involved in Problematic or Abusive Sexual Behavior.* Presentation to the Colorado Continuum Network, Denver, CO.

Dailey, L. (1996) *Adjunctive Biological Treatments with Sexually Abusive Youth.* Paper presented at the Twelfth Annual Conference of the National Adolescent Perpetration Network, Minneapolis.

Davies, D. (2004) *Child Development: A Practitioner's Guide.* New York: Guilford Press.

Faniff, A.M. and Becker, J.V. (2006) Specialized Assessment and Treatment of Adolescent Sex Offenders. *Aggression and Violent Behavior,* 11, 265–82.

Fentress, D. (2005) *The Brain's Part in Juvenile Sexual Offending.* National Adolescent Perpetration Network Conference: Denver, CO.

Finkelhor, D. (1987) The Trauma of Sexual Abuse. *Journal of Interpersonal Violence,* 2, 348–66.

Gil, E. and Johnson, T.C. (1993) *Sexualized Children: Assessment and Treatment of Sexualized Children and Children Who Molest.* Rockville, MD: Launch Press.

Glick, B. (2006) ART-A Comprehensive Intervention for Aggressive Youth. In Glick, B. (ed.) *Cognitive Behavioral Interventions for At-Risk Youth.* Kingston, NJ: Civic Research Institute.

Goldstein, A.P., Glick, B. and Gibbs, J.C. (1998) *Aggression Replacement Training: A Comprehensive Intervention for Aggressive Youth.* rev. edn. Champaign, IL: Research Press

Goldstein, A.P. and McGinnis, B. (1997) *Skill Streaming the Adolescent: New Strategies and Perspectives for Teaching Pro-social Skills.* Champaign, IL: Research Press.

Gough, H.G. (1987) *California Psychological Inventory: Administrator's Guide.* Palo Alto, CA: Consulting Psychologists Press.

Greenwood, P. (2008) *Prevention and Intervention Programs for Juvenile Offenders.*18 (2): Fall 2008 www.futureofchildren.org

Hunter, J.A. (1999) *Understanding Juvenile Sexual Offending Behavior: Emerging Research, Treatment Approaches and Management Practices.* Center for Sex Offender Management.

Hunter, J.A. (2006) *Understanding Sexually Abusive Youth: New Research and Clinical Directions.* Broomfield. nColorado Department of Human Services sponsored training.

Hunter, J.A. (2008) *Understanding Sexually Abusive Youth: New Research and Clinical Directions.* Ft. Collins: Colorado Child and Adolescent Mental Health Conference.

Hunter, J.A. and Becker, J.V. (1994) The Role of Deviant Sexual Arousal in Juvenile Sexual Offending: Etiology, Evaluation, and Treatment. *Criminal Justice and Behavior* 21, 132–49.

Hunter, J.A. et al. (2003) Juvenile Sex Offenders: Toward the Development of a Typology. *Sexual Abuse: A Journal of Research and Treatment,* 15: 1, 27–48.

Hunter, J.A., Goodwin, D.W. and Becker, J.V. (1994) The Relationship Between Phallometrically Measured Deviant Sexual Arousal and Clinical Characteristics in Juvenile Sexual Offenders. *Behavior Research and Therapy,* 32, 533–8.

Hunter, J. and Santos, D. (1990) The Use of Specialized Cognitive-Behavioral Therapies in The Treatment of Adolescent Sexual Offenders. *International Journal of Offender Therapy and Comparative Criminology,* 34, 239–47.

Kavoussi, R.J., Kaplan, M. and Becker, J.V. (1988) Psychiatric Diagnoses in Adolescent Sexual Offenders. *Journal of the American Child Adolescent Psychiatry.* 27, 241–3.

Latessa, E.J. (2005) *What Works and What Doesn't in Reducing Recidivism: The Principles of Effective Intervention.* Colorado Division of Youth Corrections Provider Council Conference, Vail.

Lerner, R.M. and Steinberg, L. (eds.) (2009) *Handbook of Adolescent Psychology (3rd Edition): Volume 1: Individual bases of adolescent development.* Hoboken, NJ: John Wiley and Sons.

Leversee, T. and Pearson, C. (2001) Eliminating the Pendulum Effect: A Balanced Approach to the Assessment, Treatment, and Management of Sexually Abusive Youth. *Journal of the Center for Families, Children, and the Courts.* 3, 45–57.

Leversee, T. (2007) Using Typologies to Individualise the Assessment, Treatment, and Supervision of Sexually Abusive Youth. In Calder, M. (ed.) *Children and Young People who Sexually Abuse: Taking the Field Forward.* Lyme Regis: Russell House Publishing.

Leversee, T. (2010a) Providing Differential Treatment and Supervision to the Diverse Population of Sexually Abusive Youth. In Schwartz, B. (ed.) Kingston, N.J. *Handbook of Sex Offender Treatment.* Civic Research Institute.

Leversee, T. (2010b) Typology Research: Refining Our Understanding of a Diverse Population. In Ryan, G., Leversee, T. and Lane, S. (eds.) *Juvenile Sexual Offending: Causes, Consequences, and Corrections.*, 3rd edn. San Francisco: Jossey-Bass Publishers.

Leversee, T. and Powell, K. (pre-print) Beyond Risk Management to a More Holistic Model for Treating Sexually Abusive Youth. In Schwartz, B. (ed.) Kingston, N.J. Civic Research Institute.

Leversee, T. and Ryan, G. (2010) Brain Development and Function: Neurology and Psychiatry in the Treatment of Sexually Abusive Youth. In: Ryan, G., Leversee, T. and Lane, S. (eds.) *Juvenile Sexual Offending: Causes, Consequences, and Corrections.* 3rd edn. San Francisco: Jossey-Bass.

Linehan, M. (1993) *Skills Training Manual for Treating Borderline Personality Disorder.* New York: Guilford Press.

Longo, R.E. (2009) *Trauma and Its Impact on the Brain.* National Adolescent Perpetration Network Conference. Tampa, FL.

Longo, R.E. (2010) Helping Body and Mind: The Use of Biofeedback, Neurofeedback, and QEEG Brain Mapping with Young People who Sexually Abuse. In Prescott, D.S. and Longo, R.E. (eds.) *Current Applications: Strategies for Working with Sexually Aggressive Youth and*

Youth with Sexual Behavior Problems. Holyoke, MA: NEARI Press.

Marshall, W.L., Barbaree, H.E. and Eccels, A. (1991) Early Onset and Deviant Sexuality in Child Molesters. *Journal of Interpersonal Violence* 6, 323–36.

Miller, A.L. et al. (1996) *A Pilot Study: Dialectical Behavior Therapy Adapted for Suicidal Adolescents.* Poster presented at the 1st annual meeting of the International Society for the Improvement and Teaching of Dialectical Behavior Therapy, New York, NY.

Miner, M. (2008) *What Attachment Theory Tells us About Unique Risks for Adolescent Boys to Sexually Offend.* Portland: National Adolescent Perpetration Network Conference.

Miner, M.H. et al. (2010) Understanding Sexual Perpetration Against Children: Effects of Attachment Style, Interpersonal Involvement and Hypersexuality. *Sexual Abuse: A Journal of Research and Treatment.*

Moffitt, T. (1993) Adolescence-Limited and Life-Course Persistent Antisocial Behavior: A Developmental Taxonomy. *Psychology Review,* 100: 4, 674–701.

National Task Force on Juvenile Sexual Offending (1993) The Revised Report from the National Task Force on Juvenile Sexual Offending. *Juvenile and Family Court Journal.* 44: 4, 69–70.

O'Brien, M. and Bera, W. (1986) Adolescent Sexual Offenders: A Descriptive Typology. *Preventing Sexual Abuse,* 1, 3.

Perry, D. (2006) Applying Principles of Neurodevelopment to Clinical Work with Maltreated and Traumatized Youth: The Neuro-sequential Model of Therapeutics. In Boyd, N. (ed.) *Working with Traumatized Children in Child Welfare,* 27–52.

Powell, K.M. (2010a) Therapeutic Relationships and the Process of Change. In Ryan, G., Leversee, T. and Lane, S. (eds.) *Juvenile Sexual Offending: Causes, Consequences, and Corrections,* 3rd edn San Francisco: John Wiley and Sons.

Powell, K.M. (2010b) Strengths-based Approaches. In Prescott, D.S. and Longo, R.E. (eds.) *Current Applications: Strategies for Working with Sexually Aggressive Youth and Youth with Sexual Behavior Problems.* Holyoke, MA: NEARI Press.

Prentky, R. (2001) *Assessing Actuarial and Dynamic Risk with Sexually Abusive Youth.* National Adolescent Perpetration Network Conference, Kansas City.

Prentky, R. and Righthand, S. (2003) *Juvenile Sex Offender Assessment Protocol: Manual.*

Washington, DC: Office of Juvenile Justice and Delinquency Prevention.

Prescott, D. and Longo, R. (2007) *Current Perspectives on Working with Youth: Where our Field has Been and Where We're Going.* National Adolescent Perpetration Network Conference. Albuquerque, NM.

Richardson, G. et al. (2004) Personality-based Classification Derived from the Personality Pattern Scales from the Millon Adolescent Clinical Inventory (MACI). *British Journal of Clinical Psychology*, 43, 258–98.

Ryan, G. (1989) Victim to Victimizer: Rethinking Victim Treatment. *Journal of Interpersonal Violence*, 4: 3, 325–41.

Ryan, G. and Lane, S. (1997) Integrating Theory and Method. In Ryan, G. and Lane, S. (eds.) *Juvenile Sexual Offending: Causes, Consequences, and Corrections.* San Francisco: Jossey-Bass.

Reitzel, L.R. and Carbonell, J.L. (2006) The Effectiveness of Sexual Offender Treatment for Juveniles as Measured by Recidivism: A meta-analysis. *Sex Abuse: A Journal of Research and Treatment*, 18, 401–21.

Saldana, L., Swenson, C.C. and Letourneau, E. (2006) Multisystemic Therapy with Juveniles who Sexually Abuse. In Longo, R.E. and Prescott, D.S. (eds.) *Current Perspectives: Working with Sexually Aggressive Youth and Youth with Sexual Behavior Problems.* Holyoke, MA: NEARI Press.

Seto, M. and Lalumiere, M. (2010) What Is So Special About Male Adolescent Sexual Offending: A Review and Test of Explanations Through Meta-Analysis. *Psychological Bulletin*, 136: 4, 526–75.

Shaw, J., Campo-Bowen, A.E., Applegate, B., Perez, D., Antoine, L.B. and Hart, E.L. (1993) Young Boys Who Commit Serious Sexual Offenses: Demographics, Psychometrics, and Phenomenology. *The Bulletin of the American Academy of Psychiatry and the Law*, 21, 399–408.

Steinberg, L. and Haskins, R. (2008) *Keeping Adolescents Out of Prison.* The Future of Children. Princeton-Brookings.

Teicher, M. et al. (2003) The Neurobiolgical Consequences of Early Stress and Childhood Maltreatment. *Neuroscience and Behavioral Reviews*, 27, 33–44.

Vance, J.E. (2001) Neurobiological Mechanisms of Psychosocial Resiliency. In Richman, G.M. and Fraser, M.W. (eds.) *The Context of Youth Violence: Resilience, Risk, and Protection.* Westport, Connecticut: Praeger.

van der Kolk, B. (2003) The Neurobiology of Childhood Trauma and Abuse. *Child and Adolescent Psychiatric Clinics of North America*, 12, 293–317.

van der Kolk, B., McFarlane, A. and Weisaeth, L. (1996) *Traumatic Stress.* New York: Guilford Press.

Veniziano, C., Veniziano, L. and LeGrand, S. (2000) The Relationship between Adolescent Sex Offender Behaviors and Victim Characteristics with Prior Victimization. *Journal of Interpersonal Violence*, 15: 4, 363–74.

Werner, E.E. and Smith, R.S. (1992) *Overcoming the Odds: High Risk Children from Birth to Adulthood.* Ithaca, NY: Cornell University Press.

Worling, J.R. (2001) Personality-Based Typology of Adolescent Male Sexual Offenders: Differences in Recidivism Rates, Victim Selection Characteristics, and Personal Victimization Histories. *Sexual Abuse: A Journal of Research and Treatment*, 13: 3, 149–66.

Worling, J.R. (2004) Essentials of a Good Intervention Programme for Sexually Abusive Juveniles: Offence Related Treatment Tasks. In O'Reilly, G. et al. (eds.) *The Handbook of Clinical Intervention with Youth People who Sexually Abuse.* Hove: Taylor and Francis.

Worling, J.R., Litteljohn, A. and Bookalam, D. (2010) 20-year Prospective Follow-Up Study of Specialized Treatment for Adolescents who Offended Sexually. *Behavioral Sciences and the Law*, 28, 46–57.

Yager, J.B. (2005) *The Brain's Part in Juvenile Sexual Offending.* National Adolescent Perpetration Network Conference: Denver, CO.

CHAPTER 4

Typologies of Juveniles who Sexually Harm: Associations With Risk Factors, Modus Operandi and Criminal Activity

Nicole Hickey

This chapter addresses the issue of typologies for young people who sexually harm; why are they investigated, which typologies currently exist, and how should we decide if they are useful in applied settings.

Throughout the chapter the term 'juvenile' will be used to refer to the total population of young people (ie pre-adolescent and adolescent), but where appropriate the ages of the samples that have been studied will be identified. Also, the term 'juveniles who sexually harm' will be used to refer to the population in question the reason being that not all the samples in the typology literature consist of individuals who had been convicted of a sex offence. Therefore it would be inaccurate to refer to them as 'sex offenders'. Similarly the behaviour will be referred to as harmful sexual behaviour (HSB).

What do we mean by 'typology'?

Typologies are a means of classifying sub-groups of a population. The aim is to identify 'types' and to try and maximise the similarities among the members of one type while maximising the differences between members of different types. The starting point for identifying typologies can be:

- conceptual, in which the basis of the typology is taken from theory or concepts that are thought to be relevant for the population
- empirical, in which the basis is derived from observed characteristics or behaviour
- a mixture of both

Why do we need typologies?

Typologies can serve a purpose in both research and applied contexts. In research contexts divining typologies can be an end in itself as a way of describing sub-groups within the population. Or they can be a step on the pathway to developing a theory by exploring the usefulness of particular concepts or classifying empirically observed phenomena. In applied contexts typologies can be used in a number of ways: to allocate scarce resources to a large heterogeneous population; to develop appropriate assessment tools for different sub-groups; and to identify the relevant intervention modules for different types. Without typologies practitioners and managers are more likely to use a random allocation of juveniles to resources which, when resources are scarce, is an inefficient method. Or they may rely on what is known about adult sex offenders to guide their service allocation and/or the content of intervention programmes; again this is likely to prove inefficient due to the differences between juveniles and adults, which means that services for juveniles should be developed on the basis of their developmental relevance.

Within the research literature concerning juveniles who sexually harm a number of typologies have been explored and have been derived from the following dimensions: victim age, criminal history, gender, and personality traits. Each of these will be reviewed with particular reference to their associations with risk factors, modus operandi and criminal activity where assessed.

Victim age typology

Classifying juveniles according to the age of the victims against which the HSB has been perpetrated (eg children versus peers/adults) is probably one of the most prevalent typologies and has received the greatest attention in the literature. The reasons for this are undoubtedly because this typology predominates within the adult sex offender literature and appears to have 'face validity'.

The studies that have explored this typology within their samples have produced varied results that make evaluating the usefulness of the typology more difficult. One of the problems is that the studies use a variety of definitions of the age ranges for 'child' and 'peer/adult' victims.

Nevertheless, this typology remains one of the most explored. One of the earliest comparisons between those who victimised children and those who victimised peers reported that the former were more likely to have suffered childhood sexual abuse (Ford and Linney, 1995). Hunter, Hazelwood and Slesinger (2000) using the definition of ≥5 years age difference to denote 'child' victims within the police records of 126 adolescent males, found a number of differences between the 'child' and 'peer' groups. For instance, those who harmed child victims were found to be more likely to have harmed male victims, to be more likely to have harmed their own siblings, and, finally, were less likely to have used physical force during the commission of the sexual harm. In contrast, those in the peer victim group were found to be more likely to harm females, more likely to harm strangers, more likely to perpetrate the sexual harm as part of a group, and were more likely to use physical force.

In a European sample of 116 adolescent males prosecuted for a sexual offence, and using the same age definition of ≥5 years age difference for the 'child' victim group, Hendriks and Bijleveld (2004) also found that those in the child victim group were more likely to have victimised males than females. Furthermore, they were also found to have more social problems, to be more likely to have a negative self-image, and more likely to have been bullied at school. Unfortunately, as this was a cross-sectional study there is no way of determining the temporal relationship between these three psychosocial factors and being in the child victim group; does the stigma of harming child victims lead to the development of a negative self-image, having social problems and being bullied, or do these types of social deficits lead to choosing child victims?

A very different definition of the victim-perpetrator age difference was used by Kjellgren et al. (2006) victims were considered 'children' if they were 11 years old or younger, and 'peer' victims were those aged 12 years or older. In their sample of 197 Swedish adolescent males referred to social services following perpetrating HSB, and despite this alternative method of categorisation, the researchers found that the child group were more likely to have experienced childhood sexual abuse, to harm siblings, and to have male victims, while those in the peer victim group were more likely to harm

strangers, and were more likely to have perpetrated the sexual harm together with accomplices.

Hunter et al. (2003) used a similar age definition in their study of 182 North American convicted male juvenile offenders from a selection of treatment facilities; victims under the age of 12 years were categorised as 'children' while those over the age of 12 were 'peers/adult'. In addition to comparing the group's offending characteristics a number of psychosocial functioning factors were also analysed. Those who offended against children were found to be significantly more likely to offend against a sibling or other relative, and to have perpetrated the offence in the victim's residence. They were significantly less likely than the peer/adult offenders to have used force or a weapon, or to have been intoxicated at the time of the offence.

In relation to psychosocial functioning Hunter et al. (2003) reported that those who offended against children had greater psychosocial deficits including a lack of social confidence, anxiety, depression, and a pessimistic outlook.

Worling (1995) also included some psychosocial functioning factors (eg self-esteem, depression, and attitudes) in his analysis comparing a sample of 90 male convicted juvenile offenders attending a community treatment service and categorised as an offender against children or an offender against peers/adult. In this study the victim-age categorisation defined 'child' as a victim at least four years younger than the perpetrator *and* still under 12 years old, all other victims were categorised as 'peer/adult'. In contrast to Hunter et al.'s (2003) findings, Worling found no differences between the child and peer/adult groups in relation to the psychosocial functioning factors. Moreover, the only significant differences found between the groups showed that those who offended against peer/adults were more likely to have experienced physical discipline, and that those who offended against children were more likely to have been sexually abused by males while those who offended against peers/adults were more likely to have been sexually abused by females.

Although not compared statistically Carpenter, Peed and Eastman (1995) reported that more of those who offended against peers/adults (from a sample of 36 male adolescent offenders attending a residential treatment facility) offended against non-relatives. In this study the groups were also compared on a number of personality traits; the results indicated that those who offended against children had higher rates of schizoid, avoidant and dependent personality traits. There were no differences in relation to antisocial, narcissistic and histrionic traits. Carpenter et al. (1995) had also used another variation of the victim-age definition in their study; child victims were under 12 years old *and* at least three years younger than the offender, while the peer/adult victims were over 13 years old and no less than two years younger than the offender.

Although the victim-age typology studies use predominantly dichotomous classifications (child or peer/adult victims) a few researchers have embraced the third potential category in such a typology: those who harm *both* children and peers/adults. Richardson et al. (1997) used a British sample of 100 male juveniles referred for assessment following perpetrating harmful sexual behaviour. The victim-age definition used in this study was that a 'child' victim had to be at least four years younger than the perpetrator whereas the 'peer/adult' victim had to be either one year younger, the same age, or older than the perpetrator. Based on a mixture of the victim's age as well as the relationship between the victim and perpetrator Richardson et al. (1997) delineated four groups; Incest, Child, Peer/Adult, and Mixed. Compared across a range of individual, family and offence factors a number of significant group differences were reported. For instance, the groups differed on the age of onset of the harmful sexual behaviour with the mixed group being the youngest and the child group the eldest, and they also differed on the mean number of victims; again the mixed group had the highest number with the child group the lowest.

In common with many of the other studies it was found that the peer/adult group were the most likely to harm strangers, as well as to victimise females; the child group was the most likely to harm male victims. The peer/adult group was also the most likely to commit the acts of sexual harm in public places whereas the incest and child groups were more likely to have harmed in residential settings including the victim's residence. The use of physical force was most characteristic of the peer/adult group although more than half of the mixed and child groups also used force. The mixed group had the highest rate of experiencing childhood sexual abuse, exposure to family violence, and

dysfunctional family backgrounds. Although not reaching statistical significance, there were differences between the groups in relation to non-sexual conduct disorder; the peer/adult group were the most likely to display other conduct disorders. This group was also found to exhibit the greatest frequency of antisocial behaviours and were the most likely to have antisocial peers.

Kemper and Kistner (2007) also used three victim-age groups in their comparison study. The North American sample of 296 male juvenile offenders represents a high-risk sample as all the young men were detained in a residential facility designated for those convicted of at least three felony offences. The allocation to one of the three victim-age groups (child offenders, peers/adult offenders, and mixed offenders) was based on the complete offence history of each individual, although the age definition used in this study was the same as that used by Worling (1995).

With regard to the details of the sexual offending, significant differences between the groups were found. The peer group was significantly most likely to offend against only female victims while the mixed group was the most likely to have a history of offending against both genders. Similarly, the mixed group was the most likely to have offended against a range of relative and non-relative victims while the peer group was the least likely to have only offended against relatives but was the most likely to have offended against only non-relatives. The mixed group was also the most likely, and the child group the least likely, to have used penile penetration against their victims. Finally, in a comparison of the officially recorded recidivism rates for the groups, over a follow-up period that averaged five years, there were no significant group differences for either the sexual or non-sexual recidivism rates of the three groups.

The study by Parks and Bard (2006) differs from other studies concerning typologies in that instead of comparing the offence characteristics of the groups it sought to compare three victim-age groups on risk assessment measures: the Juvenile Sex Offender Assessment Protocol-II (Prentky and Righthand, 2003) and the Psychopathy Checklist: Youth Version (Forth, Kosson and Hare, 2003). Among the 156 incarcerated male juvenile offenders the victim-age definitions were being at least four years younger than the perpetrator and aged 10 years or younger designated a 'child' victim, while being aged 11 years or older designated 'peer/adult' victims, but as with Kemper and Kistner (2007) the victim-age categorisation was based on the full history of adjudicated sex offences.

Across the various sub-scales of the JSOAP-II and PCL:YV there was a trend for the mixed group to have the highest scores. Moreover, there were significant differences between the three groups, predominantly accounted for by the mixed group, in relation to the JSOAP-II impulsive/antisocial behaviour scale and Total score, as well as the PCL:YV Affective, Behavioural and Total score. Thus, the mixed group were at greatest risk in terms of impulsive/antisocial behaviour, and had the highest scores on the PCL:YV indicating they possessed the greatest affective and behavioural personality trait deficits. On all of these scales the child group had the lowest scores. However, in contrast to most of the previous studies there were very few significant differences between the child and peer groups across the various comparisons in this study.

A meta-analysis, conducted on studies published between 1973–1993, by Graves, Openshaw, Ascione and Ericksen (1996) identified three juvenile offender types: 'Pedophilic youth', 'Sexual assault offender' and 'Mixed offense offenders'. The pedophilic group were reported as tending to be socially isolated, to have begun their harmful sexual behaviour before the age of 12, to show a preference for female victims, and to use verbal coercion/manipulation. The sexual assault group were more likely to have begun offending during adolescence, preferred female victims, and perpetrated sexual harm against victims of varying age, for example younger, same age and older. Finally, the mixed offense group were characterised as committing a variety of sexual acts, although they seemed to prefer considerably younger female victims, and the onset of their behaviour ranged from childhood up to mid-adolescence.

The usefulness of the results from this meta-analysis is somewhat limited given the considerable overlap between the groups on a number of the factors that contributed to the analysis.

Limitations

Despite being one of the most explored typologies within the population of juveniles who sexually harm there are a number of limitations, both methodological and conceptual, to the existing evidence base. Firstly, a range of definitions of the victim-age dimension have been used across the studies and this causes problems when trying to compare the findings between studies. This is a problem particular to the juvenile population because in the adult sex offender literature it is far easier to define 'child' and 'peer' victims using the legal definition of 'child', plus with adults it is appropriate to use the criteria of the clinical diagnosis of pedophilia in relation to some of those who offend against children, whereas there is no equivalent criteria that can be applied to juvenile perpetrators.

Secondly, the samples used in the research differ such that some include incarcerated juveniles while others employ community-based youth. As a result it becomes problematic trying to compare findings across studies because the samples differ in relation to their level of risk, and it is necessary to be sure that any application of the findings is made to a similar type of juvenile. Thirdly, the factors on which the types are compared are not consistent across studies. It is true that many have compared the groups on the modus operandi of the HSB, including the gender and type of victim, and to some extent the use of force in the commission of the behaviour. But for many of the other factors different dimensions and measures are used. Thus, there are relatively few consistent findings that can be garnered from the evidence; it appears that those in the child group are most likely to harm siblings or other relatives, and to have harmed male victims, while the peer group is most likely to have harmed strangers and to focus on female victims. When the mixed group is included in the typology they are the most likely to have perpetrated more serious HSB in that they harm victims of both genders and all ages, as well as being the most likely to use force.

Among juveniles there is less developmental likelihood that patterns of sexual arousal to a fixed type of victim have become established, unlike with adults, therefore there is a potential conceptual problem with identifying juveniles as either 'child' or 'peer/adult' abusers. Moreover, the majority of studies have categorised their samples into this dichotomous grouping by basing the categorisation on only the most recent or 'index' incidence of HSB. Consequently, it is a somewhat artificial dichotomy as it does not identify a victim-age typology based on the individual's history of HSB. Indeed, among the few studies that do base the typology groups on the full history of HSB they acknowledge the existence of a third type: the mixed group. Furthermore, in the studies that included the third group the significant group differences tend to be between the mixed group and the others, whereas the differences between the child and peer groups tend to loose their statistical significance.

Another limitation of this typology is that all the research that has contributed to the evidence has been cross-sectional in nature, which means that the temporal relationships between the group allocation and associated factors cannot be established. This has implications for aetiological theory in that it cannot be determined to what extent the group differences are related to why an individual is in one group or another rather that being an artefact of being in that group. Consequently, the typology is limited in its ability to contribute to understanding why a juvenile sexually harms a child or a peer.

Criminal history typology

Many studies have shown that juveniles convicted of sexual offences are more likely to be reconvicted of non-sexual than sexual offences (Rubenstein et al. 1993; Sipe, Jensen and Everett 1998; Worling and Curwen, 2000; Nisbet, Wilson and Smallbone, 2004) and that many convicted juvenile sex offenders have a concurrent history of non-sexual convictions (Caldwell, 2002, 2007). Consequently, in recent years researchers have begun exploring the utility of a typology based on the presence or absence of non-sexual offences. These studies have used empirical methods in testing their typologies.

Using a sample of 32 male juveniles convicted of sex offences who were undergoing mental health assessments as part of the Canadian court process, Butler and Seto (2002) were one of the first to explore this typology. The sex offender group was categorised, on the basis of official criminal charges, into a group of 22 who had only ever been charged with sexual offences (sex-only) and a group of 10 who had also incurred non-sexual offence convictions (sex-plus). The two groups were compared across a broad range of domains with the findings indicating that the sex-plus group displayed significantly more conduct problems, according to DSM-IV criteria,

than the sex-only group. Furthermore, the sex-plus group endorsed a significantly greater number of antisocial beliefs and attitudes than the sex-only group.

In this study the researchers used a standardised measure of risk for future delinquency (not specific to sex offending) the Young Offender-Level of Service Inventory (YO-LSI) (Ilacqua et al., 1999). They found that on a number of the measure's scales (ie criminal history, substance abuse, education/employment problems, family problems, and peer relation problems), as well as the Total score, the sex-plus group scored significantly higher than the sex-only group indicating that they were at higher risk on these domains for future delinquency.

In relation to the characteristics of the sexual offences committed by the sample in this study group, differences were also reported. For instance, they found that the sex-only group were more likely to have had male victims, to have offended against victims younger than six years old, and were more likely to have had multiple victims. The sex-plus group, however, were found to have offended against a greater number of victims to whom they were unrelated. Unfortunately, due to the small numbers in these groups none of these statistical comparisons reached statistical significance.

In the Netherlands, van Wijk, Mali and Bullens (2007) had access to the nationwide register of all those who come into contact with the police. Between 1996 and 2002 they identified 2,485 sex-plus and 1,945 sex-only juveniles. In contrast to most of the studies exploring typologies, van Wijk et al.'s sample included *both* male and female juveniles. Unfortunately, given the large sample in this study the lack of information contained in the register meant that the only comparisons that could be conducted between the groups was limited to the types of offences committed. Nevertheless, group differences were observed. It was found that the sex-plus group began their criminal career at a significantly earlier age than the sex-only group, and their offending career (for any type of offence) continued over a significantly longer period compared to the sex-only group. Not surprisingly, therefore, the sex-plus group had also committed a significantly greater number of offences. With respect to the first type of sexual offence committed by the groups, they were very similar. For both groups 'indecent liberties' and exhibitionism were the least likely type of offence, rape offences were the next most prevalent, while sexual assault was the most prevalent type of offence for both groups. Notably, however, the authors found no evidence that the sex-only group were more likely to be 'persistent' sex offenders, that is, to have committed a greater number of sex offences over time, with less than 20 per cent of the sex-only group having been convicted of more than one sexual offence during the study period.

Most recently Way and Urbaniak (2008) contributed to the literature on typologies based on criminal history by comparing 72 sex-plus and 80 sex-only convicted male juveniles from an American mid-western state community court. In addition to comparisons in relation to offence characteristics, this study also included factors concerning maltreatment, substance misuse, and juvenile delinquency, as well as the caregiver's criminality and substance misuse. Significant group differences were observed in a number of these domains.

The groups differed in their maltreatment experiences with the sex-plus group having significantly higher rates of physical abuse and neglect than the sex-only group, as well as being more likely to have experienced multiple types of maltreatment. Interestingly, however, the groups had very similar rates of childhood sexual abuse although the rate for the sex-plus group was marginally higher. Additionally, the sex-plus group exhibited significantly higher rates of both drug and alcohol misuse, out-of-home placements, and having received a prior mental health diagnosis (not specified). With regard to the juveniles' caregivers, there were no group differences for the fathers' substance misuse or criminal activity, but the mothers in the sex-plus group were significantly more likely to abuse alcohol and to have been arrested for an offence.

With regard to the sex offence details, the sex-only group had significantly younger victims, and were more likely to have offended against a sibling or other relative. There were no group differences in relation to the number of victims, nor were there significant differences, although the sex-only group had marginally higher rates, of having committed a penetrative sexual offence.

Finally, a regression analysis conducted to explore the variables that would predict membership of the sex-plus group found that, of all the significant factors described above, only having an out-of-home placement and a mother with a conviction history predicted being a member of the sex-plus group.

Limitations

The current criminal history or 'sex-plus/sex-only' typology evidence base has several limitations. Firstly, all samples used to test the group differences were drawn from those convicted of sex offences, thus they are not necessarily representative of all young people who sexually harm. Only some juveniles who perpetrate HSB are prosecuted through the criminal justice system, and therefore those in this select group may differ in important aspects from those who are not processed through the criminal justice system and these differences may be important for the typology. Consequently, the findings in relation to the typological differences can only be validly applied to juveniles who have been convicted of a sexual offence. The research has yet to be conducted investigating whether the group differences apply to those who have sexually harmed others but have not been convicted.

In addition, most of the studies warn that it is possible that some of those in the sex-only groups may have committed non-sexual offending behaviour but not been prosecuted within the criminal justice system; therefore, the groups may not be as 'pure' as initially thought.

Finally, the studies differ on the risk factors they explore as potential differentiators between groups. Therefore, comparing the groups to determine any consistent findings is difficult. The only factors on which at least two of the studies compared the types were the characteristics of the sex offences. Both Butler and Seto (2002) and Way and Urbaniak (2008) reported on these but the small sample numbers in the Butler and Seto (2002) study prevented statistical difference being assessed, and furthermore, while both studies reported that the sex-only group were more likely to have younger victims they had discrepant findings in relation to the number of victims; Butler and Seto (2002) reported that the sex-plus group had a greater number of victims while Way and Urbaniak (2008) reported no group differences.

Gender typology

Gender is one of the simplest conceptualisations on which to base a typology and with the emergence of empirical and applied interest in female juveniles who sexually harm the need for such a typology has increased.

Overall there are relatively few studies that have specifically addressed the characteristics of female juveniles and not all have included control samples of male juveniles. Consequently, the female juvenile typology is being developed from a mixture of conceptualisation and empirical methods.

Descriptive studies of female juveniles have tended to describe the individual and family-related characteristics of females, as well as the characteristics of the behaviour they have perpetrated (Fehrenbach and Monastersky, 1988; Johnson, 1998). Thus, large proportions of the population of female juveniles who have sexually harmed have suffered from some type of abuse, the largest proportion of which is childhood sexual abuse; most come from single-parent or reconstituted families; and many have exhibited other antisocial behaviours in addition to harmful sexual behaviour. With respect to the HSB perpetrated, characteristics that have been reported include perpetrating alone, using penetrative behaviours, harming younger children, abusing both genders, abusing victims to whom they were previously known.

Of those studies that have either directly compared males and females, or have presented descriptive data from male and female samples the findings are generally that the females are more likely to have been the victim of childhood sexual abuse, to have suffered more severe forms of childhood sexual abuse, and to have harmed younger victims than the males (Fehrenbach et al., 1986). In relation to virtually all other individual, family, and HSB characteristics the two genders rarely seem to differ.

Mathews, Hunter and Vuz's (1997) findings came from the largest comparison study involving 67 female and 70 male juveniles who sexually harmed seen in clinical settings. However, because the data for the two samples was collected using different methodologies and at different times between-group statistical comparisons were not conducted. It was reported that twice as many females than males were victims of childhood sexual abuse. Similarly, 60 per cent of the females were victims of physical abuse compared to only 45 per cent of the males. The females also had a greater mean number of sexual abusers compared to the males; were abused at an earlier age (64 per cent before the

age of five years); and were more likely to have been abused by both men and women compared to the males. Mathews et al. (1997) also reported that half the females in their sample met the clinical criteria for a diagnosis of post-traumatic stress disorder.

With regard to the characteristics of the HSB, similar proportions of the females and males were reported to have 'fondled' their victims, although only a quarter of the females, compared to half the males, had penetrated (vaginally or anally) their victims. The genders were equally likely to abuse both male and females victims and to harm children under 11 years of age. Finally, only very small proportions of either gender sexually harmed strangers.

Additional studies (Ray and English, 1995; Bumby, Halstenson and Bumby, 1997; Kubik, Hecker and Righthand, 2002; Hendriks and Bijleveld, 2006; Vandiver and Teske, 2006) also compared samples of females and males. Their findings are largely consistent with those presented above. In particular, the females were more likely to have been exposed to childhood sexual abuse than the males, while very few group differences were observed in relation to the characteristics of the HSB.

The only UK-based study to statistically contrast the characteristics of female and male juveniles compared a demographically comparable sample of 22 females and 254 males who had been referred to a community-based specialist forensic service as a result of perpetrating HSB (Hickey, McCrory, Farmer and Vizard, 2008). Confirming the findings of earlier studies, the females were significantly more likely to have been the victim of childhood sexual abuse than the males. In addition they were also more likely to have grown up in families characterised by inadequate sexual boundaries (ie inappropriate sexual expression as well as developmentally inappropriate access to sexual material). On all the other individual and family factors included in the analyses, including inconsistent parenting, physical and emotional abuse and neglect, parental supervision, and parental separation, there were no gender differences.

Moreover, when the relevant sub-groups of the two genders were compared on the characteristics of the childhood sexual abuse they had suffered, it was found that the females had experienced significantly greater number of abusers, and a greater variety of abusers, for example, both family members and friends, as well as both male and female abusers. The females were also, on average, much younger than the males (four years versus seven years, respectively) at the time of the first known incidence of childhood sexual abuse.

In comparisons on the harmful sexual behaviour perpetrated by both genders, which included the characteristics of the victims (eg gender, relationship, age) and the abuse (eg type of contact, verbal coercion, physical coercion), only three factors significantly differentiated the genders: the females were significantly younger than the males when they first began to perpetrate harmful sexual behaviour, but they were significantly less likely to have harmed any victims at least five years younger then them, and they were significantly less likely to have penetrated their victims.

This is the only study to compare the officially recorded criminal activity of male and female juveniles (Hickey, 2009). Not surprisingly males were more likely to have been convicted of criminal offences (both sexual and non-sexual) and to have committed far greater numbers of offences. However, among the females it was found that nearly two-thirds had been convicted of violent offences; a far higher proportion than the males (16 per cent). Furthermore, none of the females had been convicted of a sexual offence despite all having been referred to the forensic service as a consequence of having perpetrated act(s) of harmful sexual behaviour against another person.

Hickey et al. (2008) is the only study to have tried to statistically determine which of the variables that individually differentiates the genders can predict the gender of a juvenile who sexually harms others. Using regression analysis the only significant predictor was the total number of childhood sexual abusers a juvenile had experienced in their own victimisation. Thus, in this particular sample the single best differentiator within the typological dimension of gender was the number of sexual abusers a juvenile had suffered, with those having the greater numbers of abusers being female.

Limitations

The main limitation that also besets all research on female juveniles who sexually harm are small sample sizes which leads to the representativeness of the findings being questioned.

Personality traits typology

Using personality traits as the basis for a typology of juveniles who sexually harm has only been adopted by a few researchers and none have been extensively pursued or validated in further studies. This is surprising given that personality traits as the basis for differentiating between different sub-groups of (non-sex) juvenile offenders has proven to be a growth area in recent years (Skeem et al., 2007; Frick and White, 2008). Smith, Monastersky and Deisher (1987) were one of the first to try and develop a classification system based on the personality traits as defined by their samples' scores on the Minnesota Multiphasic Personality Inventory (Butcher et al., 1992). Using a sample of 262 male juvenile offenders and an empirical method (cluster analysis) they reported four groups: 'overcontrolled/isolated', 'narcissistic/disturbed', 'outgoing/prone to violent outbursts', and 'impulsive/undersocialised'. Interestingly it was found that these groups or 'types' were unrelated to offence factors such as the age or gender of the victims they offended against; thus, personality traits were not found to determine who was chosen to victimise. Furthermore, Smith et al. (1987) also reported, but with no accompanying detail, that the groups differed very little with respect to historical factors and clinical presentation.

Worling's (2001) study aimed to replicate Smith et al.'s (1987) study although he used a different measure of personality traits; the California Psychological Inventory (Gough, 1987). The scores from Worling's sample of 112 male juvenile offenders were again subject to cluster analysis and four factors were considered the best fit for the data; they were labelled 'antisocial/impulsive', 'unusual/isolated', 'over-controlled/reserved', and 'confident/aggressive'. As Smith et al. (1987) had previously found, there was no relationship between the personality trait types and victim age or gender. Nor was there an association with the relationship between offender and victim, or a history of childhood sexual abuse. The group differences that were observed revealed the antisocial/impulsive group to be the most likely to have suffered physical abuse and, together with the unusual/isolated group, to be the most likely to have separated or divorced parents. These two groups were also the most likely to have subsequent non-sexual offending histories.

Both Smith et al. (1987) and Worling (2001) produced empirically derived typologies, however, O'Brien and Bera (1986) had previously attempted developing a personality trait-based typology but using clinical rather than empirical methods. Seven groups were identified: 'naïve experimenters', 'undersocialised child exploiters', 'sexual aggressives', 'sexual compulsives', 'disturbed impulsives', and 'group influenced', and 'pseudo socialised'. Unfortunately the reliability and validity of this typology has not been explored and no empirical data supports these groups.

Limitations

One of the key limitations of the personality trait typology literature is the dearth of it; only two of the studies cited above used empirical measures of personality traits to develop the typologies while O'Brien and Bera (1986) relied entirely upon clinical impressions to derive their typology.

The lack of association between the typologies and the HSB characteristics will be seen by some as a limitation, but if the population of juveniles who sexually harm is viewed as having more in common with the broader antisocial juvenile population, rather than the adult sex offender population, then this typology appears to have considerable face validity. For instance, the link between personality traits and offending behaviour has been made in the wider juvenile delinquency literature and has been used to allocate sub-groups to different levels of risk for recidivism.

Miscellaneous typologies

In addition to the above typologies that have been explored by more than one group of researchers, there have also been some typologies that have only been explored by one or two groups of researchers (so far).

Offence based typology

In 2000 Langstrom, Grann and Lindblad published a typology derived by analysing a range of HSB characteristics. They used a sample of 56 Swedish juveniles (54 male and two female) who had perpetrated sexual harm and were undergoing a forensic psychiatric investigation. The typology was constructed using cluster

analysis involving 15 offence characteristics, including the type of harmful behaviour perpetrated, victim gender, number of victims, location of offence, and age of victim. Five clusters were identified, though never labelled, which makes it difficult to separate them beyond the research context and determine whether they would have utility in applied contexts. Moreover, there were no significant differences between the groups across a range of domains including previous criminal history, conduct disorder and psychopathy traits. There were, however, differences between the clusters with respect to subsequent sexual recidivism with two of the clusters being more likely to sexually recidivate than the remaining three.

The main limitation of this study lies in the methodology it uses: there are too many factors put into the cluster analysis for the small sample size which ultimately results in clusters that overlap and even one cluster that only contains three individuals. The reliability of a 'type' based on just three people is clearly questionable.

Age of onset typology

Within the general juvenile delinquency literature the age of onset of delinquent behaviour has become a key construct for classifying the population (eg childhood versus adolescent onset [Moffitt, 1993]). Surprisingly, therefore, this particular construct has not been explored with as much focus among juveniles who sexually harm. One exception is Burton (2000) who divided a sample of 263 adjudicated juveniles from a variety of North American residential and community treatment facilities into three groups: 'early offenders' who only committed sexual aggression before the age of 12, 'teen offenders' who only committed sexual aggression after the age of 12, and 'continuous offenders' who committed sexual aggression both before and after the age of 12. The age of 12 was chosen as the discriminator because it was the age of criminal responsibility in the State from where they were recruited. The groups differed significantly on a number of offence-related domains. For example, there were group differences on measures of the type of act (non-contact, contact, penetration), and severity and complexity of the acts. In both cases, the continuous offenders committed the greater number of types and the more severe/complex acts. Group differences were also reported in relation to experiences of trauma; the continuous group were the most likely to have been sexually and emotional abused while the teen group were the least likely.

One other study that has explored the differences between groups of juveniles who sexually harmed differentiated according to the age of onset of the harmful sexual behaviour was reported by McCrory et al. (2008). In contrast to Burton (2000) this study used the 'cut-off' age of 10 years (as it is the English age of criminal responsibility) to divide a sample of male and female children and adolescents referred to a community forensic service because of perpetrating HSB. Two groups were identified based on the age of the first documented act of harmful sexual behaviour; n = 100 early onset (before the age of 10) and n = 137 late onset (after the age of 10). Compared on measures of family adversity, maltreatment, psychological functioning, antisocial behaviour, and the HSB characteristics, McCrory et al. (2008) reported that the early onset group was significantly more likely to have experienced a range of family adversities including parental mental health problems, poor parental supervision, harsh parental discipline, and multiple out-of-home placements. As a group they also had higher rates of all types of maltreatment, lower levels of intellectual functioning, higher rates of pre-adolescent hyperactivity problems, and higher levels of antisocial conduct problems, particularly during the pre-adolescent period.

In terms of the characteristics of the HSB, there were many similarities between the groups but there were also some significant differences. For instance, the early onset group were more likely to have victimised both male and female victims, while the late onset group were more likely to have only victimised females, as well as being the group most likely to use verbal coercion in the commission of the HSB.

It is difficult to compare the Burton (2000) and McCrory et al. (2008) studies and draw conclusions with practical applications given that one identified three groups and the other two, and they used different ages for the age of onset differentiator. However, Burton's 'continuous' and McCrory et al.'s 'early onset' groups share some conceptual similarities and were the most likely to have experienced maltreatment and to have exhibited more complex HSB.

Global limitations of typologies

The limitations of the individual typologies have been addressed above but there are some limitations of typologies as a whole that are important, particularly when considering the practical applications of typologies in applied settings. Firstly, all typologies are based on data from groups of individuals; therefore, it can be difficult applying the typology findings to an individual. For instance, the individual may not match the typology exactly and therefore the predictions that are based on the aggregate typology profile may not translate to the individual. The individual is often more complex than the group.

Typologies offer one way of bringing order to large complex populations, such as the heterogeneous population of juveniles who perpetrate harmful sexual behaviour, and provide a way of making it easier to grasp similarities and differences between sub-groups. However, typologies are not a panacea for bring order to complexity. A typology is only as good as the dimensions on which it is based, for instance a typology based on eye colour is clinically meaningless, therefore when assessing the value of a typology the value of the determining dimensions is what should be considered.

Some of the typologies reviewed above have been subject to more empirical investigation and evaluation than others but all the typologies would benefit from further exploration. Ideally the typology groups should be identified and then prospectively followed-up to determine whether they do in fact follow different outcome paths. Perhaps more importantly, however, is that future research on typologies would benefit from closer collaboration between researchers and practitioners in order to ensure that the dimensions on which the typology is based are the most clinically relevant, and to maximise the practical application of the resultant typology.

Applications in applied settings

When it comes to applying typologies in applied settings, that is, using the typology to allocate resources, or determine assessment or intervention content for the population of juveniles who sexually harm, it is necessary to apply a couple of basic rules in order that the typology produces the best results for the setting. Therefore, firstly it is important that the individuals to whom the typology is being applied resemble the sample on which it was developed as closely as possible. Secondly, that any predictions about how the type will perform are based on actual evidence that has been demonstrated and are not inferred from what it is thought should happen. Finally, each of the typologies included in this chapter are not mutually exclusive which means that an individual could be a member of more than one type, therefore when choosing which typology to apply in a given setting that choice needs to be made on the grounds of clinical utility.

Each of the typologies reviewed in this chapter have limitations as well as applications. The victim-age typology indicates that those who sexually harm children and those who harm peers/adults have some differences and it is possible that these differences may be related to aetiological differences between the types. Consequently, individuals who fit into the child and peer victim types may require intervention programmes that focus on some different elements that are more closely aligned to the reasons for their choice of victims. In line with what the literature currently suggests those in the child type may benefit from intervention modules that address interpersonal skills in order to reduce negative self perceptions and improve the skills required to interact with others their own age.

Applying the criminal history typology would seem to suggest that those with additional non-sexual convictions will need to have their risk for all types of future offending assessed and appropriate interventions provided. If, as the current state of the evidence suggests, those in the sex-plus type are criminally versatile individuals who commit sex offences as part of a wider repertoire of offences then perhaps this group do not require a sex offender specific intervention programme, but rather would benefit more from an intervention programme that addresses the reasons for such prolific offending? Conversely the sex-only group, on the basis of the existing research, seems to consist of many juveniles with very few instances of committing HSB. Therefore, this could suggest that as a group they are relatively low-risk and do not require intensive and resource-heavy, expensive interventions, but that more basic psycho-education interventions that make it clear

what type of behaviour is acceptable and unacceptable in relation to sexual expression would be more applicable.

From the research on the gender typology, it seems that in applied settings there is no great need for very different services for male and female juveniles who sexually harm. Where the service might need to differ is in relation to addressing the group differences on their experience of childhood sexual abuse. Although it should be remembered that the relevance of this typological difference between the male and female juveniles has not yet been established. Thus, it is not yet clear how experiencing childhood sexual abuse is aetiologically important for females, or even if it is. What the typology research does indicate is that males and females are not that different and, therefore, there may not need to have different services provided for them.

Using the remaining typologies (personality traits, offence-based, age of onset) in applied settings will need to be done with caution because of the lack of empirical evidence for their reliability and validity.

Conclusions

Exploring typologies is a natural response when faced with a heterogeneous population, such as that of juveniles who sexually harm, and the need to allocate financial- and personnel-limited resources. A number of typologies have been explored, some of which have accumulated more evidence than others, and therefore their potential utility in applied settings varies.

Typologies cannot be expected to be comprehensive and explain all the different permutations of 'types' within a population, therefore it is necessary to identify appropriate dimensions on which to base typologies. Future research should aim to explore those typologies that will have the greatest utility in applied settings; this can be achieved through closer collaboration between researchers and practitioners.

Finally, a good typology should be informed by and contribute to the development of a theoretical framework that increases understanding of either why individuals start to sexually harm or maintain the behaviour once started. Such theories can then inform the types of assessments, interventions and risk evaluations that best suit different types within the population.

References

Bumby, K.M., Halstenson, N. and Bumby, N.H. (1997) Adolescent Female Sexual Offenders. In Schwartz, B.K. and Cellini, H.R. (eds.) *The Sex Offender: New Insights, Treatment, Innovations and Legal Developments.* Kingston, NJ, Civic Research Institute.

Burton, D.L. (2000) Were Adolescent Sexual Offenders Children with Sexual Behaviour Problems? *Sexual Abuse: A Journal of Research and Treatment*, 12, 37–48.

Butler, S.M. and Seto, M.C. (2002) Distinguishing Two Types of Adolescent Sex Offenders. *Journal of The American Academy of Child and Adolescent Psychiatry*, 41, 83–90.

Caldwell, M. (2007) Sexual Offense Adjudication and Sexual Recidivism Among Juvenile Offenders. *Sexual Abuse: A Journal of Research and Treatment*, 19, 107–13.

Caldwell, M.F. (2002) What we do Not Know About Juvenile Sexual Reoffense Risk. *Child Maltreatment*, 7: 4, 291.

Carpenter, D.R., Peed, S.F. and Eastman, B. (1995) Personality Characteristics of Adolescent Sexual Offenders: A Pilot Study. *Sexual Abuse: A Journal of Research and Treatment*, 7, 195–203.

Fehrenback, P.A. and Monastersky, C. (1988) Characteristics of Female Adolescent Sexual Offenders. *American Journal of Orthopsychiatry*, 48, 148.

Fehrenback, P.A., Smith, W., Monastersky, C. and Deisher, R.M. (1986) Adolescent Sexual Offender: Offender and Offense Characteristics. *American Journal of Orthopsychiatry*, 56, 225.

Ford, M.E. and Linney, J.A. (1995) Comparative Analysis of Juvenile Sexual Offenders, Violent Nonsexual Offenders, and Status Offenders. *Journal of Interpersonal Violence*, 10, 56.

Forth, A.E., Kosson, D.S. and Hare, R.D. (2003) *The Hare Psychopathy Checklist: Youth Version*, Toronto: Multi-Health Systems.

Frick, P.J. and White, S.F. (2008) Research Review: The Importance of Callous-Unemotional Traits for Developmental Models of Aggressive and Antisocial Behaviour. *Journal of Child Psychology and Psychiatry*, 49, 359–75.

Gough, H.G. (1987) *California Psychological Inventory: Administrator's Guide*, Palo Alto, CA: Consulting Psychologists Press.

Graves, R.B., Openshaw, D.K., Ascione, F.R. and Ericksen, S.L. (1996) Demographic and Parental Characteristics of Youthful Sexual Offenders. *International Journal of Offender Therapy and Comparative Criminology*, 40, 300–17.

Hendriks, J. and Bijleveld, C. (2004) Juvenile Sexual Delinquents: Contrasting Child Abusers with Peer Abusers. *Criminal Behaviour and Mental Health*, 14, 238–50.

Hendriks, J. and Bijleveld, C. (2006) Female Adolescent Sex Offenders – an Exploratory Study. *Journal of Sexual Aggression*, 12, 31–41.

Hickey, N. (2009) Typologies for Juveniles. *Nota Annual Conference*. York, UK.

Hickey, N., McCrory, E., Farmer, E. and Vizard, E. (2008) Comparing the Developmental and Behavioural Characteristics of Female and Male Juveniles Who Present with Sexually Abusive Behaviour. *Journal of Sexual Aggression*, 14, 241–52.

Hunter, J.A., Figueredo, A.J., Malamuth, N.M. and Becker, J.V. (2003) Juvenile Sex Offenders: Toward the Development of a Typology. *Sexual Abuse: A Journal of Research and Treatment*, 15, 27–48.

Hunter, J.A., Hazelwood, R.R. and Slesinger, D. (2000) Juvenile Perpetrated Sex Crimes: Patterns of Offending and Predictors of Violence. *Journal of Family Violence*, 15, 81–93.

Ilacqua, G E., Coulson G.E., Lombardo, D. and Nutbrown, V. (1999) Predictive Validity of the Young Offender-Level of Service Inventory for Criminal Recidivism of Male and Female Young Offenders. *Psychological Reports*, 84, 1214–18.

Johnson, C.T. and Berry, C. (1989) Children Who Molest: A Treatment Program. *Journal of Interpersonal Violence*, 4, 185.

Kemper T.S. and Kistner, J.A. (2007) Offense History and Recidivism in Three Victim-Age-Based Groups of Juvenile Sex Offenders. *Sexual Abuse: A Journal of Research and Treatment*, 19, 409–24.

Kjellgren, C., Wassberg, A., Carlberg, M., Langstrom, N. and Svedin, C.G. (2006) Adolescent Sex Offenders: A Total Survey of Referrals to Social Services in Sweden and Sub-group Characteristics. *Sexual Abuse*, 18, 357–72.

Kubik, E.K., Hecker, J.E. and Righthand, S. (2002) Adolescent Females Who Have Sexually Offended: Comparisons with Delinquent Adolescent Female Offenders and Adolescent Males Who Sexually Offend. *Journal of Child Sexual Abuse*, 11, 63–82.

Langstrom, N., Grann, M. and Lindblad, F. (2000) A Preliminary Typology of Young Sex Offenders. *Journal of Adolescence*, 23, 319–29.

Mathews, R., Hunter, J.A.J. and Vuz, J. (1997) Juvenile Female Sexual Offenders: Clinical Characteristics and Treatment Issues. *Sexual Abuse: A Journal of Research and Treatment*, 9, 187.

McCrory, E., Hickey, N., Farmer, E. and Vizard, E. (2008) Early Onset Sexually Harmful Behaviour in Childhood: A Marker for Life Course Persistent Antisocial Behaviour? *Journal of Forensic Psychiatry and Psychology*, 19, 382–95.

Moffitt, T.E. (1993) Adolescence Limited and Life Course Persistent Antisocial Behaviour: A Developmental Taxonomy. *Psychological Review*, 100, 674–701.

Nisbet, I., Wilson, P. and Smallbone, S. (2004) A Prospective Longitudinal Study of Sexual Recidivism Among Adolescent Sex Offenders. *Sexual Abuse: A Journal of Research and Treatment*, 16: 3, 223.

O'Brien, M.J. and Bera, W.H. (1986) Adolescent Sex Offenders: A Descriptive Typology. *Preventing Sexual Abuse*, 1, 1–4.

Parks, G.A. and Bard, D.E. (2006) Risk Factors for Adolescent Sex Offender Recidivism: Evaluation of Predictive Factors and Comparison of Three Groups Based Upon Victim Type. *Sexual Abuse*, 18, 319–42.

Prentky, R.A. and Righthand, S. (2003) Juvenile Sex Offender Assessment Protocol-II (JSOAP II). Washington DC: US Department of Justice.

Ray, J.A. and English, D.J. (1995) Comparison of Female and Male Children with Sexual Behaviour Problems. *Journal of Youth and Adolescence*, 24, 439–51.

Richardson, G., Kelly, T.P., Bhate, S.R. and Graham, F. (1997) Group Differences in Abuser and Abuse Characteristics in a British Sample of Sexually Abusive Adolescents. *Sexual Abuse: A Journal of Research and Treatment*, 9, 239–57.

Rubinstein, M., Yeager, C.A., Goodstein, C. and Lewis, D.O. (1993) Sexually Assaultive Male Juveniles: A follow-up. *American Journal of Psychiatry*, 150: 2, 262.

Sipe, R., Jensen, E. and Everett, R. (1998) Adolescent Sexual Offenders Grown Up. *Criminal Justice and Behaviour*, 25: 1, 109.

Skeem, J., Johansson, P., Andershed, H., Kerr, M. and Louden, J.E. (2007) Two Subtypes of Psychopathic Violent Offenders that Parallel Primary and Secondary Variants. *Journal of Abnormal Psychology*, 116, 395–409.

Smith, W.R., Monastersky, C. and Deisher, R.M. (1987) MMPI-Based Personality Types Among Juvenile Sexual Offenders. *Journal of Clinical Psychology*, 43, 422.

Van Wijk, A., Mali, S.R.F. and Bullens, R. (2007) Juvenile Sex-Only and Sex-Plus Offenders: an Exploratory Study on Criminal Profiles. *International Journal of Offender Therapy and Comparative Criminology*, 51, 107–419.

Vandiver, D.M. and Teske, R. (2006) Juvenile Female and Male Sex Offenders: A Comparison of Offender, Victims and Judicial Processing Characteristics. *International Journal of Offender Therapy and Comparative Criminology*, 50, 148–65.

Way, I. and Urbaniak, D. (2008) Delinquent Histories of Adolescents Adjudicated for Criminal Sexual Conduct. *Journal of Interpersonal Violence*, 23, 1197–121.

Worling, J.R. (1995) Adolescent Sex Offenders Against Females: Differences Based on the Age of their Victims. *International Journal of Offender Therapy and Comparative Criminology*, 39, 276–93.

Worling, J.R. (2001) Personality Based Typology of Adolescent Male Sexual Offenders: Differences in Recidivism Rates, Victim-Selection Characteristics and Personal Victimisation Histories. *Sexual Abuse: A Journal of Research and Treatment*, 13, 149.

Worling, J.R. and Curwen, T. (2000) Adolescent Sexual Offender Recidivism: Success of Specialised Treatment and Implications For Risk Prediction. *Child Abuse and Neglect*, 24: 7, 965.

CHAPTER 5

Specialist Intervention Services for Young People: Where are we Now and Where Can we go?

Peter Clarke

Overview – from NCH Report to today

It is approaching 20 years since the publication of the NCH *Report of the Committee of Enquiry into Children and Young People Who Sexually Abuse Other Children* (1992). This report was significant in setting the scene and context as a major overview of the emerging field of work with children and young people who have sexually harmed. At the time, it detailed key aspects of current understanding and practice for practitioners engaged in assessment and intervention work. The report highlighted a range of issues and themes that gave a structure to understanding the direction of the work at the time.

By the turn of the millennium, commentators were in a position to place the findings of the commission into a new context of a fast expanding arena of work. There had been an increasing awareness of the scale of the need due to the increasing awareness of the true prevalence of sexual harm instigated by children and young people; this was reflected in both public awareness and in an increase in the academic and professional literature (Erooga and Masson, 1999) and in the noted expansion and maturing of assessment and treatment services in the UK and elsewhere (Masson and Hackett, 2003) (McGrath, Cummings and Burchard, 2002). In addition, there was an increasing understanding as to the nature of work with young people and how it may both link with and differ from work with adults. Indeed, in describing the development of work in the US with young people who have sexually harmed, Bumby and Talbot (2007: 245) describe a process from the middle part of the 20th century where work in this field, developed from a small number of cases, came 'out of the shadows' in the 1980s and subsequently developed in the 1990s to the size of a 'cottage industry' (p246) with similar diverse and heterogeneous group characteristics. It seems timely now, therefore, to take stock again and to consider what the current issues might be and to speculate on future directions.

My main focus in this chapter will be on the higher need cases that may be accessing specialist services: either specialist residential services or specialist services working in partnership with residential services. As the field has developed in recent years, there has been a refinement of understanding relating to the therapeutic and intervention needs of all young people who enter child protection forums due to sexually harmful or sexually aggressive acts. What is emerging is a sense that there is a majority group of young people who might be best served with minimal levels of intervention. In parallel with this position is an acknowledgement that there is a significantly smaller group of young people who are in need of more intense and complex interventions. It is my intention to argue that recognising good practice through the development of a set of standards is needed. My primary focus will be on making a case for the development of specialist standards for services working with the more complex cases, and indeed as a starting point for working with young people accommodated in residential services. This is intended as an initial position, and the potential to then expand the scope of any standards developed across the field should be borne in mind.

Masson and Hackett's Delphi study – a second benchmark

As the arena of work with young people who have sexually harmed has expanded there has been a degree of diversification. The expansion of all assessment and intervention services for these young people has been mirrored by a parallel increase in residential services. In the early part of the new millennium, Masson and Hackett (2002) conducted research using the Delphi methodology that sought the opinions of a large group of practitioners and experts who were working with children and young people who had sexually harmed. The Delphi methodology can be used to obtain an understanding of levels of agreement or consensus from a group that may be diverse and geographically remote. It uses a number of rounds of questionnaires to establish opinion regarding levels of agreement for conceptual statements. Additional rounds allow a dialogue between the individual and the group to establish common understanding as to the nature of the core statements, to make additional statements if necessary and to gauge the level of agreement or disagreement from the whole group. Masson and Hackett's project included an analysis as to what the central tenets of opinion and belief were that were steering the direction of work with sexually harmful children and young people. It served as a useful benchmark and comparison with the NCH report, allowing a picture to emerge as to how the field was developing.

Perhaps the most striking aspect of the comparison between the two projects was when the prognosis for young people receiving services was considered. Masson and Hackett's update on the NCH Report noted a significant shift in understanding of the trajectory young people may be on regarding their future risk of reoffending. While the NCH Report noted that the majority view was that children and teenagers who sexually harm were at high risk of developing into adult sex offenders, that view had changed by the turn of the millennium. The consensus emerging from the work of Masson and Hackett was the opinion that young people were more than likely to 'grow out of sexually harmful behaviour' and that, with the exception of a high risk small subset, intervention should be offered at minimal levels. Although there was a reported lagging-behind of policy and the opinion of non specialist professionals, for specialist practitioners this was a significant attitudinal shift. It appears that at the heart of this ideological shift is a reinterpretation of research coming from the adult field, specifically of the findings of Abel, Mittleman and Becker (1987) who had identified a significant proportion of adult career sex offenders who reported their first concerns about their sexual behaviour during teenage years. For some time practitioners concluded that teenagers who had sexually harmed therefore had a prognosis of significant risk of developing a pathway leading towards habitual adult sexual crimes. This conclusion failed, at the time, to recognise that there may be a set of teenagers who sexually harm that would

not develop along this pathway. As prevalence data became clearer it became apparent that the numbers could not sustain the original premise regarding prognosis for teenagers who sexually harm. Although now, as a body of work, research data relating to children and young people has increased significantly, this remains a relatively new phenomenon for study and it was not uncommon, in the decade between the NCH report and the Masson and Hackett study, for practitioners to attempt to use and adapt messages from adult research to inform their practice. As there was, at the time, little else to assist practitioners, it is understandable, but as the field has now developed a more solid research base such practice should be avoided or applied with extreme caution:

> *We often think that when we have completed our study of one we know all about two, because 'two' is 'one and one'. We forget that we still have to make a study of 'and'.*
> Eddington, 2010

Masson and Hackett (2002) noted improvement in areas such as professional denial and minimisation and categorisation of what constitutes abuse. However, they highlighted continuing concerns relating to training and supervision. The issues regarding training and supervision could additionally be seen within the context of an emerging voice in the literature relating to the emotional effect of undertaking work in this field (Farmer and Pollock 1998, Banks 2006, Hackett 2006, Clarke 2008). It may be that there is a mirroring of the emotional context for the service users and practitioners working in the field. Morrison (1999) noted that practitioners often reported a sense and experience of '. . . isolation, anxiety, fear disempowerment and de skilling' (Morrison, 1999: 19).

Although in other social care settings a voice can often be found exploring the nature of the client group and the relationship between the issues generated by the client group and the issues and stresses faced by practitioners (Obholzer and Zaiger, 1994), this seems as yet to be a mostly absent voice in the field of work with sexual harm.

Picture of service accessibility and delivery

There was similar picture reported by Masson and Hackett as the picture identified in the NCH

Report relating to concerns practitioners had with the terminology used. It seems that there is a continuing tension between a desire to accurately describe behaviours without minimisation and a desire not to label young people. The largest raft of continuing concerns however, related to service provision. Masson and Hackett used the structure from the NCH report to detail a number of categories: managing young people within the child protection system, co-ordination of services, evaluation of assessment and treatment options, and the range of services offered to meet individual need. Taking these items as a whole group the picture painted was one where there were pockets of excellent practice within an overall landscape of inconsistent and deprived services; a provision that Masson and Hackett (2004: 168) described as 'chronically patchy'. The rating of 'availability of service provision' scored a minority of services as satisfactory or better (46 per cent) while, when asked about the quality of placements, a staggering 62 per cent either did not respond to or did not know about the quality and only 25 per cent of respondents scored placement provision as satisfactory or better. Indeed just four per cent of respondents rated the quality of placements as excellent. This appears to highlight both that there is a significant issue regarding how quality assurance might be judged and that there remains a significant shortfall in best practice for this challenging service user group.

Although evaluation and outcome literature is emerging (Boswell and Wedge, 2004) and evaluation and outcome research is underway (including further work by Boswell and Masson and Hackett) there is not yet enough literature to challenge the view that too much is not known or evaluated:

> Doubts are also being expressed about the appropriateness of existing assessment and treatment facilities in the context of little monitoring and evaluation of the outcomes of such services.
>
> Green and Masson, 2002: 51

Within generic residential services there has been a steady decline in numbers of young people accommodated in group living settings over the past two decades. Kendrick (2008) notes that, despite some research messages, detailing that levels of satisfaction for children in residential care is high (Save the Children, 2001) that residential care has been subject to a degree of ambivalence from policymakers who often infer

residential services should be seen as an expensive last resort. These challenging dynamics are, perhaps, compounded by increased levels of stress and the intense interpersonal dynamics present in residential work with a group who have sexually harmed (Banks, 2006). This might go some way towards understanding the phenomenon of risk identified by Green and Masson (2002) in their exploration of risk presented in non-specialised generic children's homes:

> To understand why peer sexual abuse occurs in residential homes ... its occurrence needs to be framed and contextualised within the institutionalised organisational context of the settings, grassroots staff values, attitudes and knowledge and managed responses, as well as the children's past familial and abuse histories.
>
> Green and Masson, 2002: 156

Although this implies there is much work to be done to raise standards in generic children's homes, it also forms a compelling argument for specialist services that are adequately resourced and supported through training and specialist supervision. Such services have an opportunity to build structures into the service that would enable them to address the powerful dynamics generated by working in such an intimate setting with this group and to address the shortcomings found in generic services that leave young people vulnerable.

The low ratings in Masson and Hackett's research for both service accessibility and for quality of placement suggests that although specialist services have the potential to develop environments that address the dynamic created when working with this challenging client group, there may still be some way to go if quality services are to be consistently achieved in sufficient numbers to offer the range needed to make intervention choice realistic. It is true that in the last decade the trend for service expansion has continued, however, there is little evidence that the issue of quality assurance has changed, nor that any service expansion has raised the availability of services to a level where real placement choice can be exercised. Utting (1997) expressed concerns that the number of generic children's homes at that time was at a level that suggested it was below the critical mark for real choice to be exercised in making placement, and it seems likely that this is still the case for both generic children's homes and specialist services. What is required, I believe, is a strategy that will develop services in this area to improve consistency and demonstrate quality assurance in order to enable the sector as a whole to develop and expand.

Lessons from elsewhere

When considering issues related to quality assurance and governance for specialist residential services, it may be that experiences from other forums might be of assistance to begin to think about how to develop more robust and accountable services. I believe that the experiences of Therapeutic Communities and specifically the development of the 'Community of Communities' as a support and review system might help in the process of elaborating how to move the specialist residential intervention field forward.

Setting the scene – the factors that led to the Community of Communities

Therapeutic communities offer a model of group-based intervention across a wide range of client groups including psychiatric services, the prison service, education and communities working with troubled children and young people. In the 1990s communities-working, particularly within health and prison settings, came under increasing pressure as the call for evidence-based interventions gained in popularity. At the same time Therapeutic Communities working with children and young people lobbied unsuccessfully to obtain specialist status within the standards being developed as part of the regulation and inspection of children's homes introduced through the Care Standards Act (2000). It was in this climate of the 'inevitability of regulation and accountability' (Haigh, 2004: 263) that debate was carried out within the Therapeutic Community movement as to what role regulation should take. Therapeutic Communities are a diverse group. They operate within a range of other frameworks and the pathways of accountabilities for each service differ greatly. Underpinning many of the Communities is a belief that the resources for positive development lie within their own Community itself. There were different and distinct professional bodies representing the Therapeutic Community movement – each with a

different emphasis (Association of Therapeutic Communities, Charterhouse Group, Planned Environment Therapy Trust, European Federation of Therapeutic Communities and Therapeutic Communities Open Forum). Indeed the failure of the children's communities to obtain specialised standards in the consultation with the Department of Health regarding the general standards for children's homes, appears to be partly due to the movement's inability, at that time, to self-define with a degree of consensus.

There was therefore a pressing need to stabilise the services and allow them to operate within the developing requirements of clinical governance and inspection, but the sector was struggling to do so. It was within this climate that the Community of Communities was developed. The initial process of establishing standards used a combination of open forums, 'expert groups' and a process of amalgamating existing documents to create the initial Community of Communities documents. There was an emphasis on participation and a democratic approach to generating the initial standards documents. This approach is now mirrored through the 'annual review' (Figure 5.1). This process re-evaluates the standards to ensure that they are both 'owned and understood' by participant communities, and to give the opportunity to enable developments in the field to be acknowledged within the standards structure. Amendments of the standards are made through a process of consensus where each item on the standards is assessed by each community as 'not important', 'important' or 'very important'. Low rated standards are then removed.

Moving to value-based practice and the development of peer-reviewed standards

An approach that particularly suited the Therapeutic Community movement was a move in the Health Service to combine evidence-based practice and decision-making with recognition of practice, to reflect and take into account patient values:

> *By patient values we mean the unique preferences, concerns and expectations each patient brings to a clinical encounter and which must be integrated into clinical decisions if they are to serve the patient.*
> Sackett et al., 2000: 1

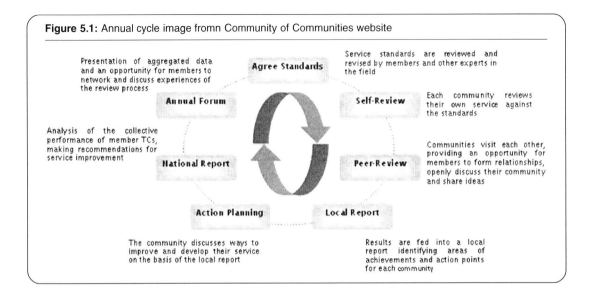

Figure 5.1: Annual cycle image fromn Community of Communities website

There appears to me to be a parallel with the development and adoption of the 'Good Lives' model of intervention stemming from humanistic and positive psychology and influencing intervention within the field of sexual harm (Ward and Stewart, 2003).

Incorporating value-based work within the health model supported the developmental process undertaken by the Community of Communities as they sought to devise and agree standards. The concept was that there should be a cyclical iterative process where standards are revised, agreed and applied both as a self-assessment and within a peer-review structure. This process is described to participants as a 'living-learning audit' and is explicit in its intention to encourage ownership through participation, to encourage reflection through self-audit, to encourage service development through supportive peer audit and through a process of supportive action planning. Overarching the individual community's audit process is an annual report that enables the whole membership (and other stakeholders) to see a more general evaluation and to inform the next round of standard reviewing. This review process is undertaken with the aim of being 'a process of engagement, and not of inspection' (Haigh, 2004: 265).

There is a set of standards developed for each distinct group within the umbrella of the Community of Communities (such as prison, addiction, children's communities, and son on)

which sits within an overarching framework of Therapeutic Community 'Core Values' and 'Core Standards'. Service Standards themselves might include quite concrete details about practice, for example in the Children and Young People standards under the heading of 'Being Healthy':

The community is involved in planning and preparation for the arrival of a new child or young person.
O'Sullivan and Paget, 2009; Standard 1.12: 10

The Children and Young People Service Standards illustrate how these standards are devised as an adjunct to the more formal inspections experiences through statutory regulation. The Children and Young People standards use, for example, the 'Every Child Matters' categories – the framework for the statutory standards.

The overarching 'Core Values' are more global in nature and serve to assist in self-definition within the wider context of Therapeutic Communities, for example:

Healthy attachment is a developmental requirement for all human beings, and should be seen as a basic human right.
Briefing Paper to Royal College of Psychiatrists, 2008,
Core Value 1

or:

Each individual has responsibility to the group, and the group in turn has collective responsibility to all individuals in it.
Briefing Paper to Royal College
of Psychiatrists, 2008, Core Value 10

Core Values then cascade down to Core Standards that make the principles and ideological aspect of the Core Values more concrete (but still general enough for the Core Standards to sit across the widely differing Communities). An example of a Core Standard is 'Power and authority in relationships is used responsibly and is open to question' (O'Sullivan and Paget, 2009 Core Standard 7: 8).

The Core Values can therefore be used as a basis to define organisations' mission statements (or to assist in organisational identity) and as a tool to facilitate self-reflection and ground that reflection within a theoretical framework and philosophical approach. They may be used to facilitate team training and to act as an indicator to new organisations who wish to work within the model. Standards act as a benchmark to review practice, and the combination of Core Values, Core Standards and Service Standards can therefore become a tool for quality assurance within the context of the annual cycle. In addition, they may act as an indicator for regulators and commissioners giving them a framework to make informed decisions regarding the suitability and efficacy of placements.

From the beginnings of the project developing the Community of Communities, there was a suggestion that they could work towards establishing a 'kite mark' for participating organisations. At this time there were significant discussions relating to the potential powers of enforcement that any standards' review process might have. The self and peer review process has been established very much within a context of support. Unless issues of 'consensually unacceptable practice' are identified, then the aim with self and peer review is to work towards improvement and in that spirit suggested changes in practice would be through mutually agreed action plans. All the members of the Community of Communities operate within other regulatory systems where external organisations hold a power of inspection and carry the weight of enforcement. The supportive nature of the self and peer review process can be understood within that context.

The concept of establishing a 'kite mark' was still present in the development of the project and so, once the annual review cycle was established and sufficiently tested, an accreditation process was agreed and established for some subsets and settings. The need for such a recognised

benchmark was more pressing within Communities working within health and prison service regulations and the fifth annual review in these two areas incorporated a pilot for accredited status for relevant services. In the eighth cycle for Therapeutic Communities working with children and young people, those communities also will pilot accreditation. This accreditation process uses the same annual cycle structure but incorporates a higher level of peer review using more external communities. This process is moderated by the Community of Communities under the umbrella of the Royal College of Psychiatry through their Research Unit. Accreditation status is regarded by the Community of Communities as recognition that the individual community is robust in its understanding and practice within the field and can act as a standard bearer for others.

The way forward

This brief account of the development of the Community of Communities project can perhaps guide the field of work with children and young people who have sexually harmed. Work with these troubled and often troubling children and young people remains very much in the early stages of its development. Although work within this field has found (or is finding) its voice we are still some way off maturation. There is a robust debate regarding the efficacy of different treatment and intervention approaches, but I believe we still have far to go before we can look at having a stable view of what appropriate intervention models might be. The field is not yet informed enough nor stable enough to have confidence that the intervention programmes currently in use will form a foundation for future interventions.

There are, however, some ways I believe to move the work forward. The experiences of the Community of Communities in devising Core Values and gradations of standards proved a valuable one for Therapeutic Communities. The concerns regarding establishing what was feared to be another set of regulations and inspections has not proved to be the reality. The process of self and peer review has proved valuable for individual organisations. The members' feedback on the Community of Communities website reinforces the supportive quality of the review experience:

I was made aware of the similarities and differences between the two communities and felt inspired. Most importantly I had a sense that we are not alone . . .

and

We look forward to the continuation and working on the improvements. It has been invaluable in having outside input . . .

The structure of developing Core Values and then placing Core Standards and Service Standards within those values, enabled the diverse group that forms the Community of Communities to develop a collective identity without compromising the unique needs of differing Therapeutic Communities who operate within vastly different settings and under differing statutory regulatory requirements. The development and review of the Core Values appears to act as a forum to enable participant organisations to reflect on their own service and also to influence the developments of that field. The Service Standards give 'flesh to the bone' of the Values and allow for practice to be reviewed and best practice to be developed and adopted. I suggest that there are a number of parallels between the profile of Community of Communities and the profile of the diverse organisations who work with children and young people who sexually harm. Organisations working with sexual harm form a diverse group that, as of yet, struggles to self-define with a strong degree of consensus. The comparison of the NCH Report and the Delphi study, undertaken some ten years later, suggests that there are still some unresolved ideological issues in the field: such as the debate and tension as to the use of terminology. Such a debate about use of language suggests some unresolved ideological issues especially if the hypothised link between thought and language is accepted (Davidson, 1983). The following analysis of the development of work with children and young people who have sexually harmed clearly identifies the need for the field to be more productive and proactive in how it self-defines and influences policy:

Indeed the history of the development of services for children and young people who have sexually abused others, or who display sexually harmful behaviours, is the history of certain committed individuals and agencies at a local level working to create coherent, child-centred and effective systems of response, despite continuing changes in philosophy, a lack of clear direction and 'joined-up'

thinking at government department levels and limited resources.

Masson and Hackett, 2004: 168

I have been particularly struck when considering the comparison regarding professional opinions relating to prognosis and the likely trajectory for young people who have sexually harmed. It was not so much the reversal of the consensus of opinion to a position where young people who have sexually harmed should be viewed within the wider context of young people with needs, but more how strong the consensus had been at the time of each report for the position held at the time and therefore how seminal the change was within a decade. I infer from that that there is still much uncertainty in the field and that a position so strongly and consistently held in other areas of the field might still be re-evaluated and radically changed. This is something resembling a 'paranoid-schizoid position' (Klein, 1946). Klein's 'paranoid-schizoid position is a schema relating to a young child and she identified this as a stage before the more sophisticated and mature 'paranoid' schema is developed – the paranoid position is one that allows an understanding with strengths and weaknesses rather than of an all encompassing 'all good' or 'all bad'.

It is both interesting and invaluable to have access to these 'benchmark' evaluations. The 'organic' growth across diverse organisations with motivated and engaged individuals reflects a field that commentators could see as something of a 'cottage industry'. Perhaps it is now time to begin a more regular process of self-reflection and self-definition? A model such as the Community of Communities annual review cycle, that encourages individual member organisations to reflect on how they compare to the agreed service standards but also allows for an annual re-evaluation of what those standards might be, seems to offer much to the field of work with sexually harmful behaviour at this time. The feedback loop created where member organisations reassess, rate and ratify the Values and Standards offers an iterative process by which changes in ideological approaches can be reflected on and analysed. This process is formalised by the creation of the annual overview report that can measure changes in the field.

We are approaching the 20th anniversary of the NCH Report, and so will be 10 years on from the Masson Hackett research. Perhaps the timing is right to undertake work to see where we are now? The Community of Communities model does not rely on researchers generating data in an 'ad hoc' manner, but rather undertakes a rolling programme of evaluation. Work in such a developmentally new field like that of interventions for children and young people who sexually harm would benefit from consistent and detailed analysis of the current thinking in the field.

There are clear benefits in considering the development of a similar model to that of Community of Communities for work with children and young people who sexually harm. The process of agreeing on the Core Values in the work would be a useful mechanism to clarify thinking. The development of Service Standards could be invaluable in terms of ensuring there is a common ground that practitioners are working from. The division of standards into subsets for different tiers and settings helps to keep the standards direct and meaningful. The annual review cycle allows individual organisations to reflect, develop and improve while it allows the field as a whole to monitor and consider the direction the work may be heading in. At this stage I would argue that treatment methodology should not necessarily be contained within Service Standards, rather the standards should focus on structures that ensure practice is both safe and considered. This is partly in recognition that intervention programmes are in their early stages of development and I would not wish an evaluation process to stifle development and originality.

There are obvious resource implications for the operation of a review system as described. The Community of Communities receives tacit support from the Royal College of Psychiatry, but operates as an independent body. It is therefore the Community of Communities organisation that has responsibility for the quality of the work it undertakes. The Community of Communities received 'pump priming' money to develop the project (from the Community Fund) but running costs are covered through membership subscription and so is self-financing. So it appears to be possible to establish a 'peer-review' based quality assurance mechanism with a potential for both longevity and the ability to move an area of work forward. Such a system carries potential to develop practice in a structured and organised manner.

Acknowledgements

I would like to acknowledge NOTA and Glebe House who are active in supporting my academic study relating to the process of developing specialist standards. I am grateful for their continued commitment.

References

Abel, G., Mittleman, M. and Becker, J. (1987) Self-Reported Sex Crimes of Non-Incarcerated Paraphiliacs. *Journal of Interpersonal Violence*, 2, 3–25.

Banks, N. (2006) Placement Provision and Placement Decisions: Resources and Processes. In Erooga, M. and Masson, H. (eds.) *Children and Young People Who Sexually Abuse Others: Current Developments and Practice*. 2nd edn. London: Routledge.

Boswell, G. and Wedge, P. (2004) A Pilot Evaluation of A Therapeutic Community for Adolescent Male Sexual Abusers. *Therapeutic Communities*, 24, 259–76.

Briefing Paper to Royal College of Psychiatrists: The Development of Core Standards and Core Values for Therapeutic Communities (2008) http://www.rcpsych.ac.uk/pdf/CSCV%20final%20briefing%20paper1.pdf

Bumby, K. and Talbot, T. (2007) Treating Juveniles Who Commit Sex Offences: Historical Approaches, Contemporary Practices and Future Directions. In Calder, M. (ed.) *Working with Children and Young People Who Sexually Abuse: Taking the Field Forward*. Lyme Regis: Russell House Publishing.

Clarke, J. (2008) Promoting Professional Resilience. In Calder, M. (ed.) *Contemporary Risk Assessment in Safeguarding Children*. Lyme Regis: Russell House Publishing.

Davidson, D. (1883) A Coherence Theory of Truth and Knowledge. Reprinted in Davidson 2001, *Subjective, Intersubjective, Objective*. Oxford: Oxford University Press.

Eddington, A. (2010) http://www.brainyquote.com/quotes/authors/a/Arthur_Eddington.html

Erooga, M. and Masson, H. (1999) (eds.) *Children and Young People Who Sexually Abuse Others: Challenges and Responses*. London: Routledge.

Farmer, E. and Pollock, S. (1998) *Sexually Abused and Abusing Children in Substitute Care*. Chichester: Wiley.

Green, L. and Masson, H. (2002) Adolescents Who Sexually Abuse and Residential Accommodation: Issues of Risk and Vulnerability. *British Journal of Social Work*, 32, 149–86.

Hackett, S. (2006) The Personal and Professional Context to Work with Children and Young People Who Have Sexually Abused. in Erooga, M. and Masson, H. (eds.) *Children and Young People Who Sexually Abuse Others: Current Developments and Practice.* 2nd edn. London: Routledge.

Haigh, R. (2004) Democratic Development of Standards: The Community of Communities-A Quality Network of Therapeutic Communities. *Psychiatric Quarterly.* 75: 3, 263–77.

Kendrick, A. (2008) (ed.) *Residential Child Care: Prospects and Challenge.* London: Jessica Kingsley.

Klein, M. (1946) Notes on Some Schizoid Mechanisms. *International Journal of Psycho-Analysis*, 27: 99–110.

Masson, H. and Hackett, S. (2003) A Decade on from the NCH Report (1992): Adolescent Sexual Aggression Policy, Practice and Service Delivery across the UK and Republic of Ireland. *Journal of Sexual Aggression.* 9: 2, 109–24.

Masson, H. and Hackett, S. (2004) The Extent and Nature of Work with Adolescents Who Have Sexual Behaviour Problems: Findings from a Survey of Youth Offending Teams in England and Wales. *Youth Justice.* 4 160–77.

Masson, H. and Hackett, S. (2006) Exploring Consensus in Practice with Youth Who Are Sexually Abusive: Findings from a Delphi Study of Practitioner Views in the United Kingdom and the Republic of Ireland. *Child Maltreatment*, 11: 2, 146–56.

McGrath, R.J., Cummings, G.F. and Burchard, B.L. (2002) *Current Practices and Trends in Sexual Abuser Management: The Safer Society 2002 Nationwide Survey.* Brandon, VT: Safer Society.

Morrison, T. (1999) Is There a Strategy Out There? Policy and Management Perspectives on Young People Who Sexually Abuse Others. In Erooga, M. and Masson, H. (eds.) *Children and Young People Who Sexually Abuse Others: Challenges and Responses.* London: Routledge.

Morrison, T. and Henniker, J. (2006) Building a Comprehensive Inter-Agency Assessment and Intervention System for Young People Who Sexually Harm: The AIM Project. In Erooga, M. and Masson, H. (eds.) *Children and Young People Who Sexually Abuse Other: Current Developments and Practice* 2nd edn. London: Routledge.

NCH (1992) *The Report of The Committee of Enquiry into Children and Young People Who Sexually Abuse Other Children.* London: NCH.

Obholzer, A. and Zaiger, V. (1994) (eds.) *The Unconscious at Work: Individual and Organisational Stress in the Human Services.* London: Routledge.

O'Sullivan, J. and Paget, S. (2009) *Service Standards for Therapeutic Communities for Children and Young People.* Community of Communities www.rcpsych.ac.uk/pdf/CYP%20stanwdards%202nd%20edition%20completed.pdf

Sackett, D. et al. (2000) *Evidence-Based Medicine: How to Practice and Teach EBM.* 2nd edn. London: Churchill Livingstone.

Save The Children (2001) *A Sense of Purpose: Care Leavers' Views and Experiences of Growing Up.* Edinburgh: Save The Children.

Utting, W. (1997) *People Like Us: Report for Review of the Safeguarding of Children Living Away From Home.* London: HMSO.

Ward, T. and Steward, C. (2003) Criminogenic Needs and Human Needs: A Theoretical Model. *Psychology, Crime and Law*, 9: 2, 125–43.

CHAPTER 6

Working Effectively With At-Risk Youth: A Strengths-Based Approach

Kevin M. Powell

Introduction

If sex offense-specific providers want youth to learn how not to be sexually abusive, they need to do more than just teach them 'what *not* to do', they must teach them 'what to do'. A strengths-based approach (SBA) emphasises pro-social behaviors and focuses attention on what is 'right' with youth rather than what is wrong with them. The field of sex offense-specific (SOS) services, both assessment and treatment, has historically placed more attention on a youth's sexually abusive acts, and on their thoughts, feelings, behaviors, and situations that increase the risk of sexual re-offending. While addressing youths' abusive behaviors is an important component of SOS services, equally, if not more important is an emphasis on youths' positive, pro-social behaviors. The purpose of this chapter is to provide information about strengths-based concepts and interventions that can assist evaluators and treatment providers in effectively working with at-risk youth including those with sexual behavior problems. Topics to be covered include: overview of SBA; strengths-based does *not* equate with being naïve to risk; empirical support for SBA; strengths-based interventions (SBIs); how to enhance youths' openness and honesty; and benefits of SBA.

Overview of a Strengths-Based Approach (SBA)

SBA is an approach that focuses on the identification, creation, and reinforcement of strengths and resources within individuals, their family, and their community. Any intervention, which emphasises strengths and the exceptions to problems and deficits, can be classified as 'strengths-based'. SBA assists youth in gaining knowledge and skills for 'how to' interact in pro-social, non-abusive ways. It emphasises the importance of forming positive therapeutic relationships and creating an environment in which youth are actively engaged in treatment. SBA can enhance youth's openness and honesty, even when addressing their abusive and problematic behaviors. It is an effective approach for working with not only youth with sexual behavior problems but *all* youth.

Although SBA has only recently been getting attention within the sex offense-specific field, it is a concept that has been evolving over the past 50 years. In the 1950s and 1960s, 'humanistic psychology' emerged as a major school of thought within psychology (eg Allport, 1961; Maslow, 1954, 1962, 1971; Rogers, 1951, 1961, 1963). Humanistic psychology emphasises the healthy attributes of the human personality and promotes optimism about human nature and our inherent potential. Although the term 'strengths-based' was not specifically used at the onset of the humanistic movement, much of today's strengths-based treatment and research developed out of this school of thought.

The study of 'resilient' youth is an area of research that has played a major role in the evolution of SBA. 'Resiliency' has been defined as an individual's successful adaptation despite risk and adversity (Masten, 1994). Resiliency research looks at what factors allow youth to develop into positive, pro-social adults even after experiencing significant adversity in life. The study of resiliency gained prominence in the 1970s and is one of the first areas of research to specifically focus attention on strengths-based concepts as it relates to at-risk youth. The utilisation of 'resiliency' as a strengths-based intervention is described later in this chapter.

A specific type of therapy that has been influential in the strengths-based movement is solution-focused therapy (De Shazer, 1985, 1988, 1994; De Shazer et al., 1986; O'Hanlon and Weiner-Davis, 1989, 2003). Solution-focused therapy emphasises a client's strengths and their capacity to help solve their own problems. Rather than delve into the details of a client's problems, this therapy approach explores the exceptions to the problems, or in other words, the solutions to problems. It is a therapy that has been quite successful in treating a variety of client populations, including at-risk youth (Berg and Steiner, 2003; Corcoran and Stephenson, 2000).

Narrative therapy (White and Epston, 1990) has also contributed to the strengths-based movement. This therapy approach encourages clients to retell their personal stories of past adversity in ways that recall their strengths as survivors rather than weaknesses as victims. It encourages clients 'to describe themselves, each other, and their relationships from a new, nonproblem-saturated perspective' (White and Epston, 1990: 39).

The field of social work has had an active role in the promotion of strengths, particularly when working with adults struggling with psychiatric disabilities. Weick et al. (1989) coined the term, 'strengths perspective' in their benchmark article and the work of Saleebey, Rapp, and many others have provided significant contributions (Saleebey, 1998, 2006; Rapp, 1998; Rapp and Goscha, 2006).

In 1998, Martin Seligman kicked off his American Psychological Association (APA) presidency by coining the term 'positive psychology', which is a movement in psychology that emphasises what is right with people rather than what is wrong with them (Seligman, 1999; Seligman and Csikszentmihalyi, 2000). Topics of study include constructs such as, happiness, optimism, interpersonal skills, altruism, and work ethic. Although the concept of positive-focused, humanistic psychology has been part of the field of psychology for many years (Taylor, 2001) Seligman's recent promotion of positive psychology has reenergised this area of research and treatment (Seligman et al., 2005; Linley and Joseph, 2004). The strengths-based interventions highlighted in this chapter are part of this positive psychology movement.

Over the past two decades, SBA has been increasingly embraced by those working with at-risk youth in the mental health and educational services field (ie Appelstein, 1998; Benard, 1991; Bohlin, Farmer and Ryan, 2001; Brendtro and Larson, 2006, Brendtro, Ness, and Mitchell, 2005; Brendtro and Shahbazian, 2004; Clark, 1998; LeBel et al., 2004; Lickona, 1991, 2004; MacKinnon-Lewis, Kaufman, and Frabutt, 2002; Murphy, 2002; Selekman, 2006; Sharry, 2004; Smith, 2006; Sugai et al., 2000). And recently, the field of sex offense-specific services has begun to consider the benefits of SBA with the Good Lives

Model of rehabilitation (Collie et al., 2007; Ward and Marshall, 2004), heightened interest in resiliency research (Gilgun, 2006; Hackett, 2006), and general interest in SBA (Powell, 2010a).

Strengths-based does *not* equate with being naïve to risk

It is important to note that being 'strengths-based' within sex offense-specific assessment and treatment does *not* mean providers are naïve to youths' risk to reoffend. Community safety is always a guiding principle of paramount importance (CSOMB, 2008). *SBA creates an atmosphere in which youth are less defensive and more open to addressing their risks and problematic behavior.* In addition to being vigilant to risk management issues, SBA focuses on strengths and protective factors which can reduce risk and increase chances of youth developing into pro-social individuals within our community.

Empirical support for a strengths-based approach

In recent years the evidenced-based practice (EBP) movement has become increasingly prominent and raised the bar regarding assessment and treatment services, to ensure that services not only do no harm but are also effective and have empirical support. A specific area of research that has received a great deal of attention in regard to services for at-risk youth is the offender rehabilitation Risk-Need Responsivity model (Andrews and Bonta, 2010). This model has identified the principles of 'Risk' (the *who* to target), 'Need' (the *what* to target) and 'Responsivity' (the *how* to target) as essential components for effective services. While these principles have been instrumental in highlighting the value in providing offenders with rehabilitation services, the 'need principle' is in direct contradiction to the strengths-based approach. This principle suggests treatment should only target 'dynamic risk factors', also referred to as criminogenic needs (Andrews and Bonta, 2010), while excluding any emphasis on other variables, which they refer to as 'non-criminogenic needs'. This recommendation purported by the 'need principle' discounts many empirically-supported variables that are *not* associated with 'risk'. These variables include *establishing positive therapeutic relationships with the use of client-centered principles* (Hubble, Duncan, and Miller, 1999; Karver et al., 2006; Norcross, 2001, 2002; Norcross and Lambert, 2006), *targeting protective factors commonly associated with 'resiliency'* (Masten and Coatsworth, 1998; Masten and Reed, 2002), *targeting developmental assets associated with positive attitudes and behaviors* (Benson, 1997, 2006; Benson, Galbraith, and Espeland, 1995; Roehlkepartain and Leffert, 2000; Search Institute, 1997), *promoting self-esteem associated with pro-social behaviors* (DuBois and Flay, 2004; Haney and Durlak, 1998; Masten and Coatsworth, 1998; Swann, Chang-Schneider, and McClarty, 2007), and *utilising solution-focused, strengths-based interventions* (Berg and Steiner, 2003; Corcoran and Stephenson, 2000; De Shazer et al., 1986; Lethem, 2002; Powell, 2010a; and Ward, Gannon, and Yates, 2008). As Ward, Gannon, and Yates (2008: 186) succinctly state, focusing on risk factors is 'necessary but not sufficient for effective treatment'.

It is important to keep in mind that some very influential psychological constructs utilised within a strengths-based approach cannot be easily studied with the use of randomised clinical trials (often viewed as the gold standard of EBP research methodology). For example, the construct of 'resiliency' cannot be studied by randomly assigning youth to various levels of neglect/abuse and intervention just so researchers can study their response. The EBP movement should rely on a broad and diverse base of evidence that includes not only randomised clinical trial methodology but also quasi-experimental designs, correlational studies, qualitative data, and single-case designs (Clay, 2010). In addition, the study of 'process variables' (what happens during the course of therapy to effect positive change) and 'moderating variables' (ie treatment setting, client characteristics, therapist skill) deserve as much attention as does 'outcome variables' (what is the result/outcome when comparing pre-treatment to post-treatment symptoms) within the EBP movement (Hall, 2008; Kopta et al., 1999; Messer, 2001). Many of the strengths-based concepts described in this chapter do have empirical support and deserve recognition. Effective SOS services, as well as mental health services in general, require an emphasis not only on risk factors but also client-centered therapeutic relationships; strengths/protective factors and many other strengths-based factors that are essential for enhancing motivation/engagement in treatment and assist youth in learning healthy alternatives to their past abusive behaviors.

Strengths-Based Interventions (SBIs)

The strengths-based interventions (SBIs) described below are organised into six categories. Each intervention is classified under the category that best describes its general emphasis/theme. The six categories are entitled:

1. Relationship development
2. Optimistic attitude development
3. Asset development
4. Pro-social development
5. Intellectual development
6. Professional/provider development.

All the SBIs described below have empirical support as it relates to their underlying components. Additional interventions associated with categories 3–6 (asset, pro-social, intellectual, and professional/provider development) can be found in Powell, 2010a.

Category 1 – Relationship development

If providers want youth to talk openly about their sexually abusive behaviors, establishing and maintaining a therapeutic relationship is absolutely essential. Establishing a positive therapeutic relationship is one of the primary objectives of SBA and an important component of sex offense-specific services (Blanchard, 1995; Marshall et al., 2002; Powell, 2010b). There is a great deal of empirical evidence highlighting how influential the therapeutic relationship is to positive treatment outcome (Hubble, Duncan, and Miller, 1999; Kazdin, Marciano, and Whitley, 2005; Norcross, 2001, 2002; Norcross and Lambert, 2006). It is estimated (averaging across hundreds of psychotherapy outcomes studies and many meta-analyses) that 18 per cent of the positive change in psychotherapy is due to factors associated with the *'therapy relationship'* (10 per cent) and the *'therapist's qualities'* (8 per cent) (Norcross and Lambert, 2006). This is a significant amount of the variance when you consider that the *specific therapeutic techniques* that are typically emphasised in the literature (eg Empirically Supported Treatments – ESTs) only account for approximately five to eight per cent of the positive change in treatment.

Although much of the research on therapeutic relationships and treatment outcome has been conducted on adults, there is increasingly more research being conducted on youth. Karver et al (2006) conducted a meta-analysis of therapeutic relationship variables and identified several factors that were associated with positive treatment outcome including:

Therapist Direct Influence Skills, which includes the therapist's active structuring of the session, and providing a clear and understandable rationale for the treatment being used.

Therapist Interpersonal Skills, which includes empathy, warmth/unconditional positive regard, and genuineness. Carl Rogers identified these three interpersonal factors as 'necessary and sufficient' for promoting therapeutic change (Rogers, 1957). When youth experience a provider as empathetic, accepting, and genuine, they become more trusting and open to forming a positive relationship, and more receptive to treatment interventions.

Youth and Parents' Willingness and Actual Participation in Treatment, which involves the youth and parents feelings of acceptability in treatment and desire/commitment to participate, as well as their involvement, collaboration, cooperation, and engagement in therapy and/or homework tasks.

Therapeutic Alliance with Youth, which includes an *emotional* connection (youth's affective bond with the therapist), a *cognitive* connection (youth's hopefulness about treatment), and/or *behavioral* component (youth's actual participation in treatment).

It is also important to be cognisant of therapist characteristics that have been found to be detrimental to therapeutic relationships. These characteristics include therapists who are perceived by their clients as 'cold', 'irritable', and 'lack collaboration' in which the therapist has a take-charge attitude in the early phase of therapy and/or prematurely offers insight or interpretation (Horvath and Bedi, 2002).

Establishing a positive relationship and communication with youth is undoubtedly one of the most critical variables for working effectively with youth who have sexual behavior problems. A brief description of two Relationship Development SBIs are described below which provide strategies for how to establish positive relationships and communication with youth and their significant others.

SBI: establish positive relationship/ communication with youth

In addition to the variables described above (Karver et al., 2006) strategies for establishing and

maintaining positive, therapeutic relationship and communication include: (1) Being patient and understanding when youth are initially defensive about treatment or the mental health 'system'; (2) Showing interest in youth by asking questions about their lives (initially excluding any focus on their sexual behavior problems); (3) Being present in the 'here and now' to ensure youth have providers' full and undivided attention; (4) Maintaining a 'staff to youth' ratio that keeps caseloads at a manageable level so providers have time to form positive relationships with youth; (5) Utilising non-verbal behaviors, such as an open posture without arms crossed, to communicate attentiveness and acceptance (Egan, 1998); and (6) Joining with youth by mimicking/matching their interpersonal style and affective range, which is a strategy referred to as 'Mimesis' (Minuchin, 1974: 128). If a provider and a youth's interpersonal style and affective range are incongruous, youth will typically feel less connected and less likely to communicate openly. For example, a youth who presents with high energy and upbeat mood typically will not be as responsive towards a provider whose mannerisms are overly reserved and serious.

SBI: establish positive relationship/ communication with youths' significant others

Another essential component to successful treatment is establishing a positive relationship and communication with youths' 'significant others'. These are the people who will be present in youths' lives long after treatment sessions have ceased (ie parents, legal guardians, extended family, or other pro-social caregivers). Strategies for connecting with youths' significant others include:

- talking to significant others about their child's strengths and when their child is doing well
- giving significant others compliments
- asking questions that place significant others in the 'expert' role
- getting significant others involved in their child's treatment activities
- asking significant others questions about their own support system to assure they are getting enough care and assistance for themselves

The stress associated with having a child with sexual behavior problems can be emotionally taxing on significant others and elicit feelings of shame, guilt, anxiety, anger, sadness, and fear. Providers can go a long way towards establishing positive relationships with significant others when they acknowledge their stress and provide support.

Category 2 – Optimistic attitude development

Enhancing optimism within youth and their families, as well as within evaluators and treatment providers, can greatly augment the effectiveness of sex offense-specific services. Working with youth who have sexual behavior problems can increase providers' exposure to the darker side of human experience involving abuse, aggression, trauma, as well as contact with youth exhibiting significant mental health problems and disorders. This kind of exposure not only can increase providers' risk of becoming negative and pessimistic, but it can also influence youth and their families to lose hope in their capacity to make positive life changes. This hopelessness and pessimism can significantly impede treatment progress. Described below is an SBI which instills hope and confidence regarding youths' capacity to make positive life changes and overcome their past sexually abusive behaviors.

SBI: promote optimism and tolerance by providing education about developmental research and statistics

There are neurophysiological and statistical reasons to remain optimistic that youths' disruptive, abusive, and impulsive behaviors will improve over time. Listed below are several reasons to remain optimistic and to share this optimism with youth, their families, and other treatment providers.

Reason for optimism – maturation of the brain's prefrontal cortex

The prefrontal cortex of the brain is located directly behind the forehead and governs our executive functions such as planning, goal setting, problem-solving, judgment, attention, and impulse control. Neurological research has identified the prefrontal cortex as one of the last regions to fully mature, not reaching full maturation until the mid-twenties (Casey, Giedd, and Thomas, 2000; Diamond, 2002; Giedd et al., 1999; Luna and Sweeney, 2004; Sowell et al., 1999a; Sowell et al., 1999b; Sowell et al., 2001;

Sowell et al., 2002; Spear, 2000). As the prefrontal cortex matures during the adolescent years (due to the myelination and synaptic pruning process) youths' ability to regulate emotions, manage sexual impulses, and think consequentially (Baird and Fugelsang, 2004) can significantly improve.

Reason for optimism – as the brain matures, it utilises the 'thinking' region (prefrontal cortex) of the brain more efficiently in coordination with the 'emotional' region

Although more research with larger subject pools and longitudinal designs are needed to gain clarity about the maturational process of the human brain, thus far it is clear that adolescents process emotions differently than adults at a neurological level, including the sometimes overutilisation of the amygdala/emotional region of the brain (Baird et al., 1999; Killgore and Yurgelun-Todd, 2007; Killgore, Oki, and Yurgelun-Todd, 2001). It is hypothesised that children and adolescents (as compared to adults) are not as proficient at simultaneously coordinating the activity between the 'thinking' and 'emotional' regions of the brain (Steinberg, 2008). The apparent lack of coordination between these two brain regions is consistent with recent findings regarding neural connections. Neuroscience studies have found that as youth mature into later adolescence and early adulthood there is an increase in neural connections *within* the 'thinking region' and *between* the 'thinking region' and 'emotional region' (subcortical areas) (Eluvathingal et al., 2007; Steinberg, 2008). As these neural connections develop, the brains capacity to utilise the 'thinking region' can greatly improve (Rubia et al., 2000). This can significantly improve youths' ability to accurately read others emotions and manage their own emotions; an improved ability to 'think before acting'.

Reason for optimism – neuroplasticity of the brain

Our brain works on a 'use it or lose it' principle. The neural pathways we use on a regular basis become strong and thrive while the pathways we do not use get pruned away or become less prominent (Bennett et al., 1996; Cicchetti and Tucker, 1994; Diamond, 2001; Nelson, 2003; Nelson and Bloom, 1997). This process is referred to as 'neuroplasticity' and it highlights the importance (on a neurological level) of youth repeatedly practicing 'healthy alternatives' to their sexually abusive behaviors in order to stimulate neural pathways and wire the brain in very positive ways.

Reason for optimism – prevalence rates for delinquent behavior dramatically decreases in late adolescence and young adulthood

Statistics on the prevalence of delinquent behaviors have found that antisocial acts peak at approximately age 17 and dramatically decrease in late adolescence and young adulthood (Caspi and Moffit, 1995; Hirschi and Gottfredson, 1983; Moffit, 1993). The large majority of youth who commit delinquent acts during their adolescent years do not continue on this path as adults.

Reason for optimism – youth recidivism rate for sexual re-offenses is low

According to the National Center on Sexual Behavior of Youth (2003), the sexual re-offense recidivism rate for youth who have committed a sexual offense is between 5–14 per cent. This low recidivism rate is another reason to be hopeful and optimistic about youths' ability to make positive life changes in treatment. The 'no cure' and 'once a sex offender, always a sex offender' belief system, which has been quite prevalent within the sex offense-specific field, is *not* supported by research (eg Langstrom and Grann, 2000; Reitzel and Carbonell, 2006; Worling and Curwin, 2000; Worling, Litteljohn, and Bookalam, 2010). *The large majority of youth who receive treatment will not sexually reoffend in the future. This is yet another reason to remain optimistic about youth with sexual behavior problems.*

Category 3 – Asset development

The word 'Asset' is defined in Webster's dictionary as a 'valuable or desirable thing to have' (Agnes, 2006). Within the field of youth services, *an 'asset' has been defined as internal qualities and external experiences/resources, which are identified as critical factors for promoting healthy youth development.* Strengths-Based Interventions (SBIs) classified under the 'Asset Development' category target assets which youth possess or have the potential to possess if providers recognise and reinforce them. The next two SBIs

are directed towards identification and reinforcement of assets/strengths commonly found within youth.

SBI: educate and promote 'developmental assets'

The Search Institute (www.search-institute.org) is a nonprofit organisation that has been conducting research, as well as providing trainings and publications on the topic of healthy youth development for many years (Benson, 1996a, 1996b, 1997, 2006; Benson, Galbraith, and Espeland, 1995; Roehlkepartain and Leffert, 2000; Search Institute, 1997). Their research findings have identified 'Forty Developmental Assets' (Fig. 6.1) that are strongly associated with healthy youth development. These developmental assets include experiences, opportunities, and internal capacities essential for health and success, which are broken down into four 'External Assets' (Support; Empowerment; Boundaries and Expectations; and Constructive Use of Time) and four 'Internal Assets' (Commitment to Learning; Positive Values; Social Competencies; and Positive Identity).

This SBA intervention involves educating youth and their significant others about the Forty Developmental Assets and highlighting how these assets can be beneficial to them. Research has consistently found that *youth who possess a greater number of these internal and external 'developmental assets', have an increased chance of developing positive attitudes and behaviors* (ie succeeds in school; values/appreciates diversity; maintains good health; delays gratification) and are at *less risk of engaging in high-risk behaviors* (ie problem alcohol use; illicit drug use; violence; depression and attempted suicide). After youth (*and their significant others) have looked over each of the 40 Developmental Assets, providers can ask them the following questions:

- How many of these Developmental Assets do you (*does your child) currently possess?
- How many of the Developmental Assets do you (*does your child) currently possess that could be made stronger?
- How many of the Developmental Assets do you (*does your child) currently *not* possess but think could have if you (*they) work on it in treatment?

These questions help target relevant 'developmental assets' that can be created and/or further enhanced within a youth's life (at school,

Figure 6.1: 40 Developmental Assets

The Search Institute has identified the following building blocks of healthy development that help young people grow up healthy, caring and responsible.

Category	Asset name and definition
External Assets	
Support	1. Family support – Family life provides high levels of love and support
	2. Positive family communication – Young person and her or his parent(s) communicate positively, and young person is willing to seek advice and counsel from parent(s)
	3. Other adult relationships – Young person receives support from three or more nonparent adults
	4. Caring neighbourhood – Young person experiences caring neighbours
	5. Caring school climate – School provides a caring, encouraging environment
	6. Parent involvement in schooling – Parent(s) are actively involved in helping young person succeed in school
Empowerment	7. Community values youth – Young person perceives that adults in the community value youth
	8. Youth as resources – Young people are given useful roles in the community
	9. Service to others – Young person serves in the community one hour or more per week
	10. Safety – Young person feels safe at home, at school, and in the neighbourhood
Boundaries and expectations	11. Family boundaries – Family has clear rules and consequences and monitors the young person's whereabouts
	12. School boundaries – School provides clear rules and consequences
	13. Neighbourhood boundaries – Neighbours take responsibility for monitoring young people's behaviour
	14. Adult role models – Parent(s) and other adults model positive, responsible behaviour
	15. Positive peer influence – Young person's best friends model responsible behaviour
	16. High expectations – Both parent(s) and teachers encourage the young person to do well
Constructive use of time	17. Creative activities – Young person spends three or more hours per week in lessons or practice in music, theatre, or other arts
	18. Youth programmes – Young person spends three or more hours per week in sports, clubs, or organisations at school and/or in the community
	19. Religious community Young person spends one or more hours per week in activities in a religious institution
	20. Time at home – Young person is out with friends 'with nothing special to do' two or fewer nights per week
Internal Assets	
Commitment to learning	21. Achievement motivations – Young person is motivated to do well in school
	22. School engagement – Young person is actively engaged in learning
	23. Homework – Young person reports doing at least one hour of homework every school day
	24. Bonding to school – Young person cares about her or his school
	25. Reading for pleasure – Young person reads for pleasure three or more hours per week

Positive values	26. Caring – Young person places high value on helping other people
	27. Equality and social justice – Young person places high value on promoting equality and reducing hunger and poverty
	28. Integrity – Young person acts on convictions and stands up for her or his beliefs
	29. Honesty – Young person 'tells the truth even when it is not easy'
	30. Responsibility – Young person accepts and takes personal responsibility
	31. Restraint – Young person believes it is important not to be sexually active or to use alcohol or other drugs
Social competencies	32. Planning and decision making – Young person knows how to plan ahead and make choices
	33. Interpersonal competence – Young person has empathy, sensitivity, and friendship skills
	34. Cultural competence – Young person has knowledge of and comfort with people of different cultural/racial/ethnic backgrounds
	35. Resistance skills – Young person can resist negative peer pressure and dangerous situations
	36. Peaceful conflict resolution – Young person seeks to resolve conflict nonviolently
Positive identity	37. Personal power – Young person feels he or she has control over 'things that happen to me'
	38. Self-esteem – Young person reports having a high self-esteem
	39. Sense of purpose – Young person reports that 'my life has a purpose'
	40. Positive view of personal future – Young person is optimistic about her or his personal future

home, and in treatment programs) in order to reduce their at-risk status and enhance healthy development. The literature linking healthy adjustment to developmental assets continues to grow (ie Guerra and Bradshaw, 2008) and undoubtedly will continue to provide valuable information for how providers can assist youth in developing into healthy, successful adults.

SBI: educate and promote 'protective factors' associated with 'resiliency'

'Resilient' individuals are those who have been exposed to significant stressors during childhood (eg abuse, neglect, poverty), yet have bounced back to lead positive, successful lives. Resiliency appears to be a common phenomenon within human beings, if enough 'protective factors' are available to reinforce healthy development (Masten, 2001). 'Protective factors' are the opposite of risk factors in that they are conditions which increase the likelihood of healthy development and outcomes, as opposed to negative outcomes. These protective

factors/assets act as a 'buffer' against biological and psychosocial risk factors. It is an area of study that appears to have significant implications for the assessment and treatment of youth with sexual behavior problems (Gilgun, 2006). This SBA intervention involves educating youth and their significant others about the definitions of 'resiliency' and 'protective factors' and then introducing them to the list of protective factors commonly linked to resiliency (Fig. 6.2).

After youth (*and their significant others) have looked over the list of protective factors (Fig. 6.2) providers can ask them the following questions:

- How many of these individual, family, community protective factors do you (*does your child) currently possess?
- How many of the individual, family, community protective factors do you (*does your child) currently possess that could be made stronger?
- How many of the individual, family, community protective factors do you (*does your child) currently *not* possess but think

Figure 6.2: Resiliency Protective Factors Checklist

Listed below are some of the most commonly reported protective factors that resilient youth possess (Masten and Coatsworth, 1998; Masten and Reed, 2002). Research has consistently found that even possessing a few of these protective factors can have a positive impact on an individual's ability to overcome hardships and develop into healthy, pro-social adults. The protective factors are listed under three categories: individual; family; and community. *Note:* Three of the 'individual' protective factors (marked with an *) have empirical support in areas of research (cited below) not included in Masten and her colleagues summary of resiliency studies.

'Individual' Protective Factors
Individual protective factors are those associated with a youth's internal, personal qualities that are influential in promoting resiliency and healthy development.

Good cognitive abilities (including problem-solving and attentional skills)
The ability to think, focus, and problem-solve when you are faced with difficult life circumstances.

Good self-regulation of emotional arousal and impulse control
The ability to control your emotions and impulses. The ability to think before you act.

Positive self-perception
Feeling good about yourself related to your positive behavior (not your negative actions).

Talents
Possessing talents that you and others value (eg, computer skills, musical abilities; writing aptitude; athletic abilities).

Self-efficacy
Believing that you can effect/influence your environment. While some youth believe they have no control over their lives (learned helplessness), resilient youth often believe in their ability to effect change within their lives.

Faith and sense of meaning in life
Believing in a 'higher power' that is watching over you.

Good sense of humor
Having a good sense of humor, which helps you manage stress and improve interactions with others.

*Coped with significant adversity in life
Have survived difficult experiences in the past (i.e., abuse; parents' divorce; death of a loved one), which has made you more skilled and confident to handle future difficult times (Affleck and Tennen, 1996; Charney, 2004; Cooper et al., 2007; Cryder, et al., 2006; Frazier and Berman, 2008).

*Good insight into problems and solutions
Having an understanding about how your problems developed and having ideas about what you need to do differently in the future to correct the problems and improve your life (Beardslee, 1989; Conte, et al., 1990; Nyklicek, Majoor, and Schalken, 2010).

*Motivated to make positive changes in life
Being committed to putting forth effort to improve your life (Miller and Rollnick, 2002; Walters et al., 2007)

'Family' Protective Factors
Family protective factors are those found within a youth's family that are influential in promoting resiliency and healthy development.

Close relationships with caregiving adults
Having a close relationship with positive, supportive adult caregivers. These caregivers are sometimes biological parents, grandparents, foster parents, adoptive parents, aunts, uncles, older siblings, or anyone else within the extended family.

Positive family climate
Living in a family environment that has positive interactions among its members and minimal parental conflict. A home that is organized, predictable, and safe.

Caregivers are involved in youth's education
Having parents/caregivers who are involved in their child's school activities (eg, regularly attend school functions; help with homework; emphasize the importance of getting an education).

Caregivers have a democratic (authoritative) parenting style
Having parents who not only set limits and provide good supervision, but are also warm, accepting, and involved. Parents who have open communication with their kids and explain (give a rationale) when they set limits and give consequences.

Family has socioeconomic advantages
Living in a family that can adequately provide/afford services for family members

Postsecondary education of parents
Parents have some level of college education

'Community' Protective Factors
Community protective factors are those found within a youth's community (within their neighborhood, peer group, and school) that are influential in promoting resiliency and healthy development.

Close relationships with competent, pro-social, and supportive adults
Having positive relationships with competent, pro-social teachers, coaches, ministers, family friends, therapists, and other community members.

Connections to pro-social, rule-abiding peers
Having relationships with positive, pro-social peers; as opposed to delinquent peers.

Connections to pro-social organizations
Being involved in pro-social activities and organizations (eg sports, band, clubs, after-school programs and jobs).

Attend an effective school
Attending a school that is well-organized and predictable; consistently enforces rules; monitors students' academic progress; and has teachers who provide high quality instruction, are positive role models, and sources of support for youth.

Live in a neighborhood with high collective efficacy
Living in a neighborhood where neighbors look out for each other and intervene if problems arise.

Live in an area with good community services
Living in an area that has access to good medical services, mental health services, and social services.

---

could have if you (*they) work on it in treatment?

These questions help to target relevant 'protective factors', which can be created and/or further enhanced within a youth's life (at school, home, and in treatment programs) in order to promote resiliency.

Category 4 – Pro-social development

Pro-social behavior can be defined as any act that is performed for the purpose of benefiting others. The promotion of pro-social skills is especially important within the field of sexual victim and sex offense-specific treatments, where too often youth regress from being a victim to a victimiser (Ryan, 1989). Described below are two SBIs that focus on youths' pro-social development.

SBI: assess and meet youth's basic human needs

A common goal when working with youth with sexual behavior problems is to enhance their pro-social actions and empathy for others; however, when a youth's most basic needs are *not* met it can significantly impede their ability to focus on anything except their own needs. It makes sense from an evolutionary perspective that when our basic needs are not being met (eg lack of food; fear for our safety; feeling socially isolated and rejected), our survival instincts kick-in and we become primarily focused on meeting our own needs while disregarding anything or anybody else. *One of the keys to enhancing pro-social behaviors is to ensure youth's basic human needs are met so they are better able to focus on the needs of others.*

Abraham Maslow's Hierarchy of Needs Theory of Motivation (Maslow, 1970) helps illustrate the potency and influence of our basic human needs. Maslow believed that humans are motivated to fulfill their unmet needs beginning with the most basic needs. Listed below is a brief description of four basic human needs that when met can be influential in boosting a youth's capacity to be pro-social.

Physiological needs: Humans most potent needs are life-sustaining processes, such as the *need for food, water, oxygen to breath, elimination of bodily waste, comfortable body temperature, and sleep.*

Safety needs: Safety needs involve the *need for stability, consistency, and protection, as well as freedom from fear, anxiety, and chaos.* There is a basic human need for a predictable, safe environment.

Social needs (belongingness and love needs): There is also a basic *need to love and be loved, to be accepted, and to belong to a group or family.* This social need also includes the desire to avoid loneliness, alienation, and rejection. Most adults have had the experience of losing a significant relationship due to breakup, divorce, or death, and have found themselves unable to focus on anything else except the lost relationship. The same holds true for at-risk youth who will have difficulty focusing on treatment topics if their basic need for love and belonging is not being met.

Competency needs (esteem and achievement needs): Competency needs involve the need for *high self-esteem, achievement, and mastery of our environment.* This need also includes the desire to be recognised by others and respected for our personal achievements and competencies.

When a youth arrives at school or a therapy session hungry (unmet physiological need); or is getting bullied on a regular basis (unmet safety need) or has no friends and feels alienated from family (unmet social need); or is struggling to learn how to read (unmet competency need), providers must identify these unmet needs and intervene accordingly. When basic human needs are fulfilled (at least to some degree), it can enhance youth's capacity to focus on the needs of others (increased pro-social and empathetic behaviors). In addition, when youth are taught how to get their basic human needs met in 'pro-social ways', they will be much less likely to resort to delinquent acts to meet these needs. Providers with a strengths-based emphasis

should begin each assessment and treatment session by asking themselves, '*What basic human needs are not being met for this youth and how can I help meet these needs?*'

It is important to note that the order and potency of Maslow's Hierarchy of Needs is not universally fixed; however, the underlying theory as it relates to fulfilling unmet needs appears to be very applicable for better understanding what motivates youth and their families (Dunlap, 2004).

SBI: educate youth about the reciprocal nature of relationships

Relationships are a two-way street. When youth have an awareness of how their behaviors influence how others respond towards them, they are more likely to interact in a pro-social manner. An effective multi-sensory method of explaining the reciprocal nature of relationships is to use the metaphor of 'throwing a ball against the wall'.

'Throwing a Ball against the Wall' Metaphor

Step 1: Have youth sit or stand approximately six to eight feet from a wall and give them a ball (a soft, hand-held ball that bounces). **Step 2:** Ask the youth to *throw the ball softly (lob the ball) against the wall and catch it.* When the youth does this, the ball bounces softly against the wall and they are able to easily catch it. **Step 3:** Then ask the youth to *throw the ball as hard as they can against the wall and catch it.* When the youth does this, the ball inevitably bounces off the wall hard and they have difficulty catching it. **Step 4:** Explain that throwing a ball against the wall is a lot like relationships. When we *throw a ball softly* against the wall (when we are open, honest and respectful in a relationship), the ball comes back softly (the other person is more likely to be open, honest, and respectful back). However, when we *throw the ball hard* against the wall (when we are disrespectful in a relationship) the ball comes back at us hard (the other person is more likely to respond back in a disrespectful manner). **Step 5:** The provider demonstrates the metaphor for the youth by first throwing the ball *hard* against the wall while yelling something like 'screw you; I don't have to listen to you'. Then throws the ball *softly* against the wall while calmly saying something like 'I hear what you are saying, lets talk about it'. The provider follows up this demonstration by facilitating a discussion about the reciprocal nature of relationships and encourages the youth to think about times when they have thrown the ball softly in relationships and when they have thrown the ball too hard.

This metaphor helps youth to better understand the reciprocal nature of relationships – what we give out in relationships influences what we get back in relationships. Respect breeds respect, while disrespect breeds disrespect. As youth begin to understand how their actions directly impact how others interact toward them, it often increases their motivation to interact respectfully in relationships. This intervention helps to open up communication in treatment about youth's interpersonal mannerisms and relationships. Youth acquire better insight into their interpersonal behavior, both pro-social and non-pro-social (ie 'I threw the ball too hard against the wall yesterday when I was talking to my teacher').

Pro-social behavior vs. grooming behavior

It is important for SOS providers *not* to assume that all 'pro-social' acts exhibited by youth are actually 'grooming' behaviors used to set up future sexual offenses. If we automatically label every pro-social behavior as 'grooming', without first assessing the situational and developmental circumstances associated with the behavior, we will be setting up a scenario in which youth are never allowed opportunities to practice pro-social actions.

Category 5 – Intellectual development

The concept of 'intelligence' embodies more than just an individual who can score high on a standardised IQ test. An individual's emotional aptitude and knowledge about the treatment they are participating in (being an informed consumer) are also forms of intelligence that can be developed.

SBI: educate and promote 'emotional intelligence'

Emotional functioning is a critical part of the human experience. This SBA intervention involves educating youth about the 'what', 'why', and 'how' of emotional intelligence (EI). Regarding '*what*' is EI, there has been an ongoing debate about the operational definition of this construct (eg Bar-On, 1997, 2002; Boyatzis, Goleman, and Rhee, 2000; Cooper and Sawaf, 1997; Goleman, 1995; Mayer, Caruso, and

Salovey, 1999; Mayer and Salovey, 1997; Mayer, Salovey, and Caruso, 2008; Neubauer and Freudenthaler, 2005; Salovey and Mayer, 1990; Weisinger, 1998); however, in general EI can be defined as *an individual's capacity to know and handle their own emotions, as well as others' emotions, and to utilise this knowledge about emotions to guide their future thoughts and actions.*

Helping youth to understand '*why*' EI is important can often enhance motivation to practice these skills in treatment. People with high EI have been linked to several positive outcomes including: enhanced competence and adaptation in social relationships (Engelberg and Sjoberg, 2005; Mayer, Salovey, and Caruso, 2008); enhanced performance in school (through the use of social and emotional learning programs) including improved academic achievement, interpersonal skills, and quality of peer/adult relationships, as well as reductions in truancy, alcohol/drug use, high-risk sexual behavior, and aggression (Greenberg et al., 2003) and improved performance on the job, including the quality of the job completed and productive working relationships related to teamwork and cohesiveness (Abraham, 2005; Carmelli, 2003; Rosete and Ciarrochi, 2005). People with low EI have been linked to several negative outcomes (compared to high EI youth) including: more interpersonal conflict, maladjustment, aggressiveness; and alcohol/drug abuse (Mayer, Salovey, and Caruso, 2008).

After youth have a good understanding of the potential benefits of EI, this intervention focuses on helping youth learn '*how*' to further develop it. Five specific EI abilities include: awareness of own emotions; regulation of own emotions; awareness of others' emotions; regulation of others' emotions; and motivation through own emotions. Each EI ability is described below, along with strategies for further enhancing these skills in youth.

Awareness of own emotions: This EI skill involves an individual's ability to accurately identify, understand, and communicate about their own internal emotional states (*self-awareness*). An awareness of emotions can aid youth in better understanding the impact of their emotions on themselves and others. **Strategies** for enhancing this skill include: writing and reading poetry/song lyrics/stories that enhance self-reflection about emotions; using biofeedback instruments to enhance physiological awareness of emotional states (Longo, 2010) and facilitating the exploration of the developmental origin and causes of problematic emotional reactions, which can assist youth in gaining awareness with less risk of becoming defensive.

Regulation of own emotions: This skill involves an individual's ability to manage and control their own emotions (*self-regulation*) including negative, extreme, and impulsive emotional reactions. **Strategies** for strengthening this ability include: teaching stress management skills (ie deep breathing/belly breathing; progressive muscle relaxation; yoga; physical exercise; journaling; reading; drawing; listening to music; and identifying a support system of adults and peers to talk to when needed); and teaching cognitive interventions (ie thought stopping; thought substitution; peaceful imagery; and positive self-talk). Our emotions are closely linked to our thoughts; therefore interrupting distressing thoughts with thoughts that are reassuring and positively reframe stressful situations, can assist youth in better regulating their emotions.

Awareness of others emotions: This component of EI involves the capacity to accurately identify and understand the feelings, needs, and concerns of others (*empathy*). That is, the ability to empathise with others through reading their emotions conveyed verbally and non-verbally. **Strategies** for enhancing this skill include: practicing non-verbal behavior exercises (ie playing feelings charades); watching movies that evoke empathy, then having discussions about how the characters in the movie must have been feeling; and putting self in others shoes who have been victimised, then exploring how it would impact your own thoughts, feelings, and behaviors as the victim. When youth are struggling with this empathy exercise it is sometimes helpful to have them imagine a loved one being victimised in a similar way (ie What if it was your mom who got assaulted, how do you think it would impact her?). In addition, exploring youth's personal history of victimisation can often enhance their insight into others' emotions.

Regulation of others' emotions: This ability involves the management of emotions in other people in order to induce desirable responses and facilitate healthy relationships. A large part of this skill is connected to the 'awareness of others'

emotions' (described above), which helps provide information about what is the most appropriate way to respond to others. When we understand others' emotions and express empathy towards them, it can positively impact how they regulate their emotions and how they reciprocally respond back towards us. **Strategies** for promoting this skill include: educating youth about good listening skills, which include paraphrasing, reflection, clarification, and summarising skills (Cormier and Cormier, 1998, p. 98); utilising a talker-listener exercise in which the youth and the provider take turns being the talker and the listener while discussing generic topics; and role-playing and discussing verbal and non-verbal behaviors that elicit positive vs. negative emotional responses from others (eg respond with a calm, soft tone of voice and respectful content vs. an escalated, loud voice, and disrespectful content; greet each other with a smile, good eye contact, and eyebrows slightly raised vs. a frown, poor eye contact, and furrowed brow).

Motivation through own emotions: This EI ability involves an individual's capacity to manage their own emotions in a manner that facilitates thinking, guides future adaptive behavior, and assists in attaining specific goals (*self-motivation*). **Strategies** for strengthening this skill include: enhancing insight about self-motivation by exploring circumstances that have motivated the youth in the past; teaching youth about goal-setting, particularly as it relates to 'approach goals' (Ward, Gannon, and Yates, 2008; Mann et al., 2004); teaching youth about self-reinforcement; and educating youth about the benefits of delayed gratification.

SBI: assist youth in being informed consumers by 'collaborating on decision-making/goal development' and providing a 'rationale for interventions'

Another SBI classified under intellectual development involves helping youth and their families to be 'informed consumers'. Most people prefer to be informed before agreeing to do something and that includes participation in SOS services. It is analogous to buying a new car. Before committing to buying a car, typically you want to find out as much as possible about the car (ie how much it costs, what kind of gas mileage it gets, will it meet your specific need for a small, gas efficient commuter car vs. a large family car). All this information is gathered in order to be an 'informed consumer' so that when a car is purchased you feel good about it and are committed to the decision made. For youth receiving SOS services, being an 'informed consumer' is equally important. When youth are provided information about the what, when, where, how, and why of SOS services and understand how these services can be beneficial to them, they are much more likely to be engaged in the process. This SBI specifically focuses on collaboration in decision-making/goal development and providing a rationale for interventions.

Collaboration in decision-making/goal development: One of the primary objectives of SBA is to explore strengths and solutions to problems. This 'exploration' is meant to be a collaborative effort between the provider, youth, caregiver, and others involved in the youth's life. Rather than providers taking on a one-sided expert role and youth being passive recipients, there is a mutual exploration of what will help youth develop into healthy successful adults. For youth who are court ordered into treatment, the coercion to fulfill the requirements of treatment can come from the court, while the role of the provider can be to collaborate with the youth in order to meet the court's requirements. 'Collaboration' and 'goal consensus' between the youth and provider enhances the effectiveness of treatment (Karver et al., 2006; Norcross, 2002). When there is agreement regarding treatment goals, it only makes sense that it will have a positive impact on services. This collaborative, team approach is an effective method of engaging youth and their families in the assessment and treatment process.

A helpful method for establishing a 'collaborative relationship' is to talk with youth, not at them, and ask questions that place them in an expert role (ie 'What do you want your life to look like in the future?' 'What do you hope to be doing one year, two years, five years from now?' 'What are the pros and cons of your behavior that has gotten you in trouble?' 'What do you think will be the most helpful thing for you to learn in treatment?' and 'What do you hope to gain from SOS treatment?'). Sometimes a youth's stated goal will simply be to 'get the system off my back'. Although this is not the most positive sounding goal, it is still relevant. That is, helping youth to develop the skills to live in the community

without intervention from the 'system' (ie legal system, social service system, school detention). It is not unusual for youth to initially be resistant to participating in SOS services; however, within the context of a strengths-based approach, the collaborative atmosphere will often improve. Not all goals need to be decided at the beginning of treatment. The identification and reassessment of goals should be revisited at various times during the course of treatment.

Providing a rationale for services provided: If a youth and/or their significant others do not understand how and why SOS services are pertinent to them, they are more likely to be resistant to participating. Conversely, when given a rationale for how SOS services will benefit them, they are much more likely to be engaged and motivated to participate. For example, a youth who regularly masturbates while thinking about abusive fantasies may not stop this practice just because a provider tells them to stop. However, when a provider helps the youth become an 'informed consumer' by giving them a rationale for why masturbating to *abusive* fantasies is bad; the youth will often be more receptive to change. Once a youth is given information about the neuroplasticity of the brain and how abusive fantasies neurologically stimulates the brain in ways that increase the risk of becoming sexually aroused to abusive acts, they are typically more motivated to stop this masturbatory practice. In addition, when youth are also educated about how *non-abusive*, *pro-social* fantasies can wire their brain in healthy ways, they are typically more motivated to develop healthy masturbatory practices. This rationale about masturbatory fantasies helps youth understand why it is important *not* to pair pleasant feelings (masturbation and orgasm) with something that gets them in trouble and causes harm to others (sexually abusive fantasies). It becomes a mutual goal of the youth and provider to assist the youth in developing pro-social fantasies that can wire the brain in healthy ways.

Youth's participation in an SOS risk assessment is another scenario in which providing a 'rationale' can be beneficial to the process. When a youth is given a rationale explaining how an accurate assessment will help them overcome their abusive behaviors and go on to live healthy successful lives, they are more likely to be open, honest, and engaged in the process. Helping youth and their families to be 'informed consumers' can increase their engagement in the process. When there is collaboration regarding decision-making/goal development and a rationale is given for why certain interventions are necessary, effectiveness of SOS services can be greatly augmented.

Category 6 – Professional/provider development

Youth cannot be expected to become actively engaged in the process of positive change if SOS providers present with a demeanor that is jaded and deficit-focused. In order to be most effective as a provider, it is absolutely essential to have good self-care and maintain a high level of optimism and positive energy while working with youth. Described below are two SBIs for enhancing providers' aptitude for working most effectively with at-risk youth.

SBI: take care of yourself/maintain a healthy balance in life

Working with youth who have committed sexual offenses can be taxing on providers (ie evaluators, therapists, direct care staff). In order for providers to be at their best when providing SOS services, good self-care is a necessity. That is, maintain a healthy balance in life, which allows time for family, friends, exercise, sleep, hobbies, and other enjoyable activities. The ability to 'compartmentalise' work can assist with this balance. Compartmentalisation involves the capacity to maintain a clear boundary between work and home life, which allows providers to 'take a break' from work not only physically but also mentally and emotionally.

SBI: self-monitor to prevent a deficit-based approach

Being exposed to delinquent behaviors and stories of abuse and trauma on a daily basis can skew perceptions and cause providers to become overly focused on problems and less optimistic about youths' capacity to make positive changes in life. This can not only impede assessment and treatment success but also lead to occupational burn-out. An effective strategy of reducing the risk of becoming deficit-based is to regularly allow time for self-reflection about working with at-risk youth. *Self-reflection time* allows providers the opportunity to step back for a moment and appraise how things are going. *Take a few minutes at the end of each work day* to ask yourself questions

such as, 'How did I come across towards youth, families, and co-workers?', 'Did I interact in a strengths-based manner?', and 'Were the concepts I discussed with the youth well received or are there better ways of delivering/teaching certain treatment concepts?'. In addition, *take a few minutes at the beginning of each work day* to ask yourself questions such as, 'How am I feeling inside right now?', 'What do I need to do to ensure I am fully present and strengths-based in my work today?', and 'How can I be most effective when working with a youth who has been struggling?' When providers regularly step back and reflect on how they are interpersonally coming across to others (ie youth, parents, colleagues) it can go a long way towards further enhancing awareness and effectiveness as a provider. Providers must always be mindful of the risk of becoming deficit-based and do everything possible to prevent it.

Enhancing youths' openness and honesty

Talking openly and honestly about their sexually abusive behaviors is not an easy task for youth. Many youth are understandably guarded and defensive when asked to talk about their delinquent and abusive behaviors. A strengths-based approach can enhance a youth's openness and honesty when providers are mindful of the youth's ego-strength and relationship connections; consider the timing and location of communication; and utilise meta-talk.

Be mindful of 'relationship connection' and 'ego-strength': When a youth's relationship connections and ego-strength are strong, they are often more receptive to addressing their problematic behaviors in an open and honest fashion. *Relationship connection* is defined as a youth's sense of trust, openness, and closeness with a particular person/provider. *Ego-strength* is defined as a youth's internal sense of security, and personal confidence to tolerate stress and frustration. Utilising a strengths-based approach can help strengthen 'relationship connections' and boost 'ego-strength'.

Be mindful of 'timing' and 'location': The timing for when to directly address a youth's delinquent behaviors is important to consider. Not only should a youth's relationship connections and ego-strength be strong, but the youth should *not* be emotionally escalated. When a youth is calm they are much more likely to be open and honest about their disruptive behaviors. Providers must also be sensitive to the location in which they discuss youth's delinquent behaviors. They must ensure youth feel safe within their surroundings. Addressing difficult issues in individual and family sessions as opposed to group settings is frequently a more optimal location. When feasible, removing the surrounding audience can often increase the chances of youth responding more openly and authentically about their present and past mistakes.

Utilise 'meta-talk': *Meta-talk* as it relates to mental health services can be defined as having discussions regarding the 'about' and 'how' of youth's potential experience in assessment and treatment before actually doing it. This is yet another strategy for enhancing youth's openness and honesty about their abusive, delinquent behaviors. Specific meta-talk strategies are described below.

Provide youth with an introduction/rationale for why it can be beneficial to talk openly and honestly. Prior to discussing youth's problem behaviors, provide youth with a rationale: (1) Explain that when you give them feedback and introduce difficult topics, it is because you 'care about them' and want them to overcome their past delinquent acts; (2) 'Normalise' the fact that we all have issues, regrets, and make mistakes in life; (3) Remind youth that their problematic behaviors do not define who they are as a person; and (4) Label a youth's 'honesty' and ability to 'take responsibility' as a strength (not a weakness) a sign of maturity, and a behavior you respect. If you provide this type of introduction and rationale, youth will often be more open to talking about their past abusive acts.

Give youth the option to talk about difficult issues at a later time. It is difficult for anybody to talk openly about his or her personal mistakes and shameful actions. For youth who have committed sexual offenses, talking openly can be extremely difficult. In addition, if a youth has not had enough time to establish rapport with an evaluator or treatment provider, they are *not* going to be as open and honest. Therefore, respect a youth's choice to discuss certain issues at a later time or to only share parts of their experience initially.

Discourage youth from lying by giving them another way to respond to difficult topics. When talking to youth about their sexually abusive acts,

many youth will be tempted to lie, minimise, or omit during their self report. In order to help reduce this risk, teach youth to say, 'I'm not ready to talk about that yet, can we talk about it later?' It is often more difficult for youth to openly admit to their past abusive behaviors if they have previously lied to us about it.

Explore censorship issues regarding why a youth is resistant to talking openly. Gather information from youth about 'what is it' that makes it hard to talk about their problems and past offenses: (1) Specifically explore what worries them about talking openly and what would be the advantages and disadvantages of talking about their issues. Youth may benefit from generating a 'pros and cons' list; (2) Youth who have committed sexual offenses often worry about how others will think and feel about them, so let them know what we (the providers) are thinking and feeling. Communicate respect and acceptance for youth who have the courage to talk about their mistakes and problems. Unconditional acceptance can go a long way towards youth talking more openly; (3) Discuss how the information they disclose will be used to help them, not hurt them; however, be sure to educate youth about mandatory reporting laws, which dictate when reports must be made to social services or law enforcement; and (4) Ask questions about youths' previous assessment and treatment services to ascertain if they had some negative experiences that may be impeding their openness. Then, utilise this information to create a therapeutic environment that does not duplicate these past negative experiences.

Benefits of a strengths-based approach

There are many benefits to utilising a strengths-based approach when assessing and treating youth with sexual behavior problems and other delinquent behaviors. These benefits include the following:

SBA increases the likelihood of 'establishing positive relationships' with youth and 'enhancing their receptiveness to SOS services': According to treatment outcome research (discussed earlier in this chapter), one of the most important components to effective treatment is the establishment of a positive therapeutic relationship. Most people will not be receptive to forming a relationship with someone who only wants to focus on their personal flaws, past mistakes, and inappropriate behaviors. The same holds true for the youth struggling with sexual behavior problems. Youth are more likely to form trusting positive relationships with providers and be open, honest, and engaged in assessment/treatment when the emphasis is on their strengths.

SBA helps create an environment that is 'emotionally safe', 'pro-social', and 'provides success experiences', which are essential components for healthy youth development: When youth feel unsafe, socially alienated, rejected and/or have failure experiences on a daily basis, they cannot be expected to be positive and pro-social. Youth will respond with defensiveness, dishonesty, irritability, aggression, and/or social withdrawal, depression, and possibly suicidal behaviors. From an evolutionary perspective, it makes sense that if a youth is placed in an environment that is unsafe, it is natural and adaptive that their responses will be more defensive, and sometimes aggressive in order to survive. SBA helps create an environment that is not only emotionally safe, but also promotes pro-social behaviors and success experiences. If we want youth to become pro-social citizens with no more sexually abusive behaviors, then we must interact with them (and our colleagues) in a pro-social, strengths-based manner.

SBA is sensitive and respectful to the diversity/heterogeneity among youth: SBA focuses on the exploration of strengths within a particular youth, their family, and their community. This exploration process is a collaborative effort between the provider, the youth, their caregiver(s), and others involved in the youth's life. This mutual exploration of strengths communicates interest and respect for values/beliefs, which are unique to a youth's: race; cultural background; gender; spirituality; religion; sexual orientation; socio-economic status; physical, emotional, and cognitive abilities/disabilities; family norms; and peer relations. This approach assists providers in connecting with and empowering youth from diverse backgrounds and affords youth opportunities to educate providers about their self-identity and personal view of the world that make them unique.

SBA directs youth toward 'what to do' rather than what not to do: Rather than just focusing on a youth's problem behaviors and what *not* to do, this approach focuses on a youth's positive behaviors and educates them on 'what to do'. It is solution-focused in that it directs services towards helping youth to be sexually healthy, pro-social citizens within our communities, which is the ultimate goal of sex offense-specific services.

Conclusion

Overly focusing on youth's problems and deficits can increase defensiveness and lead to inaccurate assessments and ineffective treatment. *A strengths-based approach (SBA) focuses on the identification, creation, and reinforcement of strengths and resources within individuals, their family, and their community.* This chapter highlighted several concepts within SBA including the importance of forming positive therapeutic relationships and creating an atmosphere in which youth are actively engaged in the assessment and treatment process. SBA is made up of an eclectic mix of interventions which all focus on 'what to do' rather than 'what not to do'. Several strengths-based interventions (SBIs) were described, which were organised into six categories entitled: relationship development, optimistic attitude development, asset development, pro-social development, intellectual development, and professional/provider development.

There is a significant body of empirical support for many SBA constructs. Relationship variables, resiliency protective factors, solution-focused interventions, and developmental assets have all been linked to positive treatment outcome and healthy youth development. SBA is also vigilant to risk management issues. A significant benefit of this approach is that it creates an atmosphere in which youth feel safe to openly address their risk factors and sexually abusive behaviors. SBA accomplishes this safe atmosphere by focusing attention on strengths and exceptions to problems, which can heighten youths' ego strength and relationship connection to providers. Establishing a strengths-based foundation can significantly enhance the effectiveness of sex offense-specific services. It targets strengths and protective factors, which not only reduce risk but increase the chances of youth developing into pro-social members of the community.

References

Abraham, R. (2005) Emotional Intelligence in the Workplace: A Review and Synthesis. In Schulze, R. and Roberts, R.D. (eds.) *Emotional Intelligence: an International Handbook.* Cambridge, MA: Hogrefe and Huber.

Affleck, G. and Tennen, H. (1996) Construing Benefits from Adversity: Adaptational Significance and Dispositional Underpinnings. *Journal of Personality,* 64: 4, 899–922.

Agnes, M. (2006) 4th edn. *Webster's New World College Dictionary.* Cleveland, OH: Wiley Publishing.

Allport, G. W. (1961) 3rd edn. *Pattern and Growth in Personality.* New York: Holt Rinehart and Winston.

Andrews, D.A. and Bonta, J. (2010) *The Psychology of Criminal Conduct.* 5th edn. New Providence: Lexis Nexis.

Appelstein, C.D. (1998) *No Such Thing as a Bad Kid: Understanding and Responding to Challenging Behavior of Troubled Children and Youth.* Weston, MA: The Gifford School.

Baird A.A. and Fugelsang, J.A. (2004) The Emergence of Consequential Thought: Evidence From Neuroscience. *Philosophical Transactions of The Royal Society of London, Biological Sciences,* 359, 1797–804.

Baird A.A. et al. (1999) Functional Magnetic Resonance Imaging of Facial Affect Recognition in Children and Adolescents. *Journal of The American Academy of Child and Adolescent Psychiatry,* 38: 2, 195–9.

Bar-On, R. (1997) *Bar-On Emotional Quotient Inventory: Short (EQ-I): Technical Manual.* Toronto, Canada: Multi-Health Systems.

Bar-On, R. (2002) *Bar-On Emotional Quotient Inventory: Short (EQ-I: S): Technical Manual.* Toronto, Canada: Multi-Health Systems.

Baumrind, D. (1978) Parental Disciplinary Patterns and Social Competence in Children. *Youth and Society,* 9, 239–76.

Beardslee, W.R. (1989) The Role of Self-Understanding in Resilient Individuals: The Development of A Perspective. *American Journal of Orthopsychiatry,* 59: 2, 266–78.

Benard, B. (1991) *Fostering Resiliency in Kids: Protective Factors in The Family, School, and Community.* Portland, OR: Northwest Regional Educational Laboratory.

Bennett, E.L. et al. (1996) Chemical and Anatomical Plasticity of Brain. *Journal of Neuropsychiatry,* 8: 4, 459–70.

Benson, P.L. (1996a) *Developmental Assets Among Minneapolis Youth.* Minneapolis: Search Institute.

Benson, P.L. (1996b) *Developmental Assets Among Albuquerque Youth.* Minneapolis: Search Institute.

Benson, P.L. (1997) *All Kids Are Our Kids: What Communities Must Do to Raise Caring and Responsible Children and Adolescents.* San Francisco: Jossey-Bass.

Benson, P.L. (2006) *All Kids Are Our Kids: What Communities Must Do to Raise Caring and Responsible Children and Adolescents.* San Francisco: Jossey-Bass.

Benson, P.L., Galbraith, J. and Espeland, P. (1995) *What Kids Need to Succeed.* Minneapolis, MN: Free Spirit.

Berg, I.K. and Steiner, T. (2003) *Children's Solution Work.* New York: W.W. Norton.

Blanchard, G.T. (1995) *The Difficult Connection: The Therapeutic Relationship in Sex Offender Treatment.* Brandon, VT: Safer Society Press.

Bohlin, K.E., Farmer, D. and Ryan, K. (2001) *Building Character in Schools: Resource Guide.* San Francisco: Jossey-Bass.

Boyatzis, R.E., Goleman, D. and Rhee, K.S. (2000) Clustering Competence in Emotional Intelligence: Insights from The Emotional Competence Inventory. In Bar-On, R. and Parker, J.D. (eds.) *The Handbook of Emotional Intelligence: Theory, Development, Assessment, and Application at Home, School, and in The Workplace.* San Francisco: Jossey-Bass.

Brendtro, L.K. and Larson, S.J. (2006) *The Resilience Revolution: Discovering Strengths in Challenging Kids.* Bloomington, IN: Solution Tree.

Brendtro, L.K., Ness, A. and Mitchell, M. (2005) *No Disposable Kids.* Bloomington, IN: Solution Tree.

Brendtro, L.K. and Shahbazian, M. (2004) *Troubled Children and Youth: Turning Problems Into Opportunities.* Champaign, Ill: Research Press.

Carmelli, A. (2003) The Relationship Between Emotional Intelligence and Work Attitudes, Behavior, and Outcomes: an Examination among Senior Managers. *Journal of Managerial Psychology,* 18, 788–813.

Casey, B.J., Giedd, J.N. and Thomas, K.M. (2000) Structural and Functional Brain Development and its Relation to Cognitive Development. *Biological Psychology,* 54, 241–57.

Caspi, A. and Moffitt, T.E. (1995) The Continuity of Maladaptive Behavior: From Description to

Understanding in The Study of Antisocial Behavior. In Cicchetti, D. and Cohen. D.J. (eds.) *Developmental Psychopathology: Vol. 2. Risk, Disorder, and Adaptation.* New York: Wiley.

Charney, D. (2004) Psychobiological Mechanisms of Resilience and Vulnerability: Implications for Successful Adaptation to Extreme Stress. *American Journal of Psychiatry*, 161: 2, 195–216.

Cicchetti, D. and Tucker, D. (eds.) (1994) Neural Plasticity Sensitive Periods and Psychopathology [Special Issue]. *Development and Psychopathology*, 6: 4.

Clark, M. D. (1998) Strength-Based Practice: The ABC's of Working with Adolescents Who Don't Want to Work with You. *Federal Probation*, 62: 1, 46–53.

Clay, R. (2010) More than one way to measure: Randomized clinical trials have their place, but critics argue that researchers would get better results if they also embraced other methodologies. *Monitor on Psychology*, 41: 8, 52–5.

Collie, R. et al. (2007) The Good Lives Model of Rehabilitation: Reducing Risks and Promoting Strengths with Adolescent Sexual Offenders. In Calder, M.C. (ed.) *Working With Children and Young People Who Sexually Abuse: Taking The Field Forward.* Lyme Regis: Russell House.

Conte, H.R. et al. (1990) Psychological Mindedness as A Predictor of Psychotherapy Outcome: A Preliminary Report. *Comprehensive Psychiatry*, 31: 5, 426–31.

Cooper, N.S. et al. (2007) Resilience and Vulnerability to Trauma Psychobiological Mechanisms. In Romer, D. and Walker, E.F. (eds.) *Adolescent Psychopathology and The Developing Brain: Integrating Brain and Prevention Science.* New York: Oxford University Press.

Cooper, R.K. and Sawaf, A. (1997) *Executive EQ: Emotional Intelligence in Leadership and Organizations.* New York: Grosset/Putnam.

Corcoran, J. and Stephenson, M. (2000) The Effectiveness of Solution-Focused Therapy With Child Behavior Problems: A Preliminary Report. *Families in Society*, 81: 5, 468–74.

Cormier, W.H. and Cormier, L.S. (1998) 4th edn. *Interviewing Strategies for Helpers: Fundamental Skills and Cognitive Behavioral Interventions.* Pacific Grove, CA: Brooks/Cole.

Cryder, C.H. et al. (2006) An Exploratory Study of Posttraumatic Growth in Children Following a Natural Disaster. *American Journal of Orthopsychiatry*, 76, 65–9.

CSOMB (Colorado Sex Offender Management Board) (2008) *Standards and Guidelines for The Evaluation, Assessment, Treatment and Supervision of Juveniles Who Have Committed Sexual Offenses.* Colorado Department of Public Safety, Division of Criminal Justice, Office of Domestic Violence and Sex Offender Management.

De Shazer, S. (1985) *Keys to Solutions in Brief Therapy.* New York: W.W. Norton.

De Shazer, S. (1988) *Clues: Investigating Solutions in Brief Therapy.* New York: W.W. Norton.

De Shazer, S. (1994) *Words Were Originally Magic.* New York: W.W. Norton.

De Shazer, S. et al. (1986) Brief Therapy: Focused Solution Development. *Family Process*, 25, 207–22.

Diamond, A. (2002) Normal Development of Prefrontal Cortex from Birth to Young Adulthood: Cognitive Functions, Anatomy, and Biochemistry. In Stuss, D.T. and Knight, R.T. (eds.) *Principles of Frontal Lobe Function.* New York: Oxford University Press.

Diamond, M.C. (2001) Response of The Brain to Enrichment. *Anais Academia Brasileira De Ciencias*, 73: 2, 211–20.

Dubois, D.L. and Flay, B.R. (2004) The Healthy Pursuit of Self-Esteem: Comment on and Alternative to Crocker and Park (2004) Formulation. *Psychological Bulletin*, 130: 3, 415–20.

Dunlap, L.L. (2004) 2nd edn. *What All Children Need: Theory and Application.* Lanham, MD: University Press of America.

Egan, G. (1998) *The Skilled Helper: A Problem-management Approach to Helping.* 6th edn. Pacific Grove, CA: Brooks/Cole.

Eluvathingal, T.J. et al. (2007) Quantitative Diffusion Tensor Tractography of Association and Projection Fibers in Normally Developing Children and Adolescents. *Cerebral Cortex*, 17: 12, 2760–8.

Engelberg, E. and Sjoberg, L. (2005) Emotional Intelligence and Inter-Personal Skills. In Schulze, R. and Roberts, R.D. (eds.) *Emotional Intelligence: an International Handbook.* Cambridge, MA: Hogrefe and Huber.

Frazier, P.A. and Berman, M.I. (2008) Posttraumatic Growth Following Sexual Assault. In Joseph, S. and Linley, P.A. (eds.) *Trauma, Recovery, and Growth: Positive Psychological Perspectives on Posttraumatic Stress.* Hoboken, NJ: John Wiley and Sons.

Giedd, J.N. et al. (1999) Brain Development During Childhood and Adolescence: A

Longitudinal MRI Study. *Nature Neuroscience*, 2: 10, 861–3.

Gilgun, J. (2006) Children and Adolescents With Problematic Sexual Behaviors: Lessons From Research on Resilience. In Longo, R.E. and Prescott, D.S. (eds.) *Current Perspectives: Working With Sexually Aggressive Youth and Youth With Sexual Behavior Problems.* Holyoke, MA: NEARI Press.

Goleman, D. (1995) *Emotional Intelligence: Why It Can Matter More Than IQ.* New York: Bantam Books.

Greenberg, M.T. et al. (2003) Enhancing School-Based Prevention and Youth Development Through Coordinated Social, Emotional and Academic Learning. *American Psychologist*, 58: 6/7, 466–74.

Guerra N.G. and Bradshaw, C.P. (eds.) (2008) *Core Competencies to Prevent Problem Behaviors and Promote Positive Youth Development. New Directions for Child and Adolescent Development,* 122. San Francisco: Jossey-Bass.

Hackett, S. (2006) Towards a Resilience Based Intervention Model for Young People with Harmful Sexual Behaviours. In Erooga, M. and Masson, H. (eds.) *Children and Young People Who Sexually Abuse Others: Current Developments and Practice Responses.* London: Routledge.

Hall, J.C. (2008) A Practitioner's Application and Deconstruction of Evidence-Based Practice. *Family in Society: The Journal of Contemporary Social Services*, 89: 3, 385–93.

Haney, P. and Durlak, J.A. (1998) Changing Self-Esteem in Children and Adolescents: A Meta-Analytic Review. *Journal of Clinical Child Psychology*, 27: 4, 423–33.

Hirschi, T. and Gottfredson, M. (1983) Age and the Explanation of Crime. *American Journal of Sociology*, 89, 552–83.

Horvath, A.O. and Bedi, R.P. (2002) The Alliance. In Norcross, J.C. (ed.) *Psychotherapy Relationships That Work: Therapist Contributions and Responsiveness to Patients.* New York: Oxford University Press.

Hubble, M.A., Duncan, B.L. and Miller, S.D. (eds.) (1999) *The Heart and Soul of Change: What Works in Therapy.* Washington, DC: American Psychological Association.

Karver, M.S. et al. (2006) Meta-Analysis of Therapeutic Relationship Variables in Youth and Family Therapy: The Evidence for Different Relationship Variables in Child and Adolescent Treatment Outcome Literature. *Clinical Psychology Review*, 26, 50–65.

Kazdin, A.E., Marciano, P.L. and Whitley, M.K. (2005) The Therapeutic Alliance in Cognitive-Behavioral Treatment of Children Referred for Oppositional, Aggressive, and Antisocial Behavior. *Journal of Consulting and Clinical Psychology*, 73: 4, 726–30.

Killgore, W.D. and Yurgelun-Todd, D.A. (2007) Unconscious Processing of Facial Affect in Children and Adolescents. *Social Neuroscience*, 2: 1, 28–47.

Killgore, W.D., Oki, M. and Yurgelun-Todd, D.A. (2001) Sex-Specific Developmental Changes in Amygdala Responses to Affective Faces. *Neuroreport*, 12: 2, 427–33.

Kopta, S.M. et al. (1999) Individual Psychotherapy Outcome and Process Research: Challenges Leading to Greater Turmoil or A Positive Transition? *Annual Review of Psychology*, 50, 441–69.

Langstrom, N. and Grann, M. (2000) Risk for Criminal Recidivism Among Young Sex Offenders. *Journal of Interpersonal Violence*, 15, 855–71.

Lebel, J. et al. (2004) Child and Adolescent Inpatient Restraint Reduction: A State Initiative to Promote Strength-Based Care. *Journal of The American Academy of Child and Adolescent Psychiatry*, 43: 1, 37–45.

Lethem, J. (2002) Brief Solution Focused Therapy. *Child and Adolescent Mental Health*, 7: 4, 189–92.

Lickona, T. (1991) *Educating for Character: How Our Schools Can Teach Respect and Responsibility.* New York: Bantam Books.

Lickona, T. (2004) *Character Matters: How to Help Our Children Develop Good Judgment, Integrity, and Other Essential Virtues.* New York: Simon and Schuster.

Linley P.A. and Joseph, S. (eds.) (2004) *Positive Psychology in Practice.* Hoboken, NJ: Wiley.

Longo, R.E. (2010) Helping Body and Mind: The Use of Biofeedback, Neurofeedback, and QEEG Brain Mapping With Youth People Who Sexually Abuse. In Prescott, D.S. and Longo, R.E. (eds.) *Current Applications: Strategies for Working With Sexually Aggressive Youth and Youth With Sexual Behavior Problem.* Holyoke, MA: NEARI Press.

Luna, B. and Sweeney, J. (2004) The Emergence of Collaborative Brain Function: Fmri Studies of The Development of Response Inhibition. *Annuals of The New York Academy of Science*, 1021, 296–309.

Mackinnon-Lewis, C., Kaufman, M. and Frabutt, J.M. (2002) Juvenile Justice and Mental Health:

Youth and Families in The Middle. *Aggression and Violent Behavior*, 7: 4, 353–63.

Mann, R.E. et al. (2004) Approach Versus Avoidance Goals in Relapse Prevention With Sexual Offenders. *Sexual Abuse: A Journal of Research and Treatment*, 16, 65–75.

Marshall, W.L. et al. (2002) Therapist Features in Sexual Offender Treatment: Their Reliable Identification and Influence on Behaviour Change. *Clinical Psychology and Psychotherapy*, 9, 395–405.

Maslow, A.H. (1954) *Motivation and Personality*. New York: Harper and Brothers.

Maslow, A.H. (1962) *Toward A Psychology of Being*. New York: Van Nostrand.

Maslow, A.H. (1970) *Motivation and Personality*. 2nd edn. New York: Harper and Row

Maslow, A.H. (1971) *The Farther Reaches of Human Nature*. New York: Viking Press.

Masten, A.S. (1994) Resilience in Individual Development: Successful Adaptation Despite Risk and Adversity. In Wang, M.C. and Gordon, E.W. (eds.) *Educational Resilience in Inner-City America: Challenges and Prospects*. Hillsdale, NJ: Lawrence Erlbaum Associates.

Masten, A.S. (2001) Ordinary Magic: Resilience Processes in Development. *American Psychologist*, 56: 3, 227–38.

Masten, A.S. and Coatsworth, J.D. (1998) The Development of Competence in Favorable and Unfavorable Environments: Lessons From Research on Successful Children. *American Psychologist*, 53: 2, 205–20.

Masten, A.S. and Reed, M-G.J. (2002) Resilience in Development. In Snyder, C.R. and Lopez, S.J. (eds.) *The Handbook of Positive Psychology*. New York: Oxford University Press.

Mayer, J.D., Caruso, D.R. and Salovey, P. (1999) Emotional Intelligence Meets Standards for A Traditional Intelligence. *Intelligence*, 27, 267–98.

Mayer, J.D. and Salovey, P. (1997) What is Emotional Intelligence? In Salovey, P. and Sluyter D.J. (eds.) *Emotional Development and Emotional Intelligence: Implications for Educators*. New York: Basic Books.

Mayer, J.D., Salovey, P. and Caruso, D.R. (2008) Emotional Intelligence: New Ability or Eclectic Traits? *American Psychologist*, 63: 6, 503–17.

Messer, S.B. (2001) Empirically Supported Treatments: What's A Nonbehaviorist to Do? In Slife, B.D., Williams, R.N. and Barlow, S.H. (eds.) *Critical Issues in Psychotherapy: Translating New Ideas Into Practice*. Thousand Oaks, CA: Sage.

Miller, W.R. and Rollnick, S. (2002) 2nd edn. *Motivational Interviewing: Preparing People for Change*. New York: Guilford Press.

Minuchin, S. (1974) *Families and Family Therapy*. Cambridge, MA: Harvard University Press.

Moffitt, T.E. (1993) Adolescence-Limited and Life-Course-Persistent Antisocial Behavior: A Developmental Taxonomy. *Psychological Review*, 100, 674–701.

Murphy, M.M. (2002) 2nd edn. *Character Education in America's Blue Ribbon Schools: Best Practices for Meeting The Challenge*. Lanham, MD: Scarecrow Press.

National Center on Sexual Behavior of Youth (July 2003) Publications, *NCSBY Fact Sheet: What Research Shows About Adolescent Sex Offenders*. Retrieved on Oct. 20, 2010 at Ncsby.Org.

Nelson, C.A. (2003) Neural Development and Lifelong Plasticity. In Learner, R., Jacobs, E. and Wertlieb, D. (eds.) *Handbook of Applied Developmental Science* (vol. 1). Thousand Oaks, CA: Sage.

Nelson, C.A. and Bloom, F.E. (1997) Child Development and Neuroscience. *Child Development*, 68, 970–87.

Neubauer, A.C. and Freudenthaler, H.H. (2005) Models of Emotional Intelligence. In Schulze, R. and Roberts, R. D. (eds.) *Emotional Intelligence: an International Handbook*. Cambridge, MA: Hogrefe and Huber.

Norcross, J.C. (ed.) (2001) Empirically Supported Therapy Relationships: Conclusions and Recommendations of The Division 29 Task Force. *Psychotherapy*, 38: 4, 495–7.

Norcross, J.C. (ed.) (2002) *Psychotherapy Relationships That Work: Therapist Contributions and Responsiveness to Patients*. New York: Oxford University Press

Norcross, J.C. and Lambert, M.J. (2006) The Therapy Relationship. In Norcross, J.C., Beutler, L.E. and Levant, R.F. (eds.) *Evidenced-Based Practices in Mental Health: Debate and Dialogue on Fundamental Questions*. Washington, DC: American Psychological Association.

Nyklicek, I, Majoor, D. and Schalken, P. (2010) Psychological Mindedness and Symptom Reduction After Psychotherapy in Heterogeneous Psychiatric Sample. *Comprehensive Psychiatry*, 51, 492–6.

O'Hanlon, W. and Weiner-Davis, M. (1989) *In Search of Solutions: A New Direction in Psychotherapy*. New York: W.W. Norton.

Powell, K.M. (2010a) Strengths-Based Approaches. In Prescott, D.S. and Longo, R.E. (eds.) *Current Applications: Strategies for Working with Sexually Aggressive Youth and Youth with Sexual Behavior Problems.* Holyoke, MA: NEARI Press.

Powell, K.M. (2010b) Therapeutic Relationships and the Process of Change. In Ryan, G., Leversee, T. and Lane, S. (eds.) *Juvenile Sexual Offending: Causes, Consequences, and Corrections.* 3rd edn. Hoboken, NJ: Wiley.

Rapp, C.A. (1998) *The Strengths Model: Case Management with People Suffering from Severe and Persistent Mental Illness.* New York: Oxford University Press.

Rapp, C.A. and Goscha, R.J. (2006) *The Strengths Model: Case Management With People With Psychiatric Disabilities.* 2nd edn. Oxford: Oxford University Press.

Reitzel, L.R. and Carbonell, J.L. (2006) The Effectiveness of Sexual Offender Treatment for Juveniles as Measured by Recidivism: A Meta-Analysis. *Sex Abuse*, 18, 401–21.

Roehlkepartain, J.L. and Leffert, N. (2000) *What Young Children Need to Succeed: Working Together to Build Assets from Birth to Age 11.* Minneapolis, MN: Free Spirit.

Rogers, C.R. (1951) *Client-Centered Therapy: Its Current Practice, Implications, and Theory.* Boston: Houghton Mifflin.

Rogers, C.R. (1957) The Necessary and Sufficient Conditions of Therapeutic Personality Change. *Journal of Consulting Psychology*, 21: 2, 95–103.

Rogers, C.R. (1961) *On Becoming a Person: A Therapist's View of Psychotherapy.* Boston: Houghton Mifflin.

Rogers, C.R. (1963) The Concept of the Fully Functioning Person. *Psychotherapy: Theory, Research, and Practice*, 1, 17–26.

Rosete, D. and Ciarrochi, J. (2005) Emotional Intelligence and Its Relationship to Workplace Performance of Leadership Effectiveness. *Leadership and Organization Development Journal*, 26, 388–99.

Rubia, K. et al. (2000) Functional Frontalisation with Age: Mapping Neurodevelopmental Trajectories With Fmri. *Neuroscience and Biobehavioral Reviews*, 24: 1, 13–19.

Ryan, G. (1989) Victim to Victimizer: Rethinking Victim Treatment. *Journal of Interpersonal Violence*, 4: 3, 325–41.

Saleebey, D. (2006) *The Strengths Perspective in Social Work Practice.* 4th edn. Boston: Pearson/Allyn and Bacon.

Salovey, P. and Mayer, J.D. (1990) Emotional Intelligence. *Imagination, Cognition and Personality*, 9, 185–211.

Search Institute (1997) *The Asset Approach: Giving Kids What They Need to Succeed* [Brochure]. Minneapolis, MN: Search Institute.

Selekman, M. (2006) *Working with Self-Harming Adolescents: A Collaborative, Strengths-Based Therapy Approach.* New York: W.W. Norton.

Seligman, M.E.P. (1999) The President's Address. *American Psychologist*, 54: 8, 559–62.

Seligman, M.E.P. and Csikszentmihalyi, M. (2000) Positive Psychology: an Introduction. *American Psychologist*, 55: 1, 5–14.

Seligman, M.E.P. et al. (2005) Positive Psychology Progress: Empirical Validation of Interventions. *American Psychologist*, 60: 5, 410–21.

Sharry, J. (2004) *Counselling Children, Adolescents, and Families: A Strengths-Based Approach.* London: Sage Publications.

Smith, E.J. (2006) The Strength-Based Counseling Model. *The Counseling Psychologist*, 34: 1, 13–79.

Sowell, E.R. et al. (1999a) In Vivo Evidence for Post Adolescent Brain Maturation in Frontal and Striatal Regions. *Nature Neuroscience*, 2: 10, 859–61.

Sowell, E.R. et al. (1999b) Localizing Age-Related Changes in Brain Structure Between Childhood and Adolescence Using Statistical Parametric Mapping. *Neuroimage*, 9, 587–97.

Sowell, E.R. et al. (2001) Mapping Continued Brain Growth and Gray Matter Density Reduction in Dorsal Frontal Cortex: Inverse Relationships During Postadolescent Brain Maturation. *The Journal of Neuroscience*, 21: 22, 8819–29.

Sowell, E.R. et al. (2002) Development of Cortical and Subcortical Brain Structures in Childhood and Adolescence: A Structural MRI Study. *Developmental Medicine and Child Neurology*, 44, 4–16.

Spear, L.P. (2000) The Adolescent Brain and Age-Related Behavioral Manifestations. *Neuroscience and Biobehavioral Reviews*, 24, 417–63.

Steinberg, L. (2008) A Social Neuroscience Perspective on Adolescent Risk-Taking. *Developmental Review*, 28, 78–106.

Sugai, G. et al. (2000) Applying Positive Behavioral Support and Functional Behavioral Assessment in Schools. *Journal of Positive Behavioral Interventions*, 2, 131–43.

Swann, W.B., Chang-Schneider, C. and Mcclarty, K.L. (2007) Do People's Self-Views Matter?

Self-Concepts and Self-Esteem in Everyday Life. *American Psychologist*, 62: 2, 84–94.

Taylor, E. (2001) Positive Psychology and Humanistic Psychology: A Reply to Seligman. *Journal of Humanistic Psychology*, 41: 1, 13–29.

Walters, S.T. et al. (2007) *Motivating Offenders to Change: A Guide for Probation and Parole*. US Dept of Justice National Institute of Corrections.

Ward, T., Gannon, T. and Yates, P.M. (2008) The Treatment of Offenders: Current Practice and New Developments With an Emphasis on Sex Offenders. *International Review of Criminology*, 15, 183–208.

Ward, T. and Marshall, W.L. (2004) Good Lives, Aetiology and the Rehabilitation of Sex Offenders: A Bridging Theory. *Journal of Sexual Aggression*, 10: 2, 153–69.

Weick, A. et al. (1989) A Strengths Perspective for Social Work Practice. *Social Work*, 34, 350–4.

Weisinger, H. (1998) *Emotional Intelligence at Work: The Untapped Edge for Success*. San Francisco: Jossey-Bass.

White, M. and Epston, D. (1990) *Narrative Means to Therapeutic Ends*. New York: W.W. Norton.

Worling, J.R. and Curwin, T. (2000) Adolescent Sexual Offender Recidivism: Success of Specialialized Treatment and Implications for Risk Prediction. *Child Abuse and Neglect*, 24, 965–82.

Worling, J.R., Litteljohn, A. and Bookalam, D. (2010) 20-Year Prospective Follow-Up Study of Specialized Treatment for Adolescents Who Offended Sexually. *Behavioral Sciences and The Law*, 28, 46–57.

CHAPTER 7

Meaningful Engagement of Adolescents in Change

David S. Prescott

Knowledge is just a rumor until it's in the muscle
New Guinea proverb

Introduction*

Before reading this chapter, it may be helpful to engage in a brief self-assessment. Put the book down and ask yourself whether there is a change you want to make in your life. Please take a moment to picture this change in your mind. It could be losing weight, stopping smoking, drinking less alcohol, reading more, calling friends and family more often, etc. Now ask yourself: For how long have you been thinking about making this change? What would be some of the good things about making this change? And, honestly, what would be some of the less desirable things about making this change? What part of you might object to making this change? If you are like many others who have asked themselves these questions, you might smile and admit you have been thinking about this change for many years. Yet you still have not made it.

The circumstances that convicted sexual offenders find themselves in are, of course, very different from yours. However, this exercise points out that there are many people who desire to change and are able to change, but don't. Many intelligent people have gone to their graves without having made necessary lifestyle changes that would have provided them with a longer life.

Next, imagine some negative experience in your life that you would not want to discuss with anyone under any circumstances. It could be something that you did to someone, or something that happened to you. Now imagine that the legal system wants you to work on it in treatment, and that failure to do so could result in significant time spent incarcerated. Imagine that you have

no choice of where to go to obtain treatment related to this issue, and that the only accepted modality is group treatment. Now, imagine yourself in a group session, surrounded by men with antisocial personality disorder. There are two therapists, each taking notes as you talk. You know that these therapists aren't perfect and that some of their notes will be incorrect. Keep in mind that all of these notes will be visible to the forces of the legal system that have taken away your liberty. It's important that you know that the disclosure of this negative experience could take several weeks, as your antisocial associates ask questions aimed at getting you to be completely honest about an experience that you don't want to talk about. Depending on the program, you may also be required to demonstrate aspects of this experience in role play.

Again, readers of this book probably don't have much in common with sexual offenders. Research has shown that adult sexual offenders themselves are clear about the need to be accountable for their actions (Levenson and Prescott, 2009; Levenson, Prescott, and D'Amora, 2010). However, it is vital to remember that no matter how important it may be, being open and honest in group therapy is not easy for any human being. It can be easy for professionals treating sexual offenders to lose sight of the client's experience of treatment (Beech and Fordham, 1997).

Historical considerations: sexual offender treatment across the life span

Many elements of sexual offender treatment remain controversial. In a recent review, Glaser (2010: 261) described it as 'a form of punishment' generally. Elsewhere in the literature, seasoned professionals (eg Chaffin, in press; Prescott, 2006; Prescott, 2010; Vess, in press) have expressed concern about the best and most ethical use of actuarial measures and polygraph examinations. Although there are plausible responses to the

*The author is grateful to many colleagues in developing these examples, including Allan Zuckoff, Yolanda Fernandez, and Ruth Mann.

argument that sex offender treatment is inherently punitive (Prescott and Levenson, 2010; Ward, 2010) there is no remaining question that entering and participating in a sexual offender treatment program can be a highly challenging experience. Despite an emerging literature regarding ethical issues in sexual offender treatment, little has been written about ethical concerns in the assessment and treatment of young people who have sexually abused (Letourneau and Miner, 2005; Zimring, 2004).

The controversies do not end there. Many professionals continue to wonder whether treatment actually works. Many cite the highly respected SOTEP study as cause for concern (Marques, Wiederanders, Day, Nelson, and van Ommeren, 2005). This study, which met a very high degree of scientific rigor, found no difference in re-offense rates between treated and untreated offenders. However, the authors were clear that the offenders who 'got it' and meaningfully completed their treatment goals did, indeed, demonstrate lower re-offense rates. To the present, no further analysis of this sub-group has occurred. Elsewhere, although meta-analyses of the past decade have provided cause for optimism (eg Hanson et al. 2002; Lösel and Schmucker, 2005) many professionals remain concerned that these studies do not account for individuals who drop out or otherwise fail to complete treatment. Fortunately, the juvenile literature is more optimistic regarding treatment outcomes (Reitzel and Carbonell, 2006; Worling, Litteljohn, and Bookalam, 2010).

Further, newcomers to the field often encounter a divergence of opinions as to the best treatment style to adopt. Much of the original literature in the field was based on populations of incarcerated adult males, and many of the first texts appeared to advocate a harsh and confrontational approach to treatment. It wasn't until within the past 10 years that research has shown what is already clear in other areas of psychotherapy research: the most effective treatment provider style is warm, empathic, rewarding, and directive (Marshall, 2005). In fact, decades of psychotherapy research shows that the most successful treatment regimes share a few vital elements. These include the therapeutic alliance, hope and expectancy, and the client's own strengths and positive attributes (Hubble, Duncan and Miller, 1999; Prescott and Levenson, 2009). Much of the juvenile literature has focused on these most important aspects (eg Ryan, Leversee and Lane, 2010).

Taken together, it seems that professionals treating sexual offenders have an obligation to recognise the ethical dilemmas inherent in this work, and – to the greatest extent possible – use therapy to invite clients to be willing partners in change, and not simply the recipients of services. This is especially true for children and adolescents. Providing services is one matter; having clients 'get it' is something else. Although critics make important points about the ethical concerns and limitations of treatment programs, the research continues to show that sexual offenders who are motivated to change and can use treatment programs build healthier lives and contribute to safer communities. The real question becomes how best to awaken the internal motivations of sexual offenders in this direction.

Getting the context right for change

Recently, Mann (2009) observed that it is also vital for treatment programs to consider and address the context in which general sexual offender treatment occurs. Describing prison-based treatment programs, she points out several obstacles to establishing an environment that is conducive to change. These include:

- *Being uninformed about treatment/believing that treatment is ineffective.* In one study, Mann and her colleagues found that about half of those interviewed after refusing treatment were uninformed about the aims of treatment and had drawn unhelpful conclusions. In contrast, most of those who accepted treatment believed that the aim of treatment was to prevent future offending. Given that adolescents are inherently more dependent on their families and other supports, this speaks to the importance of drawing family members into the treatment process.
- *Concerns about poor individual responsivity of the program.* For example, offenders who are intellectually disabled may fear that treatment will be like school, and that they will not be able to understand what they will be taught. It is easy to forget that for many clients, treatment programs can appear to be like schools where they didn't learn, with clinicians similar to teachers or mentors who somehow failed them in the past.
- *Distrust of key professionals.* It is well established in the medical literature that patients often

refuse medical treatment because they do not trust their doctors. It is easy to see the potential parallel with sexual offenders. Fortunately, recent studies (eg Levenson and Prescott, 2009; Levenson, Prescott, and D'Amora, 2010) have found that sexual offenders often perceive their treatment providers in a more favourable light than they do their legal circumstances. Similar findings have appeared in the intimate partner violence literature (eg Shamai and Buchbinder, 2010). Given the often abusive or otherwise traumatising environments that adolescents find themselves in, this distrust of adults should come as no surprise.

- *Expectation of hostile responses from others.* Typically, sexual offenders are reviled in prison, just as they are in the wider community. They face danger of physical and verbal assault because of the nature of their conviction. For this reason, it is all the more important to maintain an environment in which young people experience psychological as well as physical safety.
- *Fear of stigma.* In most situations in the western world, engaging in treatment regimens, whether medical or psychological, raises the risk of the client feeling stigmatised by his illness or condition. Sexual offender treatment is no different, even in a program that specialises in treating those who have abused.

The role of the client

The single most important factor in any treatment is the client and his or her willingness to change. Although this may appear obvious at first, it is particularly important to consider within inpatient settings. Programs for lower risk offenders frequently emphasise psychoeducational aspects and/or afford limited opportunities for clients to demonstrate change over a sufficient period of time. Although these programs may adhere to the principles of risk, need, and responsivity for the clientele they serve, it is important to note that programs treating clients with higher levels of risk and need (as well as the tendency of higher risk offenders to present with responsivity concerns) require a more comprehensive approach. There are many reasons for this.

Bem (1972) called attention to the fact that how people perceive themselves throughout the change process is critical to the success of treatment efforts, and that people develop and come to 'know' their attitudes by observing their behavior and concluding what attitudes must have caused them. His research demonstrated that people are often more convinced by what they hear themselves say than by what others say to them. Likewise, new beliefs and attitudes can result by practicing new behaviors. This is an important consideration in the treatment of sexual offenders: it is very often not enough to simply provide education or a venue for self-exploration. Rather, the client must make his own case for change within the context established by the therapist and the program beyond.

Likewise, Ryan and Deci (2000) have examined the change process extensively, noting that motivation to change often begins with outside forces (such as parents teachers and carers) which can become internalised over time. Internalised ('intrinsic') motivation refers to engaging in activities for their own sake because it is interesting and satisfying in itself, as opposed to doing an activity to obtain an external goal (extrinsic motivation). Internalisation refers to the active attempt to transform an extrinsic motive into personally endorsed values and thus assimilate behavioral regulations that were originally external. Also of note, Deci and Ryan (2002) contend there are three psychological needs that motivate people to initiate behavior, and are essential for psychological health and well-being. They argue that these needs are universal, innate, and psychological, and include the need for competence, need for autonomy, and the need for relatedness (Deci and Ryan, 2002). Treatment that enables clients to make progress towards these goals will therefore have a greater chance of being personally relevant and meaningful to the client.

Another easily overlooked element in motivating sexual offenders to change is in understanding hope. Moulden and Marshall (2009) highlight the importance of transmitting to sexual offenders a belief in the usefulness of change and a sense of ownership of that change. Snyder, Michael, and Cheavens (1999: 182) emphasise the importance of hope as a psychotherapeutic foundation, and describe it as consisting of agency thinking (believing that a goal is attainable) and pathways thinking (having ideas about how to attain it). They further emphasise that 'therapists who are burned out or otherwise fail to convey hopefulness implicitly model low agency and pathways thinking'. Given the importance of therapists within the therapeutic relationship, it is surprising that the use of hopefulness in sexual offender treatment has not received wider attention.

These are crucial considerations in the treatment of sexual offenders. It is common for outside stakeholders, the lay public, and clients themselves to view treatment programs as being entirely responsible for client change. In this mindset, treatment is something that therapists do 'to' their clients. The findings above show that although providing a sound treatment program is the responsibility of clinicians, the ultimate responsibility for committing to and maintaining change lies with the client. In this case, a better metaphor may be treatment following a heart attack. For most adults, this treatment will involve losing weight, proper exercise, and eating appropriately.

Stages of change

It is vital that treatment programs for sexual offenders take into account that not everyone who consents to treatment is ready or willing to make dramatic changes in their lives. Further, young people can change dramatically, often with little apparent notice or reason. People who succeed in making changes in their lives often proceed through five 'stages of change' (Prochaska, 1999; Prochaska, DiClemente and Norcross, 1992). It is helpful for clinicians to recognise where each client is at with respect to these stages and use relevant interventions to help the offender move to the next stage. Briefly, the five stages are:

- *Precontemplation.* Literally, this is the stage before the client begins thinking about change. At this stage, the client may not acknowledge having any need to make changes in his or her life and may deny having engaged in sexual abuse. Appropriate treatment activities can involve exploring what areas of their life the client might be interested in changing and exploring the pros and cons of both change and maintaining the status quo.
- *Contemplation.* At this stage, the offender has considered that he has a problem but may be ambivalent about change. This can appear as minimising the seriousness of his actions or reluctance to make changes in his life that

would reduce risk of re-offense. Appropriate treatment activities at this stage can include motivational enhancement, values clarification, psychoeducation, exploring and resolving ambivalence towards change, and working out what meaningful change would look like in the client's life.

- *Preparation.* As its name implies, this involves preparing to engage in action toward change. Appropriate treatment activities at this stage can include motivational enhancement, psychoeducation, and self-monitoring of areas that the client would like to change.
- *Action.* This involves the client actually taking steps to modify his or her thought patterns and behavior. It is at this stage that standard sexual offender treatment activities such as disclosure of offenses and exploration of the factors that contributed to one's offending become possible.
- *Maintenance.* This involves the client maintaining the changes made during the action stage. Treatment activities at this point involve managing the factors that contributed to one's offending in daily life, in the here and now.

Movement through these stages is typically sequential and, ideally, progressive. However, sexual offenders, like anybody else, can move back and forth among these stages in their change process. Further, they may be ready to change in some areas and not others. This can be particularly true of adolescents, who by definition are more dependent upon their environment, and for whom a willingness to change will therefore be less straightforward than for an adult. Therapists must continually assess the stage at which their clients are functioning and adjust their approach accordingly. The stages of change model is not without critics. Some have observed that it does not adequately account for situational factors and that its practical application in some situations can be limited. For that reason, it is a guiding framework but not a stand-alone treatment model.

Skill acquisition, rehearsal, and enactment

The tendency of humans to return to an earlier stage of change, or even to become ambivalent about the changes they are making, speaks to the importance of the maintenance stage of change.

Some programs for lower risk criminal offenders emphasise the acquisition and even rehearsal of skills. Because being able to maintain change is so vital to long-term risk reduction, skill *enactment* becomes particularly important in the treatment of sexual offenders. In a study of enhancing treatment fidelity in health behavior change, researchers from the National Institute for Health (Bellg et al., 2004) state that enactment of treatment skills involves self-monitoring and improving one's ability to perform treatment-related behavioral skills and cognitive strategies in relevant real-life settings.

What makes adolescents so different?

It can be easy to forget that the natural push of adolescence towards independent adulthood means additional challenges for adults attempting to guide youth in a healthy direction. While resistance may best be thought of as an interpersonal phenomenon generally (Prescott, 2009), there is much within the resistance to treatment providers by young people that is indicative of normative developmental processes. The following are a few examples of what professionals can expect to see:

'I'm not going to/you can't make me.' Inherent in this statement is the young person's drive towards independence. That very same drive is what will assist them in making their own decisions not to abuse in the future. A helpful response might be to reflect on this drive and discuss its importance. Professionals might further want to consider that protest is a basic human right (see also, Jenkins, 2006).

'It's not fair.' Similar to 'you can't make me', part of the developmental task of adolescence is to explore fairness as a part of developing their own set of values. Professionals can be more effective when they are prepared to discuss the reasons and values underlying their rules and expectations. Not doing so can replicate the often traumatic and chaotic environments where young people who have abused have lived. 'It's not fair' signals the same youthful idealism that will one day prevent the abuse of others. It may be more effective to conceptualise these young people as learning morality for themselves rather than being amoral. In this case, professionals can pursue a more nuanced path of guidance as opposed to overt direction.

'It's not like this where I'm from. You don't understand.' As mentioned elsewhere in this chapter, it can be easy to forget how dependent young people often are on their environment and family. This statement can be a clear invitation to explore further and understand. Further, if the young person's home is itself abusive, treatment may place the young client in a bind of mixed allegiances.

'I don't have a future.' Although on its surface this is a sad statement, it can also signal the fact that adolescents often have an entirely different perspective on time than adults do. It is easier for a 25-year-old to imagine the age of 40 than it is for a 15-year-old. Given the developmental tasks of adolescence, it is entirely appropriate that young people are more focused on the here and now than their adult counterparts. They are, in many ways, making their identities up as they go along.

Some principles for engaging young people who have abused meaningfully in change

To summarise to this point, programs treating sexual offenders will likely be most effective when they attend to the contextual factors that make change more difficult. For larger programs, this can involve administrators ensuring that the culture of the work environment is conducive to growth and change for their clinical staff (eg Miller, 2006). Programs can also adopt a perspective that they are building willing partnership with participants who will view themselves as responsible for their own change and maintain a hopeful approach towards it. Clinicians who consistently employ a warm, empathic, rewarding, and directive (in the sense of guiding) approach are also more likely to engage their clients meaningfully. With that, the following ideas can also help professionals build willing partners in change:

Willingness to change is different from willingness to enter a treatment program. Although clinicians can understand the expectations of their treatment program from the outset, clients often do not. Clients can often appear more ready for change than they actually are. The client does not necessarily share the clinician's view of what is important in change. Likewise, some clients are more willing to change than they are to enter a treatment program where they have to work collaboratively with others. For these reasons, it can be useful to separate treatment from change conceptually.

Focus more on awakening internal motivation to change than on imparting it. There is a time and a place for encouraging those who are attempting to change. However, active attempts to motivate others to change (eg persuasion, cajoling, and making the case why another person should consider changing) rarely work. In fact, making the case for why clients should change can create resistance. Even when clients appear to respond well to therapists leading the cheer for change, this extrinsic motivation is rarely enough to keep another person's internal motivation going, particularly in therapeutic circumstances where the treatment is one of many experiences in the client's lifetime. Both self-perception and self-determination theory (as well as the research underpinning them) illustrate the importance of the client's ability to make their own case for change. Likewise, a recent study (Amrhein, Miller, Yahne, Palmer, and Fulcher, 2003) found that client verbalisations regarding change were predictive of whether or not change occurred.

Setting the stage for someone to make their own case for change can come in many forms. The skills, principles, and mindset of motivational interviewing (Miller and Rollnick, 2002) present several stars for the clinician to steer by. A helpful strategy among these is the double-sided reflection, in which the therapist verbalises both sides of the client's ambivalence to change. Very often, these reflective statements involve 'on the one hand . . .' formats. For example, 'This is a dilemma for you. On the one hand, you would really like to complete the treatment program, and on the other hand you're not sure you can trust that others have your best interests at heart. What do you think about that? What do you think you might do?' These kinds of statements are often much more difficult to formulate than it seems. They require that the clinician have an accurate knowledge of the client's internal world. It helps to be able to use the client's own internal lexicon when making them. For example, if the client has earlier said that he doesn't want to 'take treatment,' it can be useful to use this same terminology. The exception is when by doing so the therapist appears unnatural, disingenuous, or abusive.

Another method for exploring the client's internal motivation to change is to draw a single vertical line on a chalkboard or piece of paper and ask the client first to list all the good things that making a change in a given area might bring, and writing these down on one side of the line. The clinician can next ask about what sorts of less desirable things might happen if they were to change. A variation on this involves dividing the paper or chalkboard into quadrants and exploring good and not-so-good things about change, as well as good and not-so-good things about *not* changing. In all of these activities the clinician must be careful not to impose their own agenda on the client.

Seek out 'change talk' and explore it with clients. Amrhein et al. (2003) have highlighted the importance of client verbalisations of commitment to change. These statements can be predictive of client success at change efforts. Often, change talk appears as statements indicating a desire, ability, reason, or need to change. It can also come in the form of 'commitment talk', which involves statements related to explicitly planning for change, taking steps to initiate change, or beginning a change process. One method for eliciting change talk is the use of scaling questions related to change. Two useful questions are 'On a scale of zero to ten, how important is it to you to make a change in this area?' and 'On the same scale, how confident are you that you can make a change in this area?' When the client answers, the clinician can then explore the number provided. After some discussion, the clinician next inquires as to why the client did not choose a lower number. Typically, the answer to this 'backwards question' involves some form of desire, ability, reason, or need to change. The clinician can then explore this change talk with the client.

In eliciting and exploring change talk, a key skill involves remaining focused on these self-motivating statements and less so on the resistance statements that may accompany them. There is always time to explore the reasons why a client might feel unready, unwilling, or unable to change.

Beware the righting reflex. When awakening internal motivation and eliciting change talk, it is vital to remember that expressions of each frequently occur against a backdrop of resistance. This can be a frustrating experience for clinicians who may feel they must redouble their efforts to enforce change or somehow set the record straight with their clients (Miller and Rollnick,

2002). Very often, clinicians working with young people feel this reflex particularly strongly, as they experience themselves as functioning *in loco parentis*, or as custodians responsible for the young person's best interests. Under these conditions, it can be easy to return to harsh and confrontational approaches that – research shows – are less effective. This reflexive response to make things right can serve the end of short-term compliance. However, it frequently comes at the expense of long-term change. It can be helpful for clinicians to establish ground rules for themselves to simply notice this reflex without acting on it. After all, it is a byproduct of their best wishes for the client. There is always time to provide respectful feedback later. An awareness, acceptance, and expectation of resistance can keep clinicians grounded. When working with resistant clients, it can be useful to remember the saying that very often 'the slower we go, the faster we get where we're going'.

Remember that therapeutic engagement is vital throughout the treatment experience. It can be easy to think that developing rapport takes place at the start of treatment, while forgetting how important it is to maintain that rapport. Miller, Hubble, and Duncan (2008) have demonstrated the importance of the therapeutic alliance throughout treatment, and have highlighted the importance of soliciting feedback from clients in order to make sure that they actually have the alliance in treatment that they believe is there. Like Beech and Fordham's (1997) classic study of sexual offender treatment providers, Miller, Hubble, and Duncan illustrate how psychotherapists typically view themselves as more helpful than their clients do. A therapeutic alliance is not like painkillers that prevent the patient from feeling the unpleasant effects of recovery. It is the context in which genuine change takes place.

'Treatment is just the roadmap; meaningful personal change is the goal.' These words, uttered by a civilly committed sexual offender in the Midwestern United States, are helpful to remember. Although research shows the success of cognitive-behavioral and community-based interventions in reducing sexual re-offense, more important is the actual change of cognition and behavior, preferably within the context where the client will enact new skills. Although research highlights the importance of treatment completion, it can be easy to focus too narrowly on service provision and not on the changes that the client is actually making. An unforgettable example from popular culture is in the lyrics of the song 'Rehab' by Amy Winehouse. In it, she offers roughly three minutes of repeated reasons why she does not want to enter treatment. Buried within the resistance is her internal motivation for change ('I don't ever want to drink again. I just need a friend'). Even within trainings of sexual offender treatment providers, many professionals miss these most important lyrics.

Focus on approach goals. There is a body of literature showing the importance of desirable 'approach goals' (ie goals that one can work towards rather than avoid; Emmons, 1999). Unfortunately, traditional treatment approaches have not always paid adequate attention to what offenders seek to attain or achieve through offending so that they can develop ways to achieve these ends in healthy, safe ways (Yates, Prescott, and Ward, 2010). The development of approach goals is vital to building willing partners in change and a meaningful shared vision of the future. Very often, a specific choreography takes place between the client and therapist in order to develop these goals. For example, the client may enter treatment not wanting to let little things irritate her. This avoidance of irritation focuses only on the problem itself. The clinician can then work with the client to re-cast this into an approach goal of being able to stay calm at all times. Likewise, an avoidance goal of not wanting to feel inadequate all the time can be more effective when broadened to a goal of feeling competent within relationships. Ultimately, the approach goal of building a happier and healthier life that involves satisfying relationships is likely to be more appealing than simply to stop offending.

Engage in collaborative treatment planning. In the author's experience, it is common for treatment programs to engage in a treatment planning style in which a clinician or treatment team imposes goals on the client. In inpatient settings, this can occur when representatives from each department (clinical, residential, health services, educational recreational and occupational therapy, etc.) state their goal on behalf of the client. Very often these goals are avoidance-based (eg 'John will not be belligerent about taking medication' as opposed to 'John will follow through on plans he establishes with others, including the psychiatrist and other service providers').

A more effective approach may be to listen to what the client wants from treatment, collaborate with him on crafting it into an approach goal, considering how this goal serves the purposes of meeting criminogenic needs along the way (Andrews and Bonta, 2010). Recent research has demonstrated that sexual offender treatment programs that are matched to Andrews and Bonta's principles of risk, need, and responsivity are more effective than those that are not (Hanson, Bourgon, Helmus, and Hodgson, 2009). For example, a client goal of not feeling angry might better be re-cast as developing inner peace, which in turn can be one component of the criminogenic need/dynamic risk factor of emotional regulation.

Shift the balance from command to leadership. Leadership has been defined in many ways, and for purposes of this chapter, it is most helpful to think of it as a guiding influence (Maxwell, 2007). Many professionals have viewed treatment provision as something done to clients (Glaser, 2010; Jenkins, 2006; Ward, 2010). This kind of command mentality may be less helpful than establishing a confident role of guiding influence.

All treatment providers would like nothing more than to stop offending quickly. However, the research cited throughout this chapter suggests that clinicians will be more effective in creating long-term change by amending their view of themselves from that of a commander (or perhaps a lion tamer) to that of a wilderness guide who helps a client explore how and why they might change. This requires a different perspective, away from visions akin to a surgeon who does the work so that a patient can heal. Rather, clinicians may be at their best when they view themselves as being akin to a wellness consultant. From this perspective, the clinician can help guide the client in the healthiest direction, and ultimately it is the client's responsibility to invest in their future health and well-being. It is noteworthy that this approach is not necessarily easier for the client. Moving the responsibility for change away from a commanding presence to the client him- or herself can be an entirely new experience for sexual offenders.

In the author's experience, it is all too common for professionals working with sexual offenders to confuse leadership with command. Just as employees respond poorly to supervisors directing them about in a heavy-handed fashion, a more guiding approach can build longer-lasting voluntary change. Short-term compliance is not the same thing as long-term change for either professionals or their clients.

Focus on research rather than media accounts of sexual abuse. It is easy to find pessimistic media accounts implying that treatment does not work. Sample and Kadleck (2008), for example, found that lawmakers were more likely to follow media portrayals than research in establishing policies related to sexual offenders. Elsewhere, Wilson, Leaver, and Rathjen (2008) likened media portrayals of sex crimes to news items about airplane accidents. Each account seems to negate the fact that thousands of other airplanes landed safely that day. Under these circumstances it can be easy for clinicians to lose faith in the ability of their clients to change. This, in turn, can lead to the modeling of low levels of hopefulness that can be detrimental to clients.

Keep that focused sparkle in your eye. Sexual offenders, like any other clients, are quick to notice when a professional's heart and mind are somewhere else. Just as clinicians who model low agency and pathways thinking can reduce client hopefulness, it is easy for professionals to underestimate the amount of influence they have on their clients. Although it is clear that in many jurisdictions a clinician's report can mean the difference between incarceration and community placement, it is easy for professionals to forget that often they are among the first pro-social models the client has ever known. If we are not respectful of our clients, who will be?

References

Amrhein, P.C. et al. (2003) Client Commitment Language During Motivational Interviewing Predicts Drug Use Outcomes. *Journal of Consulting and Clinical Psychology.* 71: 862–78.

Andrews, D.A. and Bonta, J. (2010) *The Psychology of Criminal Conduct, Fifth Edition.* Cincinnati, OH: Anderson.

Beech, A.R. and Fordham, A.S. (1997) Therapeutic Climate of Sexual Offender Treatment Programs. *Sexual Abuse: A Journal of Research and Treatment* 9: 219–37.

Bellg, A.J. et al. (2004) Enhancing Treatment Fidelity in Health Behavior Change Studies: Best Practices and Recommendations from the NIH Behavior Change Consortium. *Health Psychology,* 23, 443–51.

Bem, D.J. (1972) Self-Perception Theory. In Berkowitz, L. (ed.) *Advances In Experimental Social Psychology.* New York: Academic Press.

Chaffin, M. (In Press) The Case of Juvenile Polygraphy as a Clinical Ethics Dilemma. *Sexual Abuse: A Journal of Research and Treatment.*

Deci, E. and Ryan, R. (eds.) (2002) *Handbook of Self-Determination Research.* Rochester, NY: University of Rochester Press.

Emmons, R.A. (1999) *The Psychology of Ultimate Concerns.* New York: Guilford.

Glaser, W. (2010) Sex Offender Programmes: New Technology Coping With Old Ethics. *Journal of Sexual Aggression*, 16, 261–74.

Hanson, R.K. et al. (2002) First Report of The Collaborative Outcome Data Project on The Effectiveness of Treatment for Sex Offenders. *Sexual Abuse: A Journal of Research and Treatment*, 14, 169–94.

Hanson, R.K. et al. (2009) The Principles of Effective Correctional Treatment Also Apply to Sexual Offenders: A Meta-Analysis. *Criminal Justice and Behavior*, 36, 865–91.

Hubble, M., Duncan, B. and Miller, S. (1999) *The Heart and Soul of Change: What Works in Therapy.* Washington, DC: American Psychological Association.

Jenkins, A. (2006) The Politics of Intervention: Fairness and Ethics. In Longo, R.E. and Prescott, D.S. (eds.) *Current Perspectives: Working with Sexually Aggressive Youth and Youth with Sexual Behavior Problems.* Holyoke, MA: NEARI Press.

Jones, L. (2002) An Individual Case Formulation Approach to the Assessment of Motivation. In Mcmurran, M. (ed.) *Motivating Offenders to Change.* John Wiley.

Letourneau, E.J. and Miner, M.H. (2005) Juvenile Sex Offenders: A Case Against The Legal and Clinical Status Quo. *Sexual Abuse: A Journal of Research and Treatment*, 17, 293–312.

Levenson, J.S. and Prescott, D.S. (2009) Treatment Experiences of Civilly Committed Sex Offenders: A Consumer Satisfaction Survey. *Sexual Abuse: A Journal of Research and Treatment*, 21, 6–20.

Levenson, J.S., Prescott, D.S. and D'Amora, D.A. (2010) Sex Offender Treatment: Consumer Satisfaction and Engagement In Therapy. *International Journal of Offender Therapy and Comparative Criminology*, 54, 307–26.

Lösel, F. and Schmucker, M. (2005) The Effectiveness of Treatment for Sexual Offenders: A Comprehensive Meta-Analysis. *Journal of Experimental Criminology*, 1, 117–46.

Mann, R.E. (2009) Getting The Context Right for Sexual Offender Treatment. In Prescott, D.S. (ed.) *Building Motivation to Change In Sexual Offenders.* Brandon, VT: Safer Society Press.

Marques, J.K. et al. (2005) Effects of A Relapse Prevention Program on Sexual Recidivism: Final Results From California's Sex Offender Treatment and Evaluation Project (SOTEP) *Sexual Abuse: A Journal of Research and Treatment*, 17, 79–107.

Marshall, W.L. (2005) Therapist Style in Sexual Offender Treatment: Influence on Indices of Change. *Sexual Abuse: A Journal of Research and Treatment*, 17: 2, 109–16.

Maxwell, J.C. (2007) *The 21 Irrefutable Laws of Leadership*, 10th edn. Nashville, TN: Thomas Nelson.

Miller, S.D., Hubble, M. and Duncan, B. (2008) Supershrinks: What is the Secret of their Success? *Psychotherapy In Australia*, 14, 14–22.

Miller, W.R. (2006) Can Organizations Be Minty? *MINT Bulletin*, 13, 1–4. Retrieved November 14, 2010 From http://motivationalinterview.org/mint/MINT13.2.pdf.

Miller, W.R. and Rollnick, S. (2002) *Motivational Interviewing: Preparing People for Change.* New York: Guilford.

Moulden, H.M. and Marshall, W.L. (2009) A Hopeful Approach to Motivating Sexual Offenders for Change. In Prescott, D.S. (ed.) *Building Motivation to Change In Sexual Offenders.* Brandon, VT: Safer Society Press.

Prescott, D.S. (2006) *Risk Assessment of Youth Who Have Sexually Abused: Theory, Controversy, and Emerging Strategies.* Oklahoma City: Wood'N'Barnes.

Prescott, D.S. (2009) *Building Motivation to Change in Sexual Offenders.* Brandon, VT: Safer Society Press.

Prescott, D.S. (2010) Polygraphy With Youth Who Have Sexually Abused: Considerations and Cautions. In Prescott, D.S. and Longo, R.E. (eds.) *Current Applications: Strategies for Working With Sexually Aggressive Youth and Youth With Sexual Behavior Problems.* Holyoke, MA: NEARI Press.

Prescott, D.S. and Levenson, J.S. (2009) To Treat or Not to Treat: What Are the Questions? *The Forum, Newsletter of The Association for The Treatment of Sexual Abusers (ATSA)* Beaverton, OR: ATSA.

Prescott, D.S. and Levenson, J.S. (2010) Sex Offender Treatment is not Punishment. *Journal of Sexual Aggression*, 16, 275–85.

Prochaska, J.O. (1999) How Do People Change, and How Can We Change to Help Many More People? In Hubble, M.A., Duncan, B.L. and Miller, S.D. (eds.) *The Heart and Soul of Change: What Works In Therapy.* Washington, DC: American Psychological Association.

Prochaska, J.O. and Diclemente, C.C. (1992) *Stages of Change in the Modification of Problem Behaviors.* Newbury Park, CA, Sage.

Prochaska, J.O., Diclemente, C.C. and Norcross, J.C. (1992) In Search of How People Change: Applications to Addictive Behaviors. *American Psychologist*, 47: 9, 1102–14.

Reitzel, L.R. and Carbonell, J.L. (2006) The Effectiveness of Sexual Offender Treatment For Juveniles as Measured by Recidivism: A Meta-Analysis. *Sexual Abuse: A Journal of Research and Treatment*, 18, 401–21.

Ryan, G., Leversee, T. and Lane, S. (2010) *Juvenile Sexual Offending: Causes, Consequences and Correction.* New York: Wiley.

Ryan, R.M. and Deci, E.L. (2000) Self-Determination and the Facilitation of Intrinsic Motivation, Social Development, and Well-Being. *American Psychologist*, 55, 68–78.

Sample, L. and Kadleck, C. (2008) Sex Offender Laws: Legislators' Accounts of The Need for Policy. *Criminal Justice Policy Review*, 19: 1, 40–62.

Shamai, M. and Buchbinder, E. (2010) Control of The Self: Partner-Violent Men's Experience of Therapy. *Journal of Interpersonal Violence*, 25, 1338–62.

Snyder, C.R., Michael, S.T. and Cheavens, J.S. (1999) Hope as a Psychotherapeutic Foundation of Common Factors, Placebos and Expectancies. In Hubble, M.A., Duncan, B.L. and Miller, S.D. (eds.) *The Heart and Soul of Change: What Works in Therapy.* Washington, DC: American Psychological Association.

Vess, J. (in press) Ethical Practice in Sexual Offender Assessment: Consideration of Actuarial and Polygraph Methods. *Sexual Abuse: A Journal of Research and Treatment.*

Ward, T. (2002) Good Lives and The Rehabilitation of Sex Offenders. In Ward, T. and Hudson, S. (eds.) *Sexual Deviance: Issues and Controversies.* Sage Publications.

Ward, T. (2010) Punishment or Therapy? The Ethics of Sexual Offending Treatment *Journal of Sexual Aggression*, 16, 1–10.

Wilson, R.J., Leaver, W. and Rathjen, L. (2008) *Calm in the Eye of the Storm: Circles of Support and Accountability.* Plenary Address Delivered at The 27th Annual Conference of The Association for The Treatment of Sexual Abusers, Atlanta, GA.

Worling, J.R., Littlejohn, A. and Bookalam, D. (2010) 20-Year Prospective Follow-Up Study of Specialized Treatment For Adolescents Who Offended Sexually. *Behavioral Sciences and the Law*, 28, 46–57.

Yates, Prescott and Ward (2010) *Applying the Good Lives and Self-Regulation Models to Sex Offender Treatment: A Practical Guide for Clinicians.* Brandon, VT: Safer Society.

Zimring, F.E. and Allen, F.A. (2004) *An American Travesty: Legal Responses to Adolescent Sexual Offending.* Chicago, IL: University of Chicago Press.

CHAPTER 8

Emotional Intelligence and the Practitioner Working With Sexually Harmful Behaviour

Libby Ashurst

Purpose

This chapter is designed to define emotional intelligence as a personal and professional trait that is related to both the quality of professional performance and the load that is experienced by practitioners in their work. It links empathy to emotional intelligence and makes a case that emotional intelligence can be improved through personal initiatives or training. It also provides a framework that can be used to guide efforts to improve professional performance. Furthermore, it makes the case that emotional intelligence may be closely linked with personality but is different in many ways and can be used objectively in professional work to establish and maintain successful therapeutic alliances.

Introduction

Working with juvenile offenders, *and their victims*, can be difficult and stressful even at its best. When practitioners engage in therapeutic relationships with young people who harm others sexually, an emotional dimension is added to an already complex professional job. That job may expose the practitioners to the unique problem of having to bear witness to the young service users' crimes (Hermen, 1992) and connecting with issues of sex, violence and children as abusers in ways that most have not experienced directly (Hackett, 2006). While they are providing services, practitioners encounter not only the trauma experienced by the victims, who usually are other children, but also by the service users and their family members. In addition, they may discover while working with clients that some of them are caught up in a cycle of abuse that may involve them in the dual roles of victim and abuser.

In order to work successfully and effectively in this complex and stressful emotional context, practitioners will need to establish and maintain a successful therapeutic alliance with their clients

(see Fenske, 2007, and Bovard-Johns, 2009, for extensive reviews of literature documenting the importance of successful alliances). To achieve those alliances, practitioners will need not only a high level of job-related skills, but also the capacity to regulate and manage their own emotional engagement with their clients. Highest levels of success probably will come when these practitioners remain objective and act in a non-judgemental way as they analyze the tactics, motivations and grooming behaviours used by young people when they harm others sexually. Maintaining one's objectivity under such conditions is a great deal to ask of professionals and difficult for some to achieve. But that is the nature of their job, and it requires that practitioners remain aware of their own emotions and emotional responses, and also that they are able to control the responses, at least to the extent that their own emotions do not interfere with the quality of their professional practice. In a way, I think what practitioners must do is similar to what is reflected in the language I have heard from air crew as they give instructions to passengers, 'Fit your own mask before you attempt to fit someone else's.'

Some practitioners may not be successful at 'fitting their own masks,' but I recently experienced a case that reminded me about 'masks' and how important they can be while providing professional services.

An 11-year-old girl, who, for the purpose of this story, I shall call Molly, was referred to me. She came with a history of engagement in serious, violent and sexually aggressive behaviours toward other children and animals. The story of her childhood made equally sad reading.

Over the past several years, numerous social workers and health care professionals had been assigned to serve Molly and her family. However, those practitioners had come-and-gone for various reasons. Most of them had not established an effective working relationship with either Molly or her family.

For my first session with Molly, I decided to

play a picture-card game with both of us sitting on the floor. Upon arriving, she came slowly into the room, studying me as she entered, and sat on the floor opposite me. My immediate impression was of a shy, very pretty girl who was dressed immaculately. She kept her eyes focused on my face as I introduced myself and asked her whether she would like to play a game of cards that would help me get to know her and what was important to her. She agreed to play the game and selected three cards from the set that I offered. Holding the cards in her hands, and with her head down, she began to talk about her family and her life at home, and she introduced the fact that she had done some bad things. I watched and listened as she talked and held the cards.

Molly suddenly looked at me and asked, 'Why don't you have a face like my other social workers?'

I asked what she meant. She said, 'You've got a kind face, but you don't put on that face all the others put on when I talk about me. You know, like they are sad for me, or I've upset them, or something. When they put on that face, I just answer their questions. I don't tell them anything else. You don't ask many questions, do you?'

I knew what she meant by that comment. I had seen that 'social worker face' on occasions as I observed practitioners working with young people. Their expressions revealed that they were 'feeling sorry' for the young person and both their work and expressions conveyed the unspoken message, 'You poor thing!'

Objectivity in professional practice

Molly showed that she recognised the kind of therapeutic alliance she needed, but was not sure when she arrived for our session that she could get it through social health care services. She had generalised her experience with the 'social worker face' and assumed that relationships reflecting 'that face' would not be successful for her.

As I talked more with Molly, it became apparent that as she entered into a relationship with me, she wanted to know whether I could handle her problems without judging her or getting upset. She wanted me to listen to her as she told her story as she saw it. She knew and admitted that she had done some things that were unacceptable to me and to others and she

wanted me to help her solve her own problems. She did not appear to feel sorry for herself and she seemed to sense that if I felt sorry for her my feelings would get in the way of our relationship. If that happened, she would have to be very careful about what she said to me as she tried to sort out her problems. She wanted to see the face of a competent professional social health care worker and did not want to see a 'social worker mask.'

Being the kind of professional who can remain objective while establishing an effective relationship with a client presenting with sexual behaviour problems is not easy for me nor, I suspect, for many other practitioners within social health care services. Furthermore, some practitioners and writers in the field are critical of objectivity in social service practices, confusing it with cold, unconcerned or uncaring behaviour. Many seem to think that some form of emotional engagement (which some people refer to as *empathy*) with their clients is necessary to establish a successful relationship. Some assume that being warm, caring and accepting are important attributes of social health service practitioners. They may be; but care should be taken not to over-generalise this view and assume that 'taking the emotions of the client,' or 'the way of being' of the practitioner, is confused with the quality of professional services provided. My experience with Molly is just one illustration of how emotional engagement with young people should be considered very carefully when determining how best to deal with young people and personal emotions while providing professional services.

Similar advice on considering emotional engagement within sex offender treatment comes from Ashfield et al. (2010) who write, when working therapeutically with women sex offenders,

Some female practitioners in their desire to create a therapeutic alliance will strive to develop a relationship, based on friendship, that is, a 'girl's together' approach. Although the practitioner will report having a positive relationship with the female client, the client's actual experience is more likely to be one of confusion and anxiety. When this dynamic occurs female sexual offenders describe feeling uncomfortable disclosing some of the more difficult aspects of their behaviour to the practitioner due to concerns that the practitioner may perceive it as 'letting them down'.

There is a clear consensus that an effective therapeutic alliance is needed for successful client services. However, further complicating the question of how best to engage clients emotionally is the fact that there is not a consensus within the field of social services about a conceptual or operational definition of empathy or of how empathy should be revealed while providing services. Supporting that point, Hodges and Klein (2001) said that empathy is an ability with many different definitions that cover a broad spectrum, ranging from feeling a concern for other people that creates a desire to help them, experiencing emotions that match another person's emotions, knowing what the other person is thinking or feeling, to blurring the line between self and other.

Representing that broad spectrum, some practitioners may think that 'being empathetic' means being emotionally moved by the client's experiences and being able to identify their clients' emotions and accept and respond to those emotions *as their own*. They may think it is important to take on board the client's emotions (they make responses that communicate clearly, 'I *feel* your pain.')

On the other hand, some in the field support an alternative approach to emotional engagement reflected by these examples. Markakis et al. (1999) said that an empathetic professional correctly recognises and responds to the emotional state of the client *without experiencing that state personally*. Similarly, when referring to psychotherapist-patient relationships, Halpern (2003) wrote that empathy does not require that therapists vicariously experience and internalise their patients' emotions. Rather, she said that it is essential for the therapist to understand the specific ways in which emotions contribute to empathy. Using somewhat different language, Suchman et al. (1999) noted that when physicians were *attuned* to non-verbal signals and emotional conditions of their patients and paused at moments of heightened patient anxiety, the patients disclosed information about themselves and their conditions more readily. If physicians did not take the patients' emotional conditions into account in their practice the patients did not contribute critical information, even if the physicians asked appropriate and accurate questions. (In these examples, it is important that the practitioners communicated clearly, 'I hear you saying that you have these pains; let's work together so you can learn to address them.')

Empathy and authenticity in professional practice

Irrespective of those different meanings, one of the foundational descriptions of empathy seems still to be the most useful in applications for practitioners working with sexually harmful behaviour. Carl Rogers (1959) described it as:

> *Perceiving the internal frame of reference of another with accuracy and with the emotional components and meanings which pertain thereto as if one were the person, but without ever losing the 'as if' condition. Thus, it means to sense the hurt or the pleasure of another as he senses it and to perceive the causes thereof as he perceives them,* **but without ever losing the recognition that it is as if I were hurt or pleased and so forth.** *(Emphasis added by this author)*

Using this description by Rogers, the one perceiving the emotions of another does not take (adopt) those emotions as their own but, rather, recognises them and engages the other person in ways that demonstrate a full recognition of that person's emotions. For a practitioner working with sexually harmful behaviour, 'empathetic practice' would be based upon valid assessments of the emotional states of their clients and then would comprise communications, both behaviourally or verbally, that indicate that those emotions have been perceived and will be considered seriously while providing services. Elaborating this point further, Schwartz (2002) said that we recognise others as empathic when we feel that they have accurately acted on or somehow acknowledged in stated or unstated fashion our values or motivations, our knowledge, and our skills or competence, but especially as they appear to recognise the significance of our actions in such a manner that we can tolerate their being recognised.

Therefore, despite wide variations in assumptions about the meaning of empathy and 'being empathetic,' this foundational meaning from Rogers and the elaboration by Schwartz, combined with a variety of research findings about the effects of professional practices, indicate that practitioners who are 'objective' in establishing and maintaining relationships with clients can be viewed as empathetic by their clients and more successful in their practices than those who allow their own emotional responses to their clients and their conditions to become apparent in their work and relationships.

But, in this context of professional practice, what does 'being objective' mean? The two words, *objective* and *subjective*, refer to the *frame of reference* used as criteria for choices and actions, whether external to the individual or internal. For a person in a professional position, *external* referents consist of the principles and knowledge frameworks for providing service; job standards or standards for service quality; concepts, principles, methods, and models for analyzing cases and for hypothesising effects of case conditions; techniques; and information about the clients, including their emotional states, among other things. The *subjective* frame of reference comprises primarily the individual practitioner's values, beliefs, sentiments, frames of reference and patterns of responses to emotions. With that distinction between the two frames of reference, it should be absolutely clear that human service practitioners should rely most heavily on the *objective* frame. Nevertheless, the subjective frame cannot be ignored. It is always 'there' as the practitioner studies the case, interacts with the client and considers the wide range of objective referents (more about that point later). Growth in professional competence allows one to rely more on the objective frame and less on the subjective.

However, as we grow in professional competence, how do we resolve questions about 'being objective' that may be raised by some people who claim that objectivity leads to being cold, aloof, unconcerned or uncaring when it is important and even essential, that professional practitioners must be warm, caring, accepting, and emotionally engaged with their clients? How do we deal with claims by some who state, sometimes with a high degree of certainty and with little demonstrated understanding of the probabilistic nature of principles, 'They have to know that you care before they will care what you know?'

Despite the fact that these statements are found frequently in literature and in interpretations made from research evidence, professional practitioners should recognise that those arguments commonly include many words or expressions that have indefinite meaning and they may be based upon ideological propositions or conventional wisdom that have questionable or only conditional validity. Halpin (1966) introduced quite a different dimension than personality and 'ways of being' to understanding job-related actions and their interpretations. He found from his research on the effects of leader behaviour that the most critical factor in creating and sustaining effective organisational climates is not either what leaders do or how well they do it. Rather, it is the perceptions of *authenticity* of their personal and role-related behaviours and relationships – the extent to which the leaders were perceived by others as being 'for real' in their work and positions.

Halpin went on to say that there are some necessary conditions for a person to be authentic in a position. First, the person must *have something to be authentic about*. By that, he meant, among other things, that persons in positions: (a) should understand and accept their position fully including all roles to be served (b) be skilful in performing the tasks of that position, and (c) know they have the skills necessary for doing the job well. He claimed that, for example, a plumber would not be perceived as authentic in that position unless he or she was sufficiently skilful in plumbing to perform the work well. Furthermore Halpin claimed that if the plumber were not confident of his or her own skills, then work and relationships would reflect that lack of confidence and not be perceived as authentic. In other words, a necessary condition for being authentic in a position is both a high level of professional and technical competence *and* an accurate appraisal of that competence.

Next, with those *necessary* conditions for authentic behaviour met, persons who are being authentic in their position will act in ways that are not self-serving. They will act consistently to achieve organisation and position goals with no evidence that work is being done primarily to meet personal or social needs. Relationships and work will focus on position-related purposes. Indeed, few actions trigger perceptions of inauthenticity more effectively than ones that appear to be self-serving rather than role-serving. For practitioners interacting with clients this means that work is focused toward meeting organisational goals that, presumably, are to meet the clients' needs by serving them well.

Stated another way, *authentic* professional behaviour requires both competence and recognition of that competence by the person occupying the position. This has been described by Maslow (1940) as being 'consciously competent.' However, this notion of conscious competence is resisted by some who describe consciousness of one's own competence and confidence in their skills and role performance in exaggerated terms that indicate arrogance, aloofness, positioning or coldness. None of those characteristics fit within the concept of authenticity intended by this author. *Conscious competence* does not mean that a person is arrogant, cold, stuffy, aloof, or any other pejorative description that indicates that the person thinks he or she 'is better than others.' Indeed, any of those behaviours would more likely be characteristic of persons with low confidence in their own personal, social, or professional competence, therefore, perhaps, using aloofness (distancing socially) as an avoidance strategy. Such behaviours and ways of being would appear to others to be focused on maintaining a position or perceived status and serving personal or social needs rather than needs of the client or organisation. These behaviours probably would be perceived as *not authentic*. Indeed, arrogance and aloofness are totally contrary to authentic behaviour and relationships. A consciously competent person will appear confident and comfortable in work and relations, without arrogance or aloofness.

Furthermore, a large body of literature dealing with job satisfaction and work effectiveness includes the dimension of *realistic self-appraisal*. Hertzberg (1968) for example, included it as one of the dimensions of his definition and measure of job satisfaction. This use indicates his belief that realism of self appraisal is a necessary condition for satisfaction. One focus in the field of organisation development is to train staff to appraise their own work realistically using objective standards for quality.

However, we know that professional competence has many dimensions including, among others, general problem-solving and communications skills, job-specific skills, technical and professional information, habits of mind, and the personal and social skills needed to establish and maintain effective relationships. Central among these areas of professional competence for SHB practitioners is a clear understanding of the goals for their service and acceptance of those goals and responsibility for achieving them. Also important is awareness of the competence needed to provide high-quality services to the clients and 'empathy.'

As used here, empathy refers to the trait defined generally by Rogers (1959) and described more specifically for practitioners by Markakis et al. (1999) as 'correctly acknowledging the emotional state of the client without experiencing that state oneself' or by Suchman et al. (1999) as 'being attuned to the client.' These authors said, among other things, this capability (whether named empathy or attunement) can inform practice to enhance the therapeutic alliance by revealing when to ask questions, what questions to ask, how to ask them, what to say and how to say it, when to stay silent, and when and how to confirm important expressions made by clients.

Limitations on empathy in professional practice

Thus, even though we know that empathetic relations with clients are important, some researchers and practitioners warn that we should recognise that there are serious barriers to using empathy (as defined by Rogers) objectively. Practitioners may have a caseload that is so heavy that they cannot attend to all of the details of the clients' emotional states nor let the clients' conditions or interests dictate the flow of communications. Others may have difficulty becoming attuned to the conditions of the client and become annoyed or irritated when they perceive a lack of responsiveness by the young person, particularly when that person has been required to attend the services. That lack of responsiveness by the client may cloud the practitioner's willingness to appreciate the young person's perspective. But, perhaps the greatest barrier to practice of objective empathy is the one mentioned here at the outset. Working with young people charged with, or suspected of having committed sexual offences is a heavy burden, both at work and outside it, and the 'baggage' from those cases is such that the variety of experiences with them may be difficult for some practitioners to put aside.

The capacity to put one's own emotions aside while dealing with others varies significantly among the general population, just as it does among social service practitioners while they deal with their clients. The need for practitioners to develop that capacity has been addressed extensively in the literature foundations for those professions. Within this literature, it is recognised that some work is much more closely linked to high levels of emotional engagement than others. Working with young people who display SHB is among jobs placing a high level of *emotional load* on practitioners.

Some foundations for emotions, emotional labour and emotional intelligence

Emotions are complex traits of individuals that have both physical and mental dimensions. They develop or emerge as response processes that help individuals cope with changes in their relationships with their environment (Freeland, Terry and Rodgers, 2008). Generally, emotions are described as having three parts: subjective feelings; physiological (body) responses; and expressive behaviours.

The first of these parts, *subjective feelings,* cannot be observed directly, so they can only be understood by another if the person feeling the emotions describes them by using words. However, each person's descriptions and interpretations of feelings (own or of others) is a function of their general language skills and the specific vocabulary they have for describing emotions or 'feelings.' Therefore, individuals with similar feelings or emotions may describe them quite differently – both to others *and to themselves.* This is an important point that should be taken into account as practitioners think about their own feelings or emotions, talk with their colleagues about them, and ask questions and listen to descriptions of feelings or emotions of their clients. Partly because of the language limitations for describing feelings or emotions, assumption made about the feelings or emotions of another person based solely upon their descriptions, should be tentative and interpreted with care. Moreover, both clients and practitioners should be careful about interpreting their *own* feelings or emotions based on the language they use to describe them to themselves. Their self-analysis is limited inevitably to a degree by their own 'vocabulary bank account.'

Physiological responses to emotions tend to be observable *to some extent* and these responses tend to be common among people. For an example of physiological response to emotions, practitioners who are nervous prior to delivering presentations may experience a pounding heart, sweating or 'butterflies' in their stomachs. Under such conditions of nervousness the body usually releases adrenaline to help practitioners act effectively. Since these physiological responses tend to be fairly commonly experienced across people, there is a tendency for observers to

over-generalise their meaning and significance. For example, if a person waiting to make a presentation is sweating, some may assume that this person is nervous. Interpretations of these responses can be useful for providing an understanding of the emotional states of others by providing important clues to those emotions. However, it should be apparent that there are many potential causes for sweating or most other observable physiological responses. For example, it may be hot in the room. Thus, just as assumptions about emotional states from verbal descriptions should be made with care, so should assumptions about emotional states from observed physiological responses.

Expressive behaviour is an even more behavioural and observable response to emotions than physiological responses. These are outward signs, typically in the form of behaviour or action, that an emotion is being experienced. Among a number of indicators, these outward signs of emotions may include flushed face, muscle tensing, various facial expressions, shifts in tone of voice, rapid breathing, or restlessness. Since these outward signs tend to be similar across people, using them as expressions of an emotion can give other people clues about the feelings or emotions that someone is experiencing. As with the physiological responses, this tendency for people to behave in predictable ways to indicate certain emotional conditions allows others to adjust their social responses and behaviours to take into account their assumptions about the emotions of those with whom they are interacting. Molly's 'social worker face' was an example of an expressive behaviour by her practitioners, and she had responded to those emotional responses in ways that presented barriers to establishing an effective therapeutic alliance.

However, as for other emotional responses, assumptions about the meanings of expressed behaviour are prone to high levels of error and should be made very carefully. It should always be borne in mind during interactions that, while many of these expressive behaviours may reflect particular emotional states, they also may be caused by many other conditions. Using them to infer emotional states will require some form of verification of the validity of the inference, such as through confirmatory interviewing or reports of others or patterns of behaviour, if the analysis is to be used to make important judgments.

Several authors elaborate these characteristic parts of emotions. They described them as not being totally a function of the individual but also as a function of context and interactions. Mayer, Salovey, Caruso, and Sitarenios (2001), for example, claim that emotions commonly are aroused in the context of relationships or social interactions. They go on to say that during interactions both verbal and nonverbal expressions convey information about one's own and others' thoughts, intentions, and behaviours (Ekman, 1973, cited in Brackett, Rivers, and Shiffman, 2006). Additionally, Goleman et al. (2002) described how emotions may be transferable among individuals. They used the concepts of *resonance* and *dissonance* to describe the exchange of emotions, especially within work environments and organisations. In other words, they claim that emotions may be contagious, especially within work contexts. In further elaborating this notion of context importance, Lazarus (1991) concluded that when relationships among people change, so do their emotional engagements with those people. Therefore, he claims that one cannot consider the emotions of individuals except within the context of their relationships.

More particularly, Goleman et al. (2002) said that emotional environments within the workplace may be different from those outside it. The responsibility of work and the professional and hierarchical relationships within that context are clearly different from those in everyday life, and therefore likely to be associated with different emotional states and responses. Within the body of literature related to emotions, it is widely recognised that some workplaces are more emotionally loaded than others for a variety of reasons that may include, among others, the amount of work required, the working conditions, the people with whom one must work and their conditions or characteristics and the difficulty of the job. The idea of *emotional load* was described by Hochschild (1983) using the term 'emotional labour,' which she defined as:

> The paid and unpaid work that involves the use of emotions to facilitate work-related tasks required in and outside of the workplace, as well as the management of the workers' own emotions in the workplace.

This complex definition includes at least two parts: (a) attending to emotions as a necessary condition for achieving work tasks and (b) managing one's own emotions while achieving work tasks. These two parts may require employees either to express or hide their own emotions while engaging in work and recognising and responding appropriately to emotions of their colleagues or clients. This notion of emotional labour has been addressed further by other writers in this field. For example, Johnson (2001) described a particular emotional labour condition when workers must follow organisationally-sanctioned emotional responses in interactions with service users. Hochschild (1983) described the emotional rules for flight attendants and Hallett (2000) described them for restaurant waiting staff. In both of these cases the workers are expected to be pleasant and cheery irrespective of their own emotional states or of the apparent emotions of those with whom they are working. Marshall et al. (1999) described this idea of emotional labour specifically for work with young people who display SHB. In this therapeutic alliance the emotional rules for the practitioners require them to be sympathetic, warm, understanding, empathetic and confident with the ability to give advice to and direct young people. Nevertheless, terms within this expression of expectations commonly are ill-defined and may have indefinite meaning to either the speaker or listener. Therefore, these expectations may depend entirely on who is communicating the message and, thus, are arbitrary. This may leave the practitioner unclear about just what the expectations for practice really are. Irrespective of that arbitrariness of meaning, it should be clear to practitioners in this field that the emotional expectations comprise a heavy burden, one which some practitioners may not be able to carry, or can do so only with great difficulty.

But merely knowing the emotional expectations of a position or field, such as those for practitioners working with sexually harmful behaviour, is not enough either to enable or ensure conformity with those expectations. There is also a strong acknowledgement in the literature relating to this topic that *understanding the impact of emotions* (their own and those of their clients) is also essential (Mark, 2005), especially to all those involved in frontline practice with service users. Underlying the claim that understanding of emotions and their impact is important is the notion that without the understanding, practitioners cannot take expectations into account in their practices as they establish and maintain a therapeutic alliance. This potential need for the practitioner to accommodate both the emotional expectations for their position and the emotional characteristics of their clients may be a factor contributing to the load of their work. It also adds a dimension to the capabilities needed for successful practice.

The meaning and importance of emotional intelligence

The capacity that workers have for taking into account the expectations of their position, their own emotions and also the emotions of their colleagues and clients has been named 'emotional intelligence' (EI). This construct has increased in use and popularity in both mainstream media and in professional literature (Freeland, Terry and Rodgers, 2008). It has also been adapted into a wide range of professional fields including social work, clinical health care practice and counselling as an influential framework around which emotional competence can be articulated, enhanced and assessed (Kooker, Shoultz and Codier, 2007; Morrison, 2006). Nevertheless, as Morse et al. (1992) demonstrated for the field of nursing, the notions of emotional work and emotional intelligence may need to be different for various fields of professional practice depending upon the nature of their work and clients. For example, these authors demonstrated that the nurse-patient relationship is significantly different in task intensity and duration from that of a counsellor and client. The differences they described among professional occupations reveal clearly that they require different kinds of emotional engagement of the practitioner with the client.

Morrison (2006) offered evidence that EI is relevant to social workers and SHB practitioners when he described the workers who display *high* levels of EI compared to their 'emotionally-competent' colleagues:

> *Whilst highly conscientious and well organised, they (the highly competent) also bring a level of unconscious competence, expertise and effortlessness that sets them apart. These are fluent practitioners who 'fly'. Moreover, they demonstrate, under the same pressures and constraints as their 'competent' colleagues, an ability to make a positive impact above and beyond their competent colleagues.*

It should be noted here that Morrison described *highly* competent practitioners in respect of their recognition and management of emotions and emotional relations. Even though these practitioners are *unconsciously* competent,

research in other fields such as teaching demonstrate that their practices may meet the highest standards of quality within their field.

Nevertheless, one key characteristic of *a profession* is missing from the description of these 'high fliers': *conscious* recognition of decisions that are made by people occupying their positions and the technical and theoretical foundations that should be used for those decisions. Missing is a professional language that is technical and theoretical, grounded in research, common among members of the profession and used by the practitioners for decision-making, thinking and talking about their work. In other words, highly-qualified professionals are *consciously competent*, even if their practice is not higher in quality than those whom Morrison described as highly emotionally intelligent.

One consequence of this distinction between high levels of emotional intelligence and consciously-competent professionals is that by defining and making the professional foundations for practice conscious, we can treat EI as an area of competency that can be developed or improved through self-improvement, training or other professional development. We do not have to think about EI as being art, craft, or aspect or personality, or in any other way that indicates belief that it is innate and that 'some have it, some don't.'

While generally treated in research and professional literature as an important area of professional capability, definitions of EI vary widely and include characteristics and traits associated with, among others, information processing, experiential learning, environmental adaptation, thought and reasoning patterns (American Psychological Society, 2007; Mayer, Salovey, and Caruso, 2004). Others narrow the definition and focus more on the set of abilities that are linked directly to processing emotions and emotional information (Mayer and Salovey, 1997; Salovey and Grewal, 2005; Salovey and Mayer, 1990). The first definition of this construct found in the literature was made by P. Salovey and J. D. Mayer in 1990. They continued developing this conceptual framework until 1997, when they produced this definition:

> *Emotional intelligence is the ability to perceive accurately, appraise, and express emotions; the ability to access or generate feelings when they facilitate thought; the ability to understand emotions and emotional knowledge; and the ability to regulate emotions to promote emotional and intellectual growth.*

It should be noted here that the meaning of emotional intelligence is more complex than the meaning of empathy. While empathy focuses primarily on the capacity to recognise and respond effectively to the emotions of others, EI also includes the capacity to recognise and deal effectively with one's own emotions.

Using the definition above, or approximations to it, numerous researchers have documented both in commercial and scientific literature the positive influence of high levels of EI on work-based-performance and management of workplace stress (Quoidbach and Hansenne, 2009). As an example, Kunnanatt (2004) found that practitioners with a high level of EI use their own emotions and those of others to solve problems effectively in their work (Brackett et al. 2006).

Nevertheless, the empirical evidence supporting EI inclusion in professional development and practice remains somewhat murky despite the interest that media and business consultants put in it and its fast-growing use in organisation development. This lack of clarity may be a result of there being at least three different frameworks in widespread use for defining and applying the construct. Therefore, with different concepts and theoretical dimensions and different ways to measure EI, it remains controversial as a construct (Matthews et al., 2002). Nevertheless, the significance of the construct as a new area for the understanding of human performance, particularly in the workplace, appears to be overriding this controversy and resulting in effective work-based interventions that target the EI of employees as a way to improve their performance (Kunnanatt, 2004; McEnrue and Groves, 2006; Opengart, 2005; Weinberger, 2002).

One of those frameworks, developed by Salovey and Mayer (1997) and which conveys the application of their definition is referred to as the *ability-based model*. A primary assumption underlying this model is that individuals vary in their ability to process emotional information and in their ability to relate emotional processing to a wider cognitive framework. This ability to process emotional information is reflected in the adaptive behaviours of practitioners. The model identifies four factors of emotional intelligence: (a) the perception of emotion; (b) the ability to reason using emotions; (c) the ability to understand emotions; and (d) the ability to manage emotions. Salovey and Mayer claim the four branches of their model are arranged from more basic psychological processes to higher, more psychologically integrated processes. The lowest level branch concerns the (relatively) simple abilities of perceiving and expressing emotion. Whereas, the highest level branch concerns the conscious, reflective regulation of emotion.

Very similarly, but with some language differences, Goleman (1998, 2005) described EI as *a set of learned skills and personal competencies*. In this model, EI refers to the capacity for: (a) recognising our own feelings and those of others; (b) motivating ourselves; and (c) managing emotions well in ourselves and in our relationships. He described EI as the goal of emotional self-worth (Mayer et al., 2000) and suggested that emotional competency makes emotionally-intelligent individuals (Emmerling and Goleman, 2003, 2005). Goleman and colleagues also developed tools to measure emotional intelligence, which they claim provide measures that are predictive of emotional competency in the workplace.

Somewhat different in some language usage from the aforementioned two models, yet similar in final presentation, Bar-On (2005) described EI as *set of personality traits and non-cognitive capabilities* that predict emotional and social adaption within environments. Studying these traits and capabilities led him to define *Emotional Social Intelligence* (ESI) as a cross-section of interrelated emotional and social competencies, skills and facilitators that determine how effectively we understand and express ourselves, understand others, relate to them, and cope with daily demands. Bar-On (2005, 2008) affirmed Goleman's claims that emotional-social competence is a dependable predictor of human performance in the workplace and that it is both 'teachable and learnable.'

Whilst there are differences among these EI conceptualisations and language used for describing them as well as differences in their respective measures, they are more similar than different in their conceptual foundations. All conclude that the role of emotions in social relationships, health, job performance and job success is important. Furthermore, each of these writers agree that EI can be learned or enhanced by training. With that as an assumption, we might conclude also that one might become more empathetic in personal relationships and professional practice through personal initiatives or training.

Developing emotional intelligence through personal initiative and training

In the sections above, emotional intelligence was defined and documented as an important factor in the quality of professional practice. However, knowing what the construct is and knowing that it is important to quality and effectiveness of work does not necessarily provide a great deal of help for practitioners who either want or need to improve their EI. Indeed, the EI of particular individuals has developed over their lifetimes and, to some extent 'is what it is,' whether high or low, or in between. How one responds to situations and relationships emotionally has become much like many other factors that are embedded in, or closely linked to, personalities. From one perspective, it is a case of 'that's the way we are now' and it is very difficult to make changes in personality or personality-like characteristics. Without deliberate attention by the individuals or focused training, EI for most people may be similar to what is described by Bar-on (above) as personality or non-cognitive capabilities. Nevertheless, there is clear evidence in the literature on personal change that even some of the most tenacious personality characteristics can be changed by deliberate, consistent, focused attention and effort by individuals, especially if the attention and effort are supported by intensive and sustained therapeutic interventions or training.

Goleman's conceptualisation of EI as learned skills and personal competencies is perhaps the most widely used in applications to improve EI outside of academic settings. It provides definitions of various dimensions and the skills related to each of those dimensions. For that reason, and the fact that the competencies outlined in his model have direct applicability to the work of SHB practitioners, I have chosen his model to demonstrate how EI can be used in personal lives and as a tool for guiding efforts by practitioners to become more effective in their work or for providing the content areas for planning and implementing training programmes. That model and some suggestions for using it are elaborated in this section.

Goleman identified and defined four areas of competency and elaborated those to comprise his model. For each of the four areas of general competency he identified and defined several

areas of specific skills that one might develop to improve emotional intelligence. Some selected skills are listed below for illustrative purposes, but a full study of his model is recommended for anyone planning personal improvement or training programmes. These illustrative skills for the four areas of competency are:

1. Self-awareness
   - recognising own emotions
   - recognising how own emotions affect language and behaviour
   - recognising own skills, strengths and weaknesses
   - recognising own values and value systems and their foundations
   - having confidence in self
2. Self-regulation
   - maintaining control over impulses and distressful emotions
   - adapting reactions and responses to those of others and to changing situations
   - acting and relating consistently and authentically
   - managing multiple tasks and interruptions
   - recognising own mistakes and confronting mistakes of others
   - working effectively and efficiently within a schedule serving both self and others best
   - accepting accountability for own goals and task responsibilities
3. Social awareness
   - appraising the emotions of others accurately
   - responding consistently with the emotional characteristics of others
   - finding and recognising strengths of others
   - making appropriate and effective challenges to biases and intolerance of others
   - seeking and finding ways to encourage satisfaction for others
4. Social skills and management of relationships
   - listening for the intentions of others
   - building bonds with clients and colleagues
   - working collaboratively with colleagues
   - negotiating and resolving disagreements
   - modelling changes expected of others
   - adapting language and relationships to situations
   - dealing with situations and relationships objectively
   - accepting and encouraging consensus

It can be seen from this conceptual framework and the list of skills that EI includes self-awareness and self-regulation. As noted in sections above, these two dimensions are very important to objective professional practice and to authentic behaviour. Indeed, it would be very difficult for one to be authentic in a position without having at least a sufficient level of emotional intelligence. A case for the importance of empathetic practices has been made in the sections above. Within this conceptual framework for emotional intelligence, empathy can be interpreted as a combination of the third and fourth components. Thus, one conceptualisation of emotional intelligence is that it comprises self awareness and regulation plus empathy. Furthermore, it can be seen from the four components and the related skills that highly emotionally intelligent practitioners would be conscious of their own skills and practices, and conscious of the emotions of their clients and of their consequences – they would be consciously competent.

Nevertheless, it should be apparent to a reader that even this illustrative set of skills from the emotional intelligence model would be formidable to address and may seem like an impossible challenge to anyone seeking to improve their own EI. Therefore, it is not likely that practitioners who engage in self-improvement, or others who set out to improve EI by designing and implementing training programmes, would attempt to address all of these sets of skills through one intervention. It is more likely that appropriate interventions would have some methods for determining individual needs or interests for improvement and for setting priorities among the many areas for possible development. Nevertheless, it also should be apparent upon studying any one of these skill sets that people who have high levels of emotional intelligence will possess those skills and that it is possible to acquire these skills and to make the changes in practices and behaviours by using them.

Despite the plausibility of all of these skill sets and the apparent importance of being highly emotionally intelligent, overall improvement in performance will not be easy neither will it come quickly. Emotions and responses to them are too tightly embedded in personality to expect short-term or easy changes. Such a broad construct as emotional intelligence, with its broad-ranging set of dimensions and related sets of skills, cannot be changed quickly, easily, or without both continuous effort on the part of the person who is attempting to change and support from friends and colleagues.

Making changes in emotional engagement is more difficult for certain individuals than it might otherwise be, because of the fact that these traits are manifested in both patterns of behaviour and relationships with friends, colleagues and clients. As we attempt to change our emotions or responses to them, people with close associations with us will expect us to continue to respond emotionally and behaviourally as we have done previously. Therefore, old empathetic responses will be reinforced by those who interact with the persons trying to change. These social expectations may make it difficult to practice the emotional intelligence that has been acquired.

Making improvements in EI may be even more difficult for SHB practitioners than for others because of the need to work with young people from a wide range of backgrounds and who present with extreme characteristics. The values, beliefs, patterns of behaviour and moral identities of the clients may be very different from those of the practitioner. A young person's life history, family make-up, lifestyle, habits and priorities may differ significantly from those of the professional who will be providing services. These marked differences can make it difficult for the SHB practitioners to understand the young person's coping strategies and the patterns of sexual and non-sexual behaviours disclosed. These differences between the perspectives and behaviours of young clients and practitioners contribute significantly to imbuing the job with a high level of emotional load, thus making it more difficult for practitioners to achieve a high level of emotional intelligence.

Suggestions and principles for improving emotional intelligence

There are several overall approaches that practitioners might select for improving emotional intelligence through either personal initiatives or training. Among these are ones that, if successful, can reduce emotional load by changing personal perspectives and improving professional skills in negotiating positional demands. Others improve technical competency thus enabling the practitioner to work in ways that either reduce or do not trigger emotional reactions by the client or the practitioner. Nevertheless, whatever approach might be taken probably will need to begin by making a careful assessment of the capacity for self awareness and self control as outlined in the Goleman model.

Develop technical and professional skills

One of the first tasks of practitioners working with sexually harmful behaviour is to establish therapeutic relationships with the clients that enable relationships of trust with the young persons and their families to be formed. This condition of trust enables a cooperative working relationship that encourages the clients and their families to adopt the goal of changing inappropriate or problem behaviours. The primary characteristic of practitioners who can establish effective therapeutic relationships is *authenticity* in position and role. But, as has already been suggested, being authentic requires having something to be authentic about. Thus, it is essential that practitioners work deliberately and continuously to develop the technical and professional competence they need for high-quality job performance.

Be consistent

While practitioners are working to develop the professional or technical skills they need and the broader set of skills for improving emotional intelligence, they might consider making one change that, if needed, will make a major improvement in perceptions of authenticity of their performance. One characteristic of performance that shouts inauthentic behaviour loudly and clearly is *inconsistency* – for example, by saying one thing but doing another; making promises but not keeping them; predicting a definite future when those outcomes are highly uncertain or unlikely. If unreliability is a characteristic of practitioner performance, then achieving reliability must be a priority for improvement. This is an overarching factor in the interpretation of authenticity of professional performance and can overcome technical proficiency in task performance in its effect, especially in establishing a successful therapeutic alliance with clients.

Listen skilfully

An important factor in the success of establishing an effective therapeutic alliance with young people who display sexually harmful behaviour will be, perhaps, linked closely to the first task in establishing empathy with the client. It is the capacity of the practitioner to hear what the client is attempting to say in communications. Some technical techniques for listening that are rather simple to use have been built into a variety of models for which practitioners can be trained. Among those is *assertive listening*. In general, this listening model requires giving full attention to the person who is speaking and only asking for clarification when necessary. Clark (2005) demonstrated the importance of attention to listening rather than talking. In his research project which assessed the dialogue between juvenile offenders and their probation officers during scheduled visits which averaged 15 minutes each, he found that of the average 2768 words spoken the officer spoke 2017 of them. He claimed that the officers in the research were, *talking themselves out of effectiveness*.

Other studies of the impact of assertive listening practices showed that their use consistently distinguished managers, teachers, and leaders who are judged among the ones who are most effective. Similarly, among practitioners in the helping professions, including both physicians and social workers, the listening skills included in this model are among the top three abilities of practitioners who are rated as outstanding by their colleagues (Goleman, 2006). Training in the assertive listening model is available from a variety of sources and may be important to consider as a priority area of development by those seeking improvement in emotional intelligence.

Understand without agreeing or accepting

Professional practitioners with a high level of EI can understand how and why behaviour has occurred but disagree, even strongly so, with its appropriateness. These practitioners have the capacity to maintain an objective and non-judgmental approach to practice and relationships that enables them to work effectively with young persons and their families even when it is clear to all those in the relationship that the practitioners do not approve of either the patterns of behaviours, or the choices made by the client. Practitioners with high levels of EI create an environment with clients and their families in which both inappropriate behaviours and non-productive values and norms can be challenged effectively while still maintaining a productive service relationship. In other words, they achieve and maintain an effective therapeutic alliance.

Such an objective recognition and capability by

the practitioner can be achieved through personal initiative with deliberate and continuing effort concentrated toward that end. However, it will be helpful to this personal initiative if both the organisation and professional colleagues agree with this perspective, and demonstrate it through all organisational practices and professional relationships. In this initiative for improvement, practitioners will work toward an understanding that knowing the characteristics of their clients and their life histories, including their moral standards, personal values, behaviours, and current or previous criminal actions is very different from agreeing with those characteristics and accepting them as appropriate.

Reaching such an understanding and applying it in practice is no small matter. It requires clarification and adoption of one's own values and their foundations and a high level of skill in appraising the characteristics of their clients and families and communicating with them. If there is any question in the practitioner's mind about his or her own values, and their foundations, then those questions should be addressed directly. Any skills that may be weak or lacking can be addressed through other self-improvement or training initiatives focused on communications. Or, using the language of the flight attendant, put on your own mask before you attempt to put on anyone else's.

Focus on strengths

Some practices are designed to enable communication and prevent or defuse strained relationships. One of these is to *focus on strengths* of the client rather than on weaknesses or needs. A great deal of research has documented consistently that a focus on strengths can have faster and more significant effects than focus on needs or weaknesses. Yet common practice continues to focus on needs and weaknesses. Training for identification of strengths and focusing attention on them during practice is readily available. The application of this approach and set of skills by practitioners working with sexually harmful behaviour can provide effective means for overcoming some of the emotional load inherent in their positions, and help to overcome some personal emotional characteristics and patterns of responses to them. This training for strengths-based practices, and the application of the skills acquired from it, can provide significant improvements in both general

professional performance and emotional intelligence.

Plan and determine the non-negotiables

Another way that practitioners working with sexually harmful behaviour may be able to improve their practice and their emotional intelligence is to have a clear understanding of the conditions in their client relationships, and which interventions are negotiable and which are not. It is usual for the characteristics of the clients to be considered while planning interventions and, in many cases, reasonable that the clients have some participatory role in developing their own treatment plans. However, some clients may want to set goals and choose methods that are different from ones recommended by their practitioner. In these cases, the practitioner should be prepared to negotiate a compromise when it is appropriate. Some goals and methods, however, may be non-negotiable especially if they are regulated by child protection, community and or personal safety. Encountering these non-negotiable differences during therapy may strain or damage the therapeutic relationship with clients. Objective professionals can improve their emotional intelligence by anticipating these non-negotiable situations, and devising ways to exclude them from the goals and interventions that are discussed or allowed to enter into consideration. Objectively excluding them before they are introduced by the client is one approach that can prevent or significantly reduce emotional engagement or stress during the service delivery.

Use parallel problems or illustrations

A common practice in general individual problem-solving, and in providing human services, is to approach problems or needs by working directly to solve the problem that was identified. However, an alternative approach is to identify problems that are not the one confronting the person. Rather they are structurally parallel to it and ones for which the person does not have an emotional identity. By using these parallel problems, the practitioner can engage the client in learning activity for which there is no 'emotional baggage.' Once these parallel problems have been addressed and favourable therapeutic relationships are established, then the experience with the 'illustrative' problem can be transferred to the ones actually facing the client. Difficulty in solving real problems may be rooted in low understanding of the problem, low levels of skill in general problem-solving, or the choice of solutions. Working on parallel problems that have low levels of emotional baggage can help develop general problem-solving skills. It can also develop the capacity to deal with the particular problems to a point that the client and practitioner can resolve issues they encounter when they begin to work on the actual case problems.

For example, recently a young male was assigned to me. He had sexually assaulted two girls but was unable to participate in discussions in which his father was a participant. The boy and his father apparently had a long history of strong disagreements and regular arguments and fights. Rather than attempting to address their conflicts directly or to engage them in any kind of discussion related to the boy's behaviours, I introduced a game in which they used diagrammatic representations of relationships, rather than using any verbal representations. To perform tasks in this activity successfully they had to communicate slowly and clearly with each other and listen attentively. They came to understand quickly that if they argued while trying the game, they could not complete the task successfully. As they worked, I modelled some of the task until they understood it and then I raised guiding questions as they worked through it and completed it successfully. Following successful completion, we discussed how they had worked together and made plans for how they would work together over the forthcoming sessions. That practice was enough to engage them in verbal communications in other follow-up sessions without significant conflict.

Match task structure to the group maturity

As a general rule, following an objective approach can help practitioners perform in a way that is comparable to that of a practitioner who has a higher level of emotional intelligence, even while one's own emotional intelligence is being developed. One model that can be used for encouraging an objective approach is situational leadership theory, developed by Hersey and Blanchard (1977). The underlying principles of this model can be applied by practitioners working with sexually harmful behaviour who

are working with clients to develop intervention plans. In this model, the task approach that is expected to be most effective depends upon what they named *group maturity in respect to the task*. A low degree of group maturity would be characteristic of most therapeutic alliances especially early in the services and before an effective alliance has been established. According to Hersey and Blanchard, low group maturity is associated with, or can come from a lack of history of working effectively together on the types of issues which they are addressing. In other words, group maturity usually would be low if the people who are attempting to work together are new to each other. According to the situational leadership model, the therapeutic relationship for practitioners working with sexually harmful behaviour and their clients usually would be most effective if the services were designed and implemented to have a high degree of task structure and a high degree of attention to the personal and social needs of the participants. Following this guide, the practitioner would design the task tightly and fully, so that work can be effective and efficient while still being highly attentive to the personal and social needs of the client. A high degree of task structure does not mean there is little or no flexibility; neither does it mean that the practitioner is being rigid, dictatorial or controlling. Rather, the practice reflects a high degree of pre-planning and pre-structuring so that the structure not only guides the working relationship, but also enables flexibility when it is needed, or when it can be handled by the client without distractions to goal achievement.

Summary

The methods and approaches described above are not direct ways to improve emotional intelligence. Nevertheless, they offer approaches that can provide practitioners ways to work with clients to de-emphasise any direct effects of emotions on the therapeutic alliance. For the most part, these approaches use pre-planning and pre-structuring as a way to anticipate emotions and emotional reactions. They are also used to plan methods and materials that can achieve an effective therapeutic alliance, even if the practitioner does not have the full range of emotional skills that may be needed. Each of these approaches provides the practitioner with effective tools for working with clients while working on skills for improving empathy and overall emotional intelligence. They offer the practitioner approaches that can lead them toward becoming consciously competent with a high level of emotional intelligence.

Conclusion

Practitioners working with sexually harmful behaviour are often placed in the position of 'performers' who need to keep a number of plates spinning at the same time. They must protect the interest of the client while they are serving them effectively. They also must protect victims or potential victims from sexual assault whilst holding the young people accountable for their SHB. In so doing, they carry the dual burdens of community service and community safety as well as, the responsibility for the rehabilitation and well-being of the client.

Practitioners who display high levels of emotional intelligence are aware of their own values and core beliefs and they know their own emotions and their typical responses to them. Attunement to those emotions and their common responses can improve their capacity to anticipate and predict emotional 'hot spots' and plan accordingly, rather than acting impulsively when the reaction occurs. Emotionally intelligent practitioners recognise when they feel angry or resentful and they understand the cause of those emotions. They are able to control their responses in ways that do not cause barriers to but help improve relationships with clients or others. This conscious self-control, or mastery, over both positive and negative emotions, allows practitioners working with sexually harmful behaviour to tolerate the uncertainties that are associated with hypothesising and testing causal factors in their clients' sexually harmful behaviour. Additionally they are able to use that skill for professional decision-making, or for setting priorities among professional and personal needs. If practitioners react to their emotions without sufficient control over their reactions, issues may arise in the case analysis and planning that can result in inappropriate or insufficient treatment strategies. Practitioners, who have a high level of EI, along with high levels of technical and professional competence, probably will also be aware of their own strengths and weaknesses, be open to feedback and be willing to learn from experience.

As front-line practitioners working with sexually harmful behaviour, forming and maintaining relationships within emotionally charged environments is fundamental to practice. Therefore, at least a sufficient level of emotional intelligence is required for successful practice. Given the centrality of our own and clients' emotions within our jobs as practitioners working with sexually harmful behaviour, it seems imperative that we arm ourselves appropriately for providing high quality professional services by working to develop the highest level of EI and other professional skills that we possibly can.

P.S.

Molly and her mum completed work with me over two years ago. Both report a strong attachment between themselves and with Molly's sister and say they enjoy being together doing fun things. Mum is happy to be on her own with her children and is attending classes for her own personal development. There have been no reports of Molly sexually harming any other children or animals. Nevertheless, she has experienced some emotional problems and she has displayed some misbehaviour in school. She had to change schools because of her patterns of behaviour, but continues to work at controlling her temper.

As most of us know, there are few 'magic bullets' for the transformation of children who engage in sexually harmful behaviour. The case of Molly is no different, but real progress has been made. She reports that she can talk to her mum now and, when she does her mum listens. She said that she learned how to talk with her mother about problems without fighting. 'We have a right good laugh together now, me and my mum.'

References

American Psychological Association (2007) *APA Dictionary of Psychology*. Washington: Library of Congress Press.

Ashfield, S. et al. (2010) Working with Female Sexual Offenders: Therapeutic Process Issues. In Gannon, T.A. and Cortoni, F (eds.) *Female Sexual Offenders: Theory, Assessment and Practice*. Chichester: Wiley-Blackwell.

Bar-On, R. (1997) *The Emotional Quotient Inventory (EQ-I): A Test of Emotional Intelligence*. Toronto: Multi-Health Systems.

Bar-On, R. (2000) Emotional and Social Intelligence: Insights From The Emotional Quotient Inventory. In Bar-On, R. and Parker, J. (eds.) *Handbook of Emotional Intelligence*. San Francisco, CA: Jossey-Bass.

Bar-On, R. (2005) The Bar-On Model of Emotional-Social Intelligence (ESI). *Psicothema*, Special Issue on Emotional Intelligence 17, 1–28.

Bovard-Johns, R.M. (2009) *Juvenile Sex Offenders and Therapeutic Alliance: The Intricate Dynamics of Alliance in Relation to Attachment, Trauma, and Religion. Un-published study. Smith College School for Social Work, Northampton, MA.*

Brackett, M.A. et al. (2006) Relating Emotional Abilities to Social Functioning: A Comparison of Self-Report and Performance Measures of Emotional Intelligence. Journal of Personality and Social Psychology, 91, 780–95.

Clark, M.D. (2005) *Qualitative Review of Probation Officer/Offender Dialogues: Transcript Word Counts for 'Talk Time' Ratios.* Un-published study. Centre of Strength-Based Strategies.

Emmerling, R.J. and Goleman, D. (2003) Emotional Intelligence: *Issues and Common Mis-understandings*. Accessed May 31, 2007 From http://www.sciencedirect.com.ezproxy. qub.ac.uk/Science?_Ob = Redirecturland_ Method = Externobjlinkand_Locator = Urland_ Cdi = 5067and_Issn = 00207489

Emmerling, R.J. and Goleman, D. (2005) Leading With Emotion. *Leadership Excellence*, 22: 9–10.

Fenske, A.G. (2007) *Measuring Empathy, Feedback, Therapeutic Alliance and Outcome With Sexual Offenders.* Un-published study. Graduate Department of Clinical Psychology George Fox University. Newberg, OR.

Freeland, E.M., Terry, R.A. and Rodgers, J.L. (2008) Emotional Intelligence. in Cassady, J.C. (ed.) *Emotional Intelligence: Perspectives on Educational and Positive Psychology*. New York: Peter Lang.

Goleman, D. (1995) *Emotional Intelligence*. New York: Bantam Books.

Goleman, D. (1998) *Working With Emotional Intelligence*. New York: Bantam Books.

Goleman, D. (2005) *Emotional Intelligence*. New York: Bantam Books.

Goleman, D. (2006) *Social Intelligence*. New York: Bantam Books.

Goleman, D., Boyatzis, R. and Mckee, A. (2002) *Primal Leadership: Realizing The Power of Emotional Intelligence*. Boston: Harvard Business School Press.

Hackett, S. (2006) The Personal and Professional Context to Work with Children and Young People Who Have Sexually Abused. In Erooga, M. and Masson, H. (eds.) *Children and Young People Who Sexually Abuse Others: Current Developments and Practice Responses*. 2nd edn, Oxford: Routledge.

Hallett, T. (2000) *Small Group Culture and Socio Emotion Management: The Case of TD's Restaurant*. Proceedings of 95th Annual Meeting of the American Sociological Association, Washington, DC: August 12–16.

Halpern, J. (2003) What is Clinical Empathy? *Journal Intern Med*. 18: 670–4.

Halpin, A. (1966) *Theory and Research in Administration*. New York: Macmillan.

Halpin, A. (ed.) (1967) *Administrative Theory in Education*. Macmillan.

Herman, J. (1992) *Trauma and Recovery*. New York: Basic Books.

Hersey, P. and Blanchard, K.H. (1977) *Management of Organizational Behavior*. 3rd edn. NJ: Prentice Hall.

Herzberg, F. (1968) One More Time: How Do You Motivate Employees? *Harvard Business Review*, 46: 1, 53–62.

Hochschild, A.R. (1983) *The Managed Heart: Commercialization of Human Feeling*. Berkeley, CA: University of California Press.

Hodges, S.D. and Klein, K.J. (2001) Regulating The Costs of Empathy: The Price of Being Human. *Journal of Socio-Economics*, 30, 437–52.

Johnson, H. (2001) Neutral, Colluding or Subversive? Recognising The Political Implications of The Marketing Subdiscourses in English Higher Education. *Educational Management and Administration*, 29: 3, 261–74.

Kooker, B.M. et al. (2007) Identifying Emotional Intelligence in Professional Nursing Practice. *Journal of Professional Nursing*, 23, 30–6.

Kunnanatt, J.T. (2004) Emotional Intelligence: The New Science of Interpersonal Effectiveness. *Human Resource Development Quarterly*, 15: 489–95.

Lazarus, R.S. (1991) Emotion and Adaptation. in Pervin, L.A. (ed.) *Handbook of Personality: Theory and Research*. New York: Guilford.

Mark, A. (2005) Organizing Emotions in Health Care. *Journal of Health Organization and Management*, 19: 277–89.

Markakis, K. et al. (1999) *Teaching Empathy: It Can Be Done*. Working Paper Presented at The Annual Meeting of The Society of General Internal Medicine, San Francisco, CA, April 29-May 1.

Marshall, W., Anderson, D. and Ferendez, Y. (1999) *Cognitive Behavioural Treatment of Sexual Offenders.* Chichester and New York: Wiley.

Maslow, A.H. (1940) Dominance-quality and Social Behaviour in Ifra-Human Primates. *Journal of Social Psychology*, 11: 313–24.

Matthews, G., Zeidner, M. and Roberts, R.D. (2002) *Emotional Intelligence: Science and Myth.* Cambridge, MA: MIT Press.

Mayer, J.D. et al. (2001) Emotional Intelligence as a Standard Intelligence. *Emotion*, 1, 232–42.

Mayer, J.D. et al. (2003) Measuring Emotional Intelligence with the MSCEIT V2.0. *Emotion*, 3, 97–105.

Mayer, J.D. and Salovey, P. (1997) What is Emotional Intelligence? In Salovey, P. and Sluyter, D.J. (Eds.) *What is Emotional Intelligence?* New York: Basic Books.

Mayer, J.D., Salovey, P. and Caruso, D. (2000) Models of Emotional Intelligence. In Sternberg, R. (Ed.) *Handbook of Intelligence.* Cambridge: Cambridge University Press.

Mayer, J.D., Salovey, P. and Caruso, D.R. (2002) *Manual for The MSCEIT (Mayer-Salovey-Caruso Emotional Intelligence Test).* Toronto: Multihealth Systems.

Mayer, J.D., Salovey, P. and Caruso, D.R. (2004) Emotional Intelligence: Theory, Findings, and Implications. *Psychological Inquiry*, 15, 197–215.

Mayer, J.D., Salovey, P. and Caruso, D.R. (2008) Emotional Intelligence: New Ability or Eclectic Traits? *American Psychologist*, 63, 503–17.

Mayer, J.D., Salovey, P., Caruso, D.R. and Sitarenios, G. (2001) Emotional Intelligence as a Standard Intelligence. *Emotion*, 1, 232–42.

McEnrue, M.P. and Groves, K. (2006) Choosing among Tests of Emotional Intelligence: What is the Evidence? *Human Resource Development Quarterly*, 17: 1.

Morrison, T. (2006) Emotional Intelligence, Emotion and Social Work: Context, Characteristics, Complications and Contribution. *British Journal of Social Work*, March 30.

Morse, J. et al. (1992) Exploring Empathy: A Conceptual Fit for Nursing Practice? *Image J Nurs Sch*, 24: 273–80.

Opengart, R. (2005) Emotional Intelligence and Emotion Work: Examining Constructs from an Interdisciplinary Framework. *Human Resource Development Review*, 4: 1, 49–62.

Quoidbach, J. and Hansenne, M. (2009) The Impact of Trait Emotional Intelligence on Nursing Team Performance and Cohesiveness. *Journal of Professional Nursing.* 25: 1, 23–9.

Rogers, C.R. (1959) A Theory of Therapy, Personality and Interpersonal Relationships, as Developed in the Client-Centered Framework. in Koch, S. (ed.) *Psychology: A Study of Science.* New York: McGraw Hill.

Salovey, P. and Grewal, D. (2005) The Science of Emotional Intelligence. *Current Directions In Psychological Science*, 14, 281–5.

Salovey, P. and Mayer, J.D. (1990) Emotional Intelligence. *Imagination, Cognition, and Personality*, 9, 185–211.

Schwartz, W. (2002) From Passivity to Competence: A Conceptualization of Knowledge, Skill, Tolerance, and Empathy. *Psychiatry*, 65: 4, 338–45.

Suchman, A. et al. (1997) A Model of Empathic Communication in the Medical Interview. *JAMA*, 277: 678–82.

Suchman, A., Markakis, K., Beckman, H. and Frankel, R. (1999) A Model of Empathic Communication in The Medical Interview. *JAMA.* 277: 678–82.

Weinberger, L.A. (2002) Emotional Intelligence: Its Connection to HRD Theory and Practice. *Human. Resource Development* 1: 215–243.

Winstok, Z. (2009) The Relationships between Social Goals, Skills, and Strategies and their Effect on Aggressive Behavior among Adolescents. *Journal of Interpersonal Violence*, 24, 1996–2017.

CHAPTER 9

Training in Social Services

Libby Ashurst

Overview

This chapter addresses various purposes for training and the degrees of intensity and duration of training that may be needed, or appropriate, for developing job-related skills and improving performance. It also provides a summary of the foundations for design of instruction in the form of general standards for training and development regardless of the purposes to be served or the field or occupational roles. Once presented, those foundations are used to describe how training can be designed and delivered if it is expected to result in improvements in both professional skills and performance. Those standards will be used further to provide an illustration of the types of training that may be needed within social services for practitioners who work specifically in the area of sexually harmful behaviour.

Foundations for a generalised training model

Training effectiveness

Training and professional development appear to be a part of the normal life of people who are either seeking positions or currently working in professional fields. That training may range in intensity and duration from brief orientation to a new job and organisation, to workshops addressing particular job-related skills or to full courses of study leading to initial qualification for a professional position.

As a necessary basis for ensuring competence in most occupations and professions through training, practitioners are required to learn some particular job-related knowledge, skills, or sentiments *beyond* those included in the general education required as the minimum qualification for working in those fields. That training may be significant in scope and coverage or it may only be an orientation to the rules, routines, or expectations for work in a particular job (Hayes, 2007). Thus, additional job-specific training probably will be required after gaining a general qualification for learning the particulars of a new job or for continuing to improve skills and performance, to keep pace with changes in a particular job or to make job or career advancements. For example, police officers who want to be considered for positions of detective for criminal investigations may be required to complete a specialised training programme for that job even though they already hold general qualifications for their current positions.

Usually job-specific training or training designed to focus on a narrow set of skills is designed and implemented in very different ways and with different standards than a programme designed for general qualification. The targeted nature of training for development of particular job skills allows it to be designed:

- to be completed within a specific and limited time period
- to focus specifically on improving or enabling performance in the job for which one is being prepared
- to include assessments of efficiency and effectiveness in using the specific skills by trainees

Furthermore, training is usually designed based on an assumption that participants have the generalised knowledge and skills on which learning the specific skills depend and that there is some job-related need for the training and, therefore, participants are positively motivated to engage in the learning. Of course, both of these assumptions may be incorrect in any training situation and may be a cause of resistance to participation and change. Extending this point further, Tharenou, Saks and Moore (2007) say that training programmes may be used for a variety of reasons other than for improving skills or enabling job performance. Among other reasons they found from their studies of training were those needed to meet requirements for legal compliance, rewarding or retaining employees, or merely to keep up with the variety of training 'fads.'

While training has become a strategic, fundamental part of human resource development (Salas and Cannon-Bowers, 2001) it remains a topic of frequent commentary in the literature on training and professional development in which serious and compelling questions are raised about the effectiveness of training strategies. For example, training is often criticised for being faddish, too expensive, not transferring learning to the job, and not 'improving the bottom line' (cf Caudron, 2002; Kraiger, McLinden, and Casper, 2004; Salas et al., 1999; Wright and Geroy, 2001). Further criticism of training was offered by Wright and Geroy (2001) who claimed that the belief that training leads to improved organisational performance is a myth 'that equates training with "goodness".'

Furthermore, views about their training held by trainees vary widely and may range from very negative to very positive, depending upon, among other things, how the training is represented by the organisation or supervisors, the experiences of the participants during the training, their expectations about purposes and content, their motivations to engage in the training or various overall quality factors.

Elaborating this point further, Bunch (2007) said there are at least four ways training can fail at the organisation level:

- unskilled training practitioners provide flawed interventions
- skilled training practitioners provide flawed interventions because they do not have the capacity, power or influence to design valid training
- skilled training practitioners provide valid interventions, but learning does not transfer to the job
- skilled training practitioners provide valid interventions that produce positive transfer, but effectiveness is not perceived by either the practitioners or line managers. However, whilst some line managers and practitioners view *themselves* as 'master craftsmen or women,' they commonly leave others with the innovation, desperation, or responsibility to provide training even though those left with the task may not have the necessary or sufficient authority or skills to be a trainer

Under those conditions, it is probably inevitable that some training programmes will be viewed by the trainees as not delivered by an authority in their field or by a qualified trainer. These conditions and perceptions can lead to the content of training not being used in practice. Bunch (2007) recognised this dilemma when she stated, 'Ultimately, training effectiveness depends upon the power and status of the field of training being viewed as a profession.' Contributing even further to a view held by practitioners that training has low importance or value is the common practice in organisations of treating training as either a disposable or dispensable commodity when they are experiencing financial or human resource problems. Ruona, Lynham and Chermack (2003) supported this position by suggesting that organisation leaders can trivialise training through symbolic behaviour such as hiring unqualified trainers or reflexively firing trainers at the first sign of an economic slowdown.

Notwithstanding these different views of training held by participants, the varieties of questions about and criticisms of training offered in the literature, or the barriers to effectiveness either created by or found in organisations, some form of training probably is both essential and should be expected for anyone who is seeking a new professional position or who wishes to remain current and skilful within the position they have. Organisations consistently use training as a tool to improve organisational performance, whether that is an effective strategy or not.

Evidence-based professional practices

It seems reasonable to assume that all practitioners would like to believe that they are using good and effective methods in their work, and that their practice is based on the best, most sound evidence available to them. However, a variety of studies in a range of professional fields found a wide gap between actual practices and those that reflect the current best-evidence (De Laat et al., 2006; Pittet et al., 2000; Vermeulen, Meents, and Ubbink, 2007).

Some examples from nursing practice illustrate this point and show that even when there is high-quality evidence available and where it can be demonstrated that not using the information could have an adverse effect on patient safety or endanger lives, it still may not be used.

In their study of prescribed hand-hygiene in hospitals, Pittet et al. (2000) reported that less than 50 per cent of nurse practitioners were compliant on all relevant occasions. Even so, the nurses were slightly more compliant than the doctors, despite the fact that not using the prescribed hand hygiene had been shown to increase cross contamination of infection. As another example, in their study of practices known to be effective for preventing pressure ulcers, De Laat et al. (2006) found that some nurses did not use those practices regularly. Another study by Vermeulen, Meents, and Ubbink (2007) found that patients were denied nutrition for approximately four times the duration specified in new guidelines while nurses continued to follow the old practices. These studies point to both the difficulty of getting new practices adopted and to discontinuation of old practices when ones known to be more effective are presented as alternatives.

Findings from several studies indicate that the above examples of failure to use best evidence are not unique to nursing (Kitson et al. 2008). Thus, it seems essential to consider the research which documents methods and principles for promoting the uptake of findings into routines in clinical settings, community and policy when developing any new training programme or updating old ones. (The particular field of study dealing with uptake of findings is referred to by some as Implementation Science.)

Developing that issue of uptake further, and introducing another set of factors linked to use of evidence, Mykhalovskiy and Weir (2004) and Kontos and Poland (2009) said that viewing clinical practice simply as an activity that attaches research to a worksite and to work fails to recognise the profound differences among workplaces in resources, established routines and the cultural practices that influence and shape clinical practice. In other words, the professional knowledge, skills, and sentiments of the staff are not enough to ensure evidence-based practices. Other social, organisation and context factors may influence practices even more than the knowledge, skills and sentiments of practitioners. If such is the case, then significant improvements in professional practice or uptake of new practices may require significant organisation and context development and not merely training of staff.

The importance of context factors

One widely-made assumption underlying training models is that important learning can

occur directly from training (Halfens and Van Linge, 2003). More appropriately, that assumption should be that learning can occur from *well-designed* and *well-implemented* training. Also, a second underlying assumption common to training is that if learning occurs, the trainees will use the new learning to improve their performance. There is ample evidence relating to changing practices and to factors affecting change to question the validity of that second assumption (Grol and Grimshaw, 2003; Bodenheimer, 1999; Van Achterberg et al., 2008). While it is possible to change the quality of practices and job performance through training and other interventions, successful change generally requires comprehensive approaches at different organisation levels (practitioner, manager, team, organisation, wider environment), tailored to specific settings and target groups (Grol and Grimshaw, 2003).

The effects of context on implementation of evidence-based practice have been widely researched in health care services, with particular attention paid to front-line nurses. While some of these identified factors may be unique to nursing contexts, some will apply to all contexts in which practitioners are involved in front-line clinical practice. In healthcare service fields, the research by Davies et al., 2008; Dobbins et al. 2007; Estabrooks et al., 2007; Meijers et al., 2007; Ploeg et al., 2007 identified the following as being important context factors that affect implementation:

- culture and leadership
- organisation size
- staffing support
- organisation innovativeness
- administration responsiveness
- access to resources
- organisation climate
- provision of training
- access to research findings
- availability of knowledge and skills within organisations
- integration of recommendations into organisational structures and processes
- inter-organisational collaboration
- money
- workload
- resistance to change
- time.

Notwithstanding the above list of factors, research to date investigating factors affecting uptake has not established whether some of these factors have more influence on implementation than others, whether all factors are equally important, or whether it is the system as a whole determined by these factors that are the primary determinants of performance. More than likely, each of these factors is a *necessary* condition for performance but none comprises a *sufficient* condition for determining or explaining performance. If so, they must be considered as a set when planning or implementing training that is intended to improve performance.

It is clear from this small sample of research findings that successful change of professional practices depends upon more than just training in knowledge and skills linked directly to the job tasks. Improvement of practices also requires ensuring that context factors that resist or support change be addressed fully and appropriately for supporting staff learning and for using the practices, the adoption of them into their workplace, and institutionalisation of the intended practices through organisation routines and regular encouragement and support for their use.

Principles of implementation and change

A common point made by researchers in the area of change is that both the general *strategies* for change, and the specific *methods* used should be appropriate for the context and the purpose. (*Strategies* are defined in the literature on planning and change as *what will be put into place in order to achieve the intended purpose. Methods* are the ways and means to put the strategy into place.) The researchers go on to say that in order to choose the best strategy for the purpose it is crucial to identify ones that match characteristics of the specific innovation, target group, and context. Extending that idea, Van-Achterberg, Schoonhoven and Grol (2008) stated that strategies for achieving implementation are most successful when they take into account relevant change factors, are linked with relevant theoretical insights, and are supported by evidence of either the validity of the theory or the effectiveness of the strategy itself.

Describing strategies further, Van Woerkom (1990) said they are procedures or routines aimed at effecting change. He went on to say that they can be either involuntary (such as laws,

regulations or obligations) or voluntary which have different implications for change. Voluntary strategies reflect both intrinsic and extrinsic motivations for action. Intrinsic motivations are behaviour-oriented (feedback, monitoring or reminding) and competence or attitude (training, instruction and consultation). Extrinsic motivations include financial structures (rewards and penalties) and work-setting structures (such as peer reviews, audit) and are focused on the client rather than on the practitioners.

Commonly, leaders of implementations within clinical environments and health services focus on voluntary intrinsic motivations and do not consider extrinsic factors (Holleman et al., 2006 and Van Achterberg, 2006). (Having experienced first-hand the current training programmes in Northern Ireland and the UK for practitioners serving young people who have displayed sexually harmful behaviours (SHB), this author claims that this point is characteristic of SHB training, a fact that has led to the adoption of training programmes focused primarily on developing skills or attitudes and not on adoption of new or improved approaches.) One important consequence of this narrow strategic approach is that training needs that can result in changed practices are either not being addressed or, at best, are under-used (Van Achterberg, 2006).

Dall'Alba (2009) said that it is common in the literature on training as an approach to change for researchers to conclude that addressing only knowledge, skills and sentiments of the workgroup is not sufficient for improving practices. The researchers found that context variables were often equally or more important than the personal variables. While there were some disagreements among the researchers, the evidence appears compelling that if improved practices are the expected result of a training programme, then a comprehensive strategy for change must be used to address the complex set of personal, organisation and context factors that account for variance in performance. That means, among other things, that a training system may have to include methods for dealing with both personal and context variables and be prepared to conclude that in some cases training may not be appropriate without a companion or parallel programme for organisation development to achieve the necessary conditions for the trainees to use their new learnings.

Personal and context factors affecting performance

A common beginning point in the development of curriculum (defined as the organised set of learnings intended from the training) for a training model is to define the tasks for which people are to be trained and then perform learning analyses to identify the knowledge and skills that will be addressed through training. However, a large body of literature, of which only a sample is referenced in sections above, related to training effectiveness and organisation improvement indicates that merely training in the knowledge and skills necessary to perform job tasks may not be sufficient to improve performance quality. Varieties of other factors – organisation, context, personal, and work group – are known to influence performance in addition to the knowledge and skills of the workers. Thus, for the development of the curriculum for a training model that is intended to improve performance, those factors must be identified and studied to determine how, if at all, they might be addressed through training of professional staff.

A list of factors known to influence performance of health professionals was listed above. However, a more comprehensive review of literature on job performance revealed other factors not included in that list. Through further study of the literature on factors affecting performance and review by a panel of experts on training, this author has identified skills related to each of these factors that can be addressed through training. Thus, training of staff can enable practitioners to take advantage of favourable organisation and context conditions or overcome or accommodate conditions that normally comprise barriers to practitioner performance. Those factors described using language from organisation theory, are:

- autonomy over work (individual and work group)
- sense of personal welfare and security
- resources: quantity, quality, and availability for use as
- commitment to job-related goals: personal and work group
- clarity of job goals and tasks
- assumptions about role of work: personal and work group
- assumptions about work quality: personal and work group
- coping skills: personal and work group
- understanding of job tasks: personal and work group
- load (job-related and other): personal and work group
- values and beliefs: personal and work group
- perceptions of fairness
- perceived task importance: personal and work group
- organisation routines: effectiveness and efficiency
- job satisfaction
- goal and task complexity
- technology (defined as 'assumptions about how particular work should be done'): personal and work group
- job-specific knowledge and skills

It can be seen from this list that only one of the items deals directly with job-specific knowledge and skills. Others deal with the organisation and the context and may include work group characteristics as well as characteristics of the individual practitioner. Thus, the extent that these factors are real and do affect job performance either positively or negatively, then training to improve performance must take these factors into account through the application of a method-based approach. Given that proposition, curriculum for training to improve performance must go much beyond a narrow interpretation of the skills required to complete particular job tasks and include a variety of generalisable skills that allow practitioners to negotiate conditions within organisations and work effectively even when there may be a variety of important organisation or context barriers to their work. A comprehensive model for designing and implementing training to improve practitioner performance must include, or at least consider whether to include, learnings associated with each of the factors in the list above.

Once the curriculum for training is established, there remains the question of what system of instruction is appropriate to result in the intended learnings and the improved performance. The following section provides a general foundation for the kinds of instruction needed to ensure both effective learning and improved performance.

Standards for instructional design: methodological foundations for the training model

The field of instructional design provides a foundation for understanding and improving a primary part of education: the *process of instruction* (Reigeluth and Carr-Chellum, 2009). One of the fundamental realisations underlying the field of instructional design is that there are different types (varieties) of learning and, to be effective, both instruction and assessment must differ systematically to match the type of learning that is intended (Gagné, 1965, 1979; Hayes, 2007; Reigeluth and Carr-Chellum, 2009). An early leader in the development of this field, Robert Gagné (1965, 1979) made a key contribution to the development of the science and technology of instruction when he defined five general types of learning (Also referred to by him and others as types of learned capability and as domains of learning.). Those five general types of learning have no order or hierarchy implied among them; they merely are different. Consideration of these types is important for instructional decision-making, instructional design, instruction, and assessment of learning because both the standards for instruction and for the processes for assessment of learning are different among the types, as are the necessary prior characteristics of the learners. The names of those general types (domains) of learned capability are:

- attitudes
- cognitive strategies
- intellectual skills
- motor skills
- verbal information.

Although Gagné did not intend the five general types listed above to be hierarchical or subordinate, after completing further analysis of the intellectual skill domain he determined it to be both dependent and hierarchical. That is, each type is less complex than the next higher type, and the higher types require some prior learning of the types before them as a condition for acquiring the higher level learning. The types of intellectual skills defined by Gagné are (1 = lowest, 5 = highest):

1. discriminations
2. concrete concepts
3. defined concepts
4. rules
5. problem-solving

As for the five general types of learning, these five categories of intellectual skills are different as are their instructional and assessment standards. That is, to be effective, instruction and assessment for these intellectual skills must match the particular type of learning that is intended. Gagné and his colleagues continued to develop the standards for instruction and assessment for these types of intellectual skills from the time of their initial work on them throughout their professional careers. One of the most recent developments of these standards is in a working paper by Hayes (2007). Material from that paper is used extensively in the following sections with permission from the author.

An earlier project by Bloom and his colleagues (1956) attempted to classify learning into categories that could be used for instructional planning and learning assessment and devised yet another classification system. That framework, the *Taxonomy of Educational Objectives: Cognitive Domain*, commonly referred to as 'Bloom's Taxonomy,' is widely known today in education circles. There is a major difference between the intentions of Bloom and his colleagues and Gagné. Bloom et al. intended to classify varieties of *performances* that might be expected of people from an educational programme. Gagné, on the other hand, was attempting to classify varieties of *learned capability*, irrespective of the performance that might follow or be enabled. His concern was only for identifying the varieties of capabilities that required different forms of instruction and assessment since his concern was for developing the foundations for instructional decision-making. That is, one of these researchers (Bloom et al.) was seeking to classify performance or behaviour that presumably represented capability or learning and the other (Gagné) was seeking to develop a framework for classifying learning. Their purposes were different and their products were different.

However, these two classification systems are not contradictory; rather, they are complementary and both useful in developing training models. Indeed, it is useful to combine them when analyzing higher-order tasks to identify the learning requirements for performance. For example, Bloom et al. defined three categories of higher-order performance that they named *analysis*, *synthesis*, and *evaluation*. Gagné defined *problem-solving* as a category of learning that includes all three of these types of performances. It should be readily apparent that the tasks involved in analyzing, synthesising, and evaluating are quite different. Nevertheless, Gagné considered these to be similar for instructional decision-making because they require the same *general standards* for instruction and assessment. They clearly involve different types of performance, however.

Both Gagné and Bloom et al. were developing conceptual frameworks for describing learnings and performances for *general education* rather than for training. Therefore, some of their categories probably will not be addressed by training, which has a more targeted purpose than general education. For example, cognitive strategies would not be appropriate learning expectations from a training programme. These capabilities are the general ways of thinking and cognitive processing that tend to be developed over extended periods of time and remain very stable. It would be extremely difficult to affect them significantly through training. Indeed, most of the intended learnings that will be included in the curriculum for training will be verbal information and concepts, rules and problem-solving in the intellectual skill category.

Given the small number of types of learning needing to be addressed in training, a generalised model can be developed readily by designing an instructional model for each of those types and then applying it repetitively for each of those types of learning within the curriculum. More particularly, one generic instructional model can be developed for teaching verbal information (*Knowledge* in Bloom's taxonomy), another for concepts, another for rules, and one for problem-solving. These four generic models can then be applied to design the particular instruction for each item in the curriculum of the respective type.

Gagné added to his framework for instructional planning for the types of learning by identifying and defining *nine functions* that instruction must serve to be effective. While these functions apply for instruction for any type of learning, the methods and materials used to serve them effectively depend upon the particular type of intended learning. Therefore, given his overall framework of types of learning and functions of instruction, instructional planning can proceed by determining: (a) the particular learning that is intended; (b) its type, and (c) the methods and materials to be used to serve each of the nine functions. That framework provides an overarching set of standards that can be used for designing instruction or training for any type of learning. The nine functions of instruction identified and defined by Gagné are:

1. gaining learner cognitive attention to the instruction
2. informing learner of the intended capability
3. stimulating recall of prerequisite or subordinate learnings
4. presenting stimulus materials
5. providing learning guidance
6. eliciting response or performance
7. providing feedback about correctness of response or performance
8. assessing learning
9. providing for retention and transfer to the type of application or setting for which the learning is important

Using this set of nine functions to conceptualise instruction for any given learning, it is important to recognise that separate or distinct instructional actions or activities are not required to serve each of the functions. Normally, some introductory discussion or presentation can serve the first three functions well. Furthermore, it is not likely that only one example will be enough for most people to acquire an intended learning. Thus, instruction serving functions four through seven will comprise a cycle of as many examples, illustrations or practices as needed for the trainees to acquire the intended learning. Assessing learning, function eight, needs to be served within the instructional context and as close in time and experience to the instruction serving functions one to seven as possible. This learning assessment should provide both the learner and the instructor with the evidence they need to know that the learning has occurred as intended. Function nine, retention and transfer, may be served at a later time. However, if there is a delay, the stage should be set during the initial instruction for the work that will be done to extend and transfer that learning.

It is important to notice here that function nine is intended to generalise the learning to the application or setting for which the learning is intended or important. For example, if practitioners are learning some particular interviewing skill within the training context, then presumably the reason for this learning is to be able to use it in actual practice. Thus, appropriate instruction to serve this function will include a variety of simulated experiences for the initial learning and then a series of applications of that new skill in the workplace. To be appropriate, this instruction will almost certainly follow a 'plan – do – review' cycle until the skill can be used comfortably and successfully within the workplace.

It should be clear from this point about providing for retention and transfer in training that if the purpose of training is to improve practitioner performance, then the training cannot stop in a classroom or other 'workshop' setting. Some of the instruction must include application of the skills within the workplace with careful planning before application and review afterwards until the new skill is comfortable and successful to the practitioner.

Using the point made above about there being primarily four types of learning that will be of concern for training – verbal information, concepts, rules and problem-solving – a generic model can be developed for each of these types for serving each of the nine functions effectively and efficiently. Variations in the general design can be used to develop the complete training system covering the entire curriculum. While the general nature and structure of instruction will be repetitive, it will not appear repetitive to either the participants or the trainers because the content will vary among the intended learnings. The methods materials and activities for serving each of the functions can vary.

Constructing a model based on those theoretical foundations and technical models offers the advantage of being able to use the general design as a template for developing training courses in a variety of social work and similar contexts (Hayes, 2007). Once a generic skill set has been identified for the core of the curriculum, the design for instruction and for related performances to indicate learning for that generalised set can be used across other specific fields of application.

So, if we know all that, why do we still have all the questions about what types of training are needed or appropriate, whether training is effective for producing learning, or whether training 'helps the bottom line?'

As noted above, just as there are gaps between best research evidence and professional practice and there are difficulties associated with uptake, so, also, are there gaps between the best evidence

for design of training and training practices. There is a general failure to take into account systematically the variety of factors affecting performance listed above, other than job-specific knowledge and skills. Even if training is effective in producing new knowledge and skills, this tendency to overlook those factors may place the trainees in conditions in which they may not be able to use their new learning. Furthermore, within much of training design and implementation there is not a systematic distinction made among types of learning intentions and systematic matching of the intended learnings with the standards for instruction required to enable that learning. Seldom in training is there evidence that the nine functions of instruction are systematically addressed and linked to the type of learning intended for professionals. Furthermore, training usually stops at the lower levels of learning and rarely takes the learning to the level of actual professional practice through appropriate use of retention and transfer methods. But, perhaps equally important as the issues related to quality of the training design and implementation is the fact that organisations seldom adopt an overarching strategy for change and embed training into that strategy as a central component.

A training model for SHB practitioners with particular focus on northern ireland

Rationale

The National Children's Home Report (1992) '*The report of the Committee of Enquiry into children and young people who sexually abuse other children*' was one of the first to report that in the UK, children and young people who sexually harm others had emerged as a matter for concern. Some 10 years later, dealing with young people who display sexually harmful behaviour became firmly established within the professional community working in this field as an area for research. This focus identified policymaking in this field as a problem which required an urgent response (Masson and Hacket, 2003).

Other research within this field of practice also documented a need for the training of specialist practitioners. For example, Hackett and Masson (2004) reported a lack of specific staff and practitioner training for working with young people who display sexually abusive behaviour. Consequently, they advised the Home Office that in order to improve standards of practice, consideration should be given to the development and identification of different levels of accredited training.

Several years after the publication of those reports, the *Risky Children or Children at Risk* (Yiasouma, 2007) research conducted in Northern Ireland on behalf of the Department of Health, Social Services and Public Safety (DHSSPS) and the Northern Ireland Office (NIO) identified a need for professional development in this specialist area as an important issue. Despite the fact that professionals involved in this field, including police officers, specialist therapeutic practitioners and social workers, have received some training in child protection, the consensus view expressed in research reports (DHSSPS, 2006; Hacket and Masson (2004) and Yiasouma, 2007) is that the available training is insufficient to equip staff to distinguish accurately between normal and abnormal sexual behaviours by children and young people. They go on to say that the inability to distinguish normal and abnormal behaviour impedes a professional's ability to respond appropriately to the young person's needs through either the criminal justice or child protection systems. Moreover, Yiasouma (2007) and Hackett and Masson (2004) also state that the self-reported low level of capacity to identify and respond appropriately to a young person's needs has caused serious concern amongst professionals and managers within this field. This concern has resulted in practitioner anxiety about the adequacy of performance in their current roles, hesitancy about decision-making, concern about stigmatising the young people charged with sex offences, and heightened awareness of the need for appropriate intervention training and the implementation of service user risk assessment to improve procedures.

Further, the Northern Ireland Child Protection Inspection Overview Report (DHSSPS, 2006) also identified major deficiencies relating to governance for boards, trusts and key agencies to address at a number of levels. At the organisational level, they recommended implementation of a clear workforce development strategy with associated recruitment, retention and training programmes, and a uniform approach to assessment of need and risk analysis. At the practice level, they

highlighted a need for more effective risk management in fieldwork, and an appropriate range of preventative and therapeutic interventions to ensure timely and effective responses.

However, to date, there are still no validated or accredited training models within the UK for preparing these staff for professional practice in this area or for significantly improving professional performance of those in positions as SHB practitioners.

Designing the training model

This section describes the development of a training model that can respond to the challenge by first determining the general standards for training design and then applying those standards to design and implement a specific training application for SHB practitioners. This description is intended here to illustrate how the general frameworks described above can apply to training design and implementation.

It should be noted that the purpose of the project was to design, develop and validate a generalisable training model for professional case-management practitioners that has the capacity to effect *improvement of professional performance* and not merely to improve knowledge and skills. The particular application of the general model that was developed is for practitioners who work with young people, aged between 10–18 years, who display sexually harmful behaviour (SHB).

To begin developing the general standards for this professional training, the first task was to identify and document the necessary and sufficient knowledge, skills, and sentiments essential for improving performance to a level that meets standards for objective professional practice. By design and intention the general model and the application is limited to professional practitioners whose work is *case management*; that is, managing a human service case from the time it is initially referred until it is transferred to others who will implement the service plan that is developed and approved.

That case-management role was analyzed to identify key task areas for which professional knowledge and skills are required and for which training for improvement of professional performance may be needed. Those key tasks which are addressed in both the general and particular models are ones that are common to case-management practices across fields of application, and include:

- receiving and clarifying the case assignment
- assessing client conditions and contexts
- developing high-quality intervention plans
- presenting the case and service plan for critical review in case conferences or legal hearings
- documenting the case including findings, decisions and decision processes, and recommendations
- communicating the plan to practitioners who will implement it

Since curriculum (the organised set of intended learning outcomes from instruction) is a component of any educational or training programme, a model for general or particular training must specify the knowledge, skills and sentiments that will be addressed by the training – it must specify its curriculum. Once determining the overall purpose of the training and the target population, development of the curriculum is the next primary task.

A common beginning point in curriculum development for a training model is to define the tasks for which people are to be trained and then perform learning analyses to identify the knowledge and skills that will be addressed through training. That was done. However, the large body of literature related to training effectiveness and organisation improvement described above indicates that merely addressing the knowledge and skills necessary for effective job performance may not be sufficient to improve performance quality. Thus, for development of curriculum for this training model and application, the set of factors listed in a section above that are known to affect job performance was studied to determine how, if at all, they can be addressed through practitioner training. The analysis of those factors and their influences led to an extensive set of generalisable skills in areas such as communicating, negotiating, decision-making, planning, managing stress and workload, and working in teams, among others. Those skills were combined with ones directly related to task performance to comprise the curriculum for the training model.

Designing the training began from a different set of perspectives – the general standards and principles from the field of instructional systems development. As described above in that general section, there are mainly four types of learning

that will be included in most training models. Those are verbal information (more commonly known as *knowledge* as documented in Bloom's Taxonomy), defined concepts, rules and problem-solving.

But, the first task before designing instruction can begin and an understanding can be reached about what can be achieved from a training model, it is essential to achieve a clear understanding of each of those types of learning and the implications of those understandings for instruction. The following points about each of the types of learning is intended to provide content for that understanding.

It should be remembered here that verbal information is a separate domain in Gagné's classification and concepts, rules and problem-solving are in the intellectual skills domain. Therefore, despite many common assumptions to the contrary, verbal information is not subordinate to the intellectual skills. But, what are these types of learning?

Verbal information is a type of learning more commonly known as *knowledge* as defined in Bloom's *Taxonomy*. As learning, it involves only the psychological process of remembering. It does not require that one must understand or be able to apply the information. Understanding and application usually require some other form of learning than verbal information, such as concepts or rules. At its simplest, verbal information might be described as merely remembering one's birth date or the number of days one has before a report must be filed. Common errors in classifying intended learnings are the inclusion of definitions of words that people are expected to use meaningfully, or to include rules and regulations that people might be expected to follow. Almost without exception those are intellectual skills and cannot be treated merely as verbal information if they are expected to be applied.

Since remembering is the key learning that occurs for verbal information, instruction should focus on encouraging learners to remember the particular information that is to be learned. Usually that remembering is encouraged by using associations, using some form of classification system, repetition, or putting the information into some form of meaningful context. Assessment should only require the production of the information whenever remembering is stimulated by an association that is commonly linked with the need to remember.

For example, one might merely be asked to specify the number of days after an event that a particular report is required without giving any hints or clues.

Defined concepts are the classes that one knows by name and by the illustrations of the class. These concepts do not have concrete properties that can be experienced directly through one or more of the senses. For training, these concepts usually comprise the technical and professional vocabulary that we want trainees to learn. The primary reason for learning these concepts is so they can be used in professional practice. In general, once the learning has occurred, the person recognises an example of the class whenever it is encountered. While it is common in education and training to attempt to teach concepts by providing definitions, that approach, almost without exception, is inadequate and may present barriers to learning the concepts. Those definitions may be learned as verbal information that can be remembered but the class may not be understood. For example, a practitioner might be able to state the definition of *infraction* but not be able to recognise an example when it is encountered. Care should be taken in instruction and assessment not to allow defined concepts to be addressed as if they were verbal information.

Appropriate instruction for defined concept learning presents a variety of illustrations of the class while learning guidance encourages the learners to analyze illustrations and make comparisons with others that are within the class and also with others that are similar but not within the class. This cycle should continue with as many examples as needed for the learners to comprehend the class and be able to recognise illustrations whenever they encounter them. Learning assessment would present illustrations that may or may not be examples of the class and ask the learners to make the classification.

Rules are the type of learning that enables their applications whenever they should be applied. A rule as a learning can actually be stated as a rule in the form of a declarative sentence. They are not 'shoulds' or 'oughts,' however; they are definite. If they refer to social or psychological principles, they should include their probabilistic element, such as 'A person (with specified properties) who has a pattern of (specify behaviours), is more likely to respond (describe response) to intervention A than to intervention B.'

Instruction for learning rules usually includes some form of demonstration of the need for the rule and then a cycle of illustrations of the rule and application. Learning guidance focuses attention on the rule and its application without stating the rule. This cycle of applications continues until the learner can use the rule whenever it should be applied without being told or in some other way reminded to use the rule. Care should be taken in instruction not to state the rule before it has been learned as a rule. Otherwise, it is likely to be treated by the learner as verbal information and undue attention may be given to remembering the statement rather than learning to apply the rule. Assessment of rule learning requires presentation of situations in which the rule should be applied and the learner is asked to perform a task without being told to follow or use a particular rule.

Problem-solving learning includes the categories of analysis, synthesis and evaluation as described in Bloom's *Taxonomy*. This is a category of specific learning and not some broad general characteristic of individuals. It would be inappropriate to think of a practitioner or any person as, 'a good problem-solver.' This is because the capability to solve problems would enable a person to solve a particular class of problems whenever examples are encountered. Any particular class of problems can be described explicitly, but how to solve them cannot be stated explicitly. For example, a practitioner may be able to analyze a particular set of behaviours for their treatment implications but not be able to analyze a different set of behaviours. Or a practitioner may be able to judge the appropriateness of treatment plans for one class of clients but not for others. Most people cannot learn to solve a class of problems by being told how to solve them or having the problem-solving process explained to them. While those approaches may be appropriate for the most capable learners, they are significantly inadequate for most. Appropriate instruction involves ensuring that any subordinate learnings have already occurred and then presenting an example of the class of problems to the learner while then providing learning guidance while the learner works to solve the particular example. This cycle will need to be repeated with as many examples as the learners require to achieve proficiency in problem-solving.

The example training model

In a training programme for professional practitioners the curriculum will usually contain three phases that can be considered differently as phases of training. First is the foundational knowledge (verbal information) and concepts that are particular to the job or field. There may also be included in this foundational area some of the rules and regulations particular to the field that practitioners will be expected to apply in their work. Next will be the development of skills that people might be expected to apply in their work but which will only be taught to a level that is possible within a training context. Finally, there is the actual application of the new learnings within their own job and working situation. Each of these phases can be treated differently in the training model. However the particular types of learning will need to be considered carefully and taken into account in designing and implementing the training within each phase. For example, if verbal information concepts and rules are all included in the foundational phase of the training, then the instruction for the concepts and rules would need to ensure that they are treated as intellectual skills and not allowed to be addressed as verbal information.

The training model developed for SHB practitioners follows this general framework of three phases. For this occupational training course the first phase is foundational and is intended to introduce learners to their subject area. The underpinning knowledge, concepts, contextual principles, and recommended approaches for working with the client group and the standards for high quality services are addressed through instructional means that allow trainees to work outside of a training setting using highly structured materials that can be addressed by individual learners in their own time and place. Nevertheless, all of the concepts, principles and approaches require additional treatment to ensure that they are learned as intellectual skills rather than as verbal information. This instruction occurs in the second and third phases of the overall model.

One key design standard for this first phase of the model is to frame all of the learnings in the context in which they will be applied in their own work and then addressed further in the other phases of the model. Another standard is to ensure that the instruction does not encourage incorrect learning or encourage continued use of previously learned misconceptions, alternate conceptions or incorrect learnings. That standard requires giving careful attention to the type of learning intended, the general standards for instruction for that particular type of learning, and strict attention to serving each of the nine functions of instruction in ways that are appropriate for the intended learning. When it is not feasible to serve all nine functions within this first phase of the model, then the functions being served set the stage for the remainder of the instruction to come in subsequent phases. Printed materials to be studied and interactive CD-based presentations comprise most of this phase. Assessment of learning during this first phase of the model is in the form of standard pencil-and-paper task responses or interactive responses to the CD-based materials. However, all performances must match the standards for the type of learning that is intended.

The second phase of the course provides training for general professional skills, developing them as far as possible within the training context. Most of the instruction is designed around either specific tasks to be performed in the workplace, such as initial assessment of client conditions and causal structures, or general personal and professional skills, such as listening for intentions or negotiation. Within this phase, most of the final learning intentions will be problem-solving across the range of analysis, synthesis and evaluation. Thus, most of the instruction includes a variety of tasks assigned to the trainees that represent the classes of problems that they are learning to solve. Since this is done in a training context, these problems are representative of ones they might be expected to address in their own jobs. In other words, much of the instruction is simulation of real-job tasks. Each of these simulations is preceded by focused instruction to ensure that all of the concepts, rules and problem-solving that are subordinate to the intended learning for the particular simulation are addressed at least to the level that they are needed to engage effectively and efficiently in work to learn the new capability.

Of course, as with most learning, one example will not be enough for most trainees to acquire the new skill. Thus, the simulation is repeated with new examples of the class of problems for as many times as needed to develop the skill to a level that is reasonable within the training context. The simulations are designed with a variety of appropriate examples so that participants and their trainers are confident that the core set of capabilities has been learned to the standard acceptable for clinical practice which they learned in phase one.

Preparation for the final phase of the training is made during this second phase by setting the stage for serving the ninth function – extending and transferring the learning to the actual work context. Learning assessment in the second phase is done primarily by focusing on the terminal objectives represented by the simulations. Each simulation reflects a particular class of problems and performance on the examples illustrates the degree of mastery of the skill represented by the simulations. The subordinate concepts, rules and problem-solving for these terminal objectives are assessed informally within the learning context and used primarily as formative evaluation to determine readiness for engaging in the simulated experiences linked to the terminal objectives.

The third phase of the course can be thought of as supervised clinical practice in the work settings of the participants to provide further experience in using the foundational knowledge and skills acquired in phases one and two of the training. In this third phase, professional practices to be used with assigned cases are planned by the professional practitioner with supervision by the trainer, then implemented by the practitioner, and later reviewed with the trainer. This cycle continues with other cases as needed until mastery and confidence appropriate for the continued use of the new learning in ongoing work are achieved.

Ideally, this phase of the training would be organised differently. The trainer and the practitioner would work together to review the case and the learnings that applied to the new practice and then plan the work that would be done by the practitioner using the new learnings in the next working session. Then, during the working session the trainer would serve as an observer without participating in the delivery of the service. Afterward, the trainer and the practitioner would review the practice considering what had been planned, what actually was done, the reasons why changes may have been made from planned, the quality of implementation, how the practice might have been different if certain events had occurred differently or conditions might have been different, the implications for next service with this client, and implications for using this practice

with another client. This cycle would continue until the skill use meets the expectations of both trainer and practitioner.

However, observation by the trainer or an outsider is not appropriate for these SHB practitioners for a variety of privacy reasons. Thus, an approach that approximates the ideal is used. In this approach, the trainer and the practitioner review the case as described above taking into account any issues that are reasonable within the privacy standards and plan the work by the practitioner. They also plan a review session including questions they will address during the review. Following planning, the practitioner provides the service to the client. At a time and place after the service delivery the practitioner and trainer review the practice raising and addressing the questions listed above for the ideal case.

An object of this 'plan – do – review' process is to prepare the practitioners to be skilful in their planning and work and also be reflective within practice and reflective following practice. In other words, they can continue to be effective and efficient in their application of problem-solving skills and they can also continue to improve as a result of their ongoing reflection.

Assessment of performance within this third phase of training is by using three approaches. First, the trainer makes judgments of the planned practices using the standards in training. Next, the quality of practices used is judged insofar as it is revealed in the reviews. Finally, the quality of the reflections on practice is judged as it is revealed in the review. All of these judgments are made using the rubrics that were used during simulated training. If a more objective judgment of the quality of clinical practice is needed, a specialist from outside the training team might serve as the person who is leading and guiding the post-practice review.

Summary

In this chapter I have tried to make a case that training is here to stay in most organisations but has many issues associated with it which are linked to quality of training. Among these are the common failure of job-related training to take into account the variety of organisation and context factors that are known to affect job performance, the degree to which training results in improved performance, and the general requirement that training reflect the best principles from instructional design. In making this case I have tried to demonstrate that in order for training to improve performance, it must be extended to include application of skills in the workplace. I believe that it cannot stop at the training site door.

Furthermore, I have synthesised the general standards for instructional design with a particular focus on the types of learning that are likely to be the target for job-related training. Each of these types of learning has a particular form of instruction and assessment that is essential for effective and efficient acquisition of the level of capability required. The standards for this instruction provides a powerful framework for determining the kind of training that is required for the learning that is intended. By extending the standards to include the nine functions of instruction, along with the interpretation of the ninth function – providing for a retention and transfer – it can be seen clearly that if we actually want people to improve the quality of their job performance, then we must extend the instruction into the actual application in a work setting by using an approach similar to the model developed for SHB practitioners.

References

Bodenheimer, T. (1999) The American Health Care System; The Movement for Improved Quality in Health Care. *N Engl J Med*, 340, 488–92.

Bloom, B.S. et al. (1956) *Taxonomy of Educational Objectives: Handbook 1.Cognitive Domain*. New York: Mckay.

Bunch, K.J. (2007) Training Failure as a Consequence of Organizational Culture *Human Resource Development Review*, 6: 2, 142–63.

Caudron, S. (2002, June) Just Say No to Training Fads. *Personnel Management*, 56, 38–44.

Dall'Alba, G. (2009) Learning Professional Ways of Being: Ambiguities of Becoming. *Educational Phiosophy and Theory*. 1.

Davies, H., Nutley, S. and Walter, I. (2008) Why 'Knowledge Transfer' is Misconceived for Applied Social Research. *Journal of Health Services Research and Policy*. 13, 188–90.

De Laat, E.H. et al. (2006) Implementation of a New Policy Results in a Decrease of Pressure Ulcer Frequency. *International Journal of Quality Health Care*, 18: 2, 107–12.

DHSSPS (2006) Our *Children and Young People: Our Responsibility.* Northern Ireland: Social Services Inspectorate.

Dobbins, M. et al. (2007) Information Transfer: What do Decision-Makers Want and Need from Researchers? *Implementation Science*, 2: 20.

Estabrooks, C., Midodzi,W., Cummings,G. et al. (2007) Predicting Research Use in Nursing Organisations. *Nursing Research*, 56: 457–523.

Gagné, R. (1965) *The Conditions of Learning.* New York: Holt, Rinehart and Winston.

Gagné, R. and Driscoll, M. (1988) *Essentials of Learning for Instruction.* 2nd Edn. Englewood Cliffs, NJ: Prentice-Hall.

Gagné, R., Briggs, L. and Wager, W. (1992) *Principles of Instructional Design*. 4th edn. Fort Worth, TX: HBJ College Publishers.

Gagné, R.M. and Medsker, K.L. (1996) *The Conditions of Learning: Training Applications.* Fort Worth, TX: Harcourt Brace.

Grol, R. and Grimshaw, J. (2003) From Best Evidence to Best Practice: Effective Implementation of Change in Patients' Care. *Lancet*, 362: 9391, 1225–30.

Hackett, S., Masson, H. and Phillips, S. (2004) *Mapping and Exploring Services for Young People who have Sexually Abused Others: Final Report.* A two-year research project funded by Youth Justice Board, NSPCC and NOTA. Durham: University of Durham.

Halfens, R, and Van Linghe, R. (2003) Disseminatie en implementatie van kennis (Dissemination and implementation of knowledge) In Verpleging en verzorging (State of the art studies) Utrecht, The Netherlands: LEVV.

Hayes, A.E. (2007) *Types and Conditions of Learning.* Class Notes EDN 301 Instructional Design and Evaluation, University of North Carolina.

Holleman, G. et al. (2006) Promotion of Evidenced-Based Practice by Professional Nursing Associations: Literature Review. *Journal of Advanced Nursing*, 53, 702–9.

Kitson A.L. et al. (2008) Evaluating the Successful Implementation of Evidence into Practice Using the PARIHS Framework: Theoretical and Practical Challenges. *Implementation Science*, 3: 1.

Kontos, P.C. and Poland, B.D. (2009) Mapping New Theoretical and Methodological Terrain for Knowledge Translation: Contributions from Critical Realism and the Arts. *Implementation Science*, 4: 1.

Kraiger, K., Mclinden, D. and Casper, W.J. (2004) Collaborative Planning For Training Impact. *Human Resource Management*, 43: 4, 337–51.

Masson, H. and Hackett, S. (2003) A Decade on from the NCH Report (1992): Adolescent Sexual Aggression, Policy and Service Delivery across the UK and Republic of Ireland. *Journal of Sexual Aggression*, 9: 2, 1–22.

Meijer, J.M.M. et al. (2007) Assessing the Relationships Between Contextual Factors and Research Utilisation in Nursing: Systematic Literature Review. *Journal of Advanced Nursing*, 55: 5, 622–35.

Mykhalovskiy, E. and Weir, L. (2004) The Problem of Evidence-Based Medicine: Directions for Social Science. *Social Science and Medicine*, 59: 5, 1059–69.

NCH (1992) *The report of the Committee of Enquiry into Children and Young People who Sexually Abuse Other Children.* London: HMSO.

Ploeg, J. et al. (2007) Factors Influencing Best Practice Implementation: Lessons Learned from Administrators, Nursing Staff, and Project Leaders. *World Views on Evidence-Based Nursing*, 4, 210–19.

Pittet, D. et al. (2000) Effectiveness of a Hospital-Wide Programme to Improve Compliance with Hand Hygiene. Infection Control Programme. *Lancet*, 356: 9238, 1307–12.

Reigeluth, C. and Carr-Chellman, A. (2009) *Instructional Design Theories and Models: Building a Common Knowledge Base.* Volume 111. New York and London: Routledge.

Ruona, W.E.A., Lynham, S.A. and Chermack, T.J. (2003) Insights on Emerging Trends and the Future of Human Resource Development. *Advances in Developing Human Resources*, 5, 272–82.

Salas, E. et al. (1999) Training in Organizations: Myths, Misconceptions and Mistaken Assumptions. *Res Pers Hum Resour Manag*, 17: 123–61.

Salas, E. and Cannon-Bowers, J.A. (2001) The Science of Training: A Decade of Progress. *Annual Review of Psychology*, 52, 471–99.

Tharenou, P., Saks, A. and Moore, C. (2007) A Review and Critique of Research on Training and Organizational-Level Outcomes. *Human Resource Management Review*, 17: 3, 251–73.

Van Achterberg, T., Holleman, G., Van de Van, M., Grypdonck, M.H., Eliens, A. and Van Vilet, M. (2006) Promoting Evidence Based Practice: The Roles and Activities of Professional Nurses' Associations. *Journal of Advanced Nursing*, 53, 605–12.

Van Achterberg, T., Schoonhoven, L. and Grol, R. (2008) Nursing Implementation Science: How Evidence-Based Nursing Requires Evidence-Based Implementation. *Journal of Nursing Scholarship*, 40: 4, 302–10.

Van Woerkom, C. (1990) *Voorlichting als beleidsinstrument (education as a policy tool) Inaugurale rede,* universiteit Wageningen: Wageningen.

Vermeulen, H., Meents, N. and Ubbink, D. (2007) Nuchterekijk op de nuchtere maag: Onderzoek naar kennis nuchterbeleid voor OK. [Sober views on the empty stomach: A study on knowledge of fasting regimens prior to surgery], *Nursing*, 14, 20–1.

Wright, P. and Geroy, G.D. (2001) Changing the Mindset: The Training Myth and the Need for World-Class Performance. *International Journal of Human Resource Management*, 12: 4, 586–600.

Yiasouma, K. (2007) *Children at Risk/Risky Children.* DHSSPS/NIO.

CHAPTER 10

Embracing Diversity – Risk Management and Risk Reduction: A Practice Model for Children and Young People and the Systems Around Them

Ann Brady and Christine McCarlie

Introduction

Working with children and young people with problematic sexual behaviours offers many challenges to practitioners with diversity emerging as a key theme. Given the wide-ranging problem base, we have moved away from a singular assessment tool or approach and have developed an holistic model to integrate risk management, assessment and intervention.

This chapter describes a practice model drawing from work being undertaken by the authors who are currently writing a manual for managers and practitioners on risk management, assessment and intervention. The manual has integrated promising findings from research, synthesised key messages and combined this with clinical judgement to produce an accessible format that is responsive to the individual needs and circumstances of children, young people and their families. By using a wide range of evidence and approaches with a strong influence on child development the model taken from the manual can be applied to all children and young people presenting with sexual behaviour problems.

The core outcomes of our intervention are for young people to manage their own risk and meet their needs in healthier, safer, and more personally satisfying ways (Ward, 2002). While our assessments identify pathways into problem sexual behaviour, they also identify alternative pathways into a better lifestyle. This involves young people working on specific goals to meet their needs and improve their overall well-being. Following the assessment, each young person will have a Wellbeing Plan based on the following outcomes: being healthy; having people in my life; having a purpose and making a difference; being my own person; and having fun and achieving (GMAP, 2008). While these plans are strongly associated with the development of strengths they also link to risk management and the child or young person's growing capacity to

manage their own risk as they progress through a programme of work.

A systems approach

The systems around the young person have crucial roles to play in both managing their risk and in risk reduction through working with the young person to facilitate their goal development. It is essential therefore, that all of the systems involved have clarity about risk, responsibility and their respective roles and tasks; that the right people from within the different systems are meeting on a regular basis to review the ongoing manageability of risk.

Risk

To ensure that we are viewing risk as fluid and dynamic we need to understand the ever-changing internal and external factors that will be impacting on it. This naturally leads us to explore factors within the young person as well as the systems around them. It ensures that risk is understood as a tangible concept that workers can have a positive impact on.

The level of risk will vary considerably within the population of children and young people. Some may present a serious risk requiring long term interventions and high levels of supervision, while the behaviour of others may be easily redirected and changed over a shorter period of time. The practice model identifies a formal risk management process for monitoring, evaluating and managing risk while assessments and interventions are underway.

Responsibility

While the overall aim of intervention is for the young person to be able to take responsibility for managing their own risk, given the impact of trauma on many of their lives (Lyons-Ruth, 1996) it is unlikely that in the early stages of intervention many young people would have the capacity or internal resources to be able to take responsibility for managing their own risk. They have to learn this through a process of risk reduction involving building up strengths, gaining insights and learning new skills which have to be evidenced in a range of settings. For some young people this may involve work on their victimisation (Creeden, 2009). During the early stages of intervention the responsibility for risk management therefore lies mainly with the adult systems. Within this practice model the early stages of intervention often involves intensive work both within and by the systems reflecting this level of responsibility. This stance on risk and responsibility necessitates joining with the adults involved, leading to a shared consensus of viewing risk and responsibility in this way.

This is a dynamic process. As the young person is engaging in work developing insights and strengths they become more able to accept varying levels of responsibility for managing their own behaviours and risk.

The systems

In this chapter 'systems' refer to the significant people in the young person's life who will impact on risk eg parents, carers, teachers, peers. In recent years there has been an impressive body of research supporting systemic interventions (Borduin et al., 1990) and our model is strongly influenced by this approach. We consider how all the systems impact on the young person making risk more or less manageable. In practice this means considering how these systems interact with each other and with the young person on a day to day basis. By being this explicit about the impact that the systems have on risk, we naturally increase the demands and the responsibility being placed on the systems. We also recognise the potential impact that the systems can have on assisting in the skills development of young people. This requires an assessment of the systems on their capacity to both manage risk and facilitate change.

The practice model

The overall purpose of our intervention is to identify skills, strengths, concerns and areas of need within the young person and the systems in order to help them move through a process of

change and manage risk effectively. We look at this in four phases where the expectations, roles and tasks of everyone involved are clearly identified.

We recognise that the extent we can engage the young person and each system in this process will vary enormously depending on each individual's circumstance. For a significant minority of young people this process may be complex and slow requiring a substantial focus on the systems in managing risk until the young person can engage on a programme of work that will reduce risk and allow them to move through the phases.

The practice model (Figure 10.1) offers a means to hold this process and facilitates two key practice challenges:

- effective systemic work
- assessments and intervention informing risk management in an ongoing responsive way.

In the remainder of the chapter there are condensed versions of this figure with some of the boxes highlighted to illustrate which parts of Figure 10.1 are being discussed. Please refer back to Figure 10.1 at each occasion.

Effective systemic working

This model promotes a systemic approach by:

- recognising the significance and impact of the systems on risk
- identifying and targeting patterns of behaviour within and between the systems that may be maintaining the behaviours
- recognising that young people often have multiple and complex needs and that changing their behaviour often requires services of more than one agency
- recognising that effective risk management requires the involvement of all of the systems around the young person

There are considerable challenges in working effectively on an intra/inter agency level. An additional challenge is for workers to engage in a collaborative approach while simultaneously assessing the various systems involved with a young person and the attention and energy the systems require is recognised throughout the intervention process. The practice model helps workers with this, highlighting that in the initial stages of intervention work is mostly being undertaken with the systems through assessment planning meetings, group consultations and safety plans being completed.

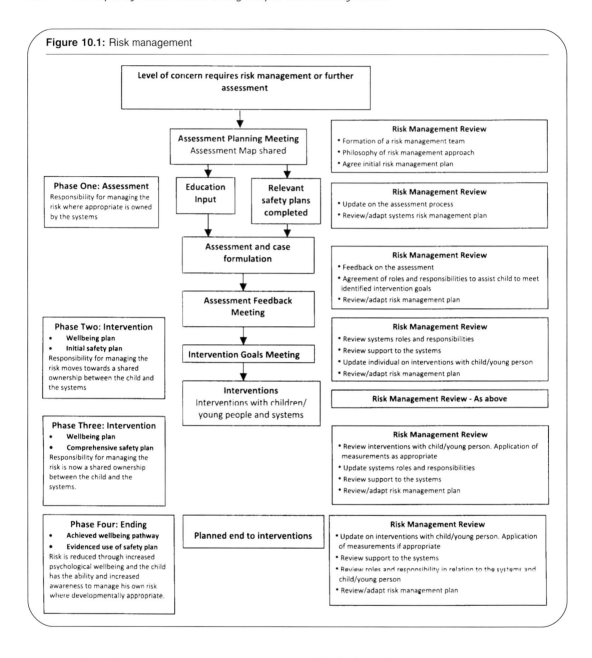

Figure 10.1: Risk management

Integrating risk management with intervention

Recent reports (HMIC and SWIA, Dec 2005) have highlighted the need for risk management to be informed by assessment and intervention and the practice model ensures this integration. In our model risk management is central, resulting in a process whereby there is a dynamic and responsive approach to risk management from beginning to end of our interventions.

To facilitate this integration a risk management team is established for every young person requiring risk management. Team membership would be relevant adults working with the young person but may also include others not directly involved eg police, head teacher, clinical manager.

This team, normally led by social work, should meet regularly throughout the intervention process to manage, evaluate and monitor risk while work is being undertaken with the young person and the systems. These risk management

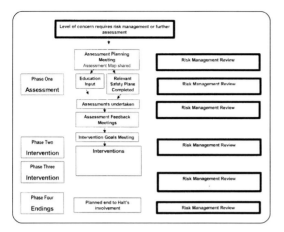

meetings/reviews provide the forum for multi agency discussion and decision-making in key areas such as safety plans, roles and tasks, third party disclosures and communication between the systems.

The Risk Management Review process can be applied in a variety of systems and procedures such as MAPPA meetings, Child Protection/Vulnerable Young Persons meetings etc. A number of authorities in Scotland have a Risk Management Protocol (McCarlie, 2007) which uses this approach to risk management.

The following describes the phases and the key components of the model to support this approach.

Phase One: Risk management and assessment

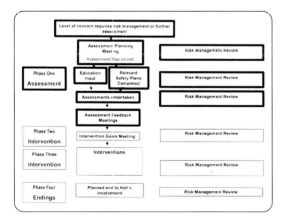

The main focus is on risk management and the systems take on most of the responsibility for this. The systems and the young person are engaged in the assessment process while the systems are also engaging in risk management activities.

Tasks:

- Establish a risk management team and risk management meetings.
- Complete initial safety plans (see Appendix 1).
- Identify the relevant areas to assess (assessment map).
- Engage the young person and the systems in the assessment process to determine needs, level of risk and capacity for risk management.
- Introduce the dual concept of risk management and improved well-being to young person in developmentally appropriate way.
- Identify and assess how the different parts of the systems are impacting on risk, making it more or less manageable.
- Use formal risk tool where appropriate eg AIM2.
- Identify specific areas for interventions within the relevant systems to impact positively on the management of risk.
- Within the assessment identify and formulate intervention goals for the child/young person to take them on their pathways to increased well-being and hence risk reduction.
- Identify work to be undertaken with the systems to enhance goal development/risk reduction.

As seen by the above, considerable emphasis is placed on the systems during this phase. Below, processes are identified that contribute to joining with the systems, ensuring an ongoing understanding of their respective roles and tasks in risk management and reduction and ensuring that their needs for support/education/ information are being attended to.

Initial risk management meeting

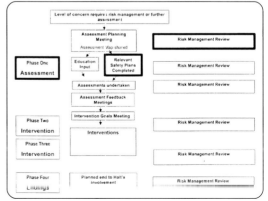

The initial risk management meeting promotes an integrated approach by:

- agreeing membership of the team
- sharing the philosophy underpinning risk management
- agreeing on terminology and definitions
- agreeing immediate risk management measures that need to be put in place
- agreeing the completion of relevant safety plan (see appendix 1)
- formalising a risk management plan
- formalising the ongoing assessment process

In our practice we have a centralised folder where all multi agency risk management activities, minutes of risk management meetings and safety plans are held. These are dynamic and responsive to the ever-changing nature of risk. As more information is gathered risk management strategies become more individualised.

Assessment mapping

Table 10.1 in Appendix 3 provides a general overview of some of the areas that may be covered in an assessment. More details for workers, including the theoretical and research based perspectives are provided on all of these areas in the manual.

It is important to note that the assessment process will be different in each case. This will be dependent on a number of factors related to the young person, for example the age and stage of development, the impact of legal processes and varying factors in their environment, for example

the extent to which the living environment can be engaged may vary from a young person residing in their own tenancy to a young child in foster care.

In planning the assessment workers need to take into account each individual's circumstances and identify the systems that need to be directly involved and the specific areas that need to be explored. Within this systemic approach the above becomes an assessment map offering clarity about the areas that will be covered with which parts of the systems, the purpose of this and why this level of service is required. Assessment mapping is a useful tool to assist workers through this complex process. The following shows examples of individualised assessment maps.

Case Study One

John is seven years old. He has been displaying reactive sexual behaviours within the school. There have been reports of sexual behaviours from age three. Parents have not been cooperating with the department and report no sexual behaviour within the home. There are child protection concerns. See Figure 10.2.

Case Study Two

Jack is a 14 year old boy currently living in a residential unit. He has exhibited a range of concerning sexual behaviours since arriving in the unit a year ago and has recently been found guilty of sexual assault. Jack has respite with carers once a month. See Figure 10.3.

Figure 10.2: John's assessment map

Systems Caring Environment; Family	Systems School	Child
1. Sexual Behaviour; capacity to manage risk 2. Parent and child history; Pathways 3. Sexual socialization; Pathways 4. Family functioning; factors contributing to the maintenance of behaviours, capacity to manage risk 5. Parent view of child	1. Sexual Behaviours; risk awareness and risk management 2. Staff and Structure; factors contributing to the maintenance of behaviours, capacity to manage risk 3. Individual work with child; capacity to join with child in implementing safety plan, capacity to meet needs of John	4. Sexual Behaviours; capacity to contribute to a safety plan. (information not necessarily collated through direct work with child)

Figure 10.3:   Jack's assessment map

Systems Caring Environment; Residential School	Systems Caring Environment; Respite carer	Systems School	Child
S1 Sexual Behaviour; capacity to manage risk **S2** Young Person's History; capacity to consider impact and meaning of life experiences on young persons present functioning; risk management capacity to assist young person address treatment goals. **S3** Sexual socialization; relevant issues within present environment; pathways **S4** Unit functioning; factors contributing to the pathway/maintenance of behaviours, capacity to manage risk **S5** Staff view of child/young person's present level of functioning; risk analysis **S6** Organisational Context	**S1** Sexual Behaviour; capacity to manage risk **S2** Family functioning; factors contributing to the maintenance of behaviours, capacity to manage risk	**S1** Sexual Behaviours; risk awareness and risk management **S2** Staff and Structure; factors contributing to the maintenance of behaviours, capacity to manage risk **S3** Individual work with child; capacity to join with child in implementing safety plan, capacity to meet needs of Jack	**S1** Assessment Foundation **S2** The child/young person's present level of functioning; **S3** Pathways **S4** Sexual behaviours

Assessment planning meeting

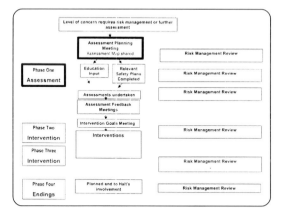

Within the Assessment planning meeting the main areas to cover are:

- sharing with the systems the assessment map; what will be asked of them in the assessment process and why
- allowing an opportunity for different views to be heard in terms level of concern
- identifying outstanding information required
- providing the opportunity to clarify what the child has been told and agree messages we

want them to have in relation to sexual behaviours and the assessment process
- sharing with systems the initial stages of the assessment process; initial home safety plan, group consultation, pre-assessment questionnaires and assessment foundation work
- identifying timescales for the above meetings

This is the first opportunity to join with, engage and motivate the systems in the assessment process. In sharing the assessment map one of the key tasks is to be able to justify why it is necessary for the systems to undergo an assessment process alongside the young person and create a sense of partnership as we move into this process. This transparency is essential as it allows the systems users an opportunity to question any areas they are unsure about and provides a foundation for collaborative working as the assessment begins.

Safety plans

During all stages of intervention it is necessary to consider and respond to a number of areas that could contribute to further sexual behaviours occurring. Safety plans are a set of external

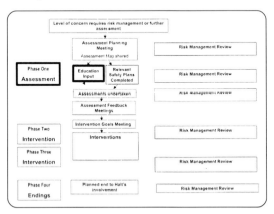

controls and limits designed to help parents, carers, young people and workers manage potential risk situations. Our safety plans have been influenced by the work of Friedrich (2007). These plans should be developed by workers in collaboration with families and other relevant professionals at the beginning of phase one. At first the safety plans will be developed for the significant adults around the child. They should be reviewed and adapted over time and in response to more information, progress or changes in situation. Given the different environments that young people are involved with, it is likely that they will require more than one safety plan, for example home, school, community and residential.

A home safety plan may include, but is not limited to, the following elements:

- level of supervision required at different times in the day and night
- bedrooms and sleeping arrangements
- access to multimedia
- privacy and dress code
- sexual dynamics within the family
- physical interactions
- specific responsibilities the child/young person has in each environment

See Appendix 1 for an example of a safety plan. It is important that these plans are informed by the guidance notes attached to them. The safety plans reflect that for some families and other systems considerable work may have to be undertaken to explore and address sexual dynamics that may contribute to risk of further behaviours happening. Exploring sex and sexuality with families takes time and sensitivity and would be part of an ongoing assessment.

As the young person moves through the

intervention process, their capacity to take more responsibility for managing their risk should increase dependent on their capacity to discuss their behaviour and risk in a meaningful way. Post assessment is a common period for an initial safety plan to be completed with them. This will detail the risk management strategies that the worker and the young person have identified in the assessment process. It is expected that the young person's plan will evolve and gain depth as they move through the intervention process. The evolving plan is shared in the risk management reviews.

A young person's safety plan may include:

- process involved in the behaviour
- external/internal triggers
- what to do when aware of trigger
- who to go to for help
- what to say to get help

Several factors will assist in the implementation, reviewing, and adjusting of the safety plans and these should be formally reviewed at risk management reviews. There may however be occasions where a young person's behaviours will require the immediate adjustment to the safety plans. In such cases the changes made should be endorsed at the following risk management review.

Group consultation

The dual role of gathering and giving information during the assessment is important, therefore at the beginning of the assessment process an extended meeting is held in order to facilitate:

- sharing information; different systems provide different dimensions of a young person to inform initial hypotheses in relation to pathways, needs being met by the behaviour and present functioning

- providing education about what we know about potential pathways and types of behaviour. This also forms a foundation for further work in the assessment, for example we begin to consider the impact and meaning of a child's experiences. Later in the assessment we explore how the carer has engaged in this process and what sense of the information has been made
- reaching an initial consensus regarding sexual behaviour
- sharing views of the child/young person; promoting a view of the child as a child first who also has problematic sexual behaviours
- forming the basis of team around a young person for future work; effective risk management.

It is recognised that different systems will need different considerations; for example, for some caring environments there may be significant impact issues and/or it may be too exposing to consider in a group setting a child's history. Where it is not appropriate to facilitate a group consultation the educative input is threaded through the assessment and risk management review meetings provide the opportunity to build consensus and team identity.

Phase One: Assessment and case formulation

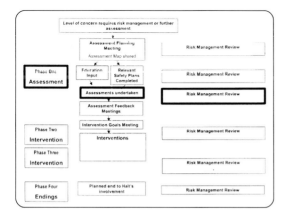

The assessment process builds up a broad based understanding of the child/young person and the systems around them. The information gathered in the assessment is pulled together to construct a case formulation. This informs risk analysis, risk management and risk reduction. This takes into account all the different strands of the assessment, including internal and external static and dynamic strengths and concerns within all the areas explored.

Assessment feedback and risk management review

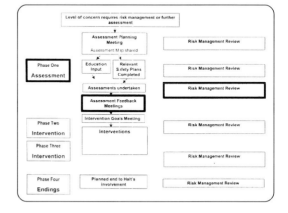

In practice the assessment feedback is incorporated into a risk management review meeting. Here the assessment report is shared and in particular the meeting considers the risk analysis. As well as reaching a consensus about risk, the risk analysis provides information to refine the risk management plan and ratify, if appropriate, the young person's initial safety plan. Consideration should be given to how to involve the young person in this process. It may be appropriate that they attend some of the meeting particularly if they have been able to contribute to a safety plan.

Intervention goals

The assessment process will have identified intervention goals for the young person to reduce their risk and improve their overall well-being. While goal attainment is often considered in the context of one to one intervention, our approach recognises that young people learn many of the skills required of them through their ongoing life experiences. This means opening up opportunities in their lives for them to develop, test and maintain these skills. Intervention goals are therefore best achieved through a combination of one to one interventions and skills training being undertaken with them by the

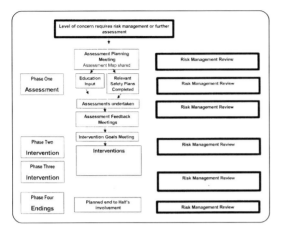

Phase Two and Three: Risk management and intervention

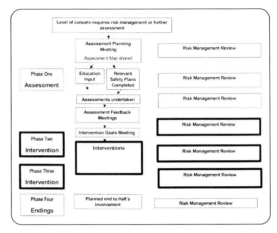

significant systems around them. Because of the multi tasks of the systems and the level of input being required of them to facilitate goals, it is recommended that a separate meeting is convened to look specifically at goal development. In this meeting the intervention goals are discussed in depth. Where possible links are made to what potential needs were being met by the sexual behaviours and how to get these needs met differently, bringing in the roles of all of the systems.

Areas to consider in this meeting are:

- identifying needs being met by behaviours
- promoting understanding/consennsus regarding intervention goals as pathway to young person's increased well-being
- prioritising goals
- identifying relevant systems to undertake goals and what support is needed to enable the systems to undertake the work
- reviewing methods to evaluate progress

The young person may or may not attend all of this meeting but it is important that they are involved when sharing the hypothesis about needs being met by behaviours and intervention goals to address this. In addition it is important that they have an understanding of how their well-being plan links to the interventions being undertaken with them, their accomplishments within this and their capacity to move towards being able to manage their risk. This can be a motivational meeting for the young person as well as promoting a collaborative strengths-based approach.

Whilst intervention is ongoing risk management and the effectiveness of interventions are reviewed within risk management reviews. These meetings will generally occur every 8–12 weeks although can be recalled at any time if required to respond to risk management issues.

During Phases Two and Three young people are acquiring strengths and learning the skills required of them through a combination of one to one interventions, structured work being undertaken within their systems and ongoing coaching/reflection/therapeutic messages. Their achievements are being recorded in their well-being plans.

In recognition of the demands being placed on the systems for goal facilitation it is important that a considerable emphasis is given to reviewing the systems roles and responsibilities and the effectiveness of their interventions. It is therefore recommended that this is given priority in the risk management review meetings and that in every third meeting the child/young person's progress in meeting their goals is reviewed. The focus for risk management reviews are:

- reviewing systems roles and responsibilities and any ongoing supports they may require
- reviewing the young person's progress
- reviewing and adapting safety plans and any other risk management activities that may be required.

In Phase Two the systems are involved in risk management and facilitating the young person's goals through a combination of intervention. Here the tasks are to:

- regularly review risk management and safety plans through ongoing work as well as in risk management meetings.
- help them take responsibility for past behaviours.
- explore processes involved in problem sexual behaviours and meaning of behaviours for the young person, and reach a shared understanding about this within the systems.
- develop and rehearse strategies for managing risk with the young person and the environment. This will include the young person's commitment to the beginnings of their safety plan.
- work with the child/young person on goals to support increased well-being.
- maintain the young person's motivation to engage in work by ensuring that they are understanding and gaining from the process.
- celebrate their successes using their well-being plans as a tool to aid this.
- maximise the levels of support and intervention provided by the systems.

By the end of this stage the young person will have been working on areas of skills development and learning how to get their needs met in healthier and more fulfilling ways. When they are able to engage in specific work on their sexual behaviours it allows for a more meaningful discussion to take place with them about their risk. This indicates that they can begin to take some responsibility for risk management therefore allows for the beginnings of their safety plans to be developed. At this stage risk management strategies are introduced and rehearsed by the child and the system. This determines their ability to move to Phase Three where the concept of risk becomes much more meaningful to them and they are becoming more responsive to interventions.

In Phase Three the responsibility for managing risk is now shared between the young person and the systems. Although risk management activity is still required, risk is now also being substantially reduced by the young person's engagement in work on their goals to facilitate their overall well-being.

Tasks:

- Regularly review risk management and safety plans through ongoing work and risk management meetings.
- Engage the young person in work towards achieving all of their intervention goals.

- The systems are now increasing and decreasing external controls from an informed perspective, knowing the factors that are impacting on the manageability of risk.
- The young person's progress is being evidenced in their well-being plan.

In Phases Two and Three intensive work is being undertaken with the young person by all the appropriate systems. However in Phase Three the young person is engaging on a higher level. The expectations of them in managing their risk are different from Phase One and Two. In Phase Three they are much more able to demonstrate in their day to day living that they are attempting to apply their learning, that they are benefiting from this in terms of improved outcomes and they are better able to manage their risk. In particular it is anticipated that they are able to do the following:

- engage in discussions about their emotions and feelings and how this might impact on risk.
- accept the fluid nature of the increase and decrease of external controls and their own internal processes.
- use the environment proactively to help them deal with challenging situations and emotions.
- evidence improvements in significant areas of their functioning.
- continue to use situations as learning processes.
- accept the guidance and controls of their environment.

During Phases Two and three young people are given well-being booklets where their achievements under the well-being section are recorded.

It is anticipated that within stage three the wording of these achievements will be changing to reflect that over time the young person has sustained significant improvements/skills in specific areas of their functioning and that their overall well-being is significantly improved.

In phase three, because they now have enough skills, capacities and insights to be able to be more actively involved in managing their own risk, they will have more detailed safety plans and more responsibility for keeping to these.

Appendix 2 highlights the interface between the young person's well-being pathway, their intervention goals and their growing capacity to manage their risk as interventions assist in their goal development.

Phase Four: Risk management and disengagement

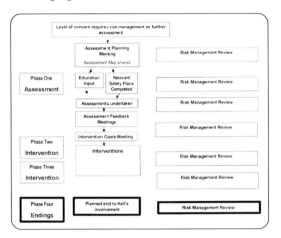

In this phase the focus is on disengagement and the risk management review considers the following:

- final review of interventions with child/young person
- completion of final risk assessment/application of measurements if appropriate
- review support to the systems
- review roles and responsibility in relation to the systems and child/young person
- review/adapt risk management plan.

In this phase it is important to use the identified individual intervention goals to determine outcome effectiveness. This includes the extent to which the young person can take responsibility for managing their own risk.

It would be expected that the achievement of their goals (a combination of strengths, skills and insights) would be evidenced in different settings. Where this is the case, it should be anticipated that risk is now reduced and the young person has the ability and increased strengths and awareness to manage their own risk where developmentally appropriate. Here the workers tasks are to:

- Complete the young person's well-being plan.
- Provide ongoing monitoring of the young person's ability to manage risk.
- Ensure that the systems will provide additional short-term supports as needed.
- Prepare for ending and disengagement from any focused intervention.

Inevitably the Fourth Phase is the shortest one. Essential to the effectiveness of the overall process however, is the need to consider how to maintain the young person in the longer term. While they will not at this stage be requiring intensive intervention on their behaviour, they may still need ongoing support and monitoring by significant systems around them. Some young people also may need to revise their strategies as they move through different developmental stages where the impact of their past experiences may be affecting them in new and sometimes difficult ways.

This chapter has extracted the practice model from the manual the authors are writing. The model provides an overall approach and within this several structures are identified to ensure the effectiveness and integration of risk management, assessment and intervention. Its benefits are:

- It can be applied to all children and young people with a range of concerning sexual behaviours who require a risk management approach recognising the individuality of each child and their circumstances.
- It takes managers and workers through a step-by-step process from beginning to end of the intervention process. This is easy to understand and provides a real clarity of respective roles and tasks in addition to providing a clarity about what we can expect from the systems and the child.
- It capitalises on the roles of all of the systems in risk management and risk reduction and in so doing, the systems are all accountable and share in the responsibility for both these tasks.
- It identifies risk management activity that can be undertaken no matter where the child is in the process, for example, where there are child protection concerns and we are unable to do direct work with the child or where the legal processes have not yet been resolved, the model provides guidance and tangible tasks that workers can address to improve risk management until the child or young person can actively become involved in work.
- It reflects the fluid and dynamic nature of risk.
- It offers an approach that is holistic, that views the child in their environmental context, bringing together a range of theories and approaches to understand and manage their behaviours.
- It offers tangible goals that enhance the child's overall well-being and which are met through a combination of transparent interventions, one

- to one, structured work and ongoing reflection/coaching.
- Most importantly, it charts a young person's journey as they engage in a therapeutic process to change their behaviours and meet their needs in healthier ways.

This model is evolving as we and other systems engage in the process. The wellness pathway in particular is in its early stages but we are finding that young people are viewing it positively. We hope the transparency and level of detail within the model serve to contribute to a greater understanding of the roles and tasks of all of the systems throughout the intervention process and contribute to improving outcomes for young people with problem sexual behaviours.

References

Borduin, C. et al. (1990) Multisystemic Treatment of Adolescent Sexual Offenders. *International Journal of Offender Therapy and Comparative Criminology*, 34: 105–13.

Creeden, K. (2009) How Trauma and Attachment can impact Neurodevelopment: Informing our Understanding and Treatment of Sexual Behaviour Problems. *Journal of Sexual Aggression*, 15: 3, 261–73.

Friedrich, W.N. (2007) *Children with Sexual Behaviour Problems: Family Based Attachment Focused Therapy.* W.W Norton and Company.

GMAP (2008) *Better Lives training.*

Lyons-Ruth, K. (1996) Attachment Relationships among Children with Aggressive Behaviour Problems: The Role of Disorganised Early Attachment Patterns. *Journal of Consulting and Clinical Psychology*, 64, 64–73. Cited in Howe, D. and Fearney, S. (1999) Disorders of Attachment and Attachment Therapy. *Adoption and Fostering*. 23; 2.

McCarlie, C. (2007) *Risk Management for Children and Young People with Problematic Sexual Behaviour.* Dumfries and Galloway Council.

Scottish Executive (2005) *Review of the Management Arrangements of Colyn Evans.* Fife Constabulary and Fife Council.

SWIA and HNIC (2005) *Review of the Management Arrangements of Colyn Evans by Fife Constabulary and Fife Council.* Scottish Executive.

Ward, T. (2002) Good Lives and the Rehabilitation of Sexual Offenders. in Ward, T., Laws, D.R. and Hudson, S.M. (eds.) *Sexual Deviance: Issues and Controversies.* Thousand Oaks, CA: Sage.

Appendix 1

Home safety plan

Name of child/young person:

Date of birth:

Worker:

Parents/carers

Date safety plan agreed:

Date of review:

The concerns:

What are the concerns? (problem sexual behaviour/access to vulnerable others)

Has this been discussed explicitly with the child/young person?
Yes – What language has been used/what was the reaction?
No – Is there need for this to be done at this stage, if so by whom?

1. Home occupancy

Who lives in the house and what are their ages?

Who are regular visitors to the home who could be in need of protecting? (include frequency of visits)

Does anyone else regularly care for this child/young person in the family home?

2. Bedrooms and sleeping

Who sleeps where in the house?

Rules required for bedroom and sleeping (see Section 2 notes)

Privacy and boundaries

Activity

Dress code

Communication of rules

How is the above communicated to the children? Is any of the above assumed or communicated non-verbally? What are appropriate consequences? Are family meetings necessary?

3. Bathroom/toilet

Rules required about bathroom/toilet activities (see Section 3 notes)

Privacy and boundaries

Activity

Dress code

Communication of rules

How are any rules communicated to the children? Is any of the above assumed or communicated non-verbally? What are appropriate consequences? Are family meetings necessary?

4. Play and other activities in the family home

Rules required for play/other activities (see Section 4 notes)

Activities:

New technologies

Communication of rules

How are any rules communicated to the children? Is any of the above assumed or communicated non-verbally? What are appropriate consequences? Are family meetings necessary?

---

5. Play and other activities outside the family home
(See community safety plan)

6. Family nudity

Rules required about nudity (see Section 6 notes)

Privacy/boundaries

Communication of rules

How are any rules communicated to the children? Is any of the above assumed or communicated non-verbally? What are appropriate consequences? Are family meetings necessary?

7. Family sexuality

Rules required about family sexuality (see Section 7 notes)

Privacy/boundaries

Access to sexual images/material

8. Risk management reviews

Are changes needing to be discussed the next risk management review

YES

NO

If yes, please identify changes needing to be discussed below:

Home safety plan: guidance notes

Introduction

During each phase of intervention it is necessary to consider and respond to a number of areas that could contribute to further sexual behaviours occurring. The home safety plan is a set of external controls and limits designed to help parents/carers manage potential risk situations.

The completion of the safety plan should be viewed as an evolving process. The core sections [S.1–S.5] should be completed in the initial stages of the process with the family. However S.6 and S.7 would potentially be completed when a relationship has been established with the parents. The timing of completing these more sensitive sections will be informed by the presenting issues at the point of disclosure.

Risk management is an ongoing process and the plan should be developed and reviewed by workers as the assessment and intervention is ongoing. There are areas of the safety plan that will be explored specifically as part of the assessment; workers are signposted to the relevant assessment section of the manual in the appendix.

Safety plans contribute to the overall risk management plan. They should be ratified and reviewed within risk management meetings.

Section 2. Bedrooms and sleeping

In considering the rules required about bedrooms and sleeping it may be helpful to consider the following:
Privacy and boundaries

- Have problem sexual behaviours occurred in any of the bedrooms in the house and if so which ones and when?
- What are the family routines around going to bed, getting up?
- When do family members tend to go to sleep and how is this known?
- Are there locks on any of the bedroom doors and, if so, are they used, when and why?
- Are siblings allowed in each other's rooms and how is this decided?
- Are children allowed in parent's bedroom and how is this decided?
- Do friends play in/hang out in bedrooms?
- Do other visitors go into bedrooms?
- Are bedroom doors open/closed/locked and how is this decided?
- If guests stay, where do they tend to sleep?

- Proximity of parent's bedroom to other bedrooms?
- Do parents hear what is going on at night in different rooms?

Activity

- Is there access to multimedia in the child/young person's bedrooms or any other bedrooms? If so, are there any rules regarding access?
- How do people spend time in bedrooms?

Dress code

- Is there a rule regarding night attire, dressing and undressing, particularly in room-sharing situations?

Section 3. Bathroom/toilet

In considering the rules required about the bathroom it may be helpful to consider the following:
  Privacy and boundaries

- Have any problem sexual behaviours occurred in the bathroom/toilet?
- If so, when and with whom?
- Has the bathroom/toilet got a working lock?
- Who uses the lock and who doesn't and are there any rules about this?
- Do people share the bathroom at the same time, if so, who tends to do this most often and what are parental views on sharing the bathroom?

Activity

- Do any family members bathe/shower together and, if so, who and in what circumstances, for example assistance to small children, sexual intimacy?
- Do older siblings help to bathe/toilet younger children?
- Can parents hear what is going on in the bathroom from other rooms in the house?
- Are family members up during the night to use the bathroom?

Dress code

- What do family members wear to and from the bathroom?

Section 4. Play and other activities in the family home

In considering the rules required about play and other activities it may be helpful to consider the following:
  Activities

- How and where does the young person spend their time at home?
- How and where do the siblings spend their time together?
- What family activities do they do together?
- Is there a lot of physical contact during play?
- Do parents know when friends are in the house?
- How does the young person spend their time with friends in the house?
- How is it negotiated for friends to be in the family home?
- What are the current levels of supervision and is this adequate?

New technologies

- Has the child access to the internet? If so is this through PC, laptop, mobile phone? Where is the PC located?
- Is there a webcam on the PC. Is there wireless connection?
- What length of time does the child spend on the computer?
- What sites does the child access?
- Are there any filters/safeguards on computer/laptop? Do parents/carers check online activity? How is this checked?

Section 6. Family nudity

In considering the rules required about nudity, it may be helpful to consider the following:
  Privacy and boundaries

- Are parents nude in front of the children, and, if so, in what context?
- Are adults naked around children, children naked around adults and children naked around other children? If so, what is the context?
- Is underwear worn around the house?

Section 7. Family sexuality

A family's sexuality is like an unwritten code from which family members understand acceptable and unacceptable ways of interacting with each other and with others outside with the family. This covers privacy, intimacy and access to sexual information as well as sexual behaviours. This helps us understand the messages a child or young person has been given about sexuality. As stated in the introduction, this is sensitive information to cover with families and this part of the safety plan is likely to evolve as workers develop closer relationships with families.
  In considering the rules required about sexuality, it may be helpful to consider the following:
  Privacy and boundaries

- How do parents show affection to each other in front of the children?
- Has the child been exposed to sexual contact between the parents?
- Do parents talk about sex or sexual acts in front of the children?
- Are children ever in the parental bedroom when they (parent's/adults) have sexual intercourse?
- Do the children touch each other in a sexualised way, and, if so, in what circumstances?
- Do the children touch the adults in a sexualised way and, if so, in what circumstances?
- Do any adult visitors touch each other in a sexualised way in front of the children?
- Do adult visitors touch the children in a sexualised way?
- Do the siblings discuss sex and sexual behaviours with each other?
- Are children potentially exposed to sexualised behaviours of older siblings?
- Are there any concerns about relationships with pets?

Access to sexual images/materials

- Are there pornographic magazines in the home and where are they kept and who has access to them?
- Are there pornographic DVDs and, if so, where are they kept and who has access to them?
- Has the child/young person unlimited access to TV? If so, what stations are available?
- Does anyone in the house have access to sexually explicit material online, use pornography or Internet-related sexual activities?

The section within the assessment on sexual socialisation will also assist workers to complete this section in more detail after the assessment process has been undertaken.

Appendix 2

The interface between the goal facilitation, risk management and wellness plans.

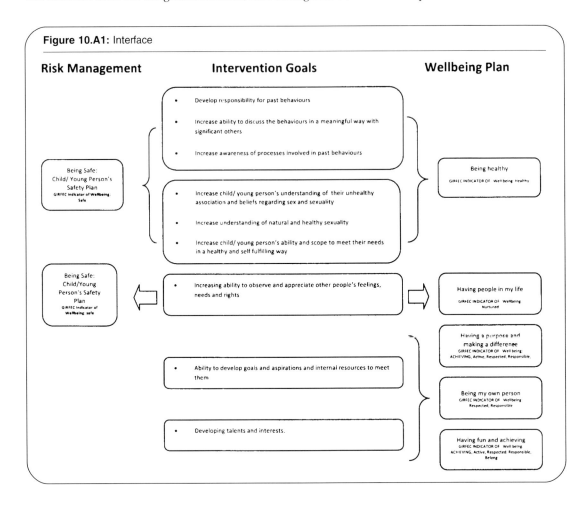

Figure 10.A1: Interface

Appendix 3

Table 10.1: Assessment areas

Caring Environment

1. Sexual behaviours
1.1 Referral behaviours and level of understanding
1.2 Carer's reaction to behaviours
1.3 Supervision: Access to potential/actual victim/s
1.4 Sexual behaviour history, Including any current concerns
1.5 Ability to discuss behaviours with child/young person and respond to any ongoing concerns
1.6 Carers ability to respond to any ongoing sexual behaviour

2. Child and Family History
2.1 Carer's knowledge and Insight regarding child/young person's history

3. Sexual Socialisation Process
3.1 Carer's knowledge and Insight regarding messages child has received about sex and sexuality.

4. Present Functioning
4.1 Attachment
4.2 Communication
4.3 Alliances
4.4 Flexibility and adaptability
4.5 Current stressors
4.6 Decision Making and Problem Solving
4.7 Guidance, Rules and Supervision
4.8 Sexual expression and culture
4.9 Boundaries
4.10 Conflict management
4.11 External relationships with extended family, school. community and helping agencies
4.12 New Technologies

5. Carer's view of Child/Young Person
5.1 Non sexual behaviours
5.2 Education
5.3 Friendship
5.4 Talents and Interests
5.5 Positive values
5.6 Social competencies

6. Organisational Context
6.1 Level and impact of external support available
6.2 Use of policies and procedures

School

1. Problem sexual behaviours
- Referral behaviours and level of understanding
- Ability to discuss the behaviour in a meaningful way with the child
- The schools reaction to the behaviour
- Access to victims/potential victims

2. Staffing and structure
- How the school reinforces positive behaviours and respect for others and creates an environment that encourages children to tell If someone Is doing anything to them that makes them uncomfortable
- Existing school policies such as bullying, equal opportunities, child protection and how children and young people with problem sexual behaviours are Incorporated
- The level of staff training on children and young people with problem sexual behaviours
- Support available to staff Including their contact points for advice
- The physical structure of the school and where sexual behaviours may occur
- How children and young people with problem sexual behaviours are identified within the school
- Liaison with other agencies and families.

3. Individual work with the child
- The ability to develop Individual programmes, e.g. problem solving, social skills
- The ability to develop safe boundaries.
- The level of assistance given to help the child integrate with other pupils and form healthy relationships.
- The ability to employ behaviour management strategies that include boundaries and consequences.
- The ability to observe and analyse the child to Inform ongoing assessment of risk
- The level of supervision and monitoring

Child/Young Person

1. Assessment Foundation Section
    1.1 Engagement: Mountain exercise
    1.2 Keeping safe
    1.3 Emotional labelling and affect regulation
    1.4 Mindfulness

The Core Assessment

2. The child/young person's present level of functioning
    2.1 Social competencies
    2.2 Secure base
    2.3 Education
    2.4 Friendships
    2.5 Talents and Interests
    2.6 Values
    2.7 Non sexual behaviours
    2.8 New Technologies
        2.8.1 Type and level of access to new technologies
        2.8.2 Level of understanding of new technologies
        2.8.3 Virtual network
        2.8.4 Functlon of use of new technologies for child/young person

3. Pathways into sexual behaviour
    3.1. Significant life events
    3.2. The child/young person's sexual socialisation
        3.2.1 Sexual development/messages about sex and sexuality
        3.2.2 Sexual knowledge, values and attitudes
        3.2.3 Sexual Interest

4. Sexual behaviours
    4.1 The child/young person's account of their sexual behaviours
    4.2 Risk awareness and risk management

Responding to Adolescent Sexual Offending: Recommendations for a Coordinated and Integrated Systemic Response

Dana Costin, Siegi A. Schuler and Tracey Curwen

Introduction

During the past several decades, the issue of adolescent sexual offending has received increased clinical, empirical, and legal attention. Research findings have demonstrated that many adults who have committed sexual offences began offending as adolescents and 50 per cent of adults who have committed sexual offences report that they experienced deviant sexual interests prior to age 18 (Barbaree, Hudson, and Seto, 1993). In Canada, 20 per cent of those charged with sexual assault are between 12 and 17 years of age (Statistics Canada, 2007) and, in the United States, adolescents have been reported to be responsible for almost half of all sexual offences that are committed yearly against children (Abel and Rouleau, 1990; Becker and Kaplan, 1993).

Research regarding sexual offending has demonstrated a relationship between sexual victimisation and subsequent sexual offending. Although most survivors of sexual abuse do not go on to commit sexual offences themselves, research findings have consistently demonstrated that significant numbers of individuals who have sexually offended were sexually victimised during childhood or adolescence (Barbaree, Marshall and McCormick, 1998; Burton and Hedgepeth, 2002; Cooper, Murphy and Haynes, 1996; Romano and De Luca, 1997; Ryan et al., 1996). Costin (2004: 3) notes that 'devoting resources to the issue of sexual offending has the potential to interrupt the victim-to-victimiser phenomenon; decreasing the frequency of offences and reoffences will reduce the number of future victims and this, in turn, will reduce the number of future sexual offenders'.

The past two decades have also seen a tremendous increase in publications on the subject of familial sexual abuse, evidently reflecting society's growing awareness and recognition of a problem previously hidden behind a veil of denial, secrecy, and disbelief. While the literature and professional community have historically focused greater attention on father-daughter incest, there is general agreement that the most prevalent type of incestuous behaviour occurs between siblings (Finkelhor, 1990; Lindzey, 1967). Furthermore, research findings and clinical experiences indicate that sibling incest can be highly intrusive and often occurs for long periods of time. For example, O'Brien (1991) found that nearly 45 per cent of sibling offenders had durations of abuse that extended beyond one year. It is also noteworthy that opportunity is an essential element in carrying out a sexual assault (Cohen and Felson, 1979). White, Kadlec and Sechrist (2006) found that sexual assaults by adolescents tended to occur immediately after school and, on non-school days, between 12pm and 1pm. Certainly, these times may correspond with limited adult supervision.

Despite increased knowledge regarding the incidence, assessment, and treatment of sexual offending by adolescents, integrated and coordinated responses by the various systems involved (eg police, child protection services, judicial services) are lacking. Clinicians, however, have long asserted that effective management of adolescents who commit sexual harm is greatly enhanced by working collaboratively with the various systems within the adolescent's circle of care.

Purpose of this chapter

This chapter evolved from a document focused on making empirically-based, best-practice guided recommendations for an integrated and coordinated response by police, child protection services, and judicial services (from the point of allegations to referral for assessment and treatment) when responding to allegations of sexual offending by adolescents. Although originally created for use in Ontario, Canada, the guidelines and recommendations provided are applicable to other jurisdictions.

The specific goals of developing the recommendations provided in this chapter are to:

- coordinate and guide a collaborative and consistent process between law enforcement/police, youth justice (ie court system, youth probation) child welfare/protection agencies, children's mental health, educators, special interest groups, and clinical experts in child sexual abuse and adolescent sexual offending when intervening in adolescent sexual offending
- implement clear and consistent best-practice standards for investigating the sexual abuse of children and adolescents when sexual offending by an adolescent has been alleged/identified
- address the removal of an adolescent who has sexually offended from the home for the purposes of assessment and/or treatment

It is expected that the proposed guidelines will:

- reduce frustration regarding the lack of appropriate or consistent responses to sexual offending by adolescents
- reduce frustration regarding poor or lack of communication between service providers
- reduce the short- and long-term impact of poor coordination of services
- effect more streamlined and collaborative approaches to allegations
- build competence in addressing safety and support issues for both victimised individuals and the public.

CSOM, 2000a

This document is intended for use by all professionals, systems, services, and agencies that may become involved when an allegation of a sexual offence has been made against an adolescent. This may include, but is not limited to, school personnel, police services, child protection services, youth justice (eg judges, probation services) and children's mental health providers. For experienced clinicians working with adolescents who have sexually offended, victimised individuals, and their families, it is hoped that this chapter can serve as a resource for educating other professionals within the systems involved (eg police, child protection, judges, probation) regarding both the significance of their role in the continuum of care and the importance of a coordinated systems response.

It is critical to note that this document is only intended for use with respect to adolescents who, in their jurisdiction, can be held criminally accountable for the sexual offence that has been alleged. For our purposes, this refers to adolescents who were 12–17 years of age at the time of commission of the sexual offence. (In Canada, a child under the age of 12 who engages in concerning sexual behaviours cannot be charged). It is important to consider that, in cases where the child is under the age of 12 at the time of the alleged sexual behaviours, protocol guidelines and recommendations may differ. This response protocol was not developed to address situations in which children under the age of 12 have engaged in concerning sexual behaviours.

It should also be noted that, in cases where the adolescent who has sexually offended is considerably delayed developmentally, it may be necessary to utilise judgment regarding the appropriateness of pursuing legal sanctions; however, it is important to note that individuals with developmental delays are also at risk of sexual recidivism and the absence of charges in such circumstances can lead to a lack of (or limited) resources being sought for these adolescents. Indeed, the decision to lay charges can be a complicated one and involves various potential risks and benefits.

With both cognitively delayed and non-delayed adolescents, in addition to addressing accountability issues, one potential benefit of laying charges against an adolescent who is alleged to have offended sexually is that this often leads to the initiation of resources (eg regarding assessment or treatment) that the adolescent (and their family) may otherwise resist or that may otherwise be difficult to obtain. Regardless of the ultimate decision that is made regarding charges, it is recommended that investigations be pursued regarding all allegations and all those involved.

It is also important to highlight that this protocol is intended to reflect best-practices and it is recognised that, in some circumstances, some of the recommendations may be difficult to implement. Although we are aware that the recommendations expressed in this chapter represent the ideal continuum of care, and that a number of communities may not have the necessary resources available to provide this scope of care or response, we believe it is vital to provide communities with information regarding best-practice of care for adolescents who have sexually offended and their families. It is hoped that this protocol will serve as a guide regarding the ideal response, and be useful both clinically and across the various systems involved, but it is certainly recognised that, where resources are limited, different and creative responses and solutions may be necessary. Nevertheless, it is our belief that implementation of an integrated and coordinated response, along the lines of that recommended in this chapter, will have a direct impact on the protection of communities through responsible and ethical treatment of adolescents who have sexually offended, victimised individuals, and their families.

Justification for a coordinated protocol

The lack of mandated response protocols results in varied and, at times, seemingly arbitrary responses to allegations. Investigation outcomes, placement/residence decisions, and dispositional outcomes are largely determined by the professional involved in a particular incident and can vary considerably, both from region to region and within regions. Given the variability in responses, decisions do not consistently integrate and reflect current best-practices. Additionally, as a result of the lack of mandated, coordinated response protocols, adolescents who offend sexually often remain in contact with the children they have victimised (or potentially vulnerable individuals) with few implemented safeguards. At times, and particularly when clinical services that are in accordance with best-practices have not been initiated, precautions are taken regarding only the *physical* safety of victimised children or adolescents, for example, by ensuring that contact is supervised. In such circumstances, however, little consideration is given to the *emotional* or *psychological* safety of the victimised individual who may then suffer further psychological impact as a result of the lack of attention to their fears, reactions, and needs. As such, a coordinated response protocol for addressing adolescent sexual offending, in both intra- and extrafamilial abuse scenarios, is much needed.

When legal or child protection sanctions include an order or request for assessment or treatment of an adolescent who has sexually offended, the implications are often farther

reaching than the adolescent alone. In particular, in cases of intrafamilial sexual abuse (ie inclusive of extended family) or, specifically, sibling incest, primary consideration must be given to the needs and wishes of the victimised individual, regardless of the adolescent's participation in, or completion of treatment. In certain families, contact with the offending adolescent may be determined (through assessment) to be appropriate for the victimised sibling or relative (eg cousin). Although contact and reintegration will be different for every family, reunification is a goal for many families when sibling incest and/or intrafamilial sexual abuse has occurred (Association for the Treatment of Sexual Abusers, 2003). However, not all victimised siblings will desire or be emotionally capable of resuming contact with the offending adolescent. As such, in addition to assessing the offending individual's risk for reoffending and progress in treatment, as well as developing appropriate safety plans for contact, the practice standards and guidelines published by the Association for the Treatment of Sexual Abusers (2003) stipulate the need for ensuring the victimised individual's interest in, and readiness for, reunification. Therefore, in cases of sibling incest and intrafamilial sexual abuse, intensive assessment and treatment services are necessary for the offending adolescent, victimised siblings/relatives and other family members.

Responding appropriately to sexual offending by adolescents is a multi-level process. This process requires involvement from the many systems that are responsible for various aspects of the response such as investigation, adjudication, assessment, treatment, and supervision (Center for Sex Offender Management, CSOM, 2008). According to Talbot et al. (2002) the primary goal of any intervention is preventing future sexual victimisation. These authors, and others, suggest that reducing recidivism requires multidisciplinary, multi-agency, and collaborative responses on both case management and policy levels. Those who should be involved in collaboration when a sexual offence has been committed by an adolescent include criminal justice system personnel such as judges, crown and defence attorneys, and law enforcement officers; corrections officials; victim advocates (CSOM, 2000a); social service providers; child protection services; and school administration (Talbot et al., 2002). However, coordinating the activities/policies of different stakeholders may be difficult. Therefore, effective intervention requires cooperation and collaboration among individuals and agencies, as well as a unified goal of protecting victimised individuals and the community (Colorado Sex Offender Management Board, CSOMB, 2003; Talbot et al., 2002).

In their writings regarding the accuracy of registered data regarding adolescent sexual offending, Worling and Langstrom (2006) have identified a number of factors that can be adapted and applied in intervening appropriately and effectively when an adolescent has been accused of a sexual offence against a sibling or relative. Specifically, appropriate intervention would require that:

- Victimised individuals are willing to report the offence.
- Adults have the ability to correctly perceive and act on information about the victimised individual.
- Child protection agencies have the ability to investigate in a timely and appropriate manner.
- Police investigate an allegation in a timely manner.
- Police notify relevant agencies.
- Investigations of both the alleged offending individual and victimised individual(s) occur (as well as family members and potential victims).

In order to effectively fulfill many of these suggested criteria, the roles and responsibilities of those involved at various levels of the system need to be delineated. Having a clear and consensus-built policy or protocol establishes the goals for the system and helps jurisdictions to clearly identify what role each system/agency will play in addressing and managing cases of sexual offending (CSOM, 2000b, 2008). Determining and implementing the various roles and responsibilities requires ongoing collaboration among those who are responsible for carrying out various parts of the process (CSOM, 2008). Clearly, a coordinated response protocol would address issues related to steps to be taken, roles, responsibilities, and collaboration.

Collaboration among agencies

Collaboration among systems/agencies is vital when an adolescent has been accused of a sexual offence. In order to implement a multi-system and multi-agency collaboration, it is important to develop functional and working relationships (CSOM, 2000a). According to CSOM, functional relationships will assist to address any misperceptions or assumptions regarding the roles of other agencies in the process and enable the clear delineation of roles for each provider involved in the process (CSOM, 2000a). To date, agency collaboration may have failed due to a lack of clarity in what others are doing and who is responsible for specific roles, the belief that collaboration may make a job more difficult, a lack of knowledge and training on issues, and the belief that collaboration will not increase efficacy of work (CSOM, 2000a). In addition, when performing a task or role, there may also be a fear of crossing role boundaries (CSOM, 2000a). Therefore, clear guidelines and/or protocols outlining the responsibility and roles of various systems/agencies should eliminate many of the above-mentioned potential detractors from successful collaboration.

According to CSOM (2000a), successful collaborative efforts involve the following key factors:

- Effective communication and cooperation among the criminal justice system and professionals.
- Assessment of collaborative needs.
- Clear definition and delineation of roles.
- Efficient and streamlined coordination of agency tasks.
- Routine and regular flow of information and data.
- Participation and accountability of all parties involved in the process.

Therefore, establishing and following guidelines regarding the management of adolescent sexual offending allegations is justified by the expectation that doing so will:

- Enhance efficient handling of all involved.
- Ensure consideration of victimised individuals and public safety.
- Consider the alleged offending individual's safety.
- Improve the overall quality and consistency of response.

The protocol

The protocol that follows includes a flow chart that is intended to serve as a quick reference for the response process. A glossary of terms is provided at the end of this chapter.

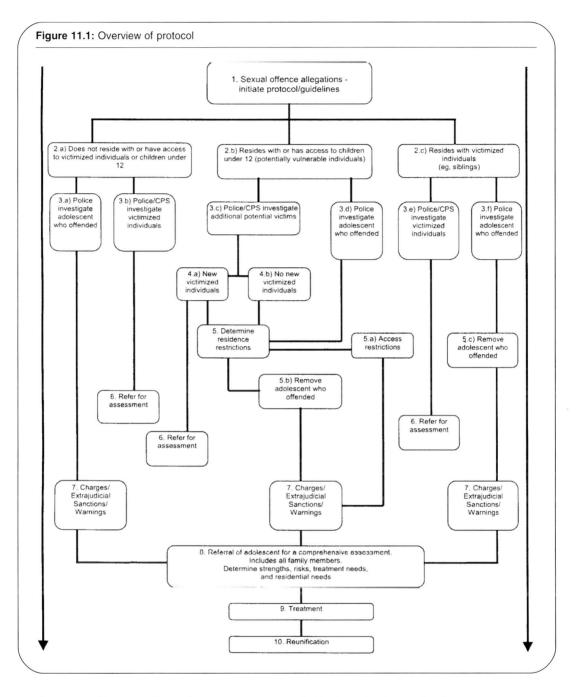

Figure 11.1: Overview of protocol

1. Sexual offence allegations – initiate protocol/guidelines

An allegation of sexual offending has been made against an adolescent, whether at home, in the community, at school, or any combination of the above. This requires the initiation of an investigation.

Initiating the investigation

When a sexual offence by an adolescent has been alleged, it is critical that an investigation be initiated immediately. Regardless of the location of the alleged offence (ie school, home, community) the investigation should be conducted by the appropriate authorities:

1. Law enforcement/police services – in all cases regardless of the age of the accused adolescent.
2. Child Protection Services (CPS) – in addition to police services, in cases where the accused is under 16 years of age and/or the victimised individual is under 16 years. (Note: this age may vary in each jurisdiction depending on child protection laws.)

Note: If the offence occurs within a school setting, it is highly recommended that school personnel make contact with the appropriate authorities in order to determine the investigation process. An internal investigation and questioning of the accused adolescent or victimised individual(s) by school personnel may influence an official investigation. School personnel should contact police services immediately and, if appropriate, child protection services as well (ie in Ontario, for example, CPS would be contacted if school personnel are aware that the alleged victimised individual is under the age of 16, the accused is under the age of 16, or the accused resides with children under the age of 16, including siblings). If the accused and the alleged victimised individual(s) are over the age of 16, only police services should be contacted. Pending the outcome of their investigation, police services should then determine if child protection services should also be contacted (eg victimised individuals under the age of 16 are disclosed; the accused resides with, or functions in a position of power or authority over children).

2. Residence of the adolescent/ access to potentially vulnerable individuals

The adolescent's access to potentially vulnerable individuals is of particular concern, both at the time of the investigation, as well as throughout the duration of assessment (and, depending on recommendations from assessment, during treatment). At the time of the investigation, it is recommended that the adolescent's access to individuals who may be victimised be addressed immediately, regardless of whether the sexual offending occurred within or outside of the home and toward younger children, peers, or adults. As sexual interest is not necessarily related to prior sexual offence history (Hunter and Lexier, 1998; Thakker et al., 2006) the residence of the adolescent must be addressed regardless of the

age of the alleged victimised individual, those with whom the adolescent is residing, or to whom the adolescent has access.

The following are of importance:

- Does the adolescent reside with, or have access to, children under the age of 12 or other potentially vulnerable individuals?
- Does the adolescent reside with the victim?

Adolescent's residence – restrictions/ removal

2 (a) The adolescent does not reside with, or have access to, children under the age of 12 and/or other potentially vulnerable individuals

Protocol: Do not remove the adolescent

The adolescent can remain in their residence as long as child protection determines that this is a safe environment (ie the adolescent is not in need of protection). In most cases, adolescents who have sexually offended outside the home (ie not against someone with whom they reside) can participate in assessment and treatment while residing with their parents (or current caregivers). It is highly recommended that caregivers be aware of the allegations and the need for supervision during the period of investigation and, if relevant, throughout the duration of a comprehensive sexual-offence-specific assessment and treatment.

Recommendation: During at least the period of investigation and assessment, the adolescent who offended sexually should not have any unsupervised contact with children under the age of 12 or other potentially vulnerable individuals. This supervision should be maintained until feedback is provided from the assessment.

Supervised contact refers to the physical presence, with direct sight of the adolescent (ie not in a different room), by an adult who is aware of the allegations of sexual offending and the supervision requirements.

2 (b) Adolescent resides with/has access to potential child victims under the age of 12 and/or other potentially vulnerable individuals

Protocol: Temporarily remove the adolescent

Once allegations have been made, until the investigation and, if relevant, a sexual offence-specific assessment has been completed, the adolescent should not reside with any children under the age of 12 or any other potentially vulnerable individuals.

Recommendation: If removal is necessary, the adolescent who offended sexually, not the children or other potentially vulnerable individuals, should be removed from the residence. In cases where the adolescent is removed, he/she should be placed in a residence in which there are no children under the age of 12 or other potentially vulnerable individuals. As well, the adult(s) in this setting must be made aware of the access restrictions and supervision needs.

Although the alleged victimised individual may not reside in the home, it is important to ensure that the adolescent is not residing with any possible previously victimised (ie by the adolescent) or potentially vulnerable individuals. Child protection should investigate the possibility that children and other potentially vulnerable individuals within the home may have also been victimised. However, as sexual assault is under-reported (Smallbone, 2006; van Dijk, Mayhew, and Killias, 1991), it is important to be aware that children and other potentially vulnerable individuals residing with the adolescent may not disclose having experienced sexual abuse, even when asked. As sexual abuse commonly occurs in secrecy and often occurs within the home (Letourneau, 2006), siblings and others within the home might be particularly hesitant to disclose past experiences of sexual abuse by the adolescent.

The issue of separating the adolescent from potentially vulnerable individuals is not confined only to protecting these individuals, but also involves addressing issues related to risk of sexual reoffending for the adolescent. Researchers suggest that adolescents' sexual interests and arousal patterns are not firmly established (Trivits and Reppucci, 2002) and patterns of offending during adolescence do not, necessarily, represent enduring behavioural tendencies (Thakker et al., 2006). As such, prior sexual assaults against only one type or group of vulnerable individuals (eg peer-aged individuals or only males) do not guarantee that the adolescent is not at risk of a sexual reoffence against another type or group of individuals (eg children or females).

Temporary removal from the home may also benefit the adolescent as he/she may reside within a family that perpetuates negative attitudes, environments, or socialisation that can be detrimental to the adolescent (White et al., 2006). In comparison to individuals who have committed nonsexual and nonviolent offences, sexually offending individuals are reported to have experienced more physical and sexual abuse as well as more violence, instability, and disorganisation in their homes (Barbaree and Langton, 2006; Ford and Linney, 1995). Therefore, removing the adolescent will not only reduce risk by eliminating access to potentially vulnerable individuals but, in certain cases, may also remove the adolescent from a negative environment that may perpetuate violence or beliefs supportive of sexual assault.

When the adolescent is not residing with children under the age of 12 or other potentially vulnerable individuals, but has access to such individuals, the appropriateness of the access must be investigated and determined by child protection. In addition, any access to children under the age of 12 or other potentially vulnerable individuals should be directly supervised during the assessment period and pending the recommendations of the assessment.

Recommendation: Regardless of the age of the alleged victimised individual, the adolescent who offended should not be permitted to reside with any children under the age of 12 or other potentially vulnerable individuals pending the outcome of both the investigation and the recommendations of a comprehensive sexual-offence-specific assessment. When exceedingly long delays are expected with respect to accessing services, strict supervision measures should be implemented regarding the adolescent's access to children and other potentially vulnerable individuals against whom he/she has not previously sexually offended (ie not known victimised individuals).

2 (c) Adolescent resides with victimised individual(s)

Protocol: Temporarily remove the adolescent

The adolescent should immediately be separated from those they victimised. If the sexual offending is alleged against an unrelated individual, but occurred within a foster home or group home setting, the adolescent should be removed from this setting pending the outcome of the investigation and the recommendations of comprehensive assessments for both the adolescent and the alleged victimised individual. If the sexual offending is alleged within the home (ie against siblings), best-practices also support separation of the adolescent from their siblings (Hodges, 2002). As indicated previously, whenever possible, this should involve removal of the adolescent from the home (ie not removing the victimised individuals).

Cautionary note regarding separation/ removal of the adolescent

Although separation of the adolescent from victimised and potentially vulnerable individuals is recommended, it is important to note that the time from investigation to the end of assessment can be lengthy. While removal from the home is often difficult for all involved, in some situations, a lengthy removal from the home can be particularly deleterious for the adolescent and the family (inclusive of victimised siblings). Therefore, it is strongly recommended that services be initiated as promptly as possible and that, wherever possible, unnecessary lengthy separations be avoided. As resources are often limited, resulting in long waiting lists for services, it is highly recommended that, once underway, assessments (for all involved) be completed as expeditiously as possible. In addition, whenever feasible, preliminary feedback should be provided by clinicians with respect to contact, residence issues, and the implementation of supervision criteria.

Recommendation: Any contact (direct or indirect) between the adolescent who offended sexually and the victimised individual should be suspended pending the outcome of the assessments and the recommendations of experienced professionals working with the adolescent who offended, the victimised individual, the parents/caregivers, and other family members.

Residential placement of adolescent

In situations when the adolescent is to be removed from the home, an appropriate placement with kin who will abide by the recommendation of no contact with victimised individuals should be the first option explored.

Other options include foster homes and group home settings. However, it is critical to ensure that, in any of the placement options pursued, there are no children under the age of 12 or other potentially vulnerable individuals, and the supervising adults are aware of the supervision requirements for the adolescent. As sexual offending often involves manipulation, secrecy, and deceit (CSOM, 2000b) those responsible for

the adolescent must closely monitor and implement restrictions to reduce the risk of re-offending (Worling and Langstrom, 2006). Visits with non-victimised family members (eg non-victimised siblings, parents) should be supported if considered safe for the adolescent (and any non-victimised siblings) by child protection services. It should be noted, however, that siblings who are believed not to have been victimised may, indeed, have been victimised as well, and investigations in this regard should be completed prior to such contact.

Victimised individual's wishes

Although it may be believed that the physical safety of the victimised individual(s) can be ensured during supervised contact, supervision cannot address the potential emotional or psychological consequences of contact and may not prevent an ongoing emotionally abusive relationship (CAPSAC). In many cases, the victimised individual may request to see the adolescent as, among other reasons, they might want to ensure that the offending adolescent is not angry, be forgiven for disclosing, or reduce the anger, sadness, and stress of other family members (CAPSAC). However, regardless of the victimised individual's wishes, it is important that assessments for the victimised individual and the adolescent who offended occur prior to any contact. In addition, it is critical that any contact and/or reunification be guided and timed by experienced treatment providers working with all of the individuals involved and only when all treatment providers are in agreement regarding such contact (CAPSAC). A good reference (Hodges, 2002) in this regard outlines five steps to reunification as follows:

1. Report the abuse and separate the victimised sibling and offending sibling.
2. Complete evaluations of family members.
3. Begin family therapy.
4. Bring victimised sibling and offending sibling together in family therapy.
5. Family therapy termination.

In addition, the Association for the Treatment of Sexual Abusers (ATSA, 2003) recommends that considerations of family reunification should be given to the wishes of victimised individuals, that contact with children should be addressed as part of a comprehensive risk management plan and linked to the offending individual's risk level and progress in treatment, and that reunification should not be recommended for individuals who deny their offences or are at moderate to high risk for re-offending, as assessed by a competent assessment (ie that follows best-practices, for example, as recommended by ATSA).

3. Investigation

It is highly recommended that trained sexual abuse investigation teams be developed within both police services and child protection. In cases where police services and child protection will both be involved, a joint investigation is recommended as this will improve consistency in investigations, adherence to protocols/guidelines, and determinations (eg charges, extrajudicial sanctions) that are made. In such cases, it would be ideal to develop a joint police-child protection investigation team within the region.

One goal of the investigation for both police services and child protection should be to identify additional potential or undisclosed victimised individuals to whom the adolescent would have immediate access. Addressing the residence of the adolescent is of immediate concern in this regard and should be a priority of the investigation.

Who is investigating?

3 (a), (d), (f) Police investigate the adolescent

Regardless of the age of the victimised individual and adolescent, the investigation and interview of the adolescent should be conducted by police services. Again, it is highly recommended that officers trained in adolescent sexual offending and issues related to sexual abuse conduct the investigation. It is critical to ensure that during this process, the rights of the adolescent are upheld (ie right to legal counsel). At the same time, child protection workers should interview any known (and potential/suspected) victimised individuals under the age of 16. (Note: The age may vary in each jurisdiction according to child protection laws.)

3 (b), (e) Interview of victimised individual

All interviews with victimised individuals should be conducted with considerable priority and concern regarding the victimised individual's emotional and psychological health.

Whenever possible, interviews of victimised individuals should not take place at a police station but, rather, at a place considered to be safe and comfortable for this individual. In addition, police officers should attend in plain clothes in order to decrease fear, anxiety, and the perspective that the victimised child or adolescent has done something wrong. Furthermore, whenever possible, consideration should be given to potential gender issues (eg individuals might be more comfortable being interviewed by an officer of the opposite gender to that of their offender; female children might prefer a female officer and male children might prefer a male officer). Whenever possible, choice should be provided in this regard.

It is also critical to consider the victimised individual's need for support while balancing this with the consideration that he/she may be unlikely to disclose information in the presence of specific individuals (eg parents, other family members). Privacy for the victim during an interview may be achieved by letting the child/adolescent know where the parent/support person is, taking necessary breaks so the child/adolescent can check in with the support person, providing snacks and/or comfort objects, etc. Ideally, a joint interview by child protection and police services should be conducted in order to prevent the victimised individual from having to endure repeated interviews.

Recommendation: A specialised team of police officers and child protection workers should be developed and trained with respect to sexual abuse-specific interviewing. These teams should investigate together in cases in which both services will be involved.

3 (c) Police/Child Protection investigate possible additional victims

As noted earlier (see 2 (b)), offending occurs in secret, often in the home, and when the opportunity is present (Cohen and Felson, 1979; CSOM, 2000b; White et al., 2006). Therefore, as much as possible/is feasible, there must be investigation of all potential unreported sexual offences against individuals of all ages. For example, if allegations are made with respect to sexual abuse of one sibling, other siblings should be interviewed. Likewise, if allegations of sexual offending against one or more foster siblings or group home residents are made, other foster siblings or group home residents should be interviewed. In addition, any child to whom the adolescent had unsupervised access should be investigated and any identified/confirmed victimised individuals should be referred for a comprehensive assessment.

Recommendation: Specially trained child protection workers and police officers conduct interviews with potentially victimised individuals in order to improve the likelihood of obtaining disclosures from undisclosed victimised individuals.

With respect to documentation of the investigation, it is recommended that detailed police records and child protection records be maintained. Detailed official documentation regarding the alleged sexual offence (ie age and gender of victimised individual; location; others present; frequency/repetitiveness; acts involved/intrusiveness; threats, coercion, force, or violence involved; how disclosed) is critical for future comprehensive assessments and treatment. Victimised individuals' version of events and impact statements should also be solicited as these can provide critical information for offence-specific assessments if consent is later obtained for release of such documents.

4. Victimised individual's status

4 (a) New victimised individuals discovered

When new victimised individuals are discovered, the residence of the adolescent must be re-visited to ensure that the adolescent is not residing with any of the newly-discovered victimised individuals. If the adolescent resides with the newly-discovered victimised individuals, it is recommended that the adolescent be removed from the residence (5 (b)). As indicated previously, the impact of the removal must be considered and unnecessary lengthy separations should be avoided. Prompt initiation of services is recommended.

Recommendation: All known/disclosed victimised individuals should be referred for a comprehensive trauma-informed assessment.

4 (b) No new victimised individuals discovered

In the case that no new victimised individuals are identified, residential criteria for the adolescent are determined based on the existing information (ie 2 (a), (b), (c)). Residential restrictions for the adolescent may still exist based on the known victimised individuals and

the adolescent's access to these or other potentially vulnerable individuals. If the adolescent is not residing with potentially vulnerable or known victimised individuals, there may be no residential restrictions.

5. Access restrictions/removal of adolescent

Residence of the adolescent for the period of assessment will be dependent upon the information gathered with respect to known and newly-disclosed victimised individuals, the adolescent's current living circumstances, and the adolescent's access to potentially vulnerable or victimised individuals.

5 (a) In some cases, the adolescent is not residing with victimised individuals, children under the age of 12, or potentially vulnerable individuals; however, he/she has access to such individuals. When this is discovered, determinations must be made regarding the adolescent's access to these individuals.

5 (b), (c) In all cases where the adolescent is residing with victimised individuals, children under the age of 12, or other potentially vulnerable individuals, it is recommended that the adolescent be separated from these individuals for the period of assessment, pending further recommendations.

Recommendations: There should be no access to known victimised individuals pending the outcome of the assessment (and, likely, the onset of treatment) of the adolescent who offended sexually and the victimised individuals.

With respect to the adolescent's access to all other children (not identified as having been victimised), this should be highly supervised during the process of assessment and pending the assessment recommendations.

6. Assessment of victimised individual

A referral for a comprehensive trauma-informed assessment is recommended for all individuals who have experienced sexual abuse as these individuals may experience a number of emotional, social, and behavioural consequences. For example, sexually victimised individuals may experience various short- and long-term effects including, but not limited to, depression, physical complaints, isolation, low self-esteem, antisocial behaviour and delinquency, post-traumatic stress, and concerning sexual behaviours (for a review, see Mendel, 1995; Beitchman et al., 1991; Beitchman et al., 1992; Finkelhor and Browne, 1986; Kendall-Tackett et al., 1993). Furthermore, individuals who have experienced sexual abuse are reported to experience relationship difficulties, sexual problems, issues with sexual orientation, addictions, and sexual aggression (see Mendel, 1995 for a review). Although one focus of the assessment should be on the sexual abuse that was experienced, it is important that other areas of the victimised individual's functioning be assessed as doing so provides considerable information regarding strengths (ie potential protective factors) and potential risks.

Specific to siblings who have been victimised, a trauma-informed assessment should also include information related to potential reunification issues. Issues related to victimisation are complicated and, therefore, the professionals involved in assessment should have specific expertise and considerable experience regarding assessing issues related to victimisation and conducting comprehensive assessments in this regard. In cases where the alleged offending adolescent is a family member or sibling, it is imperative that the assessor also be experienced regarding assessing the unique issues involved in intrafamilial sexual abuse and sibling incest, inclusive of issues that are relevant to reunification.

7. Charges/extrajudicial sanctions/warnings

Police determine the appropriateness of charges, extrajudicial sanctions (eg diversion), or warnings for the adolescent. In some circumstances, police may determine that a warning/caution is sufficient for the adolescent. Particularly in the case of nonviolent offences or intrafamilial sexual abuse, extrajudicial sanctions may also be effective and sufficient (eg mandating participation in assessment and treatment); however, these tend to be more successful if they are implemented post-charge and when the length of time involved is sufficient for appropriate resources to be obtained and interventions to be implemented. Judges and those recommending extrajudicial sanctions should consider that, given the often limited

resources, supervision for six months or one year, for example, typically will not be sufficient for the initiation of assessment and completion of treatment, particularly given that the average length of treatment is approximately 17 months (McGrath, Cumming and Burchard, 2003).

8. Referral of adolescent for a comprehensive assessment

The adolescent who is convicted of a sexual offence should be referred for a comprehensive sexual offence-specific assessment to explore treatment issues and issues related to risk of a future sexual offence. In addition to exploring various issues and areas of functioning (see Glossary regarding a comprehensive sexual offence-specific assessment), this assessment should also address risk issues and make use of available risk estimate tools such as the Estimate of Risk of Adolescent Sexual Offence Recidivism, Version 2.0 (ERASOR, 2.0; Worling and Curwen, 2001) and the Juvenile Sex Offender Assessment Protocol-II (JSOAP-II; Prentky and Righthand, 2003).

Typically, it is not recommended that an assessment be completed until a plea has been entered by the adolescent and, ideally, a finding (ie of guilt) has been determined by the courts. Not surprisingly, it is difficult for adolescents to participate openly in an assessment if a finding has not yet been determined by the courts, and lawyers often advise the adolescents not to provide detailed information regarding their offences. This is particularly true in cases where the adolescent is pleading 'not guilty'.

In the interest of making early sentencing, treatment, and placement recommendations, the sexual offence-specific assessment should be completed as part of the court process, following a plea or finding of guilt. This would typically entail an assessment being ordered by the judge. In cases where extrajudicial sanctions are pursued, the adolescent should still be referred for a comprehensive sexual offence-specific assessment. This should be completed by a professional who has experience and expertise regarding sexual offence-specific assessment and risk assessment.

Recommendation: Whenever possible, it is recommended that a professional with specialised training and expertise complete a comprehensive sexual offence-specific assessment (ie prior to sentencing but subsequent to a plea having been entered or a finding of guilt). The assessor must have familiarity with the Association for the Treatment of Sexual Abusers' (ATSA) guidelines for assessment, as well as risk assessment and available risk assessment tools (eg ERASOR 2.0; JSOAP-II). In addition, in cases of intrafamilial sexual offending or sibling incest, it is highly recommended that the assessing professional possess specific experience and expertise in assessing issues related to reunification.

Parent/caregiver/family's involvement in adolescent's assessment

Wherever possible, parents and/or caregivers for the adolescent should be included in the sexual offence-specific assessment. Involving parents and caregivers at the time of assessment increases the likelihood of engaging them successfully throughout treatment. In addition, parents and caregivers can provide considerable information regarding the adolescent's history and functioning in many areas (eg developmental, academic, social, emotional, sexual) which may help to explain the etiology of the sexual offending (CSOMB, 2003). Furthermore, parents and caregivers are often in need of support with respect to the sexual offending that has occurred, and assessing this need early on is important.

In cases of sibling incest, it is also critical for parents and/or caregivers to be involved in the assessment in order to allow the assessor to gather information on, and gain an understanding of, issues related to safety and supervision within the home. This will enhance the assessor's ability to make recommendations regarding potential future contact between the offending adolescent and their victimised and non-victimised siblings. Involvement of the parents may require encouragement and support from police services, child protection workers, and the assessing professionals.

The parents'/family's cooperation is also important with respect to informed supervision of the adolescent and his/her progress in assessment and treatment (CSOMB, 2003) as well as issues related to potential risk of sexual reoffending. Non-cooperative family members may negatively impact the adolescent's progress in assessment and treatment, as well as cooperation within a residential placement if one is sought.

Non-victimised siblings

Non-victimised siblings should also be included in assessments to explore issues related to the siblings' safety and to improve an assessor's ability to comment on residence recommendations for the adolescent. In cases where the adolescent has offended solely outside of the home, the professional might determine that (from the perspective of the siblings' safety) the adolescent might be able to reside at home during treatment because the (non-victimised) siblings are sufficiently aware of issues related to privacy, secrets, and boundaries, and are sufficiently able to assert themselves or enlist assistance from their parents. Such information is also important in cases where the adolescent has sexually offended against one or more siblings, but not all siblings. The non-victimised sibling(s) should still participate in the assessment to explore issues related to safety of contact between that sibling and the offending adolescent following the assessment (ie it may be appropriate and safe, with supervision, for contact to continue between the offending adolescent and the sibling(s) who was not victimised).

Recommendation: Additional family members participate in an assessment as needed or appropriate. Recommendations/requests for involvement of additional family members in assessment are made by experienced clinicians. Contact issues with regards to non-victimised siblings are addressed by clinicians.

9. Referral for treatment

Based on the outcome of the assessments that are completed, recommendations for the adolescent, victimised individual, and family might include various combinations of treatment modality (eg individual, family, and group therapy). Treatment must be uniquely tailored to the needs of all involved and should address the adolescent's (and other family members') unique strengths, risks, and needs.

Treatment should be delivered by degreed mental health professionals who have the training and experience necessary (as indicated in the ATSA, 2003 guidelines) to provide comprehensive treatment regarding adolescent sexual offending. For those adolescents who have also been victims of trauma, the treating professionals should have experience and training (in accordance with best-practices) in this regard as well (see Saunders, Berliner and Hanson, 2003).

It is critical to point out that, according to research findings, most adolescents who offend sexually do not continue to offend sexually as adults (Letourneau and Miner, 2005). In addition, specialised offence-specific treatment significantly reduces both sexual and nonsexual reoffending (Reitzel and Carbonell, 2006; Worling and Curwen, 2000). For example, in their 10-year (average 6.23 years) follow-up study of 148 adolescents who had sexually offended, Worling and Curwen (2000) found that 5.17 per cent of those who had participated in specialised treatment reoffended sexually in comparison to 17.8 per cent of those who had not participated in specialised treatment or had dropped out prior to one year of specialised treatment. At 20 years (average 16.23 years), only 9 per cent of the treatment group had been charged with a subsequent sexual offence, in comparison with 21 per cent of those who did not participate in treatment (Worling, Litteljohn and Bookalam, 2009). In the case of sibling incest, specialised treatment can result in successful repair of the sibling relationship and, in many cases, successful family reunification.

Recommendation: Additional family members participate in treatment as needed/appropriate. Recommendations/requests for involvement of additional family members in treatment are made by experienced clinicians and treatment for all family members is provided by clinicians experienced in this regard.

10. Reunification

In some circumstances, contact between the adolescent and the victimised individual(s) may be supported at the end of assessment (eg the adolescent is estimated to be at a low risk to reoffend sexually and has realistic safety plans; the victimised individual is not experiencing a concerning level of trauma/impact from the sexual abuse; parents/adults are aware of issues and able to supervise effectively). In most circumstances, however, it is recommended that treatment be initiated for all involved prior to contact or reunification, and that any contact or reunification be timed and guided by the recommendations of the treating professionals who are working with all involved.

In their investigation of clinicians' experiences with reunification of more than 60 sets of siblings following sibling incest, Skau, Barbour, and Falls (2008) found that more than 60 per cent reunified successfully and more than 10 per cent were still in the process of reunification. It should be noted that the intensity and duration of the adolescent's treatment, in general, will depend on the adolescent's progress and participation. In the case of reunification with the victimised individual, the intensity and duration of this process will depend, primarily, on the wishes, needs, and progress of the victimised individual, inclusive of their progress in treatment with an independent therapist. Regardless of the offending adolescent's status in treatment, reunification with the victimised individual should only occur upon the victimised individual's explicit interest and readiness in this regard, as well as the recommendations, support, and involvement of the treating professionals. When conducted by experienced clinicians, sibling and family reunification can be a positive and successful process.

Implementation and future directions

The document from which this chapter was derived was developed with the intent of providing a best-practice informed guideline for a coordinated and integrated response among the various systems involved when an adolescent is alleged to have sexually offended. Although this document is not intended as a guide regarding the specifics of clinical assessment and treatment of adolescents who have sexually offended (as well as victimised individuals and families), both procedural and clinical information and recommendations were provided in order to highlight the importance of synchronising procedural/systems issues with clinical needs and best practices. In many cases, procedural/systems issues can either directly support or challenge/impede clinical approaches and outcomes in working with these adolescents and their families.

Within the province of Ontario, the document from which this chapter was derived was provided to all child protection agencies (Children's Aid Societies) and youth justice offices, as well as to various police departments, judges, school boards/specific school personnel, numerous children's mental health agencies, community and residential programs specialising in working with adolescents who have sexually offended and those who have been victimised, advocacy groups, and private practitioners, among others. This occurred approximately one year prior to preparation of this chapter. The document has also been provided to others who have requested it and it has been made available for download on-line. To date, the authors have presented the protocol at a number of conferences, children's mental health agencies, probation offices, and child protection agencies. Reception of the protocol has been very positive, with comments generally focused on the utility of having a best-practice based document that is 'user-friendly' or 'consumable', provides a step-by-step process, and can be used to educate both parents/caregivers and individuals from the various systems involved.

Although moving toward a more formal or official implementation of the protocol has been discussed by many who have received it, and various suggestions have emerged regarding this next step, coordinating and obtaining support for this process among all of the systems involved is certain to be a considerable task. Nevertheless, many recipients from various systems have commented on smaller scale and more informal use of the protocol thus far. In many cases, this has included reviewing internal policies for consistency with the protocol recommendations, educating other professionals regarding best-practices and steps or roles within the continuum of care, and using the document to explain the process to families. Specific comments from colleagues within the various systems involved have also been received, with a sample provided below.

Responding to Adolescent Sexual Offending: Recommendations for a Regional Protocol is utilised regularly by the Sexual Abuse: Family, Education, and Treatment (SAFE-T) Program. The document is used both clinically and with collaterals involved in supporting youth towards successful outcomes. Experientially, I have learned the importance of parents, youth justice, child welfare, police, foster parents, assessors, treatment providers, etc., working collaboratively and also clearly defining our varied roles and responsibilities with youth and their families. When we have a shared understanding at the onset of intervention on how to provide safe contexts for living and the clinical interventions, I believe there are fewer dilemmas for youth and their parents, but this takes an incredible amount of work. The protocol document provides a clear road map and is shared with collaterals either prior to our first meeting or at the orientation meeting for assessment and/or treatment.

Parents appreciate how clearly the document is laid out and the document may support their advocacy in regards to the youth who offended and/or the child who was sexually abused. As well, it may also be used clinically to help parents process why certain situations or factors are presently recommended and/or stipulated.

As the community follows the guidelines set out in the protocol, I suspect evidence of successful completions of treatment, which may include reunification, will reinforce a strong commitment to the protocol. At the SAFE-T Program we have followed these standards of practice for many years; however, without a supporting document such as this protocol. I appreciate the protocol guidelines as an ideal for a continuum of care. As the manager of Treatment Services at the SAFE-T Program I encourage others to refer to this document and to adopt these standards of practice within their regions.

Alice Olsen, M.S.W., Manager of Treatment
Services, SAFE-T Program, Thistletown
Regional Centre; Toronto, Ontario;
Ministry of Children and Youth Services

In the Griffin Centre's Sexual Offending Risk/Needs Assessment and Treatment (SORNAT) Program, we continue to struggle with the challenge of explaining to youth, families, youth justice, and child welfare workers, the importance of having youth who sexually offend removed from their home during the assessment period (and perhaps longer) if there are children under 12 living there. No parent wants to believe that their adolescent could sexually harm their younger child, particularly if they have only sexually offended against extra-familial, peer-aged, or older victims. Furthermore, it is difficult for a child welfare worker to justify placing a youth in care, particularly if that youth is approaching or has reached his/her sixteenth birthday, and has not (as yet) sexually harmed their younger sibling(s). Probation officers are often reticent to implement an 'Order to Reside' condition if the youth in question is following the rules of the home and attending school. Simply referring to 'best practice guidelines' as a way of encouraging families and service providers to find a temporary home for a youth who has sexually offended is usually not enough.

Having this Protocol to refer to has provided the treatment community with a comprehensive tool to use during inter-agency meetings and counselling sessions as a psycho-educational intervention. Its step-by-step format allows clinicians to 'walk' families and other service providers through the process; from charges being laid, to assessment to treatment to termination. Because we at the Griffin Centre serve adolescents and their parents who have intellectual disabilities; having a concrete, 'black and white' document to show them is definitely a plus. While the language in the protocol might be a barrier for our clients in particular, we can certainly adapt it as necessary. We are currently in the process of using this protocol to guide us through some internal policy changes with regard to how we address adolescent sexual offending at the intake stage in terms of how we proceed from the moment of referral when youth who sexually offend are living with children under the age of twelve.

Arlene Sager, M.S.W., R.S.W., Supervisor,
SORNAT Program; Griffin Centre; Toronto, Ontario

Responding to Adolescent Sexual Offending: Recommendations for a Regional Protocol (the Protocol) is already proving to be a helpful document in many settings. The recommendations are intended to be consistent with best practice statements from the Association for the Treatment of Sexual Abusers (ATSA). This is important for those of us who work in school systems, as we are many times the first to report allegations of adolescent sexual misconduct.

The Protocol is clear about Initiating Investigations (Section 1) and dovetails well with reporting obligations in broader Education Acts (Bill 157, Ontario). It is noteworthy in the investigation phase that the Protocol says '... Youth who sexually offend should not have contact with children under the age of 12 or other potentially vulnerable individuals' (page 12). This will help strengthen the Safe School transfer process of moving the adolescent who offended to another school and making sure the responsible adults in the next setting are aware of the need to supervise and support the adolescent in a very active manner.

In cases where a school system expels a student for reasons of sexual assault under Bill 212 (Ontario) the Protocol can be especially useful. It is possible under Bill 212 to stipulate some of the non-academic conditions that need to be met in order to have an expulsion lifted. If assessment and treatment for sexual offending become part of the conditions for having an expulsion lifted, school support personnel (social workers and psychologist) can be part of the community response by making and supporting referrals to appropriate community treatment providers. The Protocol can be an effective template for mapping out such a pathway for youth who sexually offend and are part of the school system.

Brian Connelly, M.S.W., Ph.D., R.S.W., Senior
Social Worker, Support Program for
Expelled Students; Toronto District School
Board; Toronto, Ontario

As noted in the introduction of this chapter, in preparing this document and chapter, we recognise that the recommendations provided represent the ideal continuum of care and, in some circumstances, aspects of the protocol or certain recommendations may be difficult to implement. We welcome feedback and comments regarding the utility of the document, challenges and obstacles encountered regarding implementation, and creative methods that have been used to address or overcome some of these challenges and obstacles. Where aspects of the protocol have been implemented successfully, information will be particularly useful regarding the process involved in getting the various

individuals, partners, or systems on board. It is perceived that this will be an evolving document, with future updates provided regarding both informal and formal implementation of the protocol. In the interim, it is hoped that this chapter provides an effective tool in educating and guiding the various systems involved in coordinating and integrating the response when addressing adolescent sexual offending.

Glossary of terms

Adolescent: An individual between 12–17 years of age at the time of the sexual offence who (based on age) could be held legally/criminally culpable for the sexual offence that has been alleged.

Comprehensive sexual offence-specific assessment: A comprehensive assessment of the adolescent who has sexually offended. This encompasses numerous elements inclusive of, but not limited to, family history and relationships, cognitive functioning, academic functioning, social and recreational functioning, emotional functioning, victimisation history, behavioural concerns and nonsexual delinquency, physical and mental health issues, sexual development, sexual behaviour and sexual offending history, sexual interests and attitudes, and amenability to treatment. An estimate of risk of sexual reoffending utilising the best available protocols/guidelines in this regard is also included, along with comprehensive recommendations (which include specific recommendations regarding contact with children, potentially vulnerable individuals, and, if relevant, known victimised individuals).

Comprehensive trauma informed assessment: For the purpose of this document, this is included only where reunification between the offending and victimised individual(s) is a goal. In such cases, the comprehensive trauma-informed assessment encompasses numerous issues inclusive of, but not limited to, family history and relationships, cognitive functioning, academic functioning, social and recreational functioning, emotional functioning, victimisation history, behavioural functioning (inclusive of potentially concerning sexual behaviours), physical and mental health issues, and amenability to treatment. Comprehensive recommendations are provided, inclusive of addressing potential contact/reunification with the offending adolescent (or how initiating such contact should be determined, timed, and guided).

Experienced professional: A professional with a post-secondary degree who possesses specialised training and experience in the areas of sexual abuse and sexual offending. Training and experience would include comprehensive assessment and treatment, with knowledge of risk issues, risk assessment, current best-practices, and research findings. Where relevant, this would also include knowledge and experience regarding reunification issues.

Potentially vulnerable individual: Any potentially vulnerable individual who may be at risk of sexual victimisation. This may include children under the age of 12 or individuals with an intellectual or physical disability that may impact their ability to protect themselves or report victimisation.

Court-ordered assessment: An assessment that is ordered by the court and is to be completed by a qualified person who is required to report the results in writing to the court. It is recommended that these are not completed prior to a finding (ie of guilt) by the court as the adolescent's ability and willingness to speak openly would be particularly in question at that time. The assessment should include issues outlined in the definition of the comprehensive sexual offence-specific assessment, but might also include additional specific recommendations regarding placement and sentencing (eg incarceration, probation).

Sexual offence: For the purpose of this document, refers to any sexual act that is chargeable under a particular jurisdiction's Criminal Code. This may include contact or non-contact sexual offences.

Supervised contact: Contact between the adolescent and victimised individual is directly (within constant and direct sight) supervised by an adult who is aware of the sexual offending allegations and specific rules for contact and/or supervision requirements.

Unsupervised contact: Contact between the adolescent and victimised individual that is not directly supervised or that is supervised by an individual who is not aware of the sexual offending allegations and specific rules for contact and/or supervision requirements.

Victimised individual: An individual of any age who has experienced a contact or non-contact sexual offence by the adolescent.

Acknowledgements

In preparing this chapter, the authors gratefully acknowledge the ongoing support of the Halton Trauma Centre and Darryl Hall, Executive Director at the Halton Trauma Centre. As well, we are grateful to the Ministry of the Attorney General (Ontario, Canada) for funding the development of the document that preceded this chapter. Additionally, we thank Dr James R. Worling for his thoughtful review of the document from which this chapter was derived. Finally, we are grateful to the many children, adolescents, families, and colleagues from whom we have learned that much is possible when there is hope and a commitment to healing.

References

Abel, G.G. and Rouleau, J.L. (1990) The Nature and Extent of Sexual Assault. in Marshall, W.L., Laws, D.R. and Barbaree, H.E. (eds.) *The Handbook of Sexual Assault: Issues, Theories, and Treatment of The Offender.* New York: Plenum.

Association for the Treatment of Sexual Abusers (2003) *Practice Standards and Guidelines for Members of the Association for the Treatment of Sexual Abusers.* Beaverton, OR: Author.

Barbaree, H.E., Hudson, S.M. and Seto, M.C. (1993) Sexual Assault in Society: The Role of The Juvenile Offender. in Barbaree, H.E. Marshall, W.L. and Hudson, S.M. (eds.) *The Juvenile Sex Offender.* New York: Guilford Press.

Barbaree, H.E. and Langton, C. (2006) The Effects of Child Sexual Abuse and Family Environment. in Barbaree, H.E. and Marshall, W.L. (eds.) *The Juvenile Sex Offender.* 2nd edn New York: Guilford Press.

Barbaree, H.E., Marshall, W.L. and Mccormick, J. (1998) The Development of Deviant Sexual Behavior among Adolescents and its Implications for Prevention and Treatment. *Irish Journal of Psychology,* 19, 1–31.

Becker, J.V. and Kaplan, M.S. (1993) Cognitive Behavioral Treatment of the Juvenile Sex Offender. in Barbaree, H.E. Marshall, W.L. and Hudson, S.M. (eds.) *The Juvenile Sex Offender.* New York, NY: Guilford Press.

Beitchman, J.H. et al. (1991) A Review of the Short-Term Effects of Child Sexual Abuse. *Child Abuse and Neglect,* 15, 537–66.

Beitchman, J.H. et al. (1992) A Review of the Long-Term Effects of Child Sexual Abuse. *Child Abuse and Neglect,* 16, 101–18.

Burton, D.L. and Hedgepeth, M.A. (2002) *The Relationships Between Sexual Offense and Nonsexual Crimes for Sexually Abusive Youth.* Poster Presented at the 21st Conference of the Association for the Treatment of Sexual Abusers (ATSA); Montreal, Canada.

California Professional Society on the Abuse of Children (CAPSAC) *Monitored Visitation Guidelines.* Retrieved from: tcavjohn.com/guidelines.htm

Center for Sex Offender Management (2000a) *Community Supervision of the Sex Offender: an Overview of the Current and Promising Practices.* CSOM, Office of Justice Programs, Department of Justice, USA.

Center for Sex Offender Management (2000b) *Engaging Advocates and Other Victim Service Providers in the Community Management of Sex Offenders.* CSOM, Office of Justice Programs, Department of Justice, USA.

Center for Sex Offender Management (2008) *The Comprehensive Approach to Sex Offender Management.* CSOM, Office of Justice Programs, Department of Justice, USA.

Cohen, L.E. and Felson, M. (1979) Social Change and Crime Rate Trends: A Routine Activity Approach. *American Sociological Review*, 44, 588–608.

Colorado Sex Offender Management Board (2003) *Standards and Guidelines for the Evaluation, Assessment, Treatment and Supervision of Juveniles Who Have Committed Sexual Offenses.* Colorado Department of Public Safety, Denver, CO.

Cooper, C.L., Murphy, W.D. and Haynes, M.R. (1996) Characteristics of Abused and Non-Abused Adolescent Sexual Offenders. *Sexual Abuse: A Journal of Research and Treatment*, 8: 2, 105–19.

Costin, D. (2004) *The Relationship Between the Victimization History and Sexual Offences of Male Adolescent Sexual Offenders: A Focus on Sexual Victimization, and Sexual Intrusiveness and Force in Offences.* Unpublished Doctoral Dissertation. University of Toronto; Toronto, ON.

Finkelhor, D. (1990) Early and Long-Term Effects of Child Sexual Abuse: an Update. *Professional Psychology: Research and Practice*, 21: 5, 325–30.

Finkelhor, D. and Browne, A. (1986) Initial and Long-Term Effects: A Conceptual Framework. in Finkelhor, D. (ed.) *A Sourcebook on Child Sexual Abuse.* Beverly Hills, CA: Sage Publications.

Ford, M.E. and Linney, J.A. (1995) Comparative Analysis of Juvenile Sexual Offenders, Violent Nonsexual Offenders, and Status Offenders. *Journal of Interpersonal Violence*, 10, 56–70.

Hodges, C.E. (2002) A 5-Step Family Therapy Protocol to Treat Sibling on Sibling Sexual Abuse. in Calder, M.C. (ed.) *Young people who sexually abuse: building the evidence base for your practice.* Lyme Regis: Russell House Publishing.

Hunter, J.A. and Lexier, L.J. (1998) Ethical and Legal Issues in the Assessment and Treatment of Juvenile Sex Offenders. *Child Maltreatment*, 3, 339–48.

Kendall-Tackett, K.A., Williams, L.M. and Finkelhor, D. (1993) Impact of Sexual Abuse on Children: A Review and Synthesis of Recent Empirical Studies. *Psychological Bulletin*, 113: 1, 164–80.

Letourneau, E. (2006) Legal Consequences of Juvenile Sex Offending in the United States. in Barbaree, H. and Marshall, W. (eds.) *The Juvenile Sexual Offender.* 2nd edn. New York: Guilford Press.

Letourneau, E.J. and Miner, M.H. (2005) Juvenile Sex Offender: A Case Against the Legal and Clinical Status Quo. *Sexual Abuse: A Journal of Research and Treatment*, 17: 3 293–312.

Lindzey, G. (1967) Some Remarks Concerning Incest, the Incest Taboo and Psychoanalytic Theory, *American Psychologist*, 22, 1051–9.

McGrath, R.J., Cumming, G.F. and Burchard, B.L. (2003) *Current Practices and Trends in Sexual Abuser Management: The Safer Society 2002 Nationwide Survey.* Brandon, VT: Safer Society.

Mendel, M.P. (1995) *The Male Survivor: The Impact of Sexual Abuse.* London: Sage Publications.

O'Brien, M.J. (1991) Taking Sibling Incest Seriously. in Patton, M.Q. (ed.) *Family Sexual Abuse: Frontline Research and Evaluation.* Thousand Oaks, CA: Sage Publications.

Prentky, R. and Righthand, S. (2003) *The Juvenile Sex Offender Assessment Protocol (J-SOAP) Manual.* (Unpublished) Retrieved from http://www.ncjrs.gov

Reitzel, L.R. and Carbonell, J.L. (2006) The Effectiveness of Sexual Offender Treatment for Juveniles as Measured by Recidivism: A Meta-Analysis. *Sexual Abuse: A Journal of Research and Treatment*, 18: 4, 401–21.

Romano, E. and De Luca, R.V. (1997) Exploring the Relationship between Childhood Sexual Abuse and Adult Sexual Perpetration. *Journal of Family Violence*, 12, 85–97.

Ryan, G. et al. (1996) Trends in a National Sample of Sexually Abusive Youths. *Journal of the American Academy of Child and Adolescent Psychiatry*, 35: 1, 17–25.

Saunders, B.E., Berliner, L. and Hanson, R.F. (eds.) (2003) *Child Physical and Sexual Abuse: Guidelines for Treatment* Charleston, SC: National Crime Victims Research and Treatment Center.

Sexual Abuse Treatment Services City-Wide Steering Committee (2004) *Best Practice Guidelines for Working with Children, Youth and Families who have Experienced Abuse.* Toronto.

Skau, B., Barbour, H. and Falls, N. (2008) *Working with Families Where Sibling Sexual Abuse Has Occurred.* Presentation at the 2008 Conference of the Continuum of Services for Adolescents who have Sexually Offended, Toronto.

Smallbone, S.W. (2006) Social and Psychological Factors in the Development of Delinquency and Sexual Deviance. in Barbaree, H.E. and Marshall, W.L. (eds.) *The Juvenile Sexual Offender.* The New York: Guilford Press.

Statistics Canada (2007) http://www40.statcan.ca/l01/cst01/legal19a-eng.htm, Retrieved April 15, 2009.

Talbot, T. et al. (2002) *An Overview of Sex Offender Management.* Center for Sex Offender Management, Office of Justice Programs, Department of Justice, USA.

Thakker, J., Ward, T. and Tidmarsh, P. (2006) A Reevaluation of Relapse Prevention with Adolescents who Sexually Offend. in Barbaree, H.E. and Marshall, W.L. (eds.) *The Juvenile Sexual Offender.* New York: Guilford Press.

Trivits, L, C. and Reppucci, N.D. (2002) Application of Megan's Law to Juveniles. *American Psychologist*, 57, 690–704.

Van Dijk, J.J.M., Mayhew, P. and Killias, M. (1991) *Experiences of Crime across the World: Key Findings from the 1989 International Crime Survey.* Deventer, The Netherlands: Kluwer.

White, J.W., Kadlec, K.M. and Sechrist, S. (2006) Adolescent Sexual Aggression within Heterosexual Relationships. in Barbaree, H.E. and Marshall, W.L. (eds.) *The Juvenile Sexual Offender.* New York: Guilford Press.

Worling, J.R. and Curwen, T. (2000) Adolescent Sexual Offender Recidivism: Success of Specialized Treatment and Implications for Risk Prediction. *Child Abuse and Neglect*, 24: 7, 965–82.

Worling, J.R. and Curwen, T. (2001) Estimate of Risk of Adolescent Sexual Offense Recidivism (Version 2.0: The 'ERASOR') in Calder, M.C. (ed.) *Juveniles and children who sexually abuse: Frameworks for assessment.* Lyme Regis: Russell House Publishing.

Worling, J.R. and Langstrom, N. (2006) Risk of Sexual Recidivism. in Barbaree, H.E. and Marshall, W.L. (eds.) *The Juvenile Sexual Offender.* New York: The Guilford Press.

Worling, J.R., Litteljohn, A. and Bookalam, D. (2009) *20-Year Prospective Study of Specialized Treatment at the SAFE-T Program for Adolescents who Offended Sexually.* Ontario Ministry of Children and Youth Services, Toronto, ON.

CHAPTER 12

Past Caring? Issues of After Care, Attachment and Mental Health for Young People who Have Displayed Harmful Sexual Behaviour

Nicola Gilderthorp, Mette Whittaker and Julian Dunn

Brief introduction

The authors of this chapter form part of a therapeutic team working with young people who have displayed sexually harmful behaviour. The SWAAY organisation has been in existence for 21 years and has worked with approximately 150 young people from referral to after care. Working within a specialist residential facility has afforded us the luxury of being able to provide an holistic care package over an extended period, including residential care, a full education programme and a comprehensive therapeutic service. Whilst most of the young people benefit from their time in our care, we have become increasingly aware and concerned that at the point of transition into independent living the young people we work with experience significant challenges. These stem not only from their own individual difficulties and needs, but also from the systematic failings of the after care system. Whilst there are no easy answers, we seek to raise awareness of some of the issues facing the care-leaving population in general, but with specific reference to the unique problems that exist for young people who have displayed sexually harmful behaviour.

Meet 'Paul'

Paul was referred to SWAAY at the age of 14½. At the time of referral he was involved in court proceedings for several offences of rape of intrafamilial and known children. Paul, like many of these young people, had suffered significant adversity, including emotional abuse, neglect, exposure to domestic and sexual violence and sexual abuse. He was diagnosed with ADHD (Attention Deficit Hyperactivity Disorder), RAD (Reactive Attachment Disorder) and met the diagnostic criteria for conduct disorder. Paul had had a number of school exclusions and for the past six months had been attending a Pupil Referral Unit. Paul had experienced a number of foster care placements which had broken down due to his challenging behaviour, including sexual aggression. Despite concerns, he had been placed in care with his younger brother and sister. Paul's mother suffered from learning disabilities and his father had a history of non-sexual offending and non-compliance with professionals involved in the case. Despite this, it was considered important for Paul to maintain contact with his parents. Due to the high profile nature of this case, it was felt that it was not in Paul's best interests for him to return home either during contact visits with his parents, or indeed after he had completed his placement at SWAAY. Four months into his placement Paul was given a three-year Supervision Order with a condition that he undertake treatment for his sexually harmful behaviour.

Key facts

Young people in care

At any one time there are approximately 60,000 children in care, which represents roughly 0.5 per cent of all children. During the course of any one year as many as 85,000 children will spend some time in care. Of the 60,000 children in care, 71 per cent reside in foster care; 14 per cent in residential care and approximately eight per cent are placed with their families. The remainder are placed for adoption or in more specialised placements. During 2007/08, 8,300 young people over 16 years old left care (leavingcare.org, 2010).

Education, training, employment

Educational attainment of children in care is known to be poorer than that of the general population. This is evidenced by only 11 per cent of children in care gaining five good GCSEs in 2005, compared to 56 per cent of all children. At age 19 years, 28 per cent of care leavers are in further education and seven per cent are in higher education. This compares to 44 per cent of all young people in one form of education at age 19. Of those who have left care, 29 per cent are not in education, training or employment at age 19 years compared to 10 per cent of all young people (leavingcare.org, 2010).

Leaving care

In 2007/08, 24 per cent of those leaving care were aged 16 years. Those in residential care were most likely to leave at 16. This compares to an average age of leaving care of 24 years for all young people (leavingcare.org, 2010). A study conducted in 2003, showed that in a sample of 200 young people who were either in the process of leaving care, or who had recently left care, 53 per cent had used illegal drugs during the month prior to the study, while 63 per cent had used illegal drugs in the year leading up to the study. When these figures were compared to young people in the general population, this figure was much higher for the care-leaver group (Ward, Henderson and Pearson, 2003). Young women aged 15–17 years who have been in care are three times more likely to become teenage mothers than others their age (leavingcare.org, 2010). Research suggests that 23 per cent of adult prisoners and 38 per cent of young prisoners have spent time in care (DoH, 1999; in Ward, Henderson and Pearson, 2003). Between a quarter and a third of rough sleepers have been looked after by local authorities as children (Social Exclusion Unit, 2001). Up to 20 per cent of care leavers will experience some kind of homelessness within two years of leaving care (DoH, 1999; in Ward, Henderson and Pearson, 2003).

Prevalence rates of psychiatric disorder among adolescents who had been in care for an average of two years 10 months was 67 per cent compared to 15 per cent in a comparison group, which consisted of adolescents who had had no contact with any local authority. Ninety-six per cent of adolescents in residential care and 57 per cent of adolescents in foster care had psychiatric disorders (McCann, James, Wilson and Dunn, 1996).

Within the last decade, legislation such as the Children (Leaving Care) Act 2000, has attempted to address some of the concerns highlighted above. However, as can be seen from the research the needs of these young people are still not being adequately met.

Children (Leaving Care) Act 2000

The Children (Leaving Care) Act 2000 is a statutory instrument, which came into effect on 1 October 2001. The Leaving Care Act has two main aims. The first being to ensure that young people do not leave care until they are ready and secondly, to ensure that they receive more effective support once they have left.

The Children (Leaving Care) Act 2000 states the following for young people aged 16–18:

- Local authorities have a duty to undertake an assessment and to meet the needs of the young person. The young person must also be involved in the preparation and review of this assessment.
- Local authorities have a duty to ensure that a pathway plan is in place by the young persons' 16th birthday. This plan should consider the young person's need for support and assistance, as identified in the assessment. It should also look at how these needs will be met until the age of 21. Areas which are covered within this plan include:
  – accommodation
  – practical life skills
  – education and training
  – employment
  – financial support
  – specific support needs
  – contingency plans for support if independent living breaks down
- Local authorities have a duty to provide financial support to cover the cost of accommodation; food and domestic bills; pocket money; transport costs for education and training; clothing and childcare costs.
- Local authorities have a duty to provide a personal adviser, who will be involved in providing advice and support; drawing up the Pathway Plan and ensuring it addresses any changing needs; keeping in touch with the young person; co-ordinating services and linking in with other agencies.
- Local authorities have a duty to provide suitable accommodation, which must be reasonably practical for the young person given his/her needs. Bed and Breakfast accommodation is not appropriate except as an emergency measure.

For those aged 18–21:

- Local authorities have a duty to maintain contact and to provide support through the personal adviser.
- Local authorities have a duty to assist with costs of education, employment and training.
- If the young person is in full-time higher or residential further education the local authority has a duty to provide accommodation during the vacations or to pay the young person enough to secure accommodation for him/herself if the term-time accommodation is not available.

For those aged 21 and over:

- The local authority's duties remain the same as they do for 18–21 year olds if the young person is still in education or training.
- Local authorities have a duty to ensure vacation accommodation for young people in higher education.

A National Voice, 2010

Pathway Plan

The Pathway Plan is the main piece of work undertaken by the social worker with the young person to begin to make preparations for the young person's transition into independence. It should include the following:

1. Outline of the nature and level of contact and personal support to be provided, and by whom, to the child or young person.
2. Details of the accommodation the child or young person is to occupy.
3. A detailed plan for the education or training of the child/young person.
4. How the responsible authority will assist the child or young person in relation to employment or other purposeful activity or occupation.
5. The support to be provided to enable the child or young person to develop and sustain appropriate family and social relationships.
6. A programme to develop the practical and other skills necessary for the child or young person to live independently.
7. Financial support to be provided to the child or young person, in particular where it is to be provided to meet their accommodation and maintenance needs.
8. Outline the health needs, including any mental

health needs, of the child or young person, and how they are to be met.
9. Contingency plans for action to be taken by the responsible authority should the Pathway Plan for any reason cease to be effective.

DoH, *Children (Leaving Care) Act 2000*, Regulations and Guidance

Paul's placement at SWAAY

During his placement at SWAAY Paul resided in a residential home with three other young people and was under constant supervision of at least one member of staff. As is usual for young people at SWAAY, Paul was required to demonstrate his progress by applying for increasing levels of independence and responsibility. This was a graded process based on assessments of risk and vulnerability and developing levels of responsibility. This resulted in him obtaining 'full discretion' two years into his placement, which enabled him to attend a local college and to move into semi-independent accommodation (still supported by SWAAY staff) by his 17th birthday.

During his time at SWAAY, Paul engaged in full-time education and obtained Entry Level and GCSE qualifications. In addition, he completed a six-month group-work programme aimed at improving his social and emotional competencies and an 18-month offence specific programme. Although multi-modal, the main model of the therapy programmes are cognitive behavioural. After having completed this programme, Paul joined the 'Relapse Prevention – Moving On' group-work programme, which he continued to attend even after having left SWAAY. In conjunction with this, Paul attended weekly individual sessions throughout his placement. Identification of treatment needs and goals was initially established through full psychometric self-assessment and through the use of the ERASOR protocol (Estimate of Risk of Adolescent Sexual Offence Recidivism; Worling, 2004). These were reviewed throughout his placement. A final assessment was conducted just prior to his move out of SWAAY and a report outlining areas of development and ongoing need was provided to his local authority. Paul engaged well and although he formed attachments to adults within the organisation, he continued to struggle to form satisfactory relationships with his peers. As Paul obtained full independence, he became subject to Multi Agency Public Protection Arrangements

(MAPPA). Paul was reviewed on a monthly basis with reference to accommodation, education and social networks.

Needs of young people leaving care

As mentioned above, there are approximately 60,000 children in care on any given day in England. The majority (71 per cent) of these are with foster carers; 11 per cent, almost all over the age of 10, live in residential homes; eight per cent live with their parents subject to a Care Order and a small number live in secure children's homes. Of these children, 63 per cent are aged 10 or over, most of them are boys (56 per cent) and most of them are reported to be White British (74 per cent). The main reason for children of all ages becoming looked after is parental abuse or neglect. Not surprisingly then, children often enter the care system with poorer health than their non-looked after peers and the longer-term outcomes for these children remain than worse than for their peers (DCSF and DoH, 2009).

It is widely recognised that there is a high level of mental health need amongst looked after children and a national survey conducted by Meltzer et al. (2003) found that 45 per cent of looked after children were assessed as having a mental health disorder. This number rose to 72 per cent of those in residential care and compares to approximately 10 per cent of the general population aged 5–15. Even when looked after children were compared to children in a community sample from the most deprived socio-economic groups, they still showed significantly higher rates of mental health disorders (Ford et al., 2007). This corresponds with Sempik, Ward and Darker's (2008) findings in a study conducted to investigate the prevalence of emotional and behavioural difficulties among children and young people who remained in care for at least a year. They found that 72 per cent of the participants had a mental health or behavioural problem. Ford et al. (2007) found that clinically significant conduct disorders were the most common among looked after children (37 per cent), while 12 per cent had emotional disorders and seven per cent were hyperactive. Whilst this in itself is concerning, it should also be borne in mind that young people with poor health are at greater risk of lower levels of educational attainment and of failing to achieve their full potential (Department of Health, 2004). Finally, it is suggested that young people who are looked after are more vulnerable to risk taking behaviour (DFES, 2006; Meltzer et al., 2003) which, without intervention or modification, can itself increase the risk of poorer outcomes for these children.

A proportion of the children and young people in care have perpetrated sexual harm and a proportion of these have mental health problems. It is recognised that there is no 'one-size-fits-all' label for this group of young people and there is no specific or clear mental health diagnosis which would explain the sexual behaviour. It has been found, however, that a proportion of young people who sexually harm also present with co-occurring mental disorders: 10–15 per cent have been found to have some type of mood disorder, 30–15 per cent have an anxiety disorder, 10–20 per cent have ADHD, and 20–30 per cent have engaged in substance misuse (Becker et al., 1986, 1991; Kavoussi et al., 1988; Shaw et al., 1993; Leversee, 2007). Righthand and Welch (2001; in Grimshaw, 2008) suggest that schizophrenia and psychotic disorders are relatively rare among this group of young people and Lambie and McCarthy (2004, in Grimshaw, 2008), Rich (2003, In Grimshaw, 2008) and Bladon et al. (2005, in Grimshaw, 2008) assert that more relevant disorders are ADHD and PTSD. A history of nonsexual delinquency is also commonly found to be prevalent among young people who have sexually harmed, with many having been diagnosed with conduct disorder, being abusers of alcohol or drugs, and exhibiting aggressive tendencies (Boyd, Hagan and Cho, 2000). Of 128 young people referred to SWAAY, 56 per cent either had a diagnosis of or met diagnostic criteria for Conduct Disorder; 38 per cent had a diagnosis of or met diagnostic criteria for an emotional disorder; 14 per cent had ADHD; and 15 per cent PTSD (a further 20 per cent suspected).

In addition, research suggests that the families of young people who have perpetrated sexual harm are dysfunctional on a number of levels. Prentky, Knight, Straus, Rokou, Cerce and Sims-Knight (1989, in Ryan, 1998) identified 'sexual victimisation' and 'inconsistent care' as two significant developmental antecedents. Research does indeed appear to suggest that these young people commonly come from physically or sexually abusive families (eg Davis and Leitenberg, 1987; Becker, 1998, Burton, Miller and Tai Shill, 2002) or from families with low levels of positive communication (Blaske,

Borduin, Henggeler and Mann (1989); Worling, 1995). Research also indicates that witnessing family violence as a child may be a risk factor for the later development of sexually harmful behaviour in adolescence (Righthand and Welch, 2004; in Boyd and Bromfield, 2006). Several characteristics have been found to often be present in the families of young people who have sexually harmed but also in the families of children who offend more generally. Manocha and Mezey (1998) found that in their sample of 51 adolescents who had sexually harmed, were histories of abuse and victimisation, family violence, lack of sexual boundaries and a lack of parental protection. Bentovim (1991, 1995) suggests that a family climate in which these are present may serve to increase vulnerability to all types of offending behaviour. These difficulties have also been identified as risk factors for the development of mental health difficulties. The reasons for the relationship between physical or sexual victimisation and future sexual offending are still not clearly understood, and it should be noted that not all children who have experienced abuse or neglect grow up to display abusive behaviour, just as not all adolescents or adults who do display such behaviour have experienced early childhood traumas. However, it is important that these issues are borne in mind when planning treatment for this group of young people as some of these experiences may have resulted in mental health difficulties such as PTSD or Reactive Attachment Disorder, which in turn may impact on risk of future well-being and risk of relapse. The past experiences of these young people, as well as the deficits often found in their social and emotional functioning, are likely to have an impact on their ongoing need for services once they have left care.

As will be discussed in more depth later on in this chapter, periods of transition, such as leaving care, are particularly challenging for these young people. Young people leaving care do not have the same level of family support as most young people who are not in care nor are they likely to have the same level of resilience. As such, they are more vulnerable than children and young people who are not looked after, both in terms of health as well as in terms of falling through gaps between children's and adult's services. In accordance with this, Dixon (2008) found that many aspects of young people's health worsened in the year after leaving care. He found an increased level of reporting of drug and/or

alcohol use, mental health problems and 'other health problems' (eg asthma, weight loss, allergies, pregnancy) when he compared measures taken within three months of leaving care and then again a year later. Alcohol or drug use increased from 18 per cent to 32 per cent, mental health problems from 12 per cent to 24 per cent and 'other health problems' from 28 per cent to 44 per cent. Both young men and young women in care and leaving care are more likely than their peers to be teenage parents. The Guidance on Promoting the Health and Well-being of Looked After Children (DCSF and DoH, 2009) document quotes research suggesting that almost half of young women leaving care became pregnant within 18–24 months and that another quarter were pregnant or young parents within a year of leaving care. This report further suggests that this increased level of vulnerability is a result of these young people being disproportionately affected by risk factors such as experience of abuse, poor mental health and low educational attainment.

The literature pertaining to this area highlights the significant local variation in the availability of mental health services for children and young people, including those who are looked after. Additional difficulties include the level of availability of local Child and Adolescent Mental Health Services (CAMHS) assistance for those children and young people who are placed outside of their local authority, the difference in age ranges served by local CAMHS teams, as well as frequent placement changes and school absence. In order to assess the needs of their looked after children, local authorities are required to make sure that a Strengths and Difficulties Questionnaire (SDQ) is filled in for each of their looked after children aged 4–16 years. The SDQ is a valuable screening tool for mental health problems and could thus be used to support referrals to available and appropriate services. Unfortunately, experience suggests that this is not consistently done and despite the specialist nature of the SWAAY provision it is not unusual that young people are referred without having completed the SDQ or having undergone any psychiatric assessment. It has also proved very difficult for those young people who have left SWAAY to access mental health services despite their recognised vulnerabilities in this regard and despite the concerns often raised regarding their continuing level of risk post-treatment. Indeed it is noticeable that the notion of risk is more often the focus of attention for agencies when young people make the transition into independent living. It is this, rather than specific concerns for their emotional well-being, that can determine the level of ongoing support afforded to them.

As already identified, Paul came from a dysfunctional family who was unable to offer him care and support as he progressed through treatment and into independence. He was unable to return to his local area, due to the presence of past victims and the possible risk posed to Paul from others due to his offending behaviour. Paul arrived with identified and diagnosed mental health problems and behavioural difficulties and although he made a great deal of progress during his time at SWAAY, aspects of these difficulties remained. Despite Paul's high risk, high need status the Pathway Plan was completed late and no external assessment was conducted relating to his mental health. In addition, he was introduced to his leaving care worker, who was unfamiliar with the case, at age 16½ when he was going through the transition into increased independence. From our experience, this is not unusual for young people placed in residential care (out of county). This puts these young people, who are already facing more challenges than most, at an even greater disadvantage.

In recognition of Paul's ongoing needs, SWAAY proposed and provided a support package for him for six months after he left SWAAY. This included support staff helping Paul at his flat as well as Paul attending the weekly 'Relapse Prevention – Moving On' groupwork programme. During this period and after, Paul remained highly dependent on the emotional and practical support of the adults at SWAAY with whom he had made attachments.

Attachment theory

As identified above, Paul was referred to SWAAY with what was described as a Reactive Attachment Disorder. This is not unusual for young people who are referred to our service.

Insecure attachment and its causes have been identified as risk factors influencing the development of mental health problems (John, www.camhs.nhs.uk/mentalHealth/risk-and-protective-factors; Cicchetti and Toth, 2000; Dodge, Pettit and Bates, 1997; Toth and Cicchetti, 2004; Bifulco, Kwon, Jacobs, Moran, Bunn and Beer, 2006). Factors such as attachment to family,

supportive and caring family, attachment to networks in the community, access to support services and positive self-related cognitions have been identified as protective factors. Due to their past attachment experiences and significant victimisation histories the young people at SWAAY present with insecure or disorganised attachment styles and some have also been formally diagnosed with attachment disorders. As a result of this, the programme at SWAAY follows an attachment informed approach, which aims to develop the young people's abilities to form more secure attachments with individuals in the future. As will be outlined later in this chapter, attachment style has implications with regards to an individual's ability to cope and develop resilience promoting factors. It is therefore important to consider the young person's attachment style when assessing or considering their ability to cope with the transition out of the care system and when re-integrating into the community.

An in-depth description of attachment theory and research is beyond the scope of this chapter, however what is understood is that early experiences impact upon an adolescent's and adult's ability both to form healthy, intimate relationships, as well as upon their own parenting style. Rich (2006) also suggested that early attachment experiences impact upon an adolescent's self-confidence, sense of security, emotional well-being and sense of social connectedness.

One of the limitations of attachment theory is that it does not provide a clear basis by which to understand attachment in adolescence and adulthood. However the theory's concept of the Internal Working Model (IWM) is considered to address these limitations and provide an explanation of the attachment process during adolescence and adulthood. The experience of being with others and the mutual recognition and attunement, quality of interaction and reciprocal understanding that is associated with this is formed and stored in the IWM and serves as a mental representation on which ideas about the self and others are based. This also forms the basis for personality, self-image and behaviour (Johnson-Laird, 1983). The internalisation of security, incorporated into the IWM, leads to the development of resilience. A secure individual is therefore able to experience discomfort and fail to get his or her needs met and still be able to deal with the difficulties of life (Rich, 2006).

Resilience is an important concept when considering the ability of young people, such as those at SWAAY, to successfully manage transition periods, their future well-being, as well as with regards to their potential risk of re-offending (this will be discussed in further detail later in this chapter). As outlined earlier in this chapter, young people in care, including those placed at SWAAY, often present with insecure attachment styles and this therefore indicates that they are also likely to lack resilience promoting factors. Although one of the aims of the SWAAY programme is to develop the young people's abilities to form more secure attachments and thus to support them in becoming more resilient, as will be discussed later in this chapter, the nature of their transition and re-integration into the community is likely to be crucial in determining whether in fact they are able to utilise these abilities during this significant period of change.

Fonagy et al. (1997a) suggest that it is only through having a secure attachment that an individual can develop the capacity to recognise and understand another person's perspective and thus display moral social behaviour. They refer to this as mentalising. Fonagy and his colleagues (1997a, 1997b) assert that adolescents who commit crimes have inadequate mentalising capacities, ie they lack empathy and are unable to recognise or to understand other people's perspectives.

Attachment and sexual offending

Social deficits that result from attachment deficits are conceptualised as the links between attachment theory and theories of sexual offending (Rich, 2006). The broad model that links attachment deficits with sexually abusive behaviour is largely theoretical and based upon adult sexual offenders, with limited and often inconsistent evidence to support its propositions. Tracy et al. (2003; in Rich, 2006) indicate that those who have insecure attachments use sexual relationships as a means for gaining control and as a tool for getting emotional needs met, rather than having sexual romantic relationships that would be considered healthy and satisfying.

With regards to perpetrating sexually harmful behaviour, Marshall and his colleagues (Marshall, Hudson and Hodkinson, 1993; Marshall and Marshall, 2000; Marshall, Serran and Cortoni 2000, in Rich, 2006) argue that an insecure attachment style renders individuals vulnerable to sexual offending, and particularly sexual offences against children. They consider insecure attachment to be a risk factor and when individuals with this vulnerability are exposed to other predisposing or precipitating factors they suggest that they are more likely than securely attached individuals to engage in sexual abuse. One of the key variables in this attachment-linked model is that attachment deficits or weak attachment experiences make the child more susceptible to being a victim of sexual abuse. This therefore adds a significant factor to the pathway along which sexualised coping, conditioned sexualised behaviour, and sexually coercive behaviour may later develop. Marshall and Marshall (2000, in Rich, 2006) suggest that these problems lead to a primary reliance on sexualised coping, including the early onset of masturbation and sexual acts with others, thus providing the offender with a way to cope with and to avoid difficulties associated with current difficulties and frustrations as well as regarding a history of family and childhood problems.

Insecure attachment has also been linked with increased vulnerability to further victimisation in the future, including sexual. Due to his ongoing difficulties in forming and maintaining peer relationships and his desperation for emotional intimacy, Paul was exploited by more 'streetwise' young adults, both financially and sexually. He was also 'befriended' by and taken advantage of by older males. In our experience, this is not an unusual occurrence.

The treatment programme at SWAAY is an attachment-informed programme, which is designed to address the deficits highlighted in Ward's (2003) five pathways to sexually abusive behaviour model (Pathway 1: Insecure attachment driven and social deficits; Pathway 2: Deviant sexual scripts resulting from previous sexualisation; Pathway 3: Emotional dysregulation; Pathway 4: Cognitive distortions; Pathway 5: Primary deficits in all areas) and the young people work on these issues throughout the duration of their placement. Despite this, as will be discussed later in this report, the point of transition, where the young people are due to leave SWAAY, is a stressful time for them and a time when they tend to find it difficult to cope. It is thus likely to be a period of time where they will experience increased difficulties in implementing their learning and thus their risk of re-offending may increase as a result. It is therefore essential that the young people feel supported by attachment figures during this period of time so that they can utilise the skills that they have learnt in order to manage these feelings in an adaptive and pro-social manner. As mentioned earlier, ongoing attachments to networks in the community and a sense of connectedness are also considered protective factors in terms of mental health.

Neuro-developmental impact of trauma and developmental considerations

Attachment experiences have been shown to be involved in the development of the area of the brain called the pre-frontal cortex, as its development depends upon our relationship-based experiences which become amalgamated into the Internal Working Model (Balbernie, 2001). The connectors between the limbic system and the pre-frontal cortex are stimulated and strengthened by care and primary caregivers provide the skills that are acquired later in life as the pre-frontal cortex develops. Schore (2003) showed that experiencing persistent stressors in the first two years of life prunes neural connections in the pre-frontal cortex. All of the young people at SWAAY have been victimised and been subjected to significant traumatic experiences during their lives as have a large proportion of those young people not at SWAAY who have perpetrated sexual harm. These traumatic experiences, along with their attachment experiences could therefore have some impact upon the development of this area of their brain. The pre-frontal cortex is the centre for executive functions and, as such, any deficits in this area lead to difficulties in being able to effectively make decisions and solve problems. Lack of pre-frontal cortex development also affects emotional and physical regulation, attention, organisation, and cognitive flexibility (Creeden, 2008). Alongside this, research indicates that the pre-frontal cortex does not develop fully until the ages of between 22 and 25 years (Fernandes, 2006). This therefore highlights that the impact of limited development of the pre-frontal cortex and its implications should be taken into account when considering the ability of a care leaver, who will be under the age of 25 and more likely to have been subjected to traumatic experiences and negative attachment experiences, to cope effectively and be in a position to make informed decisions without support and guidance.

Paul remained highly dependent on the support of SWAAY staff to solve both interpersonal and practical difficulties which he encountered. Although, his ability to effectively self-regulate and be cognitively flexible had improved during his time at SWAAY, these difficulties continued to be evident during times of heightened levels of stress.

In addition to the structural development of the pre-frontal cortex the dopaminergic system also becomes more sensitive during adolescence, thus activities which stimulate the release of dopamines are felt as being more rewarding (Steiberg, 2008; In Kambam and Thompson, 2009). As a result of these rewarding effects, adolescents may be more inclined to engage in sensation-seeking behaviours than adults or even children. Indeed, impulsivity has been found to decrease in a linear fashion from age 10–30 (Kambam and Thompson, 2009) although, as mentioned above, trauma can have a negative impact on the development of effective self-regulation.

Adolescents are also undergoing significant physical, cognitive and emotional maturation. These factors should all be borne in mind when planning and implementing after care services for this client group. Cauffman and Steinberg (2000) found that psychosocial maturity (in the domains of responsibility, perspective and temperance/self-control) as well as antisocial decision-making improve with age. In fact they found that psychosocial maturity has more of an impact on antisocial decision-making than age, and when considering the experiences of the young people at SWAAY, or those in care with attachment difficulties or mental health problems, this is an important finding. In addition, Kambam and Thompson (2009) highlighted that adolescents are particularly susceptible to the deleterious effects of strong emotions on decision-making and Scott et al. (1995; in Kambam and Thompson) found that adolescents' decision-making capacities are also likely to be negatively impacted on by passing psychosocial characteristics such as: the need for increased conformity with peers, underestimation of risk and the greater weight placed on shorter-term versus longer-term consequences. Planning ahead is another area in which adolescents' performance is poorer than adults'. Thus, Kambam and Thompson (2009) suggest that middle adolescence (12–15 years) is a developmental period during which reckless behaviour and subsequent problematic alterations of developmental trajectories are much more likely. Thus, this is an important period in terms of intervention.

In summary, adolescence presents a number of challenges. Physical changes occur during this stage and the level of interest in sexual matters increases. Adolescents start to develop deeper moral thinking, greater appreciation of social norms and boundaries and tend to test rules and limits. As they progress through adolescence they develop an increased capacity for abstract thought and moral reasoning although a sense of self-involvement and changes in confidence persist. Not until later adolescence (19–21 years) are people likely to have mastered the ability to think ideas through and delay gratification on a consistent basis. At this point they start to experience increased emotional stability and increased concern for others. They start to experience an increased sense of independence and self-reliance and have an increased level of concern for the future. However, difficulties may persist for far longer if the individual has experienced significant trauma during childhood or has not been in an environment where normative development was possible. The young person's chronological age may thus be irrelevant in determining whether the behaviour is age-appropriate and in planning for ongoing service requirements. It is more appropriate to consider their age of emotional and cognitive functioning, however, this is inconsistent with current procedures for service implementation and planning.

Resilience

Treatment not only aims to address criminogenic factors but also to develop and improve resilience.

Resilience is the term used to describe an individual's ability to overcome stress or adversity. That is, to show resistance to psychosocial risk experiences (Rutter, 1999). Stein (2005: 1) defines resilience as being:

> ... the quality that enables some young people to find fulfilment in their lives despite their disadvantaged back-grounds, the problems or adversity that they may have undergone or the pressures that they may experience.

For some young people living in care and being removed from their family background provides them with the opportunity to develop a secure

attachment to at least one of their carers within the context of a stable environment. From this secure base they then have the opportunity, as well as the encouragement to build their confidence in the adult world and thus to develop resilience-promoting factors to help them in later life (Rutter, Giller and Hagell, 1998; Newman and Blackburn, 2002).

This is not the case, however, for some young people, due to the lack of continuity and stability that they experience while in care, which results in them continuing to be unable to form relationships or having significant difficulties in accepting other people's help. This can lead to them having difficulties in making alliances with supportive adults and peers as young adults (Stein and Carey, 1986; Downes, 1992). Thus stability while in care and/or secure attachment have been highlighted as being crucial as they result in improved life chances for care leavers and increased ability to develop resilience-promoting factors (Jackson and Thomas, 2001; Jackson, 2002).

Over the past 20 years within the general population there have been significant changes with regards to patterns of transition. This has been due to a number of reasons: firstly, the decline in the youth labour market based on manufacturing and apprenticeship training; the extension of youth training; further and higher education and reduction in entitlements to universal welfare benefits for young people. This has resulted in young people generally being more dependent upon their immediate and extended families for emotional, financial and practical support well into their early twenties (Jones, 2002).

Studies have shown that young people leaving care are generally between the ages of 16 and 17 years (Stein and Carey, 1986; Biehal et al. 1992, 1995; Dixon and Stein, 2005) and that young people leaving foster care or residential care are generally younger than their peers in the general population, which results in a *'compressed and accelerated transition to adulthood'* (Stein, 2004). Evidence also suggests that preparation for leaving care may be considered the responsibility of specialist workers as opposed to carers (Stein, 2004) which again differs from the general population where it is parents, grandparents and other relatives who occupy this role. This therefore highlights that it is those young people who are most likely to lack the range and depth of help given by families that are expected to cope with transition at a far younger age than those young people living with their families (Stein, 2004). It is also these young people who are most likely to suffer from attachment-related difficulties and to lack resilience-promoting factors.

Focal theory indicates that most adolescents cope with major life changes one at a time and over a period of time, that is dealing with one issue before moving onto the next (Coleman and Hendry, 1999). Research suggests that young people who are required to cope with the greatest amount of changes during the shortest period of time are those who experience the poorest outcomes, for example poorer mental health, lower self-esteem and less educational qualifications (Coleman and Hendry, 1999). This corresponds with the key facts presented at the beginning of this report.

An evaluation of English leaving-care services conducted in 1995 by Biehal et al. showed that specialist leaving care schemes were able to make a positive contribution with regards to improving accommodation outcomes and assisting young people in developing life skills, such as budgeting, negotiating and self-care skills, however their impact on other outcomes was limited. For example: educational outcomes were linked to placement stability, which was most often achieved in foster care placements. Success with regards to positive self image and social networks, although assisted by schemes, was mainly associated with having supportive links with family members and former carers. Stein (2004) therefore argues that *'leaving care should be reclaimed by carers'* as it is they who are able to provide the stability and continuity of care that young people need. Stein (2004) suggests that the role of specialist schemes should not be to take over from carers but to assist them in preparing and supporting the young person during their transition, thus their roles would shift to being one of servicing those who provide care. We would concur with this viewpoint, noting the importance for Paul of ongoing contact with SWAAY members of staff. Not just for Paul, but for other young people, all too often the situation arises where by their main source of support and stability is substituted with a personal adviser, with whom the young person has no relationship and who may lack in-depth understanding of the young person, including risk and vulnerability issues. Personal advisers are often, in our experience, unaware of local resources including housing, education and mental health provisions.

In order to promote resilience in care leavers,

Stein (2004) also argues that it is important to improve the quality of care, provide stability and encourage a sense of identity, assist with education and preparation and to increase the number of gradual transitions from care as well as the levels of support for young people once they have left the care system.

Coping styles

Patterson and McCubbin (1987) indicate that the development of coping styles during adolescence is a crucial process, as an adolescent is likely to be faced with a multitude of novel stressors and not have built a range of coping styles with which to manage. It is also recognised that adolescents are at high risk of displaying extreme reactions to stressors, which result from periods of great change, new demands or changing amounts of stress (Konopka, 1980; Seiffge-Krenke, 2000). Leaving care is a significant period of change for the young people leaving SWAAY and as such is likely to be highly stressful. During this time of change the young people are likely to be faced with numerous novel situations, which they are unlikely to have developed effective ways with which to cope. This coupled with the fact that they may continue to have attachment difficulties, which is also likely to influence their ability to cope, suggests that they may employ ineffective coping strategies at times of stress. Thus they are likely to display extreme reactions to stress and this may also have a negative impact upon their psychological health. For young people who have previously been involved in sexually harmful behaviour, such as those residing at SWAAY, this is thus likely to be a particularly risky period of time for them, especially if their previous ways of coping have been to become involved in antisocial or sexually harmful behaviour. It would therefore seem that the provision of support from someone whom the young person can confide in and trust, that is an attachment figure, during this transition would be essential in ensuring that they are successful in re-integrating back into the community. In addition, the availability and accessibility to services needs to be easy for these young people to negotiate as they are unlikely to have the resources required to access the systems currently in place without the help of adults.

Coping is considered to be a mediator in the relationship between stress and illness (Wong,

Figure 12.1: Coping styles

Coping style	Description
Rational	Problem-focused technique
Detached	An individual cognitively distances themselves from the problem in order to minimise the potential emotional impact.
Emotional	Re-labelling the stressor thus giving it a new meaning.
Avoidant	An individual avoids coping with the stressor

Billings and Moos, 1981; Zeidner and Endler, 1996; Roger et al., 1993

1993; Carver et al. 1993). Four different coping styles have been identified (Roger, Jarvis and Najarian, 1993; Roger, 1995). These are outlined in Figure 12.1.

Rational and detached are considered effective styles, whereas emotional and avoidant are thought to be ineffective (Roger et al., 1993). It is considered that effective styles of coping maintain the psychological health of an individual at times of stress, whereas ineffective styles are thought to lead to poorer psychological health (Ireland, Boustead and Ireland, 2005).

All the young people at SWAAY, including Paul, have survived some level of adversity and have thus developed some mechanism of coping with stress, albeit maladaptive. Changing coping styles to make these more effective is integral to the work conducted at SWAAY, but during times of stress many of the young people revert to old patterns of coping. This was evident for Paul during his transition from care into independent living, despite the continued support from SWAAY members of staff, through his avoidance in adequately managing his budgeting. This led to a crisis which had to be resolved through adult support. In addition, Paul experienced heightened levels of anxiety and stress when faced with any problems and he resorted to phoning support staff for guidance and direction many times daily. This illustrates the importance of the continued involvement of supportive individuals who are able to help the young person consolidate their learning as they negotiate the challenges of the transition into adulthood.

Focus groups

As a method of ascertaining the challenges and needs of the young people who have left SWAAY, a focus group of young people was convened as was one of staff members with experience of working with the young people during their transition from SWAAY. The aim was to listen to and learn from their own experiences and to consider how their recommendations may assist in developing a more effective after care service. A semi-structured interview was used to elicit the responses for the young people who attended the group.

What are the young people's experiences?

A focus group discussion was held with six young people who used to be at SWAAY and who left after 2001, ie once the most recent Leaving Care Act was introduced. All of the participants in the focus group left care between the ages of 17 and 18. This is thus fairly consistent with the studies outlined above which found that most young people leaving care are between the ages of 16 and 17 years (Stein and Carey, 1986; Biehal et al. 1992, 1995; Dixon and Stein, 2005). The young people involved in this focus group all had varying experiences, with some moving into independent living, and some being provided with supported living. The period of their transition out of the care system, which was defined as the time from when discussions took place regarding their move out of care, to then leaving, varied from one week to three months. Five of the young people who attended this focus group stayed in the local area, while one went back to his original home area. With regards to the amount of control that these individuals felt they had over the decisions that were made, again this varied. While this was a relatively small sample of care leavers and each person obviously had different experiences, both positive and negative, there were some challenges and difficulties which were common in each case. Some of the young people described not feeling ready to leave, however, even for those who did want to leave in order to become more independent, they all described experiencing a sudden realisation with regards to how difficult things were going to be. The main challenges that they identified were feelings of loneliness and not having anyone to talk to. There was a general view that while they were in care there was always someone there for them to turn to when they were experiencing difficulties, however when they left this was not necessarily the case. Difficulties in forming and maintaining relationships with friends and partners was also raised as a difficulty, as well as experiencing problems with landlords and neighbours. Related to this was the issue of having to tell people that they had been in care and while most of them experienced that generally people were quite sympathetic, all of them were guarded in giving too much information, due to the fact that they had been involved in sexually harmful behaviour. Another area in which all the young people identified difficulties was with money. This related to not being able to budget, as well as not having much money. One young person also stated that he did not want to apply for benefits due to the stigma associated with 'being on the dole'. Finally, a couple of the young people identified that they drank heavily, particularly when they first left care and a few of them also said that the standard of the accommodation that they were provided with was poor.

Each of the young people identified receiving differing levels of support, with some receiving no formal support once they left their placement. As it may be expected, some of the young people were more pro-active than others in asking for support, however even those who were offered support from specialist agencies found it difficult to accept and instead rejected it. This is consistent with Stein's (2004) view that care leavers should be supported by carers and not by specialist schemes. All of the young people identified having asked for some level of support from the organisation at some point to varying degrees, even if this had not been offered on a formal basis and a quote which came directly from one of the young people was 'In an emergency my first port of call would always be SWAAY'. This seemed to sum up the general view of the young people, that if they were experiencing any problems then they would decide to turn to members of staff to help them, thus highlighting the importance of the attachments that the young people had to members of staff within the organisation. Another difficulty identified, was that while the skills that the young people learnt while they were in care were useful in allowing them to be able to understand situations and other people's behaviour, that their friends would come to them with their problems due to their increased level of understanding and one of the young people described that he almost become an 'agony aunt'. The young people themselves, however, often did not feel that they had any one to help them with their problems and thus they felt overwhelmed by both their own as well as other people's difficulties.

With regards to the difficulties that they faced as a result of the fact that they had been involved in sexually harmful behaviour, there was a general consensus that they were fearful of becoming intimate with someone. This was due to the fact that they were afraid of misreading the signs and finding themselves in a position where they were accused of having committed a sexual assault. For those young people who had been in an intimate relationship, they also said that they were fearful of telling their partner about their sexually harmful behaviour and that this led to them feeling that there were barriers in their relationships. Those who did tell their partner about their background tended to wait until they had been in that relationship for a significant period of time and even then tended not to tell them everything. The young people also expressed continuing to feel guilty and ashamed of their past behaviour and that it continued to be a part of their lives. One young person described that 'it was always hanging over me and felt like someone had something against me . . . always there in the back of your head'. Finally, as a result of the space boundary at SWAAY which means that there is no touch unless in emergencies, there were several instances where the young people were in situations and someone touched them and they were unsure how to respond to this.

This therefore shows that while we do try and prepare the young people for leaving care, they continue to face significant difficulties and challenges during the transition as well as while re-integrating back into the community. As one of the young people put it 'there's room for improvement'.

During the focus group the young people were asked what advice they would give for setting up an after care package to support young people through their transition out of the care system and when re-integrating back into the community. They suggested that one of the main things that could be done would be to provide them with the opportunity to live in an independent house prior to leaving. While we are offering a semi-independent option to some of the young people, those that attended this focus group felt that this should be offered to as many people as possible and that there could be some improvements. They felt that there should still be clear boundaries, however that there should be some flexibility depending upon the people living there. They suggested that the house should be staffed for short periods at different times of the day so that there is some support from members of staff, however that, within reason, they should be able to go out and about when and where they want to. They also suggested that the house should be situated away from other staffed houses, in order to reduce the temptation for them to seek out help whenever anything went wrong. They also felt it important that they should be encouraged to resolve disagreements amongst themselves without the help of members of staff. Additionally, they suggested that it would be useful for the residents of the semi-independent house to be required to pay bills, in order that they can become used to budgeting in the same manner as they will need to when they are living on their own. They also indicated that it should be more like the 'real world' and that they should be encouraged and allowed to have friends and partners over to the house and to stay over if this was agreed. They felt that this would help them to build relationships with people prior to leaving, rather than having to wait to do this until they left. An additional suggestion was that they should be encouraged to stop using institutionalised 'lingo' when living in this house, as they found that they would use certain words with their friends which were used within the organisation and they found that their peers did not use these same words in conversation and thus they stood out as being different.

The young people also suggested that they should be given food tokens by social services rather than money to ensure that they did actually spend their money on food. While they recognised the value of being given pocket money for doing chores, they considered that as the young people progress through their

programme they should not be given as much money, due to the fact that when they left they were required to do these same chores, without the remuneration. Additionally, the young people felt that they should be encouraged to purchase less expensive items, for example when they went food shopping, in order that they could become accustomed to those items that it would be more realistic for them to buy when on a tighter budget, such as when they leave care. There was a general consensus then that they felt it important for young people in care to be given more of a realistic view of what life will be like once they have left prior to actually going through this process. Those who attended the focus group also felt that more attention should be paid to encouraging the young people to get a job and to socialise with peers in the community, in order that they may have established a friendship group and have a job prior to leaving.

The young people also highlighted the importance of ongoing support from the organisation, due to the fact that they have built up relationships with the staff. The suggestion that they proposed was that there be a specific phone number or a designated person that they could call at times when they need support, so that they know that there is always someone there who they will be able to talk to.

This group of young people was not representative of the increasing number of young people who come to SWAAY with criminal convictions for a sexual assault and the associated MAPPA listing. Additional challenges exist for these young people, which may significantly impact on their ability to reintegrate successfully into society. As a convicted sex offender, Paul was subject to MAPPA and therefore subjected to a high level of monitoring and scrutiny. At the point of moving from SWAAY semi-independence Paul encountered difficulties in securing accommodation. Not only did he have to persuade his local authority to act as guarantors but MAPPA placed restrictions on where he could live with reference to proximity to schools, local playgrounds and nurseries. This was despite Paul having successfully completed an intense and comprehensive treatment programme and him not having reoffended since his index offence which he perpetrated when he was 13 years old. In addition, when Paul started to form social relationships these too were scrutinised and he was encouraged to consider the appropriateness of the social networks he associated with. Concern from the MAPPA culminated in a proposal to seek a Sex Offender Prevention Order (SOPO). As such, it was difficult for Paul to establish normal friendships and intimate relationships with others. Although not the case for Paul, this type of scrutiny could lead to an increased sense of social isolation and frustration which in turn may increase the potential for further harm. It is of interest to note that it was the heightened concern by the various agencies that constituted the local MAPPA that led to a directive to the responsible local authority to fulfil their statutory duties towards Paul with regards to ongoing contact and support. There is no doubt that young people such as Paul require a great deal of support at the stage of establishing themselves as independent young adults. Local agencies and services need to work closely with the young person's home authority to develop more effective models for working together. Where this is achieved it offers a reduction in the potential for risk whilst catering more appropriately for the needs of the young person in transition.

What do the staff members think?

A focus group was also undertaken with members of staff who have been involved in supporting young people through their transition out of care and when re-integrating into the community in order to ascertain their views of the difficulties that the young people face. They were asked for their views on the elements which they consider important to include in an after care package designed to support the young people through this transition period. During this focus group, one of the main areas of difficulty that was highlighted related to housing and the finding of appropriate accommodation, with an adequate level of support. The feelings of uncertainty that often surround the transition period were also raised as an issue and the fact that this often impacts upon the young people's behaviour and ability to cope. This view is supported by the research discussed previously in this report, which highlights the fact that adolescents are required to deal with a number of novel stressors without having built up a range of effective coping styles and that this can result in them finding it difficult to manage. Additionally, it was acknowledged how difficult it can be for the young people to cope effectively with the level of freedom that they have once they leave

our care, having lived in an environment with a significant amount of external containment and high level of supervision. This increased level of freedom therefore tests their ability to manage and to implement the strategies that they have learnt while in care and often this leads to them making mistakes. The importance of the young people having someone to talk to about some of these issues and mistakes was raised, as was the benefit of them being able to make these mistakes while they still have support from members of staff who can support them in order to work through them. A further issue which was raised was the role of attachment during this period and what it means for the young people in terms of whether or not their relationships with attachment figures will be able to continue once their placement ends. As was highlighted in the focus group with the young people, the members of staff also recognised the problems that the young people have with regards to managing their money, forming and maintaining peer relationships, discussing their past sexually harmful behaviour and managing the issue of touch, after having lived within an environment which has a 'space boundary'.

A difficulty which was raised with regards to the level of preparation that is able to take place while a young person is living in the semi-independent house is the fact that this still has to take place within the boundaries and risk assessments and as such there is a limit to how realistic this preparation can be. Feelings of fear with regards to the impact on the organisation if one of the young people were to make a significant mistake, such as (re-)offend sexually or non-sexually, were also raised.

In terms of the support that the young people need when they leave, the importance of both practical and emotional support was highlighted. As was highlighted in the focus group with the previous residents, the members of staff who took part in this focus group highlighted the importance of the young people being encouraged to join clubs in the local community earlier in their placement, in order that they can build relationships with peers outside of the organisation. It was also felt that there should be more consistency with regards to developing the young people's independent living skills, eg budgeting prior to them reaching the transition phase.

The role of the young person's social worker with regards to how successful the transition period is, was also reiterated. The views expressed related to the fact that those young people who have a consistent social worker, who knows them and their needs well, receive more appropriate ongoing support once their placement has ended.

The fact that each of the young people are individuals and, as such, will require differing levels of support was also discussed, however it was suggested that it would be beneficial if, at the referral stage it was explicitly stated at what point the transition plan would need to begin to be discussed. This would therefore make this expectation clear at the beginning of the placement and also allow an appropriate amount of time to be able to effectively plan an appropriate transition for each young person.

The importance of having appropriately qualified staff, who understand both the emotional and practical issues, in order to support the young people through the transition period was also highlighted. Additionally, the importance of maintaining attachments and contact throughout this period of time was raised and of reducing the level of support at the appropriate time and rate for each individual. It was suggested that in order to support this process and ongoing attachment, a designated member of staff could be assigned to each young person, as a transition worker/advisor and they would be the person who would oversee that young person's transition and ongoing support package. This is again consistent with Stein's (2004) view that carers should continue to be involved in preparing and supporting a young person during their transition out of the care system.

Recommendations and conclusion

The research, as well as the experiences of staff and young people working within this field can help to highlight areas for improvement within the current provision for young people leaving care, specifically those who have displayed sexually harmful behaviour.

Each young person should be encouraged to establish relationships within the community, through attendance at clubs, obtaining part-time employment, voluntary work, or similar as soon as possible in their placement. This would need to continue to be decided on an individual basis, bearing in mind the level of risk that the young person poses as well as their level of

vulnerability, however should be encouraged as soon as is feasible and considered safe. Development of proven initiatives such as Circles of Support and Accountability (Wilson, McWhinnie and Wilson, 2010) for adolescents and young adults could provide an important resource for young people that have sexually harmed who leave care.

As highlighted by both research and the young people, support by existing attachment figures is of significant importance during the transition into full independence. As such, leaving care social workers and/or personal advisors should be introduced well in advance of the move out of care. Where supportive family members have been identified these should be included in the planning and implementation of the after care package. In addition, if the young person has been in longer term foster or residential care, attachment figures from there should be part of the planning and implementation. This would ensure that important knowledge and understanding regarding the young person's needs and risks are not lost in the process of leaving care. Individuals allocated to working with these young people should have a thorough knowledge and understanding of the challenges facing this unique group of care leavers and of working with this client group. This would further help to prevent this vulnerable group from experiencing social exclusion and isolation, mental or physical health problems and educational failure or unemployment. They would be in the best position to assist the young people in implementing the coping mechanisms and relapse prevention strategies during this time of heightened stress.

In order to ensure that the after care package meets the needs of each individual, a thorough assessment of needs, strengths and risks should be conducted. This should include an assessment of mental health for all young people leaving care conducted by an independent psychiatrist or mental health professional. This is in recognition of the significant proportion of this population who suffer from mental health difficulties and are thus likely to be in need of ongoing input in this regard. As mentioned earlier, local authorities are required to make sure that a Strengths and Difficulties Questionnaire (SDQ) is filled in for all for each of their looked after children aged 4–16. If this was done consistently it could help to provide the mental health professionals with invaluable information regarding level of need.

An assessment of attachment style may also help identify how best to engage the young people. The after care assessment could also usefully include the use of tools such as the Adaptive Behavior Assessment System II (Harrison and Oakland, 2009). This test assesses all 10 areas of adaptive behaviours as specified by DSM-IV in relation to learning difficulties: Communication; Community Use; Functional Academics; Home Living; Health and Safety; Leisure; Self-Care; Self-Direction; Social and Work. Scores allow the evaluation of functioning, as well as strengths and weaknesses in all areas. Forms are also available for teachers and parents/carers, so that their perspectives can be taken into account.

This chapter sits alongside a considerable amount of research and literature relating to the difficulties experienced by young care leavers. It is widely recognised that children and young people who enter the care system present with multiple and complex needs which are likely to continue to impact upon their future well-being and functioning unless they are provided with the highest level of stability and care. Despite being in receipt of high levels of input during their time in care, this level of support is withdrawn abruptly once they reach 16 or 18 years old. This is in spite of recognition that these young people often remain vulnerable and may continue to present some level of risk to others, particularly at times of heightened levels of stress. Whilst young people who sexually harm are a heterogeneous group, they can encounter specific challenges during their transition out of care. In addition, the potential negative consequences of failing to adequately support them during the transition stage may be significant both to themselves and to the wider community. As such, it is imperative that services involved in the care of these young people are aware of their specific needs and that adequate resources are available during the transition from care to independence. Experience and research suggests that these resources are often not provided consistently, resulting in some of our most vulnerable young people returning to a life of isolation, ill health, crime and limited opportunities.

References

A National Voice. *The Leaving Care Act*. Retrieved 4th April 2010 From http://www.anationalvoice.org/rights/clcact2.htm

Balbernie, R. (2001) Circuits and Circumstances: The Neurobiological Consequences of Early Relationship Experiences and how they shape later Behaviour. *Journal of Child Psychotherapy*, 27, 237–55.

Becker, J.V. (1998) The Assessment of Adolescent Perpetrators of Childhood Sexual Abuse. *The Irish Journal of Psychology*, 19: 1, 68–81.

Biehal, N. et al. (1992) *Prepared for Living? A Survey of Young People Leaving the Care of Three Local Authorities*. London: National Children's Bureau.

Biehal, N. et al. (1995) *Moving On: Young People and Leaving Care Schemes*. London: HMSO.

Bifulco, A. et al. (2006) Adult Attachment Style as Mediator between Childhood Neglect/Abuse and Adult Depression and Anxiety. *Social Psychiatry and Psychiatric Epidemiology*, 41, 796–805.

Blaske, D.M. et al. (1989) Individual, Family, and Peer Characteristics of Adolescent Sex Offenders and Assaultive Offenders. *Developmental Psychology*, 25: 5, 846–55.

Boyd, C. and Bromfield, L. (2006) *Young People Who Sexually Abuse: Key Issues*. Practice Brief No. 1. Australian Institute of Family Studies. National Child Protection Clearinghouse.

Boyd, N.J., Hagan, M. and Cho, M.E. (2000) Characteristics of Adolescent Sex Offenders: A Review of the Research. *Aggression and Violent Behaviour*, 5: 2, 137–46.

Burton, D.L., Miller, D.L. and Tai-Shill, C. (2002) A Social Learning Theory Comparison of the Sexual Victimization of Adolescent Sexual Offenders and Nonsexual Offending Male Delinquents. *Child Abuse and Neglect*, 26, 893–907.

Carver, C.S. et al. (1993) How Coping Mediates the Effect of Optimism and Distress: A Study of Women with Early Stage Breast Cancer. *Journal of Personality and Social Psychology*, 65, 375–90.

Cauffman, E. and Steinberg, L. (2000) (Im) Maturity of Judgment in Adolescence: Why Adolescents may be Less Culpable than Adults. *Behavioural Sciences and the Law*, 18, 741–60.

Coleman, J. and Hendry, L. (1999) *The Nature of Adolescence*. London: Routledge.

Creeden, K. (2008) *The Neuro-Developmental Impact of Trauma. What we know. What it means. How can it change what we do*. Presented at NOTA Conference 2008.

Davis, G.E. and Leitenberg, H. (1987) Adolescent Sex Offenders. *Psychological Bulletin*, 101: 3, 417–27.

DCSF and DoH (2009) *Statutory Guidance on Promoting the Health and Well-being of Looked After Children..* Nottingham: DCSF Publications.

DoH (1999) *Me Survive, Out There.* London: HMSO.

DoH *Children (Leaving Care) Act 2000, Regulations and Guidance.* Retrieved 4 April 2010 from http://www.leavingcare.org/data/tmp/1528-3901.pdf

DoH (2004) *National Service Framework for Children, Young People and Families.* HMSO.

DFES (2006) *Teenage Pregnancy Next Steps.* HMSO.

Dixon, J. (2008) Young People Leaving Care: Health, Well-Being and Outcomes. *Child and Family Social Work,* 13, 207–217.

Dixon, J. and Stein, M. (2005) *Leaving Care, Throughcare and Aftercare in Scotland.* London: Jessica Kingsley.

Downes, C. (1992) *Separation Revisited.* Aldershot: Ashgate.

Fernandes, N. (2006) *The Detection of Prefrontal Cortex Development Into Early Adulthood.* Thesis submitted to the Faculty of Marietta College.

Fonagy, P. et al. (1997a) Morality, Disruptive Behaviour, Borderline Personality Disorder, Crime, and their Relationships to Security of Attachment. in Atkinson, L. and Zucker, K.J. (eds.) *Attachment and Psychopathology.* New York: Guilford.

Fonagy, P. et al. (1997b) The Development of Violence and Crime as it relates to Security of Attachment. in Osofsky, J.D. (ed.) *Children in A Violent Society.* New York: Guilford.

Ford, T. et al. (2007) Psychiatric Disorder among British Children Looked After by Local Authorities: Comparison with Children Living in Private Households. *British Journal of Psychiatry,* 190; 319–25.

Grimshaw, R. (2008) *Young People Who Sexually Abuse.* www.yjb.gov.uk

Harrison, P.L. and Oakland, T. (2009) *Adaptive Behavior Assessment System.* 2nd edn. Los Angeles: Western Psychological Services.

Ireland, J.L., Boustead, R. and Ireland, C.A. (2005) Coping Style and Psychological Health among Adolescent Prisoners: A Study of Young and Juvenile Offenders. *Journal of Adolescence,* 28: 3, 411–23.

Jackson, S. (2002) Promoting Stability and Continuity of Care Away From Home. in McNeish, D., Newman, T. and Roberts, H. (eds.) *What Works for Children?* Buckingham: Open University Press.

Jackson, S. and Thomas, N. (2001) *What Works in Creating Stability for Looked After Children.* Illford: Barnardo's.

Johnson-Laird, P.N. (1983) *Mental Models: Towards a Cognitive Science of Language, Inference and Consciousness.* Harvard, MA: Harvard University Press.

Jones, G. (2002) *The Youth Divide: Diverging Paths to Adulthood.* York: Joseph Rowntree Foundation.

Kambam, P. and Thompson, C. (2009) The Development of Decision-Making Capacities in Children and Adolescents: Psychological and Neurological Perspectives and their Implications for Juvenile Defendants. *Behavioural Sciences and the Law,* 27, 173–90.

leavingcare.org. *Key Facts.* Retrieved 4 April 2010 from http://www.leavingcare.org/professionals/research/key_facts_for_leaving_care/

Leversee, T. (2007) Using Typologies to individualise the Assessment, Treatment, and Supervision of Sexually Abusive Youth. in Calder, M.C. (ed.) *Working with children and young people who sexually abuse: Taking the field forward.* Lyme Regis: Russell House Publishing.

Marshall, W.L., Hudson, S.M. and Hodkinson, S. (1993) The Importance of Attachment Bonds in the Development of Juvenile Sexual Offending. in Barbaree, H.E., Marshall, W.L. and Hudson, S.M. (eds.) *The Juvenile Sex Offender.* New York: Guilford.

Marshall, W.L. and Marshall, L.E. (2000) The Origins of Sexual Offending. *Trauma, Violence and Abuse,* 1, 491–503.

Marshall, W.L., Serran G.A. and Cortoni, F.A. (2000) Childhood Attachments, Sexual Abuse and their Relationship to Adult Coping in Child Molesters. *Sexual Abuse: A Journal of Research and Treatment,* 12, 17–26.

McCann, J.B. et al. (1996) Prevalence of Psychiatric Disorders in Young People in the Care System. *British Medical Journal,* 313, 1529–30.

Meltzer, H. et al. (2003) *The Mental Health of Young People Looked After by Local Authorities in England.* London: The Stationery Office.

Newman, T. and Blackburn, S. (2002) *Transitions in the Lives of Children and Young People: Resilience Factors.* Interchange 78. Edinburgh: Scottish Executive. www.scotland.gov.uk/library5/education/ic78-00.asp

Patterson, J.M. and McCubbin, H.I. (1987) Adolescent Coping Style and Behaviors: Conceptualisation and Measurement *Journal of Adolescence,* 10, 163–86.

Rich, P. (2006) *Attachment and Sexual Offending. Understanding and applying Attachment Theory to the Treatment of Juvenile Sexual Offenders.* Chichester: John Wiley and Sons.

Roger, D. (1995) The Mechanics of Stress: A Model for the Relationship between Stress, Health and Personality. *Summary of Paper Presented at the Fifth International Conference on Stress Management (ISMA-5)* Noordwijkerhout, Netherlands, April.

Roger, D., Jarvis, P. and Najarian, B. (1993) Detachment and Coping: The Construction and Validation of a New Scale for Measuring Coping Strategies. *Personality and Individual Differences*, 15, 619–26.

Rutter, M. (1999) Resilience Concepts and Findings: Implications for Family Therapy. *Journal of Family Therapy*, 21, 119–44.

Rutter, M., Giller, H. and Hagell, A. (1998) *Antisocial Behaviour by Young People.* Cambridge: Cambridge University Press.

Ryan, G. (1998) The Relevance of Early Life Experience to the Behaviour of Sexually Abusive Youth. *The Irish Journal of Psychology*, 19: 1, 32–48.

Seiffge-Krenke, I. (2000) Causal Links between Stressful Events, Coping Style and Adolescent Symptomatology. *Journal of Adolescence*, 23, 675–91.

Sempik, J., Ward, H. and Darker, I. (2008) Emotional and Behavioural Difficulties of Children and Young People at Entry into Care. *Clinical Child Psychology and Psychiatry*, 13/2, 221–33.

Social Exclusion Unit. (2001) *Preventing Social Exclusion.* p. 77. Retrieved 4 April 2010 from http://www.cabinetoffice.gov.uk/media/cabinetoffice/social_exclusion_task_force/assets/publications_1997_to_2006/preventing.pdf

Stein, M. (2004) *What Works for Young People Leaving Care?* Barkingside: Barnardo's.

Stein, M. (2005) *Resilience and Young People Leaving Care: Overcoming the Odds.* Barkingside: Barnardo's.

Stein, M. and Carey, K. (1986) *Leaving Care.* Oxford: Blackwell.

Toth, S.L. and Cicchetti, D. (2004) Child Maltreatment and its Impact on Psychosocial Child Development. in Tremblay, R.E., Barr, R.G. and Peters, R. (eds.) *Encyclopaedia on Early Childhood Development.* Montreal: Quebec.

Tracy, J.L. et al. (2003) Attachment Styles and Adolescent Sexuality. In Florsheim, P. (ed.) *Adolescent Romance and Sexual Behavior: Theory, Research and Practical Implications.* Mahwah, NJ: Erlbaum.

Ward, J., Henderson, Z. and Pearson, G. (2003) *One Problem among Many: Drug Use among Care Leavers in Transition to Independent Living.* London Home Office. Study 260. London: Home Office. Retrieved 4 April 2010 from http://www.leavingcare.org/data/tmp/3169-6734.pdf

Ward, T. (2003) The Explanation, Assessment and Treatment of Child Sexual Abuse. *International Journal of Forensic Psychology*, 1, 10–25.

Wilson J., Mcwhinnie, A. and Wilson, C. (2010) Circle of Support and Accountability: an International Partnership in Reducing Sexual Offender Recidivism 2010. *Prison Service Journal*, 178, 26–36.

Wong, P.T.P. (1993) Effective Management of Life Stress: The Resource-Congruence Model. *Stress Medicine*, 9, 51–60.

Worling, J.R. (1995) Adolescent Sibling-Incest Offenders: Differences in Family and Individual Functioning when Compared to Adolescent Non-sibling Sex Offenders. *Child Abuse and Neglect*, 19: 5, 633–43.

Worling, J.R. (2004) The Estimate of Risk of Adolescent Sexual Offence Recidivism (ERASOR): Preliminary Psychometric Data. *Sexual Abuse: A Journal of Research and Treatment*, 16: 3, 235–54.

CHAPTER 13

Dilemmas for Practitioners Working With Siblings Under 10 Years Presenting With Harmful Sexual Behaviour Towards Each Other, With Complex Trauma Histories. What are the Challenges Involved in how They Should be Placed in Local Authority Care Permanently?

Bernadette Fahy

Introduction

This chapter looks at the complexities that currently exist in England around sibling children who harm sexually and require permanent placements. It will examine the difficulties in obtaining research about these groups of children. It will highlight that these children coming into care have more complex needs as a result of attachment, trauma and maltreatment. The reader will be offered a tentative framework for thinking about what needs to be considered in assessing such children for permanent placement. The term *complex trauma* (Cook et al., 2005) describes the dual problem of children's exposure to multiple traumatic events and the impact of this exposure on immediate and long-term outcomes. Typically, complex trauma exposure results when a child is abused or neglected, but it can also be caused by other kinds of events such as witnessing domestic violence, ethnic cleansing or war. Many children involved in the child welfare system have experienced complex trauma.

Challenges of working with children presenting with sexual behaviour problems

In England there is no collective definition of harmful sexual behaviour, reflecting the lack of consensus amongst professionals working in this area of practice. Johnson (2004) talks about behaviour falling on a continuum: from natural and healthy, to children who molest other children. She divides children into children who are sexually reactive, children who engage in extensive, mutual sexual behaviours and children who molest other children. Sexually reactive

children can be distracted from engaging in this behaviour, however they often return. It is important for the multi-agency group involved with siblings to remember that when siblings come into care and continue to be looked after, the children's sexual behaviour may return intermittently due to strong emotions or stressful situations. It will be important for those involved to identify the triggers and develop strategies to manage them early on so that they don't become reinforced over a long period of time. The behaviours demonstrated are often directed towards themselves, but can be directed towards other children or adults. Children who are sexually reactive engage with other children in sexual behaviours, without the use of coercion or force. The other person on the receiving end of the behaviour is often seen as insignificant; the sexual behaviour is not directed at them in anger or out of retribution.

In talking about sexually reactive children Johnson (2004: 21) states: 'confusion, fear and anxiety about sex, which is driven by a child's history is fundamental to this type of sexual behaviour'. She explains that 'some of the children within this group report sexual arousal whilst most do not'. This is significant in thinking about siblings who may have insecure attachments and whose sexual behaviours have become habitual. They may have developed a strong sexual arousal to one another that is a strong motivating factor to repeating the behaviour.

Children who molest are described as having sexual behaviours that are repeated and persistent by Johnson. Children's chronologies will evidence a growing pattern of sexual behaviours. Such children present with extreme sexual confusion and aggression. They use coercion to gain participation in the sexual behaviours that include bribery, trickery, and manipulation. They are able to select other children who have vulnerabilities. An important part of the assessment prior to placement will include looking at the dynamics of the sibling relationship to establish if certain children are selected to engage in sexual behaviours due to perceived vulnerability, and whether there has been harm sustained.

In looking at whether sexual behaviour is harmful or not, it is important to look at the abusive dynamics described by Burton (1998) who provided guidance on interventions for parents and children. It consists of four important dynamics, which I believe are important in assessing siblings:

- power differences
- an assigned authority role
- use of manipulation and
- the use of threats, force or weapons

The first of these four dynamics is differences in power between the child who instigates the sexual behaviour and other children who are caught up in this. The child who initiates this may be larger in size, older in years or have more developed cognitive capacity. A child may target children, who are younger, or appear more vulnerable due to physical or cognitive disability. The child who initiates the behaviour may have been assigned a role within the family such as a carer or parentified child and may use this role to intimidate siblings. The use of manipulation strategies can be utilised to attract other children to participate in sexual activity. A child may use strategies such as using bribes, coaxing or games to encourage a child to participate in sexual behaviours. The fourth dynamic is that children with sexually harmful behaviour may use threats or weapons in order to secure secrecy and maintain cooperation.

Practitioner considerations

For professionals working with harmful sexual behaviour, this work takes people on the path of thinking about sex, sexuality, sexual development and sexual knowledge, gender, race and religion. It has the potential to encourage workers to think about their own sexual development and values. These self reflections could prove enlightening and rewarding or conversely expose unresolved areas.

Counter-transference is defined as the practitioner's reactions (feelings, thoughts,

statements and behaviour) directed towards the child and brought about by the practitioner's previous life experiences. A practitioner's counter-transference reactions may be created by an aspect of the child's history, the child's or children's presentation, or the interaction between the child and practitioner. The following dynamics may influence the practitioner's reactions when working with abused and neglected children:

- relationships we have with our own children
- early childhood abuse
- early relationships with family
- carers and siblings
- previous work undertaken with children

Counter-transference is significant in any therapeutic context because it can affect the quality and direction of the assessment, care planning and treatment interventions. Awareness of the issue is important in providing input to abused and neglected children, especially if the practitioner has a history of child maltreatment. Therapists must be alert to counter-transference and its impact on their practice interventions.

Hackett (2006) offers a good framework to the practitioner to critically reflect on issues such as their personal and professional experience, and how this may have an effect on how they react to others involved in this work, that is children, carers and other professionals. He encourages us, as workers, to think about our own value systems, paying particular attention to issues relating to gender, sexuality and abuse and how these influence how we work and make sense of the tasks we have as professionals. Hackett prompts us to question our levels of competence and requires us to consider what experience we have working with children who harm sexually, and what influences the models, methods and approaches we use.

This same set of questions could be related to values we hold personally and professionally about child abuse, children in care, separation and sibling relationships. What could be the potential transference reactions to these issues? Family Futures (2010) discusses the assessment of siblings placed separately or together being complex and emotive, tainted by personal thoughts, feelings, attitudes and actions. This is also echoed by Lord and Borthwick (2008); there is acknowledgement that many practitioners may have strong views, often based on their own personal experience, about whether siblings should be kept together at all costs, or should ever be separated. These authors recommend that training and supervision are both important in facilitating practitioners to share their views and consider possible choices. The importance of multi-agency working, using policies and procedures are important avenues to check and balance personal beliefs and attitudes that may get in the way of making appropriate decisions.

Paucity of data available about children who harm sexually in foster care

It is important to understand the prevalence of children who present with harmful sexual behaviour in foster care. Unfortunately to date there is no way of obtaining this data. Statistics need to be gathered from strategy meetings, case conferences, disruption meetings, and file searches. This could be complicated as children may have presented with other forms of abuse on admission to care. There have been some important community studies completed in England that contribute to developing our knowledge base about children generally that harm sexually.

Studies compiled in England

Taylor (2003) study of children and young people accused of child sexual abuse found that of the 277 children in one area, referred to children's social care, 34 per cent were children under 10. Interestingly very few of these children received a specialist service. They were more likely to have a history of alleged abuse. Twice as many had allegedly been sexually abused and three times as many had been neglected. This study and research by Johnson (1998) reveal high sexual victimisation rates for children who have displayed harmful sexual behaviour. Carson's UK 2007 study (it is unclear if any of these figures relate to children in foster care), established that a number of younger children were coming to the attention of education, children's social care services and CAMHS. The study gave the following statistics:

- Education: in one year approx 34 per cent of all calls from primary schools to the education child protection team were concerned about sexual behaviours.

- Children's social care services in a four month period: 63 per cent of the referrals to children's social care where the presenting problem was concern about the sexual behaviour of children 12 and under.
- CAMHS: 2,025 referrals over a year where there were significant problems with sexual behaviours, but concerns about sexual behaviour were often not identified as the presenting problem.

Gibb (2004) undertaking a NSPCC study showed that the number of children under 10 reported as exhibiting harmful sexual behaviour is on the rise, with 400 being referred in one year, compared to 227 from 1993–1999. The increase in figures was attributed to increased awareness and expansion of services for children who harm sexually.

Ofsted (2009) undertook a study of children aged between four years and seven years who were excluded from primary schools. This study involved visits to 69 schools and, a significant proportion of those visited discussed that they had a substantial involvement with local authorities in terms of dealing with issues pertaining to child protection, domestic violence and family breakdown. Fourteen of the 69 schools reported incidents of inappropriate sexual behaviour problems from children between four and seven years. What is interesting from this small study was that eight of these 14 schools had excluded the child for a fixed period. Two of these schools shared that even though they reported the incidents, there was a lack of response from social workers and support services. The key recommendations from this report places responsibility with various agencies such as Ofsted developing polices for identifying and responding to sexually inappropriate behaviour in young children and being clear when such situations should be referred to children's social care services. It recommends that local authorities take seriously referrals from schools if children present with sexually aggressive behaviour. It recommends that schools ensure that child protection training takes into account the reasons for young children's inappropriate sexual behaviour. It places a duty on schools to report serious incidents of sexually inappropriate behaviour to children's social care services.

The research about children within the looked after system with harmful sexual behaviour is still in its early stages, let alone research on quantative or qualitative studies on siblings who sexually harm.

American researchers Shaw et al. (2000) undertook a study of emotional and behavioural responses of children who have been victimised by juveniles 17 years of age or younger compared to child victims of adults. The sample consisted of 194 children and adolescents. They established that the sexual victims of half the sample of these children are their siblings, which was consistent with their findings that children abused by other children were more likely to be abused by siblings.

There is a paucity of research about sibling relationships and long term studies about sibling children who have stayed together or being separated as a result of harmful sexual behaviour problems. In England currently there is no research that I am aware of that focuses on sibling groups who are separated after permanent placement because of disruption due to harmful sexual behaviour.

McCormick (2010) describes how the effects of siblings' separation have been largely ignored in terms of precise research.

A literature search on siblings who present with harmful sexual behaviours in foster care was limited. Studies that have been undertaken have been by Head and Elgar (1997) which looked at the placement of sexually abused and abusing siblings. The study consisted of 85 children in 35 families. Some of the carers interviewed held the view that placing siblings together did not consistently meet the needs of both or all the children. They found that placing them together made them reticent in talking about their life experiences. A major factor of placement breakdown was the exhibition of sexualised behaviour. Some children had been observed to be re-enacting abuse from their family of origin. The authors considered that placement of children who had been exposed to interfamilial sexual abuse together may prevent children from recovering from their abuse because of the constant re-traumatisation through the reminding presence of another child. When siblings were placed together and their behaviour had become sexualised, some of the carers shared that they identified more closely with the child that had been harmed.

Research by Farmer and Pollock (2003) included a study that concentrated on substitute care for sexually abused or 'abusing children'. This research looked at the characteristics,

management and therapeutic treatment needs of such children. This study has limitations as the age of the population researched was over the age of 10 years. It highlighted the importance of effective management such as supervision, planning for safe care before placement, preparing other children in placement and careful monitoring of contact with birth family members. It illustrated the need for effective management of professionals' reactions to denial and minimisation of sexual abuse. In 53 per cent of the young people who had abused others, this information had not been shared, information that could have been shared with the foster carers. The case recordings showed a lack of information about the nature of abuse, the frequency of abuse and the duration of abuse. Information that could have been passed on when the child entered care was likely to be incomplete. This highlights the importance of good record-keeping so that people can be informed about the nature of the children's trauma and when making decisions about placement planning. A key recommendation from this research was that social services needed to ensure they passed information about children's backgrounds to relevant people and that withholding information could potentiate legal challenges.

The following study has strengths and limitations. An American study by Jones, Ownbey, Everidge, Judkins and Timbers (2006) looked at focused foster care for children with serious sexual behaviour problems over a six-year period. There are subjective accounts of important lessons learnt by staff and foster carers about working with this group of children. These included:

- It was established that although children came with serious sexual problems, they also had obvious attachment issues.
- Despite rigorous training, there was a denial about the seriousness of the children's sexual behaviour until they saw it with their own eyes.
- Professional agencies involved with the child were not initially certain that these children would engage in serious sexual behaviour unless they witnessed it or learnt it directly.
- Regarding sibling groups, the initial idea was to place those children together in the same family, with experience they stated they would not do this again. They established that siblings

engaged each other in either consensual or inappropriate sexual acts.

An Australian study by Tarren-Sweeney (2008) examined the predictors of problematic sexual behaviour among children with complex maltreatment histories. This study involved 347 pre-adolescent children in foster and kinship care. Most children presented with psychopathology, conduct problems, in-attention and attachment disturbances. Interestingly this study also revealed a high concordance of 'sexual behaviour problems in 52 sibling groups'. Attempts to contact the author to explore further details about this high prevalence proved unsuccessful. However this epidemiological study did establish the significance of increasing risk among children exposed to multiple adversities as highlighted in other recent research findings mentioned in this chapter.

It is important to understand how children develop harmful sexual behaviour

There have been various studies that have looked at how children come to develop problematic or harmful sexual behaviour such as Pither and Gray (1998). The study found that 70 per cent of the pre-adolescents who had engaged in developmentally unexpected behaviours had been abused sexually prior to the onset of their sexual behaviour problems.

Johnson (1998) calculated that less that 0.5 per cent of sexually abused children would go on to sexually abuse other children in childhood.

There are a number of factors which may enhance the risk of sexually abused children developing harmful sexual behaviour Friedrich(2001) these have included the following:

- age of the child:, the impact is greater the younger the child is
- the nature of the abuse: for example, if it is repeated, happened over a long duration and the degree of severity
- if the perpetrator has been a close relative
- following the disclosure the carer rejects or blames the child

Friedrich and Davies (2003) in looking at 'sexually intrusive behaviour' in children concluded that there were four main emerging themes:

- family adversity
- modelling coercion
- modelling of sexuality
- a vulnerable or predisposed child.

Johnson and Doonan (2005: 35) challenge the focus that has been placed on children's history of sexual abuse as a significant factor in the development of harmful sexual behaviour and encourage practitioners to be mindful of environmental factors such as family history and functioning, housing, employment, income, family social integration and community resources. They state 'whilst sexual abuse is in the history of some children with harmful sexual behaviour, there are other demographic and environmental factors that are more pervasive and which may be more instrumental in providing fodder for the development of sexual behaviour problems in children'.

Friedrich et al. (2005) undertook a year longitudinal study of adolescents with problematic sexual behaviour in the welfare system in America and established that for adolescents that presented with more severe sexual behaviours, their sexual behaviour had started when they were at a very young age.

Johnson (2005), talking about research in relation to why children molest, concurs with the findings of Friedrich and Davies. Looking at the theme of modelling of coercion and sexuality, she identifies that children have physical abuse histories and that they have universally witnessed domestic abuse. Johnson's analysis is that within this environment some children hold values, beliefs and behaviours that are predicated upon sex and aggression being allowed. Children who display problematic to harmful behaviours may have experienced a highly sexualised environment such as being exposed to information via DVDs, phone and the internet. Children can also be exposed to hearing and witnessing adults having sex. Such exposure is beyond their age and cognitive development. Parents have blurred boundaries about the child's privacy, personal space and possessions. Unpredictable families where there are impaired attachments often leave children with high levels of tension, anxiety and insecurity and psychological arousal.

I support other authors' notes of caution encouraging practitioners to remember that not all children who have been victims of sexual abuse will develop problematic or harmful behaviour. It is important to think about strength perspectives in the child's environment, such as a significant and supportive person, who models pro-social behaviours and helps the child to feel empowered and increases their self-esteem.

Heiman (2001) describes that the origin of problematic or harmful behaviour is not always due to the family and even if they are, what is crucial, is the parent or carer's ability to work with professionals to make changes for the benefit of the child. The key message here is being able to help the child survive their experience and promote change in their behaviour.

The significance of resilience in working with children presenting with harmful sexual behaviour in the looked after system

The importance of resilience, needs to be mentioned here as children may well function in certain areas and show distress in others. We know that areas of competence can change as children experience new stressors and developmental challenges.

Whilst there is often a lot of focus on adversity and risk associated with harmful sexual behaviour, it is important for practitioners to think carefully about the strengths that are available within the child, the caring environment and the wider community that can foster strong resilience to moderate or help children regain a sense of mastery over their harmful sexual behaviours. Hackett (2006) reminds us that some children who have lived in adverse environments have not gone on to harm others, others have responded well to treatment interventions. It is important to look at these resilience factors in the assessment of children who harm sexually. There are several factors that have been identified by authors such as Newman (2005) and Gilgun (2002), including positive school experience, the presence of at least one unconditionally supportive parent or parent substitute, a committed mentor or other person outside the family, a strong social support network, and the ability to express emotions. There are numerous others, such as having special talents, creativity and spirituality.

Theoretical models that help us to understand why children present with harmful sexual behaviour problems

Post traumatic stress disorder

This is when there is an identifiable stressor that would induce considerable symptoms in children such as physical victimisation and observing violence. The trauma is experienced in one of the following ways: recurring and intrusive memories, recurring nightmares or dreams, or re-experiencing the traumatic event by a stimulus in their environment. There is a numbing or limited participation in their life. Children will respond with at least two of the following symptoms: trouble concentrating, sleep disturbance, hyper-alertness or withdrawing from experiences that may potentiate memories of trauma. Within this model their harmful sexual behaviour is perceived as a trauma response. It is viewed as an attempt to recreate their own trauma abuse experience which permits them to develop control and mastery over their feelings.

Projective identification

Cunningham and MacFarlane (1996) discuss how some children have a propensity to identify with those who abused them. Projective identification shows itself in situations where anxiety is aggravated by fears of being abandoned or attacked. During original abuse experiences children may experience helplessness and being annihilated, in response they replace these with feelings with feelings of power and control.

Cunningham and MacFarlane describe how some children who do not master childhood trauma can potentiate the need to repeat and re-enact the trauma throughout developmental stages in life.

For children presenting with abuse-reactive behaviours, it is highly likely that the pain may be so intense that aggressive acting-out becomes compulsive behaviour allowing them to discharge their feelings of embarrassment and defencelessness, or to recompense for feelings associated with being inadequate. Examples of this may show itself in behaviours such as fire setting, torturing animals, physical aggression or sexual acting-out. Cunningham and MacFarlane explain how the initial response to trauma becomes cyclical; it not only becomes more problematic to extinguish, the sexual stimulation itself becomes a strong reinforcer, and it may develop into compulsivity.

Sexual abuse theory

This theory looks at how some children who harm sexually will have similar thinking to adolescents, such as antecedent thoughts, feeling and behaviours culminating in sexually harmful acts. Work with over 100 children undertaken by Cunningham and MacFarlane (1996) highlighted that these children had feelings of inadequacy and low self-esteem, and feelings of vulnerability and victimisation. They observed that these children attempted to compensate in front of others by exhibiting sexual or physically aggressive behaviour.

Finklehor's four preconditions

Cunningham and MacFarlane (1996) have adapted this to understand its relationship with children who are abusive reactive. Readers need to be mindful of how this theory assumes that children have been sexually abused. The theory does not address the function of aggression. The four preconditions are relevant however in highlighting the following:

- Motivation to abuse: this is frequently a reaction to their own abuse but may be reinforced sexually during a significant time of sexual development.
- Overcoming internal inhibitions: the majority of sexually abused children do not go on to sexually abuse others. Some may go on to develop aggressive, sexual or self-destructive thinking. The family history reveals that there were very few role models of internal control, leading to a lack of empathy and appropriate moral values.
- Overcoming external inhibitors: evidenced within these families is a lack of clear boundaries and external control which can otherwise recompense for the lack of a child's internal inhibitors. As a result the child unconsciously places themselves in situations that promote sexual acting-out or they fail to provide adequate protection for other vulnerable children.
- Overcoming victim's resistance: these children can select other children who are younger,

smaller and less powerful. They utilise coercion, bribery and threats to break the victim's resistance.

Traumagenic factors model (Finklehor and Browne, 1995)

This model looks at four traumagenic dynamics: traumatic sexualisation, betrayal, powerlessness and stigmatisation. Finklehor (1985) highlighted certain dynamics that contributed to traumatic sexualisation. Sexually abused children are compensated by perpetrators for sexual behaviours that are inappropriate for their level of development. Children thus learn to use sexual behaviour, appropriate or inappropriate, as an approach for manipulating others to get their needs met. Sexually abused children's anatomy assumes a distorted sense of importance and meaning. Children become perplexed about sexual behaviour and sexual morality as a consequence of what perpetrators tell them.

Attachment theory and trauma

Complex trauma is described as a child's exposure to multiple traumatic events. It manifests itself when a child has been abused, neglected or witnessed violence. Complex trauma interferes with the formation of an attachment bond between child and care-giver. Lack of a secure attachment may result in a loss of ability to self-regulate and relate to others. There is a growing opinion that PSTD does not encapsulate the full scope of developmental difficulties that traumatised children experience. Children who have been exposed to maltreatment and violence have been diagnosed with ADHD, depression, anxiety, eating disorders, and separation anxiety. The diagnosis just described only highlights the limited aspects of a child's complex self-regulating and relational difficulties. It is important for practitioners to think about examining the trauma impact on a child's growth and development.

Complex trauma may be activated when a child is exposed to danger which is unpredictable. The child's body as a consequence devotes its energy to survival, rather than devoting resources to growth and development. The most significant element of danger and unpredictability is the absence of a care-giver who is protective, nurturing, reliable and responsive to the child. Early care-giving affords children a context within which they can learn about themselves, their thoughts and feelings and relationships with family and community. A secure attachment supports a child's development such as their capacity to regulate emotional and physical states, safety, knowledge of how to exert influence and the capacity for communication. Care-givers that are a source of trauma then the attachment relationship is compromised. If the care-giver is abusive, erratic or hostile, this generates feelings of helplessness and rejection. As a result of this dynamic, a child tries to exert control by withdrawing or acting coercively. Children exposed to unpredictable violence or repeatedly neglected usually cope with threatening events and different feelings by restricting what they process. In challenging situations they cannot formulate an organised or coherent response. They have difficulty regulating emotions, managing stress, developing concern for others and lack language to solve problems.

Children with complex trauma histories are at risk of failing to develop brain capacities for regulating emotions in response to stress. Some children cannot access rational thought in the face of overpowering emotions. In middle childhood there is rapid brain development that is crucial for developing skills in relating to others and problem-solving. Complex trauma creates severe problems in affect regulation. Affect regulation begins with being able to identify internal emotional states: being able to identify, interpret and label states of arousal such as feeling happy, sad, scared. If children have experienced inconsistent models of affect they have no coherent framework to interpret experiences. They may experience difficulty in self-regulation and self-soothing and may even display dissociation. Disassociation is a key feature of complex trauma; it is the failure to absorb or integrate information or experiences. Thoughts, feelings and behaviours are disconnected. There may be repetitive behaviour without conscious choice, planning or self-awareness. Another key feature is that of behaviour regulation which manifests itself in under-controlled or over-controlled behaviour patterns that are the child's defensive adaptations to overwhelming stress. Re-enactment of behavioural aspects of trauma can be illustrated in children presenting with sexualised behaviours as an automatic behavioural reaction. Such behaviour is seen as gaining mastery and control over their experience. Children with neglect histories or

maltreatment histories have impaired cognitive functioning by late infancy, and demonstrate delays in expressive and receptive language development.

We know that early care-giving relationships have an intense effect on a child's development of a coherent sense of self. Early positive life experiences assist in helping a child develop a sense of themselves as competent and worthy. Children with complex trauma who have experienced harm or rejection may feel helpless, and blame themselves for negative experiences. Families and foster carers have a crucial role in how a child adapts to trauma. Their emotional functioning can mitigate the development of PSTD in children and enhance a child's capacity to resolve symptoms.

Knowledge available to the practitioner about siblings

What do we know about sibling abuse?

Caffro and Conn Caffro (1998: 9) define sibling sexual abuse as 'sexual behaviour that is not age appropriate, not transitory, and not motivated by developmentally, mutually appropriate curiosity'.

Undertaking a review of the literature in this particular area reveals that there is a scarcity of information that focuses on sibling abuse. Work by Wiehe (2002), reflecting on the narrative accounts of adult survivors of sibling abuse, noted the following characteristics:

- Adults recall sexual behaviours commencing from the age of five to seven with siblings.
- Only a few survivors stated that it was a one-off event.
- Siblings were threatened with harm or force if they did not engage.
- There was a sense of progression in the sexual behaviours over time.
- They did not tell or report their experience due to fear of consequences.
- The other sibling was left in a perceived role of authority, such as babysitting, and the control could not be argued against.
- In coping with the sexual abuse young siblings reported that they were not usually aware of what they were doing when an older sibling engaged them in sexual play. Only after the episode, sometimes many years later when

they began to experience feelings of shame and guilt, did they feel like a victim. They frequently blamed themselves for participating in the behaviour.

Assessing children in sibling groups

Lord and Borthwick recommended the following: 'It is important to do a full assessment of the individual child in a sibling group as well as an assessment of their relationships with each other and the dynamics of the group' (p 19).

Key areas of assessment are:

- Assessing individual needs should have been completed using the Framework for Assessment (2000) and the looked-after children Assessment and Action Record. These documents will link with the assessment of harmful sexual behaviour also as it will help in deciding if the combined needs of the sibling group could be met by one permanent family.
- The quality of attachment each sibling has had with their primary care-giver will affect a child's quality of relationships with siblings.
- The circumstances in which the relationships between siblings developed, such as those outlined in DoH (1991). Their gender, the extent of a shared history, position of each child in the family, the cognitive and emotional age of each child, cultural and family expectations, and the role each child is perceived to have played at home needs to be assessed.
- Within the assessment there should be an important focus on each child's temperament and the extent of resilience.
- Gathering information from the birth family, chronologies and reports may indicate that the family may have negatively influenced the relationship between siblings, such as those described by Kosonen (1994).

Assessing sibling attachment relationships

The sibling checklist produced by HMSO (1991) requires detailed observation of how the children behave with each other. It encourages a range of people in a variety of settings to observe the interactions of the siblings. These people may include birth relatives, social workers and foster carers.

Other researchers such as Buhrmester and Furman (1985), looking at the qualities of sibling relationships identified four key features that need to be assessed in a sibling relationships. These are: the degree of rivalry, the degree of warmth, the degree of conflict and the degree to which one of the siblings dominates or nurtures the other.

There is no research, studies or statistics gathered about outcomes of sibling groups who have been fostered or adopted with histories of sexual abuse and whether they go on to harm others sexually or continue harmful sexual behaviour with siblings.

The polices and legislation relating to siblings in England

The law and government guidance support the view that siblings should be placed together if possible and consistent with their welfare. There is emphasis on contact between siblings if they are looked after in separate placements.

Children Act 1989 Section 23 (7) and guidance documents supports keeping siblings together where possible: 'siblings should not be separated when in care unless this is a part of a well thought-out plan based on the child's needs'. Section 22 of the Children Act 1989 makes it clear that 'before making any decision with respect to a child whom they are looking after, or proposing to look after, a local authority shall, so far as is reasonably practicable, ascertain the wishes and feelings of the child'.

The Framework for the Assessment of Children in Need (2000) talks about the quality of relationships between siblings also being of key significance to a child's welfare

The Human Rights Act 1998 Article 8 details the right to family life and family relationships and Article 8 (1) prohibits interference unless it is a matter of protecting the rights to freedom of others. This appears to strengthen the assumption that siblings should be kept together and the Convention of Human Rights has been held to cover relationships between siblings.

The research about sibling placements that does exist is not clear-cut and reveals differing opinions and conclusions on this matter.

Wedge and Mantle (1991) found that older siblings placed in a group have a lower disruption rate than singly-placed children, but younger siblings had a higher rate than singly-placed children. They suggest that sibling placements may protect the older child but may put the young child more at risk. They concluded that whilst many sibling placements are positive, they can carry additional risks and stress for carers.

Rushton et al (2001) indicated that being parented by an older sibling can be a protective factor for younger children. Currently there are no conclusive findings on the effect this has on the parenting child.

Hegar (2005) states 'joint sibling placements are stable, or more stable, than placements of single or separated siblings, and several studies suggest that children do as well or better when placed with their brothers and sisters'.

Helen Schwenke et al. (2006) discussing sibling relationships in the care system in Australia expresses the belief that most researchers focus on what adults can offer children and that decisions do not generally incorporate the benefits of the relationship of children with their siblings.

American researcher McCormick (2010), reviewing the inadequate empirical information on siblings in foster care, highlights how sibling relationships have the possibility to be elevated to major significance in the context of child abuse and when people are considering alternative care arrangement. He also explores how the child-caretaker relationship has been a central focus for researchers and practitioners and how sibling relationships have been peripheral. While there have been studies of sibling relationships in divorce proceedings, he points out that there is still a paucity of information available about assessing the role of the sibling relationship in foster care.

The guidance produced by BAAF (2008) echoes a familiar notion that separating siblings should only take place in circumstances as listed below.

Circumstances which may indicate that siblings should be placed separately

If children are placed in the same family, it may be impossible (within a reasonable timescale) to help them recover from dysfunctional and destructive patterns of interaction from the family of origin. These patterns include:

- intense rivalry and jealousy, with each child totally preoccupied with, and unable to tolerate the attention which their siblings may be getting

- exploitation, often based on gender, for example boys may have been seen and see themselves as inherently superior to their sisters with a right to dominate and exploit them
- chronic scapegoating of one child
- maintaining unhelpful alliances in a sibling group and family-of-origin conflicts; sibling patterns of behaviour may be strongly entrenched and may prevent re-parenting or learning new cultural norms
- maintaining unhelpful hierarchical positions, for example child may be stuck in the role of victim or bully
- highly sexualised behaviour with each other
- acting as triggers to each other's traumatic material and potentially re-traumatising each other; the triggers may well be unconscious, unintentional and mundane

It should be noted that any of the above patterns and ways of relating may be transferred by a child into its new family even if separated from birth siblings and placed singularly. New parents or carers need to be made fully aware of these patterns of interaction particularly if they are also parenting other children.

Preliminary discussions with both children's social care and private fostering agencies revealed that they do not have any guidance about an assessment framework which looks at under what circumstances to separate siblings when their behaviour is deemed as 'highly sexualised with each other'.

Reviewing research on siblings who are separated, McCormick (2010) highlights that there are very few studies that consider reasons for sibling separations. McCormick advocates for a better understanding of how sibling relationships have an effect on the socialisation, development and mental health of children in care.

Although limited in sample size, a study undertaken by Smith (1996) which looked at the factors associated with separating siblings, highlighted the following reasons: one sibling sexually abusing another 38 per cent, no available space 35 per cent.

Research patterns

Research in Patterns and Outcomes in Child Placement (1991) proposed that placing siblings together in general was viewed as a protective factor for children being accommodated. This has been challenged by Burnell, Vaughan and Williams (2001) who argue that the above research was predicated on pre-Children Act, 1989 population within the care system. These particular children and young people were 'heterogeneous' and were placed in a wide variety of placements.

They believe that the implementation of the Children Acts of 1989 and 2004 have culminated in children and young people being accommodated at an older age. Sibling groups, as a result, have experienced longer periods of neglect or abusive care.

They suggest that the current criteria require higher standards of evidence for children to be subject to care orders than was previously required. Unfortunately, children remain in traumatic family environments longer and are negatively impacted as a result.

Children who are coming into care now, are often highly traumatised and have poor attachments to their parents and siblings, which in turn results in the development of trauma bonds.

Research undertaken in Australia by Tarren-Sweeney, looking at predictors of problematic sexual behaviour among children with complex maltreatment histories, established a link between children entering care with complex needs and the potential for them to exhibit problematic sexual behaviour.

The study consisted of 347 pre-adolescent children in kinship or foster care. Most of these children had conduct problems and interpersonal problems indicative of attachment disturbances. Within this sample 52 sibling dyads presented with sexual behaviour problems. Other predictive factors included children being of an older age at entry into the care system, and placement instability.

Children coming into care are highly traumatised, who have had poor attachments to their parents, and this in turn reflects in their poor attachments to siblings and the trauma bonds that develop as a consequence. Burnell, Vaughan, Williams (2007), exploring whether or not to place siblings together, stress the importance of a secure attachment to a safe caring parent figure as this is the model for attachment relationships. It is their belief that sibling relationships are of secondary significance and should be maintained. However caution is given to sibling relationships that damage, endanger or put at risk the formation of a secure attachment to a parent figure. Interestingly they would argue in terms of a child care planning process that professionals should prioritise a hierarchy of a child's needs prior to considering the complex dynamics of sibling attachments. Burnell, Vaughan, Williams (2007) state the greatest needs are identified as:

- A secure attachment to a permanent parent figure who can provide therapeutic and developmental re-parenting of an intensity and consistency that will enable the formation of a secure attachment to them over two to three years.
- Siblings should be placed together if their sibling relationship has not been severely pathologised by the previous care and birth family experiences. In this context, particular attention should be given to children whose role within the birth family has been either to be a 'parentified child' carrying an inappropriate responsibility for their sibling's well-being, or a non-preferred child who has been scapegoated in the birth family as the problem child.

Reflecting on the above information, siblings that have been traumatised may need to be separated due to the relationship dynamics, previous patterns of relating prior to care and the negative impact that this may have on them in forming an attachment to an adult.

With the lack of clarity, how do practitioners decide on what 'highly sexualised' means?

What informs practitioners about placement decisions if siblings have been harmful sexually with each other?

Consideration for the development of a framework for the assessment of children who present with sexually harmful behaviour

To date I am unaware of any assessment frameworks that particularly focus on siblings with harmful sexual behaviour living in foster placements. Another dilemma is whether these siblings are in temporary, bridged placements or permanent placements. How long have they been in these placements? Did any disrupt due to sexual behaviour problems? Did children other than siblings present with sexual behaviour difficulties?

This latter part of the chapter is intended to begin to develop an integrated framework for areas that need to be considered when placing sibling children who have, or may develop harmful sexual behaviour with complex trauma histories and maltreatment. This framework echoes the Working-Together Guidance which places an emphasis on a multi-agency approach to dealing with children who harm sexually. It builds on the Aim Assessment Model for Under 12's by Carson (2007).

Assessment needs to include:

- the attachment relationship of the care-giver that will be required for individual children
- using the sibling checklists to look at attachment relationships
- assessment of individual needs
- assessing for all areas of maltreatment of children coming into care
- assessment of the impact of trauma on each child's development, utilising the Trauma Symptoms Checklist for Children (TSCC) by Briere (2005); the TSCC assesses the specific emotional, behavioural and cognitive impact of sexual abuse, with scales for anxiety, depression, post-traumatic stress, dissociation (covert and fantasy sub-scales) anger and sexual concerns (preoccupation and distress subscales)
- assessment of harmful sexual behaviour

What risk factors need to be considered in making a decision to separate siblings in placement or keep them together?

1. the age when sexual behaviours started.
2. if siblings have been involved in this behaviour for a substantial period of time, it is difficult to stop and they may have developed a strong sexual arousal to each other that has become habitual.
3. within the family of origin a sibling may have been assigned a role of authority, such as caring for a younger sibling, which they feel is difficult to give up.
4. if the relationship between siblings is based on assumed dominance, power and control.
5. risk associated with transitions in developmental stages, such as a sibling moving from childhood to puberty.
6. if a sibling has become a parentified child.

7. trauma responses are activated in the presence of another sibling.

Within the assessment of harmful sexual behaviour there are the following areas of important risk factors.

Sexual behaviour risk factors

- There is a level of persistence in their sexual behaviour, and it is compulsive.
- The circumstances in which the behaviour is happening is secretive and planned, showing three key essential dynamics of coercion, threat and force.
- An individual sibling's reaction to being asked about their behaviour who responds with being distressed or fearful and lacks understanding is a worry. Siblings who deny or blame others for their behaviours is also a concern.
- There are clear differences in the age of siblings, size and status.
- As a result of harmful sexual behaviour a sibling may decide to avoid contact due to feeling sad, powerless and anxious.
- Recording and analysising the information from the behaviour checklist reveals that the sexual behaviour demonstrated is unequal to other areas of their lives.
- The carer's response to siblings harming sexually gives cause for concerns as they are over-identifying with one sibling denying or minimising the behaviours.

Child development risk factors

- Historical information needs to be obtained about concerns regarding wider family abuse issues.
- Whether extended family and networks supported denial of harmful sexual behaviour.
- Pre-care, the children lived in an environment where violence, child abuse and children's sexual behaviours were acceptable and not seen as a cause of concern.
- As already stated, children in care have the potential for complex trauma histories which will require a care-giver to be able to offer therapeutic and developmental parenting of such an intensity and consistency to one child over a period of two to three years to enable the development of a secure attachment. Can foster carers provide for sibling groups?
- A child is displaying post traumatic stress symptoms.

- A child has a history of emotional or behavioural problems, for example fire setting.
- A child has no understanding of personal space and privacy.
- A child has a diagnosis of conduct disorder or ADHD.
- A child has withdrawn from relationships.
- Undertaking the Strengths and Difficulties Questionnaire reveals that the child has low self-esteem and self-worth.

Risks within current foster placement

- Foster carers are overwhelmed due to activating own trauma history.
- 24-hour supervision and monitoring is too much for them.
- There is a struggle to accept the seriousness of the behaviour.
- Static risks factors known about the birth family.

Static risk factors within the family prior to children coming into care

Looking at the parenting capacity prior to care the following areas can be identified as risk factors:

- high levels of family dysfunction
- lack of boundaries and routine
- history of domestic abuse and violence
- history of mental health issues
- highly sexualised environment, with few boundaries for privacy, intimate behaviours, and sexual information; exposure to pornography and internet?
- history of parents denying observed sexual behaviours
- parents blame one of the children for the harmful sexual behaviour
- parents rejected the children or one sibling due to harmful sexual behaviour
- sexual abuse history: suspected or confirmed prior to care?
- sexual abuse history was there sadism by perpetrator, physical or emotional abuse? Were one or two children sexually aroused as a result of abuse experience?
- how long did siblings live in adverse conditions prior to care? What shared history did they have?

What strength factors which focus on building resilience can be utilised to ensure that siblings could stay together in placement?

For each child

Sexual behaviours

- Child acknowledges the impact of their sexual behaviours on others.
- Child is receptive to intervention and boundary setting around their sexual behaviour.
- Child is able to accept accountability for their sexual behaviour.
- Child is able to demonstrate genuine remorse/regrets about sexual behaviours.
- Child is concerned about their behaviour and motivated to engage in work on their sexual behaviour.

Child development

Specific to each child

- Child has no significant health problems and has appropriately met their developmental milestones.
- Child is average or above average intelligence and has good ability to reason effectively and to adapt or acquire new skills.
- Good coping strategies for dealing with difficult feelings.
- Child has good self-esteem and feels they can make things happen and influence people.
- Child has the ability to make and maintain friendships.
- Child is popular in their peer group.
- Child has at least one consistent positive attachment to an adult.
- Good problem-solving skills.
- Child is talented and interested in other activities.
- Child has good planning skills.

Children within the sibling group have the ability to communicate their feelings to others such as a foster carer or emotional confidant

- The siblings have positive talents and individual interests.
- The children accept responsibility for their sexual behaviour.

- A child/sibling is responsive to interventions and boundary-seeking around their sexual behaviour.
- There is genuine regret for their sexual behaviour and individual children are willing to work on stopping their harmful sexual behaviour.
- Children have good self-esteem.
- Children have good reasoning skills and can develop new skills.

Strengths within the foster care environment

- Foster carers can provide consistent and positive safe care for sibling group.
- The foster carers have clear rules and boundaries around privacy, intimacy and sexual behaviour. They are able to discuss sexual information with the sibling group.
- Foster carers are open to receiving information, support and guidance about management of children with harmful sexual behaviour.
- As good role models, foster carers can demonstrate good communication and express feelings appropriately.
- There are consistent positive role models and attachment figures for the children.
- The sibling group are in a stable, secure placement.
- There is network of support for the child and foster carers.
- There is a safety plan in operation that is reviewed and coordinated by regular multi-agency meetings.

Analysis of information

The placement of children together or separately will need to think about the risks and strengths identified.

Talking with other colleagues in practice, the decision needs to be undertaken on a case by case basis. An important feature in this assessment is the timescale involved in re-parenting sibling children with complex needs.

There will be times when professionals will have to decide on the best course of action with the available information. As good practitioners we must take on board the wishes and feelings of individual children; we also have a professional duty to safeguard them from further harm. Decisions to separate or place them together should be clearly recorded and evidenced. Schwenke, Hudd and Vicary (2006) discuss sibling relationships in the care system and conclude that siblings who have had early experiences which have resulted in insecure or disrupted attachments have the potential to positively attach to another carer who is able to offer a nurturing and secure environment, and sustain attachment to a sibling, even though they are in a different placement.

Future recommendations in the light of this chapter

- Ensure that a working group begins to lobby for a universal definition of harmful sexual behaviour for children.
- That staff engaged in this work receive the support, guidance and training requested in Working Together 2010.
- Researchers and practitioners begin to acknowledge the differences between children and young people who harm sexually.
- Effective supervision is available to staff to explore impact issues and issues such as transference and counter-transference, splitting, and projective identification.
- Agencies are kept accountable for responding to concerns at a low level, so that they do not only respond when high thresholds are reached.
- Professionals keep good recordings of information pre- and post-care.
- There is a rigorousness applied to keeping the professional network updated about changes in dynamic risk factors.
- That further studies are undertaken on sibling children who harm sexually in placement.
- Further research should take place to look at the role of sibling relationships while in care.
- Note of caution: just because a child had not disclosed sexual abuse pre-care, is does not mean that it has not happened.
- Data is collected from local authorities to determine the population of such children, so that they are not invisible.

References

Abrahmson, (1996) Reflections on Knowing Oneself Ethically. *Families in Society. Journal of Contemporary Human Services*, April.

BAAF (2008) *Together or Apart*. London: BAAF.

Banks, N. (2002) I'm Saying Haven't a Clue: Unconscious Process in Practitioners Who Work With Young People Who Sexually Abuse. in Calder, M.C. *Young People Who Sexually Abuse: Building the Evidence Base For Your Practice*. Lyme Regis: Russell House Publishing.

Briers, J. (2005) *Trauma Symptom Checklist For Children, Professional Manual*. Odessa, Fl: Psychological Assessment Resource.

Buhrmester, D. and Furman, W. (1985) Children's Perceptions of The Qualities of Sibling Relationships. *Child Development*, 56, 448–69.

Burnell, Vaughan and Williams (2007) Framework For Assessing Children Who Have Experienced Developmental Trauma. *Family Futures*.

Burton, J., Rasmussen, L., Bradshaw, J., Christopherson, B. and Huke, S. (1998) *Treating Children With Sexually Abusive Behaviour Problems: Guidelines For Child and Parent Intervention*. New York: Haworth Press.

Caffro, J. and Con-Cefffro, A (1998) *Siblings Abuse Trauma Assessment and Intervention*. New York: Haworth Press.

Calder, M.C. (2001) *Juveniles and Children Who Sexually Abuse, Frameworks For Assessment*. Lyme Regis: Russell House Publishing.

Calder, M.C. (ed.) *Young People Who Sexually Abuse*. Lyme Regis: Russell House Publishing.

Carson, C. (2007) *AIM and Initial Assessment and Intervention For Children Under 12 Years Who Display Sexually Harmful Behaviour*. Aim Project. *Children and Youth Services Review*, 27, 7.

Cook, A., Spinallola, J., Ford, J., Lankhee, C. et al. (2005) White Paper For National Child Traumatic Stress Network.

Cunningham, C. and Macfarlane, L. (1996) *When Children Abuse*. Brandon, VT: Safe Society Press.

Department of Health (2006) *Framework For The Assessment of Children in Need and Their Families*. DoH, DfEE.

Family Futures (2010) *Training 2010 Family Future Consortium Siblings Together or Apart*. Family Futures.

Farmer, E. and Pollock, S. (1998) *Sexually Abused and Abusing Children in Substitute Care*. John Willey and Sons.

Farmer, E. and Pollock, S. (2003) Managing Sexually Abused and/or Abusing in Substitute Care. *Child and Family Social Work*, 101–12.

Finklehor, D. and Browne, A. (1985) Sexual Abuse: Initial and Long-Term Effects. A Conceptual Framework. in Finkelhor, D.A. *Sourcebook on Child Sexual Abuse*. Beverly Hill, CA: Sage.

Finklehor, D. and Browne, A. (1985) The Traumatic Impact of Child Sexual Abuse: A Conceptualisation In America. *Journal of Orthopsychiatry*.

Friedrich, W. and Feher, E. (2004) Correlates of Behaviour Problems in a ClinicalSample of Sexually Abused Children. Manuscript Submitted For Publication.

Friedrich, W.H., Davies, W., Fehere, A., Trentham, B. and Wright, (2003) Sexual Behavioural Problems in Pre-Teen Children. *Annals of New York. Academy of Science*.

Friedrich, W.N. (1990) *Counter Transference: Psychotherapy of Sexually Abused Children and Families*. WM Norrat.

Friedrich-Baker, W., Parker, A.L., Schneiderman, M., Gnes, M. and Archer, L.M. (2005) Young People With Problems: Sexualised Behaviours in The Child Welfare System. One Year Longitudal Study. *Sexual Abuse. A Journal of Research and Treatment*, 17.

Gibe, (2004) *NSPCC Policy Summary, Children and Young People Who Display Sexually Harmful Behaviour*. NSPCC.

Gilgun, (1999) Caspars Clinical Assessments Instruments That Measure Strengths and Risk in Children and Families. in Calder, M.C. *Working With Young People Who Abuse: New Pieces of The Jigsaw Puzzle*. Lyme Regis: Russell House Publishing.

Hackett, S. (1999) *Children and Young People Who Sexually Abuse Others: Challenges and Responses* London: Brunner Routeldge.

Head, and Elgar, (1997) From Court Process to Care Plan. An Empirical Study of The Placement of Sexually Abused Children. Oxford: Centre For Sociological Studies, Wolfson College.

Hegar, (2005) Sibling Placement in Foster Care and Adoption: An Overview of International Research.

Heiman, (2001) Helping Parents and Their Children's Sexual Behaviour Problems. *Journal of Child Sexual Abuse*, 10.

HMSO (1991) *Patterns and Outcomes in Child Placement: Messages From Current Research and Their Implications*. London: HMSO.

HMSO (2010) *Working Together*. HMSO.

Human Rights Act 1998.

Johnson T C. (1988) Child Perpetrators: Children Who Molest Other Children: Preliminary Findings. *Child Abuse and Neglect*, 12.

Johnson, T.C. (1993) Childhood Sexuality. in Gil, E. and Johnson, T.C. (eds.) op cit 1–20.

Johnson, T.C. (2004) *Family Violence and Sexual Assault*. Institute San Diego.

Johnson, T.C. and Doonan, R. (2005) Children With Sexual Behavioural Problems. What Have We Learnt in The Last Two Decades? in Calder, M.C. *Children and Young People Who Sexually Abuse: New Theory Research and Practice Developments*. Lyme Regis: Russell House Publishing.

Jones, R., Ownbey, M., Everidge, J., Judkins, B. and Timber, G. (2006) Focussed Foster Care For Children With Serious Behavioural Problems. *Child and Adolescent Social Work Journal*, 23, 3.

Kosonen, M. (1994) Sibling Relationships for Children in The Care System. *Adoption & Fostering*, 18: 3, 30–5.

Kraemer, (1998) Splitting and Stupidity in Child Sexual Abuse. *Psychoanalytical Psychotherapy*, 3: 3, 247–59.

Masson, H. and Morrison, T. (1999) Young Sexual Abusers: Conceptual Framework Issues and Imperatives. *Children Society*, 13, 203–15.

Mathews, (1998) The Adolescent Offender in Canada. Old Problems – Current Issues. *Journal of Child and Young Persons Care*.

Mccormick, A. (2010) Siblings in Foster Care: An Overview of Research, Policy and Practice. *Journal of Public Child Welfare*, 4.

Newman, F. (2005) *Children and Resilience*. Bamardo's Policy, Research and Influencing Unit.

Ofsted (2009) *The Exclusion From School of Children Aged Four to Seven*. Ofsted.

Pither, A., Gray, W., Busconi, A. and Houchen, S. (1998) Children With Sexual Behaviour Problems. Identification of Five Distinct Types and Related Treatment Considerations. *Child and Maltreatment*, 3.

Rasmussen, L. (1999) The Trauma Outcome Process: An Integrated Model For Guiding Clinical Practice With Children With Sexually Abusive Behaviour Problems. *Journal of Child Sexual Abuse*, 8: 4.

Rothschild, B. with Rand, M. (2006) *Help For The Helper*. WW Norton.

Rushton, (2001) *Siblings in Late Permanent Placements*. London: BAAF.

Schwenke, H. (2006) Sibling Relationships in The Care System. *Children Australia*, 31: 1.

Shaw, J., Lewis, E., Loeb, Rosado, J. and Rodriguez, A. (2000) Child on Child Sexual Abuse: Psychological Perspectives. *Child Abuse and Neglect*, 24: 12.

Smith, M.C. (1996) An Exploratory Survey of Foster Mother and Caseworker Attitudes About Sibling Placement. *Child Welfare*, 75: 4, 357–75.

Tarren-Sweeney, M. (2008) Predictors of Problematic Sexual Behaviour Among Children With Complex Maltreatment Histories. *Child Maltreatment*, 13: 2.

Taylor, J. (2003) Children and Young People Accused of Sexual Abuse. A Study in The Community. *Journal of Sexual Aggression*, 9: 1, 57–70.

The Children's Act 1999 /2004

The Human Rights Act 1998

Wedge, P. and Mantle, G. (1991) *Sibling Groups and Social Work: A Study of Children Referred Substitute Family Placement*. Aldershot: Avebury.

Wiehe, (2002) *What Parents Need to Know About Sibling Abuse*. Bonville Books.

Working Together For Family Assessment. HMSO.

CHAPTER 14

Complementing the Comprehensive Assessment of Adolescents who Have Sexually Offended: Utility of the Schuler Adolescent Inventory of Life Experiences and Functioning

Siegi A. Schuler and Dana Costin

Adolescent sexual offending

Over the last 25 years, there has been increased clinical and research attention devoted to the issue of adolescent sexual offending (Benoit and Kennedy, 1992; Cooper, Murphy and Haynes, 1996; Smith, 1988; Veneziano, Veneziano and LeGrand, 2000; Zolondek et al., 2001) as recognition has increased that considerable numbers of sexual offences are committed by adolescents. In Canada, 20 per cent of those charged with a sexual crime are between 12–17 years of age (Statistics Canada, 2007) and adolescents are believed to be responsible for between 30 per cent and 40 per cent of the sexual offences that are committed against children (Department of Justice Canada, 1994, as cited in Carpentier and Proulx, 2002). In the United States, it has been estimated that adolescents are responsible for almost half of all sexual offences that are committed yearly against children (Abel and Rouleau, 1990; Becker and Kaplan, 1993). Additionally, research suggests that approximately 50 per cent of adult sexual offenders committed their first sexual offence during adolescence (Becker and Abel, 1985).

Research regarding adolescents who commit sexual offences has focused on a variety of issues including, but not limited to, comparing adolescents who commit sexual offences to adolescents who engage in nonsexual delinquency or commit nonsexual offences (Blaske, Borduin, Henggeler and Mann, 1989; Burton, 2000; Davis and Leitenberg, 1987; Freeman, Dexter-Mazza and Hoffman, 2005; Jacobs, Kennedy and Meyer, 1997), describing the sexual offences committed by adolescents (Boyd, Hagan and Cho, 2000; Burton, 2000; Cooper et al., 1996), identifying risk factors and rates of sexual recidivism (Caldwell, 2007; Nisbet, Wilson and Smallbone, 2004; Parks and Bard, 2006; Rasmussen, 1999; Worling and Curwen, 2001;

Worling and Langstrom, 2003, 2006) and characterising or developing personality typologies of the adolescents (Cooper et al., 1996; Hunter et al., 2003; Worling, 1995a, 2001). Some of the commonly examined characteristics and life experiences of adolescents who commit sexual offences include family structure, functioning, relationships, and violence (Benoit and Kennedy, 1992; Cooper et al., 1996; Falls, 2001; Ford and Linney, 1995; Kobayashi et al., 1995; Rasmussen, 1999; Worling, 2001), victimisation histories of adolescents who commit sexual offences (Benoit and Kennedy, 1992; Burton, 2000; Cooper et al., 1996; Ford and Linney, 1995; Veneziano et al., 2000; Way, 2002; Worling, 1995b, 1995c), antisocial behaviour/nonsexual delinquency and offending of adolescents who commit sexual offences (Caldwell, 2007; Chu and Thomas, 2010; Jacobs et al., 1997; Nisbet et al., 2004; Parks and Bard, 2006; Rasmussen, 1999; Ryan et al., 1996; Seto and Lalumiere, 2006; Worling, 1995a, 2001), social functioning and interpersonal skills (Fagan and Wexler, 1988; Cooper et al., 1996; Worling, 2001), and empathy and self-esteem (Curwen, 2003; Monto, Zgourides and Harris, 1998). Within these areas, research has demonstrated that adolescents who have sexually offended have experienced high levels of family instability and violence (Falls, 2001; Kobayashi et al., 1995; Rasmussen, 1999; Worling, 2001), evidence deficits in social competence, such as problematic social relationships, difficulty with intimacy in relationships, social isolation, and identification with younger children (Fagan and Wexler, 1988; Fehrenbach et al, 1986; Hunter et al., 2003; Letourneau, Schoenwald and Sheidow, 2004; Worling, 2001; Worling and Langstrom, 2003, 2006) and report higher levels of victimisation than is reported in the general population (Burton, 2000; Cooper et al., 1996; Fortune and Lamble, 2004; Johnson, 1988; Kobayashi et al.,

1995; Pierce and Pierce, 1987; Veneziano et al., 2000; Watkins and Bentovim, 1992; Way, 2002).

Although some common characteristics have been identified, researchers and clinicians consistently agree that adolescents who commit sexual offences are a heterogeneous group (Cooper et al., 1996; Curwen, 2003; Hunter et al., 2003; Veneziano and Veneziano, 2002; Worling, 2001; Worling and Langstrom, 2006; Zakireh, Ronis and Knight, 2008; Zolondek et al., 2001) and that adolescent sexual offending is a multi-determined phenomenon (Letourneau et al., 2004). As well, both sexual and nonsexual factors are believed to contribute to both the etiology of sexual offending and sexual recidivism by adolescents (Worling and Langstrom, 2003, 2006).

Assessment of adolescents who have sexually offended

Purpose and process

Assessment of adolescents who have sexually offended can serve many purposes, including informing judicial responses, identifying risk issues, addressing community safety and reintegration issues, determining treatment needs, plans, and amenability to treatment, and informing family reunification plans (Bonner et al., 1998). It is generally agreed that a comprehensive clinical assessment is the best-practice approach in terms of adequately identifying the individual adolescent's strengths and weaknesses, risk of sexual reoffending, and treatment needs (ATSA, 2005; CSOM, 2007b; Smith et al., 2005; Veneziano and Veneziano, 2002; Worling and Curwen, 2001; Worling and Langstrom, 2003, 2006). Recommendations regarding the process of conducting a comprehensive assessment include ensuring that the professional involved is well-trained regarding adolescent sexual offending (ie sexual and nonsexual issues involved), risk assessment (ie relevant risk factors, recidivism), and assessment of adolescents and families; that multiple sources of information are included (eg adolescent, parents/caregivers, referral sources); and that multiple approaches to collecting information (eg clinical interviews, use of questionnaires, review of official documentation and file information) are integrated into the process (Bonner et al., 1998; Worling and

Langstrom, 2006). It is also noteworthy that assessments are considered a 'point-in-time' and information can change; thus, reassessment throughout treatment and at treatment completion are recommended (CSOM, 2007b) and risk assessments regarding adolescents should be revisited every 6–12 months, or pending significant change(s) in the adolescent's circumstances and/or functioning (Prentky and Righthand, 2003; Worling and Curwen, 2001).

Comprehensive assessment: inclusion of sexual and nonsexual issues

While exploring and addressing sexual history, sexual behaviours and offending, and sexually-based risk factors are intuitive in both assessment and treatment, it is equally important to consider nonsexual influences on sexual offending and reoffending. Nonsexual factors such as family issues, social skill deficits, and antisocial values and behaviour have repeatedly been identified as important for consideration in the etiology of sexual offending behaviour (Hunter et al., 2003; Jacobs et al., 1997). Additionally, similarities have consistently been found among adolescents who commit nonsexual as opposed to sexual offences (Blaske et al., 1989; Davis and Leitenberg, 1987; Hastings, Anderson and Hemphill, 1997; Jacobs et al., 1997; Zakireh et al., 2008) and higher nonsexual recidivism rates versus sexual recidivism rates have repeatedly been reported for adolescents who have sexually offended (Caldwell, 2007; Nisbet et al., 2004; Rasmussen, 1999; Reitzel and Carbonell, 2006; Waite et al., 2005; Worling and Curwen, 2000). As well, research has demonstrated that most adolescents who commit sexual offences do not evidence primarily deviant sexual interests (Worling, 2006). More importantly, both sexual and nonsexual risk factors (eg antisocial values and behaviours/nonsexual delinquency and offending) have been identified as being of importance with respect to sexual recidivism by adolescents (Nisbet et al., 2004; Rasmussen, 1999; Waite et al., 2005; Worling and Langstrom, 2003, 2006).

Worling and Langstrom (2003, 2006) provided an overview of the various risk factors that may be considered with respect to adolescent sexual offence recidivism, classifying these as empirically-supported, promising, possible, and unlikely (for definitions, see Worling and Langstrom, 2003, 2006). The risk factors identified include both sexual and nonsexual factors. According to Worling and Langstrom (2003, 2006), empirically-supported risk factors within the sexual realm include deviant sexual interests, prior criminal sanctions for sexual assault(s), past sexual offences against more than one victim, selection of a stranger victim, and incomplete sexual offence-specific treatment (Worling and Langstrom, 2003, 2006). Sexual-specific risk factors identified as promising or possible (see Worling and Langstrom, 2003, 2006) include attitudes supportive of sexual offending, obsessive sexual interests/sexual preoccupation, selection of a male victim, an environment supporting an opportunity to reoffend, past sexual assault against a child, and threats or use of excessive violence or weapons during the sexual offence (Worling and Langstrom, 2003, 2006). Within the nonsexual domain, a lack of intimate peer relationships/social isolation has been identified as an empirically-supported risk factor and problematic parent-adolescent relationships/parental rejection is believed to be a promising risk factor (Worling and Langstrom, 2003, 2006). Nonsexual risk factors that are possibly related to risk of sexual recidivism include a high-stress family environment, impulsivity, negative peer associations and influences, interpersonal aggression, and antisocial interpersonal orientation (Worling and Langstrom, 2003, 2006). Worling and Langstrom's reviews lend support to the need to assess and address nonsexual issues and functioning, in addition to sexual issues and functioning, in attempting to reduce the risk of sexual recidivism by an adolescent.

Given empirical findings that sexual offending and reoffending are not entirely sexually determined, it is not surprising that researchers and clinicians have repeatedly recommended that, in addition to addressing sexual history, concerning sexual behaviours, sexual interests and attitudes, and sexual offence history, comprehensive assessments should also explore and address nonsexual areas of functioning (ATSA, 2005; Bonner et al., 1998; CSOM, 2007b; Worling and Langstrom, 2006; Zakireh et al., 2008). For example, the Association for the Treatment of Sexual Abusers (2005) stipulates that assessments should include assessment of nonsexual areas such as: criminal and other antisocial behaviour and values, developmental history and family background, education and employment histories, history of aggression or violence, level of cognitive functioning, medical and mental health history, and peer and romantic relationships. Similarly, in addition to gathering a detailed sexual history, Bonner et al. (1998) identified that assessments of adolescents who have sexually offended should address cognitive ability, intelligence, and academic performance; history of physical abuse, sexual abuse, and neglect; history of nonsexual delinquent or antisocial behaviour; drug and alcohol use; and history of previous mental health problems or psychiatric hospitalisations.

Consistent with recommendations regarding assessments, treatment efforts with adolescents also include addressing both sexual and nonsexual issues. In the sexual domain, treatment efforts often focus on issues such as sexual attitudes, decreasing deviant sexual arousal, addressing and disputing cognitive distortions, offence prevention and safety planning, and improving sexual health and sexual relationships. In the nonsexual realm, targets/recommendations for treatment often include enhancing social functioning and improving intimacy in relationships, addressing antisocial attitudes, resolving traumatic/victimisation histories, enhancing problem-solving skills, and improving emotional regulation and functioning (Burton, 2000; Hunter et al., 2003; Veneziano and Veneziano, 2002).

Assessing dynamic and static risk factors

Although factors that may contribute to the onset or initiation of sexual offending are of interest and importance with respect to the psychological and emotional health of the adolescent who has sexually offended, as well as primary prevention efforts, considerable attention should also be paid to the issues that may contribute to the risk of sexual recidivism. These, in turn, should inform primary treatment recommendations and goals for adolescents referred to treatment following the commission of a sexual offence.

Generally, factors identified as possibly contributing to risk of sexual reoffending are divided into two categories: static risk factors and dynamic risk factors. Static risk factors are historical risk factors that are generally stable, such as the age and gender of past victims and the characteristics of the sexual offences pre-dating the assessment (Worling and

Langstrom, 2003). Although historically described as 'unchangeable', it is noted by Mann, Hanson, and Thornton (2010) that static factors can change over time. For example, these authors point out that the age of an individual who commits sexual offences changes (ie individuals get older) and that criminal history can get worse (eg when additional sexual offences occur, different types of victims may be reported or force/violence in a sexual offence may now be reported whereas it was not in a previous offence or at a previous time). Thus, a primary descriptor of static risk factors should likely be that they are not plausible treatment targets.

Dynamic risk factors, on the other hand, are potentially changeable attributes and circumstances (Andrews and Bonta, 2006; Worling and Langstrom, 2003) and their amenability to treatment has resulted in these factors also being referred to as 'criminogenic needs' (Andrews and Bonta, 2006). It has been noted that 'the most useful dynamic risk factors are those that have the potential of responding positively to treatment' (Smith et al., 2005: 87). Although changeable overall, it has been highlighted that dynamic risk factors can also be relatively stable in that they are slower to change (CSOM, 2007b). For adolescents, some potentially stable dynamic risk factors that have been identified include deficits in social competence, social isolation, poor parent-child relationships, antisocial values and behaviours, deviant sexual interests, impulsivity, and non-compliance with treatment (CSOM, 2007b; Worling and Langstrom, 2006).

Although risk assessment tools for adults have traditionally favoured the inclusion of static risk factors (Mann et al., 2010; Worling and Langstrom, 2003) because of their empirical relationships with recidivism (Mann et al., 2010) more recent adult-focused risk tools have also included dynamic items and assessment of criminogenic needs (Mann et al., 2010). However, research regarding the effectiveness of these tools in predicting sexual recidivism is currently limited (Mann et al., 2010). On the other hand, risk assessment tools designed for use with adolescents, such as the Estimate of Risk of Sexual Offence Recidivism (The ERASOR, Worling and Curwen, 2001) and the Juvenile Sex Offender Assessment Protocol-II (J-SOAP and J-SOAP-II, Prentky and Righthand 2001, 2003), have included both static and dynamic risk factors for some time. Although research

regarding the effectiveness of the adolescent-based tools in predicting sexual reoffence risk continues, the inclusion of dynamic risk factors is based on clinical beliefs and empirical findings that adolescents are frequently changing and, thus, often amenable to treatment. Indeed, in a 20-year follow-up (average of 16.23 years) of adolescents who sexually offended, the sexual reoffence rate was found to be 9 per cent for those who participated in specialised treatment and 21 per cent for those who did not participate in treatment (Worling, Litteljohn and Bookalam, 2009). Similarly, in a recent meta-analysis of treatment studies and recidivism rates for juveniles (mean age of 14.6 years but with a possible range of 7–20 years) who sexually offended, Reitzel and Carbonell (2006) found that the overall sexual recidivism rate was 12.53 per cent (average 59-month follow-up) and, for those who had received sexual offender treatment, the sexual recidivism rate was 7.37 per cent compared to 18.93 per cent in the control groups.

Through exploration of both sexual and nonsexual issues, and both dynamic and static risk factors, comprehensive assessments should identify and clarify a client's strengths, risks, and needs. Findings from assessments should directly inform treatment recommendations and goals which both address deficits/concerns and build on the identified strengths (eg social skills/intimacy training, emotional management). Based on this information, treatment should primarily target risk factors that can change over time – that is, dynamic risk factors or criminogenic needs (ATSA, 2005) – although, addressing static or historical issues (eg resolving victimisation history – though static in nature, the impact of this may be very much dynamic) is also likely to be of importance.

The Schuler Adolescent Inventory of Life Experiences and Functioning

Introduction, clinical utility, and implementation

The Schuler Adolescent Inventory of Life Experiences and Functioning (SAILEF) is a self-report inventory intended to survey various life events/experiences and areas of functioning of adolescents. It was developed in accordance with recommendations regarding the need for comprehensive assessment and treatment of adolescents who have sexually offended. It is appropriate for adolescents who are approximately 12–18 years of age. While the SAILEF might be useful to gather certain information from adults, it was not specifically designed to consider many of the life and relationship circumstances that would be relevant for adult clients. The SAILEF can be used with both males and females; the majority of the items are applicable to both males and females, but the inventory includes some gender-specific items.

The SAILEF is a self-report questionnaire that can be completed by the adolescent at assessment, throughout treatment, and upon treatment completion, but can also be administered as a semi-structured interview. As it is based primarily on a rating scale, the inventory provides a time-effective and minimally-demanding response format for the adolescent who may find it easier to respond to certain questions in a simple manner, and through a paper-and-pencil rather than clinical interview format. Previous research has found that self-reporting through paper-and-pencil inventories can be a useful measure of past criminal and/or concerning behaviours (Daleiden et al., 1998; Smith et al., 2005; Weinrott and Saylor, 1991; Worling, 2006; Zolondek et al., 2001).

The SAILEF was developed for use in the assessment and treatment of adolescents who have sexually offended, but is intended to complement, not replace, the clinical interviews, psychometric questionnaires, and official information used in comprehensive assessments and treatment. As part of a comprehensive assessment for adolescents who have sexually offended, the SAILEF is likely to be primarily useful in identifying potentially important life events/experiences, circumstances, and functioning in a variety of areas. While a variety of sexual experiences and behaviours are included, the SAILEF is not primarily focused on the concerning sexual behaviour history or sexual offending that has occurred, nor on potential ongoing areas of sexual concern (eg deviant sexual interests/arousal, sexual attitudes). Other tools exist for assessing these areas (eg Adolescent Clinical Sexual Behavior Inventory, Friedrich et al., 1994; Hanson Sex Attitudes Questionnaire, Hanson, Gizzarelli and Scott, 1994 – modified for use with adolescents by Worling, 1998; Relationship Attitudes Questionnaire, Worling and Costin, 2007; Sexual History Form,

Kaufman, 1993a and Sexual Fantasy Questionnaire, Kaufman, 1993b; SAFE-T Sexual Offense Questionnaire, Worling, 1999). Consistent with best-practice recommendations regarding the completion of comprehensive sexual offence-specific assessments, the SAILEF provides information regarding an adolescent's cognitive and academic functioning, social relationships and functioning, emotional functioning and mental health, behaviour history/concerns and attitudes, sexual history, family functioning and relationships, physical health and medical history, and victimisation history. Given the frequent relevance of a victimisation history for adolescents who have committed sexual offences, three supplementary assessment sections provide a detailed inventory of the specific types of physical, emotional, and sexual abuse acts experienced, as well as impact-related issues related to sexual abuse. These supplementary sections may be of particular utility when using the SAILEF as part of a comprehensive assessment of trauma and/or treatment for trauma.

Many of the areas addressed in the SAILEF correspond with the empirically-supported, promising, and possible nonsexual, dynamic risk factors reported by Worling and Langstrom (2003, 2006) and risk factors included in both the ERASOR (Worling and Curwen, 2001) and J-SOAP-II (Prentky and Righthand, 2003). Thus, this inventory can inform factors that are included and assessed in an estimate of risk of sexual reoffending and, more importantly, can inform treatment goals and recommendations. Whether it is used at assessment, throughout treatment, or at treatment completion, the inventory allows clinicians to survey an adolescent's various life experiences and functioning in a variety of areas. Regardless of the point in time when the inventory is used, clinicians can go back and review with the adolescent more comprehensively, issues that emerged on the inventory.

The SAILEF was designed to be used in a clinical setting, as part of the comprehensive assessment and treatment of an adolescent. Given the sensitive and potentially distressing nature of some of the questions, it is recommended that it not be administered without clinical follow-up and clinical involvement. Although comprehensive, the SAILEF is not exhaustive and it is critical to note that it was not designed to replace a comprehensive clinical interview with adolescents who have sexually offended. Rather, it is intended to supplement the information obtained through the multiple methods of information collection involved in a comprehensive assessment (ie clinical interviews, collateral interviews and questionnaires, official documentation, past reports, questionnaires). As with any questionnaire that is completed as part of an assessment or treatment, consent and confidentiality issues (inclusive of disclosure reporting obligations) should be fully explained to the adolescent prior to administration.

Utility with sexually offending adolescent females

For many years, sexual offending by females was widely overlooked in the clinical and research literature, likely because males have been found to commit the majority of sexual offences and because of reluctance to identify females as sexual perpetrators (CSOM, 2007a; Mathews, Hunter Jr. and Vuz, 1997; Oliver, 2007; Strickland, 2008; Wijkman, Bijleveld and Hendriks, 2010). More recently, however, increased attention has been paid to the issue of female sexual offending in both the adult and adolescent literature, with attempts to provide information regarding the characteristics of the sexually offending females, their sexual offences, and their victims (Mathews et al., 1997; Moulden, Firestone and Wexler, 2007; Oliver, 2007; Strickland, 2008; Wijkman et al., 2010). Estimates of female sexual offending have ranged in the literature, but research regarding adult sexual offending suggests that approximately five per cent of sexual offences are committed by females (Cortoni, Hanson, and Coache, 2010). Although very limited research has been conducted specific to adolescent females, available information suggests that many of the characteristics identified for adult females who sexually offend are also relevant for adolescent females who sexually offend (CSOM, 2007a).

Research has demonstrated that many of the issues applicable to males who sexually offend are also relevant with respect to females who sexually offend. For example, a history of victimisation (in fact, more extensive physical, emotional, and sexual victimisation has been reported by females who commit sexual offences), dysfunctional family environments and family violence, problematic family relationships, interpersonal problems, nonsexual criminal activity, greater likelihood of nonsexual than

sexual recidivism, alcohol and drug abuse, learning disabilities, mental health concerns, emotional problems, and deviant sexual arousal/interests have been reported for adult and adolescent females who have committed sexual offences (CSOM, 2007a; Grayston and DeLuca, 1999; Mathews et al., 1997; Moulden et al., 2007). As recidivism rates for females who sexually offend are believed to be very low, it has been cautioned that risk assessments based on male-specific risk assessment tools may over estimate the risk of sexual reoffending for females (Cortoni et al., 2010).

Although best-practice standards are currently lacking with respect to the assessment and treatment of females who have sexually offended, inclusive of adolescent females, the findings to date suggest that comprehensive assessments should be completed with adolescent females who sexually offend. Like the assessments recommended for male adolescents who have sexually offended, these assessments should address various aspects of functioning (eg sexual functioning and offence history, victimisation history, family history, social functioning, academic functioning, emotional functioning, self-esteem, mental health, nonsexual delinquency) and should lead to the development of uniquely-tailored treatment recommendations (CSOM, 2007a). Given this, the Schuler Adolescent Inventory of Life Experiences and Functioning would be a useful tool in the comprehensive assessment of adolescent females who have sexually offended.

Utility with nonsexually offending adolescents

Although it was developed in the course of the author's clinical work with adolescents who have sexually offended, the exclusion of detailed questions specific to the sexual offending promotes its clinical utility of the Schuler Adolescent Inventory of Life Experiences and Functioning with adolescents who are involved in nonsexual delinquency or have committed nonsexual offences, adolescents who are in general conflict with the law, and adolescents who have experienced traumatic histories or have other clinical needs. Indeed, extensive research has demonstrated that many of the issues relevant to adolescents who sexually offend, such as family dysfunction and conflict, victimisation history, peer difficulties, emotional difficulties, and behavioural concerns, are also of importance for adolescents who are involved with the law for nonsexual delinquency or offending, or have other clinical needs (Blaske et al., 1989; Dembo, Wareham, Poythress, Meyers, and Schmeidler, 2008; Freeman et al., 2005; Hastings et al., 1997). Thus, clinicians who are working with adolescents who have not committed sexual offences may also find the SAILEF useful in their work.

Limitations and considerations

The Schuler Adolescent Inventory of Life Experiences and Functioning is a self-report inventory and, thus, limitations and risks related to self-reporting by adolescents should be considered. In particular, the issue of social desirability in responding cannot be ignored, although it is noted that theoretical understandings of social desirability issues, measurement of social desirability, and controlling for social desirability bias continue to be discussion points in forensic research, research related to sexual offending, and research specifically related to adolescents who have sexually offended (Tan and Grace, 2008).

Not surprisingly, the issue of self-reporting has been addressed in a number of writings and research regarding adolescents who have sexually offended, with conflicting results. Some researchers have reported findings that raise concerns regarding the validity of self-reporting by adolescents who have sexually offended. For example, Zolondek et al. (2001) found that those participants who were more concerned with reporting socially desirable responses also reported fewer paraphiliac behaviours. However, other researchers have found that adolescents' self-reports can provide useful and seemingly reliable information. For example, Worling (2006) found that self-reported arousal by male adolescents who had sexually offended corresponded with their choice of victims, significantly distinguishing those adolescents who assaulted a child from those who assaulted peers or adults, and those with male child victims from those who did not have male child victims. Adolescents who self-rated their sexual arousal to children (ie under the age of 12) over a '0' mark on a self-report arousal graph were significantly more likely to have offended against a single child victim, multiple child victims, or male child victims. Worling highlighted that his findings contributed to the growing evidence that

structured, self-reported methodologies can provide valuable information regarding adolescents' sexual interests. Smith et al. (2005) found that self-report instruments were useful in distinguishing between risk levels of adolescents who had sexually offended. Although the risk groups identified were not based on current sexual recidivism risk estimate tools but on the presence or absence of six static variables, those in the low risk group reported fewer problems overall than those in the medium and high risk groups. Specifically, participants identified as low risk reported greater family cohesion, less aggression, higher self-esteem, less social avoidance, and fewer sexual fantasies than did participants in the medium or high risk groups. Thus, the authors concluded that self-report data from adolescents who sexually offend (and their family members) can be useful and 'a significant source of relevant information' (p.101).

Regardless of the research supporting the utility of self-report measures, however, it is likely prudent to consider social desirability issues when assessing adolescents who have sexually offended. Understandably, issues related to shame, guilt, or fear of consequences may predispose an adolescent to minimisation or denial of a variety of information and details related to functioning and the offending that occurred. As well, limited self-insight for some adolescents will also influence the accuracy of self-reported information. Following an extensive review regarding social desirability theory, measurement, and findings related to both general offending and sexual offending populations, Tan and Grace (2008) recommended that retaining existing measures of social desirability is prudent and that caution should be exercised in interpreting the self-report of individuals with very high social desirability scores. Thus, when using the SAILEF, it is recommended that a specific social desirability measure or other questionnaires with social desirability scales also be included, and that information be included from multiple sources.

It is also important to note that, in its current form, the SAILEF is a nonstandardised inventory that does not provide sub-scale or overall/total scoring templates. For this reason, it is once again highlighted that it should be used in the context of a clinical relationship, with the opportunity for follow-up of items that are endorsed. Future development of the SAILEF may allow for scoring and the development of psychometric properties/information.

Conclusion

Adolescents who commit sexual offences are a heterogeneous group with varied experiences and needs. Although various issues related to history, experiences, and functioning have been identified as important in the empirical literature (eg family dysfunction and conflict, peer and social difficulties, emotional difficulties, academic difficulties, nonsexual behaviour concerns, victimisation history, sexual history and behaviour concerns), the relevance of these to each individual adolescent must be comprehensively assessed in order to adequately and ethically inform strengths, risks (eg mental health risks, nonsexual recidivism, and sexual recidivism), and treatment goals. This chapter introduced the Schuler Adolescent Inventory of Life Experiences and Functioning (SAILEF), a self-report inventory designed to complement and supplement the comprehensive assessment and treatment of an adolescent who has sexually offended, but that can also be used in the assessment and treatment of adolescents who have not committed sexual offences. Clinical utility, applicability to various client groups, and limitations of the SAILEF were discussed.

Acknowledgements

We would like to thank our many colleagues for their clinical insights and collaboration over the years, as well as Dr Jim Worling, Ph.D., C.Psych., for his training, support, and considerable influence on our clinical knowledge and development. We are also especially grateful to our many adolescent clients and their families, who have courageously participated in the assessment and treatment process and, in so doing, trusted us with their stories.

References

Abel, G.G. and Rouleau, J.L. (1990) The Nature and Extent of Sexual Assault. in Marshall, W.L., Laws, D.R. and Barbaree, H.E. (eds.) *The Handbook of Sexual Assault: Issues, Theories, and Treatment of the Offender*. New York: Plenum.

Andrews, D.A. and Bonta, J. (2006) *The Psychology of Criminal Conduct*. 4th edn. Newark, NJ: Lexisnexis.

Association for the Treatment of Sexual Abusers (2005) *Practice Standards and Guidelines for Members of the Association for the Treatment of Sexual Abusers*. OR: Author.

Becker, J.V. and Abel, G.G. (1985) Methodological and Ethical Issues in Evaluating and Treatment of Adolescent Sex Offenders. in Otey, E.M. and Ryan, G.D. (eds.) *Adolescent Sex Offenders: Issues in Research and Treatment*. Rockville, MD: Department of Health and Human Services.

Becker, J.V. and Kaplan, M.S. (1993) Cognitive Behavioral Treatment of the Juvenile Sex Offender. in Barbaree, H.E., Marshall, W.L. and Hudson, S.M. (eds.) *The Juvenile Sex Offender*. New York, NY: Guilford Press.

Benoit, J.L. and Kennedy, W.A. (1992) The Abuse History of Male Adolescent Sex Offenders. *Journal of Interpersonal Violence*, 7: 4, 543–8.

Blaske, D.M. et al. (1989) Individual, Family, and Peer Characteristics of Adolescent Sex Offenders and Assaultive Offenders. *Developmental Psychology*, 25: 5, 846–55.

Bonner, B.L. et al. (1998) Assessment of Adolescent Sexual Offenders. *Child Maltreatment*, 3: 4, 374–83.

Boyd, N.J., Hagan, M. and Cho, M.E. (2000) Characteristics of Adolescent Sex Offenders: A Review of the Research. *Aggression and Violent Behavior*, 5: 2, 137–46.

Burton, D.L. (2000) Were Adolescent Sexual Offenders Children with Sexual Behavior Problems? *Sexual Abuse: A Journal of Research and Treatment*, 12: 1, 37–48.

Caldwell, M.F. (2007) Sexual Offense Adjudication and Sexual Recidivism among Juvenile Offenders. *Sexual Abuse: A Journal of Research and Treatment*, 19, 107–13.

Carpentier, J. and Proulx, J. (2002) *Predictors of Criminal Career Intensity in a Sample of Juvenile Sexual Aggressors of Children*. Poster Presented at the 21st Conference of the Association for the Treatment of Sexual Abusers (ATSA); Montreal, Canada.

Center for Sex Offender Management (2007a) *Female Sex Offenders*. Available at: http://www.csom.org/pubs/female_sex_offenders_brief.pdf

Center for Sex Offender Management (2007b) *The Importance of Assessment in Sex Offender Management: An Overview of Key Principles and Practices*. Available at: www.csom.org/pubs/assessment_brief.pdf

Chu, C.M. and Thomas, S.D.M. (2010) Adolescent Sexual Offenders: The Relationship between Typology and Recidivism. *Sexual Abuse: A Journal of Research and Treatment*, 22: 2, 218–33.

Cooper, C.L., Murphy, W.D. and Haynes, M.R. (1996) Characteristics of Abused and Non-Abused Adolescent Sexual Offenders. *Sexual Abuse: A Journal of Research and Treatment*, 8: 2, 105–19.

Cortoni, F., Hanson, R.K. and Coache, M-E. (2010) The Recidivism Rates of Female Sexual Offenders Are Low: A Meta-Analysis. *Sexual Abuse: A Journal of Research and Treatment*, 22: 4, 387–401.

Curwen, T. (2003) The Importance of Offense Characteristics, Victimization History, Hostility, and Social Desirability in Assessing Empathy of Male Adolescent Sex Offenders. *Sexual Abuse: A Journal of Research and Treatment*, 15: 4, 347–64.

Daleiden, E.L. et al. (1998) The Sexual Histories and Fantasies of Youthful Males: A Comparison of Sexual Offending, Nonsexual Offending, and Nonoffending Groups. *Sexual Abuse: A Journal of Research and Treatment*, 10: 3, 195–209.

Davis, G.E. and Leitenberg, H. (1987) Adolescent Sex Offenders. *Psychological Bulletin*, 101, 417–27.

Dembo, R. et al. (2008) Psychosocial Functioning Problems Over Time Among High-Risk Youths: A Latent Class Transition Analysis. *Crime and Delinquency*, 54: 4, 644–70.

Fagan, J. and Wexler, S. (1988) Explanations of Sexual Assault among Violent Delinquents. *Journal of Adolescent Research*, 3, 363–85.

Faller, K.C. (1995) A Clinical Sample of Women who Have Sexually Abused Children. *Journal of Child Sexual Abuse*, 4, 13–30.

Falls, N. (2001) an *Empirically Derived Typology of Families of Male Adolescents who Committed Sexual Offences*. Unpublished doctoral dissertation.

Fehrenbach, P.A. et al. (1986) Adolescent Sex Offenders: Offender and Offense Characteristics. *American Journal of Orthopsychiatry*, 56, 225–33.

Ford, M.E. and Linney, J.A. (1995) Comparative Analysis of Juvenile Sexual Offenders, Violent Nonsexual Offenders, and Status Offenders. *Journal of Interpersonal Violence*, 10: 1, 56–70.

Fortune, C-A. and Lambie, I. (2004) Demographic and Abuse Characteristics in Adolescent Male Sexual Offenders with 'Special Needs'. *Journal of Sexual Aggression*, 10: 1, 63–84.

Freeman, K.A., Dexter-Mazza, E.T. and Hoffman, K.C. (2005) Comparing Personality Characteristics of Juvenile Sex Offenders and Non-Sex Offending Delinquent Peers: A Preliminary Investigation. *Sexual Abuse: A Journal of Research and Treatment*, 17: 1, 3–12.

Friedrich, W.N. et al. (2004) Assessing Sexual Behavior in High-Risk Adolescents with the Adolescent Clinical Sexual Behavior Inventory (ACSBI) *Child Maltreatment*, 9, 239–50.

Grayston, A.D. and Deluca, R.V. (1999) Female Perpetrators of Child Sexual Abuse: A Review of the Clinical and Empirical Literature. *Aggression and Violent Behavior*, 4, 93–106.

Hanson, R.K., Gizzarelli, R. and Scott, H. (1994) The Attitudes of Incest Offenders: Sexual Entitlement and Acceptance of Sex with Children. *Criminal Justice and Behavior*, 21, 187–202.

Hastings, T., Anderson, S.J. and Hemphill, P. (1997) Comparisons of Daily Stress, Coping, Problem Behavior, and Cognitive Distortions in Adolescent Sexual Offenders and Conduct-Disordered Youth. *Sexual Abuse: A Journal of Research and Treatment*, 9: 1, 29–42.

Hunter, J.A. et al. (2003) Juvenile Sex Offenders: Toward the Development of a Typology. *Sexual Abuse: A Journal of Research and Treatment*, 15: 1, 27–48.

Jacobs, W.L, Kennedy, W.A and Meyer, J.B. (1997) Juvenile Delinquents: A Between-Group Comparison Study of Sexual and Nonsexual Offenders. *Sexual Abuse: A Journal of Research and Treatment*, 9: 3, 201–17.

Johnson, T.C. (1988) Child Perpetrator: Children who Molest Other Children: Preliminary Findings. *Child Abuse and Neglect*, 12, 219–29.

Kaufman, K.L. (1993a) *Sexual History Form*.

Kaufman, K.L. (1993b) *Sexual Fantasy Questionnaire*.

Kobayashi, J. et al. (1995) Perceived Parental Deviance, Parent-Child Bonding, Child Abuse, and Child Sexual Aggression. *Sexual Abuse: A Journal of Research and Treatment*, 7: 1, 25–44.

Letourneau, E.J., Schoenwald, S.K. and Sheidow, A.J. (2004) Children and Adolescents with Sexual Behavior Problems. *Child Maltreatment* 9: 1, 49–61.

Mann, R.E., Hanson, R.K. and Thornton, D. (2010) Assessing Risk of Sexual Recidivism: Some Proposals on the Nature of Psychologically Meaningful Risk Factors. *Sexual Abuse: A Journal of Research and Treatment*, 22: 2, 191–217.

Mathews, R., Hunter Jr., J.A. and Vuz, J. (1997) Juvenile Female Sexual Offenders: Clinical Characteristics and Treatment Issues. *Sexual Abuse: A Journal of Research and Treatment*, 9: 3, 87–199.

Monto, M., Zgourides, G. and Harris, R. (1998) Empathy, Self-Esteem, and the Adolescent Sexual Offender. *Sexual Abuse: A Journal of Research and Treatment*, 10: 2, 127–40.

Moulden, H.M., Firestone, P. and Wexler, A.F. (2007) Child Care Providers who Commit Sexual Offences: A Description of Offender, Offence, and Victim Characteristics. *International Journal of Offender Therapy and Comparative Criminology*, 51: 4, 384–406.

Nisbet, I.A., Wilson, P.H. and Smallbone, S.W. (2004) A Prospective Longitudinal Study of Sexual Recidivism among Adolescent Sex Offenders. *Sexual Abuse: A Journal of Research and Treatment*, 16: 3, 223–34.

Oliver, B.E. (2007) Preventing Female-Perpetrated Sexual Abuse. *Trauma, Violence, and Abuse*, 8: 1, 19–32.

Parks, G.A. and Bard, D.E. (2006) Risk Factors for Adolescent Sex Offender Recidivism: Evaluation of Predictive Factors and Comparison of Three Groups Based upon Victim Type. *Sexual Abuse: A Journal of Research and Treatment*, 18, 319–42.

Pierce, L.H. and Pierce, R.L. (1987) Incestuous Victimization by Juvenile Sex Offenders. *Journal of Family Violence*, 2: 4, 351–64.

Prentky, R. and Righthand, S. (2001) *The Juvenile Sex Offender Assessment Protocol (J-SOAP) Manual*. Unpublished manuscript.

Prentky, R. and Righthand, S. (2003*) The Juvenile Sex Offender Assessment Protocol – II (J-SOAP-II) Manua*l. Unpublished manuscript. Available from the Office of Juvenile Justice and Delinquency Prevention's Juvenile Justice Clearinghouse.

Rasmussen, L.A. (1999) Factors Related to Recidivism among Juvenile Sexual Offenders. *Sexual Abuse: A Journal of Research and Treatment*, 11: 1, 69–86.

Reitzel, L.R. and Carbonell, J.L. (2006) The Effectiveness of Sexual Offender Treatment for Juveniles as Measured by Recidivism: A Meta-Analysis. *Sexual Abuse: A Journal of Research and Treatment*, 18: 4, 401–21.

Ryan, G. et al. (1996) Trends in a National Sample of Sexually Abusive Youths. *Journal of the American Academy of Child and Adolescent Psychiatry*, 35: 1, 17–25.

Seto, M.C. and Lalumiere, M.L. (2006) Conduct Problems and Juvenile Sexual Offending. in Barbaree, H.E. and Marshall, W.L. (eds.) *The Juvenile Sex Offender*. 2nd edn. New York: Guilford Press.

Smith, W.R. (1988) Delinquency and Abuse among Juvenile Sexual Offenders. *Journal of Interpersonal Violence*, 3: 4, 400–13.

Smith, S. et al. (2005) Differences in Self-Report Measures by Adolescent Sex Offender Risk Group. *International Journal of Offender Therapy and Comparative Criminology*, 49: 1, 82–106.

Statistics Canada (2007) http://www40.statcan.ca/l01/cst01/legal19a-eng.htm, Retrieved 15 April 2009.

Strickland, S.M. (2008) Female Sex Offenders: Exploring Issues of Personality, Trauma, and Cognitive Distortions. *Journal of Interpersonal Violence*, 23: 4, 474–89.

Tan, L. and Grace, R.C. (2008) Social Desirability and Sexual Offenders. *Sexual Abuse: A Journal of Research and Treatment*, 20: 1, 61–87.

Veneziano, C. and Veneziano, L. (2002) Adolescent Sex Offenders: A Review of the Literature. *Trauma, Violence, and Abuse*, 3: 4, 247–60.

Veneziano, C., Veneziano, L. and Legrand, S. (2000) The Relationship between Adolescent Sex Offender Behaviors and Victim Characteristics with Prior Victimization. *Journal of Interpersonal Violence*, 15: 4, 363–74

Waite, D. et al. (2005) Juvenile Sex Offender Re-Arrest Rates for Sexual, Violent Nonsexual, and Property Crimes: A 10-Year Follow-Up. *Sexual Abuse: A Journal of Research and Treatment*, 17: 3, 313–31.

Watkins, B. and Bentovim, A. (1992) The Sexual Abuse of Male Children and Adolescents: A Review of Current Research. *Journal of Child Psychology and Psychiatry*, 33, 197–248.

Way, I.F. (2002) Childhood Maltreatment Histories of Male Adolescents with Sexual Offending Behaviours: A Review of the Literature. in Calder, M.C. (ed.) *Young People Who Sexually Abuse: Building the Evidence Base for Your Practice*. Lyme Regis: Russell House Publishing.

Weinrott, M.R. and Saylor, M. (1991) Self-Report of Crimes Committed by Sex Offenders. *Journal of Interpersonal Violence*, 6, 286–300.

Wijkman, M., Bijleveld, C. and Hendriks, J. (2010) Women Don't Do Such Things! Characteristics of Female Sex Offenders and Offender Types. *Sexual Abuse: A Journal of Research and Treatment*, 22: 2, 135–56.

Worling, J.R. (1995a) Adolescent Sex Offenders against Females: Differences Based on the Age of their Victims. *International Journal of Offender Therapy and Comparative Criminology*, 39: 3, 276–93.

Worling, J.R. (1995b) Adolescent Sibling-Incest Offenders: Differences in Family and Individual Functioning when Compared to Adolescent Nonsibling Sex Offenders. *Child Abuse and Neglect*, 19: 5, 633–43.

Worling, J.R. (1995c) Sexual Abuse Histories of Adolescent Male Sex Offenders: Differences on the Basis of the Age and Gender of their Victims. *Journal of Abnormal Psychology*, 104: 4, 610–13.

Worling, J.R. (1998) *A Modified Version of the Hanson Sex Attitudes Questionnaire for Use with Adolescents.* Unpublished manuscript. Available from Worling.

Worling, J.R. (1999) *SAFE-T Sexual Offense Questionnaire.* Unpublished manuscript. Available from author.

Worling, J.R. (2001) Personality-Based Typology of Adolescent Male Sexual Offenders: Differences in Recidivism Rates, Victim-Selection Characteristics, and Personal Victimization Histories. *Sexual Abuse: A Journal of Research and Treatment*, 13: 3, 149–66.

Worling, J.R. (2006) Assessing Sexual Arousal with Adolescent Males who Have Offended Sexually: Self-Report and Unobtrusively Measured Viewing Time. *Sexual Abuse: A Journal of Research and Treatment*, 18: 4, 383–400.

Worling, J.R. and Costin, D. (2007) *Relationship Attitudes Questionnaire.* Unpublished manuscript. Available from author.

Worling, J.R. and Curwen, T. (2000) Adolescent Sexual Offender Recidivism: Success of Specialized Treatment and Implications for Risk Prediction. *Child Abuse and Neglect*, 24, 965–82.

Worling, J.R. and Curwen, T. (2001) Estimate of Risk of Adolescent Sexual Offense Recidivism (Version 2.0: The ERASOR) in Calder, M.C. (ed.) *Juveniles and children who sexually abuse: Frameworks for assessment.* Lyme Regis: Russell House Publishing.

Worling, J.R. and Langstrom, N. (2003) Assessment of Criminal Recidivism Risk with Adolescents who Have Offended Sexually: A Review. *Trauma, Violence, and Abuse*, 4: 4, 34–362.

Worling, J.R. and Langstrom, N. (2006) Risk of Sexual Recidivism in Adolescents who Offend Sexually: Correlates and Assessment. in Barbaree, H.E. and Marshall, W.L. (eds.) *The Juvenile Sex Offender.* 2nd edn. New York: Guilford Press.

Worling, J.R., Litteljohn, A. and Bookalam, D. (2009) *20-Year Prospective Study of Specialised Treatment at the SAFE-T Program for Adolescents who Offended Sexually.* Toronto, ON Ontario Ministry of Children and Youth Services.

Zakireh, B., Ronis, S.T. and Knight, R.A. (2008) Individual Beliefs, Attitudes, and Victimization Histories of Male Juvenile Sexual Offenders. *Sexual Abuse: A Journal of Research and Treatment*, 20: 3, 323–51.

Zolondek, S.C. et al. (2001) The Self-Reported Behaviors of Juvenile Sexual Offenders. *Journal of Interpersonal Violence*, 16: 1, 73–85.

Appendix 1

Schuler Adolescent Inventory of Life Experiences and Functioning (SAILEF)

Self-Report

Siegi A. Schuler, Ph.D. Candidate, RSW

Name: _____   Age _____

Today's Date: _____   Sex: M   F

Birth Date: _____/_____/_____   Current Grade: _____
         Month   Day   Year

> The information you provide here is **voluntary**. If you decide to continue, please answer the following questions to the best of your ability. The information you give here will help me understand more about you, your thoughts, and feelings. Some of these questions may be difficult to answer – this is normal. But, it is **important** that you are as honest as possible in your answers. If you have difficulty with the questions, just finish what you can.

> *Please use the following rating scale to respond to all questions:*
>   0 = Not true
>   1 = Somewhat true/sometimes true
>   2 – Very true/often true

Please circle one answer for each question

(A) Medical history

1. I have a childhood disease or illness	0	1	2
2. I have a medical condition	0	1	2
3. I have been in the hospital for more than *one* day	0	1	2
4. I have had an injury that required medical attention	0	1	2
5. I have suffered a head injury	0	1	2
6. I have had a broken bone(s)	0	1	2
7. I have suffered a poisoning	0	1	2
8. I have suffered a major burn	0	1	2
9. I currently have or have had an eating disorder	0	1	2
10. I am on medication	0	1	2
11. I have been to a psychiatrist	0	1	2
12. I have or have had a sexually transmitted infection	0	1	2

(B) Family history

13. I was born in another country	0	1	2
14. My parents are separated or divorced.	0	1	2
15. One or more of my parents has re-married/is in a relationship	0	1	2
16. I am adopted	0	1	2
17. I have lived in a group home or foster home	0	1	2
18. I had to look after my sibling(s)	0	1	2
19. I take care of my parent(s) or caregiver(s)	0	1	2
20. I did not have clean clothes	0	1	2

21. It's hard to know when my mother is in a good mood	0	1	2
22. It's hard to know when my father is in a good mood	0	1	2
23. There are too many rules in my home	0	1	2
24. There are no rules in my home	0	1	2
25. I don't get enough privacy at home	0	1	2
26. A family member is or has been seriously ill	0	1	2
27. I feel my parent(s) don't understand me	0	1	2
28. I have run away or have thought of running away	0	1	2
29. I have lived on the streets or in a shelter	0	1	2
30. I have lost my baby to foster care or given up a baby for adoption	0	1	2
31. I feel like I've lost my childhood	0	1	2
32. I get along well with my mother	0	1	2
33. I get along well with my father	0	1	2
34. My parent or a close family member has been in jail	0	1	2
35. My parent or caregiver abuses alcohol or drugs	0	1	2
36. I have been hit by a family member	0	1	2
37. A family member has died in the past three to five years	0	1	2
38. My family has moved *many* times for various reasons	0	1	2
39. My parent or caregiver is depressed or suicidal	0	1	2
40. My family has little money for food or other basics	0	1	2
41. A parent or caregiver has sent me away	0	1	2
42. I feel or have felt unsafe at home	0	1	2
43. My mother makes me feel wanted	0	1	2
44. My father makes me feel wanted	0	1	2
45. A parent or caregiver calls me hurtful names	0	1	2
46. There is/was lots of yelling or fighting at home	0	1	2
47. My family doesn't want me around	0	1	2
48. Many adults come and go in my house	0	1	2
49. I feel little support or love at home	0	1	2
50. A sibling (brother/sister) threatens or harms me	0	1	2
51. I have not seen my father in a long time	0	1	2
52. I have not seen my mother in a long time	0	1	2
53. I have been locked in a room at home	0	1	2
54. My father doesn't want me around him	0	1	2
55. My mother doesn't want me around her	0	1	2
56. A family member owns pornography at home	0	1	2
57. I have seen adults having sex at home	0	1	2
58. I have witnessed a family member get hurt or abused	0	1	2
59. A parent or caregiver at home helps me with my homework	0	1	2

(C) School history

60. I do well at school	0	1	2
61. There are subjects I like at school	0	1	2
62. I have failed a grade	0	1	2
63. I feel alone while at school	0	1	2
64. I like school	0	1	2
65. I have been suspended or expelled	0	1	2
66. I have been bullied or teased while at school	0	1	2
67. My ability to learn has been questioned by teachers	0	1	2
68. I get along with my teachers	0	1	2
69. I skip school	0	1	2
70. I plan to quit school	0	1	2
71. I have had to change schools	0	1	2

72. Thinking of going to school often makes me feel sick   0   1   2
73. I don't belong at school   0   1   2
74. School is a scary, worrisome, or unsafe place to be   0   1   2
75. I plan to finish high school   0   1   2
76. I want to go to college or university   0   1   2
77. I find it hard to pay attention and/or concentrate at school   0   1   2
78. Teachers think I'm stupid or bad   0   1   2
79. I can't keep up with school pressures or expectations   0   1   2
80. I get into trouble at school   0   1   2
81. I've had extra help at school or been in special education   0   1   2
82. I have a learning disability   0   1   2

(D) Feelings

83. I am able to tell how I am feeling   0   1   2
84. Others can usually tell what mood I'm in   0   1   2
85. I feel nothing   0   1   2
86. I am happy   0   1   2
87. I am sad   0   1   2
88. I am sad more often than others my age   0   1   2
89. I am able to cope when I feel sad   0   1   2
90. I tell someone when I feel very sad   0   1   2
91. When I am sad, I have difficulty doing anything   0   1   2
92. I have had thoughts of harming myself in the past   0   1   2
93. I currently have thoughts of harming myself   0   1   2
94. I have had thoughts of killing myself in the past   0   1   2
95. I currently have thoughts of killing myself   0   1   2
96. I have done things to try to harm or kill myself   0   1   2
97. I worry   0   1   2
98. I think I worry more than others my age   0   1   2
99. I get nervous   0   1   2
100. I think I am nervous more often than others my age   0   1   2
101. I have ways of coping when I am worried or nervous   0   1   2
102. I drink alcohol to cope with my feelings   0   1   2
103. I use drugs to cope with my feelings   0   1   2
104. I have fears   0   1   2
105. I can usually cope with or face my fears   0   1   2
106. I am shy   0   1   2
107. I am shy or nervous around people   0   1   2
108. My shyness interferes with my doing things or going out   0   1   2
109. I am angry   0   1   2
110. I become angry quite easily   0   1   2
111. I get angry at things that don't usually bother others   0   1   2
112. I think I have an anger problem   0   1   2
113. Others think I have an anger problem   0   1   2
114. I become verbally aggressive (eg yell, shout) when I am angry   0   1   2
115. I become physically aggressive (eg hit, punch) when I am angry   0   1   2
116. I have trouble calming down when I am angry   0   1   2
117. I can calm down *on my own* when I am angry   0   1   2
118. When I am angry, I can only calm down *if someone helps me* 0   1   2

(E) Peer relationships

119. I have *no* close friends who care about me	0	1	2
120. I avoid being close with people	0	1	2
121. People avoid being close with me	0	1	2
122. I am happy in my friendships	0	1	2
123. I am often changing friends or groups	0	1	2
124. My friendships don't last long	0	1	2
125. I mostly eat lunch on my own at school	0	1	2
126. Most people *do not* want me around them	0	1	2
127. Most of my friends are *not* close to my age	0	1	2
128. I get along better with younger children	0	1	2
129. My friends or people don't call/email/text me	0	1	2
130. My friends or people don't like having me around them	0	1	2
131. I get together with friends outside of school	0	1	2
132. I am teased, hurt, bullied, or used by friends/peers	0	1	2
133. My friends *rarely* come over to my house	0	1	2
134. I *never* go to my friends' houses	0	1	2
135. I feel lonely	0	1	2
136. Most of my friends are of the opposite sex	0	1	2
137. Many of my friends are in a gang	0	1	2
138. I feel under pressure around my friends	0	1	2
139. I can be myself around my friends	0	1	2
140. I have done things to be accepted by my friends	0	1	2
141. Most of my friends use drugs, alcohol, or inhalants	0	1	2
142. Many of my friends have a criminal record	0	1	2

(F) Physical health

143. I think I am in good health	0	1	2
144. I have problems sleeping	0	1	2
145. I have nightmares	0	1	2
146. I have headaches	0	1	2
147. I have stomach aches	0	1	2
148. I have wet or soiled myself (night or daytime) in the past year	0	1	2
149. I have a good appetite	0	1	2
150. I try to eat very little / I purposely limit what I eat	0	1	2
151. I overeat	0	1	2
152. I throw up after eating	0	1	2
153. I have aches and pains	0	1	2
154. I feel nauseous or throw up	0	1	2

(G) Behaviour history

155. I harm or have harmed animals	0	1	2
156. I play with or have played with fire	0	1	2
157. I have caused a large fire	0	1	2
158. I tease, bully, or hurt others	0	1	2
159. I get into a lot of physical fights	0	1	2
160. I steal	0	1	2
161. I have been charged with a criminal offence	0	1	2
162. I have friends who have a criminal history	0	1	2
163. I have damaged, broken, or vandalized someone's property	0	1	2
164. I have stolen a car	0	1	2
165. I have broken into someone's home	0	1	2

166. I have carried a weapon in the community / to school   0   1   2
167. I have used a weapon in the community / at school   0   1   2
168. I currently smoke cigarettes   0   1   2
169. I have tried alcohol more than once   0   1   2
170. I drink alcohol often   0   1   2
171. I drink alcohol when I am alone   0   1   2
172. I have taken or currently use nonprescription drugs   0   1   2
173. I use nonprescription drugs when I am alone   0   1   2
174. I have tried inhalants or solvents (eg, aerosol or glue)   0   1   2
175. I am in / have been in a gang   0   1   2
176. I have had thoughts of harming someone   0   1   2

(H) Self

177. I feel stupid or insignificant   0   1   2
178. I think I am over or under weight for my age   0   1   2
179. Most people think I'm hopeless or a "lost cause"   0   1   2
180. I think I'm unattractive or ugly   0   1   2
181. I like how I look   0   1   2
182. I am proud of myself   0   1   2
183. I am just as good as others my age   0   1   2
184. For me, the way to "measure-up" is through fighting   0   1   2
185. I have little to be proud of   0   1   2
186. I think nobody loves me   0   1   2
187. Nothing ever hurts me or sometimes I feel invincible   0   1   2
188. I like myself   0   1   2
189. I have talents or special skills   0   1   2
190. Most people are better or more talented than me   0   1   2
191. I have few or no adult role models   0   1   2
192. I hear voices or see things that others do not   0   1   2
193. People in my life are proud of me   0   1   2
194. I follow others in order to fit in   0   1   2
195. I can't figure out who I am   0   1   2
196. I have trouble telling others what I think or feel   0   1   2
197. Taking life-threatening risks helps me feel better   0   1   2
198. I feel like exploding from the inside   0   1   2
199. I am hopeful about my future   0   1   2
200. I have been to counselling   0   1   2

(I) Traumatic events – victimisation history

201. I have been physically abused   0   1   2
202. I have been emotionally abused   0   1   2
203. I have been sexually abused or forced into sex   0   1   2
204. I have witnessed a family member being abused   0   1   2
205. I have witnessed someone being killed or seriously hurt   0   1   2
206. I have been mugged or robbed in person   0   1   2
207. I have been robbed or threatened with a weapon   0   1   2
208. I have been seriously injured in a car accident   0   1   2
209. I have been in/lived in a war zone or country at war   0   1   2
210. Someone close to me has died   0   1   2
211. I have been in a natural disaster (eg earthquake, flood, fire)   0   1   2

(J) Sexual development and history

212. I consider myself: *(please circle one)* straight/bi-sexual/gay/not sure/other	0	1	2
213. Someone prepared me for puberty/sexual changes	0	1	2
214. I have had a girlfriend or boyfriend	0	1	2
215. I use sex or masturbation as a way of coping with stress	0	1	2
216. I am sexually active	0	1	2
217. I am worried about having sex	0	1	2
218. I pretend to be or dress like the opposite sex	0	1	2
219. I think masturbating is normal	0	1	2
220. Others in my family think masturbating is normal	0	1	2
221. I am concerned about puberty	0	1	2
222. I have taken money or other things for sex	0	1	2
223. I have given money or other things for sex	0	1	2
224. I feel my sexual behaviour is a problem	0	1	2
225. Others believe my sexual behaviour is a problem	0	1	2
226. I have sexually touched a child	0	1	2
227. I have had sex with adult women or men	0	1	2
228. I have used a web cam for sexual interactions	0	1	2
229. I wish I were the opposite sex	0	1	2
230. I have worries about my body or sex parts	0	1	2
231. I feel people only want me for sex	0	1	2
232. I have exposed myself or secretly watched others undress	0	1	2
233. I have worn, taken, or thought of wearing diapers	0	1	2
234. I have done sexual things with animals	0	1	2
235. I have seen/used pornography at least once	0	1	2
236. I have participated in Internet sex chat rooms	0	1	2
237. Someone on the Internet has asked me to do sexual things	0	1	2
238. I have participated in 'sexting'	0	1	2
239. I have gone to meet, in person, someone I first spoke to on the Internet	0	1	2
240. Someone has teased me about my body	0	1	2
241. I have had group sex (more than one person at a time)	0	1	2
242. I have had sex while drunk or high	0	1	2
243. My partner and I purposely hurt each other during sex	0	1	2
244. I have taken photos of my own sex parts	0	1	2
245. I have problems getting "turned on"	0	1	2
246. **Males Only:** I have trouble getting or keeping an erection	0	1	2
247. **Males Only:** I have worn or taken girls' underwear or bras	0	1	2
248. **Males Only:** I feel or worry that my penis is too small	0	1	2
249. **Males Only:** Someone has teased me about my penis	0	1	2
250. **Males Only:** I have gotten someone pregnant	0	1	2
251. **Females Only:** I have worn or taken boys' underwear	0	1	2
252. **Females Only**: I worry about/don't like the size/shape of my breasts	0	1	2
253. **Females Only:** Someone has teased me about my breasts or vagina	0	1	2
254. **Females Only:** I think menstruating (ie my period) is 'dirty' or 'gross'	0	1	2
255. **Females Only:** I am or have been pregnant	0	1	2

Supplementary assessment section (A)
Types of physical and emotional abuse experiences

> If you indicated that you were **physically or emotionally abused**, please put a *check mark* next to the types of physical or emotional abuse that happened to you. Also, indicate (if possible) how many times this occurred.

1. The abuser slapped me with their hand _____
2. The abuser kicked me _____
3. The abuser punched me _____
4. The abuser hit me with a belt or cord _____
5. The abuser hit me with a hard object (eg stick, wooden plank) _____
6. The abuser threw things at me _____
7. The abuser purposely burned me (eg cigarette, lighter, hot liquid) _____
8. The abuser tried to choke me _____
9. The abuser put something in my mouth (eg soap, hot sauce) _____
10. The abuser pushed or shoved me _____
11. The abuser pushed or shoved me down the stairs _____
12. The abuser put me in a very cold or very hot shower or bath _____
13. The abuser made me stand somewhere for hours _____
14. The abuser made me kneel on something painful (eg rice, corn kernels) _____
15. The abuser pulled my hair _____
16. The abuser chained me to something (eg chair, door) _____
17. I was locked in a room, cage, etc. _____
18. I was locked in a dark room, closet, etc. _____
19. I had bruises from the physical abuse _____
20. I had broken bones from the physical abuse _____
21. The abuser called me names, humiliated me, made fun of me, etc. _____
22. The abuser deprived me of food or water _____
23. The abuser made me stand out in the cold for long periods of time _____
24. The abuser did not allow me to use the bathroom _____
25. Other things that happened (please explain) _____

Supplementary assessment section (B)
Types of sexual abuse experiences

> If you indicated that you were **sexually abused**, please put a *check mark* next to the types of sexual abuse that happened to you. Also, indicate (if possible) how many times this occurred.

1. The abuser put their hand on my penis or vagina (masturbated me) _____
2. I touched the abuser's penis or vagina _____
3. The abuser put their mouth on my penis or vagina (oral sex) _____
4. I put my mouth on the abuser's penis or vagina _____
5. The abuser put their penis in my bum (anal sex) _____
6. The abuser put their finger in my bum _____
7. The abuser put objects in my bum _____
8. **Males Only:** I put my penis in the abuser's bum (anal sex) _____
9. **Males Only:** I put my penis in the abuser's vagina (vaginal sex) _____
10. **Females Only:** The abuser put his penis in my vagina _____
11. **Females Only:** The abuser put their finger in my vagina _____
12. **Females Only:** The abuser put objects in my vagina _____
13. I watched the abuser masturbate (male or female) _____

Schuler Adolescent Inventory of Life Experiences and Functioning © Schuler, 2011

14. I masturbated in front of the abuser
15. The abuser showed me pornography   _____
16. The abuser took pictures of me (with or without clothes)   _____
17. The abuser made me kiss them or they kissed me on the mouth   _____
18. The abuser would grab me in a sexual way   _____
19. The abuser took showers/baths with me   _____
20. The abuser said sexual things to me (ie letters/phone calls/talking)   _____
21. The abuser looked at me in a sexual way   _____
22. The abuser had secret words or signs that meant something sexual   _____
23. The abuser urinated or defecated on me   _____
24. Other adults, children, or siblings were involved in my sexual abuse   _____
25. The abuser gave me things or was extra nice to me for sex   _____
26. The abuser watched me undress or made me watch them undress   _____
27. The abuser made me sleep with them   _____
28. The abuser threatened me during or after the abuse (physical/verbal)   _____
29. The abuser made me watch them having sex with someone else   _____
30. The female abuser got pregnant after my sexual abuse   _____
31. The abuser used objects in my sexual abuse   _____
32. The abuser tied me up during the sexual abuse   _____
33. Other things that happened (please explain)   _____

Supplementary assessment section (C)

If you have been **sexually abused** please answer the following questions.

Remember: The questions here are common thoughts, feelings, and behaviours that many individuals who have been sexually abused experience – you are *NOT* alone. Some of these questions may be difficult to answer, but your answers will help me understand your sexual abuse experiences.

Because I was sexually abused

1. I feel confused about being gay or straight	0	1	2
2. I feel there is something wrong with me	0	1	2
3. I fear undressing in front of others or showering	0	1	2
4. I feel 'dirty' inside or broken	0	1	2
5. I feel confused because I *may* have liked it (sexual abuse)	0	1	2
6. I now hate my body	0	1	2
7. I worry about being sexually abused again	0	1	2
8. I worry about having a disease	0	1	2
9. By a girl/woman, that must *not* make it so 'wrong' or 'bad'	0	1	2
10. By a girl/woman, I am different from others who have been abused	0	1	2
11. I *now* feel confused when I masturbate	0	1	2
12. I have now *stopped* masturbating	0	1	2
13. I now masturbate *more often*	0	1	2
14. I think about my sexual abuse when I masturbate	0	1	2
15. I have cut (hurt) myself or thought about suicide	0	1	2
16. I have started wetting or soiling myself (night or daytime)	0	1	2
17. I feel I'm the one to blame	0	1	2
18. My family is now broken or splitting up	0	1	2
19. I feel that I am no longer a virgin	0	1	2
20. People say I'm a victim, but I feel it was *not really* sexual abuse	0	1	2
21. I have other worries that are difficult to mention	0	1	2

22. I now feel I can't have a safe or healthy sexual relationship	0	1	2
23. The person who abused me can't live with me	0	1	2
24. I feel people will only want me for sex	0	1	2
25. I worry that everyone will find out and treat me differently.	0	1	2
26. People can tell by looking at me that I was sexually abused	0	1	2
27. It doesn't mean that I won't want to see my abuser(s) again	0	1	2
28. I now have problems using the washroom (in public or private)	0	1	2
29. I think about my sexual abuse all the time	0	1	2
30. I'm now always anxious or nervous around people	0	1	2
31. I now can't sleep	0	1	2
32. I now sleep too much	0	1	2
33. I have nightmares more often than before the sexual abuse	0	1	2
34. I now want to change the way I look to prevent future abuse	0	1	2
35. I now worry that others or my parents will not like me	0	1	2
36. My parents/caregivers believe the sexual abuse was my fault	0	1	2
37. I feel no one wants to talk about my abuse or ask me questions	0	1	2
38. I now feel no one understands me	0	1	2
39. I avoid reminders of the sexual abuse	0	1	2
40. I am now afraid of males	0	1	2
41. I am now afraid of females	0	1	2
42. People treat me like I'm broken or fragile	0	1	2
43. I now try not to feel anything	0	1	2
44. **Males Only:** By a male abuser, that must make *me* gay	0	1	2
45. **Males Only:** By a male abuser, that must make *him* gay	0	1	2
46. **Males Only:** The erection ("hard-on") I had confuses me	0	1	2
47. **Males Only:** I now worry there is something wrong with my penis	0	1	2
48. **Females Only**: By a female abuser, that must make *me* gay	0	1	2
49. **Females Only**: By a female abuser, that must make *her* gay	0	1	2
50. **Females Only:** I now worry there is something wrong with my vagina	0	1	2

My feelings about my abuser are

My wish for my abuser is

My wish for my relationship with my abuser is

The questions I have about my sexual abuse are

New Technologies, New Challenges: Assessment and Treatment Guidance for Young People's Problematic/Abusive Sexual Behaviour Online

Richard Swann

Introduction

This chapter is written primarily to provide social workers and youth justice practitioners with a framework for guiding their assessments and interventions with adolescent males aged 12–18 years in mainstream educational settings who have engaged in harmful sexual behaviours online using new technologies. The guidance materials may also be relevant to practitioners working in other sectors of the children's workforce and is based upon the iAIM (Internet Assessment Intervention and Moving on) Manual written by the author in 2009.

The referral behaviours may include downloading, distributing and producing child abuse images using new technologies, for example, email, newsgroups, bulletin boards, Internet Relay Chat, peer to peer file sharing, online gaming and mobile phone technology. The guidance will assist practitioners working with young people whose Internet behaviour forms part of an overall concern regarding their harmful sexual behaviours, as well as those working with young people where this is the sole or main cause for concern.

The guidance is intended to provide a broad frame of reference to supplement structured judgement tools regarding the adolescent sexual offending population, primarily the AIM2 Initial Assessment Model (Print et al., 2007). However it may also add to other relevant assessment frameworks for young people who sexually harm, such as ERASOR-II (Estimate of Risk of Adolescent Sexual Offense Recidivism Worling and Curwen, 2001) and JSOAP-II (The Juvenile Sex Offender Protocol-II Prentky and Righthand, 2003).

What is meant by child abuse images?

The use of the term 'child abuse images' is now more generally accepted than the original term 'child pornography.' The main reason for this

change of terminology is that 'pornography' is generally associated with commercially available sexual materials involving adults. Opponents of the pornographic industry criticise the way in which it portrays the sexual subordination and objectification of women, therefore the concern about the term 'child pornography' is that it implies a justification for the portrayal of children as sexual objects and minimises the reality that the children pictured in these images have been abused and exploited. At a G8 summit in 2007 involving Home Office and Justice ministers, the delegates confirmed their dissatisfaction with the term 'child pornography':

It impedes our ability to understand the real harm that is experienced by young victims and the seriousness of the activities of those individuals that sexually exploit children in this way. This misunderstanding compromises the effectiveness of our very important efforts to protect children from this form of sexual exploitation.

G8 Press Release, 2007

Therefore throughout this chapter the preferred term will be 'child abuse images'.

In the UK *Working Together to Safeguard Children* (2010) provides a definition of child sexual abuse which acknowledges the role of new technologies:

Sexual abuse involves forcing or enticing a child or young person to take part in sexual activities, not necessarily involving a high level of violence, whether or not the child is aware of what is happening. The activities may involve physical contact, including assault by penetration (for example, rape or oral sex) or non-penetrative acts such as masturbation, kissing, rubbing and touching outside of clothing. They may also include non-contact activities, such as involving children in looking at, or in the production of, sexual images, watching sexual activities, encouraging children to behave in sexually inappropriate ways, or grooming a child in preparation for abuse (including via the Internet). Sexual abuse is not solely perpetrated by adult males. Women can also commit acts of sexual abuse, as can other children.

Working Together, 2010, para 1.35

The same document also acknowledges the role the Internet plays in the production and distribution of indecent photographs/pseudo photographs of children and advises:

> *The Internet has, in particular, become a significant tool in the distribution of indecent photographs/pseudo photographs of children. Internet chat rooms, discussion forums and bulletin boards are used as a means of contacting children with a view to grooming them for inappropriate or abusive relationships, which may include requests to make and transmit pornographic images of themselves, or to perform sexual acts live in front of a webcam. Contacts made initially in a chat room are likely to be carried on via email, instant messaging services, mobile phone or text messaging. There is also growing cause for concern about the exposure of children to inappropriate material via interactive communication technology – for example, adult pornography and/or extreme forms of obscene material. Allowing or encouraging a child to view such material may warrant further enquiry. Children themselves can engage in text bullying and use mobile phone cameras to capture violent assaults of other children for circulation.*
>
> *Working Together*, 2010, para 11.94

In reading this definition whom are we asked to be concerned about? Adults or young people? Young people do not appear to present much cause for concern. The comment at the end restricts harmful sexual behaviour to the use of 4G mobile phones and does not explicitly acknowledge that young people too may be involved in downloading, distributing and in the production of child abuse images.

This chapter therefore aims to: establish why this area of practice development is needed and explores a number of important dimensions of Internet offending which practitioners will find useful when engaging with young people and their families/carers; provide an assessment checklist on how to undertake an initial assessment of an adolescent male where there is some concern that they have been involved in accessing child abuse images using new technologies; provides examples of the iAIM Intervention Guidance for adolescents before providing a number of online resources for practitioners, including a glossary of terms. The chapter concludes with a number of appendices as follows:

- Appendix 1: iAIM Internet Time Line exercise
- Appendix 2: iAIM Internet Questionnaire for Adolescents
- Appendix 3: iAIM Concerns and Strengths Matrix
- Appendix 4: iAIM Analysis and Action Form

- Appendix 5: iAIM Audit Tool for service providers.

Setting the context

Specialist assessment and treatment providers have reported to the author that although the clinical population of young people coming to their attention because of their sexually problematic Internet related behaviours is numerically small, these Internet behaviours still pose practitioners with not inconsiderable difficult and unique challenges; for example, to what extent is this normal exploratory sexual behaviour, especially if peer related? What role does it play in 'off-line' harmful sexual behaviour? What factors may increase the likelihood of online offending? These questions may be further exacerbated if the practitioner does not feel as IT savvy as the young person they are assessing.

Data regarding the prevalence of adolescent Internet offending in the UK, that is, those cautioned or convicted for accessing child abuse images, is hard to determine as official statistics do not differentiate between adult and adolescent offenders (Gillespie, 2008). Their relative invisibility is further compounded by a dearth of empirical research studies and an absence of validated and developmentally sensitive Internet-offending assessment models. In essence the nature, extent and characteristics of adolescents displaying sexually problematic and/or abusive behaviours using new technologies is largely uncertain and unclear. Whilst this remains the case, professionals' capacity to recognise, respond to, assess and manage any perceived risk is likely to be inconsistent.

This uncertainty is contrasted by a significant increase in professional and public awareness of children and young people being sexually abused and exploited by adult sex offenders using the Internet. High publicity police investigations and Serious Case Reviews* have highlighted children and young people's vulnerability to adult offenders. For example, in November 2010 an

---

*Regulation 5 of the UK's Local Safeguarding Children Boards Regulations 2006 requires LSCBs to undertake reviews of serious cases. These reviews are known as Serious Case Reviews (SCRs). 'Chapter 8' of *Working Together to Safeguard Children* sets out the purposes of and processes for undertaking SCRs.

executive summary of a Serious Case Review in Plymouth, England, detailed how a female nursery worker made and distributed child abuse images whilst caring for very young children.*

Within the last decade there has been a notable increase in the development of investigatory, assessment and treatment provision for Internet offenders. For example, the COPINE (Combating Paedophile Information Networks in Europe) project's work in this area is internationally recognised as a key source of information regarding the characteristics of adult Internet offenders (Taylor, Holland and Quayle, 2001); CEOP (Child Exploitation Online Protection Centre) is part of UK law enforcement and provides educational information on Internet safety; Childnet International is a UK-based charity providing information for young people, carers and professionals regarding Internet safety; Stop It Now, UK and Ireland, provides confidential advice to the public and professionals regarding child sexual abuse, including those concerned about their own Internet behaviour; NPD (National Probation Directorate) has designed and implemented a Internet Sexual Offending Treatment Programme (i-SOTP) for adult male Internet offenders (Middleton and Hayes, 2006); Dr Julia Davidson provides a comprehensive research overview regarding Internet offending (Davidson, 2007) and in March 2010 the *Journal of Sexual Aggression* published a special edition entitled 'Special Issue – Child Sexual Abuse and the Internet: Offenders, Victims and Managing the Risk'.

However, there is limited knowledge regarding the characteristics of young people who access child abuse images and little published guidance for practitioners regarding the assessment and treatment issues. In preparation of this chapter the author found three chapters which specially focused on assessing young people's sexually harmful behaviours online (Longo in Calder, 2004; Quayle in Erooga and Masson, 2006 and Quayle in Calder, 2007). In UK-based peer reviewed journal articles the author found three excellent contributions, one a descriptive account of seven adolescent males referred for assessment/treatment following their arrest for possession and/or distribution of child abuse images (Moultrie, 2006), a policy discussion paper regarding the criminal justice system's

responses to adolescents who access indecent images of children (Gillespie, 2008) and a review of adolescent online behaviours and the associated safeguarding issues these behaviours provoke (Atkinson and Newton, 2010). Whilst all of these contributions are invaluable, they exist in relative isolation compared with a higher volume of published research, professional texts and resources regarding adult Internet offenders.

The one important exception to this notion of invisibility appears in a research publication commissioned by the New Zealand Department of Internal Affairs which sought to identify the characteristics of convicted Internet offenders. The research team identified that the largest age group of offenders at the time an arrest warrant was executed was the 15 to 19 year olds; the most common (mode) age of offenders was 17 years and that students were the most common occupation group. In their analysis of secondary school students' Internet offending behaviours the research team concluded that this group were, 'more likely than [other groups] to collect large volumes of images that were well indexed. They were also more frequently associated with the collection of images of older children and teenagers portrayed with other children, and much less likely to collect images of adult rape or the torture of adults or children. Their interest in objectionable material† often falls within the realm of 'age appropriateness.' However, Carr adds that half the school students convicted were found to have traded and/or possessed images of children aged between two and seven years, thus highlighting significant concerns about their use of the Internet (Carr, 2004: 136).

There is now a widely accepted clinical consensus that young people's sexually problematic and abusive behaviours can be influenced and dissuaded by professional interventions which are developmentally sensitive, family inclusive and rooted in validated and evidence-based models. There is also an acceptance that practitioners cannot simply 'graft on' adult sex offending assessment and treatment models to children and young people who display so-called 'contact' sexual offences. Perhaps then we are at a similar juncture with

---

* BBC News available at: http://www.bbc.co.uk/news/uk-england-devon-11682161

† 'Objectionable material' is defined in the New Zealand Films, Videos and Publications Classification Act 1993, Section 3 and includes material which 'promotes or supports, or tends to promote or support the exploitation of children, or young persons, or both, for sexual purposes.'

regards to adolescent Internet offending, in that we need to find a way of making what we do know about Internet offending more adolescent specific and relevant.

Therefore the guidance contained within this chapter is intended to equip practitioners with some initial ideas on how to begin assessing concerns and providing interventions for adolescents.

Young people's use of the Internet and new technologies

Understanding the evolution of how young people use the Internet and new technologies is a vital component of any assessment. It could be argued that rather than being passive recipients of the Internet, young people are influencing the development of this form of communication. A number of studies exist which explore the nature and extent of young people's use of the Internet. In 2003 Debell and Chapman undertook a survey in the United States of 28,000 children and young people aged five to 17 years, almost 60 per cent of whom used the Internet. The same survey noted some gender differences in that girls where more likely to use email and boys more likely to access games online (Debell and Chapman, 2003). In the UK, Livingston and Bober (2005) undertook a study of 1,511 children and young people aged nine to 19 years and found that 70 per cent had their own computer. In 2006 Wolak, Mitchell and Finklehor published a study in the US regarding telephone interviews of 1,500 young Internet users aged 10 to 17 years. One third of the sample reported that they had received unwanted sexual materials whilst using the Internet (Wolak, Mitchell and Finklehor, 2006).

Young people's access to the Internet is widely available and undoubtedly it provides a seemingly endless amount of educational information, and is a key source of communication and entertainment. Indeed the United Nations Convention on the Rights of the Child, Article 17, decrees that:

> Parties recognise the important function performed by the mass media and shall ensure that the child has access to information and material from a diversity of national and international sources, especially those aimed at the promotion of his or her social, spiritual and moral well-being and physical and mental health.

However, given that much of the content of the Internet is unregulated, there are dangers that some information and materials represent a risk

to children and young people. Indeed Quayle, citing Kanuga and Rosenfeld, argues that with the proliferation of information on the World Wide Web, adolescents will stumble across websites with 'nefarious intention, such as sex-seeking chat rooms and pornographic websites, while searching for answers about sexual health' (Quayle, quoting Kanuga and Rosenfeld, in Calder, 2007).

Given the physical, emotional and psychological changes that occur in adolescence, this might trigger many to have perfectly understandable questions about their bodies, relationships, identity and health. These developmental challenges, coupled with the Internet's increased accessibility, affordability and anonymity (Cooper, 2002) may leave some young people vulnerable to abuse and/or exploitation online.

Young people's vulnerability whilst online

A number of studies have highlighted children and young people's vulnerability to different forms of abuse whilst online.

Palmer's UK study *Stolen Children* identified the different ways in which children were abused using new technologies, which included children abused through prostitution using the Internet and mobile phones to contact their abusers; adults or young people who engage in cybersex with children; children groomed online for sexual abuse offline; children sold online for live sexual abuse online and children made subjects of child abuse images (Palmer, 2003). Indeed Palmer has established the Marie Collins Foundation in the UK to provide therapeutic support for young people abused via the Internet.

The SAFT study in 2003 which revealed the online behaviour of primary and post-primary students in five European countries identified that almost 20 per cent of children had been invited to a face-to-face meeting with a stranger and a third had viewed violent materials online either purposefully or by accident (SAFT, 2003).

More recently Wolak, Finklehor, Mitchell and Ybarra (2008) in their review of Internet-initiated sex crimes have identified a number of factors which heighten a young person's risk to sexual abuse online. Firstly, the age of the adolescent appears to be a relevant, in that young people aged 15 to 17 years were more prone to risk-taking behaviours online than younger children. Risk-taking behaviours online was described as sharing personal information with unknown people. One possible explanation for this is that as Internet savvy adolescents become older they engage in more complex interactive Internet use, placing them at greater risk than younger adolescents. Secondly, an older adolescent's sexual curiosity, knowledge and experience is a more active phase of their sexual development. The context is usually one of face-to-face peer contact in which young people learn to negotiate their sexual relationships. However, Internet-initiated sexual abuse will typically take place in, 'isolation and secrecy, outside of oversight by peers, family members, and others in the youth's face-to-face networks. This isolation may lead to relationships that form more quickly, involve greater self-disclosure, and develop with greater intensity than face-to-face relationships among peers' (Wolak et al., 2008: 115).

The same authors provide a helpful list of factors which may identify Internet behaviours that place young people at increased risk of harm. Importantly they make the point that the following items are neither developed nor empirically tested:

1. posting personal information online
2. interacting online with unknown people
3. having unknown people on a buddy list
4. using the Internet to make rude and nasty comments to others
5. sending personal information to unknown people met online
6. downloading images from file-sharing programmes
7. visiting pornographic and/or violent sites on purpose
8. using the Internet to embarrass or harass others they are mad at
9. talking online to unknown people about sex

In a similar way Nyman (2006) describes risky online behaviour as a 'staircase where each step leads to new dangers':

1. to reveal some personal data, like a name, passwords, phone number, address or special secrets
2. to chat about sexual matters with an unknown person
3. to upload or share sexually indicative pictures of yourself or your friends

4. to become involved in live web cam sex with an unknown person
5. to date someone offline that you have met online, without proper safety arrangements
6. to knowingly date adults offline that you have met online
7. to send pictures for payment
8. to pose live on the web cam or to have web cam sex for payment
9. to date offline someone you have met online and have sex for payment
10. to offer sex offline and online for payment

My clinical experience of working with children and young people who have displayed problematic or abusive online sexual behaviours has included the following continuum of behaviours, which illustrates the need for practitioners to track the progression and possible escalation of a young person's Internet use and sexual behaviours:

1. accidental discovery of sexual imagery whilst online
2. purposeful curiosity/searching for sexual imagery whilst online
3. searching for increasingly violent sexual imagery, including child abuse images
4. downloading, distributing and trading in child abuse images via peer-to-peer networks, newsgroups, chat rooms, etc
5. active involvement in production of child abuse images, using mobile phone technologies
6. meeting and solicitation of other young people online in order to sexually harm offline

In terms of differentiating adolescent sexually problematic behaviour online, Quayle provides a useful description of three sets of behaviours, which are not unique to young people, but should assist the practitioner in understanding the nature of these problems:

1. *Soliciting, or sexually harassing behaviours*: Children and young people may experience unwanted/aggressive sexual solicitous materials whilst online. In a 2006 study one third of young people received online solicitations whilst using chat rooms (Ybarra and Mitchell in press).
2. *Downloading, trading and production of child abuse images*: Children and young people are also known to have downloaded child images online. The Carr study of identified that 15 to 17-year-olds made up the largest proportion of

those arrested for possession of child abuse images. However, other studies illustrate a much lower rate of offending where three per cent were under 18 years of age (Wolak, el al., 2005).

3. *Self-victimising behaviours*: This set of behaviours relates especially to young people's access to the Internet via 4G (fourth generation) mobile phone technology, which includes wireless connection to the Internet. Quayle cites anecdotal examples of how young people post sexually explicit pictures of themselves or friends on the Internet.

Impact of exposure on adolescents

The risk of sexual victimisation is one potential for harm for some young people who access sexual materials online. However, to what extent does access to such materials impact in other ways? One concern might be that the exposure to deviant, violent sexual imagery may adversely effect a young person's current or future psychosexual development. At worst there may be concerns that this may trigger the abuse of a child.

Quayle (citing Greenfield, in Calder, 2007) asserts that the likely developmental effects on adolescents engaged in online sexual activity are:

1. disinhibition related to sexuality, aggression and race relations
2. early sexual priming
3. models for racism, negative attitudes towards women and homophobia

However, Quayle and others have indicated that there is little definitive empirical evidence regarding the use of pornography by young people who sexually harm.

Other authors have identified that sexual preoccupation within the adolescent sexual offending population is a risk factor. The AIM2 Initial Assessment framework identifies an 'obsession/preoccupation with sexual thoughts/pornography' as a theoretically-supported dynamic concern item (AIM2 Initial Assessment, 2005: 71). The AIM2 framework describes that although many adolescent males will have a considerable interest in sexual matters, including sexual images, those young men whose interest is so considerable that it pervades almost all that they think about could therefore be described as problematic. This is

likely to include those young men who are known to have repeatedly accessed child pornography, for example, on the Internet. In this instance, 'obsession/preoccupation' refers to recurrent thoughts, images or impulses concerning sex/pornography that may be distressing, highly frequent or come to mind despite efforts to suppress or ignore them. Some young people may self report such thoughts and for others it may be that they tend to sexualise most situations with sexual language, innuendo and comments. Authors of existing risk prediction checklists for adolescents who sexually abuse indicate that sexual preoccupation (Epps, 1997; Lane, 1997; Prentky and Righthand, 2003; Prentky et al., 2000; Steen and Monnette, 1989, cited in AIM2, 2005) and compulsive ideation concerning previous offences (Perry and Orchard, 1992) are indicative of a heightened risk of sexual recidivism. Also, this factor has been found to be associated with recidivism in adults who sexually abuse (Hanson and Harris, 2000, 2001, cited in AIM2, 2005).

Indeed the research appears to be unclear as Ford and Linney (1995) reported an elevated use of pornography among adolescents who sexually harmed, whilst O'Reilly (1998) concluded that it had little relevance. Part of the problem is that this research predates the advent of the widespread consumption of the Internet and the access this affords. Importantly, Quayle suggests that the use of pornographic materials by adolescents may 'reinforce cognitive rehearsals of sexual behaviours or aggression' (Quayle in Calder, 2007).

Internet offending: treatment issues

There appears to be little specific treatment strategies regarding children who have been sexually abused online using new technologies. However, the author has found an excellent report from a Swedish conference in 2006 which brought together international expertise in this area (Swedish Children's Welfare Service Report, 2006). One outcome of the conference was the creation of an international questionnaire regarding professional experiences in treating child and adolescent victims of online sexual exploitation (available at http://nfbo.com/questionnaire_info.htm). Wolak et al. (2008) describe the application of a change model used with drug addiction and victims of domestic violence derived from Prochaska and Prochaska (2002) in which the young person may be on a continuum of readiness to change and amend his/her Internet behaviours. The same authors make the point that other treatment modalities such as family therapy, cognitive behavioural therapy and psycho educational learning and mentoring around sexual health and relationships are also relevant.

In contrast there is substantially more information regarding the assessment and treatment of adult Internet offenders (Quayle et al., 2005, 2006 and Davidson, 2007) all of which highlight how heterogeneous this population is and that similar treatment programmes used with the general sex offender population, based upon cognitive behavioural and relapse prevention approaches, are still as efficacious. However, one identified research need described by Wolak et al. (2008) is to, 'monitor the nature and dynamics of online sexual behaviour involving youths . . . the online environment changes so quickly that formal methods of monitoring the extent and dynamics are badly needed. For example, what will be the impact of new technologies, especially cell phones and other wireless handheld devices, on dynamics and incidence of Internet-initiated sex crimes?' (Wolak et al., 2008: 124).

The COPINE unit have developed an online resource for adults worried about downloading and using illegal images and is available at http://www.croga.org/index.php.

Among the descriptions of different types of online sexually abusive behaviour Tony Krone's typology begins to elucidate the risks associated with different types of online activity. It must be noted that as these typologies are derived from data collected from adult offenders it is uncertain to what extent they can be applied to adolescents:

- *Browsers* accidentally come across indecent images and save them, in reality such images are either purchased via credit card or are swapped by collectors.
- *Private fantasisers* create digital images for their own private use.
- *Trawlers* search for indecent images through open browsers and may engage in some networking.
- *Non-secure collectors* look for indecent images in open areas of the Internet such as chat rooms, probably by networking.

- *Secure collectors* – online hidden, paedophile network. Highly organised collectors who employ sophisticated security to conceal their offending.
- *Groomers* target and groom children via peer-to-peer technology, interactive Internet games and chat rooms.
- *Physical abusers* contact abusers who have an interest in indecent images as a part of their fantasy cycle. These offenders may photograph their abusive behaviour for their own use.
- *Producers* record the sexual abuse of children for the purposes of distribution to networks and to satisfy their own fantasy.
- *Distributors* distribute indecent images either for financial gain or as part of their collecting behaviour.

Krone, 2004

Internet offending and legislative context

The COPINE project, based on a large analysis of Internet offenders, published a very influential list of typologies which described a range of Internet offending behaviours specifically in relation to child abuse images (Taylor, Holland and Quayle, 2001). Although the majority of the offenders in this study were adults, most legal systems, including the UK, have adopted this classification in terms of sentencing:

- Level 1: Indicative (non erotic/sexualised pictures).
- Level 2: Nudist (naked or semi-naked in legitimate settings, contexts).
- Level 3: Erotica (surreptitious photographs showing underwear or nakedness).
- Level 4: Posing (deliberate posing suggesting sexual content).
- Level 5: Erotic posing (deliberate sexual or erotic posing).
- Level 6: Explicit erotic posing (emphasis on genital areas).
- Level 7: Explicit sexual activity (explicit activity, but not involving an adult).
- Level 8: Assault (sexual assault involving an adult).
- Level 9: Gross assault (penetrative assault involving an adult).
- Level 10: Sadistic/bestiality (involving pain or animals).

In England and Wales the Sentencing Advisory Panel* (SAP) have adapted (and collapsed) the COPINE 10 stage typology for sentencing purposes for those in possession of indecent images of children, as follows:

- Level 1: Images depicting erotic posing with no sexual activity.
- Level 2: Non-penetrative sexual activity between children or solo masturbation by a child.
- Level 3: Non-penetrative sexual activity between adults and children.
- Level 4: Penetrative sexual activity involving a child or children, or both children and adults.
- Level 5: Sadism or penetration of or by an animal.

Whilst this framework provides a valuable structure in which to categorise sex offender's use of indecent images of children, there is no empirical evidence to suggest that the most serious Level 4 and Level 5 Internet offenders pose a greater risk to children in terms of contact offending. However, Internet offenders grooming children constitute a higher risk than those whose offending is limited to possessing indecent images, therefore practitioners should be exploring whether Level 1 offenders are engaged in contact abuse (Davidson, 2007).

In the UK, under Section 45, *Sexual Offences Act 2003* a person portrayed in an indecent image is a 'child' if that person is under 18 years of age. If the photograph (or image) is considered indecent then the person who takes, possesses or distributes it is guilty of an offence. However, Gillespie (2008) articulates how the legislation becomes more difficult when applied to adolescents in possession of such images. For example, he refers to three composite case examples described below to illustrate these difficulties:

Case Study A: Arnold aged 15

Arnold has been accessing, and downloading indecent images of children from the Internet and peer-to-peer networks. The images that he has been seeking are those of teenage girls aged 14–16.

Case Study B: Brian aged 15

Brian has been accessing, and downloading, indecent images of children from the Internet and peer-to-peer networks. The images that he has been seeking are those of teenage girls aged 14–16. However, in order to gain other images he has downloaded images of younger children and offers these as 'swaps' to others on the Internet in order to obtain pictures of his desired age-range.

Case Study C: Charlie aged 15

Charlie has taken a photograph of his girlfriend topless on his mobile telephone. His girlfriend consented to the image being taken and indeed posed for it.

Gillespie makes the point that Case Study A presents practitioners with what might be considered by some as age appropriate sexual interest, however, others may be concerned about the emotional impact on the young person of seeing the children on the images as sexual objects. Whilst Arnold may be in possession of indecent images, it is open to question whether intervention from the criminal justice system is justified.

Case Study B presents the practitioner with further challenges as Brian is clearly trading in indecent images, suggesting that he would require some specific intervention regarding his understanding of his behaviour in order to minimise any risk of repeating this behaviour online.

Case Study C is different as there is contact between the person producing the image and the person in the image. Whilst it might be argued that this image has been taken in a consensual manner, if uploaded on the Internet it could be downloaded and distributed quickly making retrieval almost impossible (Gillespie, 2008).

In the UK the SAP categorisation for possession of indecent images does not extend to Internet offenders grooming children. The concept of 'grooming' has been drawn from the sex offender literature (lead primarily by Finklehor) and has been universally absorbed into policy, legislative and crime prevention initiatives. Davidson provides an excellent definition:

Involves a process of socialisation during which an offender seeks to interact with a child (a young person under 18 in Scotland, England and Wales) possibly sharing their hobbies and interests, in an attempt to gain their trust in order to prepare them for sexual abuse. The process may also involve an attempt to normalise sexual relations between adults and children.

Davidson, 2007

This new offence category is also included in Section 15, *Sexual Offences Act 2003* (England and Wales, this section of the Act also applies to Northern Ireland) making 'meeting a child following sexual grooming' an offence and applies to the Internet and other technologies such as mobile phones and to the 'real world'. In Scotland the concept of grooming is covered within the *Protection of Children and Prevention of Sexual Offences (Scotland) Act 2005* which includes 'meeting a child following certain preliminary contact' (s1).

Despite these new range of powers Davidson (2007) referred to data which suggests that six cases of online 'grooming' have been brought under the new legislation in England and Wales since 2004. It is likely that this number will steadily increase as CEOP (Child Exploitation and Online Protection Centre), which was launched in April 2006, has a specific responsibility for investigating cases of grooming online.

iAIM Initial Assessment Checklist

Introduction

The purpose of the iAIM Assessment Checklist is to assist practitioners in their initial assessments of adolescent males aged 12 to 18 years who have accessed child abuse images using new technologies. The checklist of questions will be relevant to those young people where there are concerns about possession and/or online grooming. It is anticipated that those undertaking these assessments will be trained in and familiar with the AIM2 Initial Assessment model (2007) and this additional guidance assists with this assessment framework.

The structure of the iAIM Assessment Checklist follows the same four AIM2 domains:

1. Offence Specific Issues: nature of sexual offending, attitude to victim, offence planning, use of violence, previous professional involvement, motivation to engage with professionals.

2. Developmental Issues: early life experiences, behaviour, sexuality, health issues, resilience factors, experience of physical, sexual, emotional abuse or neglect, experience of domestic violence.
3. Family Issues: level of family functioning, attitudes and beliefs, sexual boundaries, parental competence, current parent situation.
4. Environment: opportunity for further offending, support networks, attitude of community toward the young person.

AIM2 relevant factors

The AIM2 Initial Assessment framework provides a broad, evidence-based clinical judgement tool when assessing adolescent male sexually harmful behaviours. Within the existing framework the author has identified a number of static and dynamic concerns and strengths items (listed below) which are particularly relevant to the assessment of those adolescents where there are sole and/or co-existing concerns regarding their Internet behaviours. In these circumstances the assessor/s will need to pay particular attention to the following items:

Offence specific issues

Dynamic concerns

Item 2(b) 'Sadistic or violent sexual thoughts'

Adolescents who sexually abuse who have a history of sadistic or violent sexual thoughts are likely to present a greater risk of sexual harm than those who do not. Sadistic or violent sexual thoughts involve a young person deriving pleasure or sexual gratification from fantasies or plans that involve inflicting pain or physical injury on another person during a sexual act or assault. Practitioners need to consider whether these thoughts were fuelled and/or maintained by child abuse images accessed online. The COPINE typology Levels 8 to 10 will give an indication of severity.

Item 2(c) 'Self-reported sexual interest in children'

Adolescence is a developmental stage where an individual's sexual interests are often confusing, unstable and wide-ranging. A great number of young people who sexually abuse others may have a sexual preference for an appropriately aged partner but feel unable to succeed in such a relationship and so 'resort' to sexually abusing a child. Some may have a range of sexual interests including, but not exclusively, children. A very small minority may have an apparently fixated sexual attraction solely to children. This item relates to those young people who state or clearly appear to fall in the last two of these groups as a clear sexual attraction to children is obviously an issue of concern. A child in this context means an individual that is prepubescent or at least five years younger than the young person who is the subject of the assessment. This item refers to those young people who disclose or make apparent to others that they have sexual thoughts about children or are sexually aroused by children. Such disclosure could, for example, be made as a result of known use of child abuse images, therefore practitioners will need to pay attention to whether any 'collection' of child abuse images serves to illustrate a sexual interest. Pay particular attention to the size, scale and nature of any images accessed and whether or not the young person has solicited children online, using for example chat rooms, online gaming, email, text.

Item 2(d) 'Beliefs that minimise or support sexually abusive behaviours'

Many young men who sexually abuse do so in the full knowledge that what they are doing is wrong. Some, however, attempt to minimise, justify or rationalise their behaviour by making excuses so that they can believe that what they did was not so bad. A few have a distorted belief system that leads them to consider their behaviour as justified or appropriate. Whilst some 'excuses' may be superficial and easily surrendered others are strongly held convictions and it is the latter group that are included here as concerns. This item does not apply on the basis that a young person denies their abusive behaviours. Rather it refers to those 'cognitive distortions' where a young person believes or convinces himself that his sexually abusive acts were not or not entirely wrong or his fault because he perceives his behaviour as 'invited', 'educational', 'desired', 'harmless' or otherwise welcomed by victims (Worling and Långström, 2003, cited in AIM2, 2005). Therefore it is imperative that practitioners determine whether the young person has communicated online and/or offline with others who may attempt to convince the young person that downloading, distributing and/or producing child abuse images is legitimate or is not a form of child abuse.

Item 2(e) 'Obsession/preoccupation with sexual thoughts/pornography'

Whilst many adolescent males will have a considerable interest in sexual matters, including sexual images, this item refers to those young men whose interest is so considerable that it pervades almost all that they think about and could therefore be described as problematic. This is likely to include those young men who are known to have repeatedly accessed child pornography, for example on the Internet. In this instance, 'obsession/preoccupation' refers to recurrent thoughts, images or impulses concerning sex/pornography that may be distressing, highly frequent or come to mind despite efforts to suppress or ignore them. Some young people may self report such thoughts and for others it may be that they tend to sexualise most situations with sexual language, innuendo and comments. Although much of the research regarding the role pornography has in adolescent sexual offending pre-dates the Internet, practitioners need to ascertain the extent of the young person's interest in child abuse images, paying specific attention to the frequency of their access to such materials and to what extent other areas of their lives are affected.

Developmental issues

Dynamic concerns

Item 4(h) 'Difficulties emotionally regulating'

Young people who have problems emotionally regulating, experience difficulties in controlling their feelings. They are often overwhelmed by emotion and struggle to calm themselves or control their responses. Their difficulties often emanate from traumatic experiences that can trigger emotional overloads. This item refers to young people who cope with strong, negative emotions, such as anxiety, depression or anger in maladaptive ways (eg engaging in deviant sexual fantasies, using pornography, committing abusive, aggressive or anti-social acts, or behaving in a self-isolating or self-harming manner) and tend not to use adaptive methods of emotional regulation (eg talking to others or engaging in relaxing or distracting activities).

Therefore practitioners need to be alert to the 'meaning' of the online behaviour, that is, to what extent does accessing child abuse images demonstrate a maladaptive way of coping and/or managing negative emotions.

Item 4(c) 'Emotional congruence/identification with young children'

Some young people find it more satisfying to mix with children that are considerably younger than them, that is, whilst most young people enjoy the company of peers of similar intellectual and chronological age these adolescents are more likely to view younger children as their preferred social group. The tendency for some adults who sexually abuse children to display an exaggerated cognitive and emotional affiliation with childhood/children was labelled 'emotional congruence' by Finkelhor (1984). This tendency may also be observed in adolescents who are attracted to young children (usually this would mean at least five years younger than themselves), viewing them as equals and able to meet the adolescent's emotional and social needs. The adolescent may seek children as the preferred group to meet not only his socio-psychological needs but also his sexual needs. Therefore possession of child abuse images and communicating with younger children online may also be meeting the socio-psychological needs of the young person. Practitioners need to be aware of how the young person describes either the images or their online communications with children, for example do they consider the younger children to be their equals.

Item 4(d) 'Poor general capacity for empathy'

Many young people who have sexually abused may not readily express high levels of empathy for their victims. Indeed, their initial emotional concerns may be particularly narcissistic and extend only as far as the impact of their behaviours on themselves and perhaps their parents or other family members. In most cases this will reflect something of an egocentric or defensive reaction and does not necessarily indicate a globally poor capacity for empathy but reluctance, rather than inability, to comprehend the feelings of their victim/s. 'Empathy' is defined in a number of different ways. In this instance, 'empathy' should be understood to mean the young person's ability to appreciate another person's feelings, situation or concerns. It is the ability to imagine how another might feel in a given situation at more than a superficial/intellectual level. Consideration should be given to how empathy is expressed in different cultural groups. Therefore practitioners will need to determine the extent to which the young person understands that a child abuse image is inherently abusive to the child/children portrayed.

Item 4(g) 'Generally socially isolated (emotionally lonely)'

Adolescents who are generally socially isolated (emotionally lonely) are unlikely to have close friendships with peers. They may lack the necessary skills, confidence or opportunities to form such relationships. This item refers to young people who appear unable to form or sustain emotionally intimate peer relationships (eg close friends) or are socially isolated. This would include circumstances where the young person is religiously and/or culturally isolated and would be further compounded if the young person has history of being a victim of racial abuse. This item does not apply to those young people who have historically enjoyed close friendships but have recently moved and who have not yet had the opportunity to develop such relationships. This item may be a symptom of excessive use of the Internet, in which the young person's online community becomes so important as to replace their offline relationships. Whilst social networking sites provide young people with another media to communicate with their friends and family, practitioners need to be alert to signs that their Internet use is adversely impacting on other aspects of their development.

Item 4(h) 'Unresolved trauma (eg Post Traumatic Stress Disorder)'

Psychological trauma is created by an event that emotionally, cognitively, and physically overwhelms an individual's perceived ability to cope. The circumstances of the event commonly include abuse of power, betrayal of trust, entrapment, helplessness, pain, confusion, and/or loss. It can include powerful one-time incidents like accidents, natural disasters, crimes, surgery, deaths, and other violent events. It also includes responses to chronic or repetitive experiences such as child abuse, neglect, urban violence and enduring deprivation. Whilst some young people may display high levels of resilience after experiencing a single or series of traumatic events, others may be profoundly affected, such that they suffer significant distress or lose the ability to function effectively in key areas of their lives (eg in relationships, jobs, school).

They may experience persistent symptoms, including: re-experiencing the events (eg through distressing recollections, flashbacks, dreams, feeling the event is recurring), avoiding stimuli (eg thoughts, feelings, conversations, activities, places, people) associated with the trauma; difficulty falling or staying asleep; irritability or outbursts of anger; difficulty concentrating; hyper vigilance; exaggerated startle response. Practitioners will need to be aware that some young people may have been sexually victimised using new technologies. Indeed there are accounts of how some young people have been abused using images of their own sexual abuse, the impact of which has been referred to as 'double silencing.' Equally some young people may have been encouraged by their abusers to be pro-active in the sexual abuse of other children (Palmer, 2006).

Family issues

Dynamic concern

Item 6(h) 'The most significant adults in the young person's life deny, minimise or justify the young person's abusive behaviour'

A young person's attitude towards his offence is likely to be influenced by the attitudes of the significant people in his life even if he does not live with them. Blyth, Hill, and Thiel (1982, cited in AIM2, 2005) found that about 90 per cent of teenagers identify parents as significant persons in their lives. If those individuals deny the offence, the young person may be influenced to do the same. Parents or carers who deny the young person's offence are less likely to be good protectors or supervisors as they are less likely to recognise risk. As with other types of harmful sexual behaviour, a young person's attitudes to his Internet behaviour will be influenced by his parents/carers. Practitioners are advised to expect a level of denial in the early phases of work, but that if it persists it can hinder/block effective treatment. In relation to Internet

offending, practitioners may need to exercise some caution as the 'denial' may mask the fact that the parent/carer may not fully understand the nature of the young person's online behaviour as they may not be as IT literate or aware of the serious nature of child abuse images.

Environmental issues

Dynamic concerns

Item 8(a) 'Peer group is predominately pro-criminal'

Peer culture is known to be significantly influential during adolescence. The influence of the attitudes and behaviours of pro-criminal peers is unlikely to be useful in helping a young person refrain from further illegal or anti-social behaviours. Maintaining contact with criminal/anti-social peers is widely accepted to be a risk factor for sexual (Lievore, 2004, cited in AIM2, 2007) and general reoffending in adults (Elliott, Huizinga and Ageton, 1985; Lowenkamp et al., 2001; Wrightsman and Fulero, 2005, cited in AIM2, 2007). Hunter (2002) identified associating with pro-criminal peers as a risk factor for young people who have committed sexually abusive behaviours (cited in AIM2, 2007). Therefore young people's use of the Internet as an interactive and mobile form of communication may mean that they are in frequent contact with others who may advocate pro-criminal attitudes and beliefs which support the young person's access to child abuse images. For example, they may encourage the young person to trade or produce images to 'swap' for payment.

Item 8(b) 'Local community is hostile toward young person'

A young person who does not feel safe in the community in which they live is unlikely to find it easy to fully engage in therapeutic work. In order to participate in a programme of change a young person will almost certainly benefit from feeling supported, secure and safe. For this item the local community refers to the people living in close proximity to the young person's current residence. It can include school, workplace or other environment in which the young person currently spends a lot of his time. A local community is considered hostile when the young person or his family receive threats, intimidation, aggression or violence from other individuals or families in the neighbourhood because of his sexually abusive behaviours. As with other forms of harmful sexual behaviour, if information regarding the young person's online behaviour 'leaks' to the local community and the young person is threatened and/or intimidated it is likely to reduce their capacity to accept responsibility and engage in assessment or treatment interventions. Bullying or harassment may also occur within the online community, for instance on social network sites or via text messaging.

Item 8 (c) 'Current carers are not supportive of professional intervention'

The attitudes of a young person's carers are likely to have a significant influence on him and are likely therefore to influence the level of cooperation and compliance offered by the young person. Additionally, carers that undermine the professionals involved with their child are unlikely to be relied on to safely manage or supervise the young person. Practitioners will need to feel confident that they can provide carers with clear information about Internet safety and direct carers to relevant resources.

Item 8(d) 'Young person currently has little daily structure or pro-social activities in his life'

A young person who has little routine or regular activities in their daily lives are more likely to suffer boredom, depression, poor self-esteem, isolation and other negative consequences that may serve to increase the level of concern regarding their well-being. This item is scored if the young person has no self-imposed or externally required structure to their daily routine. This will generally mean a young person who has little to occupy his time and whose days include little that would be regarded as productive activities. This can include a young person who consistently refuses to comply with a given structure as well as those young people who have no access to or provision of regular and routine activities. This item may be a symptom of an obsessive and/or compulsive use of the Internet. Practitioners will need to be aware of what the wider consequences are for the young person's use of the Internet and encourage use which leads to pro-social offline activities.

Offence specific issues

Static strengths

Item 9(a) 'Referral behaviour appears to be experimental (or non abusive)'

This item refers to occasions where the referral behaviour is considered to be motivated by curiosity/naivety or in behaviours that whilst illegal may not be seen as 'abusive'. For example, this would include two 15-year-olds engaging in sexual intercourse where both were consenting, developmentally equal and where no form of coercion was used. For the behaviour to be considered experimental the following factors must be true: both the young people involved were of similar age and intellectual developmental levels; there was no coercion involved (eg use of force, trickery, manipulation or threat); there was no real or perceived inequality in their relationship (eg by virtue of peer status, authority status, culture or race) and both of the young people involved consented (this does not include mere compliance).

Case Study C (Gillespie, 2008) referred to earlier in this chapter gives an example of how the practitioner needs to establish whether the young people involved were of a similar age, intellectual capacity, that no coercion was used and consent to take the image was established. Difficulties may arise if an image is then distributed to others, for example using mobile phones, without the knowledge or consent of the person portrayed.

Item 9(b) 'Abusive behaviour appears to be peer influenced'

This item refers to occasions when the referral behaviour was conducted in association with others and where the referred young person is considered to have been coerced into the behaviour or complied with peer pressure. Consideration should be given here to 'gang initiation' or 'rites of passage' into a gang. In these instances, the sexual behaviour is not likely to be the primary motivating factor. Indeed, the behaviour may not have occurred without the coercion of others in the group. The young person is unlikely to have a previous history of offending behaviour outside of this context. For the behaviour to be considered peer influenced the referred young man must claim to have been influenced by peer pressure or coercion; not be cited by the victim to have initiated or been influential in the referral behaviour; where there were more than two young people involved in perpetrating the referral behaviour, the young person is not identified by any of the others to have initiated or been influential in the referral behaviour; not appear to have been otherwise motivated to commit the abuse; to be considered by those who know him well (carers, teachers, social workers etc.) as likely to be vulnerable to peer pressure or coercion.

Aspects of Case Study B (Gillespie, 2008) referred to earlier in this chapter, gives an example of how a young person downloaded images of younger children in order to obtain further images of peer-aged adolescents. The issue to establish is whether the young person's primary motivation was to obtain images of younger children, that is, would the behaviour have occurred if the offer of 'swaps' had not been made? Importantly, where online chat has been engaged in, it would be useful for the practitioner to access copies of chat content from the police.

Item 10(a) 'Accepts responsibility for the referral offence'

Some level of denial is not uncommon amongst those who have been caught for sexual abuse. Very often a young person will perceive very few potential benefits in admitting to the behaviour and so a young person who is willing to some extent to accept responsibility for his referral behaviour is considered to have some strengths. Denial can take many forms. It can range from complete denial, 'I didn't do it', to blaming others, minimising what occurred, rationalising or justifying the behaviour the behaviour, 'I only did it because . . .' Accepting responsibility involves not only admitting the behaviour but not attempting to excuse or diminish the extent of the behaviour. As with other forms of harmful sexual behaviours, a young person may well struggle to perceive the benefits of admitting to all of some aspects of their online behaviour. Indeed some may 'blame' the Internet for making the images available.

Item 10(b) 'Young person regrets having sexually offended'

This item assesses the extent to which the young person expresses feelings of regret or remorse for his abusive behaviour. Genuine regret is considered to be an inhibitor to repeat behaviour.

Many young people will claim to regret their behaviour for a host of reasons. Some will have regrets about the harm or distress they have caused to others whilst some may be more upset about the consequences for themselves. In either case the young person can be considered to regret his behaviour. It is important, however, to try and distinguish whether the sentiment expressed is genuine and the young person feels bad or whether they are merely making what they consider to be socially desirable statements. Whilst this item is theoretically supported in the research field it will be imperative to establish if the young person conveys a sense of regret for the harm caused to the children in the images, or those they have communicated with online.

Item 10 (c) 'Willing to address sexual behaviour problems'

This item refers to those young people who appear motivated to engage in a programme of work to address their sexually harmful behaviour. To score on this item the young person must acknowledge his referral behaviour and express a willingness to engage in a programme of work to address these behaviours. Practitioners need to establish to what extent the young person can demonstrate a willingness to engage in work to address their harmful online behaviour. Techniques which are motivationally based may assist. Examples of intervention methods regarding Internet behaviours are provided in the following sections of this chapter.

Developmental issues

Dynamic strengths

Item 12(a) 'Positive talents and/or leisure interests'

Positive talents refer to skills or attributes that the young person possesses that will assist him in attaining his vocational, social or personal goals. The presence of these strengths may help to foster a sense of achievement and may reduce stress and increase coping strategies. These pursuits can be encouraged in order to reduce the dependency on online experiences only.

Item 12(b) 'Good negotiation/problem-solving skills'

Good problem-solving and negotiation skills are likely to increase a young person's life skills and competency in handling adverse situations. Without positive coping skills there is evidence that those that commit sexual offences are more likely than others to turn to sex as a coping mechanism. These are skills that are particularly important in managing risk. A young person with good negotiation and problem-solving skills will generally demonstrate: an ability to think logically; not usually react over-emotionally or use sex as a coping strategy; be willing to listen; often cope with difficulties by thinking things through before acting; have good communication skills; have demonstrated the use of such skills in various settings (such as at home, in school with peers). The presence and evidence of good problem-solving capacities may offset difficulties the young person may have experienced with their intimate relationships, which was compensated for by a compulsive use of child abuse images online.

Item 12(c) 'Developmentally appropriate level of sexual knowledge'

A developmentally appropriate level of sexual knowledge is an important factor in a young person's ability to form intimate relationships, avoid abusive behaviours and to maintain healthy sexual relationships. An appropriate sexual knowledge is also likely to improve self-confidence and self-esteem. It is difficult to define an appropriate level of sexual knowledge, as this will depend on a number of factors such as: age, developmental level and cultural issues. However, most adolescents should have received at least a basic level of sex education and have a reasonable understanding of the terminology and function of sexual organs, sexual acts and sexual health. Ideally they would also have an understanding of what constitutes consent and what the law defines as sexually acceptable. The presence of an appropriate level of sexual knowledge is an important factor in a young person's capacity to form intimate relationships. Some young people may use the Internet in order to explore or experiment with others (such as in chat rooms) and be able to distinguish helpful/healthy sexual knowledge.

Item 12(e) 'Good communication skills'

Good communication skills are important assets in developing relationships, emotional regulation and self-confidence. Good communication is essential to emotional resilience as it promotes positive emotions instead of negative ones. A young person who can communicate effectively will have: reasonable vocabulary; reasonable language comprehension; good listening skills; the ability to pick up social cues. Practitioners need to establish whether the young person has good levels of vocabulary, comprehension, listening and social skills in the offline world, as well as a capacity to successfully manage his online communication skills.

Family issues

Dynamic strengths

Item 14(a) 'The most significant adults in a young person's life (eg parents, foster carers) demonstrate good protective attitudes and behaviours'

Item 14(b) 'The most significant adults in a young person's life (eg parents, carers) demonstrate positive emotional coping strategies'

Item 14(c) 'The most significant adults in a young person's life (eg parents, carers) have a positive support network'

Significant adults who can demonstrate a capacity to develop risk management strategies which are effective, use their authority skilfully to assist the young person's engagement in work around their online behaviours, supervise the young person's time online and do not exhibit similar risky Internet behaviours are more likely to have a positive influence.

Environmental issues

Dynamic strengths

Item 15(a) 'The young person uses at least one emotional confidant'

A young person who has at least one person who they can trust, confide in and rely on is likely to be able to cope with stress and emotional difficulties more easily than a young person who has no confidant. Confidants can serve to model pro-social values and behaviours. A confidant can be defined as a person with whom the client has a long-term, trusting relationship in which sensitive and personal information is exchanged, and where the person has an understanding of the client's situation. They could be peers or adults of either gender. An emotional confidant may be a parent or carer who serves to model pro-social values and behaviours within the offline world. The presence of at least one person, who can demonstrate these qualities, may begin to ameliorate the difficulties some young people face, especially when placed away from home.

Item 15(b) 'Positive evaluations from work/educational staff (eg of behaviour, attendance, application to activities)'

Positive evaluations from work or educational settings represent a good prognosis for the young person's employment and leisure interests. Having positive evaluations contribute to positive self-esteem. Staff report that the young person's behaviour, attendance and application to work are positive. The presence of these positive evaluations is likely to increase a young person's sense of esteem and worth. Prior problematic use of the Internet may have been attempts to alleviate in some way difficulties associated with negative self image.

Item 15(c) 'Positive relationships with professionals'

A young person who can manage positive relationships with professionals is likely to be displaying pro-social attitudes and skills. They are also more likely to comply with a programme of intervention. Professionals in this context can include those who have a caring, therapeutic, supervisory or educational role with the young person. In order for the item to be scored, the following points must apply to the majority of professional relationships the young person currently engages in. A young person is deemed to have positive relationships with professionals if he is not known to have presented aggressive, intimidating or uncooperative attitudes to those concerned; he is able to communicate positively with professionals; he is not considered manipulative, untrustworthy or unreliable by professionals. Even where a young person may feel strongly ambivalent about engaging in work regarding their online behaviour, if they can manage a positive relationship with the service provider it is more likely that they will cooperate with assessment and treatment interventions.

Item 15(d) 'Young person feels emotionally and physically safe within their current environment'

Unless a young person feels reasonably safe in their environment they are most unlikely to engage in work to address their sexual behaviour problems. A young person who feels safe is likely to report that they feel safe; not have reported events in the establishment that are likely to have made them feel unsafe; not be suffering from psychological or emotional disturbances due to their environment; not be bullied (verbally or physically) or otherwise intimidated by peers either directly or via text or social network sites. Therefore, unless and until a young person feels physically and psychologically safe within their living and learning environments they are less likely to engage in recommended work. The attitudes, behaviours and values of those around them will shape the degree to which they feel safe and trust others.

Item 15(f) 'Current carers/living environment can maintain appropriate level of supervision'

A young person's carers will play a significant role in ensuring the safety of the young person and any potential victims. Carers who employ successful and appropriate methods of supervision are more likely to be more effective in this role. An appropriate level of supervision is one that the young person complies with; is of sufficient vigilance to effect any necessary restrictions or activities the young person is required to comply with; is consistently applied; is agreed by the professionals involved in working with the young person. Therefore supervising a young person's use of the Internet may be facilitated with the installation of security software but the capacity of parents/carers to actively oversee and educate a young person regarding the benefits and dangers of time online is an important consideration.

Gathering information

It is anticipated that assessors will use existing safeguarding arrangements for gathering and sharing information regarding young people whose Internet behaviour warrants investigation/assessment (Working Together, 2010). However, in circumstances where young people have either accessed child abuse images or have solicited other young people online, greater levels of interagency cooperation will be required.

If the young person has been arrested it is likely that their computer, mobile phone, or other wireless handheld devices will be taken by the police for forensic analysis; this process can take some time and may not fit in with timescales recommended for completion of investigations and/or assessments.

Agencies are therefore encouraged to share information regarding the nature, size, extent and level of online communication at the earliest opportunity so that a measured and balanced view can be taken. The following stages are recommended:

1. young person alleged to have downloaded/distributed/traded in child abuse images referred to police/youth justice service/social care
2. inter-agency liaison
3. workers allocated to undertake initial assessment, including collecting information
4. workers plan interviews with young person and parents or carers
5. undertake interviews
6. write report and present findings to inter-agency meeting

The following iAIM Assessment Checklist Questions (adapted from Quayle, in Calder, 2007) is a series of suggested questions designed to assist practitioners in establishing what core information is needed from other agencies, the family/carers and the young person. It is worth noting that Appendix 1 'iAIM Internet Time Line Exercise' and Appendix 2 'iAIM Internet Questionnaire' will assist practitioners with further strategies regarding how to gather some of this information from young people.

iAIM Assessment Checklist Questions

Offence specific

1. What did the young person do?
2. Where and when did it take place?
3. How often?
4. Were others involved (friends or adults) either online of offline?
5. What period of time did the behaviours occur?
6. Who discovered or reported the concerns?
7. What was the young person's response to the discovery/disclosure?

8. Were there any significant antecedents to the concerning behaviours?
9. What was the function/meaning for the online behaviour? That is, to what extent was it meeting a sex/social/emotional need?
10. How often would a young person be online for?
11. What percentage of their time was used accessing images?
12. Has there been an observed decrease in other pursuits or interests?
13. What have been the consequences for the young person, family, and community?
14. What level of knowledge does the young person have regarding new technologies?
15. What sorts of technologies are they familiar with? Email, SMS, chat rooms, social networking sites, online gaming, etc?
16. Is there any evidence of any previous sexually harmful or problematic behaviour?
17. Has the young person been sexually abused online?
18. What was the nature and context of online offending, that is, downloading images? Trading images? Producing images?
19. If downloading, how many images were accessed and from which sites? What were the images of? Were there any preferences in terms of the category of image? Did masturbation occur? What thoughts and feelings were associated with the images?
20. If trading, what images were exchanged for others? With whom and for how long? Did they meet anyone offline?
21. If producing, how were the images produced? Who were they of, particularly if images involve family members? Did they use/upload their own images?
22. What was the nature of interest: age, activities, gender, etc?
23. What was the frequency and scope of online activity: times, effects on 'real' life, compulsivity, social isolation, impact upon education and friends?
24. What was the nature of the collection: catalogued, prioritised, randomised, extent and frequency of viewing?
25. Discover if the young person ever wished to seek help for their online behaviours? If so, from whom? What was the outcome?
26. Did the young person ever try to stop accessing child abuse images themselves? If so, how? Why do they think they restarted?

NB Remember to use typologies and COPINE levels to differentiate types of Internet behaviours, but remember these were based upon adult offending populations.

Developmental issues

1. Explore early life experiences, using genograms, eco-maps.
2. Gather information regarding physical health and development, particularly any evidence of significant trauma or loss, especially sexual abuse online or offline.
3. Seek to understand young person's sexual development, knowledge and understanding: how influential was the Internet in informing the young person about these issues?
4. Consider young person's educational history and level of cognitive functioning.
5. How well can the young person regulate their emotional state, especially in times of stress? What role, if any, did the Internet play in helping to regulate their emotional state?
6. Does the young person have a supportive and pro-social peer group?
7. Check of any signs of emotional loneliness or withdrawal?

Family issues

1. What has been the response of parents/carers?
2. What is their level of understanding of their son's Internet behaviours?
3. What is their level of IT literacy?
4. What is their perception of the problem?
5. Test their ability to supervise/protect?
6. What is their attitude to the young person and victims?
7. Do family members use pornography and/or Internet-based sexual activities?
8. Have the harmful sexual behaviours online occurred in the family home and/or elsewhere?
9. What has been the impact on family members?
10. Had parents noted any previous concerns regarding the young person's Internet use? If so, what measures did they take and how effective were they?

Environmental issues

1. What opportunities are there for further Internet-related offending?

2. Test level of embeddedness within community/neighbourhood?
3. Community/school/work reaction to young person?
4. What role had the young person's e-friends/online community have in the development of pro-offending attitudes, values and beliefs?
5. Does the young person represent themselves as a different person online?
6. What were the connections with an online community: chat rooms visited, trading, sharing fantasies, ideologies etc?
7. Were there any connections with other Internet users in the offline/real world?
8. Were there any attempts to connect with and meet children, or persons assumed to be children?

iAIM Concerns and Strengths Matrix

In circumstances where the young people's online sexual behaviour is the sole cause for concern, practitioners are advised to use the following matrix. Once information is gathered practitioners can then use the iAIM Concerns and Strengths Matrix (Appendix 3) to quantify the information further and begin to identify the main causes of concern or sources of strength under each of the four domains.

In circumstances where there are additional concerns regarding 'contact' sexual offences/behaviours, practitioners are advised to complete an AIM2 Initial Assessment.

iAIM Analysis and Action Form

The next stage (Appendix 4) involves the practitioner highlighting what the key areas of concern, strengths and what is still unknown or unreported. Once this is established the assessor will need to identify key actions to address concerns, increase strengths and resolve the information gaps.

iAIM intervention guidance

Introduction

If, as an outcome of the iAIM Analysis and Action Form or the AIM2 Initial Assessment (2007), it is indicated that a young person would benefit from specific interventions aimed at addressing aspects of his online sexual behaviour the following iAIM intervention guidance may be

Figure 15.1: iAIM Concerns and Strengths Matrix

	Considerable concerns	Some concerns/ some strengths	Considerable strengths
Offence specific			
Developmental			
Family			
Environmental			

offered. The interventions described below are a sample of those contained within the *iAIM Guidance Manual* and are intended to supplement the materials already contained within the *AIM Intervention Manual* (second edition, GMAP and AIM Project, 2010) the rationale being that much of what would be relevant for other types of harmful sexual behaviour will be equally applicable for online sexual behaviour. Therefore the iAIM Intervention Guidance identifies how to make an existing framework fit for these additional types of harmful sexual offences/concerns.

Engagement of young people

Like other young people who have sexually harmed, these young people are likely to experience difficulties in addressing their online behaviour. There is a high probability that they will have experienced feelings of shame and embarrassment associated with the discovery of their behaviour and the consequences this has had on their relationships with others. Practitioners are therefore encouraged to follow

the advice given in *AIM Intervention Manual* (2010) regarding how to provide the optimal levels of physical and psychological safety to enhance the young people's motivation and capacity to change their online behaviours.

Components of iAIM Intervention Guidance

The *AIM Intervention Manual* provides an outline of the key components of a therapeutic programme designed to address an adolescent's harmful sexual behaviours. The programme modules being:

1.a. starting work – old life – new life.
1.b. starting work – six boxes.
2.a. healthy sexuality – growing up.
2.b. healthy sexuality – what is abuse?
2.c. healthy sexuality – being sexual in a safe way.
3. exploring my own abuse.
4. steps to sexual abuse.
5. exploring sexual interests.
6. the consequences of sexual abuse.
7. managing risk
8. communicating with others.

Figure 15.2: iAIM Analysis and Action Form

Identify the main concerns, strengths and areas which are unknown.

Concerns:
1.
2.
3.
4.
5.

Strengths:
1.
2.
3.
4.
5.

Information unknown/not given:
1.
2.
3.
4.
5.

Action: Identify and prioritise the main actions to address concerns, increase strengths and resolve the unknown areas.
1.
2.
3.
4.
5.

---

9. relationships with others.
10. managing anger

For each of the 10 modules the iAIM Interventions Guidance provides suggested additions and/or amendments to take into account a young person's online sexual behaviour. Outlined below are samples of some of these interventions exercises.

Starting work – six boxes

The objectives of this module are to encourage the young person to identify specific goals for change and consider the order and priority of the work. The AIM Intervention Manual uses the metaphor of 'six boxes' – each of which in turn represents six different areas of a young person's life, for example:

– facing up to problems
– family
– relationships
– sexuality

– abusive behaviour
– other difficulties

The young person is then given a series of statements (typed separately on paper), for example 'I am out of control' and asked by the practitioner to place the statement in the box dependent on what part of their live the statement affects.

In relation to harmful online behaviours any number of the statements used in response to the iAIM Internet Questionnaire (Appendix 2) can be added to the statement list. For example, 'It is not illegal to look for these pictures, lots of people do it', may encourage the young person to speculate about how this has affected his family and relationships:

● *I tried to hide/conceal my access to child abuse images.*
● *At times I wanted help with my Internet behaviour.*
● *Sometimes I pretended to be someone else online.*
● *I felt good when I accessed child abuse images.*

- *I felt bad about myself when I accessed child abuse images.*
- *At the time I knew that looking for child abuse images were wrong.*
- *I tried to be alone to use the Internet and access the images.*
- *My friends and family knew what I was doing.*
- *I have arranged to meet people whom I first had contact with online.*
- *I think about the images when I am not at my computer.*
- *Some of the images are of children I know.*
- *I am more knowledgeable than my parents/carers about the Internet.*
- *Using the Internet makes me feel important and special.*

Healthy sexuality – What is abuse?

The objectives of this model are to promote an understanding of what constitutes harmful sexual behaviours as preparation for the young person to understand their own harmful behaviours. The *AIM Interventions Manual* provides a series of hypothetical case examples which the young person is then encouraged to rate as either 'fair', 'unfair' or 'abuse'. In terms of a young person's harmful online behaviours the case examples on page 233 (Gillespie, 2008) can be used.

Steps to sexual abuse

This pivotal module forms the basis from which young people can develop an awareness of the series of 'steps' which preceded the harmful sexual behaviours and is adapted from Finklehor's (1986) Four Pre-Conditions Model. The *AIM Intervention Manual* (2010) provides a full explanation of the model and illustrates of how to practice the Four Steps with a young person. Essentially the Finklehor model provides a conceptual framework to understand the process in which sexual abuse of children occurs:

Step 1: The potential offender/abuser needs to have some motivation to abuse sexually and so may be sexually aroused by children.

Step 2: The potential offender/abuser has to overcome internal inhibitors against acting on this motivation, such as notions of conscience, morality, fear of the law.

Step 3: The potential offender/abuser has to overcome external inhibitors such as protective adults, having unimpeded access to a victim.

Step 4: The potential offender/abuser has to overcome or undermine the victim's resistance.

In order to make the model (and language) more accessible to young people the *AIM Intervention Manual* (2010) re-labels each stage as follows:

Step 1: wanting to
Step 2: making excuses (to myself)
Step 3: getting the chance
Step 4: making the person go along

In relation to possession-type Internet offences or concerns the same Four Steps model can be applied with the following additions:

Step 1: wanting to

The iAIM Internet Time Line exercise and iAIM Questionnaire may give the practitioner some early indication about the young person's motivation to access child abuse images. If possible, refer to what the young person said during their PACE interview.

Step 2: making excuses (to myself)

Explore with the young person what they found themselves saying, thinking or doing that allowed them to continue to access the materials, for example, 'looking at one more isn't going to do any harm'.

Step 3: getting the chance

Explore where and how they accessed child abuse images. If at home, how did they conceal this activity from others? Did they disable security software? Were there adults around? If so, how IT literate were they? For example, would they have known how to do a browser history search?

Step 4: making the person go along

If the young person solicited other children online, how did they turn the conversation to sexual matters? If you have text transcripts of their communications ask them to identify where they secured the victims compliance.

If the young person was in possession of child abuse images, explore how they overcame any resistance to the fact that the children in the images were being sexually abused.

The consequences of sexual abuse

The stated objectives of this module include promoting the young person's understanding of the potential consequences for their victim/s of the harmful sexual behaviours. The *AIM Intervention Manual* (2010) provides a range of exercises to enable young people to gain the perspective from the point of view of the victim, their family and others.

In relation to possession-type offences/concerns, one 'justification' might be that these offences are victimless, in that it is 'only' a picture. The following case study is suggested as an additional resource to assist the young person in thinking about the consequences or 'ripples' of accessing child abuse images; in effect it tells the story behind the image.

Case Study: Abbie aged 6

Abbie has been invited to her friend's birthday party at the local leisure centre. She has been looking forward to it for many weeks. Her friend's mother agreed to take her to the party and bring her back home afterwards. Abbie was very excited as she knew she and her friends would be able to play on the trampolines and soft play area; she had been there before with her family on many occasions.

When they got to the leisure centre two grown-ups said they were in charge; they seemed really nice and laughed and joked with Abbie and her friends. Some of the other parents went off to have a coffee whilst the children played on the trampoline. One of the grown-up helpers, a teenage boy, asked Abbie if she would help him get something out of the store cupboard. Abbie agreed and went with the boy to the room next door. The room was dark and the boy said the light did not work. He turned on his mobile phone, which lit up the cupboard. He told Abbie to take off her knickers – she was frightened but did what the boy said – he took a photo of her 'minnie' with his phone and told Abbie not to tell anyone as she would be the one in trouble.

Abbie went back to the party, but did not feel happy. When she got home she burst into tears and told her Mum what the boy had done.

Managing risk

In this module the practitioner is asked to help the young person identify key factors which may increase his risk of reoffending or repeating the harmful sexual behaviours. The *AIM Intervention Manual* outlines a series of exercises designed to assist the young person identify risky behaviours

as a basis for suggesting plans to avoid repeating the same risks. All of the illustrations and exercises used in this module are relevant to young people who have accessed child abuse images, however, suggested amendments of this exercise are given below.

The ACE exercise involves the young person using a continuum to explore different types of risky behaviours, in terms of whether they are considered 'safe', 'bit risky' or 'very risky'.

Firstly, ask the young person whether he believes the behaviours described in each case study are safe, a bit risky or very risky. If deemed to be risky, use the ACE model to ascertain what strategies the characters could deploy in order to manage the identified risk. ACE stands for Avoid, Control and Escape. Avoid refers to anything the character can do to avoid being in this situation in the first place. Control refers to any helpful strategy the character can use to take control of their thoughts and feelings. Escape refers to any last minute choices the character has in order to escape from the risky situation they find themselves in.

The following three case studies can be added in order to consider online behaviours:

Dave is 13 years old and chats about sexual matters to people he doesn't know on Facebook (social networking site). One person called 'Tracey' says she would really like to meet up and asks for Dave's email address as she has some pictures she'd like to send him. Use ACE to help Dave to decide on the best option.

Peter is 16. His parents have recently split up. At night he uses live web cams to meet others online. An adult male he has been talking to asks him to take off his clothes in exchange for money which he can pay into a PayPal account. Use ACE to help Peter to decide on the best option.

Derek is 14. He has been searching for pornographic images of girls his own age, using peer-to-peer file-sharing software. Derek knows that if he downloads images of younger children he can offer these as 'swaps' to others on the Internet in order to obtain pictures of his desired age-range. Use ACE to help Derek to decide on the best option.

Conclusion

Over the last 10 years the influence of the Internet on sexual offending behaviours within the adult male population has been widely researched, with an exponential growth of publications, research articles and significant developments in assessment and treatment models. However, the needs of the adolescent Internet offenders are still relatively unknown and obscured from most criminal statistics, rendering their specific needs largely unknown and invisible.

As developments in information technology gather pace, there is now a greater need to understand how advancements in new technologies may leave some young people vulnerable to exploitation and abuse as well as increasing their risk-taking behaviours online.

This chapter has therefore sought to provide frontline practitioners with some clinical footholds to understand the scale of influence the Internet may have on vulnerable adolescent populations and set out how existing assessment and intervention frameworks can be adapted to suit this small but ever-concerning number of young people.

Online resources for young people, parents and practitioners

For reporting illegal material/child abuse images or other abusive Internet related sexual offending, the following organisations will assist:

- www.internetwatch.org.uk
- www.virtualglobaltaskforce.com
- www.ceop.gov.uk

Online resources for practitioners relating to Internet offending can be accessed at:

- www.stopitnow.org.uk – provides a confidential helpline for people who suspect that others may be a sexual risk to a child, or they themselves are a risk. Professionals too can contact the helpline to discuss their concerns.
- www.copine.ie – provides information on a self-help website for people worried about their own online behaviour.
- www.childnet-int-org – UK-based charity which provides wide-ranging advice and online educational materials for professionals, including teachers, to use with children and young people about their online behaviours.

Educational Materials for young people and parents/carers on Internet safety can be accessed at:

- www.childnet-int-org
- www.childline.org.uk
- www.bbc.co.uk/cbbc/help/safesurfing
- www.thinkuknow.co.uk
- www.webwise.ie
- www.parentscentre.gov.uk/usingcomputersandtheinternet

Glossary of terms

Administrator: *The computer user who can manage the access rights of other users of that computer.*

Avatar: *A digital icon or cartoon that represents a real person in the online world, for example in Second Life.*

Blog: *Short for Weblog or online journal which can be used to create profiles and share interests with others on the Internet.*

Bluetooth: *A short-wave transmission of files or information using digital devices, such as mobile phones, laptops etc.*

Broadband: *Describes a generally quicker connection to the Internet than dial-up connections.*

Browser: *A programme which allows the user to navigate around the World Wide Web, examples include Microsoft Internet Explorer.*

Chat rooms: *An online discussion group in which the users can correspond via text in real, rather than retrospective time.*

Download: *Describes how the user can transfer a copy of a file from another computer via the Internet.*

Desktop: *Refers to a computer made for use on a desk and is distinguished from more portable computers such as laptops or PDAs.*

Filter: *A computer programme designed to monitor what is being accessed on to a web browser or email account and can block certain types of information.*

Email: *Short for electronic mail and is a store and forward method of corresponding over the Internet.*

Firewall: *Computer software or hardware designed to prevent unauthorised access to a computer.*

Friend-to Friend (F2F): *Is a type of peer-to-peer network in which users make connections with people they know. Passwords can be used to ensure authentication.*

Grooming: *The term used to describe how sex offenders gain trust and access to victims. This process can occur online in which children and young people are exploited by those pretending to be a friend with the intention of meeting them offline with the intention of committing a sexual assault.*

Hardware: *The physical components of a computer system.*

Instant Messaging (IM): *Describes text-based communication in real time over the Internet.*

Internet Service Provider (ISP): *A company which provides a connection to the Internet.*

Laptop: *A small mobile computer.*

MP3: *MPEG-1 Audio Layer-3 describes a device which compresses data such as music and video files.*

Peer-to Peer: *A network in which users are connected to one another's computer for purposes of file sharing, typically music files. Less secure than F2F.*

PDAs: *Personal Digital Assistants are handheld computers.*

Social Networking sites: *Places where users can create and share with others a personalised page on the web relating to their interests, hobbies, lifestyle, views etc.*

Software: *Refers to computer programs that perform a task on a computer system.*

Spyware: *Computer software installed without the users knowledge to gain access or to control the computer. Anti-Spyware software can be bought and installed to counter Spyware threats.*

Pop-Up: *A small window which appears on a computer screen to display an advert.*

User account: *A collection of rules which governs the user's access to files and systems on a computer that is specific to any given individual.*

Username: *A code or password which allows access to a user account.*

Webcam: *A digital camera which can transmit images over the Internet to other users.*

References

Carr, A. (2004) *Internet Traders or Child Pornography and other Censorship Offenders in New Zealand*. Dept of Internal Affairs.

Cooper, A. and Griffin-Shelly, E. (2002) The Internet: The Next Sexual Evolution. In Cooper, A. (ed.) *Sex and the Internet. A Guidebook for Clinicians*. New York: Brunner Routledge.

Calder, M.C. (2007) *Working with Children and Young People Who Sexually Abuse: Taking the Field Forward*. Lyme Regis: Russell House Publishing.

Calder, M.C. (2004) *Child Sexual Abuse and the Internet: Tackling the New Frontier*. Lyme Regis: Russell House Publishing.

Debell, M. and Chapman, C. (2003) *Computer and Internet Use by Children and Adolescents in 2001*. Washington, DC: US Dept of Education, National Centre for Education Statistics.

Davidson, J. (2007) *Current Practice and Research into Internet Sex Offending*. Scotland: Risk Management Authority Research.

Davidson, J. et al. (2010) Editorial. *Journal of Sexual Aggression*, 16: 1, 1–4.

Erooga, M. and Masson, H. (ed.) (2006) *Children and Young People who Sexually Abuse Others: Current Developments and Practice Responses*. Routledge.

G8 (2007) Justice and Interior Ministers Meeting Press Release, 24 May 2007. Available at: http://www.bmj.bund.de/files/-/2131/Ministers'%20Declaration%20Child%20Pornography.pdf

Gillespie, A. (2008) Adolescents Accessing Indecent Images of Children. *Journal of Sexual Aggression*, 14: 1–12.

Greenfield, P.M. (2004a) Developmental Considerations for Determining Appropriate Internet Use: Guidelines For Children and Adolescents. *Applied Developmental Psychology*, 25: 751–62.

Henniker, J. and Morrison, T. (2004) *AIM: Setting up AIM Service in a Local Context*. AIM Publication.

Krone, T. (2004) *A Typology of Online Child Pornography Offending*. Australian Institute of Criminology. Available on: http://www.aic.gov.au/publications/tandi2/tandi279.pdf

Livingstone, S. and Bober, M. (2005) *UK Children Go Online: Final Report of Key Project Findings*. Available on: http:/www.children-go-online.net

Morrison, T. et al. (2010) 2nd edn. *AIM Intervention Manual: Adolescents and Families: A guide produced for the AIM Project by staff working at, or in association with G-MAP*. G-MAP and AIM Publication.

Moultrie, D. (2006) Adolescents Convicted of Possession of Abuse Images of Children: A New Type of Adolescent Sex Offender? *Journal of Sexual Aggression*, 12: 2, 165–74.

Nyman, A. (2006) Risky Behaviour on the Internet. In *Children and Young Persons with Abusive and Violent Experiences Connected to Cyberspace: Challenges for Research, Rehabilitation, Prevention and Protection*. Swedish Children's Welfare Foundation and Council of the Baltic Sea States.

Palmer, T. (2003) *Stolen Childhood*. UK: Barnardo's.

Palmer, T. (2006) Sexual Exploitation via the Internet: The Clinical Challenges. In *Children and Young Persons with Abusive and Violent Experiences Connected to Cyberspace: Challenges for Research, Rehabilitation, Prevention and Protection.* Swedish Children's Welfare Foundation and Council of the Baltic Sea States.

Print, B. et al. (2007) *AIM2: An Initial Assessment Model for Young People who Display Sexually Harmful Behaviour.* UK: AIM Publication.

Quayle, E. and Taylor, M. (2006) *Young People who Sexually Abuse: The Role of the New Technologies.* In Erooga, M. and Masson, H. (eds.).

Quayle, E. and Taylor, M. (2003) *Child Pornography: An Internet Crime.* New York: Brunner-Routledge.

SAFT (2003) *Children's Study: Investigating Online Behaviour.*

Swann, R. (2009) *Internet Assessment Intervention and Moving On: iAIM Practice Guidance for Young People who Display Harmful Sexual Behaviour Online Using New Technologies.* UK: AIM Publication.

Taylor, M., Holland, G. and Quayle, E. (2001) Typology of Paedophile Picture Collections. *The Police Journal*, 74, 97–107.

Ward, T. (2002) Good Lives and the Rehabilitation of Offenders: Promises and Problems. *Aggression and Violent Behaviour*, 7, 513–28.

Wolak, J., Mitchell, K. and Finklehor, D. (2006). *Online Victimisation: 5 Years Later.* Alexandria, VA: National Center for Missing and Exploited Children.

Wolak, J. et al. (2008) Online 'Predators' and Their Victims: Myths, Realities, and Implications for Prevention and Treatment. *American Psychologist*, 63: 2, 111–28.

DfES (2010) *Working Together to Safeguard Children.* Available on: http://www.everychild matters.gov.uk/workingtogether/

Appendix 1: Internet Time Line

This exercise will assist the practitioner's understanding of the development of a young person's Internet use over time. The time required to undertake the exercise will depend upon the young person's needs, level of engagement and motivation as well as the practitioner's time and availability.

1. Start with a large piece of paper and some pens and ask the young person to draw a line along the middle, with one end representing their birth and the other end the future. Ask where and how they would like the present to be marked or represented.

2. Ask them to start with a significant memory or event in their lives; note that this need not be the first memory. Continue to encourage the young person's description of the events, turning points, significant transitions and experiences. Be curious and asked open-ended questions. Don't just do for a list of events but fill the page with memories, feelings, emotions associated with the experiences. Ask what other significant people were doing at the time? How they would have experienced the young person, what would they have noticed? If a young person is struggling with words or spelling, assist them, suggest they use different colours or pictures to represent events, people, emotions etc.

3. Start to chart their first experience or memory of the Internet/computers/mobiles phones/cameras etc. Where were they? What was it like? Who first showed them how to use a computer? Explore the associated feelings.

4. What were they first using the Internet for? What were their family and family using it for? What were the rules around their Internet use? For example was it different between school, home, Internet cafe?

5. When did they start to view pornographic websites? What were they looking for? What did they find? Did anything worry or frighten them?

6. Did they talk to others either online of off line about their use of Internet pornography? Track this against other sexual experiences and consider to what extent the Internet might have been a source of information and curiosity about sex, sexual relationships, sexual orientation.

7. When did this begin to involve children or other young people? What happened when they accessed material? Was it used for masturbation? Which type of image did they prefer? Did they catalogue or store the images? Share with other users?

8. How did they keep it a secret from others? Did other people know? What was their reaction? Who else were they communicating with online? Did correspondence contain a sexual element? Have they planned to meet online friends off line?

9. What were the consequences for other areas of their life? For example, did this mean that they gave up other activities/friendships?

10. How would they like to be using the Internet in the future? How could this be safe? If unsafe, what would they do and who would they talk to?

Appendix 2: iAIM Internet Questionnaire for Adolescents (adapted from O'Brien and Webster, in Davidson, 2007)

This questionnaire can be used with a young person either during, or as preparation for an assessment appointment.

Please use the rating scale to evaluate the following statements.
1. disagree strongly
2. disagree to some extent
3. agree to some extent
4. agree strongly

I tried to hide/conceal my access to child abuse images
    1   2   3   4

At times I wanted help with my Internet behaviour
    1   2   3   4

I contacted others online to talk about or share other child abuse images
    1   2   3   4

I was always clear what I was looking for
    1   2   3   4

I used more than one computer/handheld device to access child abuse images
    1   2   3   4

I made contact with adults online about child abuse images
    1   2   3   4

Sometimes I pretended to be someone else online
    1   2   3   4

I felt good when I accessed child abuse images
    1   2   3   4

I felt bad about myself when I accessed child abuse images
    1   2   3   4

At the time I knew that looking for child abuse images were wrong
    1   2   3   4

I organised the images into folders on my computer
    1   2   3   4

I planned my day around when I found access child abuse images
    1   2   3   4

My friends and family knew what I was doing
    1   2   3   4

I have arranged to meet people whom I first had contact with online
    1   2   3   4

I have paid for some child abuse images
  1   2   3   4

I think about the images when I am not at my computer
  1   2   3   4

I have sent child abuse images to other children
  1   2   3   4

I have traded in child abuse images with others for payment
  1   2   3   4

I have produced my own child abuse images
  1   2   3   4

Some of the images are of children I know
  1   2   3   4

Please comment on anything else about your Internet behaviour which is important for others to know:

I am more knowledgeable than my parents/carers about the Internet
  1   2   3   4

Using the Internet makes me feel important and special
  1   2   3   4

The children in the images often smiled, so it didn't harm them
  1   2   3   4

It is not illegal to look for these pictures, lots of people do it
  1   2   3   4

I think about sex frequently
  1   2   3   4

I have fewer friends in the offline world than the online world
  1   2   3   4

Sometimes I have wanted to have sexual contact with a child after looking at the images
  1   2   3   4

I have masturbated to images of children
  1   2   3   4

My family think I have done nothing wrong
  1   2   3   4

I would like some help with my Internet behaviours
  1   2   3   4

Please comment on anything else about your attitudes and beliefs about child abuse images which are important for others to know:

Appendix 3: iAIM Concerns and Strengths Matrix

	Considerable concerns	Some concerns/ some strengths	Considerable strengths
Offence specific			
Developmental			
Family			
Environmental			

Appendix 4: iAIM Analysis and Action Form

Identify the main concerns, strengths and areas which are unknown.

Concerns
1.
2.
3.
4.
5.

Strengths
1.
2.
3.
4.
5.

Information unknown/not given
1.
2.
3.
4.
5.

Action: Identify and prioritise the main actions to address concerns, increase strengths and resolve the unknown areas.

1.
2.
3.
4.
5.

Appendix 5: iAIM Audit Tool (adapted from Morrison and Henniker, 2004)

Purpose and aims

To provide local authorities and safeguarding boards with a practice and service development tool to gather information regarding the nature and extent of adolescent harmful online sexual behaviour.

It is hoped that the iAIM Audit Tool will assist with:

1. an initial understanding of the scope and prevalence of children and young people who have come to the attention of local agencies because of their use of and access to child abuse images on the Internet
2. an understanding of current service arrangements regarding the reporting, referral and management of this population
3. an understanding of practitioners' experiences of the engagement of children, young people and their parents and carers
4. the development of an inter-agency model for the identification, referral and management of these young people in local areas
5. informing the development of practice guidance materials for local clinicians

It is anticipated that the audit tool will be initially completed by senior representatives from youth justice and social care.

Mapping exercise

An important early step to the development of an audit tool is to establish a baseline picture in terms of assets and gaps in the arrangements for assessing children and young people who have accessed child abuse images. In the following sections you are invited to consider one of three areas:

1. the scope and prevalence of children and young people who have come to the attention of local agencies because of their use of and access to child abuse images on the Internet
2. understanding current service arrangements and policies regarding the reporting, referral and management of children and young people who have accessed child abuse images
3. practitioners' experiences of the engagement of children, young people and their parents and carers

For each domain there are a number of items which you are invited to score/rate using a continuum of strengths-weaknesses. Space is provided to make additional comments. Lastly you are invited to identify key areas for development in this field and what other actions may be required.

1. The scope and prevalence of children and young people who have come to the attention of local agencies because of their use of and access to child abuse images on the Internet

Please rate items in terms of the availability of the information.

0. No information and very difficult to obtain
1. Minimal or unreliable information but possible to obtain
2. Some useful information but patchy and/or largely anecdotal
3. Comprehensive information available

1.1. Number of children and young people coming to your agency's attention over last two years because of a reported concern that they have accessed child abuse images on the Internet.

0	1	2	3
Information and comments:			

1.2. Number of children and young people receiving final warnings, reprimands or referral orders.

0	1	2	3
Information and comments:			

1.3. Number of children and young people convicted of downloading and/or distributing child abuse images, including where possible COPINE levels.

0	1	2	3
Information and comments:			

1.4 Number of Section 47 inquiries conducted where a child or young person is suspected to have accessed child abuse images.

0	1	2	3
Information and comments:			

1.5. Availability of demographical data regarding children and young people, such as age, gender, ethnicity, disability, looked after status and whether subject to a Child Protection Plan.

0	1	2	3
Information and comments:			

1.6. Nature and type of online behaviour causing concern, for example, downloading and distributing child abuse images using mobile phone technology, voyeuristic videoing.

0	1	2	3
Information and comments:			

Action planning

Given your responses to the above what are the three most important gaps in information and how might these be addressed.

> *Information need 1:*
> *Action required.*
>
>
> *Information need 2:*
> *Action required:*
>
>
> *Information need 3:*
> *Action required.*
>
>
> *What other information/data needs can you identify?*

2. Understanding current service arrangements and policies regarding the reporting, referral and management of children and young people who have accessed child abuse images

Please rate items in terms of the availability of the information.

0. no arrangements exist
1. informal arrangements exist
2. single agencies have formal arrangements
3. bi-lateral arrangements exist, that is, between two agencies/services
4. comprehensive inter-agency arrangements exist.

2.1. Inter-agency strategic leadership for the development/commissioning of services and inter-agency policies for children and young people who have accessed child abuse images.

0	1	2	3	4
Information and comments:				

2.2. Inter-agency arrangements exist with specific regard to the thresholds for referral, information sharing, assessment, planning and review of children and young people who have accessed child abuse images.

0	1	2	3	4
Information and comments:				

2.3. An agreed multi-disciplinary assessment protocol for children and young people who have accessed child abuse images covering both needs and risks, which is linked to Common Assessment Framework* and ASSET.†

0	1	2	3	4
Information and comments:				

2.4. Standards exist for residential, foster care services and others who have responsibility for managing children and young people.

0	1	2	3	4
Information and comments:				

---

*The CAF is a standardised approach to conducting assessments of children's additional needs and deciding how these should be met. It can be used by practitioners across children's services in England.
†The ASSET is the primary assessment method for young people at risk of involvement in offending or young people who have offended in England by youth justice services.

2.5. Arrangements exist for identifying, funding and co-ordinating services and responsibilities for children and young people who access child abuse images where it is identified that external residential/therapeutic placements are required.

0	1	2	3	4
Information and comments:				

2.6. Practice guidance exists for assessment/intervention work with these young people and their parents/carers.

0	1	2	3	4
Information and comments:				

2.7. Multi-disciplinary training for practitioners on assessment and intervention exists.

0	1	2	3	4
Information and comments:				

2.8. Awareness and initial response training is available for teachers, early years staff, foster and residential workers etc.

0	1	2	3	4
Information and comments:				

Action Planning

Given your responses to the above what are the three most important management and inter-agency arrangement requiring attention and the first actions to address these needs:

Management/inter-agency need 1:
Action required:

Management/inter-agency need 2:
Action required:

Management/inter-agency need 3:
Action required:

Please identify other medium- to longer-term management/inter-agency arrangements which you feel are important:

---

3. Practitioners' experiences of the engagement of children, young people and their parents and carers.

Please rate items as follows.

0. Very low
1. yes, but only applies to individual practitioners
2. yes, but only in specialist agencies/teams
3. some of the practitioners some of the time
4. most of the practitioners most of the time

3.1. Practitioners are aware of the current policies/protocols affecting the management of children and young people who have accessed child abuse images.

0	1	2	3	4
Information and comments:				

3.2 Practitioners have a shared definition and understanding of what constitutes abusive/problematic Internet behaviour by children and young people.

0	1	2	3	4
Information and comments:				

3.3. Practitioners believe that assessment and intervention should focus on needs, concerns, and strengths as opposed to focusing exclusively upon risk.

0	1	2	3	4
Information and comments:				

3.4. Practitioners see that working alongside parents/carers is an integral part of the assessment/intervention task.

0	1	2	3	4
Information and comments:				

3.5. Practitioners believe that they can, with training and support, deliver assessment and therapeutic interventions with children and young people who have accessed child abuse images as opposed to seeing such work as belonging *only* to specialist services/teams.

0	1	2	3	4
Information and comments:				

3.6. Practitioners believe that the services for these young people should be multi-disciplinary rather than the responsibility of a sole agency.

0	1	2	3	4
Information and comments:				

3.7. There are informal pockets of good practice and knowledge to build on with practitioners with some experience in this field.

0	1	2	3	4
Information and comments:				

Action planning

Given your responses to the above what are the three most important areas in relation to improving practitioners' confidence and competence and the first actions to address these needs:

Practitioner confidence/competence need 1:
Action required:

Practitioner confidence/competence need 2:
Action required:

Practitioner confidence/competence need 3:
Action required:

Please identify other medium to longer term actions which you feel would improve practitioner confidence and competence:

CHAPTER 16

A Framework to Assist in Assessing Children's Risk to Repeat Concerning Sexual Behaviour

Tracey Curwen

Introduction

In recent years, considerable attention has been paid to the characteristics of children who engage in concerning sexual behaviours. Much of the literature to date has focused, very importantly, on the etiology and treatment of these children and their behaviours. Although incidence rates of repeated problematic sexual behaviours by children are unknown, there is some evidence that many adolescents commenced their sexual offending behaviours as children (Burton, 2000; Wieckowski et al., 1998; Zolendek et al., 2001). Rich (2009) suggests problematic sexual behaviour that commences in childhood and continues uninterrupted into adolescence may be important to adolescent sexual recidivism. The evidence of a childhood history of sexual behaviours for many adolescents indicates that some children engaging in concerning sexual behaviours will continue these behaviours into adolescence. Such evidence supports the need to ensure identification of children with concerning sexual behaviours who may continue these problematic behaviours.

In prospective investigations of children demonstrating concerning sexual behaviours, there is some discrepancy in how many perpetuate these behaviours. Treatment outcome studies have been conducted on children whose treatment focused on their sexual behaviours (primary) or on the affects of sexual abuse which include sexual behaviour (secondary). Short-term studies (ie pre-post treatment) using children whose problematic sexual behaviour was either a primary or secondary focus have demonstrated improvement on measures of sexual behaviour (see Cohen and Mannarino, 1996, 1997; Stauffer and Deblinger, 1996; Silovsky et al., 2007).

Others have investigated long-term follow-up (ie one to ten years) of children with concerning sexual behaviours and results have been mixed. On one hand, a number of researchers, including those on the ATSA Task Force on Children with Sexual Behavior Problems, report that few children continue concerning sexual behaviours over time (see ATSA, 2006; Chaffin, Letourneau and Silovsky, 2002) however, others have revealed that up to 30 per cent of samples have repeated their sexual behaviour problems post-identification and post-treatment (see Bonner, Walker and Berliner, 1999, Carpentier, Silovsky and Chaffin, 2006; Prentky et al., 2009). Importantly, differences in the percentage of those who repeated in long-term studies have been linked to the type of treatment received. In addition most follow-up studies were devised to investigate treatment efficacy and therefore include children receiving treatment. It is possible that some of these treated children would not have repeated concerning sexual behaviours regardless of whether or not they received intervention. Until evidence is available to assist in determining which children are likely to continue, providing treatment to most children referred for concerning sexual behaviour may be an appropriate response.

Clinicians are asked to assess risk and the field must move towards applying knowledge to assist in this (Curwen and Costin, 2007). A method to assist assessors who must rely on speculation and anecdotal evidence to identify children likely to continue their sexual behaviours would be beneficial. In addition, frameworks for risk assessment will aid in identifying those children who may not require intensive intervention and assist in circumventing mistaken decisions that treatment is not warranted. Ultimately, it is clear that some children do pose a risk to continue concerning sexual behaviours and with a method to assist in identifying which child is at risk and why, treatment providers will be able to appropriately direct intervention efforts.

Although there is general consensus in the field that children with concerning sexual behaviours must be viewed differently than adolescents and adults who have sexually offended, sexual behaviours by children do cause heightened concern and the potential for overestimating risk (Curwen and Costin, 2007). Intervention decisions should be based on current knowledge regarding each child's risk factors and not on formulaic and rigid treatment recommendations. The goal of this chapter is to present a framework to aid assessors and treatment providers in assessing a child's risk and to provide a discussion of how the framework could be used as part of a larger comprehensive assessment.

Risk assessment

Intervention decisions are based on adults' concerns regarding whether or not a child is likely to re-engage in concerning sexual behaviours once identified. As such, intervention decisions are usually based on whether or not the child seems to pose a risk to continue the behaviours. Assessors and treatment providers are charged with determining specific intervention needs and such decisions will certainly impact multiple individuals including the referred child, his or her primary and extended family, peers, teachers, community, etc.

Intervention decisions will vary from no intervention to severe restrictions on the child. There are many cases of children who have been subjected to interventions (ie sex offender registration) similar to those of adult sex offenders (Chaffin, Letourneau and Silovsky, 2002) and there will no doubt be children whose sexual behaviour is ignored and ultimately repeated. When such critical decisions are based on the risk a child is believed to pose, it is important that an assessor not rely on intuition and speculation with respect to risk. Of course, there are seasoned clinicians with many years of experience and anecdotal evidence to draw from when deciding whether one child may be more concerning than another; however, there may not be consistency in the opinions of these assessors and important decisions may be based on conflicting factors. For those without long-term experience assessing and treating children with concerning sexual behaviours, issues of risk and methods to reduce risk may have little basis in their current knowledge or experience.

The framework proposed in this chapter was designed to assist in the assessment of a child's risk, and ultimately how concerned adults should be regarding repeat behaviours. The framework is based on both empirical and non-empirical (ie professional consensus) evidence. With children, an accurate assessment of risk will benefit those

responsible for making key decisions regarding almost every aspect of intervention. For example, the ATSA Task Force on Children with Sexual Behavior Problems (ATSA, 2006) state that clinical assessments, amongst other things, should provide knowledge of the appropriateness of specific interventions, intervention needs, level of service required, who must be involved in the intervention (ie parents, siblings, etc.) as well as who must be informed of the child's risk (ie school personnel, babysitters, etc.). As part of this decision-making process, the risk a child may pose should be considered when determining intervention strategies. In addition, given the age and developmental stage of these children, it is *vital* that the child's best interests – as well as those of other children, the community, and the family – are considered in intervention decisions (ATSA, 2006) Assessment of risk should be one component of a comprehensive assessment to ensure that the best interests of all are considered and safeguarded.

With no empirically validated factors to assist in understanding why some children repeat their problematic sexual behaviours, assessors must rely on clinical speculation when deciding which child requires a specific intervention plan and what that plan should encompass. Although clinical predictions are usually based on accumulated knowledge and experience, there is evidence to indicate that unstructured clinical prediction is only slightly better than chance (Hanson and Bussière, 1998). With limited knowledge and evidence regarding children who stop or continue, it is concerning that clinical predictions regarding risk are used to justify, or at least support, imposing limitations or alterations to the child's daily activities. Having a framework to aid in assessing risk will promote consistency in decisions, highlight the factors that contribute to such decisions, and will provide evidence upon which decision-makers can justify their conclusions. Accurate risk assessment would help ensure that the rights of low risk children are minimally impacted, that higher risk children receive appropriate intervention and monitoring, and that a child's risk will be addressed with the necessary treatment intensity and resources. In addition, risk assessment will assist to ensure that appropriate resources are allocated to address dynamic risk factors (ie social skills) that if left untreated may increase risk.

Methods for assessing risk

Risk assessment protocols fall into three categories: Unstructured/Unaided Clinical Judgment, Actuarial, and Empirically-Guided Clinical Judgment. With Unstructured/Unaided methods, the assessor relies on interviews, test data, other clinical reports, and their own clinical opinion to determine risk (Bonta, 2002; Grove and Meehl, 1996). Several concerns have been raised regarding unstructured risk assessments, which include: the likelihood of seeking information consistent with expectations, an inconsistency in how historical (static) factors are weighted in decisions, and the tendency to overestimate risk for fear of being wrong (Bonta, 2002; Grove and Meehl, 1996). To date, this is the method utilised by many of those making decisions about the risk and needs of children with concerning sexual behaviours.

Another risk assessment method is Actuarial. Using Actuarial methods, risk is based on a score obtained from a fixed number of factors. Actuarial methods do have an objective scoring system and the resulting score indicates the probability of repeated behaviours (ie sexual offending in adult populations) within a specified time frame (Bonta, 2002; Worling and Curwen, 2001). This method is used primarily with adults as a great deal of evidence has supported specific factors in this population. Developing such a method for use with children would be, justifiably, controversial; actuarial methods are generally based on historical (static) factors and therefore the risk level will never change resulting in little benefit of intervention to reduce risk.

The third method, Empirically-Guided Clinical Judgment (EGCJ) seems most appropriate for assessing risk for children. Decisions using the EGCJ approach are determined from a number of fixed factors believed to be related to repeated behaviour as evidenced through research, professional opinion, and empirical support. EGCJ methods include both static (historical and unchangeable such as gender or age of first behaviour) and dynamic (changeable, such as self-esteem or residence) factors and each factor is considered in determining level of concern, or risk (Boer et al., 1997; Hanson, 1998; Worling and Curwen, 2001). There are a number of concerns with this method, which include: different evaluators can reach diverse conclusions and that reliance on clinical judgment is ultimately

required. Aside from these, there are also benefits to applying such a method: the assigned level of risk can change with improvements on dynamic risk factors. Ultimately, decisions are based on a set of factors supported by evidence instead of on speculation, anecdotal evidence, and personal beliefs regarding issues that impact risk.

Considering both static and dynamic factors is important when determining which child is at risk and why they are at risk to continue concerning sexual behaviour. Static factors are those based on a child's history and therefore cannot be changed. In adult and adolescent samples, static factors have demonstrated utility in differentiating recidivists from nonrecidivists (Harris et al, 2003; Worling and Curwen, 2000). Therefore, it is possible that static factors are also important when identifying children at risk to repeat sexual behaviours. Although static factors may be important, these factors do not account for the developmental, behavioural, emotional, psychological, and environmental changes that take place during childhood. Dynamic factors, on the other hand, are those that can change over time. As such, the inclusion of dynamic factors in a risk assessment framework for children could assist clinicians in determining an appropriate treatment plan. As has been noted, the 'most effective assessments are likely to be those that identify clear risks and needs that become the subject of relevant and effective interventions' (Grimshaw, 2008: 12) and dynamic factors can be targeted in interventions. Dynamic factors also afford flexibility in the level of concern when information about a child changes, should that information be important to his or her potential to repeat concerning sexual behaviours.

Given that assessors and treatment providers would benefit from methods to reduce their reliance on unstructured predictions, caution must be exercised when deciding which method to apply. Developmentally, there are vast differences between children and adolescents/adults; this justifies the need to consider risk assessment methods utilised in older populations as unlikely to be relevant to children. For example, sexual interest in children, targeting a child, and penetration of a victim are risk factors noted for adolescents (ie Epps, 1997; Kahn and Chambers, 1991; Lane, 1997; Ross and Loss, 1991; Worling and Curwen, 2001) that may not be relevant to children. Similarly, there may be specific factors that increase a child's risk that are not found in adolescent protocols. Since clinical decisions should be based on empirical evidence and with the availability of adolescent and adult risk assessment tools, it is important to stress that these methods *should not* be applied to a child without evidence that the risk factors are useful for this population. Instead, identifying and applying factors that have shown evidence regarding a child's risk, and then using those factors to assist in treatment planning is a more appropriate method to conduct an assessment of risk.

Applying risk assessment methods to children under 12?

To date, and until evidence suggests otherwise, EGCJ is the most appropriate method to implement to assess whether or not a child may be at risk to repeat concerning sexual behaviours. There have been a number of empirically guided protocols devised specifically for children to assess their risk of engaging in or continuing a variety of antisocial or inappropriate behaviours. For example, single protocols have been developed to assess risk for a variety of behaviours, of which sexual behaviour is one (see Augimeri et al., 2000; Gilgun, 2001; Levene et al., 2000) while others focus on evaluating risk and protective factors specifically for children identified for problematic sexual behaviours (see Henniker, 2007; Rich, 2002). Each of these protocols was developed specifically for children under age 12. Recently, a risk assessment tool purported by its authors to be useful with children as well as younger and older adolescents, males and females, and children and adolescents with developmental delays has been discussed (see Rasmussen and Miccio-Fonseca, 2007). Based on documented information, each of these assessment protocols follow an empirically guided format and inclusion of each variable has been supported by empirical findings, professional opinion, or both. Future investigations of these tools will indicate their utility and predictive ability. The remainder of this chapter will present a discussion of another ECGJ protocol developed specifically to assist assessors in determining whether and why a child may be at risk to repeat previously identified concerning sexual behaviours.

Assessing Risk to Repeat Sexual Behaviour Problems (AR-RSBP under 12)

Based on the increased need to understand which children (under 12 years of age) may continually engage in concerning sexual behaviours and which children will desist once they are identified and cautioned by an adult (ie adult warning, reprimand) the AR-RSBP <12 (RSBP) was developed. The following discussion will not include detailed information regarding each specific risk factor, as this has been provided elsewhere. (See Curwen and Costin, 2007). Instead, the remainder of the chapter will present an overview of the development of the RSBP, how this framework may be incorporated into a comprehensive assessment, and how risk based on the RSBP should be communicated. An overview of current evidence regarding the RSBP will also be provided. For referral, the RSBP is provided in the appendix to this chapter.

Development

The first version of the RSBP was completed in 2006. Since its inception it has undergone some minor revisions. The development of this risk assessment tool followed a thorough review of literature to inform which factors must be considered in assessments of risk for male and female children identified with concerning sexual behaviours. A review of the literature occurred in 2005 and focused on five primary areas:

1. children known to have continued their concerning sexual behaviours
2. children believed likely to continue engaging in concerning sexual behaviours
3. treatment goals for children identified as having concerning sexual behaviours
4. assessment tools designed to assess children at risk for general antisocial behaviours which include sexual behaviours
5. research specific to sexually offending adolescents who initiated concerning sexual behaviours during childhood

Due to the limited evidence on this population, the criteria for inclusion in the final list of risk factors was based on any mention that a specific behaviour or characteristic *could* contribute to a child repeatedly engaging in concerning sexual behaviours. This nonrigorous methodology was necessary due to the lack of empirical evidence on factors that differentiate children known to have repeated and not repeated concerning sexual behaviours after being identified by an adult. The review of literature revealed 31 factors and of these 31 factors, 12 were static and 19 were dynamic. Many of the dynamic factors included in the RSBP were identified from the treatment goals of programs designed to desist concerning sexual behaviours.

Although 31 factors were identified while defining the variables, it seemed apparent that one factor, which related to the child's family environment (ie factor entitled Family Environment: Residing in a negative, unstable, and sexualised family environment) was, in essence, tapping three diverse family issues. Therefore, the original Family Environment factor was split into three separate factors: Poor family sexual boundaries, Negative home environment, and Family instability. The first version of the RSBP therefore contained a total of 33 risk factors.

The initial risk factors and their descriptors were reviewed and considered with respect to a few recently assessed children. This initial application of the factors to a specific clinical sample was completed to ensure face validity and the applicability of each factor to the population it was intended for. Four assessors, including the author, had conducted sexual behaviour specific assessments with a small number of children identified as engaging in concerning sexual behaviour on school property. In pairs, the assessors provided an assessment that included interviews and psychometric measures with the identified child, the child's parent or guardian, and the child's teacher. Also, where possible, school reports and documented accounts of sexual and concerning nonsexual behaviour were collected. The four assessors reviewed and discussed each factor as it related to a specific child recently assessed; the assessors discussed the relevance of the factor names, the factor descriptions, as well as the ease of determining each factor's applicability to each child. Following these discussions, some additional examples were included in the factor descriptions to increase ease and accuracy in factor coding. Once the final list of factors were identified and descriptors of each factor had been finalised, they were sent to experts in the field with a request for feedback to determine professional substantiation.

The final list of risk factors with the descriptive information for each was distributed to seven experts with extensive experience conducting assessments, treatment, and research on children with concerning sexual behaviours. Of the six who responded, two suggested slight changes or additions to the descriptors for two of the factors. Additionally, one respondent suggested including sexual contact with an animal (Gil, personal communication, 2005) as an additional behaviour that had been shown clinically to be related to children who continued engaging in concerning sexual behaviour. Because no documented evidence was found for this, the variable was investigated, but not as part of the 33 risk factors. Ultimately empirical and clinical evidence supported the sexual contact with animals, and it was included as a static factor in a later version of the RSBP.

Upon completion of the first study, the risk factors were used to produce a research version of the risk assessment framework, which was entitled Risk for Sexual Behaviour Perpetuation (RSBP) however, over time, it was evident that perpetuation was being mistakenly referred to as perpetration. As this framework was in no way related to adolescents, and with the belief that the trem perpetration connotes offending, the title of the framework was altered to reflect its intended purpose as a method to assist in assessing risk in continued sexual behaviour problems and not 'sexual offending'. Therefore, the name of the framework was changed to Assessing Risk to Repeat Sexual Behaviour Problems, which allowed for the acronym RSBP to be retained. Research regarding the RSBP commenced in 2006 and continues; this work has informed the factors and the structure of the RSBP, as presented in this chapter.

AR-RSBP structure

The structure for the RSBP follows that of other risk assessment protocols used for similar purposes and with similar age groups (see Augimeri et al., 2001; Gilgun, 2001; Levene et al., 2001; Worling and Curwen, 2001). The 34 risk factors (the original 33 plus contact with animals) are grouped into overriding categories. Originally, the 33 risk factors were organised under 6 categories which have been reorganised based on evidence and utility. Originally, the main categories under which the risk factors were organised included: Sexual Behaviour Characteristics (12 factors) Victimization (7 factors) Personal Characteristics (3 factors)

Interpersonal Characteristics (4 factors) Family Environment (5 factors) and Intervention (2 factors). Following further investigation, the current version of the RSBP has 6 general categories, which were altered slightly from the previous version, that encompass the 34 risk factors as follows: Sexual Behaviour Characteristics (13 factors) Victimization Experiences (7 factors) Family Environment (5 factors) Violence and Control (4 factors) Personal and Interpersonal Characteristics (3 factors) and Intervention (2 factors). As previously noted, the factors are categorised as static and dynamic: 13 factors reflect prior behaviours or situations that have *ever* occurred (static factors) while 21 dynamic factors reflect behaviours and situations that may change over time. Dynamic factors are coded for a specific time frame, such as the past six months or the next six months. All but one (2.1: Victim of sexual abuse which is coded dichotomously as Yes or No) is responded to (ie coded) by choosing one of three options. Based on the information provided at assessment, clinicians would determine whether each factor is either (a) definitely present (*Yes*) (b) partially/possibly present (*PP*) or (c) not present (*No*) for the child.

Within each factor, there is a description of what the factor is addressing, along with examples that would qualify for the factor being present or not. For example, the factor regarding Coercion/manipulation (factor 1.2) is described as whether or not the child has '*ever* used nonviolent means to attain cooperation during sexual behaviours,' indicating that this may have occurred on one or more occasions and that the goal of the behaviour *must* have been to obtain the other's involvement. The specific criteria as outlined for each factor must be considered in coding decisions. For example, if the only suspected use of coercion or manipulation occurred while one child was tickling and ultimately touched the genitals of the other, it is important to establish whether a 'tickling game' resulted in an accidental touch or was used to create the opportunity to touch. In addition, behaviours such as *bribes, tricks, manipulation*, and *coercion* are listed as examples that would qualify for a coding under the Coercion/manipulation factor; prior to coding the factor, determine whether specific behaviours do indeed reflect the specified criterion. Additionally, examples provided for many of the factors are not exhaustive, and it is incumbent upon the assessor

to determine whether the information does fit the criteria for the respective factor. Therefore, clinical judgment is an integral component of determining the appropriate coding for each factor on the RSBP. As such, it is recommended that, where possible, two individuals complete the RSBP for each child to ensure that assessment information is being accurately interpreted and that the possibility in coding bias is minimised.

As noted, each individual risk factor and the evidence supporting inclusion has been discussed in detail elsewhere (see Curwen and Costin, 2007), and this discussion assists to ensure that any decisions based on the RSBP are qualified within the limitations of current evidence.

Utilising the AR-RSBP

The RSBP as a guide to risk assessment

The intended purpose of the RSBP is to assist in collecting specific information that *may* be important to understanding which child may and may not continually engage in concerning sexual behaviours and why. As such, the RSBP is to be used as only one dimension of a comprehensive assessment. The RSBP should be used *only* with children who have *previously* been identified for concerning sexual behaviour and with justification that the sexual behaviour is, without a doubt, inappropriate. The RSBP should never be used to assist in assessing children where no known concerning sexual behaviours have been identified. Therefore, it is incumbent upon those working in this field to understand child development, as well as developmentally appropriate sexual behaviour.

The factors on the RSBP can be used to guide some of the information to be collected during an assessment. With knowledge of the factors that may increase risk, the assessor can ensure that the information necessary to comment on risk is collected during the assessment. Therefore, the RSBP can be used to both guide and establish consistency in the information collected during an assessment. It is also important to note that the examples of issues that qualify for a specific coding (Yes/PP/No) are not limited to those provided. If used as part of a comprehensive assessment, it is likely that examples not specified in the RSPB will also be important to consider when coding each factor. In addition, it may be that factors not included in the RSBP are important to a child's risk. If the assessor believes a specific piece of information may be important to the child's risk, then this too must be documented. A provision for 'other' is provided in the summary coding form, which will be discussed shortly.

Information should be collected that informs the coding of each RSBP factor; however, the terminology and language used in defining and describing each factor is not necessarily the language that should be applied in a clinical setting. For example, to code the Sexual thoughts/fantasies (factor 1.9) factor requires knowledge of the child's sexual thoughts; however, it would not be appropriate to ask a nine-year-old 'what are your sexual thoughts and fantasies?' Instead, the assessor should collect such information using age and developmentally appropriate language and activities. In this example, Costin (2010) suggests that asking the child 'How much time do you think about touching other people's private parts?' may be more appropriate. With younger children, the child and assessor could draw pictures of different times of day (ie getting ready for school, in the morning at school, lunch time) and then the child could place stickers on each picture to represent when they have certain thoughts – both age and developmentally appropriate and inappropriate. Similar methods could be used to obtain information on other issues identified on the RSBP such as how often they think of their own victimisation (factor 2.5) or how their body felt when they were touched by someone else (factor 2.2). To determine how often the child thinks about touching (or any other issue being assessed), the assessor could also have the child indicate when and how often they play with their toys or do homework. By putting a child's sexual thoughts and behaviours in the context of age appropriate thoughts and behaviours, the assessor will obtain the necessary information to allow for RSBP factors to be coded.

Due to the developmental level and needs of children younger than 12 years of age, it is important that more information than is presented on the RSBP be collected to ensure that the child's needs and strengths are identified. To date, no clear profile regarding concerning sexual behaviours has been established; it is not yet known whether specific factors or patterns distinguish children with and without concerning sexual behaviours or between children whose concerning sexual behaviours occurred over

longer or shorter time frames, with more or less severity, etc. (ATSA, 2006; Chaffin et al., 2002). Therefore, in order to determine the unique needs and strengths of the child and his or her family, a comprehensive assessment is essential, and an assessment of risk is only one component of that. Understanding the needs of the child must reflect their general development and not be limited to sexual behaviour.

The ATSA Task Force on Children with Sexual Behavior Problems (ATSA, 2006) recommends that, among other things, the assessment of the caregiver-child relationship, role models, discipline and consequences, boundary violations, and factors related to resilience be assessed. Other areas such as academic needs and functioning, recreational interests, as well as physical health are also important to assess (Costin, 2010). As these and many other areas of functioning are not reflected on the RSBP and, therefore, to date, have not been linked to increased risk, the RSBP is certainly not a general assessment tool. It is likely that with continued research, factors other than those included in the RSBP will prove important to risk and, a comprehensive assessment may reveal unique risk factors for a particular child that are not reported for others. Additionally, information not outlined in the RSBP (ie academic needs) may be useful in determining how to implement appropriate treatment and intervention plans.

Of note, the RSBP does not include areas of strength and factors that may be protective. Furthermore, there is no evidence that *not* having one of the RSBP factors present is protective against risk (Curwen and Costin, 2007). An assessor must also be aware of the possible limitations of their knowledge of the child; this lack of knowledge may result in factors seemingly not being present when, in fact, they are (Curwen and Costin, 2007). Until more evidence is presented, a comprehensive assessment must be conducted and should be considered in determining the future clinical and nonclinical needs of the child and his or her family.

Coding the AR-RSBP

Once a comprehensive assessment has been completed and all relevant information has been collected (ie school reports, Child Welfare reports, any prior assessment and/or treatment reports) the RSBP may then be coded by an assessor – or any other individual who was significantly involved in the assessment of the child and his or her family. Only after *all* of the required information has been collected would an assessor be in a position to complete the RSBP. Without collecting as much detail as possible, any assessment would be incomplete and decisions regarding would not likely accurately reflect the child's needs.

Upon completion of an assessment, the assessor would read the description and examples listed for the factor specific to each coding option, and then select the coding option that is most reflective of the information collected. It is important that the assessor pay particular attention to the time frame specified in each factor. A number of factors are limited to the past six months or the next six months and it is important that only information regarding this time frame be used to determine its coding. Additionally, the number of issues that must be present for a coding to be assigned is stated and should be adhered to. For example, to code Family instability (factor 3.3) as Yes (or present) the evidence uncovered through the assessment must indicate conclusively that *two or more* indicators were present within the past six months.

If information collected through the assessment indicates that the specific factor was definitely true for the child, the Yes option should be coded. If the factor is potentially true or true but to a lesser extent than is outlined in the descriptors of the Yes categorisation, the code of *Partially/possibly present* (*PP*) is appropriate. The PP coding may be appropriate under circumstances where limited details of the factor are provided (ie other professionals alluded to a problem, or the child/family suggested that there was a problem but did not indicate any details). Otherwise, if all information collected during the assessment indicates that the factor is not possibly or definitely true for the child, the factor should be coded as No. When the information necessary to code a specific factor is not collected or is unknown, all coding options for that factor should be left blank and not considered in any decisions that utilise the RSBP.

Once each of the factors has been read and coded, the assessor would then transfer their responses to the RSBP summary page (see p. 290–1). The summary page lists each of the factors organised into categories as well as into the static and dynamic types. It is important that the assessor not complete the summary until they have ensured that the assessment information is accurately represented in their coding of each factor. Once each coding is transferred to the summary page, the assessor will be able to easily view which factors are present, which dynamic factors may require intervention to impact risk, and which factors to use in determining intervention recommendations. As shown on the summary sheet, there are two columns entitled Assessment 1 and Assessment 2. Originally, the two columns were provided to allow a comparison of the initial assessment using the RSBP to a later assessment; however, the two columns may also be useful for comparing the independent coding of dual assessors for the same child.

As noted, clinical judgment is a component of empirically guided risk assessment; it is incumbent upon an assessor to accurately reflect their knowledge of a child in their coding of the RSBP and in any subsequent decisions. It is recommended that two individuals independently complete the coding of a child and then compare and discuss any differences, it is possible that both do not have similar knowledge of the child, or that some issues may be viewed as relevant to a coding for one but not for the other assessor. Although dual coding is not always possible it would benefit clinicians to discuss how the factors and risk should be considered. Periodic comparisons of dual completions of the RSBP will ensure consistency and objectivity in determining a child's needs and appropriate intervention strategies.

Determining and communicating risk using the RSBP

To date, there is no evidence to support assigning a specific level of risk (eg low, moderate, or high) for continued concerning sexual behaviours and there is no evidence to indicate whether the presence of one or more specific factors is more or less concerning. Considering these knowledge and research limitations, the assessor is required to rely on their clinical judgment in determining the extent of the assessors concerns and the specific strategies needed to reduce risk.

It is suggested that the issue of risk be addressed through recommendations that are based on the assessment (Curwen and Costin, 2007). By producing specific redommendations to address concerns that are believed to increase risk, the overall risk of continued problematic sexual behaviour will be reduced (Curwen and Costin, 2007). Completing the RSPB allows assessors to identify which factors should be targetted to address issues of risk.

Great care must be exercised when communicating the results of a risk assessment for children. There is always concern that the information will be provided to individuals with little training or knowledge regarding children with concerning sexual behaviours. Without the appropriate background, individuals receiving assessment reports may consequently use information from a risk assessment in an eroneous manner. Providing assessment information along with the caveats of current knowledge is important for ensuring that any risk assessment is utilised for the purpose it was intended.

The primary goal of an assessment is to determine the most appropriate intervention plan (ATSA, 2006). A risk assessment report must be one aspect of a comprehensive assessment and must be discussed in terms of the current and future issues to be addressed. As such, those reporting on risk must be mindful about incorporating open-ended or unexplained comments that could be misconstrued. Those writing risk reports must be conscious of how the information may be used and ensure that any assessment report never includes simply 'risk' statements (Curwen and Costin, 2007). A number of recommendations and cautions in writing risk assessment reports for children and adolescents have been documented elsewhere (Curwen and Costin, 2007, Curwen and Costin, 2010, Worling and Curwen, 2000) but are relevant to reporting on the RSBP and are therefore reiterated below.

Risk assessment reports based on the RSBP should be written to assist in treatment and intervention planning and, as such, should include the following:

- Specific information regarding issues that may increase risk should be provided. Specifically, the report should include a complete discussion of the RSBP factors found to be concerning along with the details of why these factors are present for a child. By providing sufficient detail, treatment plans can focus on addressing any specific factors that may require attention to decrease any chance that a child will repeat concerning sexual behaviours.

- A discussion of specific circumstances that may exacerbate risk or alter the child's current status on dynamic factors should be provided. For example, if the child is being moved from one school to another and that child has concerns regarding social skill (factor 5.1) and/or affective coping skill deficits (factor 5.2) a caution should be included that such a change may impact his or her social functioning or affective coping. Documented information should note that social and effective coping should be considered when determining how such a move should occur and whether specific interventions can assist to counter any potential risk.

- There should be appropriate notation regarding circumstances that could increase risk, it is also important to provide strategies to manage risk.

- When providing strategies, a number of specific recommendations, as in the above example, as well as general recommendations, should be provided. By reviewing and including individual risk factors for a child, specific recommendations then become possible. Recommendations regarding which intervention is appropriate and why, certain treatments or interventions that may or may not be appropriate and why, the level of service required, who and how others should be involved, and whether and how specific individuals must be informed of the child's behaviours are some of the general recommendations that could assist in protecting the child and others.

- Equally important, is the inclusion of a discussion regarding how to implement specific recommendations that are based on the identified RSBP factors. To ensure that the report is used for the purpose it was intended, it should include specific information as well as individualised recommendations regarding how to reduce a child's risk.

- According to the ATSA Task Force, a 'good assessment should attempt to identify situations or circumstances under which (sexual behaviour problems) seem to occur' (ATSA, 2006: 9). Specifically, risk assessment reports should specify any circumstances and situations that may increase risk; these reports should be sufficiently detailed with recommendations provided to manage a child's risk. Where possible, details of when, why, with whom, and where the child's risk may be increased should be provided, as well as which circumstances reduce risk. Much of this information may be obtained via a completed RSBP.

Along with providing details and recommendations based on the risk assessment, a number of caveats must also be included in the report to ensure accurate interpretation and use of the information. Firstly, and of importance, risk assessment reports based on the RSBP must include a warning regarding the limitations of knowledge. To date, empirical evidence regarding the predictive utility of any one or combination of factors on the RSBP is unknown. As noted, the RSBP is an empirically-guided method to assist in assessment of factors believed important to risk, but until further evaluation of the RSBP and/or specific factors on the RSBP provides evidence of predictive validity, caution must be taken to stress that the factors used to assess risk are still under investigation. As has been provided elsewhere, the following statement is recommended prior to any discussion (report or verbal feedback) of a risk assessment based on the RSBP.

Currently there are no empirically validated methods for determining the risk of continued inappropriate sexual behaviours by children under 12 years of age; however, clinical and empirical evidence is emerging with respect to a number of potential risk factors. Recommendations for treatment based on these factors can be made in an attempt to reduce the likelihood of further concerning sexual behaviours.

Curwen and Costin, 2007

In addition, the information in the risk assessment report should be time restricted. Given the potential for children to experience significant developmental, environmental, familial or circumstantial changes in short periods, it is recommended that the risk factors be reassessed at six-month intervals; any report based on the RSBP should include a statement indicating that the information is relevant for the next six-months only or unless circumstances warrant a reassessment sooner. One final caveat to include in a report based on the RSBP is the acknowledgement that evidence regarding risk is evolving and new factors may be found to be pertinent, while some of the factors believed important to risk may no longer be valid. Therefore, reports based on the RSBP should include the caution that the information provided is limited to the current knowledge available to clinicians.

Current evidence

To date, a number of agencies have used the RSBP either as part of an assessment or for research purposes. Since investigation of the RSBP is ongoing, its utility in predicting or assisting to identify children who may be at risk to repeat concerning sexual behaviours is not yet known. However, preliminary investigations within a few different samples suggests this framework may aid with intervention recommendations that help reduce a child's risk to continue engaging in concerning sexual behaviours. Various investigations which include inter-rater agreement measuring information discriminant utility of total scores and individual risk factors, child gender, and the coding scheme have provided some evidence regarding the RSBP.

Inter-rater agreement

In an early investigation of the RSBP, inter-rater agreement was conducted to determine whether dual assessors of the same child were consistent in their coding of each factor (see Curwen, 2007; Curwen, Jenkins and Worling, 2009 for a full discussion). Dual codings were provided on 12 children by seven assessors. To investigate agreement, the two assessors discussed the information and details collected as part of an assessment and then independently coded whether each factor was: present (Yes) partially/possibly present (PP) or not present (No) for the child. The assessors then returned the completed factors to the researcher without discussing their individual coding.

The intraclass correlation coefficient (ICC) was used to investigate inter-rater agreement. Of the original factors, 27 achieved acceptable inter-rater agreement (ie ICC above .61; Shrout, 1998) and most ($n = 20$) were substantial (ie ICC above .81). All of the factors that did *not* reach a moderate level (ie below .61) of agreement between the coders were dynamic and included: Opportunities for sexual behaviour (ICC = .53; factor 1.13) Family in denial (ICC = .59; factor 3.2), Aggressive thoughts/fantasies (ICC = 43; factor 4.3) Power-based beliefs (ICC = .32; factor 4.4); Affective coping skills (ICC = − .29; factor 5.2), and No guardian treatment involvement (ICC = .52; factor 6.2). Of note, most of these factors did meet fair agreement (ICC between .4 and .6; Shrout, 1998); therefore only two factors were of concern. The lower agreement on some dynamic factors as compared to static factors is not surprising; dynamic factors require a judgment by the coder regarding the presence or absence of the factor. Reasons for poor inter-rater agreement on these factors could include a lack of information, differing interpretations of the information between coders, or simply differing opinions on the presence of the factor. Where agreement was not shown, these may also be a result of the small sample size and the impact on detecting true reliability (Shrout, 1998).

Regardless of the reasons for less than moderate inter-rater agreement, important decisions based on clinical judgment may not be reliable given the issues with dual coding of some factors. Again, dual coding will help to ensure that assessment information is accurately and appropriately applied to the RSBP risk factors before specific decisions are made. In addition, the results suggest that individuals involved in an assessment often agree on how most RSBP factors should be coded, suggesting clarity of factor descriptions and appropriateness of the factors for children.

Missing information

Another method to assist in evaluating the usefulness of the RSBP would be a review of the complete and incomplete (ie missing) coding on each factor. If many assessors are not coding specific factors, this could imply that the information collected during the assessment did not include details necessary to code specific factors, or that certain factor descriptions are not clear enough to permit coding (ie not clear what qualifies as being present on the factor).

Missing data has been found in a number of samples; however, the consistency in where the data is missing differs based on the sample. Completed RSBPs have been obtained from three different samples. For two of these samples, the RSBP information was presented to and coded by assessors *after* the assessment was completed (Sample 1 = Canadian and American assessors; Curwen, 2007; Curwen, Jenkins and Worling, 2009; Curwen, 2011 and Sample 2 = Brazilian assessors; Curwen, Do Coutto Monni and Temponi dos Santos, 2008; Curwen, 2011). In other words, the assessors were not aware of what was to be coded at the time they were conducting the assessment. The third sample (Canadian assessors) was presented with the RSBP prior to their assessment (Curwen, 2011).

Any differences in missing data between these samples may reflect the benefits of using the RSBP to assist in identifying information to be collected.

In reviewing the missing data in the three groups, it appears that the majority of factors missing a coding were those specific to the details of the child's own victimisation (ie 2.2 Arousal during own sexual victimisation; 2.5 Trauma from own sexual victimisation, and 2.6 Arousal to memories of own sexual victimisation). Although improvement was shown in factor 2.5 between those who coded without knowledge compared to with knowledge the factors on the RSBP 31 per cent and 0 per cent missing respectively; other victimisation factors were similar on missing data. Improvement with knowledge of RSBP was shown between the two North American samples regarding factor 4.3 Aggressive thoughts/ fantasies and 4.4 Power-based beliefs which were both missing five per cent in Sample 1 but none missing in Sample 3. Specific to the child's sexual behaviours, only Coercion/manipulation and Sexual thoughts/fantasies were missing data in Sample 1 (3.2 and 8.1 respectively) and both had no missing data in Sample 3. Overall no missing data was found in Sample 1 and 3 and improvement in the number of missing codings was found for four factors. These results suggest that there was improvement in completing some of the factors on the RSBP when the assessor had this tool to guide their assessment.

Factors for which differences in response rates were found between those who did and did not have knowledge of the RSBP highlight the need for continued exploration. There are a number of reasons that could explain differences in response rates. For example, if certain issues are not usually assessed as part of a comprehensive assessment, then clinicians may not have the resources that would assist them to collect such information (ie creative methods such as games, activities, etc.), which could cause assessors to avoid collecting such details. Depending on the age of the child, language and comprehension difficulties may impact whether certain information can be collected. It is also possible that some clinicians are not comfortable discussing certain issues or cannot find an appropriate way in which to ask a question. Finally, the level of experience of the assessor may also impact missing information. Only with time and continued investigation will the causes of missing information be understood.

Some of the above results were not discussed with respect to a sample of 16 children in Brazil. Within this sample, approximately half of the factors regarding sexual behaviours were not missing data and where data was missing it was for few of the children; however, all of the Interpersonal, Personal, and Family factors were missing a coding for between seven per cent and 42 per cent of the children. The missing coding of certain factors for the Brazilian children likely reflects the resources of the country and the assessor's ability to conduct comprehensive assessments with minimal support. Instead, children in the Brazilian sample may have received assessments specifically for the most pertinent behaviours or concerns ie sexual behaviour and not necessarily for other factors (Curwen, Do Coutto Monni, and Temponi dos Santos, 2008).

The review of missing information suggests that many of the factors on the RSBP can be and are assessed in North American samples. Where missing data was prominent, having knowledge of the RSBP factors did improve response rates, suggesting that having knowledge of the issues for risk allows assessors to ensure they collect such information. Conversely, even though some factors are believed important to a child's risk, information to allow each factor to be regularly coded may not be assessed for a number of reasons. Therefore, further investigation of methods and resources to assist assessors to collect pertinent information to assess risk is warranted. Overall, the RSBP appears to be useful in guiding the information important to assess the level of concern a chld poses.

Discriminant utility

In order to determine the predictive use of the RSBP, or any other risk protocol for children with concerning sexual behaviours, a prospective study of children reprimanded for their first concerning sexual behaviour and then followed over time is necessary. However, given that this design is costly and time-consuming and due to the fact that little evidence of risk in this population exists, other methods to identify risk factors provide clinicians with a good starting point.

By applying a method used in adolescent and adult populations, the factors of the RSBP can be investigated for their use in differentiating children who have, and have not, repeated concerning sexual behaviours after being identified. By comparing those who were reprimanded (eg caught) for sexual offences and repeated (recidivists) to those who did not repeat (nonrecidivists), some insight into factors has been found for both adult (Thornton, 2002) and adolescent (Kenny, Keogh and Seidler, 2001; Worling, 2004) sexual offending populations. This same method was applied to children who have been identified and reprimanded (ie warned, punished) by an adult and then either repeated their sexual behaviours or did not. Of note, the children in both groups had an average of six different victims, showing that this was not an investigation of children caught or not for their first concerning sexual behaviour.

By comparing the Total RSBP score (a sum of the RSBP coding where No $= 0$, PP $= 1$, Yes $= 2$) for all children on whom the data has been collected, those who had been reprimanded and had repeated concerning sexual behaviour had a significantly higher Total RSBP score than those who had not repeated (Curwen, 2011). In addition, an earlier study revealed that a Total score based on a combination of eight specific RSBP factors (see Curwen, 2007; Curwen, Jenkins and Worling, 2009) and non-repeaters. Receiver operating characteristic curves revealed moderate accuracy of the eight-factor total score in predicting group membership (ie 86 per cent of the time, a randomly selected child from the repeated group would have a higher eight-factor Total score than a randomly selected child from the non-repeated group). In addition each of the eight individual factors were found to differ between those for the repeated and non-repeated groups. These results provide early support of the RSBP in differentiating children who do and do not repeat concerning sexual behaviours.

Gender

Although the development of RSBP was based on evidence from research and clinical opinion regarding both gender, much of the current evidence has been found in samples of predominantly male children. In the three samples discussed above, females accounted for 14 per cent to 26 per cent of the children. Investigations of gender and the RSBP have revealed that male and female children do not differ in age, in the coding received on each risk factor, or on the Total RSBP score (Curwen, 2007, 2011). To date, there has been no evidence to suggest that the RSBP is not applicable to both male and female children; however, since similar numbers of males and females have been reported in sexual behaviour samples (Friedrich et al., 2003), it seems that females are underrepresented in studies of the RSBP. Investigation of gender of the child and the RSBP is on going.

Coding scheme

To ensure that the three-point coding scheme is necessary, investigations into the outcomes for a two-point coding scheme (ie present or not present) have been conducted (Curwen, 2011). The possibly/partially present (*PP*) response was recoded: first into the Yes category and then into the No category. Recoding resulted in dichotomised factors the first method indicating that the factor was either *definitely* present or not (recoding PP into the No category) and the second resulted in *some* indication that the variable was present or was *definitely not* a problem (recoding PP into the Yes category). Regardless of the coding scheme, the repeated group (as discussed above) obtained significantly higher total RSBP scores than the non-repeated group (Curwen, 2011).

RSBP evidence

The results of a number of investigations suggest that the RSBP may be useful in aiding in the assessment of risk for children with concerning sexual behaviours. Support for the RSBP has been shown in investigations of inter-rater agreement, missing data, discrimination between groups, child gender, and the coding scheme. Although the results of various investigations suggest that the RSBP may aid in assessing risk, caution must be taken in how such results are used in assessments. At this point, it is recommended that all factors be coded and that the assessor use clinical judgment regarding each RSBP factor, and the combination of factors, to determine whether the child may be at risk to repeat problematic sexual behaviour and where intervention efforts may aid in reducing risk.

Summary and limitations

The goal of this chapter was to provide an overview of the RSBP as a method to assist in assessing risk to repeat concerning sexual

behaviour by children previously identified. Rich (2009) rightly cautions that the lack of empirical evidence for any specific risk factors requires that assessors use such information to help in their evaluation of issues that *may* be related. As such, the RSBP should be used to aid in the assessment of risk and not to be *the* risk assessment.

This chapter provided an overview of the RSBP and how to apply this risk assessment framework as part of a comprehensive assessment. It is important to reiterate that the RSBP was not designed for identification of a child's potential to start engaging in any concerning sexual behaviour. Before applying the RSBP, it is important to ensure that the sexual behaviours engaged in are indeed inappropriate. Children with concerning sexual behaviours may or may not have other nonsexual behavioural, emotional, and environmental issues; therefore, risk is only one issue that should be explored in the assessment of a child with concerning sexual behaviour.

Until there is further evidence of the RSBP and its risk-related factors, it is necessary to stress the need for caution when interpreting the results of an assessment that incorporates it; utilising results of an assessment guided by the RSBP in a clinical setting must be done with prudence. It is important to stress that the RSBP, as outlined in this chapter, is still under investigation and to employ the RSBP in establishing risk ratings and risk labels (ie high risk). Factors outlined in the RSBP should be considered *potentially* important until further validated. Even with validation, the goal in conducting this type of assessment should be accurate identification of children who may benefit from additional intervention and *not* for the purpose of making risk statements alone, or to segregate children demonstrating concerning sexual behaviour.

Assessors using the RSBP must ultimately rely on their clinical judgment in establishing the level and intensity of intervention required to assist in reducing the likelihood of repeated concerning sexual behaviour. Until further empirical evidence of the RSBP and its utility in predicting repeated sexual behaviours is provided, clinicians should not rely on total scores as an indication of risk; instead, a discussion of the factors that may impact risk and specific recommendations to address these factors should be one dimension of a comprehensive assessment report. Ultimately, the purpose of the RSBP is to aid assessors and treatment providers in identifying personal and environmental characteristics that may increase a child's risk and to develop intervention strategies to reduce the likelihood repeated concerning sexual behaviour.

Acknowledgements

The author is grateful to Dr G. Sharpe and K. Morgan for their feedback on an earlier draft of this chapter.

References

Association for the Treatment of Sexual Abusers (2006) *Report of the Task Force on Children with Sexual Behavior Problems.* Beaverton, OR. From http://www.atsa.com/pdfs/report-TFCSBP.pdf

Augimeri, L.K. et al. (2001) *Early Assessment Risk List for Boys. EARL-20B (Version 2).* Toronto, ON: Earlscourt Child and Family Centre.

Boer, D.P. et al. (1997*) Manual for the Sexual Violence Risk-20.* Burnaby, British Columbia: The Mental Health, Law, and Policy Institute, Simon Fraser University.

Bonner, B.L., Walker, C.E. and Berliner, L. (1998) *Children with Sexual Behaviour Problems: Assessment and Treatment.* National Centre on Child Abuse and Neglect. US Department of Health and Human Services.

Bonta, J. (2002) Offender Risk Assessment: Guidelines for Selection and Use. *Criminal Justice and Behavior,* 29, 355–79.

Burton, D.L. (2000) Were Adolescent Sexual Offenders Children with Sexual Behaviour Problems? *Sexual Abuse: A Journal of Research and Treatment,* 12: 1, 37–48.

Carpentier, M. Silovsky, J. and Chaffin, M. (2006) Randomised Trial of Treatment for Children with Sexual Behaviour Problems: Ten Year Follow-up. *Journal of Consulting and Clinical Psychology,* 74: 3, 482–8.

Chaffin, M., Letourneau, E. and Silovsky, J. (2002) Adults, Adolescents, and Child who Sexually Abuse Children: A Developmental Perspective. In Byers, J.E.B. and Berliner, L. (eds.) *APSAC Handbook on Child Maltreatment.* Thousand Oaks, CA: Sage.

Cohen, J.A. and Mannarino, A.P. (1996) A Treatment Outcome Study for Sexually Abused Preschooler Children: Initial Findings. *Journal of the American Academy of Child and Adolescent Psychiatry,* 35: 1, 42–50.

Cohen, J.A. and Mannarino, A.P. (1997) A Treatment Study of Sexually Abused Preschool Children: Outcome During One Year Follow-Up. *Journal of the American Academy of Child and Adolescent Psychiatry,* 6: 9, 1228–35.

Costin, D. (2010) Conducting an Assessment. In Curwen, T. and Costin, D. *Concerning Child Sexual Behaviour: Empirically-Based Identification, Assessment, and Intervention.* Workshop, Toronto, ON.

Curwen, T. (2007) *Assessing Risk for Continued Sexual Behaviour Problems by Children.* Paper Presented at the International Family Violence and Child Victimization Research Conference, Portsmouth, NH.

Curwen, T. (2011) *Current Evidence Regarding the Utility of a Framework to Assess Risk to Repeat Concerning Sexual Behaviour (RSBP)* Unpublished manuscript.

Curwen, T. and Costin, D. (2007) Toward Assessing Risk for Repeated Concerning Sexual Behaviour by Children with Sexual Behaviour Problems: What We Know and What We Can Do with this Knowledge. In Prescott. D.S. (ed.) *Knowledge and Practice: Challenges in the Treatment and Supervision of Sexual Abusers.* Oklahoma City: Wood'N'Barnes.

Curwen, T and Costin, D. (2010) *Concerning Child Sexual Behaviour: Especially based identification assessment and intervention.* Toronto ON.

Curwen, T., Do Coutto Monni, M. and Temponi Dos Santos, A. (2008) *Comparison of Canadian and Brazilian Children on Factors of Risk for Sexual Behaviour Perpetuation.* Final Report for the Provincial Centre of Excellence, Ottawa, Ontario.

Curwen, T., Jenkins, J.M. and Worling, J.R. (2009) *Differentiating Children with and without a History of Repeated Sexual Behaviours Following Adult Reprimand.* Manuscript under review.

Epps, K.J. (1997) Managing Risk. In Hoghughi, M.S., Bhate, S.R. and Graham, F. (eds.) *Working with Sexually Abusive Adolescents.* London: Sage.

Gilgun, J.F. (2001) CASPARS Instruments. In Calder, M.C. et al. (eds.) *Juveniles and children who sexually abuse: Frameworks for assessments.* 2nd edn. Lyme Regis: Russell House Publishing.

Grimshaw, R. (2008) *Young People who Sexually Abuse: Source Document.* London: Youth Justice Board.

Grove, W.M. and Meehl, P.E. (1996) Comparative Efficiency of Informal (Subjective, Impressionistic) and Formal (Mechanical,

Algorithmic) Prediction Procedures: The Clinical-Statistical Controversy. *Psychology, Public Policy, and Law*, 2, 293–323.

Hanson, R.K. (1998) What Do We Know about Sex Offender Risk Assessment? *Psychology, Public Policy and Law*, 4, 50–72.

Hanson, R.K. and Bussière, M.T. (1998) Predicting Relapse: A Meta-Analysis of Sexual Offender Recidivism Studies. *Journal of Consulting and Clinical Psychology*, 66, 348–62.

Harris, G. et al. (2003) A Multisite Comparison of Actuarial Risk Instruments for Sex Offenders. *Psychological Assessment*, 15: 3, 413–25.

Henniker, J. (2007) *An inter-agency project working with children and young people who display sexually harmful behaviour: policies and procedures.* 4th edn. AIM Project, London. Retrieved From http://www.Gmsafeguardingchildren.Co.Uk/Wp-Content/Uploads/Aim-Procedures.Doc

Kahn, T.J. and Chambers, H.J. (1991) Assessing Reoffense Risk with Juvenile Sexual Offenders. *Child Welfare*, 70, 333–45.

Kenny, D.T., Keogh, T. and Seidler, K. (2001) Predictors of Recidivism in Australian Juvenile Sex Offenders: Implications for Treatment. *Sexual Abuse: A Journal of Research and Treatment*, 13: 2, 131–48.

Lane, S. (1997) Assessment of Sexually Abusive Youth. In Ryan, G. and Lane, S. (eds.) *Juvenile Sexual Offending: Causes, Consequences, and Correction.* San Francisco: Jossey-Bass Publishers.

Levene, K.S. et al. (2001) *Early Assessment Risk List for Girls. EARL-21G (Version 1 – Consulting Edition)* Toronto, Ontario: Earlscourt Child and Family Centre.

Prentky, R.A. et al. (2009) Predicting Risk of Sexual Recidivism in Juveniles: Predictive Validity of the J-SOAP-II. In Beech, A.R., Craig, L.A. and Browne, K.D. (eds.) *Assessment and Treatment of Sexual Offenders: A Handbook.* Chichester: John Wiley and Sons.

Rasmussen, L.A. and Miccio-Fonseca, L.C. (2007) Paradigm Shift: Implementing MEGA, a New Tool Proposed to Define and Assess Sexually Abusive Dynamics in Youth Aged 19 and under. *Journal of Child Sexual Abuse*, 16, 85–106.

Rich, P. (2002) *LA-SAAT: Latency Aged-Sexual Adjustment and Assessment Tool, Assessment of Sexual Behaviour and Adjustment in Children.* Barre, MA: Stetson School.

Rich, P. (2009) *Juvenile Sexual Offenders: A Comprehensive Guide to Risk Evaluation.* Hoboken, NJ: John Wiley and Sons.

Ross, J. and Loss, P. (1991) Assessment of the Juvenile Sex Offender. In Ryan, G.D. and Lane, S.L. (eds.) *Juvenile Sexual Offending: Causes, Consequences, and Correction.* Lexington, MA: Lexington Books.

Shrout, P.E. (1998) Measurement Reliability and Agreement in Psychiatry. *Statistical Methods in Medical Research*, 7, 301–17.

Silovsky, J. et al. (2007) Treatment for Preschool Children with Interpersonal Sexual Behavior Problems: A Pilot Study. *Journal of Clinical Child and Adolescent Psychology*, 36, 378–91.

Stauffer, L. and Deblinger, E. (1996) Cognitive Behavioral Groups for Nonoffending Mothers and their Young Sexually Abused Children: A Preliminary Treatment Outcome Study. *Child Maltreatment*, 1, 65–76.

Thornton, D. (2002) Constructing and Testing a Framework for Dynamic Risk Assessment. *Sexual Abuse: A Journal of Research and Treatment*, 14: 2, 139–53.

Wieckowski, E. et al. (1998) Deviant Sexual Behaviour in Children and Young Adolescents: Frequency and Patterns. *Sexual Abuse: A Journal of Research and Treatment*, 10, 1998.

Worling, J.R. (2004) The Estimate of Risk of Adolescent Sexual Offence Recidivism (ERASOR): Preliminary Psychometric Data. *Sexual Abuse: A Journal of Research and Treatment*, 16: 3, 235–54.

Worling, J.R. and Curwen, T. (2000) Adolescent Sexual Offender Recidivism: Success of Specialized Treatment and Implications for Risk-Prediction. *Child Abuse and Neglect*, 24: 7, 965–82.

Worling, J.R. and Curwen, T. (2001) Estimate of Risk of Adolescent Sexual Offence Recidivism (ERASOR: Version 2.0) In Calder, M.C. et al. (eds.) *Juveniles and children who sexually abuse: Frameworks for assessments.* 2nd edn. Lyme Regis: Russell House Publishing.

Zolendek, S.C. et al. (2001) The Self-Reported Behavior of Juvenile Sexual Offenders. *Journal of Interpersonal Violence*, 16, 73–5.

Appendix – AR-RSBP

Coding Guidelines

Assessing Risk to Repeat Sexual Behaviour Problems <12 AR-RSBP <12)
Version 2.1: 2010

Tracey Curwen, PhD
Nipissing University, Psychology Department
100 College Drive, North Bay, ON
Canada P1B 8L7
traceyc@nipissingu.ca
© 2006, 2007, 2010 T. Curwen

Static variables

Static factors are those that cannot change/alter.
  *These risk factors include issues/ characteristics that have **ever** happened or been true for the child.*

1.0 Characteristics of sexual behaviours

1.1. Use of force/threat/violence

Yes	During any sexual behaviour or in an attempt to keep any of the sexual behaviours a secret, the child has ever: • Used excessive force or violence. • Used intimidation against the victim. • Threatened to use force or violence. • Used physical strength to gain compliance.
Possibly/ Partially	During any sexual behaviour or in an attempt to keep sexual behaviour a secret, the child *may* have used force, threat or violence as outlined above.
No	Has *never* used any of the force, threat or violence methods outlined above.

1.2. Coercion/manipulation

Yes	Child has ever used non-violent means to attain cooperation during sexual behaviours, which could have included, but are not limited to: • Bribes. • Tricks. • Manipulation. • Coercion.
Possibly/ Partially	*May* have used nonviolent means to attain cooperation during sexual behaviours as outlined above.
No	Has *never* used nonviolent means to attain cooperation during sexual behaviours as outlined above.

1.3. Pattern of sexual behaviours

Yes	Child has ever engaged in prior sexual behaviours which could be indicated by: • One victim on multiple occasions. • Pattern of inappropriate sexual behaviours/ • Multiple victims. repetitive.
Possibly/ Partially	*May* have history of sexual behaviours as outlined above.
No	*No* known history of prior sexual behaviours as outlined above.

1.4. Penetration

Yes	Child has ever penetrated or attempted to penetrate another (includes penetration with penis, object, finger): • *Attempted* vaginal, oral, anal penetration. • *Completed* vaginal, oral, anal penetration.
Possibly/ Partially	*May* have penetrated or attempted to penetrate another (includes penetration with penis, object, finger).
No	Has *never* engaged in vaginal, oral, or anal penetration or attempted penetration of another.

1.5. Sophisticated sexual behaviours

Yes	Child has ever employed sophisticated means to engage in sexual behaviours with others. Sophisticated means may include, but are not limited to, sexual behaviours that were: • Strategic. • Highly planned. • Well thought out. • Offered drug/alcohol to victim.
Possibly/ Partially	*May* have employed sophisticated means to engage in sexual behaviours with others.
No	Has *never* used sophisticated means used to engage in sexual behaviours.

1.6. Multiple types of sexual behaviours

Yes	Child has ever engaged in more than one type of sexual behaviour. Can include, but not limited to, two or more of the following: • Sexual touching over clothes. • Vaginal penetration. • Sexual touching under clothes. • Penetration with penis. • Sexual touching above waist. • Viewed pornography. • Sexual touching below waist. • Show pornography to victim. • Exhibitionism. • Excessive masturbation. • Stalking. • Cross-dressing. • Male and Female Victims. • Voyeurism. • Frottage. • Internet sex rooms/chat lines. • Kissing. • Obscene phone calls. • Victims from multiple age groups. • Bestiality. • Oral penetration. • Forcing victim to sexually touch self. • Anal penetration. • Sexual behaviour not listed. • Penetration with object.
Possibly/ Partially	*May* have engaged in more than one type of sexual behaviour.
No	Has *never* engaged in more than one type of sexual behaviour.

1.7. Victim selection based on vulnerability

Yes	Child has ever chosen at least one victim because of specific characteristics, which made them appear vulnerable. Victim characteristics were known to the child and may include, but are not limited to: ● Those who are easy to fool, bribe, or force. ● A person with no verbal ability to report. ● A person with intellectual deficits. ● A person who was vulnerable. ● Person with trauma history. ● A less assertive person. ● A person with a known sexual victimization history. ● A person who was asleep. ● A person who was not physically able to protect self. ● A person under the influence of alcohol/drugs.
Possibly/ Partially	*May* have selected at least one victim because of their vulnerability.
No	*Did not* choose any victim based on their vulnerability.

1.8. Sexual behaviours with animal

Yes	Child has ever engaged in sexual contact with one or more animals on one or more occasions.
Possibly/ Partially	*May* have history of sexual behaviours with animals as noted above.
No	*No* known history of prior sexual behaviours with animals.

2.0. Victimization history

2.1. Victim of sexual abuse

Yes	Child *has* a history of sexual abuse.
No	Child *is not* a victim of sexual abuse.

2.2. Arousal during own sexual victimization

Yes	Child experienced sexual arousal during own sexual abuse.
Possibly/ Partially	*May* have experienced sexual arousal during own sexual abuse.
No	*Did not* experience sexual arousal during own sexual abuse.

2.3. Multiple sexual offenders

Yes	Child has ever been sexually abused (any unwanted sexual contact/s) by more than one person. Offenders need not have been charged or been of a chargeable age. Offenders were: • Multiple male offenders. • Both male and female offenders. • Multiple female offenders.
Possibly/ Partially	*May* have been sexually abused by more than one person as outlined above.
No	Has been sexually abused by *one person only*.

2.4. Witnessed violence

Yes	Child has witnessed, been exposed to, or been privy to violence as noted by, but not limited to: • Family violence (seen or heard). • Witnessed violence between real people outside of the family. • Friends/ peers have been harmed by violence.
Possibly/ Partially	*May* have witnessed, been exposed to, or been privy to violence as outlined above.
No	Has *never* witnessed, been exposed to, or been privy to violence as outlined above.

3.0. Family and environment

3.1. Poor family sexual boundaries/ sexualized family environment

Yes	Child has ever been exposed to poor sexual boundaries in the home. Poor boundaries may include, but are not limited to: • Family nudity. • History of prostitution in family. • Lack of privacy (eg bathroom, changing). • Knowledge of adult sexual behaviours (hearing/seeing). • Child used to meet parents sexual needs. • Has received age inappropriate sexual knowledge. • Perpetration in family (not including child's sexual behaviours) • Inappropriate displays of affection • Exposure and/or access to explicit media • Sexual talk in family that is denigrating, objectifying, disrespectful • More than one child sexually abused in family (not by this child) • Guardians confused about sexual boundaries/ sexuality • Photographed in nude or engaging in sexual acts.
Possibly/ Partially	*May* have been exposed to inappropriate sexual boundaries within the family as outlined above.
No	Child *has not* been exposed to poor sexual boundaries within the family.

Dynamic variables

Dynamic factors are those that can change. Items are specific to situations/circumstances for the **previous six months**, **currently**, or for the **next six months**.

Please note the time frame for each item.

1.0. Characteristics of sexual behaviours

1.9. Sexual thoughts/fantasies (past 6 months)

Yes	Over the *past six months*, the child has had inappropriate sexual thoughts or fantasies. Age inappropriate sexual fantasies/thoughts about things outside of what is natural and expected sexual behaviour for each age group.** Inappropriate sexual thoughts/fantasies may be demonstrated through, but are not limited to: • Adult themes (e.g. a six year-old fantasizing about intercourse)**. • The urge to sexually abuse during self-stimulation. • Thoughts/fantasies of sexual violence. • Thoughts/fantasies of sexual coercion. • Thoughts/fantasies of sexual aggression. • Fantasies/thoughts include age, size, or status differences**. • Sexual fantasies/thoughts, which include themes of power and control.
Possibly/ Partially	Over the past six months *may* have had an inappropriate sexual thought/fantasy as outlined above.
No	Has *never* had an inappropriate sexual thought/fantasy, over the past six months.

**Refer to documented age appropriate sexuality information, eg Gil, E. (1993). Age appropriate sex play versus problematic sexual behaviours. In E. Gil and T.C. Johnson (Eds.), *Sexualized children: Assessment and treatment of sexualized children and children who molest* (pp. 21-40). Rockville, MD: Launch Press.

1.10. Distorted sexual beliefs (current)

Yes	*Currently* the child has distorted sexual beliefs that are demonstrated through, but not limited to: • Justifying own sexual behaviours. • Confusion about sexual issues. • Anxiety regarding sexuality. • Sees own sexual behaviours as 'normal'. • Confusion about own sexuality. • Confusion about appropriate and. • Anger regarding sexuality. inappropriate sexual behaviours.
Possibly/ Partially	*May currently* have distorted sexual beliefs as demonstrated through those issues as demonstrated above.
No	*Does not currently* experience distorted sexual beliefs as demonstrated above.

1.11. Denial (current)

Yes	Child *currently* denies: • Any involvement in sexual behaviours. • Any problem with sexual behaviours.
Possibly/ Partially	*Currently* acknowledges involvement for *some*, but not all sexual behaviours. **May** acknowledge having some problem with sexual behaviour.
No	Acknowledges involvement in *all* sexual behaviours, even if does not accept full responsibility. Recognizes inappropriateness of sexual behaviours.

1.12. Lacks understanding of consequences of sexual behaviours (current)

Yes	*Currently* the child *lacks understanding* of consequences of behaviours as demonstrated through, but not limited to: • Does not understand the consequences of sexual behaviours to self. • Does not understand the consequences of sexual behaviours to other. • Does not think of consequences to self or other. • Is not concerned about the consequences to self or other. • Does not have age appropriate empathy for other.
Possibly/ Partially	*May not currently* **consider** the consequences to self *or* other. May not currently be concerned about consequences to self *or* other.
No	*Currently* **able to understand** consequences of sexual behaviours to self and other and is concerned about consequences to self and other.

1.13. Opportunities for sexual behaviour* (next 6 months)

Yes	Over the *next six months*, **child will have the opportunity** to engage in continued sexual behaviours with others. Opportunities can include, but are not limited to: • Living with and/or allowed access to potential victims. • Guardians who are unable to control child. • Child will not receive adequate supervision. *Consider all areas of life, eg school, extracurricular activities, and home. Child will rarely be monitored by people who are aware of the sexual behaviours.
Possibly/ Partially	Over the *next six months*, child *may* have opportunity to engage in continued sexual behaviours with others. Therefore, child will be monitored often, but not all of the time, by people aware of the sexual behaviours.
No	Over the *next six months*, child *will not* have the opportunity in all realms (school, home, etc) to engage in continued sexual behaviours with others. Therefore, child will be monitored all the time by people who are aware of the sexual behaviours.

2.0. *Victimization history*

If the child is not a victim of sexual abuse, skip to item **2.7.**

2.5. Trauma from own sexual victimization (current)

Yes	Child *currently* has unresolved trauma related to *own sexual victimization* history. Trauma may be displayed by intrusive thoughts or memories, dissociation, nightmares, sleeping difficulties, emotionality, feelings of helplessness, etc. Child has not received required treatment for victimization.
Possibly/ Partially	*May currently* have unresolved trauma related to own sexual victimization history. Child *might* require treatment for sexual victimization.
No	• *Has received treatment* for own sexual victimization history. • *Does not* indicate unresolved trauma from own sexual victimization.

2.6. Arousal to memories of own sexual victimization (current)

Yes	Child **currently** sexually aroused to thoughts or discussion of own sexual victimization experiences.
Possibly/ Partially	*May currently* experience sexual arousal to thoughts of own sexual victimization.
No	*Does not currently* experience sexual arousal to thoughts of own sexual victimization.

2.7. Impact of nonsexual victimization (current)

Yes	Child *is the victim* of a nonsexual abuse (ie physical, emotional abuse, neglect, or other nonsexual abuse) and *currently experiences* the negative emotional impact from this abuse (eg trauma, sadness, anxiety, etc.).
Possibly/ Partially	*May currently* experience the negative emotional impact of past nonsexual abuse, as outlined above.
No	*Is not currently* experiencing the negative emotional impact of nonsexual abuse or trauma history.

3.0. Family and environment

3.2. Family in denial (current)

Yes	*At least one* legal guardian who has contact with the child denies the child's sexual behaviours. Denial may be demonstrated through, but is not limited to: • Do not acknowledge problem sexual behaviours. • Unwilling to cooperate with treatment. • Do not take responsibility for changes that need to happen. • Know little about the sexual behaviours. • Not willing to supervise the child. • Do not believe the sexual behaviours took place. • Do not believe the behaviours were sexual in nature.
Possibly/ Partially	*At least* **one** legal guardian who has contact with the child *may* deny the child's sexual behaviours as listed above.
No	*No* legal guardians who have contact with the child deny the child's sexual behaviours as listed above. All legal guardians acknowledge the child's sexual behaviours.

3.3. Family instability (past 6 months)

Yes	Over the *past six months, two or more* indicators of family instability were present. Instability can include, but is not limited to: • A history of protective services. • Family disruptions (eg divorce, out of • Multiple parental figures. home placements). • Unexplained absent parent. • Strangers in and out of home. • Frequent residential moves. • Economic stressors. • No sense of predictability/orderliness.
Possibly/ Partially	Over the *past six months*, *one* family instability indicator was definitely present OR *two or more* indicators *may* have been present as outlined above.
No	Over the *past six months*, *no* family instability indicators were present.

3.4. Negative home environment (past 6 months)

Yes	Over the *past six months, two or more* factors indicating a negative home environment were present. A negative home environment may include, but is not limited to: • Unresolved abuse/trauma history. • Police involvement. • Poor housing. • Isolation from extended family. • Age inappropriate expectations. • Poor parenting. • Inadequate parenting. • Impaired attachment. • Stress. • Poor anger management. • Poor child management. • Inconsistent discipline/rules. • Alcohol/drug abuse. • Social services involvement. • Cultural conflicts. • Parents isolated from each other. • Child is caretaker. • Family turmoil/arguments/violence. • No sense of orderliness/predictability. • A guardian with psychiatric/emotional difficulties. • Poor communication.
Possibly/ Partially	Over the *past six months, one* negative home environmental factor was definitely present OR two or more factors *may* have been present as outlined above.
No	Over the *past six months, no* negative home environmental factors were present.

3.5. Parental/guardian rejection (past 6 months)

Yes	Rejecting behaviours have been directed at child by a parent/guardian, over the *past six months*. Rejecting behaviours may be indicated by, but are not limited to: • At least one guardian dislikes child. • Another child is favoured. • Guardian projects negative attitudes on to child. • Guardian is not involved in child's life. • Child is isolated within family. • No apparent emotional connection to any guardian. • Child told they are moving to another placement.
Possibly/ Partially	*May* have experienced rejecting behaviours over the *past six months*, as outlined above.
No	*No* known rejecting behaviours were present over the *past six months*, as outlined above.

4.0. Violence and control

4.1. Impulsivity (past 6 months)

Yes	Over the *past six months*, child has been impulsive or demonstrated poor self-control. Impulsivity and poor self-control can include, but are not limited to: • Acting before thinking. • Interrupting others. • Unable to wait turn.
Possibly/ Partially	Over the *past six months*, child *may* not have had very good self-control.
No	Over the *past six months*, child *has shown* good self-control.

4.2. History of nonsexual aggression (past 6 months)

Yes	Over the *past six months* child has been aggressive in a nonsexual manner. Nonsexual aggression can include, but is not limited to: • Poor anger control (ie rage, explosive, unpredictable anger, etc.). • Threatening. • Oppositional behaviours. • Demanding. • Cruelty towards people or animals. • Manipulative. • Age inappropriate temper tantrums. • Attacking others/fighting/hitting.
Possibly/ Partially	Over the *past six months*, child *may* have engaged in nonsexual aggression as outlined above.
No	Over the *past six months*, child *has not* engaged in nonsexual aggression.

4.3. Aggressive thoughts/fantasies (past 6 months)

Yes	Over the *past six months* child had aggressive (nonsexual) thoughts and/or fantasies. Thoughts and fantasies may be demonstrated through, but are not limited to: • Role-play of an aggressive fantasy. • Thoughts/fantasies of harming another. • Thoughts/fantasies of controlling others. • Thoughts/fantasies of aggressive retaliation. • Thoughts/fantasies of violent retaliation. • Play that suggests thoughts/fantasies of harming and/or aggression towards others.
Possibly/ Partially	Over the *past six months*, child *may* have had aggressive nonsexual fantasies or thoughts.
No	Over the *past six months*, child has *no known* aggressive nonsexual fantasies or thoughts.

4.4. Power-based beliefs (past 6 months)

Yes	Over the *past six months*, child has held views that support power-based beliefs and/ or behaviours. Power-based beliefs/behaviours could include, but are not limited to: • Believes that strength equals power. • Feels sense of entitlement due to gender. • Feels sense of entitlement due to strength. • Bullying. • Solves problems with power/strength. • Self-esteem is based on being powerful. • Feels that a lack of power is a negative trait. • Power/control/domination is important.
Possibly/ Partially	Over the *past six months*, *may* have held views that support power-based beliefs and/or behaviours as outlined above.
No	Over the *past six months*, *has not* held views that support power-based behaviours (outlined above).

5.0. Personal and interpersonal characteristics

5.1. Social skill deficits (past 6 months)

Yes	Over the *past six months*, child has experienced multiple (two or more) social skill problems/ deficits. Social skill problems may be evident through, but are not limited to: • Difficulties interacting with peers. • Few, if any, age appropriate friends. • Poor communication. • Socially inept. • Social isolation. • Age inappropriate interests. • Friends who get into trouble. • Lacks social confidence and/or competence.
Possibly/ Partially	Over *past six months*, child *may* have had a number of social skill problems or *definitely has* at least one social skills problem/deficit.
No	Over *past six months*, child has had *no* social skill deficits/problems.

5.2. Affective coping skill deficits (past 6 months)

Yes	Over the *past six months*, child has experienced affective coping-skills deficits. Deficits may include, but are not limited to: • Poor problem solving skills. • Poor emotion regulation. • Poor conflict management. • Cannot express emotions. • Withdrawing. • Easily frustrated. • Using aggressive or manipulative methods to solve problems. • Sexual self-stimulation following negative emotions.
Possibly/ Partially	Over *past six months* child may have had or has had some affective coping-skills deficits (see above).
No	Over *past six months* child has not demonstrated poor affective coping-skills and does not display deficits or behaviours noted above.

5.3. Poor self-esteem (past 6 months)

Yes	Over the *past six months*, child has had low-self esteem. Low self-esteem could be demonstrated through, but not limited to: • Negative self-statements. • Lacking goals. • Interpreting situations with negative self-conclusions. • Negative self-talk. • Lack of assertiveness. • No understanding of own needs. • No internal sense of self. • Feels incapable of positive or consistent action.
Possibly/ Partially	Over the *past six months*, child *may* have demonstrated low-self esteem. Low self-esteem may be demonstrated through, but is not limited to, those issues listed above.
No	Over the *past six months*, the child has *not* demonstrated poor self-esteem.

*Consider the next six months when answering the following intervention questions.

6.0. Intervention

6.1. Treatment/intervention* (next 6 months)

Yes	In the *next six months*, concerning treatment/intervention, child: • Has not responded to sexual behaviour specific intervention to date. • Will not engage in intervention sexual behaviour specific intervention. • Does not have access to sexual behaviour specific intervention. • Is or has been resistant to sexual behaviour specific intervention.
Possibly/ Partially	In the *next six months* child *may* be resistant to treatment/intervention as demonstrated above.
No	In the *next six months* child will *not* be or is not resistant to treatment/intervention as outlined above.

6.2. No parent/guardian treatment involvement* (next 6 months)

Yes	Over the *next six months*, no legal guardians/parents will be involved in child's sexual behaviour specific intervention/treatment.
Possibly/ Partially	Over the *next six months*, at least *one* guardian/parent will or might engage in their child's sexual behaviour specific intervention.
No	*All* legal guardians/parents are willing and interested in involvement in child's sexual behaviour specific intervention.

RSBP <12 summary coding form

Child ID _____

	Assessment 1 Date:			Assessment 2 Date:		
Static factors	Yes	PP	No	Yes	PP	No
1.0 Sexual behaviour characteristics						
1.1 Use of force/threat/violence						
1.2 Coercion/manipulation						
1.3 Pattern of sexual behaviours						
1.4 Penetration						
1.5 Sophisticated sexual behaviours						
1.6 Multiple types of sexual behaviours						
1.7 Victim selection based on vulnerability						
1.8 Sexual behaviour with animal						
2.0 Victimisation						
2.1 Victim of sexual abuse						
2.2 Arousal during own sexual victimisation						
2.3 Multiple sexual offenders						
2.4 Witnessed violence						
3.0 Family environment						
3.1 Poor family sexual boundaries/sexualised family environment						
Dynamic factors						
1.0 Sexual behaviour characteristics						
1.9 Sexual thoughts/fantasies						
1.10 Distorted sexual beliefs						
1.11 Denial						
1.12 Lacks understanding of consequences of sexual behaviours						
1.13 Opportunities for sexual behaviour						
2.0 Victimisation						
2.5 Trauma from own sexual victimisation						
2.6 Arousal to memories of own sexual victimisation						
2.7 Impact of nonsexual victimisation						

3.0 Family environment						
3.2 Family in denial						
3.3 Family instability						
3.4 Negative home environment						
3.5 Parental/guardian rejection						
4.0 Violence and control						
4.1 Impulsivity						
4.2 History of nonsexual aggression						
4.3 Aggressive thoughts/fantasies						
4.4 Power-based beliefs						
5.0 Personal and interpersonal characteristics						
5.1 Social skill deficits						
5.2 Affective coping skill deficits						
5.3 Poor self-esteem						
6.0 Intervention						
6.1 Treatment/intervention						
6.2 No parent/guardian treatment involvement						
Other:						
Other:						

**PP = partially/possibly present

Add any important information or more details regarding any of the above factors and the child.

CHAPTER 17

Biofeedback, Neurofeedback and Self Regulation

Robert E. Longo

This chapter has also appeared in the *International Journal of Behavioral Consultation and Therapy* under the title The Use of Biofeedback, CES, Brain Mapping and Neurofeedback With Youth who Have Sexual Behavior Problems, May 2011.

This chapter will address the use of Biofeedback, Cranial Electrotherapy Stimulation (CES), qEEG Brain Mapping, and Neurofeedback with young people who have sexual behavior problems. Current knowledge in neuroscience, trauma, theory, rational, and case examples will be addressed. The chapter will review selected biofeedback and neurofeedback protocols and their use in treating conditions common to young people with sexual behavior problems. Implications for the future will be discussed.

Introduction

During the early part of this decade, an increasing number of researchers, practitioners, and clinicians, within the field of assessing and treating sexually abusive and sexually aggressive behavior, among others, have begun to address the impact of trauma on the brain, especially in young people with sexual behavior problems, for example, Teicher (2007) Creeden (2006) Bengis and Cunningam (2006). This information and knowledge also has direct application to those young people who also have histories of abuse and/or neglect (see Ziegler (2002) Ogden, Minton and Pain (2006)). In particular the professionals listed above and others have addressed the impact on youth with sexual behavior problems and those who have been sexually abused. This is important because many young people with sexual behavior problems have a history of abuse and neglect.

Teicher (2008) notes that exposure to childhood abuse, particularly childhood sexual abuse, is a risk factor for development of impulse control disorders, and can lead to a cycle of violence and perpetration. Exposure to early stress can exert enduring effects on brain development that may underlie many of the consequences of exposure to

sexual abuse. Research indicates there are negative effects of childhood sexual abuse on development of the hippocampus, corpus callosum, prefrontal cortex and visual cortex.

Martin Kafka, MD, Clinical Associate Professor of Psychiatry at Harvard Medical School notes that the following are risk factors for sexual recidivism in adult males: negative mood states, mood disorder, ADHD combined subtype, PTSD, Conduct Disorder, and BiPolar Dysthymic Disorder. Kafka notes that 10–15 per cent of males with anxiety and/or depression had sexual risk-taking behaviors; and that 'mood and anxiety disorders may be so common among sexual offenders, that these conditions and their associated effects are not distinctly identified as correlated with recidivism'.

Trauma and its impact on the brain

Trauma resulting from early childhood abuse and neglect impacts the brain in a variety of ways. The Training and Research Institute, in Albuquerque, NM (2004) notes that childhood physical, emotional, sexual abuse and neglect can cause antisocial behavior by over-excitation of the limbic system; the primitive midbrain region that regulates memory and emotion, and the prefrontal cortex, which is associated with judgment, consequential thinking, and moral reasoning. They note, for example:

1. The left hemisphere is responsible for regulation and oversight of logical responses to a situation, and control and mediation of emotional responses generated by the right hemisphere.
   The impact of childhood abuse or neglect results in diminished control of emotional response, resulting in poor or inappropriate reactions to emotional situations, angry outbursts, self-destructive or suicidal impulses, paranoia, psychosis, and a tendency to pursue intense, ultimately unstable, relationships.
2. The prefrontal cortex is the internal editor of emotional states, consequential thinking,

moral reasoning, and reactions to emotional crisis.

The impact of childhood abuse or neglect results in increased potential for depression and delinquent and criminal behavior.

3. The corpus collosum creates communication between the right and left hemispheres.

   The impact of childhood abuse or neglect results in a significantly smaller corpus collosum, causing nonintegrated, inappropriate responses to everyday situations.

4. The temporal lobes regulate emotions and verbal memory.

   The impact of childhood abuse or neglect results in poor modulation of emotions, and an increased chance for temporal lobe epilepsy.

5. The hippocampus (part of the limbic system) is responsible for the formulation and retrieval of verbal and emotional memories.

   The impact of childhood abuse or neglect results in lower performance on verbal memory tests, possible continued mental problems, and concerns during the adult years.

6. The amygdale (also part of the limbic system) creates emotional content for memories, mediating depression, irritability, and hostility/aggression, and governing reaction and responses to fear.

   The impact of childhood abuse or neglect results in a significantly smaller amygdala raising the risk for depression, irritability and hostility/aggression, and is also responsible for incorrect emotional 'memories', absence of fear conditioning, and an increased chance of psychopathic tendencies.

7. The purpose of the cerebellar vermis is to modulate production and release of neurotransmitters, and has a significant number of receptor sites for stress-related hormones.

   The impact of childhood abuse or neglect results in an increase in potential risk for psychiatric symptoms such as depression, psychosis, hyperactivity, and attention deficits, and in rare cases, psychotic symptoms are possible.

For patients who suffer from trauma, depression, and other mental disorders, we now know that we can use cognitive behavioral therapy (CBT) and trauma-focused cognitive behavioral therapy (TFCBT) to reduce or even eliminate the need for psychotropic medications (Begley, 2007). CBT can:

(a) mute over-activity in the frontal cortex (while antidepressants often raise activity there)

(b) raise activity in the limbic system

(c) 'rewire' the brain to adopt new 'thinking circuits'.

In other words, one's own thoughts can virtually reshape one's emotions by redirecting one's own thought process, which in turn opens pathways for people to change their perceptions about themselves and others. This process is often referred to as 'mindfulness' (Siegel, 2007; Kabat-Zinn 2005).

The brain is often negatively impacted when a person is traumatised. Trauma can result from a variety of experiences, which include, but are not limited to:

- actual physical injury to the head or traumatic brain injury (TBI)
- neglect, physical abuse, sexual abuse
- exposure to traumatic events such as the death of a sibling or parent, the killing of a family pet or farm animal, natural disasters
- life-threatening experiences, among others

The use of effective treatments, however, helps the brain's response to trauma, and problematic thoughts, feelings, and behaviors that can be altered and changed from unhealthy responses to healthy ways of coping. When patients are diagnosed with PTSD, they are likely to have experienced terror and affect dysregulation (dissociation) immediately after the trauma (Siegel, 1999).

Biofeedback and self regulation

When using trauma-focused cognitive behavioral therapy, the treatment goal is to first teach affect regulation, and then begin Narrative Therapy with a focus on internal states awareness.* Traumatised patients and patients who suffer from stress-related disorders including insomnia, anxiety and depression can benefit from participation in peripheral biofeedback. Peripheral biofeedback may include learning self-regulation skills through the measurement and monitoring of breathing/respiration rate (RR), heart rate (HR), heart rate variance (HRV), skin conductivity level (SCL), and body temperature (thermofeedback).

Self regulation is important in working with traumatised patients because as the patient works through the trauma and works towards creating a

*http://tfcbt.musc.edu/

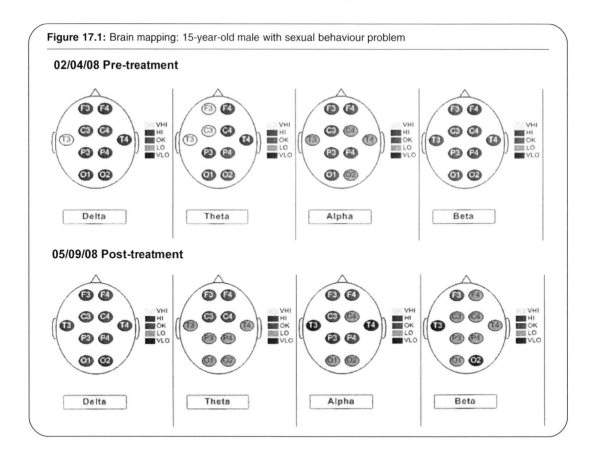

Figure 17.1: Brain mapping: 15-year-old male with sexual behaviour problem

new narrative, retrieving such memories can create both a psychological and physiological response. These responses can result in the patient shutting down during the session and not making further progress (Ogden, Minton, and Pain, 2006). The use of biofeedback, and self-regulation techniques assist the patient in coping with trauma and developing the skills that are necessary to remain in the 'Window of Tolerance' (Ogden, Minton, and Pain, 2006).

Figure 17.1 illustrates how peripheral biofeedback and cranial electrotherapy stimulation (CES) assisted a 15-year-old male patient who was diagnosed with ADHD and ODD (in addition to sexual behavior problems), and quantitative electroencephalograph brain mapping (qEEG)* revealed the patient had

---

*qEEG stands for quantitative electroencephalograph. Recorded from either 12 or 19-channels. The resulting EEG data are computer processed to provide a statistical analysis of brain electrical activity. In turn, these data are presented in various visual forms such as 'brain maps' and other images which can show the ways in which different areas of the brain are functioning.

ADHD, moderate depression, severe anxiety, and moderate learning disability.

The above figure is from pre-post brain mapping on a 15-year-old male with sexual behavior problems also diagnosed with ADHD and Oppositional Defiant Disorder (ODD). The patient participated in weekly biofeedback and CES sessions over a three-month period. Of significance is the lowering of Delta and Theta brain wave magnitude.

Biofeedback, cranial electrotherapy stimulation (CES), brain mapping and neurofeedback

Treatment benefits

Biofeedback has been around for approximately 40 years, and in recent years has gone through a 'renaissance' or resurgence. Many major hospitals and clinics, ie Harvard's Brigham and Women's Hospital and Duke University Medical Center now offer biofeedback to patients with a variety of physical and/or mental health concerns.*

Whether biofeedback actually teaches permanent skills remains unproven. However, the evidence and studies do suggest that therapy works to lower stress-related problems, including physical aches and pains. Evidence also indicates that biofeedback helps with non-stress-related conditions as well. A newer technique, neurofeedback or EEG biofeedback, appears promising for restoring normal brain wave function that has been disrupted by TBI, PTSD, severe migraines, and other disorders.

There is even some evidence that biofeedback and neurofeedback (a subset of biofeedback) can work with attachment disordered children, and that underdiagnosis of a mood or developmental disorder can lead to ineffective treatment. Anxiety disorders, traumatic disorders, and physiological factors must also be taken into account. Many of these patients are misdiagnosed with ADHD instead of addressing what may very well be behavioral disorders.†

The use of biofeedback to impact heart rate variability (HRV) through the practice of controlled breathing is becoming more popular and has a growing body of research and clinical evidence to support its benefits. Striefel (2008) notes, 'HRV serves as both a diagnostic marker of adaptability and health and as a treatment approach for a wide variety of client problems'.

The ethics of most, if not all mental health and physical health disciplines and those practitioners of biofeedback, are (and in most cases, state and/or federal regulations mandate as a patient's right) that patients have the right to be free from pain and anxiety in the shortest amount of time and through the use of the least intrusive methods. Thus these issues must be addressed in the patient's treatment plan.

More recently HRV has been used to reduce trauma-related symptoms, including depression in patients (Gevirtz and Dalenberg, 2008). The Trauma Research Institute protocol for Post Traumatic Stress Disorder (PTSD) treatment includes psychoeducation, Cognitive Behavioral Therapy (CBT), Acceptance and Commitment Therapy (ACT) and HRV Biofeedback. Karavidas

(2008) notes, 'autonomic nervous system (ANS) dysfunction is thought to play a significant role in depression. Prior research indicates that individuals suffering from depression often show decreased vagal tone, increased heart rate, fatigue, sleep disturbance, and sympathetic arousal.' Karavidas (2008) states:

> Biofeedback techniques are known to facilitate treatment for a wide variety of disorders with a psychosomatic component, including asthma, cardiovascular disorders, hypertension, cephalopathies, anxiety, and duodenal ulcers . . . Nevertheless, it remains unclear how the patient who has undergone training with such biofeedback techniques learns how to control his or her autonomic responses . . . Generally, the instructions given to such patients have been aimed at achieving a general state of relaxation in many cases by using progressive muscle relaxation . . . Some studies are now highlighting the importance of respiration in order to improve learning of biofeedback techniques.

What is biofeedback?

'Biofeedback is a non-invasive form of treatment. The therapist attaches sensors or electrodes to the body and these sensors provide a variety of readings – *feedback* – which is displayed on the equipment for the patient to see. The signals typically measure skin temperature, muscle tension and/or brainwave function. With this information, patients can learn to make changes so subtle that at first they cannot be consciously perceived. With practice, however, the new responses and behaviors can help to bring relief and improvement to a variety of disorders.'‡

Peripheral biofeedback is a non-medical technique in which people learn to use their own body's signals to improve their health. Biofeedback training teaches how to consciously change and control the body's vital functions that are normally unconscious, such as breathing, heart rate, blood pressure, and temperature through information provided by electronic devices/sensors that take readings through a software program. The process of learning to control these body functions gives the patient moment by moment information about their physiological conditions, of which they are normally unaware.

Biofeedback has been shown to be effective with many stress-related disorders and conditions that may be made worse under stress such as high blood pressure, muscle pain,

---

*The Benefits of Biofeedback. www.wilddivine.com newsletter 8/27/08. Wild Divine newsletter@wilddivine.com
†Alston, J.F. The complex issue of attachment disorders http://www.psychiatrictimes.com/display/article/10160/543268/26/08

‡Definition adopted by BCIA, AAPB and ISNR May 18, 2008.

migraine and tension headaches, and anxiety disorders, such as panic attacks, phobias, and obsessive–compulsive disorder. The biofeedback professional serves as a coach and the patient as the trainee. By teaching the patient the process of self-monitoring (becoming sensitive to and aware of one's stress patterns and symptoms), the patient develops skills for self-regulation (changing responses to decrease or eliminate discomfort and unpleasant sensations), which in turns results in the skill of self-regulation, providing the patient with a sense of self-control.

Patients are provided with the opportunity to learn basic biofeedback techniques through the use of biofeedback hardware and software (ie the Wild Divine Project® Healing Rhythms®*). The *Healing Rhythms* software guides the patient through 15 biofeedback and relaxation steps. Patients place sensors on the fingers of one hand which measure HR and SCL; both of which increase when the patient is stressed or anxious, and decrease as he/she becomes more relaxed. Another probe placed on the *middle section* of the *middle finger* measures skin temperature, which increases as the patient becomes more relaxed and less anxious. When training down headaches and migraines, for example, the thermometer probe is placed on the *middle section* of the *middle finger* of the *hand on the opposite side of the head/body where the patient is experiencing headache pain*. Patients are expected to practice their breathing and relaxation techniques each day.

How biofeedback works

Sensors are placed on the patient's fingers (an ear-clip sensor may also be used (ie with HeartMath) and the patient is then instructed to use relaxation, meditation, or visualisation to bring about the desired response, whether it is muscle relaxation, lowered heart rate, slower breathes, or lower temperature. The biofeedback device reports progress by changes in the vital signs being monitored. Peripheral biofeedback includes physical responses:

- thermal – skin temperature (thermofeedback) measured on hand or foot
- sweat gland activity – electrical conductivity of the skin, galvanic skin response (SCL, SCR, GSR)

*www.wilddivineproject.com

- heart rate – with an electrocardiograph (ECG) (HR)
- heart rate and blood pressure (heart rate variability (HRV)
- brain-wave activity, with an electroencephalograph (EEG)
- respiratory sinus arrhythmia is a noninvasive measure of vagal cardiac input, or RSA feedback (respiratory sinus arrhythmia feedback (RSA)†
- respiration – respiratory function-breathing patterns and rate, breaths per minute (BPM)
- muscular reactivity and tension, electromyography (EMG)

Biofeedback measures

Breathing rates, breaths per minute (BMR):

- Normal 12 BPM
- Range 4 (relaxed)–18 (tense/anxious) BPM
- Normal resting adult 10–18 BPM
- Anxiety 20–30 BPM
- Hyperventilation 57 BPM

Thermofeedback temperature: The measure of body temperature via the finger in degrees Fahrenheit or Celsius.

- 95 + F/35 + C is very relaxed
- 90–94/32.2–34.3 is calm/relaxed
- 80–90/26.6–32.2 is nervous
- 75–80/23.8–26.6 is tense/stressed
- <75/23.8 is very stressed and tense

Skin Conductivity Level (SCL) Galvanic Skin Response (GSR) or Skin Resistance Level (SRL): The measure of sweat and moisture in the fingers, the lower the measure the more calm and less anxious/stressed. Sweat glands are surrounded by blood vessels.

- Range: 2–100 microhms
- Stressed out: 20 microhms
- Relaxed baseline: 2–5 microhms

Coherence (Coh): Coherence is the interaction of the body's heart rate, SCL, and breathing which then registers in the brain as a relaxed state. To achieve good coherence the patient needs to have a Coh of .80 or higher, up to 1.00

†RSA is the natural cycle of arrhythmia that occurs through the influence of breathing on the flow of sympathetic and vagus impulses to the sinoatrial node (http://bio-medical.com/news_display.cfm?newsid=63)

Heart Rate Variance (HRV): During biofeedback when the heart rate becomes rested and even between beats; the body and mind are more relaxed and a smooth sinusoidal rhythm appears.

Conditions treated by biofeedback

Peripheral biofeedback is particularly useful and can help with stress-related conditions where there is sympathetic or adrenal stress. It is also useful for conditions where there is inadequate control over muscle groups or muscle dysfunction. Conditions treated with biofeedback include but are not limited to: stress, anxiety, depression, sleep disorders, headaches, asthma, muscle injury, pain relief, insomnia, TMJ, high blood pressure, digestive disorders, attention deficit disorder, irritable bowel syndrome, hyperactivity.

Cranial Electrotherapy Stimulation (CES)*

What is Cranial Electrotherapy Stimulation (CES)?

Cranial Electrotherapy Stimulation (CES) involves the use of the Alpha Stim 100®, a small hand-held device that delivers small electrical pulses, one milliampere (mA) or less, directly to the brain. Pulses are used to promote relaxation, sleep, and relieve some psychological and emotional conditions like depression and anxiety. CES electro-technology causes production or reduction of certain neurochemicals in the brain. For example, levels of norepinephrine and dopamine (that reflect relaxed mental and emotional states) can increase using CES technology, and biochemical compounds related to emotional stress can be seen to decrease. Cortisol is an important hormone (also know as the stress hormone) in the body and is secreted by the adrenal glands and involved in many functions including regulation of blood pressure. Cortisol is an important and helpful part of the body's response to stress. Higher and more prolonged levels of cortisol in the bloodstream (like those associated with chronic stress) have been shown to have negative effects. Cortisol† is involved in the following functions and more:

- proper glucose metabolism
- regulation of blood pressure
- immune function
- inflammatory response
- insulin release for blood sugar maintenance

Normally, it is present in the body at higher levels in the morning and at its lowest at night. Although stress isn't the only reason that cortisol is secreted into the bloodstream, it has been termed 'the stress hormone' because it's also secreted in higher levels during the body's 'fight or flight' response to stress, and is responsible for several stress-related changes in the body. Small increases of cortisol have some positive effects:

- heightened memory functions
- a burst of increased immunity
- lower sensitivity to pain
- helps maintain homeostasis in the body
- a quick burst of energy for survival

While cortisol is an important and helpful part of the body's response to stress, it's important that the body's relaxation response is activated so the body's functions can return to normal following a stressful event. Unfortunately, in our current high-stress culture, the body's stress response is activated so often that the body doesn't always have a chance to return to normal, resulting in a state of chronic stress. Higher and more prolonged levels of cortisol in the bloodstream (like those associated with chronic stress) have been shown to have negative effects, such as:

- impaired cognitive performance
- suppressed thyroid function
- blood sugar imbalances such as hyperglycemia
- higher blood pressure
- decreased bone density
- decrease in muscle tissue
- lowered immunity and inflammatory responses in the body, slowed wound healing, and other health consequences
- increased abdominal fat, which is associated with a greater amount of health problems than fat deposited in other areas of the body. Some of the health problems associated with increased stomach fat are heart attacks, strokes, the development of, higher levels of 'bad' cholesterol (LDL) and lower levels of 'good' cholesterol (HDL) which can lead to other health problems.

To keep cortisol levels healthy and under control the body's relaxation response should be

---

*http://alpha-stim.com/default.htm
†http://stress.about.com/od/stresshealth/a/cortisol.htm

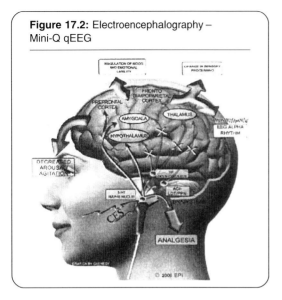

Figure 17.2: Electroencephalography – Mini-Q qEEG

Beta) in various parts of the brain. The EEG is a recording of the electrical activity of the brain from the scalp. Quantitative Electroencephalography (qEEG) is the measurement, using digital technology, of electrical patterns at the surface of the scalp which primarily reflect cortical activity or 'brainwaves'. A multi-electrode recording of brain wave activity is recorded and converted into numbers by a computer. These numbers are then statistically analyzed and are converted into a color map of brain functioning. qEEG provides a method to take EEG recorded from a variety of locations and statistically analyze the data to provide topographical maps as illustrated in the figures below. This output can be used to assess clients and develop Neurofeedback protocols. Learning to process and read qEEG reports typically takes years of experience.†

activated after the fight or flight response occurs. Patients can learn to relax their body with various stress management techniques (ie biofeedback) and through making lifestyle changes in order to keep their bodies from reacting to stress in the first place.

How does CES work?

The Alpha Stim 100®, has the proven ability to alter brain wave patterns through electronic stimulation. This stimulation is delivered through two small earclips (electrodes) attached to the ear lobes. The micro-current stimulation coaxes the brain into the desired state. Effectively, CES offers many benefits. All of these benefits are centered around the brain, which is in control of the rest of the body.* Figure 17.2 below illustrates how the *Alpha Stim 100* CES current enters, stimulates and activates the brain.

Electroencephalography – Mini-Q qEEG

Mini-Q qEEG

Electroencephalography (e-lec-tro-enceph-a-lo-graphy – EEG) is a neurological diagnostic procedure that records the changes in electrical potentials (brainwaves, Delta, Theta, Alpha and

Neurofeedback

Zalaquett and Bell (2008) note that neurofeedback, unlike medicines, when done properly has no negative physical side effects and the training appears to produce permanent alterations in learning and behavior. Some studies have shown that neurofeedback is linked to improved IQ scores‡ (see Fig. 17.3 below).

Figure 17.3 shows pre-post treatment mapping of a 51-year-old female with a recent TBI, and who was suffering with depression, mild anxiety and learning disability. After 26 sessions of neurofeedback, the patient had reduced magnitude. Pre-post IQ testing revealed that the patient had an IQ increase of 12 points. Elevated Beta at C3 and C4 (sensory and motor functions) reflect pain the patient has from a lower back injury. Elevated Beta at P3 and P4 likely indicate problem areas with self-boundaries, excessive thinking, vigilance personality, excessive self-concern, and victim mentality based upon the recent departure from an abusive relationship.

Neurofeedback, also called neuro-biofeedback or EEG biofeedback is a therapy technique that presents the patient with realtime feedback on brainwave activity, as measured by sensors on the scalp, typically in the form of a video display, and sound. When brain activity changes in the direction desired by the neurofeedback protocol,

---

*http://www.alpha-stim.com/default.htm

†https://www.newmind-apps.com/
‡http://www.coedu.usf.edu/zalaquett/n/neurofeedback.htm 8/26/08

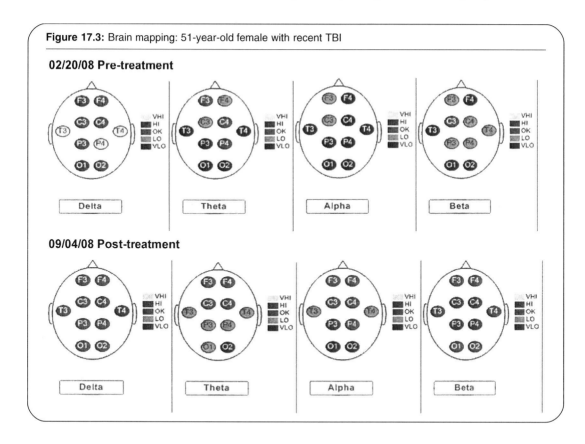

Figure 17.3: Brain mapping: 51-year-old female with recent TBI

a positive 'reward' feedback is given to the patient. Rewards/reinforcements can be as simple as a change in pitch of a tone or as complex as a certain type of movement of a character in a video game.

The most common and well-documented use of neurofeedback is in the treatment of attention deficit hyperactivity disorder. Multiple studies have shown neurofeedback to be useful in the treatment of ADHD. Other areas where neurofeedback has been researched include treatment of substance abuse, anxiety, depression, epilepsy, obsessive compulsive disorder (OCD) learning disabilities, bipolar disorder, conduct disorder, anger and rage, cognitive impairment, migraines, headaches, chronic pain, autism spectrum disorders, sleep dysregulation, post traumatic stress disorder (PTSD) and mild traumatic brain injury (MTBI).

Below are pre-post measures of magnitude qEEG. In qEEG brain mapping:

> ... the magnitude analysis system provides a reference database system that is tailored specifically for clinicians instead of researchers. Instead of using standard devi-

ations, the maps provide simple output indicating whether EEG is high or low in the various dimensions of analysis. The cognitive output automatically flags areas of possible problems based on correlations between map output and MRI research. Emotional output information provides similar information based on MRI research and standard neurology texts as well as clinical experience. Clinicians can see at a glance the salient issues likely to be present due to the EEG distribution as well as being provided with an appropriate protocol option.*

Magnitude is the most important reading, as it is the power of individual brain waves:

> Magnitude is used instead of power because most neurofeedback practitioners work with magnitude. Professionals feel it is important that they be able to easily refer to their statistics and see what the actual microvolt value when an area is indicated as high on the map. Magnitude is merely the average amplitude over time. The magnitude values in brain maps are based on a statistical sample in addition to being cross validated with the major databases. The meaning of high or low magnitudes varies with location and distribution. Learning to interpret their meaning takes considerable experience.†

---

* https://www.newmind-apps.com/
† https://www.newmind-apps.com/

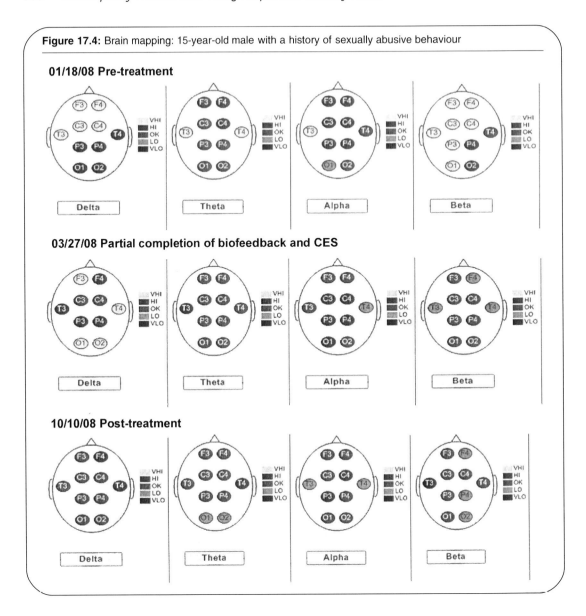

Figure 17.4: Brain mapping: 15-year-old male with a history of sexually abusive behaviour

01/18/08 Pre-treatment

Delta   Theta   Alpha   Beta

03/27/08 Partial completion of biofeedback and CES

Delta   Theta   Alpha   Beta

10/10/08 Post-treatment

Delta   Theta   Alpha   Beta

Figure 17.4 shows the brain mapping of 15-year-old male with a history of sexually abusive behavior and an admitting diagnosis of ADHD, PTSD, ODD. Patient completed 15 sessions of biofeedback with CES and 20 sessions of neurofeedback.

Figure 17.5 shows pre-post treatment effects of a 16-year-old male sexual abuser with an admitting diagnosis of PTSD and conduct disorder, after completing 15 sessions of biofeedback, CES, and nine sessions of neurofeedback.

Brain waves

Delta waves

Delta brainwaves are of the greatest amplitude and slowest frequency. They are typically irregular, and center around the range of 1.5 to 3 cycles per second. Deep dreamless sleep would take the patient down to the lowest frequency, typically, two to three cycles a second. These brainwaves occur during coma. Delta brainwaves are normally found in deep sleep and in 'normal' infants, and young children. Unhealthy Delta

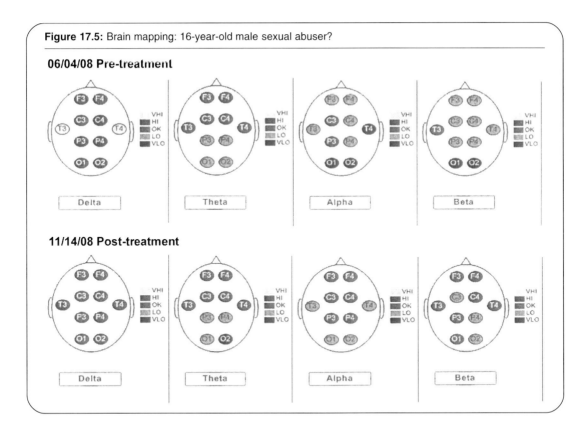

Figure 17.5: Brain mapping: 16-year-old male sexual abuser?

brainwave patterns often reduce one's ability to focus and maintain attention. They indicate an abnormality in an awake adult.

Theta waves

Theta brainwaves are typically of greater amplitude than Delta and are slow frequency. This frequency range is normally between 4–7 Hz, with a sinusoidal rhythm or/square top. Theta waves are usually suggestive of creativity, spontaneity, and distraction/daydreaming. A person who begins to daydream is often in a Theta brainwave state.

Alpha waves

Alpha brainwaves are the second highest frequency brainwave category (in order of frequency – the highest frequency being Gamma waves), and typically occur in a pattern of 8–12 cycles per second. Alpha represents non-arousal. Alpha brainwaves are slower and higher in amplitude. When an adult's eyes are closed, Alpha has the highest amplitude. Most of the recorded waves in a normal adult's EEG are the occipital Alpha waves, which are best obtained from the back of the head when the adult is resting quietly with the eyes closed but not asleep.

Beta waves

Beta brainwaves are present in normal waking consciousness. When the brain is aroused and actively engaged in normal mental activities, it generates Beta waves. Beta waves are of relatively low amplitude, and are the fastest of the five different brainwaves ranging from 13–30 Hz. Healthy levels of Beta enable analytical problem-solving, decision-making and sound judgments, and are characteristics of a strongly engaged mind. Some neurotherapists have observed that SMR (LoBeta) brain wave frequencies (12–15 cycles per second) make individuals feel more present, and in the moment.

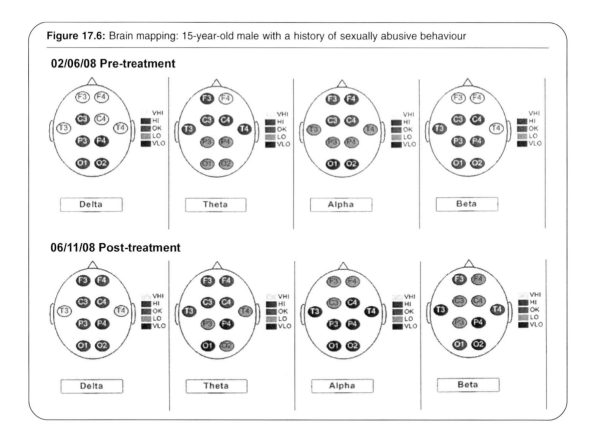

Figure 17.6: Brain mapping: 15-year-old male with a history of sexually abusive behaviour

The application of biofeedback, CES, and neurofeedback with sexually abusive youth

Working with young people who have sexual behavior problems is no different than working with other patients when the practitioner is considering the use of biofeedback, CES, qEEG brain mapping, and/or neurofeedback. The majority of patients coming into our stress reduction clinic and biofeedback lab are residential male adolescent patients between the ages of 11 and 17 who have sexual behavior problems. As noted above, most of these patients have attentional problems, learning disabilities, depression and/or anxiety.

To date our clinic has conducted over 110 brain mapping sessions on 85 patients of which 63 are adolescents and over 35 are young people with sexual behavior problems. Every brain map conducted on a young person with sexual behavior problems has revealed that the patient suffers from either depression, anxiety or both.

While biofeedback and neurofeedback hold much promise for working with this population, no one therapy, treatment or intervention can claim a perfect success rate. The case illustrations (Figs 17.6 and 17.7) below, demonstrate some of the differences between patients.

Figure 17.6 illustrates pre and post treatment mapping on a 15-year-old male with a history of sexually abusive behavior and an admitting diagnosis of ADHD, PTSD, ODD, and CD. At the onset of treatment and during the first several months, the patient demonstrated non-compliant behavior and severe acting-out behavior resulting in the need to place him in therapeutic holds. Towards the end of treatment the patient was engaged in intensive therapy dealing with family issues related to his being adopted. Patient completed 15 sessions of biofeedback and CES and approximately 12 sessions of neurofeedback.

Patient completed 15 sessions of biofeedback and CES and 9 sessions of neurofeedback, prior to dropping out of neurofeedback. Patient's behavior continued to worsen and he requested to be reinstated in neurofeedback. The first brain map revealed that the patient had mild attentional problems, severe depression, and

Figure 17.7: Brain mapping: 15-year-old male with a history of sexually abusive behaviour

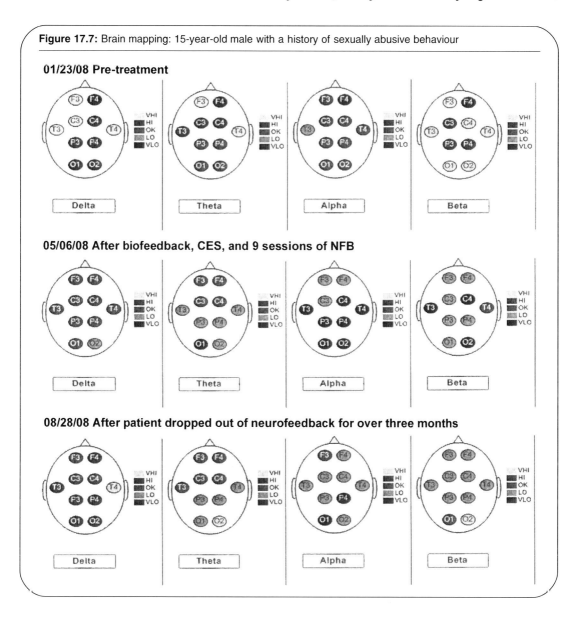

moderate anxiety. Follow-up mapping after biofeedback, CES and 9 sessions of neurofeedback revealed that he had no attentional problems, however his depression and anxiety remained the same at that time. The third mapping on 08/28/08 shows how the patient relapsed due to a variety of emotional problems that occurred prior to his request to re-enter treatment.

Implications for the future

The US Food and Drug Administration (FDA) notes that biofeedback is a standard relaxation 'therapy'. Biofeedback and neurofeedback are primarily operant conditioning, and reinforcement of a naturally occurring event. Patients can reinforce the desired brain activity with EEG biofeedback. When patients participate in neurofeedback, they often experience significant change in 15–40 sessions and the average change occurs in 20–25 sessions.

Neurotherapists and other mental health professions are turning to the above discussed treatments and therapies in increasing numbers. Some in psychiatry are suggesting that brain mapping is so important, that patients should not be prescribed psychotropic medications until a qEEG brain map has been conducted (Walker, 2008). While brain mapping cannot be considered as diagnostic at this time, those working in this field are increasingly hopeful that brain mapping diagnostics is not too far from being a reality. Given the benefits of biofeedback and the treatments discussed above, there is no good reason why these treatments should not be used with any youth who has emotional, cognitive and/or behavioral problems. Ethically, we will become more challenged by our disciplines and specialties if we do not turn to these methods of helping others.

Combining therapies

Combining therapies to assist patients in learning to relax and decrease stress-related responses including anxiety and depression can further facilitate recovery. For example, patients who received a combination of EMG biofeedback and CES showed greater improvement that those who underwent biofeedback alone.* Neurofeedback should generally not be done without other supportive therapies.

Generally, there are no contraindications for using any of the above treatments and therapies with adults, young people, and specifically young people with sexual behavior problems. There are benefits to combining CES and biofeedback and combining biofeedback with neurofeedback. Any of these treatments and therapies will enhance sex offense specific treatments as well as the use of CBT, TFCBT and other treatment modalities and therapies as described above.

Summary

While this chapter has limits to the degree to which any of the above treatments and therapies can be described in detail, it serves as an

overview and hopefully an impetus for professionals who treat young people with sexual behavior problems to consider expanding their practice and services to include them.

Research has shown that the majority of young people who have sexual behavior problems do not differ significantly from those youth who become involved in the juvenile justice system and/or have other delinquent behaviors (Hunter (2006); Chaffin and Longo (2004); Longo (2003); Longo and Calder (2004); Prescott and Longo (2006)). However, research does show that many of these young people do suffer from depression and anxiety among other mental health concerns and problems. The use of biofeedback, CES, brain mapping and neurofeedback can further assist these patients in working toward healthier lifestyles and full recovery.

References

Begley, S. (2007) *Train Your Mind Change Your Brain: How a New Science Reveals Our Extraordinary Potential to Transform Ourselves.* New York: Ballentine Books.

Bengis and Cunningam (2006) Beyond Psychology: Brain-Based Approaches that Impact Behavior, Learning and Treatment. In Longo, R.E. and Prescott, D.S. (eds.) *Current Perspectives: Working With Sexually Aggressive Youth and Youth with Sexual Behavior Problems.* Holyoke, MA: NEARI Press.

Chaffin, M. and Longo, R.E. (2004) Guidelines for Placement within a Continuum of Care for Adolescent Sex Offenders and Children with Sexual Behavior Problems. *Family Violence and Sexual Assault Bulletin.* 20: 3.

Creeden, K. (2006) Neurological Impact of Trauma and Implications. In Longo, R.E. and Prescott, D.S. (eds.) *Current Perspectives: Working with Sexually Aggressive Youth and Youth with Sexual Behavior Problems.* Holyoke, MA: NEARI Press.

Gevirtz, R. and Dalenberg, C. (2008) Heart Rate Variability Biofeedback in the Treatment of Trauma Symptoms. *Biofeedback.* 36: 1, 22–3.

Hunter, J.A. (2006) Understanding Diversity in Juvenile Sexual Offenders: Implications for Assessment, Treatment and Legal Management. In Longo, R.E. and Prescott, D.S. (eds.) *Current Perspectives: Working with Sexually Aggressive Youth and Youth with Sexual Behavior Problems.* Holyoke, MA: NEARI Press.

---

*Biofeedback and electromedicine reduce the cycle of pain spasm pain in low back patients. Research abstracts http://wwwbiof.com/onlinestore/alpha/zimmerman-spasm.asp 8/26/08

Kabat-Zinn, J. (2005) *Coming to Our Senses: Healing Ourselves and the World through Mindfulness.* New York: Hyperion.

Kafka, M.P. April 10, 2008. *Hypersexuality and Sexual Offending.* MASOC/MATSA Joint Conference, Marlboro, MA.

Karavidas, M. (2008) Heart Rate Variability Biofeedback for Major Depression. *Biofeedback.* 36: 1, 18–21.

Longo, R.E. (2003) Emerging Issues, Policy Changes, and the Future of Treating Children with Sexual Behavior Problems. In Prentky, R.A., Janus, E.S. and Seto, M.C. (eds.) *Sexually Coercive Behavior: Understanding and Management.* Annals of the New York Academy of Sciences. Vol. 989.

Longo, R.E. and Calder, M.C. (2004) The Use of Sex Offender Registration with Young People who Sexually Abuse. In Calder, M.C. (ed.) *Children and young people who sexually abuse: New theory, research and practice developments.* Lyme Regis: Russell House Publishing.

Longo, R.E. (2004) An Integrated Experiential Approach to Treating Young People who Sexually Abuse. In Geffner, R. (ed.) *Sex Offenders: Assessment and Treatment.* San Diego, CA: Family Violence and Sexual Assault Institute.

Longo, R.E. and Prescott, D.S. (2006) Introduction. In Longo, R.E. and Prescott, D.S. (eds.) *Current Perspectives: Working with Sexually Aggressive Youth and Youth with Sexual Behavior Problems.* Holyoke, MA: NEARI Press.

Ogden, P., Minton, K. and Pain, C. (2006) *Trauma and the body: a sensorimotor approach to psychotherapy.* New York: W.W. Norton.

Pastor, M.C. et al. (2008) The Influence of Respiration on Biofeedback Techniques. *Applied Psychophysiology and Biofeedback.* 33: 49 51.

Prescott, D.S. and Longo, R.E. (2006) Current perspectives: Working with young people who sexually abuse. In Longo, R.E. and Prescott, D.S. (eds.) *Current Perspectives: Working with Sexually Aggressive Youth and Youth with Sexual Behavior Problems.* Holyoke, MA: NEARI Press.

Siegel, D.J. (1999) *The developing mind: toward a neurobiology of interpersonal experience.* New York: Guilford Press.

Siegel, D.J. (2007) *The mindful brain: reflection and attunement in the cultivation of well-being.* New York: W.W. Norton.

Striefel, S. (2008) Ethical Aspects of Heart Rate Variability Biofeedback. *Biofeedback,* 36: 5–8.

Training and Research Institute (2004) The Neurobiology of Child Abuse (Poster) Albuquerque, NM.

Teicher, M.H. (2007) *Keynote: Childhood Abuse, Brain Development and Impulsivity.* MASOC/MATSA Joint Conference, 12 April 2007, Marlboro, MA.

Teicher, M.H. (2008) *Keynote: Child Abuse, Brain Development, and Impaired Impulse Control.* NAPN 2008 Conference. Rocking the Boat without Sinking the Ship: Integrating the New into Existing Systems. 19 May 2008. Portland, OR.

Walker, J. (2008) The Value of Quantitative EEG in Clinical Psychiatry. Letter from AAPB Neurofeedback Division President. *Neuroconnections,* October, p. 4.

Ziegler, D. (2002) *Traumatic Experience and the Brain: A Handbook for Understanding and Treating those Traumatized as Children.* Phoenix, AZ: Acacia Publishing.

CHAPTER 18

Responding Early to Concerning Sexual Behaviour in Children and Young People With Learning Disabilities: A Step by Step Approach to Initial Assessment

Joanne Butterworth and Tim Plant

Introduction

Our experience suggests that change is required at both a procedural and practice level, in order to better respond to the needs of children and young people with learning disabilities presenting with potentially harmful sexual behaviour. In a climate where practitioners are feeling vulnerable about secured employment, funding is being withdrawn and specialist services decommissioned, it is important that we have a clear pathway for the identification, assessment and intervention of this vulnerable group. We need to accurately identify those young people who require help and services to address their concerning sexual behaviour at the earliest opportunity, rather than simply defer until it has become more acute and problematic and the child protection and/or criminal processes invoked. In order to achieve this goal we have to collate and organise the evidence which requires much more than a trawl of the available research. We have to draw upon the practice wisdom of frontline staff dealing with such issues on a daily basis. It also requires a much more strategic inter-agency approach that moves beyond the common practice of excluding young people from individual agency remits. This occurs when young people are under the umbrella of children's services and can also extend to the transition from children to adult services. All agencies have a duty of care and are responsible for safeguarding children and young people, which is why a multi disciplinary approach is required, whether we work in health, education or social care.

A typical scenario

In our experience, caregivers are often unprepared for the young person's chronological sexual development. The young person is not prepared for the physical and emotional changes they are experiencing and neither is prepared for how this affects the child/young person's behaviour. Care provision comes from a number of different agencies who may not respond with appropriate and/or consistent boundaries and support, and subsequently it gets framed as a behavioural issue. Alternatively, it may be framed as a health issue, with referrals to health professionals who may explain sexual development to parent/carers, but may not have the capacity or skills to intervene. This results in the young person not having access to the information they need to learn appropriate behaviour and their right to sexual identity/expression not being affirmed. They are not able to learn via their peers and may pick up developmentally inappropriate information from visual media. Sex education is not accessed from a young age in schools, due in part because its delivery remains controversial and risky; parent/carers are not confident/comfortable/prepared in how to approach sex education in a way the young person with learning disabilities will understand. Ultimately the behaviour is not viewed as a developmental need, or as a cue to provide information, guidance and support. The behaviour presenting as inappropriate or concerning then continues through puberty and early adolescence; as a result of their developmental delay, parents/carers may not foresee the risks inherent in allowing unsupervised contact between learning disabled adolescents and younger children; 'normal' curiosity is aroused in the learning disabled adolescent and sexual exploration occurs with a chronologically younger child. They may then come to the attention of services, but there is still no appropriate and consistent response. Opportunities are often missed to take appropriate actions regarding assessment, risk management, parental guidance and tailored education, and the problem becomes chronic as the behaviour continues. 'Victims' are likely to be younger or other vulnerable children with whom the adolescent has contact and a chronic pattern of behaviour could subsequently be established. A contributory factor here may again lie in the lack of self-protection knowledge and skills amongst this population. There are likely to be no legitimate outlets for healthy sexual expression because this is not recognised as normal in children and young people with learning disabilities, so the behaviour escalates. An incident then takes place that registers the behaviour as a safeguarding or criminal matter; the behaviour then becomes labelled as abusive. Outside assessment is sought due to the lack of local capacity and appropriate interventions; further assessment and specialist treatment is recommended which brings with it a hefty cost implication. When this crosses over between children's and adult's services, the issue of who takes responsibility for funding may also lead to inaction.

Cross-agency issues

Literature has identified that there is a variation in views and responses of professional services working with this population and a lack of consistency in responding to 'risky' behaviours. Sexual behaviour (of people with learning disabilities) can be misunderstood, minimised or ignored depending on the context and attitudes of the professionals responding (Vail, 2002). It has been documented that although in some cases early warning signs had been noted by schools, no intervention was forthcoming until a criminal act of abuse had been committed (see Fyson, 2007). This has also been replicated in statutory services, which often only become aware of incidents once an alleged 'victim' has been in contact with the police (see Fyson, 2007a). Others by way of contrast emphasise the tendency of some, to see all sexual behaviour of people with learning disabilities as inherently problematic (Heyman and Huckle, 1995) and subsequently service intervention is requested at a much earlier stage than for the non-disabled population. It has long been our view that the child/young person is not helped by a strategy of ignoring the concerns until they go away because they rarely do. In addition, the impact of the behaviour on others most certainly cannot be ignored. A lack of appropriate responses to initial concerns relating to sex and sexuality of children and young people with learning disabilities can potentially result in the following:

- An escalation of the behaviour causing concern
- the behaviour being perceived as normal by the individual (and others).
- An avoidance of care-givers (in the various environments) taking responsibility.
- Responses to behaviour(s) becoming more punitive as the individual gets older and makes the transition into adulthood, when such behaviour is perhaps less tolerated.

Many assessment models are 'offence focused', with their starting point being that an offence has already been committed. We would advocate the use of a process which seeks to explore and understand any emerging behaviours in children relating to sex and sexuality, which are of concern. Such early identification lends itself to a preventative option. It is not designed to dismiss such behaviours or conversely over-react or respond punitively, but rather to be a more proactive approach designed to address the behaviour of concern, whilst also avoiding unnecessary labelling wherever possible. It is likely to be detrimental to outcomes for the young person in the long run if an assessment framework is applied which has been developed from an evidence base of adult sexual offending behaviour. Applying offending models to vulnerable young people who have not been convicted of sexual offences is likely to begin a labelling process. Evidence of this came to light during the course of our involvement with one particular young person for whom the label 'offender' had a serious detrimental impact. Whilst there had not actually been any criminal proceedings, case files stated that he had 'committed sexual offences'. This had been drawn from an assessment carried out initially which stated that he had had sex with a sibling on many occasions. Here, 'sex' had been used interchangeably with 'intercourse'. During our work with this young person it was also established that he did not fully understand what sex actually was. Subsequent assessments took this as fact and therefore the starting point upon which to base their interventions. Even so the consequences for this young person included the following:

- Exclusion from school (due to decisions about risk and supervision).
- Period of time out of formal education.
- Adverse affect on subsequent educational opportunities.
- Restricted access to 'youth' and 'housing' services.

- Contact with sibling curtailed.
- Interventions restricted to working on a one to one basis with adults only.

In addition, it has been documented that children and young people with learning disabilities are more vulnerable to experiencing abuse for a whole host of reasons (see Westcott and Cross, 1996 for a detailed discussion). And whilst there is no direct or linear relationship between experiencing abuse and going on to perpetrate acts of sexual abuse, it should be noted that high levels of abuse are evidenced in almost all samples of sexual abusers (Vail, 2002). In light of this, researchers have highlighted that there is a need for earlier and more effective intervention for both children and young people with learning disabilities who have been victims of abuse and for any who show signs of developing sexually inappropriate behaviour (Keeling, Beech and Rose, 2007).

Current assessment challenges

Further to the issues raised via our earlier scenario, Brown and Barrett (1994) have highlighted a series of dilemmas practitioners are faced with when considering such situations. These are noted below, along with additional challenges we have encountered in our practice and which we aim to tackle through an initial assessment of sexual concerns:

- What is our starting point, bearing in mind that some children/young people look highly pathological on paper? Has the individual already been labelled as a 'perpetrator' or 'predator' for example?
- What is 'sexual' behaviour?
- Which of the behaviours are in the person's control?
- What is difficult (concerning/problematic) and for whom?
- Is there agreement about what healthy sexuality might look like?
- Is some behaviour considered a 'problem' because the person has a learning disability?
- How do we involve the child/young person meaningfully in the assessment process?
- How do we achieve the balance between rights and protection?
- What is our duty of care, remembering we are accountable for acts of commission and omission?

- Have assumptions been challenged?
- How do we achieve a balance between under- and over-responding?
- Are definitions and language used precise and clearly delineated?
- Are concepts derived from adult sex offender behaviour being applied to interpret a child/young person's behaviour?
- Has safety planning been based in a developmental context?
- Has consideration been given to the particular adversities the individual may experience during the transition to sexual maturity?

Development of the I-ASC (Initial Assessment of Sexual Concerns)

With the above in mind, we have developed the I-ASC in response to situations we have been asked to address in our practice.

- It is a guide for health and social care practitioners to plan initial responses to concerning sexual behaviour in children and young people with learning disabilities. By this we refer to children and young people with a full scale IQ of 70 or below. We feel it is complimentary to and can be used alongside existing child protection procedures and the Common Assessment Framework (CAF). We foresee it being used by experienced health or social care professionals who have a lead role in case-working with children and young people with learning disabilities. It does not require specialist training or knowledge in sexual offending.
- It is a combined assessment and planning tool. It follows a step by step approach through which the concerning behaviour is explored in the context of the young person's development and their home, education and wider community environments. The I-ASC may prove sufficient to address the issues, provided that the behaviour(s) present risks that can be managed within existing resources.
- It is designed to establish the reason/s that may underlie these behaviours and the factors that may sustain them; the reasons for concerns where the behaviour is developmentally normal, consensual and non abusive; and support needs that are sexual in nature, producing an action plan to address them.
- It is designed to help identify gaps in service provision and the individual's support

networks and also the impact these have on that person, in order to build upon the capacity of existing local services and supports. We feel strongly that local resources and existing local services should be used wherever possible.

- It is suggested that the I-ASC should be completed within four to six weeks wherever possible and should enable teams to establish facts, reach reasoned conclusions and take appropriate actions.
- It is intended that information gathered via the I-ASC would clearly highlight the need for further assessment where appropriate. Again it is worth noting, that if behaviour has been left to develop into something more chronic or intransigent, this is more likely.
- It is part of a process that can move beyond the I-ASC to initiate more detailed assessments where needed, which we are developing concurrently: ASC (Assessment of Sexual Concerns) and BASK (Baseline Assessment of Sexual Knowledge).

The following circumstances should warrant consideration for initiating the I-ASC:

- As a response to the earliest signs of 'problematic' sexual behaviour.
- As a response to low-level 'nuisance' sexual behaviour.
- As a response to an emerging pattern of problematic sexual behaviour.
- Where a team is looking for specific direction within a local safeguarding process.
- Where concerns may have been investigated by the police but where it is viewed as not being in the public interest to prosecute.
- As a response to anxieties about sexual development where the behaviour is developmentally appropriate and non-harmful.
- As a response to early indications of sexual maturity that raise concerns for others, for example not knowing how to explain andr deal with menstruation, wet dreams or masturbation.

Overview of the I-ASC process

Step One – Defining the problem

1. Checklist

One of the first things that needs to happen, is to establish whether the behaviour in question is likely to be normal and healthy, concerning, or

abusive, with reference to objective standards (an evidence base). The concern for example may be related to an underlying fear or anxiety on behalf of a parent/carer, that relates to their own cultural or religious beliefs. Our standards and values, however, are the same for all children and young people, regardless of their culture or religion. Similarly, concerns may relate to misunderstandings about children's sexual development and/or negative attitudes and values about the rights of children with learning disabilities. There also appears to be limited understanding amongst practitioners about what is or is not normal or healthy for different ages (Calder, 1997, 2001). Our starting point was therefore to trawl the existing evidence-base, to identify whether any useful assessment tools were already available. We located the following instruments that have been developed specifically to assess the sexual behaviour of children and young people: the Child Sexual Behaviour Inventory (CSBI) (Friedrich, 1997) and the Child Sexual Behaviour Checklist (CSBCL) (Johnson, 1998). Hackett (2001) has also written about a continuum of sexual behaviours covering four stages of children/young people's sexual development, from young preadolescence through to older adolescence. For ease of reference, we have attempted to combine the above to form a checklist covering ages from birth to 18. It is intended as a guide only; children develop at different rates and sexual behaviour needs to be placed in a context. We hope to offer the assessor some starting points in relation to what may be considered 'normal' sexual behaviour. This stated, as Johnson highlights, 'If a child (or young person) engages in most or all of the behaviours, (listed below as 'normal') this may raise concern'. In the absence of checklists researched/designed specifically for application to children and young people with learning disabilities, we are left with a default position which has its advantages and disadvantages. On the one hand, we should exercise caution when making direct comparisons between the two populations. For example, we speculate that significant differences between young people with learning disabilities and their non-learning disabled peers are likely with regard to consenting sexual relationships as they reach sexual maturity. On the other hand, we feel the way in which all children and young people explore/experience their bodies physically is comparable. We recommend the assessor consults the chart that depicts the child's chronological age initially, but if their behaviour does not fit at all with those described reference be made to the checklist prior to that. This should give a better sense of the child's behaviour in a developmental context.

Checklist of normal sexual behaviour – children (0–5 yrs)

- explores own and other children's bodies
- age two or above, touches/simulates their own genitals in private
- age two to four, interest in looking at other children's genitals
- age two to four, touches own and other children's bodies in play/games (eg doctors and nurses)
- touches private parts of familiar adults and children other than in play/games
- likes being nude and showing own genitals to others
- takes advantage of opportunities to look at naked people
- boys have erections
- general interest in differences between the sexes
- touch between children is light-hearted and unplanned (may giggle if an adult enters the room)
- touch between children is easily distracted by adult redirection
- asks parents/carers where babies come from; interested in having/birthing a baby
- interested in bathroom/toilet activities of others
- age four to five, can become shy/embarrassed about bodies/sex
- age four to five, may demand more privacy
- uses 'rude' words for toileting/sexual functions
- interested in own faeces
- puts something into genitals/anus once for curiosity/exploration
- acts out roles of mum/dad

Checklist of concerning sexual behaviour – children (0–5 yrs)

- touches body parts of children of different ages/sizes/stages of development
- use of coercion/force/manipulation in touch
- sexual interest predominates over other interests

- touches/stimulates own genitals in public after being told repeatedly to stop
- child shows worry, fear, anger or shame about touching behaviour
- hurts own genitals by touching them
- continued interest in genital differences despite all questions being answered at the child's level
- touches private parts of unfamiliar children/adults and continues to touch despite being told not to
- asks/demands children/adults touch the child's genitals
- tries to disguise genital touching of others as accidental
- stares at nude people despite being told not to
- asks/forces others to undress
- sexual knowledge too great for their age
- boys with continuous/painful erections
- repeated public nudity/refusing to put clothes on
- secretly exposes private body parts in public
- unusual/obsessive interest in toilet/bathroom activities
- interest in having/birthing a baby persists after several weeks; fear/anger expressed in relation to babies/birthing/intercourse
- persistent use of rude words for bathroom/sexual function after being told to stop and repeated reprimands
- repeatedly smears/plays with faeces despite reprimands
- puts objects into own genitals/anus more than once; puts objects into the genitals/anus of others; force or coercion associated with this behaviour to self/others
- simulated sexual intercourse with other children clothed; simulated or real sexual intercourse with other children unclothed; oral sex

Checklist of normal sexual behaviour – children (6–10 yrs)

- both interest and embarrassment about sexual matters
- age five or more, private masturbation
- plays 'sex' games with peers in school, eg kiss – catch
- asks questions about genitals/breasts/intercourse/babies
- age eight or more, interest in mechanics of sexual intercourse
- interest in bathroom/toilet activities of others
- uses 'rude' words for bathroom/sexual functions

- interested in others bodies, eg playing doctors
- interested in having/birthing a baby
- shows genitals to other children
- interested in urination/defecation
- touches/stimulates own genitals when going to sleep/tense/excited/afraid
- acts out roles of mum/dad
- thinks children of opposite gender are 'gross'/'smelly'
- talks about sex/sexuality with friends and talks about having boy/girlfriends
- wants privacy in bathroom or when changing
- likes to hear/tell jokes and obscenities (within cultural norms)
- looks at nude pictures
- sex/sexuality are features of play with same age friends
- draws genitals on pictures of human nude figures
- pretends to be opposite gender
- compares genitals with peer-aged friends
- interest in touching private parts of same age children or being touched by same age children
- kisses familiar adults/children
- looks at others' private parts
- boys have erections
- puts objects in to own genitals/rectum for the physical sensation/curiosity/exploration
- interest in animals' sexual reproduction
- age nine plus, boys may ejaculate (depending on development/onset of puberty).

Checklist of concerning sexual behaviour – children (6–10 yrs)

- fear/anxiety expressed regarding sexual topics; repeated questions about sex; sexual knowledge too great for age
- spying on others; use of bathroom/toilet; refusing to leave others alone in bathroom
- continues to use 'rude' words for bathroom/sexual functions following parent/carers attempts to stop this
- plays 'doctors and nurses' games repeatedly even if told not to – forcing others to play or remove clothes
- boy continues to make believe he is having a baby; fear/anxiety regarding babies/intercourse
- wants to be nude/expose self in public places and this persists following attempts to stop it
- repeated play/smearing with faeces; purposely urinating on furniture/floor
- continues to touch/stimulate genitals following attempts to stop it; rubs genitals on furniture or

objects or people; touches/stimulates genitals to exclusion of normal childhood activities
- imitates sexual intercourse with other children/dolls/toys whilst clothed
- simulates sexual intercourse unclothed with other child; actual sexual intercourse with another child; forcing sexual intercourse with another child
- hurts other gender children; uses 'bad language' against other child's family
- gets in trouble due to repeated sexual talk
- becomes very upset if observed changing clothes; aggressive/fearful in demand for privacy
- telling sexual/obscene jokes repeatedly; making sexual sounds repeatedly
- continued fascination with nude pictures; viewing nude pictures whilst masturbating
- plays sex/sexual games with older/younger children; any element of force or coercion in such play
- drawing genitals on clothed figures; large genitals depicted; depictions of sexual intercourse, group sex, sadism, masochism
- plays male/female roles in sad/angry/aggressive manner; 'hates' own/other sex
- stares at nude people; asking others to take clothes off; attempts to forcibly undress others
- child appears unable to stop self doing sexual things
- child's sexual behaviour directed towards adults
- other children complain about child's sexual behaviour
- sexual behaviour in public
- threats/anger associated with sexual behaviour
- shame/anxiety/guilt associated with sexual behaviours

Checklist of normal sexual behaviour – children (10–14 yrs)

- masturbation with orgasm and, age 13+, sexual fantasies; frequent masturbation in young men
- confusion/anxiety/embarrassment related to sexual matters/puberty
- increasing sexual attraction to same/opposite sex
- increasing interest/consciousness of own appearance
- wide range of sexual behaviours ranging from holding hands to sexual intercourse within boyfriend/girlfriend relationships

(remembering, however, that intercourse is illegal for under 16s and therefore local policy/guidelines will need to be applied)

Checklist of normal sexual behaviour – children (14–18 yrs)

- consensual sexual relationships between young people are common, in stable relationships/'one night stands'
- approximately 50 per cent of this population are sexually experienced/active sexually
- may experience overwhelming sexual feelings
- sexual talk with friends/same age peers
- use of sexual swear words/jokes
- interest in erotic material and use of this to masturbate
- consensual kissing, fondling, touching genitals
- mutual masturbation with same/opposite sex
- consenting sexual intercourse with partner around same age
- confusion/worry about sexual matters
- anxiety about own bodies
- anxiety about own masturbation habits.

Checklist of concerning sexual behaviour – children (10–18 yrs)

- indiscriminate sexual behaviour (ie makes no distinction about when/where/who with)
- compulsive sexual behaviour
- violence/aggression accompanying sexual behaviour
- indecently exposing self to others and where this continues after attempts to stop it
- sexually rubs self against others bodies
- makes obscene phone calls
- public masturbation
- excessive masturbation that stops them doing day to day tasks
- exposes other young person's genitals following attempts to stop it and where this involves force
- uses pornographic material depicting violence/children/animals
- has sexual conversations or sexual contact with younger or vulnerable children
- touches/tries to touch another person's genitals without consent
- sexual threats to another person
- forces another to engage in sexual behaviour, sexual assault, rape
- any sexual contact with animals
- genital injury to self or others.

2. Chronology

The chronology should give detail of formative events in the child/young person's life to date. It should provide a historical context to the current concerns and should therefore include all concerns expressed about their sexual development, physical development (including evidence of puberty where appropriate) and behaviour relating to sex and sexuality. Note, too, any other significant behavioural concerns and all the sources providing information, including the nature of the concerns and subsequent responses. It is also useful to highlight interventions that have previously been implemented to help establish what worked/did not, in order to inform the best way forward. The chronology will be significant in helping to identify whether the behaviour is new or part of an established pattern and help inform appropriate interventions. This chronology can also be used as an 'easy reference' at the interim multi-disciplinary meeting (see Step Six).

Established or chronic behaviours are more difficult to address through behavioural or therapeutic interventions and may highlight historical child protection concerns or help indicate the effectiveness of an intervention.

3. Statement about the behaviour

By pulling together factual information from the checklist and chronology, a definitive statement can now be produced regarding the concerns. This will help set the agenda for the interim planning meeting. This statement should only use objective and factual language that can be backed up by evidence. Subjectivity and conjecture should be avoided. If information cannot be supported with evidence, or if it is in dispute or is simply unknown, then this should be documented. In our experience, factual evidence is often missing or incomplete. If facts are not established at the time, it is often very difficult thereafter to pull evidence together. People should be prompted to describe only what they saw and not the reason why they thought it was happening. Where an account has been given second-hand, this should be recorded and clearly distinguished from first-hand accounts. How this information was disclosed and to whom must also be noted. Factors such as the comprehension, memory or suggestibility of witnesses with learning disabilities for example, must be taken into account. If there are any doubts at all about the information or how it was elicited, including the skills of the interviewer, it is important to go back and check. Legally, special provision has to be made for the communication needs of a witness or alleged victim lacking capacity. However, when the alleged perpetrator has a learning disability there is no similar requirement for provision to be made. It is important to be mindful that information drawn from interviews may be made under duress or coercion for example.

Obtaining the perspectives of the key people involved is essential. It is extremely important to record, with dates, who provided the evidence, their name, title and relationship to the child/young person. Any discrepancies between sources, with particular reference to those from the same environment, should also be noted.

The statement should include:

- A description of the behaviour; where and when it happened/happens; how long it has been happening for; how often it happens and how long it lasts.
- Whether the behaviour is developmentally normal or concerning (from the checklist).
- Antecedents to the behaviour, that is, what happened immediately before the behaviour took place; information should be included about the environments in which the behaviour happens; for example, other people present, what was going on at the time and information about the child/young person's physical/emotional and behavioural state immediately before the behaviour occurred; a review of antecedents may indicate what factors are significant to triggering the concerning behaviour.
- Consequences, that is, what happened immediately after the behaviour; for example, what was said to the child/young person by way of a response; behaviours can be reinforced by positive consequences. Also, how the young person presented and their reaction afterwards.
- Any previous or current management strategies used; the level of success and any reason for discontinuing/amending them.

4. Initial risk assessment

Applying a risk assessment framework will help to establish a baseline against which the efficacy of subsequent interventions can be judged. All the information needed for the risk assessment comes from the previous steps. A risk assessment should be completed for each concern as below, using a standard risk assessment framework. We have adapted a standard risk assessment format to include concerns about sexual behaviours. The main elements are as follows:

- Identify the impact of the behaviour for the child/young person themselves (and others). The impact can be represented by physical, psychological or financial harm; by loss of amenities/opportunity and by social stigma. Rate the severity and score it on a scale of 1–3 with 1=low, 2=medium 3=high.
- Assess the likelihood of the behaviour happening again with the current levels of support and score it on a scale of 1–3 as above.
- Multiply the two values to give a score between 1 and 9, with 1–3=low risk, 4–6=medium risk and 7–9=high risk.

Step Two – Identifying what support is available, as represented by professionals, existing assessment and frameworks

1. Who can help?

In any local authority there is a wealth of specialist knowledge to be utilised, from health, education and social care. As a result, a range of theoretical perspectives, including psychodynamic, developmental, cognitive and behavioural, can be drawn upon. The list below includes professionals whose training and experience reflects these diverse perspectives and it has been our experience that most practitioners are keen to share their expertise for this purpose:

- education – teachers, educational psychologists, special educational needs co-ordinators (SENCOs)
- health – clinical psychologists, learning disabilities nurses, psychiatrists, community paediatricians, psycho-sexual counsellors, young persons' sexual health services
- allied health professionals – speech and language therapists, occupational therapist/physiotherapist
- social care – social workers

2. What guidance or information is needed from them?

A number of education, health or social care professionals will either currently be working with the child/young person or will have been involved in assessing them in the past. Written permission will be required from parents/carers to allow them to share this information. A list of professionals should be compiled who are then contacted and asked for help in completing the initial assessment and consideration of what information is shared at this point and issues of confidentiality discussed. It should be ascertained that information from their assessments is up-to-date and that they still feel it is valid. Where necessary, reassessment should be requested. The attendance and/or contribution of a specific person at the interim planning meeting may also be important in order to contribute to the decision-making process. There will be a range of formal assessments and reports, including Common Assessment Frameworks (CAFs), core assessments, Statements of Special Educational Needs (SSENs), Individual Education Plans (IEPs), care plans, psychometric assessments etc. If the reports are complex and technical, individual practitioners should be asked to provide an explanation in lay terms such that the child/young person's parent/carer could understand. A bullet-pointed summary may also be requested if reports are extensive.

3. Existing policy/procedure

Processes that devalue people with learning disabilities are evident during childhood. Practitioners will benefit in this regard from having a policy framework for reference to statements about rights and values. It will be necessary to include consideration of all environments that the child/young person accesses.

Consideration of inter-agency governance is needed. If key members of the multi-disciplinary team have different governance arrangements for example, and these are not mutually compatible, this needs to be highlighted as an organisational risk through appropriate governance arrangements (such as Local Safeguarding Children's Boards). It is important to be clear about child protection procedures and policy on sexuality specifically; for example, the child/young person's school should have a policy on sex and relationship education. If there are no organisational or local policies providing guidance for practitioners, it may be necessary to seek good practice advice from national bodies and this should also be highlighted as an organisational risk as above.

Step Three – Understanding the capability of the child/young person

It is important to explore what the diagnostic label of learning disabilities means for the particular child as it relates specifically to their capabilities. Each child is unique. Every child with a learning disability has a different pattern of strengths, abilities and needs and they have all had different formative experiences cumulating in different potentials for learning, growth and development. Implicit in the label 'learning disability' is the fact that they have significantly impaired ability to learn new and complex information and achieve independence in social functioning when compared with their age equivalent peers. In an attempt to understand the child/young person's capability, the I-ASC includes the following:

- The child/young person's learning disability as described in the formal assessments (noted above): it is common for children to be described as having a spiky developmental profile, characterised by a pattern of relative strengths and weaknesses. It should not be assumed that competence in one area of functioning will be mirrored in others. Many children and young people with learning disabilities also have other physical disabilities or sensory impairments; it is also helpful to summarise these in lay terms.
- Details about how the child/young person communicates; this is often explained as expressive (what they communicate to others) or receptive (what they can understand from others' communication). Methods may include spoken language, sign language or standardised alternative communication systems, whilst some communicate through idiosyncratic gesture and behaviour and may be very reliant on others to interpret or anticipate their needs. This is one area where expert advice from a speech and language therapist is likely to be necessary. Teachers and parents should also be asked to add information about the child's communication in school and at home. It is often the case in our experience, that the same communication support is not available across all the environments the child accesses. Speech and language therapy is in short supply nationally and alternative communication systems used at school may not necessarily be used at home. It

is also our experience that children/young people often do not have a sufficient vocabulary to allow them to explain what has happened or indeed is happening to them, particularly where they use alternative communication systems. This is of great concern and must be addressed when taking steps to keeping children and young people safe; this includes for instance, feelings and emotions, the names of private body parts and sexual behaviours ranging from normal/healthy through to abusive.

- Details of how the young person describes and explains the behaviour about which there are concerns: the young person's own account of the behaviour and the reasons/explanations for it should be included where this has already been established. We would not recommend that assessment with the young person is undertaken at this stage, however, unless this has been carefully planned. The BASK (Baseline Assessment of Sexual Knowledge) which we are also developing, is a detailed individual assessment involving the young person from the outset. It is useful early on in the BASK process, to check that accounts provided by key people in the I-ASC correspond and are not in conflict with those shared by the young person. It is also important to ascertain the outcomes the young person would want to see happen.
- Identification of chronic or current health problems that may be relevant to understanding the sexual behaviour: for example, bladder or bowel problems and/or pain or discomfort in the genitals, anus or breasts. One should be aware that some medications prescribed to manage behaviours in children with learning disabilities may affect sexual function.
- Questions relating to what is known about the young person's social skills: how they express their feelings and emotions and their ability to recognise and understand the emotions of others. Cognitively, many children with learning disabilities will struggle to understand another person's perspective. Interpersonal relationships rely on emotional feedback from others. Children on the autistic spectrum in particular may have a significantly impaired social functioning and be unable to recognise and interpret peoples' facial expressions. We should not attribute negative intentions to children who are not able to show empathy to

the emotional distress of others, but rather seek to understand their need for support to negotiate such difficult interactions.
- Information about the young person's knowledge of:
  - their own bodies in relation to important abstract concepts such as public and private
  - social and legal rules like 'right and wrong'
  - consent – including their ability to understand and give consent to touching, both with regard to self and others
- Details too about what opportunities, both formally and informally, the child/young person has, which enables them to learn healthy and appropriate sexual behaviour: it is important to guard against making children/young people feel it is wrong to show interest in this area of their development, which is after all, a natural experience of childhood.
- Consideration of whether there is evidence or indication that the child has been exposed to any form of abuse or neglect, which includes any experience of bullying or victimisation.
- Exploration of what the parents/carers and other key people feel the child/young person is gaining from the behaviours. It also encourages the person completing the assessment to compare and contrast their explanations. Differences in attitudes may already have impacted on how the parent/carers support the child and subsequently have already played a role in shaping the concerning behaviours. It would be useful to record if there is any recognition of what different needs the behaviour meets and if any particular practitioner or care-giver offers insights that could be followed up as part of the action planning.

Step Four – Understanding the capacity of the child/young person's family

We need to understand the concerning sexual behaviour in the context of the child/young person's family life. Key to this is the parent/carer's understanding of the child/young person's developmental support needs and their capacity to address the behaviours. The following questions have been included by way of addressing this:

- How do the parent/carers describe and explain the concerning behaviours?

- Do they share the same degree of concerns with each other and the wider team surrounding the child?
- What have they done so far to address the concerning behaviours and what measures have they taken to keep the young person and others safe?
- What do the parent/carers do to help the child/young person learn appropriate personal, social and sexual behaviour and self-care, taking into account the child/young person's disabilities?
- Is there any history of sexual/domestic abuse or drug/alcohol/substance misuse within the family, including the parent/carer's own experience?
- Where relevant, how is the relationship described between the child/young person and their siblings and are there any concerns in relation to the development and/or behaviour of the siblings?
- Are there any issues affecting the capacity of the parents to work with the wider team to address the behaviours?
- What outcomes would the parent/carers want to see happen in response to the concerning behaviour?
- Do the parent/carers have/feel they have sufficient information, resources and support in order to meet the sexual health needs of the child/young person? If not, what do they need and how will this be provided?

Step Five – Understanding the capacity of the child/young person's wider support networks

An understanding of the behaviour within the wider community and other environments frequented by the young person will also help to contextualise it. School staff and religious/youth leaders, for example, will have key information about the range of behaviours presented by the young person in each setting. It is also imperative that consistent messages are received by the young person with learning disabilities across the different environments they access. Differences in sexual behaviour between environments may be significant in indicating causative factors and perpetuating/maintaining factors. If a young person does not display the behaviour in one environment, reasons for this will require explanation in order that lessons can be learned by establishing the factors that promote positive

behaviour. Differences could indicate, for example, the ability of the young person to learn or apply rules about social behaviour. Through assessment a better understanding of the dynamic relationship will be gained, between the child, their environment and behaviours presented. It is therefore essential that the capacity of all agencies/establishments to meet the sexual health needs of the young person should be addressed. We have included the questions below in an attempt to do this:

- How do the young person's school teachers and key people from other agencies describe and explain the concerning behaviours that have happened whilst the young person has been in their care?
- What have they done so far, both proactively and reactively, to address the concerning behaviours and what measures have they taken to keep the young person, and others safe?
- As an organisation, what does each agency do to proactively manage interpersonal behaviour and promote appropriate sexual behaviour by young people with learning disabilities?
- Are there any religious and/or cultural beliefs which may have an impact on the young person's sexual behaviour?
- What outcomes would people from school/agencies involved want to see happen in response to the concerning behaviour?
- Do individual people/agencies involved have/feel they have sufficient information, resources and support in order to meet the sexual health needs of the young person? If not, what do they need and how will this be provided?

Interaction between the young person and their environment

To understand the behaviour, we need to understand individual and environmental factors and the interaction between the two. If an environment works to effectively meet needs, then it is less likely for the problematic behaviour to occur. Environments can enable or disable people with learning disabilities, so it is important to include analysis of those the young person accesses. Characteristics of positive enabling environments include:

- parents/staff feel confident and competent to respond to a young person's sexual development

- evidence of policies, procedures and training
- supportive culture from management and colleagues to address issues
- commitment to affirm or support safe and healthy sexual development
- young person's developmental needs are understood
- inter-agency agreement with young person's family about their needs and how to meet them
- rules about public and private behaviour are clear and explicit
- access to privacy is acknowledged as a basic need
- attempts to enquire about or explore own sexuality are responded to in safe and developmentally appropriate ways

Characteristics of negative or disabling environments include:

- uncertainty about how to respond to needs relating to sexuality, sexual development or interpersonal behaviour
- no evidence of policies, procedures and training
- unsupported staff
- negative attitudes about rights to sexual personhood
- limited understanding about young person's developmental needs
- culture of high tolerance to risk and/or poor practice
- lack of understanding regarding age/developmentally appropriate material
- confusion/disagreements between carers about young person's abilities and developmental needs
- families set inappropriate boundaries
- unhealthy/problematic behaviour is tolerated, reinforced or even encouraged
- rules about privacy are not taught and young person has limited access to privacy

Individual characteristics vary from person to person and include cognitive, physical, psychological, emotional, attitudinal and experiential elements. Some of these elements are more likely to be associated with negative or unhealthy behaviour, including:

- negative experiences, including abuse/victimisation
- low expectations of interactions with others
- poor attachment
- poor adult role models

- relatively poor communicative/interpersonal skills
- lack of empathy or understanding of other's viewpoints
- inability to comprehend abstract social and legal rules
- limited ability to retain information in memory
- poor self-esteem
- limited ability to inhibit impulses

Other elements are likely to be associated with positive or healthy behaviour and include:

- positive experiences
- positive expectations of interactions with others
- positive/healthy attachment
- positive adult role models
- relatively good communicative/interpersonal skills
- able to empathise or understand others' viewpoints
- ability to comprehend abstract social and legal rules
- ability to retain information in memory
- high self-esteem
- ability to inhibit impulses

Step Six – Interim planning meeting

At this point, sufficient information ought to have been gathered to enable the questions, 'should we be concerned?' and 'what do we need to do next?' to be answered. We advocate holding an interim planning meeting with the parent/carers and key people from the multi-agency team. The goals of the meeting are to draw conclusions about:

- the nature of the concerns
- the efficacy of responses to the concerning behaviour
- the impact on those involved
- the implication/s of any differences in perspective
- the support available and any gaps in provision

Through sharing the assessment information we can draw on the skills, experience and knowledge of multi-agency/disciplinary colleagues to help reach conclusions about the behaviours and to gain everyone's cooperation and support to address them. The people invited to the meeting should provide varied personal/professional perspectives and a working knowledge of the young person. The outcome of the meeting should be to agree an interim support plan that manages risks and affirms rights as below.

Take actions to protect from harm

Workers need to review the risk assessment and identify any areas of highest risk as well as identifying all people at risk. From the risk assessment you will have identified the personal and environmental setting conditions in which the behaviour is most likely to occur. These need to be addressed and in the short turm this may mean reducing the young person's opportunities. The balance you should find is having more proactive strategies in place than reactive strategies. Have plans for how you will manage at the first point where you feel that the concerning behaviour is likely to occur (for example, re-direction, distraction, stimulus change, incompatible alternative activity). Have any outstanding issues affecting inter-agency governance been highlighted? And what actions are to be taken and by whom to address these where there are general child protection issues that may affect others?

Take actions to affirm rights

Important issues for all parties to consider include:

- How are the young person's needs for an appropriate sexual outlet being supported?
- How is the young person going to be supported to develop the knowledge, skills and attitudes they need in order to express their sexuality in healthy and appropriate ways?
- How will the rights of vulnerable young people be maintained in relation to confidentiality?
- Have we effectively found a balance between promoting the young person's rights (to sexual expression) and managing the risks that their behaviour presented to themselves and others?

Share the responsibility

All efforts should be made to reach a consensus of opinion about the behaviour and its management. However, if this cannot be achieved and there remain significant differences of opinion, it may be necessary to seek further consultation. As a group and based on the information available, there is a need to make a statement about the level of concern and the probable explanation/s. These statements must be reviewed/revised according to changes in evidence. Below are some possibilities:

- The child/young person's behaviour is of high concern because it is sexually abusive to other children, for example.
- The child/young person's behaviour is of medium concern because there is an established pattern of problematic sexual behaviour, for example.
- The child/young person's behaviour is of low concern because it is developmentally normal, for example.

This is not an exclusive or exhaustive list but the following may help to frame explanations for the behaviours of concern:

- The child has/may have been sexually abused and they are acting out/modelling the behaviour of others ('abuse-reactive').
- They have/may have been exposed to age/developmentally inappropriate experiences and are acting them out.
- They have/may have seen or heard age/developmentally inappropriate material and are acting this out.
- Their family or other carers have/may have set inappropriate boundaries and this behaviour is ignored, tolerated or even encouraged.
- They have/may have been discouraged from developing healthy and appropriate behaviours in response to sexual maturation and a pattern of problematic behaviour has become established.
- The young person is sexually maturing and this is an early attempt at expressing this in the absence of adequate support.
- The behaviour is developmentally normal and is appropriate, but it
  - transgresses the social or religious beliefs of others
  - challenges attitudes about the sexuality of children/young people
  - challenges attitudes specifically about the sexuality of children/young people with learning disabilities.

Conclusion

Empowering children and young people to achieve a positive identity is the goal of any organisation and this should include 'sexual' identity. The way in which agencies, practitioners, and parent/carers interpret their role with regard to this, significantly influences the opportunities that are available to children and young people. Addressing issues relating to sex and sexuality continues to present many challenges, particularly when it relates to children and young people with learning disabilities. We have highlighted the need for a specific response by practitioners to this challenging area of practice where we understand a gap in provision currently exists. We have advocated a role for initial assessment as a reactive response within a wider proactive strategic framework. The approach outlined, offers a way through which these aims can be achieved within existing resources. Services for children and young people should do more to anticipate the specific developmental needs of this population and should be commissioned and reviewed on this basis. There are likely to be sufficient resources in every area represented by the skills and knowledge of front line practitioners. It is our view that Local Safeguarding Children's Boards (LSCB) should be instrumental in setting a strategy; that resolves multi-agency governance issues such as policy, training and supervision for practitioners as well as support for parent/carers.

References

Brown, H. and Barrett, S. (1994) Understanding and Responding to Difficult Sexual Behaviour. In Craft, A. (ed.) *Practice Issues in Sexuality and Learning Disabilities*. London and New York: Routledge.

Calder, M.C. (1997) *Juveniles and Children Who Sexually Abuse: A Guide to Risk Assessment*. Lyme Regis: Russell House Publishing.

Calder, M.C. (2001) *Juveniles and Children Who Sexually Abuse: Frameworks For Assessment*. 2nd edn. Lyme Regis: Russell House Publishing.

Friedrich, W. (1997) *Child Sexual Behaviour Inventory Professional Manual*. Odessa, FL: Psychological Assessment Resources.

Fyson, R. (2007) Young People with Learning Disabilities who Sexually Harm Others: The Role of Criminal Justice within a Multi-Agency Response. *British Journal of Learning Disabilities*, 35, 181–6.

Fyson, R. (2007a) Young People with Learning Disabilities who Sexually Abuse: Understanding, Identifying and Responding from within Generic Education and Welfare Services. In Calder, M.C. (ed.) *Working with Children and Young People Who Sexually Abuse: Taking The Field Forward*. Lyme Regis: Russell House Publishing.

Hackett, S. (2001) *Facing The Future: A Guide for Parents of Young People Who Have Sexually Abused*. Lyme Regis: Russell House Publishing.

Heyman, B. and Huckle, S. (1995) Sexuality as a Perceived Hazard in the Lives of Adults with Learning Difficulties. *Disability and Society*, 10: 2, 139–55.

Johnson, T.C. (1998) *Understanding Children's Sexual Behaviours: What's Natural and Healthy*. 1101 Fremont Avenue, Suite 101, South Pasadena, CA 91030.

Johnson, T.C. and Doonan, R. (2005) Children with Sexual Behaviour Problems: What Have We Learned in the Last Two Decades? In Calder, M.C. (ed.) *Children and Young People Who Sexually Abuse. New Theory, Research and Practice Developments*. Lyme Regis: Russell House Publishing.

Keeling, J.A., Beech, A.R. and Rose, J.L. (2007) Assessment of Intellectually Disabled Sexual Offenders: The Current Position. *Aggression and Violent Behaviour*, 12, 229–41.

Vail, B. (2002) An Exploration of the Issue of Sexuality and Abusive Behaviour Amongst Adolescents who have a Learning Disability. *Child Care in Practice*, 8: 3, 201–15

Westcott, H. and Cross, M. (1996) *This Far and No Further: Towards Ending the Abuse of Disabled Children*. Birmingham: Venture Press.

CHAPTER 19

Reducing Shame and Increasing Guilt and Responsibility With Adolescents who Have Offended Sexually: A CBT-Based Treatment Approach

James R. Worling, Nina Josefowitz and Melissa Maltar

Introduction

Shame that is often experienced by adolescents who offend sexually can be detrimental to the treatment process. Heightened shame can lead to increased defensiveness, denial, victim-blaming, anger, and social isolation. Shame can also interfere with the adolescent's capacity to examine the sexual offending and accept responsibility. Although most authors stress the need to reduce the debilitating levels of shame experienced by youth who offend sexually, there is little guidance in the literature for how this can be accomplished. In this chapter, we present a four-stage approach to reducing shame that is based on cognitive behavioural therapy (CBT) principles. The goal is to help adolescents move from a position of shame (eg 'I am a horrible person') to a position of guilt and responsibility (eg 'I did a horrible thing'). The four stages of treatment include building trust, differentiating between the person and the behaviour, processing the sexual offending, and developing guilt and responsibility.

Shame vs. guilt

Given the understandably negative societal view of sexual offending, it is not surprising that many adolescents who have offended sexually will feel some degree of shame and guilt as a result of their offending behaviours; particularly once the behaviour has been brought to light. Shame and guilt are negative emotions that share a number of common features. For example, both are self-conscious emotions, involve negative evaluations of the self, and typically result from a personal failure or the transgression of a moral code (Lewis, 1971; Tangney, 1995; Tangney and Dearing, 2002). Furthermore, shame and guilt both originate from an individual's negative evaluation of their behaviour in specific situations that are usually interpersonal (Covert et al., 2003; Tangney and Dearing, 2002).

Despite these similarities, shame and guilt are distinct emotions that differ considerably with respect to the thoughts, feelings, and underlying motivating factors (Tangney, 1995; Tangney and Dearing, 2002). Guilt is an emotion that occurs when you evaluate your behaviour (or failure to act) negatively (Tangney, 1995; Tangney and Dearing, 2002). Although guilt can lead to considerable personal discomfort, one's overall sense of self is not negatively impacted. The focus of guilt is on the behaviour that one engaged in – not on the self. Guilt-based cognitions following the commission of a sexual offence may include thoughts such as, 'I have really hurt him', 'I made a big mistake again', or 'I did something really disgusting'. Guilt is frequently associated with a sense of regret and remorse. There is often a focus on how others may have been impacted by the behaviour, and there is motivation to acknowledge responsibility and repair the damage (Tangney and Dearing, 2002).

Shame, on the other hand, involves a negative evaluation of the whole self – not just the behaviour (Lewis, 1971; Tangney and Dearing, 2002). Shame is typically characterised by a global negative self-evaluation that involves (i) intense pain, discomfort, and anger (ii) a desire to avoid further exposure, and (iii) a feeling of being inadequate and unworthy (Blum, 2008). Shame-based cognitions following a sexual offence may include thoughts such as, 'I am a pervert', 'I'm a disgusting person', or 'I am a failure'. Feelings of shame involve an assumption that others will negatively evaluate both the behaviour as well as the whole person and that the individual would no longer be accepted into their social community if the behaviour were known. Heightened levels of shame are associated with a number of psychological difficulties including depression, hostility (directed at self and/or others) social anxiety, self-harm, and reduced self-efficacy (Covert et al., 2003; Stuewig and McClosky, 2005). Furthermore, given that shame is fuelled by real or imagined negative appraisals by others, shame motivates individuals to deny, avoid, or hide (Tangney and Dearing, 2002) and interferes with an individual's capacity for intimacy and empathy (Nathanson, 1992).

Shame and guilt in individuals who offend sexually

Previous treatment approaches with individuals who offend sexually have been based on the belief that shame could actually serve as an aversive stimulus to punish deviant sexual fantasies and urges (eg Maletzky, 1991; Server, 1970). Although there is no empirical evidence that shame-based interventions are efficacious with adolescents who offend sexually, approximately 18 per cent of treatment programs in North America (surveyed in 2000) indicated that they used shame-based approaches to address deviant sexual arousal (McGrath, Cumming, Burchard, Zeoli and Ellerby, 2010).

There is a general consensus in the literature, however, that the shame experienced by individuals who have committed a sexual offence actually *inhibits* the treatment process (Association for the Treatment of Sexual Abusers, 2003; Bumby, 2000; Bumby, Marshall and Langton, 1999; Jenkins, 2005; Marshall, Anderson and Fernandez, 1999; Proeve and Howells, 2002; Ward et al., 2004). Indeed, shame following sexual offending is frequently associated with victim-blaming, retaliatory anger, decreases in self-esteem, reduced victim empathy, social withdrawal (Bumby et al., 1999), minimisation and denial, and self-harming behaviours (Jenkins, 2005). It is very difficult in therapy to help an adolescent to examine the situations, thoughts, feelings, and body responses that were occurring both prior to and during the sexual offending if they are also experiencing heightened shame. To reduce the risk of a sexual reoffence, adolescents need to examine their sexual offending in therapy so that sexual offence-prevention plans can be tailored to their unique risk factors. Heightened levels of shame can interfere considerably in this process and, ultimately, perpetuate the risk of reoffending.

By contrast, guilt is seen by most theorists to be a protective factor for individuals who have offended sexually. In particular, guilt – the belief that one has done something wrong and caused harm – will motivate the individual to take corrective steps and repair the damage. Several authors have stressed the need to help those who have offended sexually to separate their behaviour (committing the sexual offences) from their overall sense of identity (Bumby et al., 1999; Jenkins, 2005; Marshall et al., 1999; McAlinden, 2005). In this way, treatment assists the individual to move from a position of shame to a position of guilt (Proeve and Howells, 2002).

Despite this consensus in the literature, however, there is very little guidance for how clinicians can address the shame related to sexual offending. Although Jenkins (2005) does not differentiate between shame and guilt, he described an approach to working with youth who have offended sexually that involves highlighting differences between their actions and their personal ethics. Jenkins stressed the need for therapists to be supportive, patient, and affirming, and he stressed the need to work with the shame experienced by family members. In their article regarding shame and guilt in those who sexually assault children, Proeve and Howells (2002: 664) suggest that it would be 'important in therapy to reduce the focus on the self through the eyes of others and to increase self-esteem'.

Treatment overview

The treatment approach to reduce shame experienced by adolescents who have offended sexually is outlined below. The treatment approach is based on cognitive behaviour therapy (CBT). CBT is currently the dominant orientation of the majority of treatment programs for adolescents who have offended sexually (McGrath et al., 2010). For example, CBT is used to address a number of treatment targets including social skills development, affect regulation and expression, and posttraumatic distress (Worling, 2004). One of the main principles of CBT is that individuals' emotional and behavioural reactions to situations are mediated, or influenced, by their thoughts. The client and therapist collaboratively explore the relationship between feelings, physical reactions, behaviours and thoughts and use the understanding to develop and implement treatment goals. Treatment typically targets either cognitive or behavioural interventions (see Friedberg and McClure, 2002, for a more

---

Figure 19.1: Stages of therapy to address shame in adolescents who have offended sexually

---

Stage 1: Building trust and developing a collaborative therapeutic relationship

Stage 2: Differentiating the behaviour and the person
      (a) Education regarding normative adolescent sexual behaviours and development
      (b) Thought records
          (i) Everyday difficult situations
          (ii) Sense of self connected to sexual offending
      (c) 'A day when I sexually offended' exercise
      (d) Promoting prosocial peer and family relationships
          (i) Enhancing peer relationships
          (ii) Working with parents

Stage 3: Processing the sexual offending
      (a) Understanding that sexual offending was a choice
      (b) Altering distorted cognitions and underlying beliefs that support sexual offending

Stage 4: Developing guilt and responsibility
      (a) Education regarding the impact of sexual offending
      (b) Writing a letter of responsibility

---

complete description of CBT with adolescents). Of course, the treatment of shame is just one of many potential treatment goals for adolescents who have offended sexually, and it is one component of the overall treatment. Although treatment is tailored to meet the individual needs, strengths and risks presented by each adolescent and his or her family, common treatment goals include the development and practice of offence prevention plans, enhancing affective expression and social functioning, and building skills for healthy sexual futures, for example.

The overall goal of treatment for reducing shame is complex and involves developing an alternative cognitive framework for understanding the sexual offending that minimises shame while encouraging feelings of guilt and personal responsibility. The goal is for the adolescent to experience a sense of responsibility for the acts without generalising the sense of responsibility to a global negative self-evaluation. The experience of shame inhibits the ability to focus on and understand the sexual offending, as shame-based feelings lead to avoidance and a sense of hopelessness regarding the capacity to prevent a reoffence. The assumption is that the adolescent needs to develop an understanding of the circumstances of the offending to understand their own role and responsibility. This understanding then forms the basis for a greater sense of self-efficacy for preventing a reoffence, a better understanding of the harm caused by their offending, and a

capacity to experience regret and attempt to repair the damage. The avoidant behaviour and poor problem solving that results from shame-based cognitions is also directly addressed.

As noted in Figure 19.1, the treatment approach consists of four stages. Although the order in which these stages are addressed can vary with each adolescent, they are often addressed sequentially. In our experience, adolescents cannot start to examine the sexual offending, accept responsibility for offending sexually, and examine the impact of their offending on the victim until they no longer feel overwhelming shame and a global negative self-evaluation. Indeed, if adolescents are asked too early in treatment to look at the harm that they have caused their victims, this can lead to increased feelings of shame. Increased feelings of shame, in turn, can lead to increased defensiveness, denial, and victim blaming. It should also be stressed that these stages are not mutually exclusive. For example, the therapeutic relationship is continually enhanced throughout all stages of treatment, and there is a focus on differentiating between the person and the behaviour throughout the treatment process.

Although some of this work can be done in a group therapy format, therapists should be cautious that some group discussions could inadvertently increase shame for individuals who have offended sexually (Proeve and Howells, 2002). For example, group discussions regarding issues such as an adolescent's sexual interests and fantasies, and the specific details regarding his or her past sexual offences, could inadvertently increase the shame experienced by group members. These issues are typically best addressed in individual therapy. However, group therapy can provide an excellent forum for discussions regarding many issues, including normative adolescent sexual development, formation of healthy sexual attitudes and relationships, development and practice of offence-prevention plans, social skill development, affect expression and management, development of support networks, family relationships, the impact of sexual offending on victims and family members, and many other issues. Parent groups can also be a powerful intervention for addressing the shame and guilt that may be experienced by parents.

Stage 1: Building trust

For interventions to be effective, they need to occur within the context of a trusting and collaborative therapeutic relationship (Marshall et al., 2003). The nonspecific aspects of therapy, such as careful listening, summarising, reflection, and a generally caring stance can assist the youth to overcome feelings of shame and promote self-acceptance and self-valuing (Jenkins, 2005; Josefowitz and Myran, 2005). Aside from the professionals who investigated the offending, the therapist is often the first person who knows about the sexual offending and does not react in a negative, blaming, shame-inducing manner. The therapist's stance, combined with the adolescent's ability to enter into a positive relationship with someone who knows about the offending, starts to address the feeling of shame. The relationship becomes an experience whereby the adolescent can have a positive relationship with a new person who can value them as a person – despite knowing about the sexual offending (Jenkins, 2005; Proeve and Howells, 2002). The attitudes and behaviours of the support staff are also important, as the adolescents and their families are well aware of the reason that they are attending the therapy office. When they are treated with dignity and respect from the outset, this begins the process of reducing shame.

Stage 2: Differentiating the behaviour and the person

The goal in this stage is to expand the adolescents' beliefs about themselves so that they view the sexual offending as a behaviour that they engaged in rather than as a defining personal feature. In this stage, the two central beliefs that underlie shame are addressed specifically. The first belief consists of: 'Because I have done **X** (sexual offending), that means that I am **Y** (a global negative evaluation of the self, such as ''worthless'', ''perverse'', or ''disgusting'').' The second belief consists of: 'Because I did **X** (sexual offending) that means I am **Y** (global negative evaluation of self) and no one will ever be able to care about me or want me as a friend or family member.' The shame connected to the sexual offending is frequently so intense that it defines the youth, and any other activities or relationships that they engage in are minimised. The first goal is to expand the definition of self so that the adolescents do not view themselves, primarily or solely, as individuals who have offended sexually. In our clinical experience, as the adolescent's sense of self expands, he or she is more able to explore the actual sexual offending without becoming overwhelmed with shame. Four components of treatment are designed to assist adolescents to expand their definitions of self subsequent to the sexual offending. These include education regarding normative adolescent sexual behaviours and development, thought records, promoting prosocial peer and family relationships, and an exercise called 'A day when I sexually offended'.

A. Education regarding normative adolescent sexual behaviours and development

Early in the treatment process, adolescents are provided with information regarding normative adolescent sexual behaviours and the differences between normative and abusive sexual behaviours. The focus in the early stages of education, as it relates to the reduction of shame, is to demonstrate that sexual offending is a behaviour – not a personality characteristic. Adolescents also start to develop an understanding of what is normal sexual development and what is considered a sexually offensive behaviour. The clinician needs to monitor that the increased understanding of the legal ramifications of sexual offending does not increase the adolescent's sense of shame. Another important educational component at this stage of treatment is to inform adolescents that successful treatment has been shown to significantly decrease the risk of reoffending sexually (see Reitzel and Carbonell, 2006, for review). In addition to providing hope, this also helps to reinforce the notion that sexual offending – and continued sexual offending – is not something that is inevitable but, rather, a behaviour that can be altered. Education in this phase of treatment can be provided during individual, group, and/or family therapy formats. As adolescents increasingly understand that the offending was morally and legally wrong, they may also feel ashamed of the sexual pleasure that they experienced while offending. Adolescents may feel ashamed of their bodies and worry that they are not 'normal'. An understanding of normal adolescent sexual development may assist with the feelings of shame associated with the pleasure in the act.

B. Thought records

(i) Thought records of everyday difficult situations

The adolescent's emotional experience of shame, associated global negative self-evaluation, and fear of rejection by others manifests itself in difficulties in everyday interactions. The clinician starts by using a CBT model to understand these everyday difficulties. Working collaboratively with the adolescent, the clinician identifies difficult situations and helps the adolescent explore his or her feelings, physical reactions, behaviours, and thoughts. The clinician uses CBT techniques to help the adolescent identify thoughts that are related to self, other, and the future. The clinician pays particular attention to thoughts that are related to global negative evaluations of the self such as, 'I'm no good', 'I'm stupid', 'I'm sick and perverted', and thoughts related to expected rejection, such as, 'No one likes me', or 'No one would want to be my friend'. Initially, these may be difficult to identify, as the negative cognitions are often so automatic that the adolescent is unaware of them. It can take patient exploration to identify meaningful thoughts. Once the thoughts related to a global negative evaluation of self and expected negative

judgment are identified, the clinician engages the adolescent in an examination of the evidence that would confirm or disconfirm these thoughts. For example, if the adolescent's thought is 'I'm no good', the evidence for this thought is examined. Frequently, the fact that the adolescent has offended sexually is perceived as convincing evidence for the global negative self-evaluation or expectation of rejection. When examining the evidence for the negative beliefs, if the adolescent does not mention the sexual offending, the clinician can ask about the impact of the sexual offending on the adolescent's negative beliefs about self. When examining the evidence, the clinician starts by examining the evidence that would support the global negative self-evaluation or, in this example, the evidence that would support the belief that 'I'm no good'. The clinician needs to acknowledge the sexual offending, but encourage the adolescent to examine if there is any other evidence to support the global negative self-evaluation or expectation of rejection. When examining the evidence for the belief, the therapist's attitude indicates that the sexual offending is one behaviour that the adolescent engaged in and, therefore, just one piece of evidence; the therapist conveys the attitude that the adolescent has engaged in other behaviours besides the sexual offending.

Next, the clinician and adolescent examine any evidence that does not support the negative beliefs. In this example, the clinician and client would examine evidence against the belief that the client is 'no good'. This work is usually initiated after the clinician has a sufficient relationship with the adolescent that the clinician knows about events in the adolescent's life that do *not* support a global negative self-evaluation or expectation of rejection. The clinician can, therefore, assist the adolescent to focus on this evidence. After an examination of the evidence, the clinician assists the adolescent to develop a more balanced self-evaluation that takes into account all of the evidence.

Although the above work can be done as part of a therapeutic conversation, thought records can be useful in providing a structure for helping the adolescent explore the basis for their global negative beliefs and to develop a more realistic, evidence-based self-evaluation. This process may sound relatively straightforward; however, it requires a trusting therapeutic relationship, can take a number of therapy sessions, and requires a great deal of skill on the clinician's part. Basic texts on providing CBT therapy can be very helpful in suggesting ways of exploring youth's thoughts and the evidence for and against the thoughts (see Beck, 1995, or Persons, Davidson and Tomkins, 2001).

Figure 19.2 shows an example of the use of a thought record with an adolescent named 'Michael'.* Michael is a 16-year-old male who was in counselling because of his sexual interest in prepubescent children, making child abuse images available on the Internet, and his significant social anxiety. During a session focused on issues related to enhancing his social skills and addressing his social anxiety, Michael and his therapist completed a thought record regarding a recent social situation that caused strong emotional reactions. Michael described a situation where he was rollerblading with friends. He did not know what to say to his friends or how to continue the conversation. Michael experienced this situation as extremely distressing. In the process of completing the thought record, Michael was able to identify feeling nervous, which made him respond to his friends by withdrawing from the conversation, lagging behind the group, and not speaking to his friends for the remainder of their outing, so much so that his friends questioned, 'What's wrong with you?' Michael also recalled feeling confused and becoming sweaty and red in the face. Although Michael identified a number of automatic thoughts, he decided that 'I'm a weird person' was the one thought he wanted to work on given that it related to the situation and accounted for the intensity of his mood. The therapist identified Michael's 'I'm a weird person' thought as his 'hot thought' (ie the automatic thought that is most connected to the intensity of the mood). The therapist explained to Michael that it made sense that, if he was thinking that he was a 'weird person', he would be feeling nervous, and this would validate the relationship between his automatic thought and his feeling.

Michael was then invited to step back and look at the evidence that supported his 'I'm a weird person' thought and the evidence that did not support this thought in order to provide a basis for evaluating his automatic thought. To assist Michael, he was asked to think about his automatic thought ('I'm a weird person') as a

hypothesis that deserved testing, and he was supported in gathering objective data and facts for/against his automatic thought. Michael initially found this process difficult and required support from his therapist, as it was easier for him to mix facts with interpretations. Michael found that evidence disputing his hot thought ('I'm a weird person') was difficult to uncover, especially when he was experiencing a strong mood. The therapist used her previous knowledge of Michael to focus his attention on events or facts that did not support the hot thought. Michael was then invited to put all the evidence he gathered into a more realistic perspective. It is important for the therapist to have a realistic expectation. This thought record was the beginning of a process of shifting Michael's perspective and was only one of many thought records completed in the course of therapy.

(ii) Thought records regarding sense of self connected to sexual offending

In addition to examining how shame manifests itself in difficulties in everyday interactions, it is integral that the adolescent's global negative self-evaluation is addressed directly. Figure 19.3 shows an example of the use of a thought record to examine the impact of the sexual offending on an adolescent's negative beliefs about self to develop a more realistic, evidence-based self-evaluation. 'Sam' is a 15-year-old male who was in counselling because of sexual offences against his six-year-old female cousin. Sam was not particularly hopeful about his personal ability to solve problems connected to his sexual offending, and he believed that something was intrinsically wrong with him. Although Sam often said that he wanted to ensure that he never offended again, he often reverted to extreme devaluing and deprecating self-statements when asked to confront his behaviours, often leaving him immobilised. This made it extremely difficult for Sam to engage in the necessary work related to sexual offence-specific treatment. Sam's primary coping strategy for such instances was to avoid anything that reminded him of his past offending behaviours. Although this initially minimised the distress he associated with his past offending behaviours, his avoidance invariably led to his reminders remaining vivid and intrusive. This, in turn, served to reinforce his belief that something was wrong with him and

---

† Please note that pseudonyms were used for all examples in this chapter.

Figure 19.2: Example of thought record of an everyday, difficult situation

Situation	Feelings	Body response	Behaviours	Automatic thoughts	Evidence for the hot thought	Evidence against the hot thought	Balanced thought	Feelings after
With friends rollerblading down a park trail and I didn't know what to say to them or continue the conversations	Nervous (75%)	Sweaty. Red in face	Very quiet	People don't like hanging out with me I always sound stupid if I express myself I'm a loser **I'm a weird person**	I smoke a lot of weed and, when I do, I sound stupid in front of friends – it slows me down and sometimes I don't make any sense Kids at school sometimes don't accept me and they ignore me at lunch I act immature when I'm nervous and I don't act my age	I started a new school last year and I met two new people who I still hang out with People talk to me all the time at school during class The things I say around real friends never sound stupid to me	I'm capable about having intellectual conversations My brain trips me up sometimes, and I need to remind myself to think realistically	Nervous (25%)

that it would be better to avoid anything that reminded him of his sexual offending. As such, thought records were used with Sam, because his experience of shame was causing him to ignore any experiences that were not consistent with his global negative self-evaluation of, 'I'm a sick and disgusting person'.

Identifying alternative beliefs about the self that are more realistic and evidence-based usually takes time. Adolescents may require a significant amount of evidence and repetition to change their negative absolute beliefs about themselves that developed in relation to the sexual offending. As in Sam's case, it is often very easy for youth to miss facts that do not fit their expectations and, thus, ignore evidence which contradicts the negative global self-evaluation. Identifying and strengthening the evidence that his global negative self-evaluation was not 100 per cent true and strengthening the more realistic, evidenced-based beliefs was necessary for Sam to begin to tolerate his offence-specific work.

C. Overview of 'A day when I sexually offended' exercise

Just as the experience of shame can cause adolescents to minimise or ignore any experiences that are not consistent with a global negative self-evaluation, shame can also cause adolescents to minimise or ignore anything else that occurred during a day when they sexually offended. This particular exercise assists adolescents in two ways: first, to understand that the sexual offending was only one behaviour that occurred on a particular day and, second, to notice behaviours, thoughts, and motivations that are related to personal strengths and positive personality attributes. This exercise involves describing an entire day when the adolescent sexually offended. When completing this exercise, it is important that the clinician focus the adolescent's attention on positive aspects of their behaviour, even if the adolescent considers the behaviour routine. For example, if the adolescent got to school on time that day, this takes planning and a certain amount of self-discipline; if the adolescent spent lunchtime at school with friends, this means that there are peers who like them. Typically, youth are surprised at how much else occurred during the day and what a small amount of the day was occupied by the sexual offending. When working

on this exercise, it is often helpful to use a visual cue, such as a timeline of the entire day. As adolescents notice all of the other activities and experiences that occurred during a day when they sexually offended, they also start to expand their self-concept to include these other behaviours. For example, rather than seeing themselves as 'just a sex offender', they begin to see that they are also a student, a friend, a child in the family, and a sports team member, for example. Prior to engaging in this exercise, however, the clinician needs to have developed a good therapeutic relationship, and the clinician and adolescent need to have processed a number of difficult situations using thought records so that the adolescent has started expanding his or her self-evaluation. In addition, the clinician needs to have sufficient knowledge of the adolescent so that the clinician can assist the adolescent to notice aspects of the day that had been ignored and that indicate positive personality characteristics.

D. Promoting prosocial peer and family relationships

(i) Enhancing peer relationships

The feeling of shame, and the associated beliefs, frequently causes the adolescent to withdraw from normal peer activities and avoid social contact. The adolescent may need to be encouraged to participate in normal, age-appropriate activities. This can be addressed through a combination of activity scheduling and cognitive interventions. It is important to start with small steps and increase the adolescent's social contacts in a hierarchical, stepwise progression. As the adolescent increases social contact, obstacles can be examined and dealt with using a variety of cognitive interventions, such as thought records or self-talk. As the adolescent starts to experience some social success, these experiences are further evidence against global negative self-evaluations and predictions of social rejection. At this stage, skills such as relaxation, self-talk, visualisation, and social problem-solving are frequently taught to enhance prosocial behaviour. Furthermore, specific social skills, such as starting a conversation, can be targeted and addressed using modeling, role playing, reverse role playing, and rehearsal (see Goldstein and McGinnis, 1997).

Figure 19.3: Example of thought record to address sense-of-self and shame connected to sexual offending

Situation	Feelings	Body response	Behaviours	Automatic thoughts	Evidence for the hot thought	Evidence against the hot thought	Balanced thought	Feelings after
Every time I remember the sexual offending	Anger (40%) Crappy (30%) Cranky (30%) Shame (110%)	I get a vomit-like taste in my mouth Stomach drops Butterflies in stomach	Avoidance Take it out on others (brothers/parents) I isolate myself (I do stuff by myself)	I'm a really bad person I'm not deserving of being around people People are scared of me **I'm a sick and disgusting person**	I committed a sexual offence against a child	I help other people at school in English Class I help people at soccer practice by showing them how to be a better player and help them when they are struggling I'm a fair and honest referee during soccer games I'm a respectful person by listening to my parents and I do what I'm told I respect other people's boundaries, property, rights (I don't believe breaking the law is OK) I gave a homeless person the rest of my popcorn after I went to a soccer game with my Dad	I'm not a sick person, there's not enough evidence I'm not a bad person; I made a wrong choice	Anger (2%) Crappy (10%) Cranky (5%) Shame (5%)

(ii) Working with parents

Family attitudes can influence the adolescent's thoughts, feelings, attitudes, and behaviours and can impact directly on the degree of shame and guilt experienced by the adolescent (Barnes and Hughes, 2002; Jenkins, 2005). Parents may react to the news that their child has offended sexually with a number of reactions such as anger, shock, disbelief, guilt, and confusion. It is not uncommon for adolescents to withdraw from the family and/or for the family to withdraw from the adolescent. Parental reactions should be addressed within the context of treatment for the adolescent (Rich, 2003; Thomas, 1997). Ideally, parents will need to develop an understanding of their child's sexual offending that focuses on separating the negative evaluation of the sexual offending from a global negative evaluation of their child. It should be pointed out that directly involving parents in treatment with adolescents in the criminal justice system significantly reduces recidivism; particularly when parent-child communication is targeted (Latimer, Dowden, Morton-Bourgon, Edgar, and Bania, 2003).

Stage 3: Processing the sexual offending

This stage has two main goals. The first goal for this stage is for the adolescent to understand that the sexual offending was a behaviour that the adolescent chose to engage in and, therefore, has control over in the future; rather than believing that the sexual offending is an indication of a fixed trait. Once there has been some progress in expanding the youth's global self-evaluation, and expectation of rejection, with a concomitant reduction in shame, therapy can start to address the adolescent's shame regarding past sexual offences by exploring the sexual offending specifically. The second goal for this stage is to reduce feelings of shame while increasing feelings of guilt and responsibility. This stage of treatment involves two interventions: (i) identifying moments when the adolescent made a conscious choice that lead to the sexual offending, and (ii) identifying cognitions that enabled the sexual offending and then modifying the beliefs that underlie these cognitions.

A. Understanding that sexual offending was a choice

Adolescents often experience the sexual offending as something that 'just happened' as opposed to a choice that they made. The role of the therapist is to provide the adolescent with a structure for starting to explore the sexual offending in a way that leads to an understanding that the offending was a choice and that they are responsible for the choice (Steen, 2005). Before actually exploring the sexual offending, it can be helpful to introduce the adolescent to the model of sexual offending as a choice. For example, therapy might proceed as in the following transcript with Michael:

Therapist: We've been talking about a lot of events in your life over the past few weeks. I was wondering if it was time to try and understand the sexual offending. You've talked about wanting to figure out why this happened.

Michael: Yeah, it just sort of happened; like, I'm just a creep. I must be a sick person.

Therapist: I know it must feel like it just 'sort of happened' (the therapist acknowledges the adolescent's experience but focuses on the task); but often, when we look closely at behaviours that feel like they just sort of happen, we can see that we actually made some choices.

Michael: I don't know.

Therapist: Let's talk about some of the choices you made during a regular activity you do every day, like getting ready for school in the morning (therapist and Michael breakdown all the behaviours required to get ready for school in the morning and the choices he made such as eating breakfast, brushing teeth, having a shower, choosing clothes, packing his books, and making a lunch – in this manner, therapist assists Michael to see that 'automatic' and simple activities actually involve thinking, planning, and choices). You know the way we looked at the trouble you were having with your friends when you were rollerblading, and we separated out your feelings, behaviours, and thoughts, and looked at how they went together?

Michael: Yeah, that was sort of cool.

Therapist: Well, I would like to take a look at your feelings, behaviours, and thoughts in relation to the sexual offending and see if we can understand what was going on a bit more. Would that be OK with you?

Michael: Yeah, but I'm just a pervert.

Therapist: I know it must feel like you're just a pervert (the therapist acknowledges the youth's experience, but continues to focus on the task), but I think it would be really helpful for us to explore what was actually going on inside of you when you offended (the therapist tries to use language that describes the sexual offending as a behaviour rather than a personality trait). Would you be willing to try?

Michael: Yeah, OK, I guess.

The CBT model of exploring experience by separating feelings, body reactions, behaviours, and thoughts and examining their interdependence forms the theoretical basis of this stage of therapy. The adolescent's experience prior to the sexual offending, during the offending, and subsequent to the offending is examined. This approach has a number of advantages. First, the experience is slowed down so that each phase can be explored in detail. This enables the adolescent to feel more in control and less overwhelmed. Second, exploring the preoffence experiences first tends to be less shameful and frightening. This enables adolescents to learn that they can disclose and explore the details of their experience without being shamed by the clinician or overwhelmed by their own affect.

The clinician's task is to slow down the events in each phase and elicit the feelings, thoughts, body responses, and behaviours with a view towards listening for and eliciting thoughts that indicate that a choice was made. Sometimes the choice is made very quickly, under conditions of heightened sexual arousal; other times, there is a process of planning for the opportunity to offend to occur. However, in both cases, there is a moment of choice. The clinician needs to reinforce the identification of thoughts that indicate that a choice was made and, at the same time, indicate that these thoughts can be examined and changed so that the adolescent can make different choices in the future. Take, for example, the following example with a young man called 'Sam', whom we discussed earlier. Sam had committed sexual offences against his younger cousin.

Therapist: I know it feels like the sexual offending just happened, but when we look at it carefully, when you left the computer room after viewing the sexual images on the Internet, what was your brain saying to you?

Sam: I remember thinking everyone is asleep and it's late at night.

Therapist: Where did you go after you left the computer room?

Sam: I went to Kimberly's room.

Therapist: So, help me understand why Kimberly's room and not your room?

Sam: Because I was turned on and I thought this would make me feel good, and Kimberly is so young, so she won't know what I'm doing to her.

Therapist: So it sounds like there was this moment when you made a choice to go ahead by telling yourself that it would be OK because everyone was sleeping, you were turned on, and Kimberly was too young to notice, is that right?

Sam: I see what you're saying.

Therapist: You have a choice about whether to act or change your thoughts and that's why it's so important for us to figure out your thoughts and have you become more aware of the choices you are actually making because you don't always have control of the consequences of your choices (eg charges, probation) but you have control of your thoughts, feelings, and behaviours. Now, lets break this down even further and add to the thoughts you had before, during and after the sexual offence.

During this discussion, Sam identified the following:

Thoughts before the sexual offence:
'This would make me feel good'; 'Everyone is sleeping so I won't get caught'; 'I was already turned on from watching the website'; 'I don't think Kimberly would know what I'm doing to her because she is really young'.

Thoughts during the sexual offence:
'She's a girl, I'm not gay, so I wouldn't do that with my brothers'; 'My brain knew that if I did penetrate her, she would cry, I would get caught, so I just rubbed up against her'.

Thoughts after the sexual offence:
'I don't think I'll get caught 'cause everyone is asleep'; 'She's so young, she won't tell, I won't get caught, it would be an easy way out'; 'I didn't do it (I know the consequences)'.

B. Altering distorted cognitions and underlying beliefs that support sexual offending

Adolescents who have offended sexually frequently display distorted cognitions and beliefs that may rationalise past sexual offending and/or support further sexual offending (eg Rich, 2003; Steen, 2005). It is not surprising, therefore, that most treatment programs for this population currently target cognitive distortions (McGrath et al., 2003). Once the clinician and adolescent have identified the typical thoughts that occurred prior to, during, and after the sexual offending, the clinician and adolescent can explore the cognitive distortions that are involved in these thoughts and the underlying beliefs that enabled the offending. An excellent approach to deconstructing cognitive distortions and their underlying beliefs is presented by Richardson, Bhate and Graham (1997). The four steps outlined by these authors are:

1. Identify the unique self-statements that reflect the cognitive distortions (eg 'If the child had said "No", I wouldn't have done it').
2. Identify the underlying beliefs that contribute to the distorted self-statement (eg 'A young child is able to consent to sexual contact with a teen'; 'if a child does not say "No", then they have agreed').
3. Make the belief statement explicit and understand how it supports sexual offending (eg 'If I believed that young children would want to have sex with a teenager, then this would make it easier for me to make the choice to offend').
4. Develop a new belief by examining the accuracy of the original belief and constructing alternative statements that contradict the abuse-supportive belief statements (eg 'Young children are way too young to be even thinking about sex yet', or 'Young children sometimes don't say "No" because they don't feel they can disagree with an older person').

The dialogue, below, between Sam and his therapist, illustrates how this process can be started:

Therapist: So, Sam, lets take one of the thinking errors you identified, 'My brain knew that if I did penetrate her, she would cry, I would get caught, so I just rubbed up against her', and let's figure out the beliefs behind this thought.
Sam: What do you mean?

Therapist: Well, by 'beliefs' I mean, what are you accepting to be true about the self-statement? Lets take a common example of a thinking error that lots of guys and girls your age have – downloading music from Limewire (pirating) is OK. Many people I work with say that pirating music isn't that bad because no one gets hurt and people post it to be downloaded anyway, so it's no big deal.
Sam: Yeah, I do that all the time.
Therapist: So, what is the *belief* behind the statement, 'it's not that bad, no one gets hurt, and people post it to be downloaded anyway, it's no big deal'.
Sam: That it's OK to do?
Therapist: Yes, but give me a little more about *what* exactly is OK to do. What are you actually doing when you are downloading music from Limewire?
Sam: Stealing? Pirating music?
Therapist: Yes!! So what's the belief?
Sam: That there are good reasons to steal and break the law.
Therapist: Exactly! This belief supports the self-statement. So, now lets do the same thing to figure out the beliefs behind the abuse-supportive thinking error. What are we saying to be true if we believe, 'If I did penetrate her, she would cry, I would get caught, so I just rubbed up against her'.
Sam: Ummm (Sam takes some time thinking and eventually comes up with the following list): 'I'm not doing too much harm, so it's not so bad'; 'She didn't cry, so I didn't hurt her'; 'It's easier to get away with it if I keep the sexual behaviours minimal'; 'When kids don't cry or resist, it means it doesn't hurt them'; 'Kids only get hurt if they get injured'; 'Children don't have good memories, and this won't affect her and she won't tell'.
Therapist: OK, good job. Now, tell me how do these beliefs support sexual offending behaviours?
Sam: Well, isn't it obvious, they are giving the thinking error evidence that this is true.
Therapist: What do you think about that?
Sam: It's not true.
Therapist: Then lets come up with some true statements to combat these abuse-supportive thoughts and beliefs. Why is this not true?

Eventually Sam came up with the following list:

'All sexually abusive behaviour impacts kids negatively and I cannot say that one has a greater effect over another – I still sexually abused her'; 'Kids find it very difficult to say "No" or "Stop" to things they don't understand'; 'Older people are supposed to be good role models and protect younger kids – kids deserve protection and safety not abuse'; 'I knew what I was doing was against the rules and I tried to get away with it – I broke rules and laws'; 'There are laws against bigger people being sexual with smaller people because kids can't consent to sex, so they are protected.'

Frequently, additional education will be provided at this point – particularly when adolescents struggle to come up with evidence to counter their faulty beliefs. For example, if an adolescent believes that the victim liked the sexual offence because he or she did not yell or actively resist, the clinician may provide information on typical victim responses. Ideally, this information would be presented in an interactive format. Adolescents are asked to think about their own reactions to different situations and relate them to the victim's response. For example, in understanding how a victim might not be acquiescing even though they were not actively resisting, it might be helpful to ask the adolescent to think about a time when they did not want to go along with a situation, but did not actively resist. The following dialogue between 'Sarah' and her therapist shows an example of this process. Sarah sexually assaulted a young child in the neighbourhood:

Therapist: Tell me about a time when you did things, or went along with something, you didn't want to do, but went along with it anyway and didn't say anything.

Sarah: Well, I hate writing book reports, especially when we are doing a unit on Shakespeare.

Therapist: What happens?

Sarah: I do it because I don't want to get into trouble with my teacher.

Therapist: Do you say anything or resist?

Sarah: No, I do it anyway, and I usually don't question the assignments my teacher gives me.

Therapist: Why is that?

Sarah: Because I don't want to get in trouble with my teacher; I don't want to cause trouble, because that might make them unhappy, and it will probably affect my mark. Sometimes you just go along with things that adults tell you to do and you don't say anything – even if you don't want to do it.

Therapist: So what can we say about your belief that, if a child doesn't say 'No', then they must be OK with sexual touching with a teen?

Sarah: It's wrong. Sometimes children just go along with things that older people tell them and they don't say anything – even if they really don't want to do it.

Stage 4: Developing guilt and responsibility

By this stage of therapy, adolescents are normally experiencing a great deal less shame in relation to the sexual offending and are feeling more responsibility and guilt. They have shifted to see the past sexual offending as a behaviour that they chose to engage in rather than as a defining personal feature. At this point, they are ready to start to focus on the impact of the offending on their victims and attempt to make reparation. As noted earlier, guilt feelings that develop as a result of an individual committing a wrong will motivate the individual to acknowledge responsibility for their behaviour and correct the harm that has been done. Two main interventions are used at this stage: education regarding the impact of sexual abuse and letters of responsibility.

A. Education regarding the impact of sexual offending

The goal is to assist adolescents to understand the short- and long-term impact that their sexual offending had on others. As noted previously, it is critical that this work is not attempted until such time that the adolescent has significantly reduced their feelings of shame, as shame can result in victim-blaming and denial of negative impact. Using a variety of materials, such as poetry, songs, movies, television shows, or stories written about surviving sexual abuse, adolescents are encouraged to examine the negative impact for victims. Some adolescents also find it helpful to look at times in their own lives when others have abused them. We find it advantageous for the adolescents to examine how their sexual offending has impacted their victim's subsequent thoughts, feelings, behaviours, and body responses. It is also important to help the adolescents to learn how others (eg parents, siblings, friends, and neighbours) have been negatively impacted by their sexual offending.

B. Writing a letter of responsibility

After adolescents have developed a good understanding of the harm that they have likely caused as a result of their sexual offending, a useful next step is a letter of responsibility that is addressed to those who have been harmed. These letters are not typically sent; rather, they are used to process thoughts and feelings regarding personal responsibility and encourage the adolescent to attempt to repair the damage that has been done. Therapeutic sessions with the adolescents and their parents are also arranged such that the adolescents can begin to take responsibility for their decision to engage in sexual offending behaviours and address the negative outcome for their family.

Conclusion

Feelings of shame are common for individuals who have offended sexually, and these feelings can interfere significantly in successful treatment. In particular, heightened shame can lead to denial, resistance, victim-blaming, depression, and retaliatory hostility. Increased shame also makes it difficult for adolescents to examine their sexual offending, to take responsibility for their behaviours, and to devise prevention strategies to reduce their risk of reoffending. High levels of shame can also result in the adolescent withdrawing from social situations for fear of being exposed as an individual who has offended sexually. This, of course, makes it difficult for the adolescent to engage in normative social activities and to build the capacity for more healthy interpersonal relationships. Parents of adolescents who offend sexually may also experience shame as a result of their son's or daughter's decision to commit sexual offences, and this shame is likely to exacerbate their child's shame and negative affect.

We have presented a CBT approach to reducing feelings of shame, and enhancing feelings of guilt and responsibility, for adolescents who have offended sexually. We have demonstrated how common CBT approaches, such as education and thought records, can be used to impact on feelings of shame. In our approach, we have provided a number of examples of how a therapist might work with an adolescent to separate the behaviour from a global evaluation of the self and how the adolescent could begin to see that their sexual offending was the result of a choice to act and not an immutable personality characteristic. As is typical with other CBT approaches with

youth (eg Friedberg and McClure, 2002) our interventions also directly involve the parents, as parental attitudes and behaviours will undoubtedly impact on the adolescent's feelings of guilt and shame.

Research regarding specialised treatment for adolescents who offend sexually is certainly encouraging (Reitzell and Carbonell, 2006) however, very little is known about the specific mechanisms or approaches to enhancing the well-being of these adolescents and their families. It would be ideal for researchers to more closely examine how specific therapeutic interventions impact adolescents who sexually offend. Given the debilitating impact of heightened shame, this is an important area for future study.

References

Association for the Treatment of Sexual Abusers (2003) *Practice Standards and Guidelines for Members of the Association for the Treatment of Sexual Abusers.* Beaverton, OR: Author.

Barnes, C. and Hughes, G. (2002) Family Work with Adolescent Sex Offenders. in Calder, M.C. (ed.) *Young People Who Sexually Abuse: Building the Evidence Base for Your Practice.* Lyme Regis: Russell House Publishing.

Beck, J. (1995) *Cognitive Therapy: Basics and Beyond.* New York: Guilford Press.

Blum, A. (2008) Shame and Guilt, Misconceptions and Controversies: A Critical Review of the Literature. *Traumatology,* 14, 91–102.

Bumby, K.M. (2000) Empathy Inhibition, Intimacy Deficits, and Attachment Difficulties in Sex Offenders. in Laws, D.R., Hudson, S.M. and Ward, T. (eds.) *Remaking Relapse Prevention with Sex Offenders.* Thousand Oaks, CA: Sage.

Bumby, K.M., Marshall, W.L. and Langton, C.M. (1999) A Theoretical Model of the Influences of Shame and Guilt on Sexual Offending. in Schwartz, B. and Cellini, H. (eds.) *The Sex Offender* (Vol. 3). Kingston, NJ: Civic Research Institute.

Cohen, J.A., Mannarino, A.P. and Deblinger, E. (2006) *Treating Trauma and Traumatic Grief in Children and Adolescents: A Clinician's Guide.* New York: Guilford.

Covert, M.V. et al. (2003) Shame-Proneness, Guilt-Proneness, and Interpersonal Problem Solving: A Social Cognitive Analysis. *Journal of Social and Clinical Psychology,* 22, 1–12.

Deblinger, E. and Runyon, M.K. (2005) Understanding and Treating Feelings of Shame in Children who Have Experienced Maltreatment. *Child Maltreatment*, 10, 364–76.

Feiring, C., Taska, L. and Chen, K. (2002) Trying to Understand why Horrible Things Happen: Attribution, Shame, and Symptom Development Following Sexual Abuse. *Child Maltreatment*, 7, 25–39.

Friedberg, R.D. and Mcclure, J.M. (2002) *Clinical Practice of Cognitive Therapy with Children and Adolescents: The Nuts and Bolts*. New York: The Guilford Press.

Goldstein, A.P. and Mcginnis, E. (1997) *Skillstreaming the Adolescent (revised edition): New Strategies and Perspectives for Teaching Prosocial Skills*. Champaign, IL: Research Press.

Jenkins, A. (2005) Knocking on Shame's Door: Facing Shame without Shaming Disadvantaged Young People who Have Abused. in Calder, M.C. (ed.) *Children and Young People Who Sexually Abuse: New Theory, Research and Practice Developments*. Lyme Regis: Russell House Publishing.

Josefowitz, N. and Myran, D. (2005) Towards a Person-Centred Cognitive Behaviour Therapy. *Counselling Psychology Quarterly*, 18, 329–36.

Latimer, J. et al. (2003) *Treating Youth in Conflict with the Law: A New Meta-Analysis*. Ottawa: Youth Justice Research, Department of Justice.

Lewis, H.B. (1971) *Shame and Guilt in Neurosis*. New York: International Universities Press.

Maletzky, B.M. (1991) *Treating the Sexual Offender*. Newbury Park, CA: Sage.

Marshall, W.L., Anderson, D. and Fernandez, Y. (1999) *Cognitive Behavioural Treatment of Sexual Offenders*. West Sussex: John Wiley and Sons.

Marshall, W.L. et al. (2003) Process Variables in the Treatment of Sexual Offenders: A Review of the Relevant Literature. *Aggression and Violent Behavior*, 8, 205–34.

Mcalinden, A. (2005) The Use of 'Shame' with Sexual Offenders. *British Journal of Criminology*, 45, 373–94.

McGrath, R.J., Cumming, G.F. and Burchard, B.L., Zeoli, S. and Ellerby, L. (2010) *Current Practices and Emerging Trends in Sexual Abuser Management: The Safer Society 2009 North American Survey*. Brandon, VT: Safer Society Press.

Nathanson, D.L. (1992) *Shame and Pride: Affect, Sex and the Birth of the Self*. New York: Norton.

Persons, J.B., Davidson, J. and Tompkins, M.A. (2001) *Essential Components of Cognitive-Behavior Therapy for Depression*. Washington, DC: American Psychological Association.

Proeve, M. and Howells, K. (2002) Shame and Guilt in Child Sexual Offenders. *International Journal of Offender Therapy and Comparative Criminology*, 46, 657–67.

Reitzel, L.R. and Carbonell, J.L. (2006) The Effectiveness of Sexual Offender Treatment for Juveniles as Measured by Recidivism: A Meta-Analysis. *Sexual Abuse: A Journal of Research and Treatment*, 18, 401–21.

Rich, P. (2003) *Understanding, Assessing, and Rehabilitating Juvenile Sexual Offenders*. Hoboken, NJ: Wiley.

Richardson, Bhate and Graham (1997) Cognitive-Based Practice with Sexually Abusive Adolescents. in Hoghughi, M.S. (ed.) *Working with Sexually Abusive Adolescents*. London: Sage.

Server, M. (1970) Shame Aversion Therapy. *Journal of Behavior Therapy and Experimental Psychiatry*, 1, 213–5.

Steen, C. (2005) Cognitive-Behavioral Treatment under the Relapse Prevention Umbrella. in Calder, M.C. (ed.) *Children and Young People Who Sexually Abuse: New Theory, Research and Practice Developments*. Lyme Regis: Russell House Publishing.

Stuewig, J. and McCloskey, L.A. (2005) The Relation of Child Maltreatment to Shame and Guilt among Adolescents: Psychological Routes to Depression and Delinquency. *Child Maltreatment*, 10, 324–36.

Tangney, J.P. (1995) Shame and Guilt in Interpersonal Relationships. in Tangney, J.P. and Fischer, K.W. (eds.) *Self-Conscious Emotions: Shame, Guilt, Embarrassment, and Pride*. New York: Guilford.

Tangney, J.P. and Dearing, R.L. (2002) *Shame and Guilt*. New York: Guilford.

Thomas, J. (1997) The Family in Treatment. in Ryan, G. and Lane, S. (eds.) *Juvenile Sexual Offending: Causes, Consequences, and Correction*. San Francisco: Jossey-Bass.

Ward, T. et al. (2004) The Multifactor Offender Readiness Model. *Aggression and Violent Behavior*, 9, 645–73.

Worling, J.R. (2004) Essentials of a Good Intervention Programme for Sexually Abusive Juveniles. Part Two: Offence Related Treatment Tasks. in O'Reilly, G. et al. (eds.) *The Handbook of Clinical Intervention with Young People who Sexually Abuse*. Hove: Brunner-Routledge.

CHAPTER 20

A Brief CBT Programme for Low Risk Adolescent Sex Offenders

Nicholas A.J. Bankes

Introduction

Over the past 18 years of providing therapeutic treatment for adolescents who sexually abuse I have increasingly come to realise that there are some adolescents who, whilst being assessed as 'low' risk of committing further abuse and therefore not in need of longer term therapeutic treatment, nevertheless would benefit from a more limited therapeutic intervention in order to help them gain an understanding of why they sexually abused in the first place, why they continued to abuse after a first offence and what the effects of their abusive behaviour were, are, and will be in the future. Consequently I began to offer these young people the opportunity to engage in a time-limited programme, usually consisting of 10 to 16 sessions, to achieve these aims. As an external consultant to a youth offending team I presented this model to youth justice practitioners and they have found it particularly useful in the light of the brief duration of time with which they are able to work with many of these adolescents.

The model is intended for adolescents who have committed more than one sexual offence but who are deemed to be at 'low' risk of committing further sexual offences. Typically they would be at the higher end of the 'low' risk scale. These adolescents demonstrate guilt and remorse for their offending and are motivated to engage in therapeutic treatment.

The model is not for adolescents with learning disabilities, mental health problems or disorders, or who have therapeutic needs other than their sex offending unless these therapeutic needs are being met elsewhere. For example, adolescents who have generalised low self esteem (ie not just because of the discovery of their offending) who have a history of dysfunctional family problems, severe anger management problems (conduct disorder), attachment difficulties or a history of experiencing significant trauma, would not be suitable candidates for this model of therapeutic intervention. In some cases, where the risk is low but there are some other limited therapeutic needs which can be met by other practitioners, this model can be used in conjunction with another intervention such as bereavement counselling or family therapy. However, some caution needs to observed when attempting this. Firstly, it is important that the model is not used as an adjunct to a vast array of other therapeutic needs that the adolescent has. In such cases it is my experience that a single practitioner is better placed to provide an holistic therapeutic treatment programme, including the sex offence specific treatment, which is likely to entail a much longer period of time. Secondly, if a practitioner is using this brief CBT model in conjunction with a separate intervention provided by another practitioner, then it is important that these two practitioners liaise frequently to compare notes and discuss the case as there is usually a cross-over between the sex offending and the adolescent's other therapeutic needs.

For example, in a recent case a 16-year-old boy, 'Fred', who had been sexually abusing his 11-year-old sister, was assessed as low risk. His parents had moved him to live with grandparents and his mother would have no contact with him at all. The abuse had a traumatic effect, not only on his sister, but on the parents as well who could not agree on what was in their children's best interests. The assessment recommended family therapy for the parents, psychotherapy for the sister and a brief CBT intervention for Fred. All three therapists worked together with the aim of healing the rifts in the family that the disclosure of the abuse had caused with the ultimate goal of facilitating an apology session between Fred and his parents and, separately, with his sister.

Some of the approaches, techniques and skills described in this chapter will be familiar to practitioners working in this field. It is hoped, however, that some of the approaches, techniques and skills which I have developed over the years may be useful to the reader. Whilst the approaches, techniques and skills are described here in the context of a brief intervention, they can also be transferred to longer-term work with adolescent sex offenders.

Approach

It is essential to meet with the adolescent and his parents or carers at the beginning of any intervention. The purpose of this is to briefly explain the process and likely duration of the intervention, to arrange dates, times and venues for subsequent sessions, explain the limits of confidentiality and to provide an opportunity for questions. It is also the practitioner's first opportunity to 'engage' with the adolescent and his parents or carers and enlist their cooperation and motivation. I also have found that this initial meeting provides an opportunity for the family to meet me prior to engaging in the 'work' itself thus reducing tensions and anxieties that they may have. With this in mind, the approach which the practitioner uses at this stage is of vital importance. Providing a pleasant room with the correct number of seats, refreshments and a genuine welcome and thanks for them attending are all beneficial at this stage. Of course, this initial meeting *is* part of the 'work' itself and is the beginning of the therapeutic process but it is likely that it will not be perceived this way by the family. For the adolescent it takes the 'sting' out of the first therapeutic session.

Whilst the adolescent will be motivated to attend the therapeutic treatment programme, he is also likely to want to minimise some aspects of his offending due, usually, to shame or embarrassment. A useful technique/metaphor which I use during this initial meeting, as an attempt to overcome this, is to explain to the adolescent that if he goes to see his GP complaining of a headache, but omits to mention his stomach ache, then he will be prescribed aspirin. However, when his appendix later bursts he will realise that he should have mentioned the stomach ache. I stress that, in the same way, I can only help him if he is open about all aspects of his sexual behaviour problem. It is also important to explain to his parents or carers that they should reinforce this message to their son throughout the programme.

Therapeutic relationship – use of self

It is encouraging that the last decade has increasingly recognised the importance of

adopting an holistic approach to the therapeutic treatment of adolescent sex offenders (Letourneau and Borduin, 2008; Ryan et al., 2010). Between 1995 and 2001 I undertook a research project investigating therapeutic work with adolescents who sexually abuse (Bankes, 2002a: 2002b: 2006). A major finding of this research was that 'therapists who are perceived by the client as warm, empathic, honest, respectful, non-judgemental and who maintain clear and safe boundaries, produce the most successful outcomes irrespective of theoretical orientation' (Bankes, 2002b: 57). I also recently conducted a research study investigating what adult sex offenders found useful or helpful in their therapeutic treatment (Bankes, 2010). A major finding from this research was that all the research participants valued the therapeutic relationship above all else in their therapy and it was this that fostered trust in the therapist, thereby enabling them to be open and honest about all aspects of their lives including their sex offending. In my experience I have found that this is also the case when working with adolescent sex offenders.

Curiosity and active listening

Two very useful and related skills to adopt in working with this client population are 'curiosity' and 'active listening'. For example, the adolescent says something along the lines of 'sometimes she started it'. The practitioner is aware that this may be true given that the child may have become adapted to the abuse by the adolescent, but the practitioner is curious to understand how the adolescent conceptualises this and may say something like 'Ah, that's interesting. Tell me how that works then?' without a trace of sarcasm!

Active listening is a therapeutic skill or technique which has been widely written about (see: Rogers, 1986). Essentially it involves listening intently to the client and reflecting back to the client what the practitioner's understanding is of what the client has said. This induces a sense of being heard by the client. This then paves the way for a challenge. For example, following on from the previous example, the adolescent may say 'well I remember one time she said "can we play monsters?" and then she got undressed'. The practitioner may then say 'I see, so one time she wanted to play the "monster" game and asked you to play it with her and got undressed. What do you make of that

Peter?' Later the practitioner may ask something along the lines of 'do you think that she wanted to play the "monster" game because she just wanted to play with you without the sexual stuff, but didn't really know how to ask you for that?' if the adolescent has not already worked this out for himself.

Allowing space in the session

My previous research demonstrated that practitioners engaged in therapeutic work with adolescent sex offenders spoke twice as much as the adolescent, interrupted the adolescent frequently and did not allow silences to develop in the session (Bankes, 2006). In my experience some of the most illuminating statements by clients (adolescents and adults) take place after a silence. The use of silence as a therapeutic tool and the meaning of silence in a therapeutic encounter are well established (Hooper and Koprowska, 2000; Rober, 2002; Vas Dias, 2000).

The ability of the practitioner to tolerate silence in a session gives the adolescent the space to get in touch with and process thoughts or feelings that they may be experiencing. It also allows the adolescent to verbalise these thoughts or feelings in their own time. Thus the ability of the practitioner to tolerate silence in a therapeutic session indicates that the practitioner is not attempting to impose their own agenda on the session but is enabling the adolescent to control the agenda. As Peter Rober observes: 'silence is full of unspoken stories and reasons why they are kept unspoken' (Rober, 2002: 193). He goes on to advocate the importance of being curious about silences in therapy as a means of enabling the client to 'talk about their more vulnerable stories' thereby creating a more collaborative therapeutic relationship. Hooper and Koprowska (2000) however, remind us that silence can also be used by the practitioner, or experienced by the client, as a punitive intervention.

In the most extreme examples the adolescent begins a statement after a silence only to be interrupted by the practitioner. The following is an example of this from my previous research (Bankes, 2002a: 155–6):

Practitioner: So it's not going to be easy for you to stop that behaviour.
Adolescent: (four seconds silence) Um . . .
Practitioner: (interrupting) Do you think? Or do you disagree with that?   What I want you to do first is just spend a minute or so thinking

about the time, a time, a time you remember quite clearly, perhaps not too long ago, but a time you remember quite clearly when you sexually abused a girl. OK? So spend a minute thinking about that.
Adolescent: (19 seconds silence) Yeah . . .
Practitioner: (interrupting) Is that hard to do?

In this research it was usually the practitioners who broke the silences. I have found that it is usually more therapeutically beneficial to wait for the adolescent to break the silences.

An example of how the use of silence can be used to positive effect concerns an adolescent who I found very difficult to work with. I had shared my countertransference with him: that I felt helpless in knowing how to help him because he seemed to always dismiss my suggestions or tried to anticipate my next question, making it difficult for me to have any sort of meaningful dialogue with him. For a long moment neither of us spoke and then he blurted out 'it's always like that – even with my fucking girlfriend!' This eventually and slowly paved the way to exploring the way he used defence mechanisms in his relationship with me, his girlfriend and 'significant others' and the possible meanings of this. Over the course of the remainder of our sessions together he was able to get in touch with the helplessness he had felt as a child when he was emotionally abused by his stepfather and the powerlessness and helplessness he had felt because of his inability to protect his older sister from being sexually abused by the same man (which he had projected onto me) and how this had played a significant part in his own sexual offending.

Non judgemental

Adopting a non-judgemental approach towards clients in therapy is a well established therapeutic skill. In Rogers' 'Person Centred' therapeutic tradition, for instance, the concepts of 'congruence' and holding the client in 'unconditional positive regard' are considered to be two of the core skills in the therapist's kit-bag which facilitate trust in the therapeutic relationship (Rogers, 1957). By congruence Rogers means 'putting up no professional front or personal façade' (Rogers, 1986: 135). By holding the client in unconditional positive regard Rogers means 'when the therapist is experiencing a positive, non-judgemental, accepting attitude toward whatever the client *is* at that moment'

(Rogers, 1986: 136). In the research referred to above (Bankes, 2010) with adult sex offenders, all of the research participants referred to this approach (which they perceived the therapist to demonstrate) as being one of the most important factors in helping build trust between the therapist and client. Again, this is also the case when working with adolescent sex offenders (Bankes, 2002a, 2002b, 2006). It is particularly relevant in therapeutic work with sex offenders due to the immense shame, in the current climate, which these clients experience in relation to their offending.

Reassurance

In line with the 'Good Lives' approach to working with both adolescent and adult sex offenders (Ward and Stewart, 2003), which stresses the value of working with the clients' strengths in order to foster a sense of meaningful purpose and value for their future, it is useful to bear in mind that reassurance will go a long way to both fostering a strong therapeutic relationship and to facilitating self-belief in the client. It is 20th-century sociologist Robert K. Merton (1957) who is credited with coining the expression 'self-fulfilling prophecy' and formalising its structure and consequences. Essentially this means that if someone expects to fail or succeed at a particular task, then they will. Furthermore, the person's belief in their ability to succeed, or lack of it, is strongly affected by other people's expectations of them. Hence, if the therapist demonstrates a 'can do' expectation with an adolescent sex offender this will help foster a 'can do' attitude in him.

Countertransference

Countertransference is a concept derived from psychoanalysis. The concept has gone through various interpretations but nowadays it is generally held to mean the totality of the practitioner's experience within a therapeutic session. This could be an activation of the practitioner's own 'baggage' being triggered by something the adolescent has said. These are thoughts and feelings which originate in, and belong to, the practitioner. Alternatively it could be a reaction to something the adolescent has said which originates in, or belongs to, the adolescent. The practitioner should be aware of both of these

types of countertransference reaction and whether they belong to themselves or are being projected by the adolescent. In the case of the former the practitioner should attempt not to let their own baggage influence how they are interacting with the adolescent. In the latter case the countertransference provides the practitioner with a rich source of information about the adolescent which can be used therapeutically.

Campbell (1994) and Hodges et al. (1994) comment, from their own clinical experience as psychotherapists, on the potentially destructive impact of unconscious processes such as countertransference reactions and projective identification in psychotherapeutic assessments of adolescents who sexually abuse. In my own research (Bankes, 202a) I discovered the following behavioural and communicative indicators that practitioners may be experiencing countertransference reactions and acting these out unconsciously in their therapeutic work or assessments with adolescent sex offenders:

- talking more than the client
- not allowing silences to develop or breaking the silences
- interrupting the client
- controlling the agenda of the session
- not responding to the client's inputs other than discussion of their sexual abuse
- boundary violations
- an interrogative style of questioning
- a tendency towards using the sessions to educate the clients as opposed to creating a therapeutic dialogue
- avoiding sessions or write-ups of sessions
- health and/or sleep disturbance
- adverse or compulsive reactions to own sexuality
- stress or anxiety

These affective, behavioural and communicative indicators are not necessarily, in themselves, indicative of countertransference reactions and I am not advocating that they should never take place. They are merely clues to alert the practitioner to reflect on their practice for the possible existence and meaning of countertransference reactions. If particular styles of intervention are, or become, habitual for practitioners, either in a general sense or with a particular adolescent, this may be the practitioner's preferred conscious style. However, it may alternatively be an unconscious enactment of a countertransference, particularly if it is a reaction to a specific client. It behoves the practitioner, therefore, to reflect on their feelings, thoughts and behaviour in their sessions and contemplate their meaning. For example, providing the adolescent with knowledge may be best achieved by means of an educative session and this could well be conceptualised as part of the therapeutic process of change. In such an instance, however, the practitioner should be clear that this is what they are undertaking for that session and still be alert to other possible indicators of countertransference reactions such as interrupting or talking more than the adolescent. Paying attention to one's own feelings, thoughts and behaviours as a therapist and contemplating the possible meaning of these usually leads the therapy into new and more meaningful domains and this is at the core of emotionally competent practice.

Case study 'John'

John (aged 16) came to the attention of the local social work department when they were informed by the mother of a young girl in the care of John's mother of inappropriate sexual touching by John of this four-year-old child ('Sally'). It was reported that Sally said that John had touched her bottom and that she had touched his penis. The social worker met with John and his family and John stated that he had put his hand down the back of the Sally's trousers inside her underwear. He told the social worker that it had happened five or six times and that he had once shown her his penis. John also acknowledged touching another two children in a similar manner whilst being child-minded by his mother.

John was clinically assessed as posing a 'low' risk of re-offending and this was confirmed by the ERASOR (Worling and Curwen 2001) and the AIM2 (Print et al. 2007) assessment tools. Given his secure family and educational background and normal level of self-esteem John had no psychotherapeutic needs other than a brief CBT therapeutic intervention.

Treatment programme

This section will present a brief outline of the programme which I used with John. As I had not done the assessment with him it was necessary to

spend some time building a rapport with him and the construction of the Genogram and lifeline assisted this process. A fuller description of these topics and others will be found in the following section. Flexibility is required: some topics may not be applicable to every adolescent or may be covered in one session, whereas some adolescents may take several sessions to cover one topic. Let the adolescent work at his own pace. I find it useful to briefly ask the adolescent what he can recall from the previous session and to briefly review this.

Session 1 – Building rapport – Genogram

- Re-clarify treatment aims and process.
- How are you feeling?
- Tell me about your family.
- Explain family tree and construct genogram.

Session 2 – Building rapport – Lifeline

- What do you remember from last week's session?
- Tell me about your life.
- Explain 'lifeline' and construct.

Session 3 – Building rapport – Feelings, thoughts and behaviour

- What do you remember from last week's session?
- Educational input regarding connection between feelings, thoughts and behaviour.
- Feelings, thoughts and behaviours 'card sort' exercise.
- Homework   feelings diary.

Session 4 – Controlling deviant fantasies

- What do you remember from last week's session?
- Explore feelings diary.
- Fantasy pie chart.
- Aversive scenario.

Session 5 – Cognitive distortions – 'Yes/No' thoughts

- What do you remember from last week's session?
- Explore feelings diary.
- Clarify names, ages of victims and timescale.
- 'Yes' thoughts and 'No' thoughts.

Session 6 – Pathway into abuse (causation) – The jigsaw

- What do you remember from last week's session?
- Explore feelings diary.
- Explain concept of the jigsaw.
- Construct jigsaw.
- Homework – think of any other things you might want to put on the jigsaw.

Session 7 – Pathway into abuse (causation) – The jigsaw continued

- What do you remember from last week's session?
- Explore feelings diary.
- Continue to construct jigsaw.

Session 8 – Pathway into abuse (process) – The cycle

- What do you remember from last week's session?
- Explore feelings diary.
- Explain concept of cycle.
- Construct cycle.
- Homework – think of any other things you might want to put on to the cycle.

Session 9 – Pathway into abuse (process) – The cycle and power, consent, coercion

- What do you remember from last week's session?
- Explore feelings diary.
- Complete cycle.
- Explain power, consent, coercion concept.
- Explore power, consent, coercion in relation to offending.

Session 10 – Pathway into abuse (process) – Finkelhor's 4-Step building blocks

- What do you remember from last week's session?
- Explore feelings diary.
- Explain building blocks concept (Finkelhor).
- Construct building blocks.

Session 11 – Victim empathy – Ecomap

- What do you remember from last week's session?
- Explore feelings diary.
- Explore empathy questions.

- Explain ecomap.
- Construct ecomap.
- Check how John is feeling.

Session 12 – Victim empathy – Victim letter

- What do you remember from last week's session?
- Explore feelings diary.
- Using ecomap ask John to write letter from Sally to him.
- Revise letter.
- Homework – letter of apology to Sally.
- Check how John is feeling.

Session 13 – Victim empathy – Apology to victim letter

- What do you remember from last week's session?
- Explore feelings diary.
- Revise apology letter.
- Write letter of apology to Sally's parents.
- Revise letter.
- Homework – letter of apology to John's parents.
- Check how John is feeling.

Session 14 – Victim empathy and relapse prevention

- What do you remember from last week's session?
- Explore feelings diary.
- Revise apology letter to John's parents.
- Review work so far and construct relapse prevention plan.
- Check how John is feeling.

Session 15 – Review and relapse prevention with parents

- John explains work he has undertaken and shows his parents examples.
- John reads letter of apology to Sally, her parents and his own parents.
- John and parents discuss and agree relapse prevention plan.
- Endings.

Topics

In this section I will describe some of the topics which I have found useful in conducting this brief CBT programme with adolescent sex offenders. These topics are also transferable to longer-term work and are part of the standard CBT approach to working with adolescent sex offenders. However I have also included some specific approaches and techniques which I have developed over the years. Firstly it is important to memorise these topics: don't go into a session with notes or questions written down as 'aide memoirs'. These can sometimes make the practitioner look as if they either don't know their subject too well and thereby do not inspire confidence, or can serve to distance the practitioner from the adolescent by making the adolescent perceive the practitioner as too 'official'. It is important to remember that the most effective tool in your repertoire is you and how you foster a trusting relationship with the adolescent.

Genogram

Constructing a genogram (family tree) with the adolescent, if this has not been done as part of the assessment, is a particularly good way of engaging the adolescent and demonstrating your interest in him as a person. It also helps the practitioner and the adolescent to see links and family 'patterns'. Explore who is close to who and who is not: eg who is mum's favourite, dad's, gran's. Look for intergenerational patterns (eg mum's relationship with her daughter mirrors her relationship with her own mother); roles within the family (scapegoat, joker, protector); family 'scripts'; myths or belief systems (eg you're just like your real father, women are victims); losses (separation or death). For instance, in John's genogram, we were able to see that, despite the fact that his parents were loving and supportive, he had not felt able to talk to them about his worries or anxieties.

Lifeline

There are several methods of doing this but my preferred method is to draw a line horizontally in the centre of a piece of paper and mark along the line from 0 to however old the adolescent is. Then explain to the adolescent that you and he are going to map out the main events and memories that he has experienced in his life. The good/happy events go above the line and the not so good/unhappy events go below the line. Start with what he knows about his birth and early childhood which he has been told about or seen

photos of and then move on to his earliest memories.

Useful prompts are: first day at nursery/playschool/primary school (how separation was experienced); memories about birthdays, holidays, Christmases, change of home/school, losses, who taught adolescent to swim, tie his shoelaces, ride a bike etc.

Feelings, thoughts and behaviour

It is an important aspect of any therapeutic treatment work with adolescents who have sexually offended to help them identify the difference between feelings, thoughts and behaviour, particularly for boys as they are frequently socialised to suppress their feelings, especially feelings associated with vulnerability: 'big boys don't cry'. This understanding paves the way for the more sex offence specific work. I have found it useful to ask the adolescent to keep a feelings diary which they bring to the session each week to read out and discuss with the practitioner. They thus learn the language of emotions. In explaining the difference between feelings, thoughts and behaviour the adolescent needs to understand how this applies in every day life. For example, John was keen on playing football so we examined the various feelings, thoughts and actions that would take place in a split second as the ball is coming towards him and he has a clear shot at the goal: anticipation, excitement, some fear or nervousness etc, all accompanied by rapid thoughts about what to do and then making a decision and carrying out the action. We also explored what his feelings, thoughts and actions would be if he scored, or did not score a goal. Another useful exercise is to use a card sorting procedure in which the adolescent has to sort cards with words on them into behaviours, feelings or thoughts.

Sexual history

This topic was not undertaken with John as it had already been covered in the assessment. I find it particularly useful to chart the sexual history on to the lifeline as frequently clusters of either positive or negative life experiences will be closely aligned to positive or negative sexual experiences. It also helps the practitioner and the adolescent to contextualise their sexual offending within their lives as a whole, including their sexual development. Whether as part of an assessment or therapeutic treatment, this topic is best covered after the adolescent has built up some trust in the practitioner and has begun to experience some therapeutic gains.

A sexual history starts when a child realises that girls are different to boys, usually between the age of two to four, possibly because 'girls wore dresses and had long hair' or because of sharing a bath with siblings or seeing a younger child having its nappy changed. Also at this stage the child realises that girls grow into women and boys into men. From the age four plus, children become aware of the physical differences between males and females and they may ask a parent or older sibling about this. Many children discover that pleasurable sensations can be derived from rubbing their genitalia: again they may ask about this. The response they get usually defines the family 'rules' about sexual matters. Is it a 'taboo' or shameful subject or is it acceptable for the child to voice his curiosity about sexual matters? During primary school years an increasing amount of knowledge about sex is gained. A child comes to realise that their genitalia is not just for urinating, but that there is something called 'sex' which involves genitalia, and also kissing. Children will typically play games such as 'kiss-chase', 'mums and dads', 'doctors and nurses' or 'spin the bottle' as a way of discovering and experimenting with sexual differences and potential relationships. By the time a child is reaching puberty they usually have a rudimentary knowledge of the 'facts of life'.

From puberty onwards adolescents discover masturbation, if they hadn't done so before. They begin to have sexual fantasies, view pornography and become more intent on having a boyfriend or girlfriend. Recently the internet and mobile phones have greatly increased adolescents' access to pornography. This can be a particularly difficult time for adolescents whose primary sexual interest is towards their own gender, as adolescents can be highly homophobic. It is also important to bear in mind that adolescents may engage in sexual behaviours with members of the same sex even though that is not their primary sexual orientation. For boys who have been sexually abused by a male this may be particularly confusing. A simple way of helping an adolescent to clear up any confusion they may have about their sexual orientation is to ask them what their sexual fantasies consist of (see description of fantasy pie chart below).

When asking about negative sexual experiences bear in mind that it is not just whether the person has been sexually abused or exploited or not. There may be other unpleasant, confusing or distressing experiences that the adolescent has had, such as feeling rejected, humiliated or embarrassed due to their own or others' behaviour.

Controlling deviant fantasy

The adolescent needs to be helped to understand the presence of deviant fantasies as a common feature of sexually abusive behaviour and enabled to see that there is a way of controlling fantasies. He is more likely then to be honest about their occurrence. Initial work has to be educational and should be undertaken fairly early on in a programme before extensive denial sets in on the issue. Educational input should include the definition and role of sexual fantasy in general, the connection between a fantasy and masturbation, which fantasies are acceptable and which need to be controlled. A simple thought stopping technique using an aversive scenario can be introduced as one control method. Help the adolescent to understand at what point an aversive scenario should be employed: ie once a deviant fantasy has begun but before it leads to masturbation or orgasm. The adolescent must then construct his own aversive scenario, which is essentially the most terrible thing that could happen (in the fantasy) whilst fantasising about a child. Once the scenario has been written out, the individual has to read it through and underline the most emotionally painful parts. This will give the practitioner some insight into the young person's emotional language, repertoire and responsiveness.

It is also important to help the adolescent learn to recognise when he is seeing children in a sexualised context, for example, when at the swimming pool. Getting the adolescent to practice imagining who the child's mother, father or siblings are, or what other non-sexual aspects of the child they can think of will help the adolescent not to see the child (and children generally) in a sexualised manner.

I find it is helpful to ask the adolescent to help me construct a 'pie chart' of their different types of fantasy, both at the time of the offending and in the present. For example, with John, he described that when he was offending about half of his sexual fantasies were about the children he was abusing, about 25 per cent were about peer-aged girls he found attractive that he knew and the remaining 25 per cent were of female celebrities. Since the abuse came to light he told me that only about 5 per cent of his sexual fantasies were about the children he abused, the remaining 95 per cent being equally divided between peer-aged girls he found attractive and female celebrities.

John then identified an aversive scenario for the sexual fantasies about the children he had abused which he agreed to use if he began to have one of those fantasies.

The pathway or why I did what I did – Yes/No thoughts

There are thoughts which impede abuse, described as break thoughts: eg 'someone may find out', or 'I am hurting them'. There are also thoughts which are reality-based and accelerate abuse, described as a dangerous thoughts: eg 'I want to do it again'. Finally there are thoughts which are not reality-based and accelerate abusive behaviour described as distorted thoughts eg 'they want me to do it'. There is a considerable difference between someone who has a mixture of break, dangerous and distorted thoughts, thus revealing some internal capacity to critically and morally review their abusive actions, and someone who only possesses dangerous and distorted thoughts that contain little or no appreciation of the impact of their behaviour. The adolescents who are suitable for a brief CBT programme are the former of these two types.

The adolescent must evaluate and restructure his distorted thoughts. This can be achieved by testing out each thought against reality, highlighting the contrasts between distorted and reality based thinking and then generate an alternative thought which serves as a break: eg 'I am harming this person' or 'they cannot give consent to what I want to do'. The more empathic the break thoughts the better. Good verbal skills often mask poor cognitive skills therefore it should not be assumed that in addressing cognitive distortions, an individual's understanding of thoughts, feelings and behaviours are equivalent to their verbal abilities.

I have found that a useful way to help the adolescent conceptualise cognitive distortions is to remind him that after each occasion of abuse he would have felt bad about what he did: these are 'No' thoughts and feelings (break thoughts). Ask the adolescent to tell you what 'No' thoughts

he had and write them down. Then say to the adolescent that these are powerful thoughts and feelings and so there must have been some even more powerful thoughts and feelings that made him commit a further offence: these are the 'Yes' thoughts and feelings. Again, ask the adolescent to tell you what these were and write them down. Often, a 'Yes' thought will be linked to a 'No' thought. For example, in John's list (Figure 20.1), the 'No' thought 'After getting one victim to touch my penis I worried it was getting worse' was countered by the 'Yes' thought of 'Decided not to do that again – just the other stuff'.

The jigsaw

It is useful to explain to the adolescent that there is never one reason why he committed the sexual offence: there is a collage of different reasons. I find it useful to liken this to a jigsaw where each piece contributes to the overall picture of why they committed a sexual offence. This is where the information gained in the genogram, lifeline and sexual history will be pertinent. In John's case he identified the following pieces of the jigsaw. Frequently some of the 'Yes' thoughts will be part of the jigsaw:

- It felt good.
- Other lads were bragging about sexual experiences – I was feeling left out and embarrassed.
- I'm not embarrassed with them (the victims) because they were too young.
- Feeling left behind/different (John started puberty later than his peers).
- Feeling stupid and 'small'.
- I'm not good enough to get a girlfriend.
- I can't get a girlfriend.
- Feeling bad about myself.
- Feeling aroused/sexual.
- What does it (sex) feel like?
- They (the victims) were there and I was already friendly with them.
- They trusted/looked up to me.
- I could control them.
- They made me feel big.
- They won't know what's going on so won't tell and it won't hurt them.

The cycle or 'why I didn't stop after the first time'

This is a familiar concept for practitioners who work with adolescent sex offenders originally

Figure 20.1: No and Yes thoughts

NO thoughts	YES thoughts
Victims parents might find out	It feels good
My parents might find out	Blanked out 'no' thoughts
Embarrassed/ashamed	They don't know what's happening so it doesn't matter
I shouldn't do this – it's wrong	
Whole village could find out	One more time won't hurt
How would villagers react?	They never said stop so they didn't mind
Victims probably didn't like it	Decided not to do that again – just the other stuff
Mustn't do it again in case it gets worse	I'm under-age so can't be convicted as a child molester
After getting Sally to touch my penis I worried it was getting worse	
Am I becoming 'one of them?' ie a 'pervert'	Told them not to tell so it should be OK
Police might be told – prison	Better not do anything to her again only the other two girls
Feeling guilty	
One victim wriggled away – she knew it was wrong	

described by Gail Ryan and Sandy Lane (1991). It is important to remind the adolescent the link between feelings, thoughts and behaviour and it may be necessary to give some examples. For instance: if I *feel* hungry I will *think* about food and how or where to get some; then this combination of a feeling and thoughts will influence what I *do* (eg go to the fridge/eat some food).

Again, some of the thoughts and feelings in the cycle will have already appeared in the previous exercises but understanding the cyclical nature of their offending will deepen the adolescent's understanding of why he continued to offend and reinforces the previous learning.

In introducing this topic I find it helpful to describe the stages of the cycle in general terms to the adolescent and ask if this makes any sense to him in terms of his own offending. Usually they will say that it does make sense, or some of it does. It may be necessary to go over the parts which do not make sense to them to make sure they understand them. For example, some adolescents may struggle with the idea of the 'Withdrawal' stage and you may have to explore this, again in general terms, looking for ways of describing it which do make sense to the adolescent.

John's cycle (Figure 20.2) was constructed over two sessions and focused on Sally as she was the child whom he had abused more frequently and whom he had got to touch his penis which he had not done to the other children. It is important to help the adolescent to differentiate between feelings, thoughts and behaviour on the cycle.

Power, consent and coercion

This concept, originally described by Gail Ryan and Sandy Lane (1991) will also be familiar to practitioners working with adolescent sex offenders. It is useful to explore with the adolescent the following questions under each heading. Then explore the ways in which the adolescent had more power than his victim, why his victim did not consent and how he got the victim to engage in the behaviour.

1. *Power*
   What is healthy power?
   Who are your heroes or role models who use healthy power?
   hat is unhealthy power?
   Who can you think of who uses unhealthy power?
   Describe ways you use healthy power.
   Describe ways you use unhealthy power.

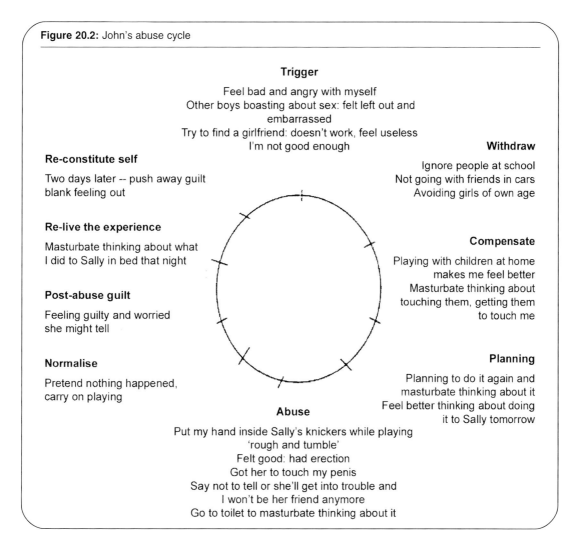

Figure 20.2: John's abuse cycle

Trigger

Feel bad and angry with myself
Other boys boasting about sex: felt left out and
embarrassed
Try to find a girlfriend: doesn't work, feel useless
I'm not good enough

Withdraw

Ignore people at school
Not going with friends in cars
Avoiding girls of own age

Re-constitute self

Two days later -- push away guilt
blank feeling out

Compensate

Playing with children at home
makes me feel better
Masturbate thinking about
touching them, getting them
to touch me

Re-live the experience

Masturbate thinking about what
I did to Sally in bed that night

Post-abuse guilt

Feeling guilty and worried
she might tell

Planning

Planning to do it again and
masturbate thinking about it
Feel better thinking about doing
it to Sally tomorrow

Normalise

Pretend nothing happened,
carry on playing

Abuse

Put my hand inside Sally's knickers while playing
'rough and tumble'
Felt good: had erection
Got her to touch my penis
Say not to tell or she'll get into trouble and
I won't be her friend anymore
Go to toilet to masturbate thinking about it

2. *Consent or 'agreement'*
   For each victim say how much (0–10) you were responsible for the sexual behaviour and how much they were responsible for it. Was any one else responsible for it?

3. *Coercion or 'getting the other person to do something they don't want to do or don't understand'*
   Describe how you got them to go along with the sexual behaviour (bribes, threats, force, promises, games etc).

In John's case he acknowledged that he was bigger and older than the victims and that he had a position of responsibility towards them. He also acknowledged that they trusted him. He also acknowledged that they were too young to understand what was going on and that therefore they did not consent to the abuse even though they agreed to play 'rough and tumble' games with him. Finally he realised how he had exploited his position of trust and responsibility towards them in order to entice them into playing the 'rough and tumble' game under which guise he abused them.

Finkelhor's four step model

Practitioners will be familiar with Finkelhor's Four-Step model of how sexual abuse takes place (Finkelhor 1986). This is a useful way of drawing together and reinforcing the topics already covered.

Firstly explain the Finkelhor model then see how it applies to the adolescent.

1. What was your motivation? (*the jigsaw*)
    *   Emotional needs (eg lonely, can't make friends, bullied, insecure, angry, want power or control).
    *   Sexual arousal to children (eg thoughts, fantasies, games, play fighting, being abused, pornography, comfort).
    *   Blockage (eg can't get age-mate to have sex with, masturbation is dirty, shy or embarrassed with age-mates).
    *   Disinhibitors (eg alcohol, drugs, cognitive distortions, opportunity).

2. What did you tell yourself to overcome your internal barriers (cognitive distortions and feelings)? (*'Yes' thoughts and feelings*)
    *   Get past fear of getting caught.
    *   Decide victims' feelings don't matter.
    *   Ignore the fact you know it's wrong.

3. How did you overcome the external barriers (planning)? (*Jigsaw and 'Yes' thoughts and feelings*)
    *   Choose victim.
    *   Create opportunity.

4. How did you overcome his/her resistance (grooming behaviours)? (*Power/consent/coercion*)
    *   bribes
    *   threats
    *   force
    *   promises
    *   games

Victim empathy or 'understanding how the abuse affected them'

This is usually the most distressing aspect of the therapeutic treatment for the adolescent as he begins to understand the real effects of the offending on the victim and their parents as well as the effect on the adolescent and his family. It is important to help the adolescent understand that what they did was wrong and harmful but that this does not make them a 'bad' person. Also it is good practice to ask the client how he is feeling at the end of victim empathy sessions and offer reassurance as appropriate.

Four general empathy skills have been noted:

*   Perspective-taking is a cognitive ability to look at someone else's point of view.
*   Empathic concern is the effective ability to feel compassion for others encountering negative experiences.

*   Fantasy is an imaginative capacity to place oneself in the role of a character in fantasy.
*   Personal distress is the degree to which one shares the negative emotions of another.

In order to help the adolescent develop these skills the reader may find the following questions useful:

1. How did the victim react during the sexual behaviour (what they said or did, what their faces looked like, how they held their bodies)?
2. Describe how you think they felt:
    *   before
    *   during
    *   after the abuse
3. What were the effects of the sexual behaviour on them at the time?
4. What may the effects be on them in the future?
5. What were the effects of the sexual behaviour on their family at the time of disclosure?
6. What may the effects be on their family in the future?
7. What were the effects of the sexual behaviour on your family at the time of disclosure?
8. What may the effects be on your family in the future?

Having considered these questions I have found it useful to construct an 'ecomap' listing all those affected by the abuse then write down the effects on the different people on the ecomap. First, ask the adolescent where, in relation to him and the others affected by the abuse, they will go on the sheet of paper. Then, starting with the adolescent ask how the abuse affected them. For the adolescent and the victim this will include 'at the time of the abuse, since disclosure and in the future'. For the others it will include 'since disclosure and in the future'. In John's ecomap (Figure 20.3) notice how he placed Sally's mum and dad close together in front of Sally as a protective barrier and his own mum and dad not so close with his sister at some distance. This provided an opportunity for John to talk about how the abuse had affected people in different, and sometimes, similar ways.

Considering the effects, not only on the victim, but on all those affected (the 'ripple effect') paves the way to writing the apology letters. Before the apology letters, however, ask the adolescent to write a letter from the victim to him about how he thinks they felt when the abuse was taking place, how they might feel now and how the abuse may be affecting them now and in the future. The

Figure 20.3: John's eco map

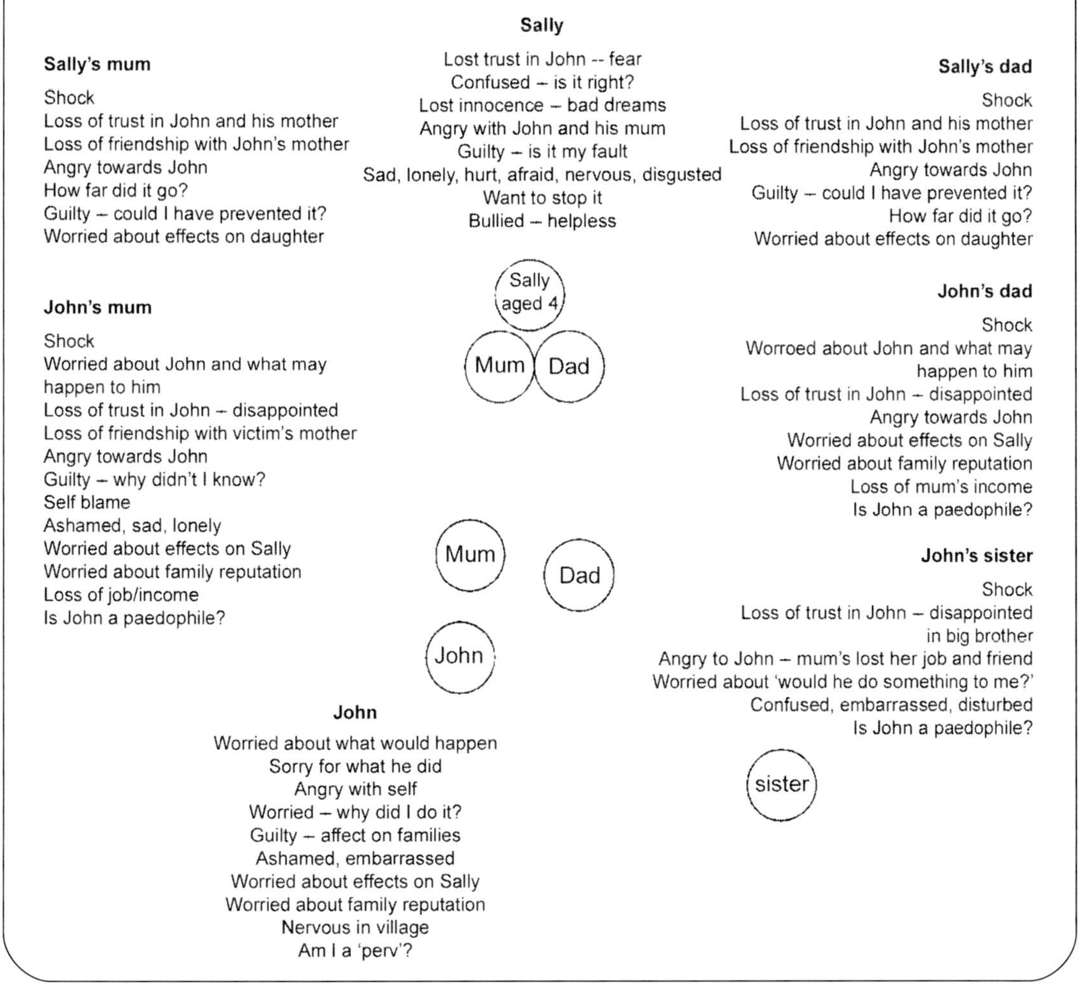

Sally

Lost trust in John -- fear
Confused – is it right?
Lost innocence – bad dreams
Angry with John and his mum
Guilty – is it my fault
Sad, lonely, hurt, afraid, nervous, disgusted
Want to stop it
Bullied – helpless

Sally's mum

Shock
Loss of trust in John and his mother
Loss of friendship with John's mother
Angry towards John
How far did it go?
Guilty – could I have prevented it?
Worried about effects on daughter

Sally's dad

Shock
Loss of trust in John and his mother
Loss of friendship with John's mother
Angry towards John
Guilty – could I have prevented it?
How far did it go?
Worried about effects on daughter

John's mum

Shock
Worried about John and what may happen to him
Loss of trust in John – disappointed
Loss of friendship with victim's mother
Angry towards John
Guilty – why didn't I know?
Self blame
Ashamed, sad, lonely
Worried about effects on Sally
Worried about family reputation
Loss of job/income
Is John a paedophile?

John's dad

Shock
Worroed about John and what may happen to him
Loss of trust in John – disappointed
Angry towards John
Worried about effects on Sally
Worried about family reputation
Loss of mum's income
Is John a paedophile?

John's sister

Shock
Loss of trust in John – disappointed in big brother
Angry to John – mum's lost her job and friend
Worried about 'would he do something to me?'
Confused, embarrassed, disturbed
Is John a paedophile?

Sally aged 4

Mum Dad

Mum   Dad

John

sister

John

Worried about what would happen
Sorry for what he did
Angry with self
Worried – why did I do it?
Guilty – affect on families
Ashamed, embarrassed
Worried about effects on Sally
Worried about family reputation
Nervous in village
Am I a 'perv'?

adolescent will most likely need to make more than one attempt at this. The letter writing tasks can be undertaken as 'homework' but the first attempts are best undertaken in the session. The following are examples of John's first and third attempt. In between attempts I read, as Sally, the letter to him and asked him how he felt. I also told John how I, as Sally, might feel hearing the letter.

Dear John (Version 1)

Today I had a really bad experience at my childminder's as I was playing in the sitting room with all the other kids and John. John is a very friendly boy and I always loved playing with him. Today he put his hand down my pants. I thought it was an accident. It was probably a mistake as John does get very enthusiastic when throwing pillows and wrestling with us. I have never seen him doing this before therefore I genuinely think it was a mistake. It probably just happened as he was playing with me.

Dear John (Version 3)

I am writing to you to tell you how I feel about what happened to me when I was at your mother's house. When this all happened at first I was too young to know what you were doing to me. Now that I am older I can understand what happened. Thinking back on it I don't like the feeling of your hand being down my pants as I was only four. And I think that it was disgusting touching your penis. There was 11 years in the difference of our ages which means that I would not have had any notion of what you were doing to me. I hate you for what you done to me and I guess that you probably hate yourself. I hope that there was a good explanation for what you done to me. But what's done is done and there is no going back on it, but I will never forget what you done to me and hope that you have realised how wrong it is. I can never forgive you and I don't think you would blame me for that.

Next, ask the adolescent to write a letter of apology to the victim. It is often useful to ask the adolescent to write a letter of apology to the victim's parents as well. These letters are not intended to be given to the victim or the parents, they are exercises to help the adolescent develop empathy. Ask the adolescent to read out the letters to you. Again more than one attempt is likely to be necessary. The following are John's first and third attempt at an apology letter.

Dear Sally (Version 1)

I am writing this letter as an apology to my incident I got you involved in last year. I'm sorry I done such a disgusting thing to you and how it affected you and your family. You were only a child and I was almost an adult, I was totally out of line. I can never forgive myself for doing this to you. I didn't think at the start of it all and then I couldn't stop what I was doing. I'm sorry for what I put you through and I hope you are getting better. I'm ashamed at what I done and I apologise how I affected your life. I know this will have a terrible influence on you for the rest of your life and if I could take it back how I hurt you and your parents I would, but there is no way back. I'm very sorry.

Dear Sally (Version 3)

I am writing to you to apologise to you for what I done to you last year. I can understand that you don't want anything to do with me but I am writing to apologise. Last year, when you were at my mother's house I put my hand down your pants a few times and touched your vagina and I got you to touch my privates. As I look back on this it is terrible what I did. I should have never have done this. You must be so angry at me for doing this to you. I know that children have nightmares and you would have had them for what I done to you. You were only a child and I was almost an adult, I was totally out of line. It was all my fault, not yours. This will have a terrible influence on you for the rest of your life and if I could take it back how I hurt you and your parents I would, but there is no way back. I also know that your parents are hurt and angry and disappointed with me as well. I took advantage of you as I wasn't able to get a girl of my own age. I know that this doesn't excuse how I hurt you but I thought I would just let you know. You didn't deserve this to happen to you. You were so playful, kind and funny and had friends at my mother's house. I can never forgive myself for taking all this away from you. I wanted to write this

letter to you to apologise to you for hurting you this way.

The apology letter may also be a useful starting point if it is planned to facilitate an apology session with the victim and his/her parents.

Relapse prevention

Relapse prevention comprises the following four elements:

- Review the work so far.
- Identify the high risk states, triggers, feelings, thoughts, behaviours, places etc.
- Work out an exit strategy.
- Work out a support network – who to talk to.

It is useful to include the parents in some way in the relapse prevention session/s as they are likely to be an important part of the adolescent's support network. Encourage the adolescent to go through the work that has been done with his parents. For example he may read the final versions of the letter from the victim and the apology letter.

In John's case he explained to his parents how he had felt left behind in relation to other boys who were boasting about their sexual exploits and how, when he played with the children who his mother childminded, it made him feel better about himself. He told them about the 'Yes' and 'No' thoughts and about how he had convinced himself the children would not understand what was happening. He showed them the ecomap we had constructed and he read the final versions of the letters he had written to Sally, her parents and his parents. His parents assured him that if he was feeling bad about himself and emotionally withdrawing he could share these feelings with them and he agreed that he would, saying that he now knew how to recognise his feelings.

Conclusion

This chapter has presented a brief CBT therapeutic intervention for adolescent boys who have been assessed as posing a low risk of re-offending. A case study has been used to exemplify the model. The therapeutic approaches described in the first part of the chapter are applicable to this model, but also to longer-term interventions. The topics in the latter part of the chapter have described possible components for a brief intervention as a guideline, but it is important to bear in mind that each adolescent will have different therapeutic needs and the topics should be tailored to suit these needs. It is hoped that the reader will take from these topics whatever they find useful or interesting, try them out, adapt them or abandon them. Each of us has our own way of being a therapist and it is important that the therapist is 'real' in their work with adolescent sex offenders.

References

Bankes, N. (2002a) *Unconscious Processes in Practitioners who Work Therapeutically with Children and Young People who Sexually Abuse.* PhD thesis: Sussex University.

Bankes, N. (2002b) I'm Sorry I haven't a Clue: Unconscious Processes in Practitioners who Work with Young People who Sexually Abuse. in Calder, M.C. (ed.) (2002) *Young People Who Sexually Abuse: Building The Evidence Base For Your Practice.* Lyme Regis: Russell House Publishing.

Bankes, N. (2006) The Responsibility Avoidance Syndrome: Unconscious Processes in Practitioners' Therapeutic Work with Children and Young People who Sexually Abuse. in Erooga, M. and Masson, H. (eds.) *Children and Young People who Sexually Abuse Others: Current Developments and Practice Responses.* 2nd edn. UK: Routledge.

Bankes, N. (2010) *What Can Sex Offenders Tell Us About What Was Helpful or Unhelpful to Them in Their Psychotherapy?* MA thesis. University College Cork, Ireland.

Campbell, D. (1994) Breaching the Shame Shield: Thoughts on the Assessment of Adolescent Child Sexual Abusers. *The Journal of Child Psychotherapy.* 20: 3, 309–26.

Finkelhor, D. (1986) *A Sourcebook on Child Sexual Abuse.* London and New York: Sage.

Hodges, J., Lanyado, M. and Andreou, C. (1994) Sexuality and Violence: Preliminary Clinical Hypotheses from Psychotherapeutic Assessments in a Research Programme on Young Sexual Offenders. *The Journal of Child Psychotherapy.* 20: 3, 283–308.

Hooper, C. and Koprowska, J. (2000) Reparative Experience or Repeated Trauma? Child Sexual Abuse and Adult Mental Health Services. in McCluskey, U. and Hooper, C. (eds.) *Psychodynamic Perspectives on Abuse: The Cost of Fear.* London and Philadelphia: Jessica Kingsley.

Letourneau, E.J. and Borduin, C.M. (2008) The Effective Treatment of Juveniles who Sexually Offend: An Ethical Imperative *Ethics and Behavior,* 1532–7019, 18: 2, 286–306.

Merton, R.K. (1957) *Social Theory and Social Structure.* New York: The Free Press.

Print, B. et al. (2007) The AIM2 Model of Initial Assessment. Manchester: GMap.

Rober, P. (2002) Some Hypotheses about Hesitations and their Nonverbal Expression in Family Therapy Practice. *Journal of Family Therapy,* 24: 187–204.

Rogers, C.R. (1957) A Theory of Therapy, Personality and Interpersonal Relationships as Developed in the Client-Centred Framework. in Koch, S. (ed.) (1959) *Psychology: A Study of Science,* Vol. 3, *Formulations of the Person and the Social Context.* New York: McGraw-Hill.

Rogers, C.R. (1986) A Client-centred/Person-centred Approach to Therapy. in Kirschenbaum, H. and Henderson, V.L. (1989) (eds.) *The Carl Rogers Reader: Selections from the Lifetime Work of America's Preminent Psychologist.* New York: Houghton Mifflin.

Ryan, G. and Lane, S. (1991) *Juvenile Sexual Offending: Causes, Consequences and Correction.* Lexington Books.

Ryan, G., Leversee, T.F. and Lane, S. (2010) *Juvenile Sexual Offending: Causes, Consequences and Correction.* New Jersey: John Wiley and Sons.

Vas Dias, S. (2000) Inner Silence: One of the Impacts of Emotional Abuse upon the Developing Self. in McCluskey, U. and Hooper, C. (eds.) *Psychodynamic Perspectives on Abuse: The Cost of Fear.* London: Jessica Kingsley.

Ward, T. and Stewart, C.A. (2003) The Treatment of Sex Offenders: Risk Management and Good Lives. *Professional Psychology: Research and Practice,* 34: 353–60.

Worling, J.R. and Curwen, T. (2001) *Estimate of Risk of Adolescent Sexual Offence Recidivism.* Canada: Safe-T Programme.

■ Other books by Martin Calder

For earlier books by Martin Calder about children and young people who sexually abuse, please see detailed listings of contents and contributors on pages xi to xvi of this book. The books listed there, and these books by Martin Calder on other topics, can be obtained:
- in North America from www.isbs.com
- in Australia and New Zealand from www.psychotherapy.com.au
- in the rest of the world from www.russellhouse.co.uk.

Contemporary risk assessment in safeguarding children
Edited by Martin C. Calder
'Provides a lot of information . . . the topics are well presented and can be read in chapters or as a whole . . . a useful training resource.' *Rostrum*. 'An absorbing and exciting read . . . A broad perspective of thinking about risk and the challenge of interpreting information gathered from and about children's lives . . . extremely useful.' *Children & Young People Now*. 'Gems that will be a real boon to practice . . . tablets of wisdom set as a feast before you.' *PSW*
978-1-905541-20-1

Sexual abuse assessments
Using and developing frameworks for practice
Edited by Martin C. Calder
'Comprehensive . . . coherent . . . all chapters make for interesting and useful reading . . . This book will be a much mined source for social work, health and criminal justice professionals in both training and direct practice.' *BJSW*
978-1-905541-28-7

Assessment in child care
Using and developing frameworks for practice
Edited by Martin C. Calder and Simon Hackett
Over 6,000 copies sold. 'Covers all aspects of how to assess, when to assess and what to assess . . . The strength of this book is in the range of perspectives about assessment theory and practice, which are supported by good evidence bases and interesting examples.' *Community Care*
978-1-903855-14-0

Children living with domestic violence
Towards a framework for assessment and intervention
By Martin C. Calder
'Contains a mass of research findings along with indicators of domestic violence, a screening assessment and principles and engagement issues for working separately with perpetrators, mothers and children . . . This is all essential information that hopefully will be well used.' *Young People Now*
978-1-903855-45-4

The carrot or the stick?
Towards effective practice with involuntary clients in safeguarding children work
Edited by Martin C. Calder
For work with children and young people, men and women, fathers and mothers in all relevant circumstances. 'The carefully selected chapters in this book offer systematic and evidence-based approaches.' *ChildRIGHT*. They are 'no-nonsense' approaches that will fit with practice wisdom and practice realities of work. 'Engaging, well structured, disciplined and encouraging.' *Rostrum*
978-1-905541-22-5

What I did on my summer vacation
Surviving and helping others learn from a boyhood of sexual abuse
By Paul M. Hambke with Martin C. Calder
'As a victim myself, and having counselled hundreds of other victims . . . everything he said was instantly recognisable, to the extent that, at times, I found myself saying out loud what was coming next . . . This book tells it like it is . . . Having said that, you don't have to be a victim to benefit from this book. The author's courage in sharing his profound and thought-provoking disclosure will be of significant value to a wide range of individuals working with victims of psychosexual trauma in children and young people.' *Child Abuse Review*. Contains graphic language and illustrations that may be upsetting to some people. For a full commentary by the author on the issues raised by this book, please visit www.russellhouse.co.uk.
978-1-905541-59-1

Becoming ethical
A parallel, political journey with men who have abused
By Alan Jenkins
By the author of 'Knocking on shame's door: facing shame without shaming disadvantaged young people who have abused' in Martin C. Calder's *Children and Young People who Sexually Abuse* (RHP, 2005). This major new book is a practical guide for anyone who works in the field of interventions with men who have engaged in violence or sexual abuse towards partners and family members. 'This is an intriguing read . . . It will definitely be added to my library of must have books.' *Addiction Today*. It 'extends Jenkins's wisdom regarding ethical relationships, towards the development of a restorative position for abusers that can lead to a sense of integrity . . . a 'must read' for practitioners who work with issues relating to domestic abuse.' *Healthcare Counselling and Psychotherapy Journal*
978-1-905541-40-9.

Making sure children get 'HELD'
Ideas and resources to help workers put Hope, Empathy, Love and Dignity at the heart of child protection and support
By Nicki Weld
By the author of 'The three houses tool: building safety and positive change' in Martin C. Calder's *Contemporary risk assessment in safeguarding children*. 'Not only are we offered concepts and ideas but clear tools and resources which can be drawn on in day to day practice.' *Professor Nigel Parton*. 'A good, strong and engaging workbook . . . provides invaluable and sophisticated assessment questions for professionals seeking guidance in gaining clarity and depth of understanding.' *Child Abuse Review*
978-1-905541-55-3

■ The following books are available from:

The **NEARI Press**
New England Adolescent
Research Institute
70 North Summer Street Holyoke. MA 01040 888.632.7412
603.448.0317
www.nearipress.org

An Introduction to Autism Spectrum Disorders, Sexual Behaviors, & Therapeutic Intervention
by Gary D. Blasingame.
NEARI Press. Paperback, 157 pages.
ISBN 978-1-929657-50-6

Assessing Youth Who Have Sexually Abused: A Primer
by David S. Prescott.
NEARI Press. Paperback, 98 pages.
ISBN 978-1-929657-27-8

Current Applications: Strategies for Working with Sexually Aggressive Youth and Youth with Sexual Behavior Problems
by David S. Prescott and Robert E. Longo, (Editors).
NEARI Press. Hardcover, 368 pages.
ISBN 978-1-929657-43-8

Current Perspectives: Working with Sexually Aggressive Youth and Youth with Sexual Behavior Problems
by Robert E. Longo and David S. Prescott (Editors).
NEARI Press. Hardcover, 720 pages.
ISBN 978-1-929657-26-1

Enhancing Empathy
by Robert E. Longo and Laren Bays.
NEARI Press. Paperback, 80 pages.
ISBN 978-1-929657-04-9

Evicting the Perpetrator: A Male Survivor's Guide to Recovery from Childhood Sexual Abuse
By Ken Singer.
NEARI Press. Paperback, 268 pages.
ISBN 978-1-929657-46-9

Evolving Residential Work with Children and Families
by James R. Harris, Jr.
NEARI Press. Paperback, 160 pages.
ISBN 978-1-929657-36-0

Growing Beyond: A Workbook for Teenage Girls
by Susan L. Robinson.
NEARI Press. Paperback, 216 pages.
ISBN 978-1-929657-17-9

Growing Beyond Treatment Manual: A Workbook for Sexually Abusive Teenage Girls
by Susan L. Robinson.
NEARI Press. Paperback, 42 pages.

Lessons from the Lion's Den: Therapeutic Management of Children in Psychiatric Hospitals and Treatment Centers
by Nancy S. Cotton.
NEARI Press. Paperback, 316 pages.
ISBN 978-1-929657-24-7

Men & Anger: Understanding and Managing Your Anger
by Murray Cullen and Robert E. Longo.
NEARI Press. Paperback, 125 pages.
ISBN 978-1-929657-12-4

Moving Beyond Sexually Abusive Behavior: A Relapse Prevention Curriculum
by Thomas F. Leversee.
NEARI Press. Paperback, 88 pages.
ISBN 978-1-929657-16-2

Moving Beyond: Relapse Prevention Student Manual
by Thomas F. Leversee.
NEARI Press. Paperback, 52 pages.
ISBN 978-1-929657-18-6

New Hope For Youth: Experiential Exercises for Children & Adolescents
by Robert E. Longo and Deborah P. Longo.
NEARI Press. Paperback, 142 pages.
ISBN 978-1-929657-20-9

Paths To Wellness
by Robert E. Longo.
NEARI Press. Paperback, 144 pages.
ISBN 978-1-929657-13-1

Paths To Wellness en Espanol!
by Robert E. Longo.
NEARI Press. Paperback, 144 pages.
ISBN 978-1-929657-31-5

The Prevention of Sexual Violence: A Practitioner's Sourcebook
by Keith L. Kaufman (Editor).
NEARI Press. Hardcover, 536 pages.
ISBN 978-1-929657-45-2

Promoting Healthy Childhood Development Today
by James R. Harris, Jr.
NEARI Press. Paperback, 92 pages.
ISBN 978-1-929657-30-8

RESPECT: A Professional Manual by Tom Keating.
NEARI Press. Paperback, 216 pages.
ISBN 978-1929657-47-1

RESPECT: Student Workbook
by Tom Keating.
NEARI Press. Paperback, 136 pages.
ISBN 978-1-929657-48-3

Responsibility And Self-Management: A Client Workbook of Skills to Learn
by Jack Apsche and Jerry L. Jennings.
NEARI Press. Paperback, 224 pages.
ISBN 978-1-929657-29-2

Responsibility And Self-Management: A Clinician's Manual and Guide for Case Conceptualization
by Jack Apsche and Jerry L. Jennings.
NEARI Press. Paperback, 118 pages.
ISBN 978-1-929657-28-5

Smoothies For The Brain: Brain-Based Strategies To Defuse Behavior Problems in the Classroom
by Penny Cuninggim and Shannon Chabot.
NEARI Press. Paperback, 48 pages.
ISBN 978-1-929657-35-3

Strong at the Broken Places: Building Resiliency in Survivors of Trauma
by Linda T. Sanford.
NEARI Press. Paperback, 208 pages.
ISBN 978-1-929657-25-4

The Safe Workbook for Youth: New Choices for a Healthy Lifestyle
by John McCarthy and Kathy MacDonald.
NEARI Press. Paperback, 210 pages.
ISBN 978-1-929657-14-8

Stages of Accomplishment
by Phil Rich.
NEARI Press.

Clinician's Manual Paperback, 96 pages.
ISBN 978-1-929657-41-4

Introduction to Treatment, Stage I
Paperback, 72 pages.
ISBN 978-1-929657-37-7

Understanding Yourself, Stage 2
Paperback, 96 pages.
ISBN 978-1-929657 38 4

Understanding Dysfunctional Behavior, Stage 3
Paperback, 120 pages.
ISBN 978-1-929657-39-1

Hitting the Target: Making Change Permanent, Stage 4
Paperback, 168 pages.
ISBN 978-1-929657-40-7

The Thursday Group
by Peggy Ellen Kleinleder and Kimber Everson.
NEARI Press. Paperback, 280 pages.
ISBN 978-1-929657-44-5

Try and Make Me! Power Struggles: A Book of Strategies for Adults Who Live and Work with Angry Kids
by Penny Cuninggim.
NEARI Press. Paperback, 112 pages.
ISBN 978-1-929657-23-0

Using Conscience as a Guide: Enhancing Sex Offender Treatment in the Moral Domain
by Niki Delson.
NEARI Press. Paperback, 104 pages.
ISBN 978-1-929657-22-3

Using Conscience as a Guide: Student Manual
by Niki Delson.
NEARI Press. Paperback, 52 pages.
ISBN 978-1-929657-19-3

Who Am I and Why Am I In Treatment?
by Robert E. Longo with Laren Bays and Steven Sawyer.
NEARI Press. Paperback, 96 pages.
ISBN 978-1-929657-01-8

Why Did I Do It Again & How Can I Stop?
by Robert E. Longo with Laren Bays.
NEARI Press. Paperback, 184 pages.
ISBN 978-1-929657-11-7

For prices and shipping information, or to order any of the books on this or the previous page, please call: (USA) **888.632.7412** Find us online at: **www.nearipress.org**